WHAT'S NEW?

Shigechiyo Izumi of Japan became the oldest human ever, when he celebrated his 114th birthday in June, 1979.

Sebastian Coe of England set three major track and field records in a three-month span, including the first new record for the mile in over four years.

Actor James Coburn was paid $250,000 per syllable to speak two words in a television commercial for a brand of beer.

"Hercules" John Massis held a helicopter down using only his teeth.

**AND THAT'S NOT ALL! THOUSANDS OF NEW ENTRIES!
THOUSANDS OF BROKEN MARKS!
EVERY ACHIEVEMENT IMAGINABLE!**

GUINNESS BOOK OF WORLD RECORDS.

THE LARGEST VOLCANO—THE SMALLEST FLEA—THE OLDEST WOMAN—THE FATTEST MAN—THE BIGGEST PIZZA—THE FASTEST HUMAN—THE LONGEST HOME RUN—THE TALLEST TREE

Guinness titles by Bantam Books
Ask your bookseller for the books you have missed

ABOUT THE EDITOR

NORRIS McWHIRTER was born in London in 1925. Educated at Trinity College, Oxford University, he received an M. A. in Economics. He has been a television and radio commentator, a newspaper columnist, a contributor to the *Encyclopaedia Britannica* and a candidate for the British Conservative Party in the 1964 General Election. In 1955, Norris and his twin brother Ross edited the first *Guinness Book of World Records*. They continued to do so together annually until Ross' death in 1975. Norris is married and has a son and daughter.

NEW! 1980 EDITION
GUINNESS
BOOK OF
WORLD
RECORDS

Editors and Compilers

NORRIS McWHIRTER
(ROSS McWHIRTER 1955–1975)

Sports Editor
STAN GREENBERG

American Editor
DAVID A. BOEHM

Associate American Editor
STEVE MORGENSTERN

BANTAM BOOKS
TORONTO · NEW YORK · LONDON

GUINNESS BOOK OF WORLD RECORDS

A Bantam Book / published by arrangement with
Sterling Publishing Company, Inc.
PRINTING HISTORY OF AMERICAN EDITION
American Guinness edition published October 1956
Sterling edition published April 1962

3rd edition	.............September 1963	9th edition	.....................May 1970
4th edition	...............January 1964	10th edition	...................April 1971
5th edition	................October 1965	11th edition	...........November 1972
6th edition	............September 1966	12th edition	...............October 1973
7th edition	.................January 1968	13th edition	...........September 1974
Book Club edition	.... Sept. 1969	14th edition	...............October 1975

Bantam edition / October 1963
4 printings through February 1964

Revised Bantam edition / April 1964
8 printings through February 1966

Revised and enlarged Bantam Special edition / June 1966
7 printings through July 1967

Revised and enlarged new Bantam edition / March 1968
9 printings through October 1969

Revised and enlarged new Bantam edition / May 1970
6 printings through December 1970

Revised and enlarged new Bantam edition / April 1971
17 printings through September 1972

Revised and enlarged new Bantam edition / March 1973
17 printings through December 1973

Revised and enlarged new Bantam edition / February 1974
10 printings through November 1974

Revised and enlarged new Bantam edition / February 1975
13 printings through August 1975

Revised and enlarged new Bantam edition / March 1976
10 printings through October 1976

Revised and enlarged new Bantam edition / January 1977
10 printings through September 1977

Revised and enlarged new Bantam edition / March 1978
2 printings through November 1978

Revised and enlarged new Bantam edition / March 1979
7 printings through October 1979

Revised and enlarged new Bantam edition / March 1980

ISBN 0-553-13300-4

Published simultaneously in the United States and Canada

PRINTED IN THE UNITED STATES OF AMERICA

0 9 8 7 6 5 4 3 2 1

CONTENTS

FOREWORD

By Senator the Right Honourable the Earl of Iveagh

The book that you hold in your hands is the eighteenth American edition. It was first designed in 1956 to record the then extremes in, on and beyond the Earth—notably in human performance and of the natural world. The name "Guinness" derives from the Guinness Brewery in Dublin which is Ireland's largest Company. In Ireland people, as everywhere else, are always arguing about the largest, the longest, the heaviest, the hottest, the coldest, the wettest, the mostest, etc., and some authoritative reference work was needed to settle such arguments. We realise, of course, that much joy lies in argument, but how exasperating it can be if there is no ultimate means of finding out the correct answer. The Guinness Book has rather proved this point, since it has now succeeded to the title of the fastest selling book ever published anywhere in the world.

While the exports of Guinness Stout from Dublin to the rest of the world make the Guinness Brewery the largest exporter of beer in the world we never expected that the Guinness Book would become the runaway best seller that it now is. It is now published all over the world in twenty-three different languages. We are proud to have made the world more aware of the records that it is continually setting.

Iveagh.
[BENJAMIN GUINNESS]
EARL OF IVEAGH, Chairman
Arthur Guinness, Son & Co. (Dublin) Ltd.,
St. James's Gate Brewery, Dublin, Ireland.

September, 1979

PREFACE

This eighteenth U.S. edition has been brought up to date and provided with new illustrations. We wish to thank correspondents from most of the countries of the world for raising and settling various editorial points. Strenuous efforts have been made to improve the value of the material presented and this policy will be continued in future editions.

NORRIS D. MCWHIRTER
General Editor

Guinness Superlatives, Ltd.,
Main Editorial Office,
2 Cecil Court,
London Road, Enfield,
Middlesex, England.

See the GUINNESS Book Come Alive
at
THE GUINNESS EXHIBIT HALLS

Now, in five different locations, you can **see** world records—on video tape as they were set, real record objects, three-dimensional replicas, and color and monochrome photographs. More than 200 exhibits are housed in each of the five Exhibit Halls, which are open long hours 7 days a week during the warm weather months and all year round in New York. Admission prices are reasonable, with special rates for children and school groups. Some of the records in this edition of the book were set in personal appearances at the Exhibit Halls, and some are pictured in this book. Here are the exact addresses:

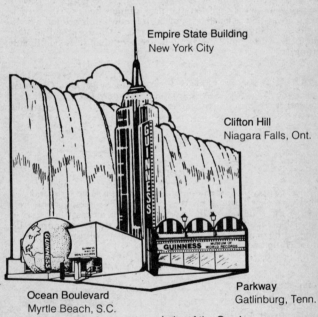

Empire State Building
New York City

Clifton Hill
Niagara Falls, Ont.

Ocean Boulevard
Myrtle Beach, S.C.

Parkway
Gatlinburg, Tenn.

Lake of the Ozarks
Missouri

IS IT A RECORD?

We are likely to publish only those records which improve upon previous records or which are newly significant in having become the subject of widespread and preferably international competitiveness.

It should be stressed that unique occurrences and interesting peculiarities are not in themselves necessarily records. Records in our sense essentially have to be both measureable and comparable. Records which are *qualified* in some way, for example, by age, day of the week, etc. cannot be accommodated in a reference work so general as *The Guinness Book of World Records.*

The authors and publishers reserve the right to determine in their sole discretion the record to be published and the name of the record holder for purposes of inclusion in the book. The publishers do *not* supply personnel to invigilate record attempts but reserve the right to do so.

Claimants should send independent corroboration in the form of local or national newspaper cuttings, radio or TV coverage reports and signed authentication by independent adult witnesses or representatives of organizations of standing in their community. Signed log books should show there has been unremitting surveillance in the case of endurance events.

There has been in recent years a marked increase in efforts to establish records for sheer endurance in many activities. In the very nature of record breaking the duration of such "marathons" will tend to be pushed to greater and greater extremes and it should be stressed that marathon attempts are not without possible dangers. Organizers of marathon events would be well counselled to seek medical advice before and surveillance during marathons which involve extended periods with little or no sleep. (See below for notes on rest periods.)

Five-minute rest intervals (optional but aggregable) are *permitted* after each completed hour in marathon events except for those few "non-stop" categories in which minimal intervals may be taken only for purposes other than for resting.

Notwithstanding the best efforts of the editors, errors in publication, while rare, may occur. In the event of such errors, the sole responsibility of the publishers will be to correct such errors in subsequent editions of the book.

If there are discrepancies between entries in one edition and another, it may be generally assumed that the *later* entry is the product of the more up-to-date research.

If an activity is one controlled by a recognized world or national governing body that body should be consulted and involved in ratifying it.

Finally the editorial office, which is concerned with maintaining and improving the quality of each succeeding edition, is unable to perform also the function of a free general information bureau for quiz competitions and the like, by telephone or by correspondence.

FASTEST MILE RUN: England's Sebastian Coe broke the four-year-old world record for the mile with a time of 3 minutes 49 seconds on July 17, 1979. This was the 33rd world track and field record set at Bislet Stadium, Oslo, Norway. During the summer, Coe also set new world records at 800 and 1,500 meters.

Chapter One

THE HUMAN BEING

1. Dimensions

Tallest Giants

The height of human giants is a subject in which accurate information is frequently obscured by exaggeration and commercial dishonesty. The only admissible evidence on the true height of giants is that collected in the last 100 years under impartial medical supervision. Some medical papers have themselves, however, published fanciful, as opposed to measured, heights as recently as 1962.

The biblical claim that Goliath of Gath (*c.* 1060 B.C.) stood 6 cubits and a span (9 feet 6½ inches) suggests a confusion of units or some over-enthusiastic exaggeration by the Hebrew chroniclers. The Hebrew historian Flavius Josephus (born in 37 or 38 A.D., died after 93 A.D.) and some of the manuscripts of the Septuagint (the earliest Greek translation of the Old Testament) attribute to Goliath the quite credible height of 4 Greek cubits and a span (6 feet 10 inches).

Extreme medieval data, taken from bone measurements, invariably refer to specimens of extinct whale, giant cave bear, giant ape, mastodon, woolly rhinoceros or other prehistoric non-human remains.

Paul Topinard (1830–1911), a French anthropometrist, stated that the tallest man who ever lived was Daniel Mynheer Cajanus (1714–49) of Finland, standing 9 feet 3.4 inches. In 1872 his right femur, now in the Leyden Museum, in the Netherlands, was measured by Prof. Carl Langer of Germany and indicated a height of 7 feet 3.4 inches. Pierre Lemolt reported in 1847 that Ivan Stepanovich Lushkin (1811–44), a drum major in the Russian Imperial Regiment of Guards at Preobrazhenskiy, measured 3 arshin 9¼ vershok (8 feet 3¾ inches) and was "the tallest man that has ever lived in modern days." However, his left femur and tibia, which are now in the Museum of the Academy of Sciences in Leningrad, U.S.S.R., indicate a height of 7 feet 10¼ inches.

An extreme case of exaggeration concerned Siah Khan ibn Kashmir Khan (born 1913) of Bushehr (Bushire), Iran. Prof. D. H. Fuchs showed photographs of him at a meeting of the Society of Physicians in Vienna, Austria, in January, 1935, claiming that he was 10 feet 6 inches tall. Later, when Siah Khan entered the Imperial Hospital in Teheran for an operation, it was revealed that his actual height was 7 feet 2.6 inches.

The tallest recorded "true" (non-pathological) giant was Angus MacAskill (1825–63), born on the island of Berneray, in the Sound of Harris, in the Outer Hebrides, Scotland. He stood 7 feet 9 inches and died in St. Ann's, on Cape Breton Island, Nova Scotia, Canada.

Modern opinion is that tne tallest recorded man of whom there is irrefutable evidence was the pre-acromegalic giant Robert Pershing Wadlow, born in Alton, Illinois, on February 22, 1918. Weighing 8½ lbs. at birth, his abnormal growth started at the age of 2, following a double hernia operation. His height progressed as follows:

Age in Years	Height ft.	in.	Weight in lbs.	Age in Years	Height ft.	in.	Weight in lbs.
5	5	4	105	15	7	8	355
8	6	0	169	16	7	10½	374
9	6	2½	180	17	8	0½	315*
10	6	5	210	18	8	3½	—
11	6	7	—	19	8	5½	480
12	6	10½	—	20	8	6¾	—
13	7	1¾	255	21	8	8¼	491
14	7	5	301	22.4†	8	11.1	439

* Following severe influenza and infection of the foot.
† He was still growing during his terminal illness.

Dr. C. M. Charles, Associate Professor of Anatomy at Washington University School of Medicine, in St. Louis, and Dr. Cyril MacBryde measured him at 8 feet 11.1 inches, on June 27, 1940. He died 18 days later, on July 15, 1940, in Manistee, Michigan, as a result of cellulitis of the right ankle aggravated by a poorly fitted brace, which had been fitted only a week earlier. He was buried in Oakwood Cemetery, Alton, Illinois, in a coffin measuring 10 feet 9 inches in length, 32 inches in width, and 30 inches in depth.

His greatest recorded weight was 491 lbs., on his 21st birthday. He weighed 439 lbs. at the time of his death. His shoes were size 37AA (18½ inches long) and his hands measured 12¾ inches from the wrist to the tip of the middle finger. His arm span was 9 feet 5¾ inches and he consumed 8,000 calories daily. At the age of 9 he was able to carry his father, the mayor of Alton, who stood 5 feet 11 inches tall and weighed 170 lbs., up the stairs of the family home.

The only other men for whom heights of 8 feet or more have been reliably reported are the eight listed next. In six cases gigantism was followed by acromegaly, a disorder which causes an enlargement of the nose, lips, tongue, lower jaw, hands and feet, due to renewed activity by an already swollen pituitary gland, which is located at the base of the brain.

		ft.	in.
John F. Carroll (1932–69) of Buffalo, New York	(a)	8	7¾
John William Rogan (1871–1905), of Gallatin, Tennessee	(b)	8	6
Don Koehler (1925–fl. 1979) of Denton, Montana, now living in Chicago (see photo, page 19)	(c)	8	2
Bernard Coyne (1897–1921) of Anthon, Iowa	(d)	8	2
Vainö Myllyrinne (1909–63) of Helsinki, Finland	(e)	8	1.2
Patrick Cotter O'Brien (1760–1806) of Kinsale, County Cork, Ireland	(f)	8	1
"Constantine" (1872–1902) of Reutlingen, West Germany	(g)	8	0.8
Sulaiman 'Ali Nashnush (1943–fl. 1979) of Tripoli, Libya	(h)	8	0.4

TALLEST MAN:
Robert Wadlow, the tallest man in history, is shown here with his brothers Eugene and Harald. Robert is the one wearing glasses.

(a) Carroll was a victim of severe kypho-scoliosis (two-dimensional spinal curvature). The figure represents his height with assumed normal spinal curvature, calculated from a standing height of 8 feet 0 inches, measured on October 14, 1959. His standing height was 7 feet 8¼ inches shortly before his death.

(b) Measured in a sitting position. Unable to stand owing to ankylosis (stiffening of the joints through the formation of adhesions) of the knees and hips.

(c) Some spinal curvature. Recent standing height c. 7 feet 10 inches. He has a twin sister who is 5 feet 9 inches tall. His father was 6 feet 2 inches tall, his mother 5 feet 10 inches. He lives a normal life.

(d) Eunuchoidal giant ("daddy-longlegs" syndrome). He was rejected by the U.S. Army in 1918 when he stood 7 feet 9 inches.

(e) Stood 7 feet 3½ inches at the age of 21 years. Experienced a second phase of growth in his late thirties and may have stood 8 feet 3 inches at one time.

(f) Revised height based on skeletal remeasurement in 1975.

(g) Height estimated, as both legs were amputated after they turned gangrenous. He claimed a height of 8 feet 6 inches. Eunuchoidal.

(h) Operation in Rome in 1960 to correct abnormal growth was successful.

Circus giants and others who are exhibited are normally under contract not to be measured and are, almost traditionally, billed by their promoters at heights up to 18 inches in excess of their true heights. Notable examples of such exaggeration are:

Name	Dates	Country	Claimed Height ft. in.	Actual Height ft. in.
Gerrit Bastiaansz	1620–68	Netherlands	8 3	7 1
Cornelius Magrath	1736–60	Ireland	8 6	7 2½
Bernardo Gigli	1736–62	Italy	8 0	7 6½
Charles Byrne	1761–83	Ireland	8 4	7 7
Sam McDonald	1762–1802	Scotland	8 0	6 10
"Lolly"	1783–1816	Russia	8 4½	7 3
James Toller	1795–1819	England	8 6	7 6
Arthur Caley	1829–53	Isle of Man	8 4	7 6
Patrick Murphy	1834–62	Ireland	8 10	7 3.4
Martin van Buren Bates	1845–1919	U.S.	7 11½	7 2½
Chang Wu-gow	1846–93	China	9 2	7 8¾
Joseph Drazel	1847–86	Germany	8 3½	7 6.5
Paul Henoch	1852–76	Germany	8 3	7 2
Franz Winkelmeier	1867–89	Austria	8 9	7 5.7
Lewis Wilkins	1873–1902	U.S.	8 2	7 4½
John Turner	1876–1911	U.S.	8 3	7 3
Baptiste Hugo	1879–1916	France	8 10	7 6.5
Fyodor Machnov	1880–1906	Russia	9 3½	7 9.7
Johnny Aasen	1890–1937	U.S.	8 0	7 0
Albert Johann Kramer	b. 1897	Netherlands	9 3½	7 8½
Clifford Thompson	b. 1904	U.S.	8 8	7 5
Jacob Ehrlich, *alias* Jack Earle	1906–52	U.S.	8 7	7 7½
Aurelio Tomaini	1912–62	U.S.	8 4½	7 4
Henry Mullens, *alias* Henry Hite	b. 1915	U.S.	8 2	7 6½
Rigardus Riynhout	b. 1922	Netherlands	9 1½	7 8.1
William Camper	1924–42	U.S.	8 6	7 2
Edward Evans	1924–58	England	9 3	7 8½
Poolad Gurd	b. 1927	Iran	8 2	7 3
Max Palmer	b. 1928	U.S.	8 0½	7 7
Eddie Carmel	1915–1978	Israel/U.S.	9 0¾	7 6⅜

NOTE: The actual heights given above for John Turner, Clifford Thompson and Max Palmer are estimated from photographs. Each of the other heights given in the last column above was obtained by an independent medical authority, the first deduced from evidence of his leg bones.

Gabriel Estevao Monjane (born 1944) of Monjacaze, Mozambique, has been credited with a height of 8 feet 6 inches, but this measurement has not been confirmed. Photographic evidence suggests he may have reached 8 feet. Eunuchoidal giants sometimes grow well into their fourth decade.

Tallest Giantesses

Giantesses are rarer than giants but their heights are still spectacular. The tallest woman in medical history was the acromegalic giantess Jane ("Ginny") Bunford, born on July 26, 1895, at Bartley Green, Northfield, West Midlands, England. Her abnormal growth started at the age of 11 following a head injury, and on her 13th birthday she measured 6 feet 6 inches. Shortly before her death on April 1, 1922, she stood 7 feet 7 inches tall, but she had severe kypho-scoliosis (curvature of the spine) and would have measured about 7 feet 11 inches with assumed normal spinal curvature. Her skeleton, now preserved in the Anatomical Museum in the Medical School at Birmingham University, England, has a mounted height of 7 feet 4 inches.

TALLEST WOMAN: Sandy Allen, who stands 7 feet 7¼ inches tall, visits with Doug Birrell, manager of the Guinness Museum of World Records at Niagara Falls

Anna Hanen Swan (1846–88) of Nova Scotia, Canada, was billed at 8 feet 1 inch but actually measured 7 feet 5½ inches. In London, on June 17, 1871, she married Martin van Buren Bates (1845–1919), of Whitesburg, Letcher County, Kentucky, who stood 7 feet 2½ inches, making them the tallest married couple on record. The eunuchoidal giantess Ella Ewing (born March, 1872) of Gorin, Missouri, was billed at 8 feet 2 inches and reputedly measured 6 feet 9 inches at the age of 10 (*cf.* 6 feet 5 inches for Robert Wadlow at this age). She measured 7 feet 4½ inches at the age of 23 and may have attained 7 feet 6 inches before her death in January, 1913.

Living. The tallest living woman is Sandy Allen (born June 18, 1955, in Chicago), who lives in Shelbyville, Indiana, and has been working in Indianapolis. On July 14, 1977, she measured 7 feet 7¼ inches at age 22, when she underwent a pituitary gland operation to inhibit further growth. A 6½-lb. baby, her acromegalic growth began soon after birth. She now weighs 440 lbs. and takes a size 22 shoe.

Shortest Dwarfs

The strictures which apply to giants apply equally to dwarfs, except that exaggeration gives way to understatement. In the same way 9 feet may be regarded as the limit toward which the tallest giants tend, so 23 inches must be regarded as the limit toward which the shortest mature dwarfs tend (*cf.* the average length of new-born babies is 18 to 20 inches). In the case of child dwarfs the age is often enhanced by their agents or managers.

There are many forms of human dwarfism. Ateliotic dwarfs, known as midgets, have essentially normal proportions but suffer from a deficiency of growth hormone. Such dwarfs tended to be even shorter when human stature was generally shorter due to lower nutritional standards.

Midgets seldom grow to more than 40 inches tall. The most famous midget in history was Charles Sherwood Stratton, *alias*

MOST FAMOUS DWARF: Not the shortest but surely the most famous dwarf of modern times, "General Tom Thumb" poses with his wife for a formal portrait.

"General Tom Thumb," born on January 4, 1838. When he came into the clutches of the circus proprietor P. T. Barnum, his birth date was changed to January 4, 1832, so that when he was billed as standing 30½ inches at the age of 18 he was in fact only 12 years old. He died of apoplexy on July 15, 1883 at his birthplace of Bridgeport, Connecticut, aged 45 (not 51), and was then 3 feet 4 inches tall.

Another celebrated midget was Józef ("Count") Boruwalaski (born November, 1739) of Poland. He measured only 8 inches long at birth, growing to 14 inches at the age of one year. He stood 17 inches at 6 years, 21 inches at 10, 25 inches at 15, 35 inches at 25 and 39 inches at 30. He died near Durham, England, on September 5, 1837, aged 97.

The shortest mature human of whom there is independent evidence was Pauline Musters ("Princess Pauline"), a Dutch midget. She was born at Ossendrecht on February 26, 1876, and measured 12 inches at birth. At the age of 4 she was only 15 inches tall. At the age of 9 she was 21.65 inches tall and weighed only 3 lbs. 5 oz. She died, at the age of 19, of pneumonia, with meningitis, in New York City on March 1, 1895. Although she was billed at 19 inches, she had earlier been medically measured and found to be 23.2 inches tall. A *post mortem* examination showed her to be exactly 24 inches (there was some elongation after death). Her mature weight varied from 7½ lbs. to 9 lbs. and her "vital statistics" were 18½–19–17, which suggests she was overweight.

The Italian girl Caroline Crachami, born in Palermo, Sicily, in 1815, was only 20.2 inches tall when she died in London, England, in 1824, aged 9. At birth she measured 7 inches long and weighed 1 lb. Her skeleton, measuring 19.8 inches, is now part of the Hunterian collection in the Museum of the Royal College of Surgeons, London.

Male. The shortest recorded adult male dwarf was Calvin Phillips, born in Bridgewater, Massachusetts, on January 14, 1791. He weighed 2 lbs. at birth and stopped growing at the age of 5. When he was 19 he measured 26½ inches tall and weighed 12 lbs. with his clothes on. He died two years later, in April, 1812, from progeria, a rare disorder characterized by dwarfism and premature senility.

William E. Jackson, *alias* "Major Mite," born on October 2, 1864, in Dunedin, New Zealand, measured 9 inches long and weighed 12 oz. at birth. In November, 1880, he stood 21 inches and weighed 9 lbs. He died in New York City, on December 9, 1900, when he measured 27 inches.

Another notable case was Max Taborsky, *alias* "Prince Kolibri," born in Vienna, Austria, in January, 1863. He measured 13.8 inches at birth and stopped growing at the age of 9. When he died, aged 25, in 1888, he stood 27.2 inches tall and weighed 11 lbs.

The shortest living mature human reported is Nruturam (born May 28, 1929), a rachitic dwarf of Naydwar, India, who measures 28 inches. Süleyman Eris (born January 24, 1955), a circus acrobatic dancer from Turkey now living in West Germany, was medically measured on March 3, 1977, and found to be 30.1 inches tall. He weighs 25 lbs. 2 oz. He, his brother and his sister are all primordial dwarfs.

Oldest Dwarf. There are only two centenarian dwarfs on record. The first was Miss Anne Clowes of Matlock, Derbyshire, England, who died on August 5, 1784, at the age of 103. She was 3 feet 9 inches tall and weighed 48 pounds. On April 6, 1979, Hungarian-born Miss Susanna Bokoyni ("Princess Susanna") of Newton, New Jersey, celebrated her 100th birthday. She is 3 feet 2 inches tall and weighs 40 lbs.

Most Variable Stature. Adam Rainer, born in 1899 in Graz, Austria, measured 3 feet 10.45 inches at the age of 21. But then he suddenly started growing upwards at a rapid rate, and by 1931 he had reached 7 feet 1¾ inches. He became so weak as a result that he was bedridden for the rest of his life. He died on March 4, 1950, aged 51. By constant practice in muscular manipulation of the vertebrae, the circus performer Clarence E. Willard (1882–1962) of the U.S. was, at his prime, able to increase his apparent stature from 5 feet 10 inches to 6 feet 4 inches at will.

Greatest Height Differential. When Don Koehler, at 8 feet 2 inches the world's tallest living man, met Mihaly Meszaros (known as "Mishu"), at 32⅝ inches one of the world's smallest living men, the difference in their heights was 65⅜ inches. The occasion was the taping of the TV special, "The Second David Frost Presents the Guinness Book of World Records," on April 5, 1974.

Tribes

Tallest. The world's tallest major tribe is the Tutsi (also called Batutsi, Watutsi, or Watussi), Nilotic herdsmen of Rwanda and Burundi, Central Africa, whose young males *average* 5 feet 10¾ inches

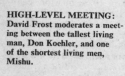

HIGH-LEVEL MEETING: David Frost moderates a meeting between the tallest living man, Don Koehler, and one of the shortest living men, Mishu.

in height. A tribe with an average height of more than 6 feet reported from the inland region of Passis Manua of New Britain in December, 1956 may be wholly discounted.

Shortest. The smallest pygmies are the Mbuti, with an average height of 4 feet 6 inches for men and 4 feet 5 inches for women, with some groups averaging only 4 feet 4 inches for men and 4 feet 1 inch for women. They live in the forests near the river Ituri in Zaire.

Weight

Lightest Humans. The lightest recorded adult was Lucia Zarate, born in San Carlos, Mexico, on January 2, 1863. At birth she weighed 2½ lbs. This emaciated ateliotic dwarf of 26½ lbs. weighed 4.7 lbs. at the age of 17. She "fattened up" to 13 lbs. by her 20th birthday. She died in October, 1889.

The thinnest recorded adults of normal height are those suffering from Simmonds' disease (Hypophyseal cachexia). Losses up to 65 per cent of the original body weight have been recorded in females, with a "low" of 45 lbs. in the case of Emma Shaller (1868–1890) of St. Louis, Missouri, who stood 5 feet 2 inches tall. In cases of anorexia nervosa, weights of under 70 lbs. have also been reported.

It was recorded that the American exhibitionist Rosa Lee Plemons (born 1873) weighed 27 lbs. at the age of 18. Edward C. Hagner (1892–1962), *alias* Eddie Masher, is alleged to have weighed only 48 lbs. at a height of 5 feet 7 inches. He was also known as "the Skeleton Dude." In August, 1825, the biceps measurement of Claude-Ambroise Seurat (born April 10, 1797, died April 6, 1826), of Troyes, France, was 4 inches and the distance between his back and his chest was less than 3 inches. He stood 5 feet 7½ inches and weighed 78 lbs., but in another account was described as 5 feet 4 inches and only 36 lbs.

Heaviest Man. The heaviest medically weighed human was the 6-foot-0½-inch tall Robert Earl Hughes (born 1926) of Monticello, Missouri. An 11¼-lb. baby, he weighed 203 lbs. at 6 years, 378 lbs. at 10, 546 lbs. at 13, 693 lbs. at 18, 896 lbs. at 25, and 945 lbs. at 27. His greatest recorded weight was 1,069 lbs. in February, 1958, and he weighed 1,041 lbs. at the time of his death. His claimed waist of 122 inches, his chest of 124 inches and his upper arm of 40 inches were the greatest on record. Hughes died of uremia (condition caused by retention of urinary matter in the blood) in a trailer at Bremen, Indiana, on July 10, 1958, aged 32, and was buried in Binville Cemetery, near Mount Sterling, Illinois. His coffin, as large as a piano case measuring 7 feet by 4 feet 4 inches and weighing more than 1,100 lbs., had to be lowered by crane. It was once claimed by a commercial interest that Hughes had weighed 1,500 lbs.—a 40 per cent exaggeration.

The greatest weight attributed to any human by a member of the medical profession is 1,400 lbs. for John Brower Minnoch (b. 1941) whose height was measured to be 6 feet 1 inch lying down. He was carried into University Hospital, Seattle, Washington, on planking

HEAVIEST HUMAN OF ALL TIME: This is Robert Earl Hughes when he weighed only 700 lbs. He later reached a top weight of 1,069 lbs. He was buried in a coffin the size of a piano case.

in March, 1978. His weight by July, 1979, was down to a measured 475 lbs. His peak weight was "conservatively" estimated at "more than 1,400 lbs." by the endocrinologist Dr. Robert Schwartz, who arrived at this figure by extrapolating the differential between his daily fluid intake and output. At his peak, however, he was never weighed.

Greatest Weight Loss. The greatest weight loss by a human being has been approximately 900 lbs. by John Brower Minnoch (see above).

The only other men for whom weights of 800 lbs. or more have been *reliably* reported are listed below:

John Lang, *alias* Michael Walker (b. 1934) U.S. (6 ft. 2 in.)	1,187 lbs (d)
Mills Darden (1798–1857) U.S. (7 ft. 6 in.)	1,020
John Hanson Craig (1856–94) U.S. (6 ft. 5 in.)	907 (c)
Arthur Knorr (1914–60) U.S. (6 ft. 1 in.)	900 (a)
Toubi (b. 1946) Cameroon	857½
T. A. Valenzuela (1895–1937) Mexico (5 ft. 11 in.)	850
David Maguire (1904–*fl.* 1935) U.S. (5 ft. 10 in.)	810
William J. Cobb (b. 1926) U.S. (6 ft. 0 in.)	802 (b)
Unnamed Patient (b. 1936) Richmond, Virginia (August, 1973)	800¼

(a) Gained 300 lbs. in the last 6 months of his life.
(b) Reduced to 232 lbs. by July, 1965.
(c) Won $1,000 in a "Bonny Baby" contest in New York City in 1858.
(d) Independent authentication of this claim is still lacking.

HEAVIEST TWINS: Benny and Billy McCrary together weighed almost 1,500 lbs. Billy died in July, 1979, while making a personal appearance at Niagara Falls, Ontario, Canada.

Heaviest Twins. The heaviest ever were the performers Billy Leon and Benny Loyd McCrary, *alias* Billy and Benny McGuire (born December 7, 1946) of Hendersonville, North Carolina. In November, 1978, they were weighed at 743 lbs. (Billy) and 723 lbs. (Benny) and had 84-inch waists. Billy died of heart failure on July 14, 1979. He was buried in a square coffin with a total weight of over 1,000 lbs. in Hendersonville. A hydraulic lift was needed to lower the coffin to its final resting place.

Heaviest Woman. The heaviest woman ever recorded was the late Mrs. Percy Pearl Washington (born Louisiana, 1926) who died in a hospital in Milwaukee, on October 9, 1972. The hospital scales registered only up to 800 lbs., but she was believed to weigh about 880 lbs. The previous weight record for a woman was set 84 years earlier at 850 lbs. although a wholly unsubstantiated report exists of a woman, Mrs. Ida Maitland (1898–1932) of Springfield, Mississippi, who reputedly weighed 911 lbs.

A more reliable and better documented case was that of Mrs. Flora Mae (or May) Jackson (*née* King), a 5-foot-9-inch woman born in 1930 at Shuqualak, Mississippi. She weighed 10 lbs. at birth; 267 lbs. at the age of 11; 621 lbs. at 25; and 840 lbs. shortly before her death in Meridian, Mississippi, on December 9, 1965. She was known in show business as "Baby Flo."

Greatest Weight Differential. The greatest weight differential recorded for a married couple is 922 lbs. in the case of Mills Darden (1,020 lbs.) of North Carolina and his wife Mary (98 lbs.). Despite her diminutiveness, however, Mrs. Darden bore her husband at least three (and possibly five) children before her death in 1837.

Slimming

The greatest recorded slimming feat was that of William J. Cobb (born 1926), *alias* "Happy Humphrey," a professional wrestler of Macon, Georgia. It was reported in July, 1965, that he had reduced from 802 lbs. to 232 lbs., a loss of 570 lbs., in 3 years. His waist measurement declined from 101 inches to 44 inches. In October, 1973, "Happy" was reported back to a normal 650 lbs.

The U.S. circus fat lady Mrs. Celesta Geyer (born 1901), *alias* Dolly Dimples, reduced from 553 lbs. to 152 lbs. in 1950–51, a loss of 401 lbs. in 14 months. Her vital statistics diminished *pari passu* from 79–84–84 to a *svelte* 34–28–36. Her book "How I Lost 400 lbs." was not a best seller. In December, 1967, she was reportedly down to 110 lbs.

The speed record for slimming was established by Paul M. Kimelman, 21, of Pittsburgh, Pennsylvania, who from December 25, 1966, to August, 1967, went on a crash diet of 300 to 600 calories per day to reduce from 487 lbs. to 130 lbs., a total loss of 357 lbs. He has now stabilized at 175 lbs. Between February 4th and 8th, 1951, Mrs. Gertrude Levandowski of Burnips, Michigan, successfully underwent a series of operations to reduce her weight from 616 lbs. to 308 lbs.

Weight Gaining

A probable record for gaining weight was set by Arthur Knorr (born May 17, 1914), who died on July 7, 1960, aged 46, in Reseda, California. He gained 300 lbs. in the last 6 months of his life and weighed 900 lbs. when he died. Miss Doris James of San Francisco is alleged to have gained 325 lbs. in the 12 months before her death in August, 1965, aged 38, at a weight of 675 lbs. She was only 5 feet 2 inches tall.

2. Origins

EARLIEST MAN

Earliest Primate

The earliest known primates appeared in the Paleocene period of about 80,000,000 years ago. The sub-order of higher primates, called Simiae (or Anthropoidea), evolved from the catarrhine or old-world sect more than 40,000,000 years later in the Lower Oligocene period. During the Middle and Upper Oligocene the super-family Hominoidea emerged. This contains three accepted families, *viz.* Hominidae (bipedal, ground-dwelling man or near man), Pongidae (brachiating forest apes) and Oreopithecidae.

The earliest known hominoid (man-like) fossil found is the *Oligopithecus savagei*, found in El Faiyum, Egypt, dated to *c.* 33,000,000 years ago.

Earliest Hominid (Near Man)

The characteristics of the Hominidae, such as a large brain, very fully distinguish them from any of the other Hominoidea. Evidence published in August, 1969, indicated that *Ramapithecus*, discovered by G. Edward Lewis at Siwalik Hills in northern India in 1932, can be dated from 8,000,000 to 13,000,000 years ago.

Earliest Genus Homo (True Man)

The greatest age attributed to fossils of the genus *Homo* is for the remains of 8 adults and 3 children discovered in the summer of 1975 at Laetolil, Tanzania, by Dr. Mary Leakey, and dated by the University of California at Berkeley to between 3,350,000 and 3,750,000 B.C. An arm-bone fragment from Kanapoi has been tentatively regarded as from *Homo* and has been dated from *c.* 4,000,000 years ago.

The most complete of the earliest skeletons of *Homo* is that of "Lucy" (40% complete) found by Dr. Donald C. Johanson and named *Australopithecus afarensis*, found in the Afar region of Ethiopia in November, 1974, and dating 3–4 million years before the present day.

Earliest Homo Sapiens

Man (*Homo sapiens*) is a species in the sub-family Homininae of the family Hominidae of the super-family Hominoidea of the sub-order Simiae (or Anthropoidea) of the order Primates of the infra-class Eutheria of the sub-class Theria of the class Mammalia of the sub-phylum Vertebrata (Craniata) of the phylum Chordata of the sub-kingdom Metazoa of the animal kingdom.

The earliest recorded remains of the species *Homo sapiens*, variously dated from 300,000 to 450,000 years ago, in the middle Pleistocene period, were discovered on August 24, 1965, by Dr. Lászlo Vértes in a limestone quarry at Vértasszöllös, about 30 miles west of Budapest, Hungary. The remains, designated *Homo sapiens palaeo-hungaricus*, comprised an almost complete occipital bone, part of a skull with an estimated cranial capacity of nearly 1,400 cubic centimeters (85 cubic inches).

Earliest man in the Americas dates from at least 50,000 B.C. and "more probably 100,000 B.C." according to the late Dr. Louis Leakey after the examination of some hearth stones found in the Mojave Desert, California, and announced in October, 1970. The earliest human relic is a skull found in the area of Los Angeles, California, dated in December, 1970, to be from 22,000 B.C.

Scale of Time

If the age of the earth-moon system (latest estimate at least 4,700 million years) is likened to a single year, Handy Man appeared on the scene at about 8:35 p.m., on December 31, Britain's earliest known inhabitants arrived at about 11:32 p.m., the Christian era began about 13 seconds before midnight and the life span of a 114-year-old man (see Oldest Centenarian) would be about three-quarters of a second. Present calculations indicate that the sun's increased heat, as it becomes a "red giant," will make life insupportable on earth in about 10,000,000,000 years. Meanwhile there may well be colder epicycles. The period of 1,000,000,000 years is sometimes referred to as an eon.

3. Longevity

Oldest Centenarian

No single subject is more obscured by vanity, deceit, falsehood and deliberate fraud than the extremes of human longevity. Extreme claims are generally made on behalf of the very aged rather than *by* them.

Many hundreds of claims throughout history have been made for persons living well into their second century and some, insulting to the intelligence, for people living even into their third. The facts are that centenarians surviving beyond their 110th year are of the extremest rarity and the present absolute limit of proven human longevity does not admit of anyone living to celebrate a 115th birthday.

It is highly significant that in Sweden, where alone proper and thorough official investigations follow the death of every allegedly very aged citizen, none has been found to have surpassed 108 years. The most reliably pedigreed large group of people in the world, the British peerage, has, after ten centuries, produced only two peers who reached their 100th birthdays, and only one reached his 101st. However, this is possibly not unconnected with the extreme draftiness of many of their residences.

Scientific research into extreme old age reveals that the correlation between the claimed density of centenarians in a country and its regional illiteracy is 0.83 ± 0.03. In late life, very old people often tend to advance their ages at the rate of about 17 years per decade. This was nicely corroborated by an analysis of the 1901 and 1911 censuses of England and Wales. Early claims must necessarily be without the elementary corroboration of birth dates. England was among the earliest of all countries to introduce local registers (1538) and official birth registration (July 1, 1837), which was made fully compulsory only in 1874. Even in the United States, 45 per cent of births occurring between 1890 and 1920 were unregistered.

Several celebrated super-centenarians are believed to have been double lives (father and son, relations with the same names or successive bearers of a title). The most famous example is Christian Jakobsen Drackenberg, allegedly born in Stavanger, Norway, on

November 18, 1626, and died in Aarhus, Denmark, aged seemingly 145 years 326 days on October 9, 1772. A number of instances have been commercially sponsored, while a fourth category of recent claims are those made for political ends, such as the 100 citizens of the Russian Soviet Federated Socialist Republic (population about 132,000,000 at mid-1967), claimed in March, 1960, to be between 120 and 156. From data on documented centenarians, actuaries have shown that only one 115-year life can be expected in 2,100,000,000 lives (cf. world population was estimated to be 4,205,000,000 at mid-1978).

The height of credulity was reached on May 5, 1933, when a news agency solemnly filed a story from China with a Peking dateline that Li Chung-yun, the "oldest man on earth," born in 1680, had just died aged 256 years (sic). Recently the most extreme case of longevity claimed has been 168 years for Shirali Mislimov of Azerbaijan, U.S.S.R., who died on September 2, 1973 and was reputedly born on March 26, 1805. No interview with this man has ever been permitted to any Western journalist or scientist. He was said to have celebrated the 100th birthday of his third wife, Hartun, in 1966 and that of one of his grandchildren in August, 1973. It was reported in 1954 that in the Abkhasian Republic of Georgia, U.S.S.R., where aged citizens are invested with an almost saint-like status, 2.58 per cent of the population was aged over 90—some 25 times the proportion in the U.S.

Dr. Zhores A. Medvedev, the exiled Soviet gerontologist, on April 30, 1974, in Washington, D.C., referring to the claims of the U.S.S.R. stated:"The whole phenomenon looks like a falsification . . . He (Stalin) liked the idea that (other) Georgians lived to be 100 or more . . . Local officials tried hard to find more and more cases for Stalin." He points out that the *average* life span in the regions claiming the highest incidence of centenarians is lower than the U.S.S.R.'s average, and that the number of centenarians claimed in the Caucasus has declined rapidly, from 8,000 in 1950 to 4,500 in 1970. Dr. I. M. Spector, of the Institute of Traumatology, Kazan, U.S.S.R., quoted the maximum lifespan of man in April, 1974, as "110–115 years," though Dr. Medvedev in December, 1977, put the *proven* limit in the U.S.S.R. as low as 108 years.

After 4 years the Andean valley of Vilcabamba in Ecuador has ceased to be the source of highly publicized and uncritical reports about very aged humans. These, it was said, lived up to 25 years beyond the so far acceptable limit of about 115 years. The discovery by Mazess and Forman, published in March, 1978, that inhabitants had been pointing to baptismal entries of their fathers, and even their grandfathers, as their own reduced the age of the valley's oldest man from 140 to 96. The lucrative income from tourism is expected to decline to a similar degree.

Charlie Smith of Bartow, Florida obtained a Social Security card in 1955, claiming to have been born in Liberia on July 4, 1842. The U.S. Dept. of Health, Education and Welfare states that they are "unable to disclose the type of evidence used" to determine Mr. Smith's age because such disclosure "would infringe on the confidentiality of the individual's record." He celebrated what he

OLD BEFORE HIS TIME: The U.S. Social Security office believes that Charlie Smith is 137 years old, but research shows him to be 104.

reckoned to be his 136th birthday on July 4, 1978. However, a reference to the county records at Arcadia, Florida (Book 2, page 392) reveals a marriage contracted at age 35 on January 8, 1910, and hence an exaggeration of some 33 years, making him 104 in 1979.

George Fruits was reputedly a veteran of the American Revolution, born in Baltimore, Maryland, on February 2, 1762, who died on August 6, 1876, at Alamo, Indiana, aged 114 years. However, new research, released by A. Ross Eckler in 1978, has shown him to be 17 years younger than the age shown on his gravestone.

The 1900 U.S. Federal census for Crawfish Springs Militia District of Walker County, Georgia, records a Mark Thrash aged 77. If the Mark Thrash (reputedly born in Georgia in December, 1822) who died near Chattanooga, Tennessee on December 17, 1943, was he, then he would have survived for 121 years.

Mythology often requires immense longevity; for example, Larak the god-king lived according to Sumerian mythology 28,800 years and Dumuzi even longer. The most extreme biblical claim is that for Methuselah at 969 years (Genesis V, verse 27).

Oldest Authenticated Centenarian

The greatest authenticated age to which a human has ever lived is over 114 years in the case of Shigechiyo Izumi of Tokunoshima, Kagoshima Prefecture, Japan. He was born on June 29, 1865, and recorded as a 6-year-old in Japan's first census of 1871. He watches television and says the best way to a long life is "not to worry."

The following national records can be taken as authentic:

AUTHENTICATED NATIONAL LONGEVITY RECORDS

	Years	Days		Born	Died
Japan	114	0	Shigechiyo Izumi	June 29, 1865	fl. June 29, 1979
U.S. (d)	113	214	Delina Filkins (née Ecker)	May 4, 1815	Dec. 4, 1928
Canada (a)	113	124	Pierre Joubert	July 15, 1701	Nov. 16, 1814
U.K. (c)	112	39	Alice Stevenson	July 10, 1861	Aug. 18, 1973
Morocco	112	+	El Hadj Mohammed el Mokri (Grand Vizier)	1844	Sept. 16, 1957
Ireland	111	327	The Hon. Katherine Plunket	Nov. 22, 1820	Oct. 14, 1932
France	111	v. 210	Virginie Duhem	Aug. 1866	May 1, 1978
S. Africa (b)	111	151	Johanna Booyson	Jan. 17, 1857	June 16, 1968
Czecho-slovakia	111	+	Marie Bernatkova	Oct. 22, 1857	fl. Oct., 1968
Channel Islands	110	321	Margaret Ann Neve (née Harvey)	May 18, 1792	Apr. 4, 1903
Northern Ireland	110	234	Elizabeth Watkins (Mrs.)	Mar. 10, 1863	Oct. 31, 1973
Yugoslavia	110	150+	Demitrius Philipovitch	Mar. 9, 1818	fl. Aug., 1928
Netherlands	110	113	Geert Adrians Boomgaard	Sept. 23, 1788	Feb. 3, 1899
Australia (f)	110	39	Ada Sharp (Mrs.)	Apr. 6, 1861	May 15, 1971
U.S.S.R. (i)	110	+	Khasako Dzugayev	Aug. 7, 1860	fl. Aug., 1970
Tasmania	109	179	Mary Ann Crow (Mrs.)	Feb. 2, 1836	July 31, 1945
Italy	109	179	Rosalia Spoto	Aug. 25, 1847	Feb. 20, 1957
Scotland	109	14	Rachel MacArthur (Mrs.)	Nov. 26, 1827	Dec. 10, 1936
Norway	109	+	Marie Olsen (Mrs.)	May 1, 1850	fl. May, 1959
Belgium	108	327	Mathilda Vertommen-Hellemans	Aug. 12, 1868	July 4, 1977
Germany (g)	108	128	Luise Schwarz	Sept. 27, 1849	Feb. 2, 1958
Portugal (e)	108	+	Maria Luisa Jorge	June 7, 1859	fl. July, 1967
Finland	107	221	Amalia Wallenius (Mrs.)	Aug. 6, 1867	Mar. 24, 1975
Sweden	107	94	Anna Johansson	Nov. 21, 1865	Feb. 23, 1973
Austria	106	231	Anna Migschitz	Feb. 3, 1850	Nov. 1, 1956
Spain (h)	106	14	José Palido	Mar. 15, 1866	Mar. 29, 1972
Malaysia	106	+	Hassan Bin Yusoff	Aug. 14, 1865	fl. Jan., 1972
Isle of Man	105	221	John Kneen	Nov. 12, 1852	June 9, 1958

(a) Mrs. Ellen Carroll died in North River, Newfoundland, Canada, on December 8, 1943, reputedly aged 115 years 49 days.

(b) Mrs. Susan Johanna Deporter of Port Elizabeth, South Africa, was reputedly 114 years old when she died on August 4, 1954. Mrs. Sarah Lawrence of Cape-town, South Africa, was reputedly 112 on June 3, 1968.

(c) London-born Miss Isabella Shepheard was allegedly 115 years old when she died at St. Asaph, North Wales, on November 20, 1948, but her actual age was believed to have been 109 years 90 days. Charles Alfred Nunez Arnold died in Liverpool, England, on September 15, 1941, reputedly aged 112 years 66 days (based on a baptismal claim in London on November 10, 1829). Mrs. Elizabeth Cornish (née Veale), who was buried at Stratton, Cornwall, on March 10, 1691 or 1692, was reputedly baptized on October 16, 1578, 112 or 113 years 4 months earlier.

(d) The U.S. Veterans Administration was in March, 1974, paying pensions to 272 women attested to be widows of veterans of the Civil War (1861–65), the last soldier having died in 1959. The oldest of these widows is Angela Felicia Virginia Davalos (Mrs. Harry Harrison Moran), who filed a claim dated 1928 with a baptismal certificate showing she was born in Morelia, Mexico, on May 17, 1856.

(e) Senhora Jesuina da Conceicao of Lisbon was reputedly 113 years old when she died on June 10, 1965.

(f) Reginald Beck of Sydney was allegedly 111 years old when he died on April 13, 1928.

(g) Friedrich Sadowski of Heidelberg reputedly celebrated his 111th birthday on October 31, 1936. Franz Joseph Eder died in Spitzburg on May 3, 1911, allegedly aged 116.

(h) Juana Ortega Villarin, Madrid, was allegedly 112 years in February, 1962. Ana Maria Parraga of Murcia was reportedly 107 in November, 1969.

(i) There are allegedly 21,700 centenarians in the U.S.S.R. compared with 7,000 in the U.S. Of these, 21,000 are ascribed to the Georgian S.S.R., or one out of every 232 people. In July, 1962, it was reported that 128, mostly male, resided in the one village of Medini.

OLDEST AMERICAN: Delina Filkins of Herkimer County, New York, lived to the age of 113 years 214 days.

In the face of the above data the claim published in the April, 1961 issue of the Soviet Union's *Vestnik Statistiki* ("Statistical Herald") that there were 224 male and 368 female Soviet citizens aged in excess of 120 recorded at the census of January 15, 1959, indicates a reliance on hearsay rather than evidence. Official Soviet insistence on the unrivalled longevity of the country's citizenry is curious in view of the fact that the 592 persons in their unique "over 120" category must have spent at least the first 78 years of their prolonged lives under Czarism. It has recently been suggested that the extreme ages claimed by men in Georgia, U.S.S.R., are the result of attempts to avoid military service when younger, by assuming the identities of older men.

4. Reproductivity

MOTHERHOOD

Most Children. The greatest officially recorded number of children produced by a mother is 69 by the first of the two wives of Feodor Vassilyev (b. 1707–*fl.* 1782), a peasant from Shuya, 150 miles east of Moscow, who, in 27 confinements, gave birth to 16 pairs of twins, 7 sets of triplets and 4 sets of quadruplets. The children were born in the period *c.* 1725–1765. At least 67 survived infancy, and nearly all survived to their majority. The case was reported to Moscow by the Monastery of Nikolskiy on February 27, 1782, and Empress Ekaterina II (The Great) was reputed to have evinced interest.

Currently the highest reliably reported figure is a 32nd child born to Raimundo Carnauba and his wife Madalena, of Ceilandia, Brazil. She was married at 13 and so far has had 24 sons and 8 daughters. In May, 1972, the mother said "They have given us a lot of work and worry but they are worth it," and the father "I don't

MOST DESCENDANTS (left): When Capt. Wilson Kettle died at age 102, he left 582 living descendants. **OLDEST MOTHER** (right): Mrs. Ruth Alice Kistler was over 57 years old when she gave birth to her daughter Suzan.

know why people make such a fuss." The figures given here are tentative, however, since no two published interviews with this family produce entirely consistent data.

Oldest. Medical literature contains extreme but unauthenticated cases of septuagenarian mothers such as Mrs. Ellen Ellis, aged 72, of Four Crosses, Clwyd, Wales, who allegedly produced a stillborn 13th child on May 15, 1776, in her 46th year of marriage. Many early cases were cover-ups for illegitimate grandchildren. The oldest recorded mother of whom there is certain evidence is Mrs. Ruth Alice Kistler (*née* Taylor), formerly Mrs. Shepard, of Portland, Oregon. She was born at Wakefield, Massachusetts, on June 11, 1899, and gave birth to a daughter, Suzan, in Glendale, California, on October 18, 1956, when her age was 57 years 129 days.

The incidence of quinquagenarian births varies widely, with the highest known rate in Albania (nearly 5,500 per million).

Descendants

In polygamous countries, the number of a person's descendants soon becomes incalculable. The last Sharifian Emperor of Morocco, Moulay Ismail (1672–1727), known as "The Bloodthirsty," was reputed to have fathered a total of 548 sons and 340 daughters.

Capt. Wilson Kettle (born 1860) of Grand Bay, Port Aux Basques, Newfoundland, Canada, died on January 25, 1963, aged 102, leaving 11 children by two wives, 65 grandchildren, 201 great-grandchildren, and 305 great-great-grandchildren, a total of 582 living descendants. Mrs. Johanna Booyson (see table, page 28), of Belfast, Transvaal, was estimated to have 600 living descendants in South Africa in January, 1968.

Multiple Great-Grandparents

Theoretically a great-great-great-great-grandparent is a possibility, although, in practice, countries in which young mothers are common generally have a low life expectancy.

At least eleven cases of great-great-great-grandparents have been reported in the last 20 years. Of these cases the youngest person to learn that her great-grandaughter had become a grandmother was Mrs. Ann V. Weirick (1888–1978) of Paxtonville, Pennsylvania, who received news of her great-great-great-grandson Matthew Stork (b. September 9, 1976) when aged only 88. She died on January 6, 1978.

Most Ascendants

In July, 1978, six-week-old Kurt Diekrager of Winona, Minnesota, was photographed with a complete set of parents, grandparents, and great-grandparents, and his great-great-grandmother Mrs. Anna Meyers, making 15 ascendants in all. This is believed to be the greatest assemblage of its kind (see photo below).

Multiple Births

It was announced by Dr. Gennaro Montanino of Rome that he had removed the fetuses of ten girls and five boys from the womb of a 35-year-old housewife on July 22, 1971. A fertility drug was responsible for this unique and unsurpassed instance of quindecaplets.

FAMILY PORTRAIT: Kurt Diekrager is shown at six weeks of age with all of his parents, grandparents and great-grandparents and his great-great-grandmother, for a total of 15 ascendants.

MULTIPLE BIRTHS

Highest number reported at single birth (Decaplets):		10 (2 male, 8 female), Bacacay, Brazil, April 22, 1946 (also report from Spain, 1924, and China, May 12, 1936).
Highest number medically recorded (Nonuplets):		9 (5 male, 4 female), to Mrs. Geraldine Broderick at Royal Hospital, Sydney, Australia, June 13, 1971. 2 males were stillborn. Richard (12 oz.) survived 6 days.
		9 (all died), to patient at University of Pennsylvania, Philadelphia, May 29, 1972.
		9 (all died) reported from Bagerhat, Bangladesh, c. May, 1977, to 30-year-old mother.
Highest number surviving:		6 out of 6 sextuplets (3 males, 3 females), to Mrs. Susan Rosenkowitz (*née* Scoones) at Capetown, South Africa, January 11, 1974. In order of birth they were: David, Nicolette, Jason, Emma, Grant and Elizabeth. They totaled 24 lbs. 1 oz.
Quintuplets	(Heaviest):	25 lbs., to Mrs. Lui Saulien, Chekiang, China, June 7, 1953.
		25 lbs., to Mrs. Kamalammal, Pondicherry, India, December 30, 1956.
	(Most sets):	No recorded case of more than a single set.
Quadruplets	(Heaviest):	21 lbs. 9 oz. to Mrs. David Bergquist, Mountain Iron, Minneapolis, at University of Minnesota Hospital (4 girls), September 7, 1975.
	(Most sets):	4, to Mme. Feodor Vassilyev (d. *ante* 1770), of Shuya, Russia.
Triplets	(Heaviest):	26 lbs. 6 oz. (unconfirmed), Iranian case–(2 male, 1 female), March 18, 1968.
	(Most sets):	15, to Maddalena Granata (1839–*fl.* 1886), Nocera Superiore, Italy.
Twins	(Heaviest):	35 lbs. 8 oz. (live-born), Warren's case (2 males, 17 lbs. 8 oz. and 18 lbs.), reported in *The Lancet* from Derbyshire, England, December 6, 1884.
		27 lbs. (surviving), 14 lbs. and 13 lbs. 12 oz., to Mrs. J. P. Haskin, Fort Smith, Arkansas, February 20, 1924.
	(Most sets):	16, to Mme. Vassilyev (see above).
		15, to Mrs. Mary Jonas (d. December 4, 1899), of Chester, England—all sets were boy and girl.
		Mrs. Barbara Zulu of Barbeton, South Africa, bore 3 sets of girls and 3 mixed sets in 7 years (1967–73).

GREATEST GATHERING OF MULTIPLE BIRTHS: Shown here are nine sets of triplets (four of which are identical) and one set of identical quadruplets, brought together and photographed at St. Paul, Minnesota, on July 30, 1973, by "super-twinologist" Lani Pettit.

Earliest Surviving Quintuplets. The earliest set of quintuplets in which all survived were the Dionnes: Emilie (died August 6, 1954, aged 20), Yvonne (now in a convent), Cecile (now Mrs. Philippe Langlois), Marie (later Mrs. Florian Houle, died February 28, 1970) and Annette (now Mrs. Germain Allard), born in her seventh pregnancy to Mrs. Olivia Dionne, aged 25, near Callander, Ontario, Canada, on May 28, 1934 (aggregate weight 13 lbs. 6 oz. with an average of 2 lbs. 11 oz.).

Oldest Surviving Triplets. The longest-lived triplets were Faith, Hope, and Charity Caughlin, born on March 27, 1868, in Marlboro, Massachusetts. Mrs. (Ellen) Hope Daniels was the first to die, on March 2, 1962, when she was 93.

Fastest. The fastest recorded natural birth of triplets has been 2 minutes in the case of Mrs. James E. Duck of Memphis, Tennessee (Bradley, Christopher and Carmon) on March 21, 1977.

Twins

Lightest. The lightest recorded birth weight for surviving twins is 2 lbs. 3 oz. in the case of Mary (16 oz.) and Margaret (19 oz.) born to Mrs. Florence Stimson of Peterborough, England, delivered by Dr. Macaulay, on August 16, 1931.

Oldest. The oldest recorded twins were Eli and John Phipps, born on February 14, 1803, in Affington, Virginia. Eli died at the

SIAMESE TWINS: Elisa and Lisa Hansen, Siamese twins joined at the tops of their heads, were separated in a pioneering 16½-hour operation on May 31, 1979. The first successful operation to separate Siamese twins was performed 24 years earlier.

age of 108 years 9 days on February 23, 1911, in Hennessey, Oklahoma, at which time John was still living, in Shenandoah, Iowa.

The chances of identical twins both reaching 100 are said to be one in 700 million.

"Siamese." Conjoined twins derived this name from the celebrated Chang and Eng Bunker, born at Maklong, Thailand (Siam), on May 11, 1811. They were joined by a cartilaginous band at the chest and married in April, 1843, the Misses Sarah and Adelaide Yates. They fathered ten and twelve children respectively. They died within three hours of each other on January 17, 1874, aged 62.

The earliest successful separation of Siamese twins was performed on Prisna and Napit Atkinson (b. May, 1953, in Thailand) by Dr. Dragstedt at the University of Chicago on March 29, 1955.

The rarest form of conjoined twins is Dicephales tetrabrachius dipus (two heads, four arms and two legs) of which only two examples are known today. They are the pair Masha and Dasha, born on January 4, 1950, in the U.S.S.R., and an unidentified pair separated in a 10-hour operation on June 23, 1977, in Washington, D.C.

BABIES

Largest. The heaviest normal newborn child reported in modern times was a boy weighing 24 lbs. 4 oz., born on June 3, 1961, to Mrs. Saadet Cor of Cegham, southern Turkey. It was revealed in January, 1978, however, that although this report was relayed by a major news agency, it cannot be considered reliable.

Mrs. Anna Bates, *née* Swan (*see* Tallest Giantesses) produced a baby weighing 23 lbs. 12 oz. according to a report in the *New York Medical Record* of March 22, 1879. A deformed baby weighing 29¼ lbs. was born in May, 1939, in a hospital at Effingham, Illinois but only lived for two hours.

Most Bouncing Baby. The most bouncing baby on record was probably James Weir (1819–1821) whose headstone in the Old Parish Cemetery, Wishaw, Strathclyde, Scotland, lists him at 112 lbs., 3 feet 4 inches in height, and 39 inches around the waist at the age of 13 months.

Therese Parentean, who died in Rouyn, Quebec, Canada, aged 9, on May 11, 1936, weighed 340 lbs.

Smallest. The lowest birth weight for a surviving infant, of which there is definite evidence, is 10 oz. in the case of Marion Chapman, born on June 5, 1938, in South Shields, northwest England. She was 12¼ inches long. By her first birthday her weight had increased to 13 lbs. 14 oz. She was born unattended, and was nursed by Dr. D. A. Shearer, who fed her hourly through a fountain pen filler. Her weight on her 21st birthday was 106 lbs.

The smallest viable baby reported born in the United States has been Jacqueline Benson, who was born in Palatine, Illinois, on February 20, 1936, weighing 12 oz.

A weight of 8 oz. was reported on March 20, 1938, for a baby born prematurely to Mrs. John Womack, after she had been knocked down by a truck in East St. Louis, Illinois. The baby was taken alive to St. Mary's Hospital, but further information is lacking. On February 23, 1952, it was reported that a 6 oz. baby only 6¼ inches in length lived for 12 hours in a hospital in Indianapolis. A twin was stillborn.

Longest Pregnancy. Claims of pregnancies lasting up to 413 days have been widely reported, but accurate data are bedevilled by the increasing use of oral contraceptive pills, which is a cause of amenorrhea. Some women on becoming pregnant erroneously add some preceding periodless months to their pregnancy. In the pre-pill era, English law had accepted pregnancies with extremes of 174 days (1939), and 349 days (1949).

Coincidental Birth Dates. The only verified example of a family producing five single children with coincidental birthdays is that of Catherine (1952), Carol (1953), Charles (1956), Claudia (1961) and Cecilia (1966), born to Ralph and Carolyn Cummins of Clintwood, Virginia, all on February 20th.

The random odds against five such births occurring singly on the same date would be 1 to 17,797,577,730—almost 4 times the world's population.

Most Proximate Births and Shortest Pregnancies. Mrs. Wendra Orr of East Kilbride, Strathclyde, Scotland, gave birth to a son, Calum-Stewart, on March 3, 1967, and twin daughters, Susan Wendra and Sandra Carol, on October 16, 1967, only 227 days later.

Most Southerly. Emilio Marcos Palma, born January 7, 1978, at the Sargento Cabral Base, Antarctica, is the only infant who can now claim to be the first born on any continent.

Earliest Test Tube Baby. Louise Brown (5 lbs. 12 oz.) was delivered by Caesarean section from Lesley Brown, 31, in Oldham General Hospital, Lancashire, England, at 11:47 p.m. on July 25, 1978. She was externally conceived on November 10, 1977.

5. Physiology and Anatomy

Hydrogen (63%) and oxygen (25.5%) are the commonest of the 24 elements in the human body. In 1972, four more trace elements were added—fluorine, silicon, tin and vanadium. The "essentiality" of nickel has not yet been finally pronounced upon.

Bones

Longest. Excluding a variable number of sesamoids, there are 206 bones in the human body. The thigh bone or *femur* is the longest. It constitutes usually 27½ per cent of a person's stature, and may be expected to be 19¾ inches long in a 6-foot-tall man. The longest recorded bone was the *femur* of the German giant Constantine, who died in Mons, Belgium, on March 30, 1902, aged 30. It measured 29.9 inches. The *femur* of Robert Wadlow, the tallest man ever recorded, measured an estimated 29½ inches.

Smallest. The *stapes* or stirrup bone, one of the three auditory ossicles in the middle ear, is the smallest human bone, measuring from 2.6 to 3.4 millimeters (0.10 to 0.17 of an inch) in length and weighing from 2.0 to 4.3 milligrams (0.03 to 0.065 of a grain).

Muscles

Largest. Muscles normally account for 40 per cent of the body weight and the bulkiest of the 639 muscles in the human body is the *gluteus maximus* or buttock muscle, which extends the thigh.

Smallest. The smallest muscle is the *stapedius*, which controls the *stapes* (see above), an auditory ossicle in the middle ear, and which is less than 1/20th of an inch in length.

Smallest Waists

Queen Catherine de Medici (1519–89) decreed a standard waist measurement of 13 inches for ladies of the French court. This was at a time when females were more diminutive. The smallest recorded waist among women of normal stature in the 20th century is a reputed 13 inches in the cases of the French actress Mlle. Polaire (1881–1939) and Mrs. Ethel Granger (born April 12, 1905) of Peterborough, England, who reduced from a natural 22 inches over the period 1929–39.

Largest Chest Measurements

The largest chest measurements are among endomorphs (those with a tendency toward globularity). In the extreme case of Robert Earl Hughes of Monticello, Missouri (the heaviest recorded human), this was reportedly 124 inches, but in the light of his known height and weight a figure of 104 inches would be more supportable.

Among muscular subjects (mesomorphs) of normal height *expanded* chest measurements above 56 inches are extremely rare. Louis Cyr (1865–1912), the famous French-Canadian strongman, had a chest measurement of 59 inches at his best weight of 300 lbs. Arnold Schwarzenegger (born 1948) of Graz, Austria, former Mr. Universe and called "the most perfectly developed man in the history of the world," has a chest measurement of 58 inches at a bodyweight of 252 lbs. He also boasts a 22-inch upper arm.

BRAINS? (above): Anatole France, Nobel Prize winner for literature, reportedly had the smallest human brain ever measured. BRAWN! (right): The unique physique of Arnold Schwarzenegger has been called "the most perfectly developed" in the history of the world.

Brain

The brain has 10×10^{10} nerve cells or neurons interconnected by dendrites or filaments and 10×10^{11} glia. Some of the brain's chemical reactions require only one millionth of a second. After the age of 18 the brain loses some 10^3 cells every day.

Largest. The brain of an average adult male (30–59 years) weighs 3 lbs. 1.73 oz., falling to 2 lbs. 4.31 oz. The heaviest brain ever recorded was that of a 50-year-old white male which weighed 4 lbs. 8.29 oz., reported by Dr. Thomas F. Hegert, Chief Medical Examiner for District 9, State of Florida, October 23, 1975. The brain of Oliver Cromwell (1599–1658) reputedly weighed 4 lbs. 14.8 oz., but the size of his head in portraits does not support this extreme figure. The brain of Lord Byron, who died in Greece in 1824, aged 36, reportedly weighed 6 Neapolitan pounds (4 lbs. 3.86 oz.), but this figure also included a certain amount of blood. In January, 1891, the *Edinburgh Medical Journal* reported a case of a 75-year-old man in the Royal Edinburgh Asylum whose brain weighed 4 lbs. 0.5 oz.

Smallest. The non-atrophied brain of the writer Anatole France (1844–1924) weighed only 35.8 oz. without the membrane. Brains in extreme cases of microcephaly may weigh as little as 10.6 oz. (*cf.* 20 oz. for the adult male gorilla, and 16–20 oz. for other anthropoid apes).

Longest Necks

The maximum measured extension of the neck by the successive fitting of copper coils, as practiced by the Padaung or Karen people of Burma, is 15¾ inches. From the male viewpoint the practice serves the dual purpose of enhancing the beauty of the female and ensuring fidelity. The neck muscles become so atrophied that the removal of the support of the rings produces asphyxiation.

Most Fingers

In 1938, the extreme case of a baby girl with 14 fingers and 12 toes was reported by St. George's Hospital, Hyde Park, London.

Longest Finger Nails

The longest finger nail ever grown is one of 25½ inches, grown in 13 years by Romesh Sharma of Delhi, India, measured on February 15, 1979.

The longest known set of nails now belong to the left hand of Shridhar Chillal, 41, of Poona, India. The 5 nails have been uncut since 1952, and by February 23, 1979, they had reached a total measured length of 92½ inches, including a thumb nail 23.2 inches long. Human nails normally grow from cuticle to cutting length in from 117 to 138 days.

Longest Hair

Swami Pandarasannadhi, the head of the Tirudaduturai monastery, India was reported in 1949 to have hair 26 feet in length. From photographs it appears that he was afflicted with the disease Plica caudiformis. The hair of Jane Bunford (see page 14), which she wore in two plaits, reached down to her ankles, indicating a length in excess of 8 feet.

Longest Moustache

The longest moustache on record was that of Masuriya Din (born 1908), a Brahmin of the Partabgarh district in Uttar Pradesh, India. It grew to an extended span of 102 inches between 1949 and 1962. The longest known moustache on a living man belongs to Karna Ram Bheel (b. 1928), who was granted permission by a New Delhi prison governor in February, 1979, to keep his 7-foot-10-inch moustache, grown since 1949, during his life sentence.

Longest Beard

The longest beard preserved was that of Hans Langseth (1846–1927) of Norway, which measured 17½ feet at the time of his death after 15 years residence in the U.S. The beard was presented to the Smithsonian Institution, Washington, D.C. in 1967.

The beard of the bearded lady Janice Deveree (born in Bracken County, Kentucky, in 1842) was measured at 14 inches in 1884.

Touch Sensitivity

The extreme sensitivity of the fingers is such that a vibration with a movement of 0.02 of a micron can be detected. On January 12, 1963,

LONGEST FINGERNAILS: The nails on the left hand of Shridhar Chillal reached a total length ot 92½ inches in 1979.

the Soviet newspaper *Izvestia* reported the case of a totally blindfolded girl, Rosa Kulgeshova, who was able to identify colors by touch alone. Later reports confirmed in 1970 that under rigorous test conditions this claimed ability totally disappeared.

Commonest Diseases

The commonest non-contagious disease is dental caries or tooth decay, known to afflict over 53 per cent of the population of the U.S. During their lifetime few completely escape its effects. Infestation with pinworm (*Enterobius vermicularis*) approaches 100 per cent in some areas of the world.

The commonest contagious illness in the world is coryza (acute nasopharyngitis) or the common cold.

MOUSTACHE AT LEAST 102 INCHES LONG: The longest moustache on record belongs to Masuriya Din of India.

Rarest Disease

Medical literature periodically records hitherto undescribed diseases. Kuru, or laughing sickness, afflicts only the Fore tribe of eastern New Guinea and is 100 per cent fatal. It is transmitted by the cannibalistic practice of eating human brains.

The only recorded case of congenital agammaglobulinaemia was reported from Houston, Texas, in February, 1972. A disease as yet undescribed but predicted by a Norwegian doctor is podocytoma of the kidney—a tumor of the epithelial cells lining the glomerulus of the kidney.

Highest Mortality

Rabies in humans has been regarded as uniformly fatal when associated with the hydrophobia symptom. A 25-year-old woman, Candida de Sousa Barbosa of Rio de Janeiro, Brazil, was believed to be the first ever to survive the disease in November, 1968. Some sources give priority to Matthew Winkler, 6, on October 10, 1970, who was bitten by a rabid bat. Once common, rabies is now rare.

Most and Least Infectious Diseases

The most infectious of all diseases is the pneumonic form of plague, with a mortality rate of 99.99 per cent. Leprosy transmitted by *Mycobacterium leprae* is the least infectious and most bacilliferous of communicable diseases.

Leading Cause of Death

The leading cause of death in industrialized countries is arteriosclerosis (thickening of the arterial wall), which underlies much coronary and cerebrovascular disease.

Most Notorious Carrier

The most notorious of all typhoid carriers was Mary Mallon, known as Typhoid Mary, of New York City. She was the source of the 1903 outbreak with 1,300 cases. Because of her refusal to leave employment, often under assumed names, involving the handling of food, she was placed under permanent detention from 1915 until her death in 1938.

Parkinson's Disease

The most protracted case of Parkinson's disease is 55 years in the case of Frederick G. Humphries of Croydon, Greater London, England, whose symptoms became detectable in 1923. The disease was named after Dr. James Parkinson's essay of 1817, and the earliest treatments were not published until 1946.

Most Durable Cancer Patient

The most extreme recorded case of survival from diagnosed cancer is that of Mrs. Winona Mildred Melick (*née* Douglass) (b. October 22, 1876) of Long Beach, California. She had four cancer operations, in 1918, 1933, 1966 and 1968, but celebrated her 102nd birthday in 1978.

Blood Groups

The preponderance of one blood group varies greatly from one locality to another. On a world basis Group O is the most common (46 per cent), but in some areas, for example Norway, Group A predominates.

The rarest blood group on the ABO system, one of 14 systems, is AB, which occurs in about 4 per cent of the population. The rarest type in the world is a type of Bombay blood (sub-type A-h) found so far only in a Czechoslovak nurse in 1961 and in a brother (Rh positive) and sister (Rh negative) named Jalbert in Massachusetts, reported in February, 1968. The brother has started a blood bank for himself.

Champion Blood Donor

Ed "Spike" Howard (1877–1946), the professional strongman from Philadelphia, during his life is said to have donated a total of 1,056 pints of blood. The present-day normal limit on donations is 5 pints a year.

Warren C. Jyrich, a 50-year-old hemophiliac, required 2,400 donor units (2,283 pints) of blood when undergoing open heart surgery at the Michael Reese Hospital, Chicago, in December, 1970.

Richest Natural Resources

Joe Thomas of Detroit was reported in August, 1970, to have the highest known count of Anti-Lewis B, the rare blood antibody. A U.S. biological supply firm pays him $1,500 per quart. The Internal Revenue Service regards this income as a taxable liquid asset.

Largest Vein

In the human body, the largest is the vein known as the inferior *vena cava*, which returns most of the blood from the body below the level of the heart.

Longest Coma

The longest recorded coma was that of Elaine Esposito (born December 3, 1934) of Tarpon Springs, Florida. She never stirred after an appendectomy on August 6, 1941, when she was six, in Chicago. She died on November 25, 1978, aged 43 years 357 days, having been in a coma for 37 years 111 days.

Body Temperature

Highest. Sustained body temperatures of much over 109°F. are normally incompatible with life, although recoveries after readings of 111°F. have been noted. Marathon runners in hot weather attain 105.8°F.

In a case reported in the British medical magazine *Lancet* (October 31, 1970), a woman following halothane anesthesia ran a temperature of 112° F. She recovered after a procainamide infusion.

A temperature of 115°F. was recorded in the case of Christopher Legge in the Hospital for Tropical Diseases, London, England, on February 9, 1934. A subsequent examination of the thermometer disclosed a flaw in the bulb, but it is regarded as certain that the patient sustained a temperature of more than 110°F.

Lowest. There are two recorded cases of patients surviving body temperatures as low as 60.8°F. Dorothy Mae Stevens (1929–74) was found in an alley in Chicago on February 1, 1951, and Vickie Mary Davis of Milwaukee, Wisconsin, at age 2 years 1 month was admitted to the Evangelical Hospital, Marshalltown, Iowa, on January 21, 1956, each with a temperature of 60.8°F. The little girl had been found unconscious on the floor of an unheated house and the air temperature had dropped to —24°F. Her temperature returned to normal (98.4°F.) after 12 hours and may have been as low as 59°F. when she was first found.

Pulse Rate

A normal adult pulse rate is 70–72 beats per minute at rest for males, and 78–82 for females. This can increase to 200 or more during violent exercise or drop to as low as 12 in the extreme case of Dorothy Mae Stevens (see Lowest Body Temperature).

Heart Stoppage

The longest recorded heart stoppage is a minimum of 3 hours 32 minutes in the case of Miss Jean Jawbone, 20, who was revived by a team of 26, using peritoneal dialysis, in Winnipeg Medical Centre, Manitoba, Canada, on January 19, 1977.

In February, 1974, Vegard Slettmoen, 5, fell through the ice on the River Nitselv, Norway. He was found 40 minutes later, 8 feet down, but was revived in Akerhaus Sentral Hospital without brain damage.

The longest recorded interval in a post-mortem birth was one of at least 80 minutes in Magnolia, Mississippi. Dr. Robert E. Drake found Fanella Anderson, aged 25, dead in her home at 11:40 p.m. on October 15, 1966, and he delivered her of a son weighing 6 lbs. 4 oz. by Caesarean operation in the Beacham Memorial Hospital at 1 a.m. on October 16, 1966.

Largest Stone

The largest stone or vesical calculus reported in medical literature was one of 13 lbs. 14 oz., removed from an 80-year-old woman by Dr. Humphrey Arthure at Charing Cross Hospital, London, England, on December 29, 1952.

Fastest Reflexes

The results of experiments published in 1966 have shown that the fastest messages transmitted by the human nervous system travel as fast as 180 m.p.h. With advancing age, impulses are carried 15 per cent more slowly.

Most Alcoholic Person

It is recorded that a hard drinker named Vanhorn (1750–1811), born in London, England, averaged more than four bottles of ruby port per day for 23 years prior to his death at 61. He is believed to have emptied 35,688 bottles.

The youngest recorded death from alcoholic poisoning was that of a 4-year-old boy, Joseph Sweet, in Wolverhampton, England, in 1827, reported in the Stafford Assizes case *R. v. Martin.*

HEART STOPPAGE:
Vegard Slettmoen survived a
40-minute submersion in the icy
waters of the Nitselv River
in Norway.

Hiccoughing

The longest recorded attack of hiccoughs is that afflicting
Charles Osborne (b. 1894) of Anthon, Iowa, from 1922 to date. He
contracted it when slaughtering a hog. His first wife left him and he
is unable to keep in his false teeth.

The infirmary at Newcastle upon Tyne, England, is recorded to
have admitted a young man from Long Witton, Northumberland,
on March 25, 1769, suffering from hiccoughs which were reportedly
audible at a range of more than a mile.

Sneezing

The most chronic sneezing fit ever recorded was that of June
Clark, aged 17, of Miami, Florida. She started sneezing on January
4, 1966, while recovering from a kidney ailment in the James M.
Jackson Memorial Hospital, Miami. The sneezing was stopped by
electric "aversion" treatment on June 8, 1966, after 155 days. The
highest speed at which expelled particles have been measured to
travel is 103.6 m.p.h.

Loudest Snore

Research at the Ear, Nose and Throat Department of St. Mary's
Hospital, London, published in November, 1968, shows that a
rasping snore can attain a loudness of 69 decibels, as compared to
70 to 90 decibels for a pneumatic drill.

Yawning

In a case reported in 1888, a 15-year-old female patient yawned
continuously for a period of five weeks.

Swallowing

The worst reported case of compulsive swallowing was an insane woman, Mrs. H., aged 42, who complained of a "slight abdominal pain." She was found to have 2,533 objects in her stomach, including 947 bent pins. They were removed by Drs. Chalk and Foucar in June, 1927, at the Ontario Hospital, Canada.

The heaviest object ever extracted from a human stomach was a 5-lb. 3-oz. ball of hair, from a 20-year-old woman at the South Devon and East Cornwall Hospital, England, on March 30, 1895.

Sword "Swallowing"

The longest length of sword able to be "swallowed" by a practiced exponent, after a heavy meal, is 27 inches. Alex Linton (born in Ireland on October 25, 1904, later from Sarasota, Florida) has swallowed four 27-inch blades at one time.

King Daredevil (real name Larsson) swallowed nine 23-inch blades below the xiphisternum.

Pill Taking

The highest recorded total of pills swallowed by a patient is 331,211 from June 9, 1967 to January 1, 1979, by C. H. A. Kilner (born 1926) of Malawi, following a successful pancreatectomy.

Most Injections

Mrs. Evelyn Ruth Winder, a diabetic from Invercargill, New Zealand, injected herself with insulin an estimated 52,730 times over 48 years to May, 1979.

Most Tattoos

Vivian "Sailor Joe" Simmons, a Canadian tattoo artist, had 4,831 tattoos on his body. He died in Toronto on December 22, 1965, aged 77. George Zastrow of Justice, Illinois, is believed to be the most illustrious example of the art now living.

The most decorated woman is Rusty Skuse (née Field) (born 1944) of Aldershot, Hampshire, England, who, after 12 years under the needle of tattoo artist Bill Skuse, came within 15 per cent of totality. He stated that he always had designs on her. (See photo, page B.)

Dentition

Earliest. The first deciduous or milk teeth normally appear in infants at five to eight months, these being the mandibular and maxillary first incisors. There are many records of children born with teeth, the most distinguished example being Prince Louis Dieudonné, later Louis XIV of France, who was born with two teeth on September 5, 1638. Molars usually appear at 24 months, but in Pindborg's case published in Denmark in 1970, a 6-week premature baby was documented with 8 natal teeth of which 4 were in the molar region.

Most. Cases of the growth in late life of a third set of teeth have been recorded several times. A reference to an extreme case in

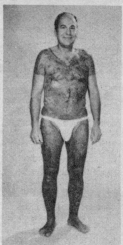

HUMAN FLAMETHROWER (above): Fire-eater Jack Sholomir extended his record to 23 feet of flame in 1977. ILLUSTRATED MAN (right): George Zastrow models his tattoo "suit" with 130 individual designs and extensive scrollwork.

France of a fourth dentition known as Lison's case was published in 1896. A triple row of teeth was noted in 1680 by Albertus Hellwigius.

Most Dedicated Dentist. Brother Giovanni Battista Orsenigo of the Ospedale Fatebenefratelli, Rome, Italy, a religious dentist, conserved all the teeth he extracted in three enormous boxes during the time he exercised his profession from 1868 to 1904. In 1903, the number was counted and found to be 2,000,744 teeth.

Fire-Eating

Jack Sholomir of Great Britain blew a flame from his mouth to a distance of 23 feet at the Eardisley & District Royal Legion Stampede at Kinnersley, Hereford and Worcester, England, on June 6, 1977.

Mrs. Jean Chapman successively extinguished 1,921 flaming torches in her mouth in 120 minutes on October 29, 1977 in Stoke Poges, Buckinghamshire, England. (See photo, page B.) Fire-eating is potentially a highly dangerous activity.

Fire-Walking

The highest temperature endured in a fire-walk is 1,494°F. by "Komar" (Vernon E. Craig) of Wooster, Ohio, at the International Festival of Yoga and Esoteric Sciences, Maidenhead, England, on August 14, 1976. The temperature was measured with a pyrometer.

Smallest Visible Object

The resolving power of the human eye is 0.0003 of a radian or an arc of one minute (1/60th of a degree), which corresponds to 100

microns at 10 inches. A micron is a thousandth of a millimeter, hence 100 microns is 0.003937, or less than four thousandths of an inch. The human eye can, however, detect a bright light source shining through an aperture of only 3 to 4 microns across. In October, 1972, the University of Stuttgart, West Germany reported that their student Veronica Seider (b. 1953) possessed a visual acuity 20 times better than average. She could identify people at a distance of more than a mile.

Color Sensitivity

The unaided human eye, under the best possible viewing conditions, comparing large areas of color, in good illumination, using both eyes, can distinguish 10,000,000 different color surfaces. The most accurate photo-electric spectrophotometers possess a precision probably only 40 per cent as good as this.

Color Blindness. The most extreme form of color blindness, monochromatic vision, is very rare. The highest rate of red-green color blindness exists in Czechoslovakia and the lowest rate among Fijians and Brazilian Indians. About 7.5 per cent of men and 0.1 per cent of women are color blind.

Voice

Highest and Lowest. The highest and lowest recorded notes attained by the human voice before this century were a staccato E in *alt-altissimo* (*e''''*) by Ellen Beach Yaw (U.S., 1869–1947) in Carnegie Hall, New York City, on January 19, 1896, and an *A'* (55 cycles per second) by Kaspar Foster (1617–73). Since 1950 singers have achieved high and low notes far beyond the hitherto accepted extremes. Notes, however, at the bass and treble extremities of the register tend to lack harmonics and are of little musical value. Fräulein Marita Günther, trained by Alfred Wolfsohn, has covered the range of the piano from the lowest note *A"* to *č''''*. Of this range of 7¼ octaves, 6 octaves are considered to be of musical value. Mr.

Roy Hart, also trained by Wolfsohn, has reached notes below the range of the piano. Barry Girard of Canton, Ohio, reachéd the e (4,340 Hz) above the piano's top note in May, 1975.

Madeleine Marie Robin (1918–60), the French operatic coloratura, could produce and sustain the B flat above high C in the Lucia mad scene in *Lucia di Lammermoor*.

The lowest note put into song is D'' by the singer Tom King, of King's Langley, Hertfordshire, England. The highest note put into song is G'''' twice occurring in *Popoli di Tessaglia* by Mozart.

Stephan Zucker sang A in *alt-altissimo* for 3.8 seconds in the tenor role of Salvini in the world premiere of Bellini's *Adelson e Salvini* in Carnegie Hall, New York City, on September 12, 1972.

Greatest Range. The normal intelligible outdoor range of the male human voice in still air is 200 yards. The *silbo*, the whistled language of the Spanish-speaking Canary Island of La Gomera, is intelligible across the valleys, under ideal conditions, at 5 miles. There is a recorded case, under freak acoustic conditions, of the human voice being detectable at a distance of $10\frac{1}{2}$ miles across still water at night. It was said that Mills Darden (see Heaviest Man) could be heard 6 miles away when he shouted at the top of his voice.

Lowest Detectable Sound. The intensity of noise or sound is measured in terms of pressure. The pressure of the quietest sound that can be detected by a person of normal hearing at the most sensitive frequency of *c.* 2,750 Hz (cycles per second) is 2×10^{-5} pascal. One tenth of the logarithm to this standard provides a unit termed a decibel. Prolonged noise above 150 decibels will cause immediate permanent deafness while 200 decibels may be fatal. A noise of 30 decibels is negligible.

Highest Detectable Pitch. The upper limit of hearing by the human ear has been regarded as 20,000 Hz (cycles per second), although children with asthma can often detect a sound of 30,000 cycles per second. It was announced in February, 1964, that experiments in the U.S.S.R. had conclusively proved that oscillations as high as 200,000 cycles per second can be heard if the oscillator is pressed against the skull.

Shouting. At the "World" Shouting Competition at Scarborough, Yorkshire, England, held on February 17, 1973, the title was taken by Skipper Kenny Leader with 111 decibels at a distance of $2\frac{1}{2}$ meters. Mrs. Grace Hall hit the feminine record of 110 decibels on November 19, 1976 at Exeter, Devon, England.

Longest Survival in Iron Lung

The longest recorded survival by an iron lung patient is 31 years 9 months by Howard Lee Hale (born 1912) of Crockett, Virginia, from August, 1944, until his death on May 10, 1976.

Operations

Longest. The most protracted operations are those involving brain surgery. Such an operation lasting 31 hours was performed on Victor Zazueta, 19, of El Centro at San Diego Hospital, California, by Drs. John F. Alksne and Randall Smith on January 17–18, 1972.

Most Major. On August 20, 1975, Charles Hill (born 1914) of Sydney, Australia, underwent his 87th major operation. Most of the surgery has been abdominal.

Oldest Subject. The greatest recorded age at which a person has been subjected to an operation is 111 years 105 days in the case of James Henry Brett, Jr. (born July 25, 1849, died February 10, 1961) of Houston, Texas. He underwent a hip operation on November 7, 1960.

Heart Transplants

The first human heart transplant operation was performed on Louis Washkansky, aged 55, at the Groote Schuur Hospital, Capetown, South Africa, between 1:00 and 6:00 a.m. on December 3, 1967, by a team of 30 headed by Prof. Christiaan N. Barnard (born 1922). The donor was Miss Denise Ann Darvall, aged 25. Washkansky died on December 21, 1967.

The longest surviving heart transplant patient has been Emmanuel Vitria, 57, of Marseilles, France, who received a heart transplant on November 28, 1968, and entered the tenth year of his new life in 1977.

Kidney Transplants

R. H. Lawler (b. 1895, U.S.) performed the first transplantation of a human kidney in 1950. The longest survival, as between identical twins, has been 20 years.

Laryngectomy

On July 24, 1924, John I. Poole of Plymouth, England, then aged 33, after diagnosis of carcinoma, underwent total laryngectomy in Edinburgh, Scotland. In July, 1978, he entered his 55th year as a "neck-breather."

Earliest Appendectomy

The earliest recorded successful appendix operation was performed in 1736 by Claudius Amyand (1680–1740). He was Serjeant Surgeon to King George II (reigned 1727–60) of Great Britain.

Earliest Anesthesia

The earliest recorded operation under general anesthesia was for the removal of a cyst from the neck of James Venable by Dr. Crawford Williamson Long (1815–78), using diethyl ether ($(C_2 H_5)_2$ O), in Jefferson, Georgia, on March 30, 1842.

Surgical Instruments

The longest surgical instruments are bronchoscopic forceps which measure up to $23\frac{1}{2}$ inches over-all. Robot-retractors for abdominal surgery made by Abbey Surgical of England weigh 11 lbs. The smallest is Elliot's eye trephine which has a blade 0.078 of an inch in diameter, and "straight" stapes picks with a needle-type tip or blade 0.013 inches long.

Fastest Amputation

The shortest time recorded for the amputation of a leg in the pre-anesthetic era was 13 to 15 seconds by Napoleon's chief surgeon, Dominique Larrey. There could have been no ligation.

Fasting

Most humans experience considerable discomfort after an abstinence from food for even 12 hours, but this often passes off after 24–48 hours. Records claimed without unremitting medical surveillance are of little value.

The longest period for which anyone has gone without solid food is 382 days by Angus Barbieri (born 1940) of Tayport, Fife, Scotland. He lived on tea, coffee, water, soda water and vitamins from June, 1965, to July, 1966, in Maryfield Hospital, Dundee, Angus, Scotland. His weight declined from 472 lbs. to 178 lbs.

Sister Therese Neumann survived 35 years on the "bread" of the Holy Eucharist at mass each morning at Konnersreuth, Germany.

The longest recorded case of survival without food *and* water is at least 321 hours (13 days 9 hours) by U.S. Army Privates Randy Boutaain and Dennis E. Feathers, stowaways in Container No. 303454 aboard S.S. *Sea-Land Economy* from Rotterdam, Netherlands, to Houston, Texas, December 7–22, 1977.

Hunger Strike

The longest recorded hunger strike was one of 94 days by John and Peter Crowley, Thomas Donovan, Michael Burke, Michael O'Reilly, Christopher Upton, John Power, Joseph Kenny and Sean Hennessy in Cork Prison, Ireland, from August 11 to November 12, 1920. These nine survivors owed their lives to expert medical attention.

Fastest Talker

Extremely few people are able to speak *articulately* at a sustained speed above 300 words per minute. The fastest broadcaster has usually been allowed to be Gerry Wilmot, the Canadian ice hockey commentator in the post World War II period. Raymond Glendenning (1907–74) of the British Broadcasting Corp. once spoke 176 words in 30 seconds while commentating on a greyhound race. In public life the highest speed recorded is a 327-words-per-minute burst in a speech made in December, 1961, by John Fitzgerald Kennedy (1917–63), then President of the U.S. Tapes of attempts to recite Hamlet's 262-word soliloquy in under 24 seconds (655 w.p.m.) have proved indecipherable. Patricia Keeling-Andrich delivered 403 words from W. S. Gilbert's "The Nightmare" in a test in 60 seconds at Chabot College, Hayward, California, on March 16, 1978.

Human Memory

Mehmed Ali Halici of Ankara, Turkey, on October 14, 1967, recited 6,666 verses of the Koran from memory in six hours. The recitation was followed by six Koran scholars. Rare instances of eidetic memory, the ability to reproject and thus "visually" recall material, are known to science.

HUMAN COMPUTER: Willem Klein of the Netherlands took only 3 minutes 51 seconds to extract the 13th root of a 100-digit number in 1978.

Highest I.Q.

On the Terman index for Intelligence Quotients, 150 represents genius level. The indices are sometimes held to be immeasurable above a level of 200, but a figure of 210 has been attributed to Kim Ung-Yong of Seoul, South Korea (born March 7, 1963). He composed poetry and spoke four languages (Korean, English, German and Japanese), and performed integral calculus at the age of 4 years 8 months on television in Tokyo on "The World Surprise Show" on November 2, 1967. Both his parents are university professors and were both born at 11 a.m. on May 23, 1934. The International Society for Philosophical Enquiry has 140 members, of whom 22 per cent have an I.Q. above 160 and none below 148. Only 100 persons in a million have I.Q.s above 160.

The highest mean I.Q. published for a national population is 106.6 for the Japanese.

Human Computer

The fastest extraction of a 13th root from a 100-digit number is in 3 minutes 51 seconds by Willem Klein (b. 1914, Netherlands) in Stockholm, Sweden, on November 8, 1978.

Memorizing Pi

The greatest number of places to which π (Pi) has been memorized and recited is 15,151 by Hideaki Tomoyori, an electronics company worker from Yokohama, Japan, on June 4, 1979. (Note: The approximation of π at $\frac{22}{7}$ repeats after its sixth decimal place and can, of course, be recited *ad nauseam*. It deviates from the true value after only the second decimal place.)

Isolation

The longest recorded period for which any volunteer has been able to withstand total deprivation of all sensory stimulation (sight, hearing and touch) is 92 hours, recorded in 1962 at Lancaster Moor Hospital, England.

The farthest distance that any human has been isolated from all other humans has been when the lone pilots of the lunar command modules were antipodal to their Apollo missions, 2,200 miles away.

Motionlessness

The longest that any person has voluntarily remained motionless is 6 hours 31 minutes by William Fuqua at Dillard's Department Store, Fort Worth, Texas on July 22, 1978.

Staff Sgt. Samuel B. Moody, U.S.A.F., was punished by being forced to stand at attention for 53 hours in Narumi prison camp, Nagoya, Japan, in the spring of 1945. He survived to write *Reprieve from Hell.*

Highest Temperature Endured

The highest dry-air temperature endured by naked men in U.S. Air Force experiments in 1960 was 400°F. and for heavily clothed men 500°F. (Steaks require only 325°F.) Temperatures of 284°F. have been found quite bearable in sauna baths.

Longest Dream

Dreaming sleep is characterized by rapid eye movements (called REM). The longest recorded period of REM is 2 hours 23 minutes, set by Bill Carskadon on February 15, 1967, at the Department of

LIVING STATUE: William Fuqua (right) required the services of a bodyguard in his 1978 record attempt. In a 1975 personal appearance he was stabbed in the back by a man who could not believe that he was real.

Psychology, University of Illinois, Chicago. His previous sleep had been interrupted.

Sleeplessness

Researches indicate that the peak of efficiency is attained between 8 p.m. and 9 p.m., and the low comes at 4 a.m.

The longest recorded period for which a person has voluntarily gone without sleep is 449 hours (18 days 17 hours) by Mrs. Maureen Weston of Peterborough, England, in a rocking chair marathon from April 14 to May 2, 1977. Though she tended to hallucinate toward the end of this surely ill-advised test, surprisingly, she suffered no lasting aftereffects.

Extrasensory Perception

The highest consistent performer in tests to detect powers of extrasensory perception is Pavel Stepánek (Czechoslovakia), known in parapsychological circles as "P.S." His performance in correctly naming hidden white or green cards from May, 1967, to March, 1968, departed from a chance probability yielding a Chi^2 value corresponding to $P < 10^{-50}$ or odds of more than 100 octillion to one against the achievement being one of chance. One of the two appointed referees recommended that the results should not be published.

The highest published scores in any E.S.P. test were those of a 26-year-old female tested by Prof. Bernard F. Reiss of Hunter College, New York City, in 1936. In 74 runs of 25 guesses each, she scored one with 25 all correct, two with 24, and an average of 18.24, as against a random score of 5.00. Such a result would depart from chance probability by a factor $>10^{700}$. This produced the comment that there might be a defect in the theory of probability.

EXTRAORDINARY EXTRASENSORY PERCEPTION: Pavel Stepánek of Czechoslovakia named hidden cards' colors for almost a year, and the results were 100 octillion times better than chance.

G FORCE SURVIVAL: David Purley is shown here seated on the wreckage of the race car he was driving at 108 m.p.h. when he crashed, stopping in a distance of 26 inches.

g Forces

The acceleration due to gravity (g) is 32 feet 1.05 inches per second per second at sea level at the Equator. A *sustained* force of 25 g was withstood in a dry capsule during astronautic research by Dr. Carter Collins of California.

The highest g force endured was 82.6 g for 0.04 of a second on a water-braked rocket sled by Eli L. Beeding, Jr., at Holloman Air Force Base, New Mexico, on May 16, 1958. He was put in the hospital for three days.

Race car driver David Purley survived a deceleration from 108 m.p.h. to zero in 26 inches in a crash at the Silverstone circuit, Northamptonshire, England, on July 13, 1977, which involved a g force of 180.

A man who fell off a 185-foot cliff has survived a *momentary* g force of 209 in decelerating from 68 m.p.h. to stationary in 0.015 of a second.

The land divers of Pentecost Island, New Hebrides, dive from 70-foot-high platforms with liana vines attached to their ankles. The resulting jerk can transmit a momentary force in excess of 100 g.

Underwater

The world record for voluntarily staying underwater is 13 minutes 42.5 seconds by Robert Foster, aged 32, an electronics technician of Richmond, California, who stayed under 10 feet of water in the swimming pool of the Bermuda Palms at San Rafael, California,

UNDERWATER LONGEST: Robert L. Foster of California, while he held his breath for a record 13 minutes 42½ seconds in a swimming pool. Record-breaking of this kind is extremely dangerous.

on March 15, 1959. He hyperventilated with oxygen for 30 minutes before his descent. It must be stressed that record-breaking of this kind is *extremely* dangerous.

Electric Shock

Excluding lightning bolts, the highest reported voltage electric shock survived was one of 230,000 volts by Brian Latasa, 17, on the tower of an ultra-high-voltage power line in Griffith Park, Los Angeles, November 9, 1967. Highly insulated individuals have touched 1,200,000-volt cables in barehand live cable work without harm.

Most Durable "Ghosts"

Ghosts are not immortal and, according to the *Gazetteer of British Ghosts*, seem to deteriorate after 400 years. The most outstanding exceptions to this normal "half-life" are the ghosts of Roman soldiers three times reported still marching through the cellars of the Treasurer's House, York Minster, England, after nearly 19 centuries. The book's author, Peter Underwood, states that Britain has more reported ghosts per square mile than any other country with Borley Rectory near Long Melford, Suffolk, the site of unrivaled activity between 1863 and its destruction by fire in 1939.

Chapter Two

THE ANIMAL AND PLANT KINGDOMS

ANIMAL KINGDOM (ANIMALIA)

Largest and Heaviest Animal

The largest and heaviest animal is the blue or sulphur-bottom whale (*Balaenoptera musculus*), also called Sibbald's rorqual. The largest accurately measured specimen on record was a female landed at the Cia Argentina de Pesca shore station, South Georgia, *c.* 1904–20 which measured 110 feet $2\frac{1}{2}$ inches in length. Another female measuring $96\frac{3}{4}$ feet brought into the shore station at Prince Olaf, South Georgia, Falkland Islands, off Argentina, in *c.* 1931 was calculated to have weighed 183.34 tons, exclusive of blood, judging by the number of cookers that were filled by the animal's blubber, meat and bones. The total weight of the whale was believed to have been 195 tons. On the principle that the weight should vary as the cube of the linear dimensions, a 100-foot blue whale in good condition should weigh about 179 tons, but in the case of pregnant females the weight could be as much as 200 or more tons, equivalent to 35 adult bull African elephants.

BIGGEST BEAST: Blue whales have been accurately measured at over 110 feet in length and weighing nearly 200 tons. This life-sized model measures 92 feet long.

Longest Animal

The longest animal ever recorded is the ribbon worm *Lineus longissimus*, also known as the "boot-lace worm," which is found in the shallow coastal waters of the North Sea. In 1864 a specimen measuring more than 180 feet was washed ashore at St. Andrews, Fifeshire, Scotland, after a storm.

Tallest Animal

The tallest living animal is the giraffe (*Giraffa camelopardalis*), which is now found only in the dry savannah and semi-desert areas of Africa south of the Sahara. The tallest ever recorded was a Masai bull (*G. camelopardalis tippelskirchi*) named "George," received at Chester Zoo, England on January 8, 1959 from Kenya. His head *almost* touched the roof of the 20-foot-high Giraffe House when he was 9 years old. George died on July 22, 1969. Less credible heights of up to 23 feet between taxidermist's pegs have been claimed for bulls shot in the field.

Longest-Lived Animal

Few non-bacterial creatures live longer than humans. It would appear that tortoises are the longest-lived such animals. The greatest authentic age recorded for a tortoise is 152-plus years for a male Marion's tortoise (*Testudo sumeirii*), brought from the Seychelles to Mauritius in 1766 by the Chevalier de Fresne, who presented it to the Port Louis army garrison. This specimen (it went blind in 1908) was accidentally killed in 1918. When the famous Royal Tongan tortoise "Tu'malilia" (believed to be a specimen of *Testudo radiata*)

TALLEST ANIMAL: George, the tallest giraffe ever held in captivity, liked to lick the telephone lines which ran past his pen, disrupting the system. Officials had to raise the wires.

MOST VALUABLE ANIMAL:
After his Triple Crown triumph in 1978, *Affirmed* was sold in syndication for a record $14.4 million.

died on May 19, 1966, it was reputed to be over 200 years old, having been presented to the then King of Tonga by Captain James Cook (1728–79) on October 22, 1773, but this record may well have been compiled from two (or more) overlapping residents.

The bacteria *Thermoactinomyces vulgaris* has been found alive in cores of mud taken from the bottom of Windermere Lake, northern England, which have been dated to 1,500 years before the present.

Fastest Flying Animal

The fastest reliably measured speed of any animal is 106.25 m.p.h. (air) for a spine-tailed swift (*Chaetura caudacuta*), reported from the U.S.S.R. in 1942. In 1934, ground speeds ranging from 171.8 to 219.5 m.p.h. were recorded by stopwatch for spine-tailed swifts over a 2-mile course in the Cachar Hills of northeastern India, but scientific tests since have revealed that this species of bird cannot be seen at a distance of 1 mile, even with standard binoculars. This bird is the fastest-moving living creature and has a blood temperature of 112.5°F. Speeds even higher than a free-fall maximum of 185 m.p.h. have been ascribed to peregrine falcons (*Falco peregrinus*) in a stoop, but in recent experiments in which miniature air speedometers were fitted, the maximum recorded diving speed was 82 m.p.h.

Most Valuable

The most valuable animals in cash terms are thoroughbred race horses. It was announced in November, 1978, that Triple Crown winner *Affirmed* would be syndicated for $14.4 million. The most valuable zoo exhibits are Giant Pandas (*Ailuropoda melanoleuca*) for which the San Diego Zoological Gardens offered $250,000 in 1971 for a fertile pair. The most valuable marine exhibit is the killer whale (*Orcinus orca*). In September, 1975, the 6,500 lb. female "Newtka" was flown from Dallas, Texas, to Niagara Falls insured for $150,000.

LARGEST FISH EGG: This unique photograph shows the young and the egg of the largest fish, the whale shark, which weighs as much as 45 tons when fully grown.

Commonest Animal

It is estimated that man shares the earth with 3×10^{33} (or 3 followed by 33 zeros) other living things. The number of nematode sea-worms, probably the commonest animal, has been estimated at 4×10^{25}.

Rarest Animal

The best claimants to the title of the world's rarest land animal are those species which are known only from a single (type) specimen. One of these is the tenrec *Dasogale fontoynonti*, which is known only from the specimen collected in eastern Madagascar (Malagasy Republic) and now preserved in the Paris (France) Museum of Natural History.

Longest Gestation

The viviparous amphibian Alpine black salamander (*Salamandra atra*) can have a gestation period of up to 38 months when living above 4,600 feet in the Swiss Alps, but this drops to 24–26 months at lower altitudes.

Fastest and Slowest Growth

The fastest growth in the animal kingdom is that of the blue whale calf. A barely visible ovum weighing 0.000035 of an ounce grows to a weight of *c.* 29 tons in $22\frac{3}{4}$ months, made up of $10\frac{3}{4}$

months gestation and the first 12 months of age. This is equivalent to an increase of 30,000 million fold.

The slowest growth in the animal kingdom is that of the deep-sea clam (*Tindaria callistiformis*) of the North Atlantic, which takes an estimated 100 years to reach a length of 0.31 inches (8 mm.).

Largest Egg

The largest egg of any living animal is that of the whale shark (*Rhiniodon typus*). One egg case measuring 12 inches by 5.5 inches by 3.5 inches was picked up by the shrimp trawler "Doris" on June 29, 1953, at a depth of 186 feet in the Gulf of Mexico, 130 miles south of Port Isabel, Texas. The egg contained a perfect embryo of a whale shark 13.78 inches long.

Greatest Size Difference Between Sexes

The largest female deep-sea angler fish of the species *Ceratias holboelki* on record weighed half a million times as much as the smallest known parasitic male. It has been suggested that this fish would make an appropriate emblem for Women's Lib.

Heaviest Brain

The sperm whale (*Physeter catodon*) has the heaviest brain of all living animals. The brain of a 49-foot-long bull processed aboard the Japanese factory ship *Nissin Maru No. 1* in the Antarctic on December 11, 1949, weighed 9,200 grams (20.24 lbs.), compared to 6,900 grams (15.38 lbs.) for a 90-foot blue whale. The heaviest brain recorded for an elephant was an exceptional 16.5 lbs. in the case of a 2.17-ton Asiatic cow. The normal brain weight for an adult African bull is 9¼–12 lbs.

Largest Eye

The giant squid *Architeuthis sp.* has the largest eye of any living animal. The ocular diameter may exceed 15 inches, compared to less than 12 inches for a 33⅓-r.p.m. long-playing record.

Highest g Force

The highest g force encountered in nature is the 400 g *averaged* by the click beetle (*Athous haemorrhoidalis*), a common British species, when jackknifing into the air to escape predators. One example measuring 0.47 inch in length and weighing 0.00014 ounce which jumped to a height of 11¾ inches was calculated to have endured a peak brain deceleration of 2,300 g at the end of the movement.

1. Mammals (Mammalia)

Largest and Heaviest is the blue whale (see page 55). One whale, a female taken by the *Slava* whaling fleet of the U.S.S.R. in the Antarctic on March 17, 1947, measured 90 feet 8 inches in length. Its tongue and heart weighed 4.73 tons and 1,540 lbs. respectively.

Blue whales inhabit the colder seas and migrate to warmer waters in winter for breeding. Observations made in the Antarctic in

1947–8 showed that a blue whale can maintain speeds of 20 knots (23 m.p.h.) for 10 minutes when frightened. This means a 90-foot blue whale traveling at 20 knots would develop 520 horsepower. The young measure up to 28.5 feet long at birth and weigh up to 3.1 tons.

It has been estimated that there were between 17,500 and 19,000 blue whales living throughout the oceans in 1977. The species has been protected *de jure* since 1967 although non-member countries of the International Whaling Commission (Chile and Peru) are not bound by this agreement.

The greatest recorded depth to which a whale has dived is 620 fathoms (3,720 feet) by a 47-foot bull sperm whale (*Physeter catodon*) found with his jaw entangled with a submarine cable running between Santa Elena, Ecuador, and Chorillos, Peru, on October 14, 1955. At this depth he withstood a pressure of 1,680 lbs. per square inch.

On August 25, 1969, a sperm whale was killed 100 miles south of Durban, South Africa, after it had surfaced from a dive lasting 1 hour 52 minutes, and inside its stomach were found two small sharks which had been swallowed about an hour earlier. These were later identified as *Scymnodon sp.*, a species found only on the sea floor. At this point from land the depth of water is in excess of 1,646 fathoms (10,476 feet) for a radius of 30–40 miles, which now suggests that the sperm whale sometimes may descend to a depth of over 10,000 feet when seeking food.

Largest on Land. The largest living land animal is the African bush elephant (*Loxodonta africana africana*). The average adult bull stands 10 feet 6 inches at the shoulder and weighs $6\frac{1}{2}$ tons. The largest specimen ever recorded, and the largest land animal of modern times, was a bull shot 25 miles north-northeast of Mucusso, southern Angola, on November 7, 1974. Lying on its side this elephant measured 13 feet 8 inches in a projected line from the highest point of the shoulder to the base of the forefoot, indicating that its standing height must have been about 13 feet. Other measurements included an over-all length of 35 feet (tip of extended trunk to tip of extended tail) and a forefoot circumference of 5 feet 11 inches. The weight was computed to be 26,328 lbs. (see also Shooting, Chapter 12).

Smallest. The smallest recorded mammal is the rare Kitti's hog-nosed bat (*Craseonycteris thonglongyai*) or bumblebee bat, which is restricted to two caves near the forestry station at Ban Sai Yoke on the Kwae Noi River, Kanchanaburi, Thailand. Mature specimens of both sexes have a wing span of about 6.29 inches and weigh between 0.062 and 0.071 oz.

The smallest totally marine mammal is probably Heaviside's dolphin (*Caephalorhynchus heavisidei*) of the South Atlantic. Adult specimens have an average length of 4 feet and weigh up to 90 lbs. The sea otter (*Enhydra lutris*) is even smaller, weighing from 55 to 81.4 lbs., but this species sometimes comes ashore during storms.

Fastest. The fastest of all land animals over a short distance (*i.e.* up to 600 yards) is the cheetah or hunting leopard (*Acinonyx*

FASTEST AND SLOWEST MAMMALS: The cheetah (left) has been clocked at over 60 m.p.h., a figure 353 times faster than the top speed attained by the three-toed sloth (right).

jubatus) of the open plains of East Africa, Iran, Turkmenia and Afghanistan, with a probable maximum speed of 60–63 m.p.h. over suitably level ground. Speeds of 71, 84 and even 90 m.p.h. have been claimed for this animal, but these figures must be considered exaggerated. Tests in London in 1937 showed that on an oval greyhound track over 345 yards a female cheetah's average speed over three runs was 43.4 m.p.h. (compare with 43.26 m.p.h. for the fastest race horse), but this specimen was not running at its best.

The fastest land animal over a sustained distance (*i.e.* 1,000 yards or more) is the pronghorn antelope (*Antilocapra americana*) of the western United States. Specimens have been observed to travel at 35 m.p.h. for 4 miles, at 42 m.p.h. for 1 mile and 55 m.p.h. for half a mile. On August 14, 1936, at Spanish Lake, Lake County, Oregon, a hard-pressed buck was timed by a car speedometer at 61 m.p.h. over 200 yards.

Slowest. The slowest moving land mammal is the ai or three-toed sloth (*Bradypus tridactylus*) of tropical America. The usual ground speed is 6 to 8 feet a minute (0.068 to 0.098 m.p.h.), but in the trees it can "accelerate" to 15 feet a minute (0.170 m.p.h.). (Compare these figures with the 0.03 m.p.h. of the common garden snail and the 0.17 m.p.h. of the giant tortoise.)

Tallest is the giraffe (see page 56).

Longest-Lived. No other mammal can match the proven age of 114 years attained by man (*Homo sapiens*). It is probable that the closest approach is among blue and fin whales (*Balaenoptera musculus* and *B. physalas*). Studies of the annual growth layers or laminations found in the wax-like plug deposited in the outer ear indicate a maximum life span of 90–100 years.

The longest-lived land mammal, excluding man, is the Asiatic elephant (*Elephas maximus*). The greatest age that has been verified with certainty is 70 years in the case of a bull timber elephant "Kyaw Thee" (Tuskar 1342), who died in the Taunggyi Forest division, southern Shan States, Burma, in 1965. The age of 78 years attributed to "Modoc," the circus cow elephant, who died in Santa Clara, California, on July 17, 1975, has not yet been fully authenticated.

Rarest Mammal. The rarest placental mammal is the tenrec *Dasogale fontoynonti* (see page 58). Among subspecies, the Javan tiger (*Panthera tigris sondaica*) was reduced to 4 or 5 specimens by 1977, all of them in the Meru Betiri reserve in eastern Java. The Arabian oryx (*Oryx leucoryx*) has not been reported in the wild since 3 were killed and 4 captured in South Oman in 1972.

Longest Hibernation. The common dormouse (*Glis glis*) spends more time in true hibernation than any other mammal. The hibernation usually lasts between 5 and 6 months (October to April), but there is a record of an English specimen sleeping for 6 months 23 days without interruption.

Highest Living. The highest-living wild mammal in the world is probably the yak (*Bos grunniens*), of Tibet and the Szechwanese Alps, China, which occasionally, when foraging, climbs to an altitude of 20,000 feet. The Bharal (*Pseudois nayaur*) and the Pika or Mouse hare (*Ochotona thibetana*) may also reach this height in the Himalayas. In 1890, the tracks of an elephant were found at 15,000 feet on Mt. Kilimanjaro, Tanzania.

Largest Herd. The largest herds on record were those of the South African springbok (*Antidorcas marsupialis*) during migration in the 19th century. In 1849, Sir John Fraser of Bloemfontein reported seeing a herd that took three days to pass through the settlement of Beaufort West, Cape Province. Another herd seen in the same province in 1888 was estimated to contain 100,000,000 head, although 10,000,000 is probably a more realistic figure. A herd estimated to be 15 miles wide and more than 100 miles long was reported from Karree Kloof, Orange River, South Africa, in July, 1896.

The largest concentration of wild mammals found living anywhere in the world today is that of the guano bat (*Tadarida mexicana*) in Bracan Cave, San Antonio, Texas, where twenty million animals assemble after migration from Mexico.

Longest and Shortest Gestation Periods. The longest of all mammalian gestation periods is that of the Asiatic elephant (*Elephas maximus*), with an average of 609 days (or just over 20 months) and a maximum of 760 days (2 years and 30 days)—more than 2½ times that of a human.

The shortest gestation period is that of the American opossum (*Didelphis marsupialis*), also called the Virginian opossum, normally 12 to 13 days, but it may be as short as 8 days.

LONGEST-LIVED ELEPHANT: The female Asiatic elephant "Modoc" may have lived to age 78, but there is some confusion regarding her birth date.

The gestation periods of the rare water opossum or Yapok (*Chironectes minimus*) of Central and northern South America (average 12–13 days) and the Eastern native cat (*Dasyurus viverrinus*) of Australia (average 12 days) may also be as short as 8 days.

Largest Litter. The greatest recorded number of young born to a wild mammal at a single birth is 32 (not all of which survived), in the case of the common tenrec (*Centetes ecaudatus*), found in Madagascar and the Comoro Islands. The average litter is 12 to 16.

In March, 1961, a litter of 32 was also reported for a house mouse (*Mus musculus*) at the Roswell Park Memorial Institute in Buffalo, N.Y. (average litter size 13–21). (See also Chapter 9, prolificacy records—pigs.)

Youngest Breeder. The streaked .tenrec (*Hemicentetes semispinosus*) of Madagascar is weaned after only 5 days, and females are capable of breeding 3–4 weeks after birth.

Carnivores

Largest. The largest living terrestrial member of the order Carnivora is the Kodiak bear (*Ursus arctos middendorffi*), which is found on Kodiak Island and the adjacent Afognak and Shuyak islands in the Gulf of Alaska. The average adult male has a nose-to-tail length of 8 feet (tail about 4 inches), stands 52 inches at the shoulder and weighs 1,050–1,175 lbs.

In 1894, a weight of 1,656 lbs. was recorded for a male shot at English Bay, Kodiak Island, whose *stretched* skin measured 13 feet 6 inches overall. This weight was exceeded by a "cage-fat" male in the Cheyenne Mountain Zoological Park, Colorado Springs, which scaled 1,670 lbs. at the time of its death on September 22, 1955.

The Peninsular brown bear (*Ursus arctos gyas*), also found in Alaska, is almost as large, adult males measuring 7¾ feet nose-to-tail length and weighing about 1,100 lbs. A specimen 10 feet long with an estimated weight of between 1,600 and 1,700 lbs. was shot near Cold Bay, Alaska, on May 28, 1948.

Weights in excess of 1,600 lbs. have also been reported for the male polar bear (*Ursus maritimus*), which has an average nose-to-tail length of 7¾ feet and weighs 850-900 lbs. In 1960, a polar bear allegedly weighing 2,210 lbs. was shot at the polar entrance to Kotzebue Sound, northwest Alaska. In April, 1962, the over-mounted specimen, measuring 11 feet 1½ inches, was put on display at the Seattle World's Fair.

Smallest. The smallest living carnivore is the least weasel (*Mustela rixosa*), also called the dwarf weasel, which is circumpolar in distribution. Four races are recognized, the smallest of which is the *M. r. pygmaea* of Siberia. Mature specimens have an overall length (including tail) of 6.96–8.14 inches and weigh between 1¼ and 2½ oz.

Largest Marine. The largest toothed mammal ever recorded is the sperm whale (*Physeter catodon*), also called the cachalot. The average adult bull is 47 feet long and weighs about 37 tons. The largest specimen ever to be measured accurately was a bull 67 feet 11 inches long captured off the Kurile Islands, in the northwest Pacific, by a U.S.S.R. whaling fleet in the summer of 1950.

Rarest. The rarest land carnivore is probably the red wolf (*Canis niger*) of Texas, of which no more than 50–70 survive. Of subspecies, there are only 20–30 Mexican grizzly bears (*Ursus arctos nelsoni*) left in the Sierra Madre in California.

Largest Feline. The largest member of the cat family (Felidae) is the long-furred Siberian tiger (*Panthera tigris altaica*), also known as the Amur or Manchurian tiger. Adult males average 10 feet 4 inches in length (nose to tip of extended tail), stand 39–42 inches at the shoulder, and weigh about 585 lbs. A male weighing 846.5 lbs. was shot in the Sikhote Alin Mountains, Maritime Territory, U.S.S.R. in 1950. In November, 1967, an 857-lb. Indian tiger (*Panthera tigris tigris*) was shot in northern Uttar Pradesh by David H. Hasinger of Philadelphia. It measured 10 feet 7 inches long (between taxidermist's pegs), or 11 feet 1 inch over the curves, compared with 9 feet 3 inches and 420 lbs. for the average adult male. It is now on display in the Smithsonian Institution, Washington, D.C.

The average adult African lion (*Panthera leo*) measures 9 feet overall, stands 36–38 inches at the shoulder, and weighs 400–410 lbs. The heaviest recorded specimen found in the wild was one weighing 690 lbs., shot near Hectorspruit, in the eastern Transvaal, South Africa, in 1936. In July, 1970, a weight of 826 lbs. was reported for an 11-year-old black-maned lion named "Simba" at the Colchester

Zoo, Essex, England. He died on January 16, 1973, at Knaresborough Zoo, North Yorkshire, England, where his stuffed body is currently on display.

Smallest Feline. The smallest member of the cat family is the rusty-spotted cat (*Felis rubiginosa*) of southern India and Ceylon. The average adult male has an overall length of 25–28 inches (tail 9–10 inches) and weighs about 3 lbs.

Pinnipeds (Seals, Sea Lions and Walruses)

Largest. The largest of the 32 known species of pinnipeds is the southern elephant seal (*Mirounga leonina*) which inhabits the sub-Antarctic islands. Adult bulls average 16½ feet in length (tip of inflated snout to tip of the outstretched tail flippers), 12 feet in maximum body girth and weigh 5,000 lbs. The largest accurately measured specimen on record was a bull killed in Possession Bay, South Georgia, on February 28, 1913, which measured *c.* 22½ feet in length or 21 feet 4 inches after flensing and weighed at least 9,000 lbs. There are old records of bulls measuring 25, 30 and even 35 feet, but these figures must be considered exaggerated.

Smallest. The smallest pinniped is the Baykal seal (*Pusa sibirica*) of Lake Baykal, U.S.S.R., and the ringed seal (*Pusa hispida*) of the Arctic. Adult specimens measure up to 5 feet 6 inches and weigh up to 280 lbs.

Fastest and Deepest. The highest speed measured for a pinniped is 25 m.p.h. for a California sea lion (*Zalophus californianus*). The deepest dive recorded for a pinniped is 1,968 feet for a bull Weddell seal (*Leptonychotes weddelli*) in McMurdo Sound, Antarctica, in March, 1966. At this depth, the seal withstood a pressure of 875 lbs. per square inch.

The exceptionally large eyes of the southern elephant seal (see above) point to a deep-diving ability, and unconfirmed measurements down to 2,000 feet have been claimed.

Longest-Lived. A female gray seal (*Halichoerus grypus*) shot at Shunni Wick in the Shetland Islands, Scotland, on April 23, 1969,

HIGHEST-PITCHED HEARING: Fruit bats can hear frequencies 7½ times as high as the human limit.

was believed to be at least 46 years old, based on a count of dental annuli.

Rarest. The Caribbean or West Indian monk seal (*Monachus tropicalis*) was last seen on the beach of Isla Mujeres off the Yucatan Peninsula, Mexico, in 1962, and is now believed to be on the verge of extinction.

Bats

Largest. The only flying mammals are bats (order Chiroptera), of which there are about 1,000 living species. The bat with the greatest wing span is the Kalong (*Pteropus vampyrus*), a fruit bat found in Malaysia and Indonesia. It has a wing span of up to 5 feet 7 inches and weighs up to 31.7 oz.

Smallest. The smallest species of bat is the rare Kitti's hog-nosed bat (see page 60).

Fastest. Because of the great practical difficulties, little data on bat speeds has been published. The greatest speed attributed to a bat is 32 m.p.h. in the case of a free-tailed or guano bat (*Tadarida mexicana*). This speed is closely matched by the noctule bat (*Nyctalus noctula*) and the long-winged bat (*Miniopterus schreibersi*), both of which have been timed at 31 m.p.h.

Longest-Lived. The greatest age reliably reported for a bat is "at least 24 years" for a female little brown bat (*Myotis lucifugus*) found on April 30, 1960, in a cave on Mount Aeolis, East Dorset, Vermont. It had been banded at a summer colony in Mashpee, Massachusetts, on June 22, 1937.

There is an unconfirmed French report of a 26- to 27-year-old greater horseshoe bat (*Rhinolophus ferrumequinum*).

Highest Detectable Pitch. Because of their ultrasonic echolocation bats have the most acute hearing of any land animal. Vampire bats (*Desmodontidae*) and fruit bats (*Pteropodidae*) can hear frequencies as high as 150,000 cycles per second (compare with 20,000 cycles per second for the adult human but 153,000 cycles for the bottlenosed dolphin (*Tursiops truncatus*).

Primates

Largest. The largest living primate is the eastern lowland gorilla (*Gorilla gorilla graueri*) which inhabits the lowlands of the eastern part of Zaïre and southwestern Uganda. The average adult bull stands 5 feet 9 inches tall (including crest) and measures 58–60 inches around the chest and weighs about 360 pounds. The greatest height (top of crest to heel) recorded for a mountain gorilla (*Gorilla gorilla beringei*) is 6 feet 2 inches for a bull shot in the eastern Congo *c*. 1921.

The heaviest gorilla ever kept in captivity was a bull of the eastern lowlands named "Mbongo," who died in San Diego Zoological Gardens, on March 15, 1942. During an attempt to weigh him shortly before his death, the platform scales "fluctuated from 645 pounds to nearly 670." This specimen measured 5 feet 7½ inches in height and 69 inches around the chest.

The heaviest gorilla living in captivity today is the western lowland (*Gorilla gorilla gorilla*) bull "Samson" (born 1949) of Milwaukee County Zoological Park. He has weighed as much as 658 lbs. but is now down to 485 lbs.

Smallest. The smallest known primate is the rare feather-tailed tree shrew (*Ptiolcercus lowii*) of Malaysia. Adult specimens have a total head and body length of 3.9–5.5 inches and a tail of 5–7.5 inches. The weight varies from 1.23 to 1.76 oz. The mouse lemur

OLDEST PRIMATE MATES: Gaus (right) lived to be 57 years old, and his mate Guarina (left) reached 56.

OLDEST LIVING PRIMATE: "Massa," now over 48 years old, has lived at the Philadelphia Zoo since 1935.

(*Microcebus murinus*) of Madagascar is approximately the same length (10.8–11.8 inches overall) but heavier, adults weighing 1.58 to 2.82 oz.

Longest-Lived. The greatest irrefutable age reported for a primate (excluding humans) is 57 years in the case of the male orangutan (*Pongo pygmaeus*) "Guas," who was received by the Philadelphia Zoo on May 1, 1931, after having been kept in Cuba for several years, and died on February 9, 1977.

The world's oldest living primate is the western lowland gorilla "Massa" of the Philadelphia Zoological Garden, a bull who was still alive in March, 1979, aged 48 years 3 months. He was received as a 5-year-old on December 30, 1935.

Rarest. The rarest primate is the hairy-eared mouse lemur (*Cheirogaleus trichotis*) of Madagascar, which was known, until fairly recently, only from a type specimen and two skins. However, in 1966 a live one was found on the east coast near Mananara.

Strength. "Boma," a 165-lb. male chimpanzee at the Bronx Zoo, New York City, in 1924 recorded a right-handed pull (feet braced) of 847 lbs. on a dynamometer (compare with 210 lbs. for a man of the same weight). On another occasion an adult female chimpanzee named "Suzette" (estimated weight 135 lbs.) at the same zoo registered a right-handed pull of 1,260 lbs. while in a rage. A record of a 100-pound chimpanzee achieving a two-handed dead lift of 600 pounds with ease suggests that a male gorilla could, with training, raise 1,800 pounds!

Largest and Smallest Monkeys. The largest monkey is the mandrill (*Mandrillus sphinx*) of equatorial West Africa, weighing up to 119 lbs. An unconfirmed weight of 130 lbs. has been reported.

The smallest monkey is the pygmy marmoset (*Cebuella pygmaea*) of Ecuador, northern Peru and western Brazil. Mature specimens have a maximum total length of 12 inches, half of which is tail, and weigh 1.7 to 2.81 oz. which means it rivals the mouse lemur for the title of *Smallest Living Primate*.

Rodents

Largest. The world's largest rodent is the capybara (*Hydrochoerus hydrochaeris*), also called the carpincho or water hog, which is found in tropical South America. Mature specimens have a head and body length of 3¼ to 4½ feet and weigh up to 174 lbs.

Smallest. The smallest rodent is the Old World harvest mouse (*Micromys minutus*), of which some forms weigh between 4.2 and 10.2 grams (0.15 to 0.36 of an ounce) and measure up to 5.3 inches long, including the tail. It was announced in June, 1965, that an even smaller rodent had been discovered in the Asian part of the U.S.S.R., probably a more diminutive form of *M. minutus*, but further information is lacking.

Rarest. The rarest rodent in the world is believed to be the James Island rice rat (*Oryzomys swarthi*). Four were collected on this island in the Galápagos group in the eastern Pacific Ocean in 1906. The next trace was in January, 1966, when a recent skull was found.

Fastest Breeder. The female meadow vole (*Microtus agrestis*), found in Britain, can reproduce from the age of 25 days and have up to 17 litters of 6 to 8 young in a year.

Longest-Lived. The greatest reliable age reported for a rodent is 22 years 10 months for a female bushtailed porcupine (*Atherurus africanus*), which died in the Philadelphia Zoological Garden on May 6, 1933. It was received as a young adult on July 5, 1910.

Insectivores

Largest. The largest insectivore (insect-eating mammal) is the moon rat (*Echinosorex gymnurus*), also known as Raffles' gymnure, found in Burma, Thailand, Malaysia, Sumatra and Borneo. Mature specimens have a head and body length of 10.43–17.52 inches, a tail measuring 7.87–8.26 inches, and weigh up to 3.08 lbs. Although anteaters feed on termites and other soft-bodied insects, they are not insectivores, but belong to the order Edentata which means "without teeth."

Smallest. The smallest insectivore is Savi's white-toothed pygmy shrew (*Suncus etruscus*), also called the Etruscan shrew, which is found along the coast of the northern Mediterranean and southwards to Cape Province, South Africa. Mature specimens have a head and body length of 1.32–2.04 inches, a tail length of 0.94–1.14 inches, and weigh between 0.052 and 0.09 oz.

Longest-Lived. The greatest reliable age recorded for an insectivore is 10½ years for a hedgehog tenrec (*Setifer setosus*), which died in the London Zoo in 1971. There is an unconfirmed record of a hedgehog (*Erinaceus europaeus*) living for 14 years.

LARGEST AND SMALLEST ANTELOPES: The rare Derby eland may weigh over a ton, while the Royal antelope weighs less than 8 lbs.

Antelopes

Largest. The largest of all antelopes is the rare Derby eland (*Taurotragus derbianus*), also called the giant eland, of west and north-central Africa, which may surpass 2,000 lbs. The common eland (*T. oryx*) of east and south Africa has the same shoulder height of up to 70 inches, but is not quite so massive, although there is one record of a 65-inch bull being shot in Nyasaland (now Malawi) *c.* 1937 which weighed 2,078 lbs.

Smallest. The smallest known antelope is the Royal antelope (*Neotragus pygmaeus*) of West Africa, measuring only 10 to 12 inches at the shoulder, and weighing only 7 to 8 lbs. The slenderer Swayne's dik-dik (*Madoqua swaynei*) of Somalia, East Africa, when adult, stands about 13 inches at the shoulder, weighs only 5 to 6 lbs.

Rarest. The rarest antelope is probably Jentink's duiker (*Cephalophus jentinki*), also known as the black-headed duiker, which is found only in a restricted area of tropical West Africa. There are only four in captivity, "Alpha," a female born on December 1, 1971; "Beta," and their two offspring, in the Gladys Porter Zoo, Brownsville, Texas.

LARGEST DEER: The Alaskan moose has been reliably weighed at 1,800 lbs.

Deer

Largest. The largest deer is the Alaskan moose (*Alces alces gigas*). A bull standing 7 feet 8 inches at the withers, and weighing 1,800 lbs., was shot in 1897 in the Yukon Territory, Canada. Unconfirmed measurements of up to $8\frac{1}{2}$ feet at the withers and 2,600 lbs. have been claimed. The record antler span is $78\frac{1}{2}$ inches.

Smallest. The smallest true deer (family Cervidae) is the pudu (*Pudu mephistophiles*) of Ecuador, the male of which stands 13–15 inches at the shoulder and weighs 18–20 pounds. The smallest known ruminant is the lesser Malayan chevrotain or mouse deer (*Tragulus javanicus*) of southeastern Asia. Adult specimens measure 8–10 inches at the shoulder and weigh 6–7 lbs.

Rarest. The rarest deer in the world is Fea's muntjac (*Muntiacus feae*), which is known only from two specimens collected on the borders of Tenasserim (in Burma) and Thailand.

Oldest. The greatest reliable age recorded for a deer is 26 years 6 months and 2 days for a red deer (*Cervus elephus*), which died in the National Zoological Park, Washington, D.C., on March 24, 1941.

Tusks and Horns

Longest. The longest recorded elephant tusks (excluding prehistoric examples) are a pair from the eastern Congo (Zaïre)

LONGEST TUSKS:
Weighing 293 lbs. and
each measuring 11
feet or more, this
pair of elephant tusks
is in the Bronx Zoo.

preserved in the National Collection of Heads and Horns, kept by
the New York Zoological Society in New York City. The right
tusk measures 11 feet 5½ inches along the outside curve and the
left measures 11 feet. Their combined weight is 293 lbs. A
single tusk of 11 feet 6 inches has been reported, but details are
lacking.

Heaviest. The greatest weight ever recorded for one elephant tusk
is 258 lbs. for a specimen collected in Benin (formerly Dahomey),
western Africa, and exhibited at the Paris Exposition in 1900.

Longest Horns. The longest recorded animal horn was one
measuring 81¼ inches on the outside curve, with a circumference of
18¼ inches, found on a specimen of domestic Ankole cattle (*Bos taurus*)
near Lake Ngami, Botswana (formerly called Bechuanaland).

The largest head (horns measured from tip to tip across the
forehead) is one of 13 feet 11 inches on a wild buffalo (*Bubalus
bubalus*) shot in India in 1955. The maximum for a Texas longhorn
steer is 9 feet 9 inches tip to tip.

The longest recorded anterior horn of a rhinoceros is one of 62¼
inches, found on a female southern race white rhinoceros (*Cerato-
theriam simum simum*) shot in South Africa *c.* 1848. The interior horn
measured 22¼ inches. An unconfirmed length of 81 inches for an
anterior horn has also been once reported.

Blood Temperatures

The highest mammalian blood temperature is that of the domestic
goat (*Capra hircus*) with an average of 103.8°F., and a normal range
of from 101.7° to 105.3°F. The lowest mammalian blood temperature is that of the spiny anteater (*Tachyglossus aculeatus*), a
monotreme found in Australia and New Guinea, with a normal
range of 72° to 87°F. The blood temperature of the golden hamster

(*Mesocricetus auratus*) sometimes falls as low as 38.3°F. during hibernation, and an extreme figure of 29.6°F. has been reported for a myotis bat (family Vespertilionidae) during a deep sleep.

Most Valuable Furs

The highest-priced animal pelts are those of the sea otter (*Enhydra lutris*), also known as the Kamchatka beaver, which fetched up to $2,700 each before their 55-year-long protection started in 1912. The protection ended in 1967, and at the first legal auction of sea otter pelts in Seattle, Washington, on January 31, 1968, Neiman-Marcus, the famous Dallas department store, paid $9,200 for four pelts from Alaska.

In May, 1970, a Kojah (mink-sable cross) coat costing $125,000 was sold by Neiman-Marcus to Welsh actor Richard Burton for his then wife, Elizabeth Taylor.

Ambergris

The heaviest piece of ambergris (a fatty deposit in the intestine of the sperm whale) on record weighed 1,003 lbs. and was recovered from a sperm whale (*Physeter catodon*) on December 3, 1912, by a Norwegian whaling company in Australian waters. The lump was sold in London for £23,000 (then $111,780).

Marsupials

Largest. The largest of all marsupials is the red kangaroo (*Macropus rufus*) of southern and eastern Australia. Adult males or "boomers" stand 6–7 feet tall, weigh 150–175 lbs. and measure up to 8 feet 11 inches in a straight line from the nose to the tip of the extended tail.

Smallest. The smallest known marsupial is the rare Kimberley planigale or flat-skulled marsupial mouse (*Planigale subtilissima*), found only in the Kimberley district of Western Australia. Adult males have a head and body length of 1.75 inches, a tail length of 2 inches and weigh about 0.141 oz. Females are smaller than males.

Rarest. The rarest marsupial is probably the thylacine (*Thylacinus cynocephalus*), also known as the "Tasmanian tiger," the largest of the carnivorous marsupials, which reportedly became extinct some time in the mid-1930's. The last captive specimen died in the Hobart Zoo, Tasmania, in 1934. However, in 1961, a fisherman at Sandy Cape, western Tasmania, accidentally killed a young male, and in July, 1977, a positive sighting was made of another specimen near Derby on the northwestern side of the island.

Longest-Lived. The greatest reliable age recorded for a marsupial is 19 years 7 months for a South Australian wallaroo (*Macropus robustus erubescens*), which died at the New York Zoological Park (Bronx Zoo) in 1968.

Highest and Longest Jump. The greatest measured height cleared by a hunted kangaroo is a pile of timber 10 feet 6 inches high. The longest recorded leap was reported in January, 1951, when, in the course of a chase, a female red kangaroo (*Macropus rufus*) made a series of bounds which included one of 42 feet. There is an unconfirmed report of a great gray kangaroo (*Macropus canguru*) jumping nearly 44 feet 8½ inches on the flat.

DOMESTICATED ANIMALS

Horses and Ponies

Horse Population. The world's horse population is estimated to be 75,000,000.

Age. The greatest reliable age recorded for a horse is 62 years in the case of "Old Billy" (foaled 1760), believed to be a cross between a Cleveland and an Eastern blood, who was bred by Edward Robinson of Wild Grave Farm in Woolston, Lancashire, England. In 1762 or 1763, he was sold to the Mersey and Irwell Navigation Company and remained with them in a working capacity, marshalling and towing barges, until 1819 when he was retired to a farm, where he died on November 27, 1822. The skull of this horse is preserved in the Manchester Museum, and his stuffed head is now on display in the Bedford Museum.

The greatest reliable age recorded for a pony is 54 years for a stallion owned by a farmer in central France which was still alive in 1919.

The greatest age recorded for a thoroughbred racehorse is 42 years in the case of the bay gelding "Tango Duke" (foaled 1935), owned by Mrs. Carmen J. Koper of Barongarook, Victoria, Australia. The horse died on January 25, 1978.

Largest. The heaviest horse ever recorded was "Brooklyn Supreme," a pure-bred Belgian stallion weighing 3,200 lbs. and standing 19.2 hands (6 feet 6 inches). He died on September 6, 1948, aged 20, in Callender, Iowa. In April, 1973, the Belgian mare "Wilma du Bos" (foaled July 15, 1966), owned by Mrs. Virgie

LARGEST HORSE: At the height of her pregnancy, "Wilma du Bos" reportedly equalled the all-time equine weight record.

TALLEST HORSE: "Firpon" stood 7 feet 1 inch high and weighed 2,976 lbs. The same height was also claimed for a Clydesdale, "Big Jim."

Arden of Reno, Nevada, was reported to weigh slightly more than 3,200 lbs. when in foal and being shipped from Antwerp. The mare stands 18.2 hands (6 feet 2 inches) and normally weighs about 2,400 lbs.

The tallest horse ever documented was the Percheron-Shire cross "Firpon" (foaled 1959) owned by Julio Falabella which stood 21.1 hands (7 feet 1 inch) and weighed 2,976 lbs. He died on Recco de Roca Ranch in Argentina on March 14, 1972. A height of 21.1 hands was also claimed for the Clydesdale gelding "Big Jim" (foaled 1950), bred by Lyall M. Anderson of West Broomley, Montrose, Scotland. "Big Jim" died in St. Louis in 1957.

A claim of 21.2 hands (7 feet 1½ inches) was made in 1908 for "Morocco" of Allentown, Pennsylvania, weighing 2,835 lbs.

Smallest. The smallest breed of horse is the Falabella, bred by Julio Falabella (see *Largest*), developed over a period of 45 years

SMALLEST HORSE: This Falabella from Argentina stands less than 8 hands high.

GREATEST LOAD HAULED: These fifty logs, weighing 48 tons, were pulled 275 yards across snow by two Clydesdale horses in 1893.

by crossing and recrossing a small group of undersized English thoroughbreds with Shetland ponies. Adult specimens range from 15 inches to 30 inches at the shoulder and weigh from 40 to 80 lbs. Foals standing 3 hands (12 inches) have been recorded twice by Norman J. Mitchell of Glenorie, New South Wales, Australia, in the cases of "Tung Dynasty" (February 8, 1978) and "Quicksilver" (1975).

The upper accepted limit for the American Miniature Horse Breeders Association is 34 inches.

Heaviest Load Hauled. The greatest load hauled by a pair of Clydesdale draught horses (with a combined weight of 3,500 lbs.) was 50 pine logs comprising 36,055 board-feet of lumber (48 tons) hauled on a sledge litter 275 yards *across snow* on the Nester Estate at Ewen, Michigan, on February 26, 1893.

A pair of shire geldings owned by Liverpool Corporation registered a much more impressive *maximum* pull equivalent to a starting load of 56 tons on a dynamometer at the British Empire Exhibition at Wembley, London, on September 4, 1924.

Dogs

Dog Population. In 1979 there were an estimated 41,000,000 dogs in the United States, compared to 5,500,000 in the United Kingdom.

Oldest. Dogs of over 20 are very rare but even 34 years has been accepted by one authority. The greatest reliable age recorded for a dog is 29 years 5 months for a Queensland "heeler" named "Bluey," owned by Les Hall of Rochester, Victoria, Australia. The dog was obtained as a puppy in 1910 and worked among cattle and sheep for nearly 20 years. He was put to sleep on November 14, 1939.

Most Popular. The breed with the most American Kennel Club new registrations for the year 1978 was the poodle, with 101,100. The earliest dog show was held in The Town Hall, Newcastle upon Tyne, England, June 28–29, 1859, with 23 pointers and 27 setters.

Rarest. The rarest breed of dog is the Tahl-Tan bear dog of Canada. In May, 1978, there were reportedly only 3 purebred examples still living, all of them in Atlin, British Columbia.

The rarest breed recognized by any national kennel club is the Portuguese water dog (*Cao de Agua*). The world population in March, 1978 was 237, including 213 in the U.S. and only 17 in Portugal.

Largest. The heaviest breed of domestic dog (*Canis familiaris*) is the St. Bernard. The heaviest example is "Schwarzwald Hof Duke" owned by Dr. A. M. Bruner of Oconomowoc, Wisconsin. He was whelped on October 8, 1964, and weighed 295 lbs. on May 2, 1969. He died in August, 1969.

Tallest. The tallest breeds of dog are the Irish wolfhound and the Great Dane, both of which can exceed 39 inches at the shoulder. The Irish wolfhound "Broadbridge Michael" (whelped in 1920), owned by Mrs. Mary Beynon of Sutton-at-Hone, Kent, England, stood 39½ inches at the age of two years. The Great Dane "Shamgret Danzal" (whelped in 1975), owned by Mrs. G. Comley of Milton Keynes, Buckinghamshire, England, stands 40½ inches and weighs 224 lbs.

Smallest. The smallest breeds of dog are the Yorkshire terrier, the short-haired Chihuahua and the toy poodle, miniature versions of which have been known to weigh less than 16 oz. when fully grown. In April, 1971, a weight of 10 oz. was reliably reported for an adult Yorkshire terrier named "Sylvia," owned by Mrs. Connie Hutchins of Walthamstow, Greater London, England.

Strength and Endurance. The greatest load ever shifted by a dog was 6,400½ lbs. of railroad steel pulled by a 176-lb. St. Bernard named "Ryettes Brandy Bear," at Bothell, Washington, on July 21, 1978. The 4-year-old dog, owned by Douglas Alexander of Monroe, Washington, pulled the weight on a four-wheeled carrier across a cement surface for a distance of 15 feet in less than 90 seconds.

In the annual 1,049-mile dog sled race from Anchorage to Nome, Alaska, the record time is 14 days 14 hours 43 minutes, by "Emitt Peters" in the 1975 race.

Fastest. The fastest breed of dog (excluding the greyhound and possibly the whippet) is the saluki, also called the Arabian gazelle hound or Persian greyhound. Speeds up to 43 m.p.h. have been claimed, but tests in the Netherlands have shown that it is not as fast as the present-day greyhound which has attained a measured speed of 41.7 m.p.h. on a track.

TALLEST DOG: This three-year-old Great Dane stands over 40 inches tall.

Largest Litter. The largest recorded litter of puppies is one of 23 thrown on June 9, 1944, by "Lena," a foxhound bitch owned by Commander W. N. Ely of Ambler, Pennsylvania. On February 6–7, 1975, "Careless Ann," a St. Bernard owned by Robert and Alice Rodden of Lebanon, Missouri, produced a litter of 23, of which 14 survived.

Most Prolific. The dog who has sired the greatest recorded number of puppies was the greyhound "Low Pressure" whelped in 1957 and owned by Mrs. Bruna Amhurst of Regent's Park, London. From December, 1961 until he died in November, 1969, he had fathered 2,414 registered puppies, with at least 600 others unregistered.

Most Valuable. Mrs. Judith Thurlow of Great Ashfield, Suffolk, England, turned down an offer of £14,000 ($35,000) in 1972 for her racing greyhound "Super Rory" (born October, 1970). Show dogs have also fetched extremely high prices. In July, 1976, Mrs. Eiselle Banks of Rayleigh, Essex, England, turned down an American offer of $20,000 for her international champion Lowchen "Cluneen Adam Adamant" (born August 13, 1969).

LARGEST LITTER: All 23 puppies shown here were born in a single litter to a foxhound in 1944.

"Top Dog." The greatest altitude attained by a mammal other than man is 1,050 miles by the Samoyed husky (Russian, *laika*) bitch fired as a passenger in *Sputnik II* on November 3, 1957. The dog was variously named "Kudryavka" (feminine form of Curly), "Limonchik" (diminutive of lemon), "Malyshka," "Zhuchka" or by the Russian breed name for husky "Laika."

Top Show Dog. The record number of "Best in Show" awards won by any dog in all-breed shows is 127, compiled from January, 1957, to February, 1960, by the Pekinese International Champion "Chik T'Sun of Caversham," owned by Mr. and Mrs. Charles C. Venable of Marietta, Georgia.

Police Dog. The world's top police dog is "Trep" of the Dade County Crime Force, Florida, who has sniffed out $63,000,000 worth of narcotics. In a school demonstration looking for 10 hidden packets, Trep once found 11.

In January, 1977, a "contract" worth $10,000 was put out on the life of a very successful drug-sniffing police dog named "Sergeant Blitz" by the underworld in Savannah, Georgia. Shortly afterwards, an 8-foot-high concrete wall was built around the dog's kennel as a precautionary measure.

Guide Dog. The longest reported period of active service for a guide dog is 13 years 2 months, in the case of a Labrador retriever bitch named "Polly" (whelped October 10, 1956) owned by Miss Rose Resnick of San Rafael, California. The dog was put to sleep on December 15, 1971.

Ratting. James Searle's bull terrier bitch "Jenny Lind" killed 500 rats in 1 hour 30 minutes at "The Beehive" in Liverpool, England, in 1853. Another bull terrier named "Jacko," owned by Mr. Jemmy Shaw, was credited with killing 1,000 rats in 1 hour 40 minutes, but the feat was performed over a period of ten weeks in batches of 100 at a time. The last 100 were accounted for in 5 minutes 28 seconds in London on May 1, 1862.

Tracking. The greatest tracking feat recorded was performed by the Doberman "Sauer" trained by Detective-Sergeant Herbert Kruger. In 1925, he tracked a stock thief 100 miles across the Great Karroo, South Africa, by scent alone.

In 1923, a collie named "Bobbie," lost by his owners while they were on vacation in Wolcott, Indiana, turned up at the family home in Silverton, Oregon, six months later, after having covered a distance of close to 2,000 miles. The dog, later identified by people who had cared for him along the route, had apparently wandered back through Illinois, Iowa, Nebraska, and Colorado, before crossing the Rocky Mountains in the depths of winter and then continuing through Wyoming and Idaho.

Highest and Longest Jump. The canine "high jump" record is held by a German shepherd named "Crumstone Danko" owned by the De Beers mining company, who, without a springboard, scaled a wall of 11 feet 3 inches in Pretoria, South Africa in May, 1942.

GREATEST CANINE LEAPER: "Crumstone Danko" was able to scale walls over 11 feet high in a single bound.

He was also credited with a jump of 16½ feet off a springboard. The longest recorded canine long jump was one of 30 feet by a greyhound named "Bang" made in jumping a gate in coursing a hare at Brecon Lodge, Gloucestershire, England, in 1849.

Greatest Dog Funeral. The greatest dog funeral on record was for the mongrel dog "Lazaras" belonging to the eccentric, Emperor Norton I of the United States, Protector of Mexico, held in San Francisco, in 1862, which was attended by an estimated 10,000 people.

Top Trainer. The most successful dog trainer in the world—and the fastest—is Mrs. Barbara Woodhouse of Rickmansworth, Hertfordshire, England, who has trained 16,867 dogs to a high standard from 1951 to March 19, 1979. Her record for a single day is 80 dogs in June, 1973, in Denver, Colorado.

Cats

Oldest. Cats are longer-lived animals than dogs and there are a number of authentic records over 20 years. Information on this subject is often obscured by two or more cats bearing the same nickname. Probably the oldest cat ever recorded was the tabby "Puss," owned by Mrs. T. Holway of Clayhidon, Devon, England. He was 36 on November 28, 1939 and died the next day. A more recent and better documented case was that of the female tabby "Ma," owned by Mrs. Alice St. George Moore, of Drewsteignton, Devon, England. She was put to sleep on November 5, 1957, aged 34.

Heaviest. The heaviest domestic cat (*Felix catus*) on record is a 9-year-old long-haired part-Persian named "Tiger," who consistently weighs 42–43 lbs., with a 12½-inch neck, a 33-inch waist and a 37-inch length. He is owned by Mrs. Phyllis Dacey of Billericay, Essex, England. In December, 1978, an unconfirmed weight of 44 lbs. was reported for a 6-year-old male cat named "Tiddles" living in Cardiff, South Wales. (See photo, page C.)

Largest Litter. The largest litter ever recorded was one of 19 kittens (4 stillborn) delivered by Caesarean section to "Tarawood Antigone," a 4-year-old brown Burmese, on August 7, 1970. Her owner, Mrs. Valerie Gane of Oxfordshire, England, reported that the litter was the result of mismating with a half-Siamese. Of the 15 survivors, 14 were male.

The largest live litter of which all survived was one of 14 kittens born in December, 1974, to the Persian cat "Bluebell," owned by Mrs. Elenore Dawson of Wellington, South Africa.

Most Prolific. A cat named "Dusty," aged 17, living in Bonham, Texas, gave birth to her 420th kitten on June 12, 1952.

Richest. Dr. William Grier of San Diego, California, died in June, 1963, leaving his entire estate of $415,000 to his two 15-year-old cats, "Hellcat" and "Brownie." When the cats died in 1965 the money went to George Washington University, Washington, D.C.

Most Valuable. In 1967, Miss Elspeth Sellar of Grafham, England, turned down an offer of 2,000 guineas (then $5,880) from an American breeder for her 2-year-old champion copper-eyed white Persian tom, "Coylum Marcus" (born March 28, 1965, died April 14, 1978).

Mousing. The greatest mouser on record was a tabby named "Mickey," owned by Shepherd & Sons Ltd. of Burscough, Lancashire, England, which killed more than 22,000 mice during 23 years with the firm. He died in November, 1968.

Cat Population. The largest cat population is in the U.S.— 23 million. Of Britain's cat population of 4,900,000, an estimated 100,000 are "employed" by the civil service.

Rabbits

The largest breed of domestic rabbit (*Oryctolagus cuniculus*) is the British giant. Adult specimens average 18–20 lbs., but weights up to 30 lbs. have been reliably reported for bucks.

The heaviest recorded wild rabbit is one of 6 lbs. 12 oz., shot by Mr. Monty Forest on the Swinford Estate, Burford, Oxfordshire, England, in February, 1976.

The smallest breeds of domestic rabbit are the Netherlands dwarf and the Polish, both of which average 2½ lbs. at maturity.

Oldest. The greatest reliable age recorded for a domestic rabbit is 18 years for a European rabbit which was still alive in August, 1977. An age of 18 years is also recorded for a doe which was alive in 1947.

Most Prolific. The most prolific domestic breeds are the New Zealand white and the Californian. Does produce 5 to 6 litters a year, each containing 8–12 young (compare with 5 litters and 3 to 7 young for the wild rabbit).

Hares

In November, 1956, a brown hare (*Lepus europaeus*), weighing 15 lbs. 1 oz., was shot near Welford, Northamptonshire, England.

Guinea Pigs

The greatest recorded age for a domestic guinea pig (*Cavia porcellus*) is 14 years 10½ months for "Snowball," owned by M. A. Wall of Nottinghamshire, England, who died on February 14, 1979.

Gerbil

The greatest recorded age for a gerbil (*Gerbillus gerbillus*) is 7 years 9½ months in the case of "Squirt," owned by Tom Clouser of Brookfield, Wisconsin. The pet died on September 22, 1977.

House Mouse

The oldest house mouse (*Mus musculus*) was "Hercules," who lived to be 5 years 11 months old. Owned by R. Hair of Purley, Surrey, England, the mouse lived from January, 1971, to December 26, 1976.

Hamster

A report of 10 years 2 months has been published for the oldest hamster but details are lacking.

Rat

The oldest recorded rat (*Rattus sp.*) lived to be 5 years 8 months old in Philadelphia, Pennsylvania, *c.* 1924.

For auction prices, milk yield and prolificacy records for cattle, sheep and pigs, see Agriculture, Chapter 9.

2. Birds *(Aves)*

Largest. Of the 8,650 known living species, by far the largest is the North African ostrich (*Struthio camelus camelus*) which lives south of the Atlas Mountains from Upper Senegal and Niger across to the Sudan and central Ethiopia. Male examples of this flightless or ratite subspecies reach 345 lbs. in weight and stand 9 feet tall.

The heaviest flying bird, or *carinate,* is the Kori bustard or paauw (*Otis kori*) of East and South Africa, which has a wing span up to 8 feet 4 inches. Weights up to 40 lbs. have been reliably reported for cock birds shot in South Africa. The mute swan (*Cygnus olor*) can also reach 40 lbs. on occasion, and there is a record from Poland of a cob weighing 49.5 lbs. which was probably too heavy to fly.

The heaviest flying bird of prey is the Andean condor (*Vultur gryphus*), which averages 20–25 lbs. as an adult. An exceptionally large specimen of the rare California condor (*Gymnogyps californianus*), now preserved in the California Academy of Sciences, Los Angeles, reputedly weighed 31 lbs.

Smallest. The smallest bird in the world is Helena's humming-bird (*Mellisuga helenae*) found in Cuba and the Isle of Pines. An average male adult has a wing span of 3 inches and weighs only 2 grams or 1/18th of an ounce (0.070 oz.). This is less than a sphinx moth. It has an overall length of 2.28 inches, the bill and tail accounting for about 1.7 inches.

The smallest bird of prey is the 1¼-oz. Bornean falconet (*Microhierax latifrons*), which is about the size of a sparrow.

The smallest sea bird is the least storm petrel (*Halocyptena microsoma*), which breeds only on San Benito Island in Lower California. Adult specimens average 5½ inches in total length.

Largest Wing Span. The wandering albatross (*Diomedea exulans*) of the southern oceans has the largest wing span of any living bird, adult males averaging 10 feet 4 inches with wings tightly stretched. The largest recorded specimen was a male measuring 11 feet 10 inches caught by banders in Western Australia *c.* 1957, but some unmeasured birds may exceed 13 feet.

The only other bird reliably credited with a wing spread in excess of 11 feet is the vulture-like marabou or adjutant stork (*Leptoptilus crumeniferus*) of Africa. A 12-foot specimen has been reported, and there is an unconfirmed claim of 13 feet 4 inches for a stork shot in Central Africa in the 1930's. The species rarely exceeds 9 feet.

Most Abundant. The most abundant of all birds is the red-billed quelea (*Quelea quelea*) of the drier parts of Africa south of the Sahara with a population estimated at 10,000,000,000 of which a tenth are destroyed each year by pest control units.

The most abundant domesticated bird is the chicken. the domesticated form of the wild red jungle fowl (*Gallus gallus*) of Southeast Asia. There are believed to be about 4,000,000,000 chickens in the world, or nearly one chicken for every member of the human race.

The most abundant sea bird is Wilson's petrel (*Oceanites oceanicus*). No population estimates have been published, but the number runs into the hundreds—possibly thousands—of millions.

LARGEST WING SPAN: This wandering albatross had a wing span of 11 feet 4 inches.

MOST ABUNDANT BIRD: About 10 billion red-billed queleas, shown alone and in a more social situation, inhabit sub-Saharan Africa.

Rarest. Great practical difficulties attend the identification of the rarest species of bird in the wild. One of the strongest candidates, however, must be the Kauai O-o (*Moho braccatus*) of Kauai, Hawaii, of which only a single pair survived in 1976. The white-winged guan (*Penelope albinennis*), thought to have become extinct about 100 years ago, was rediscovered in considerable numbers in northwestern Peru in December, 1977. In January, 1978, a New Zealand ornithological expedition exploring Chatham Island positively identified and photographed three magenta petrels (*Pterodroma magentae*). The only previous claimed sighting had been in 1868, about 500 miles east of the island.

The world's rarest raptor (bird of prey) is the Mauritius kestrel (*Falco punctatus*). In December, 1978, the total wild population was 18, with another 5 being raised in captivity.

Longest-Lived. The greatest irrefutable age reported for any bird is 72 years in the case of a male Andean condor (*Vultur gryphus*) named "Kuzya," which died in Moskovskii Zoologicheskeii Park, Moscow, in 1964. This bird had been received there as an adult in 1892. Other records which are regarded as probably reliable include 73 years (1818–91) for a greater sulphur-crested cockatoo (*Cacatua galerita*), 72 years (1797–1869) for an African gray parrot (*Psittacus erithacus*), 70 years (1770–1840) for a mute swan (*Cygnus olor*), and 69 years for a raven (*Corvus corax*). In 1972, a southern ostrich (*Struthio camelus australis*) aged 62 years 3 months was killed in the Ostrich Abattoir at Oudtshoorn, Cape Province, South Africa.

"Jimmy," a red and green Amazon parrot owned by Mrs. Bella Ludford of Liverpool, England, was allegedly hatched in captivity on December 3, 1870, and lived 104 years in his original brass cage. He died on January 5, 1975.

Fastest-Flying. The spine-tailed swift (see page 57) is the fastest bird.

The bird which presents the hunter with the greatest difficulty is the red-breasted merganser (*Mergus serrator*). On May 29, 1960, a specimen flushed from the Kukpuk River, Cape Thompson, northern Alaska, by a light aircraft recorded an air speed of 80 m.p.h. in level flight for nearly 13 seconds before turning aside.

Fastest and Slowest Wing Beat. The fastest recorded wing beat of any bird is 90 beats per second by the hummingbird *Heliactin cornuta* of tropical South America. This rate is probably exceeded by the bee hummingbirds *Mellisuga helenae* and *Acestrura bombus*, but figures have not yet been published.

Large vultures (family Vulturidae) and albatrosses (family Diomedeidae) can soar for hours without beating their wings, and sometimes exhibit a flapping rate as low as one beat per second.

Fastest Swimmer. A small group of Gentoo penguins (*Pygoscelis papua*) were timed at 22.3 m.p.h. underwater near the Bay of Isles, South Georgia. This is a respectable flying speed for some birds.

Deepest Diver. The emperor penguin (*Aptenodytes forsteri*) of the Antarctic can reach a depth of 870 feet and remain submerged for as long as 18 minutes.

Longest Flights. The greatest distance covered by a ringed bird during migration is 12,000 miles by an Arctic tern (*Sterna paradisaea*), which was banded as a nestling on July 5, 1955, in the Kandalaksha Sanctuary on the White Sea coast of the U.S.S.R., north of Archangel, and was captured alive by a fisherman 8 miles south of Fremantle, Western Australia, on May 16, 1956.

Highest-Flying. The celebrated example of a skein of 17 Egyptian geese (*Alopochen aegyptiacus*), photographed by an astronomer from Dehra Dun, India, on September 17, 1919, as they crossed the sun at a height estimated at between 11 and 12 miles

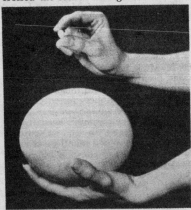

EGG EXTREMES: The eggs of the ostrich (below) and the hummingbird (top) are the largest and smallest known.

NIGHT OWL: The barn owl boasts night vision 2-5 times as great as a human being's.

(58,080–63,360 feet), has been discredited by experts. The highest acceptable altitude is 26,900 feet by a small group of alpine choughs (*Pyrrhocorax graculus*) which followed the British expedition up Mount Everest to Camp V in 1924. On May 23, 1960, a steppe eagle (*Aquila nipalensis*) and two other raptors were found dead at nearly 26,000 feet on the South Col of Mount Everest.

On three separate occasions in 1959, a radar station in Norfolk, England, picked up flocks of small passerine night migrants flying in from Scandinavia at up to 21,000 feet. They were probably warblers (*Sylviidae*), chats (*Turnidae*) and fly-catchers (*Muscicapidae*).

Most Airborne. The most airborne of all land birds is the common swift (*Apus apus*) which remains aloft for at least nine months of the year, but the sooty tern (*Sterna fuscata*) remains continuously aloft for three or four years after leaving the nesting grounds before it returns to the breeding grounds.

Most Acute Vision. Birds of prey (*Falconiformes*) have the keenest eyesight in the avian world. Their visual acuity is at least 8–10 times stronger than that of human vision. The golden eagle (*Aquila chrysaetos*) can detect an 18-inch-long hare at a range of 2,150 yards (possibly even 2 miles), and a peregrine falcon (*Falco peregrinus*) can detect a pigeon at a range of over 3,500 feet.

Eggs—Largest. Of living birds, the one producing the largest egg is the ostrich (*Struthio camelus*). The average egg weighs 3.63 to 3.88 lbs., measures 6 to 8 inches in length, 4 to 6 inches in diameter and requires about 40 minutes for boiling. The shell is 1/16th of an inch thick and can support the weight of a 280-lb. man.

Eggs—Smallest. The smallest egg laid by any bird is the egg of Helena's hummingbird (*Mellisuga helenae*), the world's smallest bird. One measuring 0.45 of an inch long and 0.32 of an inch wide is now

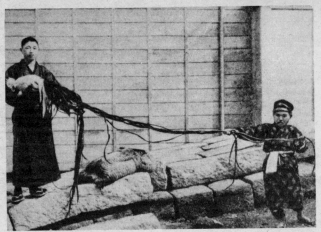

LONGEST FEATHERS: Tail feathers on the cock birds of the onagadori have been known to measure more than 34 feet long.

in the Smithsonian Institution in Washington, D.C. This egg, which weighs 0.176 oz., was collected at Boyate, Santiago de Cuba, on May 8, 1906.

Incubation. The longest incubation period is that of the wandering albatross (*Diomedea exulans*), with a normal range of 75 to 82 days. There is one case recorded of an egg of the mallee fowl (*Leipoa ocellata*) of Australia taking 90 days to hatch. Its normal incubation period is 62 days. The shortest incubation period is the 10 days of the great spotted woodpecker (*Dendrocopus major*) and the black-billed cuckoo (*Coccyzus erythropthalmus*). The idlest of cock birds are hummingbirds (family Trochilidae), eider ducks (*Somateria mollissima*) and golden pheasants (*Chrysolophus pictus*), among whom the hen bird does 100 per cent of the incubation, whereas the female common kiwi (*Apteryx australis*) leaves this entirely to the male for 75 to 80 days.

Largest Nests. The largest bird's nest on record is one 9½ feet wide and 20 feet deep built by bald eagles (*Haliaeetus leucocephalus*) near St. Petersburg, Florida, reported in 1963 and estimated to weigh more than 2¼ tons. The incubation mounds built by scrubfowl (family Megapodidae) have, however, been measured up to 50 feet in diameter and 20 feet in height.

Longest Feathers. The longest feathers known are those of the cock birds of the Japanese long-tailed fowls, or onagadori (a strain of *Gallus gallus*), which have been bred in southwestern Japan since the mid-17th century. In 1973, a tail covert measuring 34 feet 9½ inches was reported by Masasha Kubota of Kochi, Shikoku.

The tail feathers of the flying Reeve's pheasant (*Syrmaticus reevesi*) of north and east China can exceed 8 feet.

Most Feathers. In a series of "feather counts" on various species of birds, a whistling swan (*Cygnus columbianus*) was found to have 25,216 feathers. A ruby-throated hummingbird (*Archilochus colubris*) had only 940, although hummingbirds have more feathers per area of body surface than any other living bird.

Champion Bird-Watcher

The world's leading bird-watcher is G. Stuart Keith, an Englishman who works at the American Museum of Natural History, New York City. In the 32 years to March, 1979, his score is 5,450 species of the 8,650 known species.

Domesticated Birds

Largest Turkey. The greatest *live* weight recorded for a turkey (*Meleagris gallopavo*) is 75 lbs., reported in December, 1973, for a "holiday" turkey reared by Signe Olsen, Salt Lake City, Utah.

Most Expensive Turkey. The record price reached at auction for a turkey was £1,300 ($2,600) paid by Thornhill Poultry Packers of Great Longstone, Derbyshire, England, for a 72-lb. stag at The Glazier's Hall, London, on December 8, 1978.

Largest Chicken. The heaviest chicken on record is "Weirdo," a 22-pound white Sully reported in Calaveras County, California in January, 1973. "Weirdo" was so ferocious that he crippled a dog and killed two cats. The white Sully breed was developed by Mr. Grant Sullens of West Point, California.

The record flight by a chicken is 297 feet 2 inches by "Kung Flewk" at the International Chicken Flying Association meet at Rio Grande, Ohio, on May 21, 1977.

Most Talkative Bird. The world's most talkative bird is a male African gray parrot (*Psittacus erythacus*) named "Prudle," owned by

MOST SIGHTINGS: G. Stuart Keith of the American Museum of Natural History, shown here with a Fiji lory, has sighted over 63 per cent of all the known bird species in the world.

Mrs. Lyn Logue of Golders Green, London, England, which won the "best talking parrot-like bird" title at the National Cage and Aviary Bird Show in London for 12 consecutive years before retiring undefeated in 1977. Prudle, who has a vocabulary of nearly 1,000 words, was taken from a nest in a tree about to be felled at Jinja, Uganda, in 1958.

Longest-Lived. The longest-lived small cage bird is the canary (*Serinus canaria*). The oldest example on record was a 34-year-old cock bird named "Joey," owned by Mrs. K. Ross of Hull, England. The bird was purchased in Calabar, Nigeria, in 1941, and died on April 8, 1975.

The longest-lived domesticated bird (excluding the ostrich) is the domestic goose which normally lives about 25 years. A gander named "George," owned by Mrs. Florence Hull of Lancashire, England, died on December 16, 1976, aged 49 years 8 months. He was hatched in April, 1927.

On June 20, 1977, a budgerigar (parakeet) hen named "Charlie," owned by Miss J. Dinsey of Stonebridge, London, England, died aged 29 years 2 months, to set a record for the oldest bird of its species.

3. Reptiles *(Reptilia)*

(Crocodiles, snakes, turtles, tortoises and lizards)

Largest and Heaviest. The largest reptile in the world is the estuarine or salt-water crocodile (*Crocodylus porosus*) of Southeast Asia, northern Australia, New Guinea, the Philippines and the Solomon Islands. Adult bulls average 12–14 feet in length and scale about 1,100 lbs. In 1823 a notorious man-eater measuring 27 feet in length and weighing an estimated 4,400 lbs. was shot at Jala Jala on Luzon Island in the Philippines after terrorizing the neighborhood for many years. Its skull, the largest on record (if we exclude fossil remains) is now preserved in the Museum of Comparative Zoology at Harvard University, Cambridge, Massachusetts. Another outsized example with a reputed length of 33 feet and a maximum bodily girth of 13 feet 8 inches was shot in the Bay of Bengal, India, in 1840, but the dimensions of its skull (preserved in the British Museum of Natural History, London) suggest that it must have come from a crocodile measuring about 24 feet. In 1957, an unconfirmed length of 28 feet 4 inches was reliably reported for an estuarine crocodile shot by Mrs. Kris Pawlowski on MacArthur Bank in the Norman River, in northwestern Queensland, Australia.

The holder of the "official" record is a 20-foot 2-inch bull harpooned by Mr. Keith Adams in the MacArthur River near Borroloola in northern Australia on June 26, 1960.

Smallest. The smallest species of reptile is believed to be *Sphaerodactylus parthenopion*, a gecko found only on the island of Virgin Gorda, British Virgin Islands in the Caribbean. It is known from 15 specimens, including some gravid females, found between August 10 and

SPEEDY REPTILE: The six-lined race runner has been clocked at 18 m.p.h.

16, 1964. The three largest females measured 0.71 of an inch from snout to vent, with a tail of approximately the same length.

It is possible that another gecko, *Sphaerodactylus elasmorhynchus,* may be even smaller. The only specimen ever discovered was an apparently mature female, with a snout-vent length of 0.67 of an inch and a tail of the same length, found on March 15, 1966, among the roots of a tree in the western part of the Massif de la Hotte in Haiti.

A species of dwarf chameleon, *Evoluticauda tuberculata,* found in Madagascar, and known only from a single specimen, has a snout-vent length of 0.71 inch and a tail length of 0.55 inch. Chameleons, however, are more bulky than geckos, and it is not yet known if this specimen was fully grown.

Fastest. The highest speed measured for any reptile on land is 18 m.p.h. by a six-lined race runner (*Cnemidophorus sexlineatus*) pursued by a car near McCormick, South Carolina, in 1941. The highest speed claimed for any reptile in water is 22 m.p.h. by a frightened Pacific leatherback turtle (see *Largest Chelonians*).

Largest Lizard. The largest of all lizards is the Komodo monitor or Ora (*Varanus komodoensis*), a dragon-like reptile found on the Indonesian islands of Komodo, Rintja, Padar and Flores. Adult males average 8 feet in length and weigh 175–200 lbs. Lengths up to 23 feet (*sic*) have been quoted for this species, but the largest specimen to be accurately measured was a male presented to an American zoologist in 1928 by the Sultan of Bima which then taped 10 feet 0.8 inches. In 1937, this animal was put on display in the St. Louis Zoological Gardens for a short period. It then measured 10 feet 2 inches in length and weighed 365 lbs.

The longest lizard in the world is the slender Salvadori dragon (*Varanus salvadori*) of New Guinea, which has been reliably measured up to 15 feet 7 inches long.

Oldest. The greatest age recorded for a lizard is more than 54 years for a male slow worm (*Anguis fragilis*) kept in the Zoological Museum in Copenhagen, Denmark, from 1892 until 1946.

Chelonians

Largest. The largest of all chelonians is the Pacific leatherback turtle (*Dermochelys coriacea schlegelii*). The average adult measures 6–7 feet in overall length (length of carapace 4–5 feet) and weighs between 660 and 800 lbs. The greatest weight reliably recorded is 1,908 lbs. for a specimen captured off Monterey, California, in 1961, which is now on permanent display at the Wharf Aquarium, Fisherman's Wharf, Monterey. Its length was 8 feet 4 inches overall.

The largest living tortoise is *Geochelone* (*Testudo*) *gigantea* of the Indian Ocean islands of Aldabra, Mauritius, Réunion and Seychelles (introduced 1874). Adult males sometimes exceed 350 lbs. in weight, and a specimen weighing 900 lbs. was allegedly collected in Aldabra in 1847. The largest desert tortoise is the protected *Gopherus agassizi* of the southwestern United States, which normally weighs about 10–12 lbs. when fully grown. In January, 1976, a weight of 23 lbs. 14 oz. was recorded for a huge male with a shell 15 inches long, found in the Mojave Desert, California.

Longest-Lived. Tortoises are the longest-lived of all vertebrates. Reliable records over 100 years include a common box tortoise (*Testudo carolina*) of 138 years and a European pond tortoise (*Emys orbicularis*) of 120+years. The greatest proven age of a continuously observed tortoise is 116+years for a Mediterranean spur-thighed tortoise (*Testudo graeca*) which died in Paignton Zoo, Devon, England, in 1957.

Slowest-Moving. In a recent "speed" test carried out in the Seychelles Islands, a male giant tortoise (*Geochelone gigantea*) could only cover 5 yards in 43.5 seconds (0.23 m.p.h.) despite the enticement of a female tortoise.

Snakes

Longest. The longest of all snakes (average adult length) is the reticulated python (*Python reticulatus*) of Southeast Asia, Indonesia and the Philippines, which regularly exceeds 20 feet. In 1912, a specimen measuring exactly 32 feet 9½ inches was shot near a mining camp on the north coast of Celebes in the Malay archipelago.

Lengths up to 45 feet have been claimed for the anaconda (*Eunectes murinus*) of tropical South America, but these extreme measurements were probably based on stretched skins. The greatest authenticated length recorded for an anaconda is 27 feet 9 inches for a female killed in Brazil *c.* 1960.

The longest snake living in captivity today is probably a female reticulated python named "Cassius" owned by Mr. Adrian Nyoka of Knaresborough Zoo, North Yorkshire, England, which measures about 27 feet and weighs 240 lbs. It was collected in Malaysia in 1972.

A long-standing reward of $5,000, offered by the New York Zoological Society, Bronx Park, New York City, for a living specimen of any snake measuring more than 30 feet has never been collected.

The longest venomous snake in the world is the king cobra (*Ophiophagus hannah*), also called the hamadryad, of Southeast Asia

LONGEST VENOMOUS SNAKE: The king cobra, 18 feet 9 inches long.

and the Philippines. A specimen was collected near Port Dickson in Malaya in April, 1937, and grew to 18 feet 9 inches in the London Zoo. It was destroyed with the outbreak of war in 1939.

Shortest. The shortest known snake is the thread snake *Leptotyphlops bilineata*, found on the Caribbean islands of Martinique, Barbados and St. Lucia. It has a maximum recorded length of 4.7 inches.

The shortest venomous snake is the striped dwarf garter snake (*Elaps dorsalis*) of South Africa. Adults average 6 inches in length.

Heaviest. The heaviest snake is the anaconda (*Eunectes murinus*), which is nearly twice as heavy as a reticulated python of the same length. The specimen shot in Brazil *c.* 1960 (see p. 92) was not weighed, but based on its maximum bodily girth of 44 inches, it must have weighed nearly 500 lbs.

The heaviest venomous snake is the Eastern diamondback rattlesnake (*Crotalus adamanteus*), found in the southeastern United States. A specimen 7 feet 9 inches in length weighed 34 lbs. Less reliable weights up to 40 lbs. and lengths up to 8 feet 9 inches have been reported.

A posthumous weight of 28 lbs. was reported for a king cobra (*Ophiophagus hannah*) 14 feet 5 inches long at the New York Zoological Park (Bronx Zoo) in February, 1973.

Oldest Snake. The greatest irrefutable age recorded for a snake is 40 years 3 months and 14 days in the case of a common Boa (*Boa constrictor constrictor*) at Philadelphia Zoological Gardens. Named "Popeye," he was purchased from a London dealer in December, 1936, and his life was humanely ended on April 15, 1977, because of medical problems associated with advanced age.

Fastest-Moving. The fastest-moving land snake is probably the slender black mamba (*Dendroaspis polylepis*). On April 23, 1906, an angry black mamba was timed at a speed of 7 m.p.h. over a measured

SERPENTINE SPEEDSTER: The slender black mamba may reach a speed of 15 m.p.h.

distance of 47 yards near Mbuyuni on the Serengeti Plains, Tanzania. Stories that black mambas can overtake galloping horses (maximum speed 43.26 m.p.h.) are wild exaggerations, though a speed of 15 m.p.h. may be possible for short bursts over level ground.

Most Venomous. The world's most venomous snake is now believed to be the sea snake *Hydrophis belcheri* which has a venom one hundred times as toxic as that of the Australian taipan (*Oxyuranus scutellatus*). The snake abounds around Ashmore Reef in the Timor Sea, off the coast of northwestern Australia.

The most venomous land snake is the small scaled or fierce snake (*Parademansia microlepidotus*) of southwestern Queensland and northeastern South Australia and Tasmania. One specimen yielded 0.00385 oz. of venom after milking, a quantity sufficient to kill at least 125,000 mice. Until 1976, this 6-foot-6-inch-long snake was regarded as a western form of the taipan, but its venom differs significantly from the latter.

It is estimated that between 30,000 and 40,000 people (excluding Chinese and Russians) die from snakebite each year, 75 per cent of them in densely populated India. Burma has the highest mortality rate with 15.4 deaths per 100,000 population per annum.

Longest Fangs. The longest fangs of any snake are those of the Gaboon viper (*Bitis gabonica*), of tropical Africa. In a 6-foot-long specimen, the fangs measured 1.96 inches. A Gaboon viper bit itself to death on February 12, 1963, in the Philadelphia Zoological Gardens. Keepers found the dead snake with its fangs deeply embedded in its own back.

4. Amphibians *(Amphibia)*

(Salamanders, toads, frogs, newts, caecilians, etc.)

Largest

The largest species of amphibian is the Chinese giant salamander (*Megalobatrachus davidianus*), which lives in the cold mountain streams and marshy areas of northeastern, central and southern China. The average adult measures 39 inches in total length and weighs 24 to 28 lbs. One huge individual collected in Kweichow (Guizhou) Province in southern China in the early 1920's measured 5 feet in total length and weighed nearly 100 lbs. The Japanese giant salamander (*Megalobatrachus japonicus*) is slightly smaller, but one captive specimen weighed 88 lbs. when alive and 100 lbs. after death, the body having absorbed water from the aquarium.

Newt. The largest newt in the world is the pleurodele or ribbed newt (*Pleurodeles waltl*), which is found in Morocco and on the Iberian Peninsula. Specimens measuring up to 15.74 inches in total length and weighing over 1 lb. have been reliably reported.

Frog. The largest known frog is the rare Goliath frog (*Rana goliath*) of Cameroon and Equatorial Guinea. A female weighing 7 lbs. 4.5 oz. was caught in the rapids of the River Mbia, Equatorial Guinea, on August 23, 1960. It had a snout-vent length of 13.38 inches and measured 32.08 inches overall with legs extended. In December, 1960, another giant frog known locally as "agak" or "carn-pnag" and said to measure 12–15 inches snout to vent and to weigh over 6 lbs. was reportedly discovered in central New Guinea, but further information is lacking. In 1969, a new species of giant frog was discovered in Sumatra.

Tree Frog. The largest species of tree frog is *Hyla vasta*, found only on the island of Hispaniola (Haiti and the Dominican Republic) in

LARGEST FROG (left): The Goliath frog of West Africa can be over 32 inches long and weigh up to 7¼ lbs. LARGEST AMPHIBIAN (right): The Chinese giant salamander can grow to a length of 5 feet.

the West Indies. The average snout-vent length is about 3.54 inches, but a female collected from the San Juan River, Dominican Republic, in March, 1928, measured 5.63 inches.

Toad. The largest toad in the world is probably the marine toad (*Bufo marinus*) of tropical South America. An enormous female collected on November 24, 1965, at Miraflores Vaupes, Colombia, and later exhibited in the Reptile House at the Bronx Zoo, New York City, had a snout-vent length of 9.37 inches and weighed 2 lbs. 11¼ oz. at the time of its death in 1967.

Smallest

The smallest species of amphibian is believed to be the arrow-poison frog *Sminthillus limbatus*, found only in Cuba. Fully-grown specimens have a snout-vent length of 0.44–0.48 inches.

Newt. The smallest newt in the world is believed to be the striped newt (*Notophthalmus perstriatus*) of the southeastern United States. Adult specimens average 2.01 inches in total length.

Tree Frog. The smallest tree frog in the world is the least tree frog (*Hyla ocularis*), found in the southeastern United States. It has a maximum snout-vent length of 0.62 inches.

TINY TOAD: The largest *Bufo taitanus beiranus* yet discovered measured less than an inch.

Toad. The smallest toad in the world is the sub-species *Bufo taitanus beiranus*, first discovered in *c.* 1906 near Beira, Mozambique, East Africa. Adult specimens have a maximum recorded snout-vent length of 0.94 inches.

Salamander. The smallest species of salamander is the pygmy salamander (*Desmognathus wrighti*), which is found only in Tennessee, North Carolina and Virginia. Adult specimens measure from 1.45 to 2.0 inches in total length.

Longest-Lived. The greatest authentic age recorded for an amphibian is about 55 years for a male Japanese giant salamander (*Megalobatrachus japonicus*) which died in the aquarium at Amsterdam Zoological Gardens on June 3, 1881. It was brought to Holland in 1829, at which time it was estimated to be 3 years old.

Highest and Lowest. The common toad (*Bufo vulgaris*) has been found at an altitude of 26,246 feet in the Himalayas, and at a depth of 1,115 feet in a coal mine.

Most Poisonous. The most active known venom is the batracho-toxin derived from the skin secretions of the kokoi (*Phyllobates latinasus*), an arrow-poison frog of northwestern Colombia, South America. Only about 1/100,000th of a gram (0.0000004 of an ounce) is enough to kill a man.

Longest Frog Jump. The record for three consecutive leaps is 33 feet 5½ inches by a female South African sharp-nosed frog (*Rana oxyrhyncha*) named "Santjie" at a frog derby held at Lurula Natal Spa, Paulpietersburg, Natal, on May 21, 1977.

At the annual Calaveras County Jumping Frog Jubilee at Angels Camp, California, in 1975, "Ex Lax" made a *single* leap of 17 feet 6¾ inches for its owner Bill Moniz.

LARGEST CARNIVOROUS FISH: The fearsome jaws of the great white shark have become a popular nightmare in recent years.

5. Fishes *(Pisces, Bradyodonti, Selachii and Marsipoli)*

Largest—Sea. The largest species of fish is the whaleshark (*Rhiniodon typus*) first discovered off Capetown, South Africa, in April, 1828. It is not, however, the largest aquatic animal, since it is smaller than the larger species of whales (mammals). A whaleshark measuring 60 feet 9 inches long and weighing about 90,000 lbs. was caught in a bamboo fish-trap at Koh Chik, in the Gulf of Siam, in 1919.

The plankton-feeding whaleshark, grayish or dark brown with white or yellow spots, is extremely docile and lives in the warmer areas of the Atlantic, Pacific and Indian Oceans. Unlike mammals, fish continue to grow with age.

The largest carnivorous fish (excluding plankton-eaters) is the great white shark (*Carcharodon carcharias*), also called the man-eater, which ranges from the tropics to temperate zone waters. In June, 1930, a specimen measuring 37 feet in length was reportedly trapped in a herring weir at White Head Island, New Brunswick, Canada, but this may have been a wrongly identified basking shark (*Cetorhinus maximus*). In May, 1948, a great white shark measuring 21 feet in length was captured after a fierce battle by fishermen off Havana, Cuba. It weighed 7,302 lbs.

The longest of the bony or "true" fishes (Pisces) is the Russian sturgeon (*Acipenser huso*), also called the Beluga, which is found in the temperate areas of the Adriatic, Black and Caspian Seas, but enters large rivers like the Volga and the Danube for spawning. Lengths up to 26 feet 3 inches have been reliably reported, and a gravid female taken in the estuary of the Volga in 1827 weighed 3,250 lbs.

The heaviest bony fish in the world is the ocean sunfish (*Mola mola*), which is found in all tropical, sub-tropical and temperate waters. On September 18, 1908, a huge specimen was accidentally struck by the S.S. *Fiona* off Bird Island about 40 miles from Sydney, New South Wales, Australia, and towed to Port Jackson. It measured 14 feet between the anal and dorsal fins and weighed 5,017 lbs.

Largest—Fresh-water. The largest fish which spends its whole life in fresh or brackish water is the rare Pa Beuk or Pla Buk (*Pangasianodon gigas*), a giant catfish found in the Mekong River of Laos and Thailand. Adult males average 8 feet in length and weigh about 360 lbs. This size was exceeded in fresh water by the European catfish or Wels (*Silurus glanis*). In the 19th century lengths of up to 15 feet and weights up to 720 lbs. were reported for Russian specimens, but today anything over 6 feet and 200 lbs. is considered large. The arapaima (*Arapaima glanis*), also called the pirarucu, found in the Amazon and other South American rivers and often claimed to be

LARGEST FRESH-WATER FISH (left): This European catfish measured up to 11 feet long and weighed 565 pounds. **LARGEST FISH (above):** The whale-shark (not a mammal) grows up to 59 feet long and lays the largest eggs of any living creature. (See page 57.)

FASTEST FISH: Some experts believe the swordfish is capable of speeds nearing 60 m.p.h.

the largest fresh-water fish, averages 6½ feet and 150 lbs. The largest "authentically recorded" measured 8 feet 1½ inches and weighed 325 lbs. It was caught in the Rio Negro, Brazil, in 1836. In September, 1978, a Nile perch (*Lates niloticus*) weighing 416 lbs. was netted in the eastern part of Lake Victoria, Kenya.

Smallest—Sea. The smallest recorded marine fishes are the Marshall Islands goby (*Eviota zonura*), measuring 0.47 to 0.63 of an inch, and *Schindleria praematurus* from Samoa, measuring 0.47 to 0.74 of an inch, both in the Pacific Ocean. Mature specimens of the latter, largely transparent and first identified in 1940, have been known to weigh only 2 milligrams, equivalent to 17,750 to the ounce—the lightest of all vertebrates and the smallest catch possible for any fisherman.

The smallest known shark is the long-faced dwarf shark (*Squaliolus laticaudus*) of the western Pacific. Adult specimens measure about 4.33 inches long.

Smallest—Fresh-water. The shortest recorded fresh-water fish and the shortest of all vertebrates is the dwarf pygmy goby (*Pandaka pygmaea*), almost transparent and colorless, found in streams and lakes on Luzon, the Philippines. Adult males measure only 0.28 to 0.38 of an inch long and weigh only 4 to 5 milligrams (0.00014 to 0.00017 of an ounce).

Fastest. The sailfish (*Istiophorus platypterus*) is generally considered to be the fastest species of fish, although the practical difficulties of measurement make data extremely difficult to secure. A figure of 68.1 m.p.h. (100 yards in 3 seconds) has been cited for one off Florida. The swordfish (*Xiphias gladius*) has also been credited with very high speeds, but the evidence is based mainly on bills that have been found deeply embedded in ships' timbers. A speed of 50 knots (57.6 m.p.h.) has been calculated from a penetration of 22 inches by a bill into a piece of timber, but 30 to 35 knots (35 to 40 m.p.h.) is the most conceded by some experts. Speeds in excess of 35 knots (40 m.p.h.) have also been attributed to the marlin (*Tetrapturus sp.*), the wahoo (*Acanthocybium solandri*), the great blue shark (*Prionace glauca*), and the bonefish (*Albula vulpes*); and the bluefin tuna (*Thunnus thynnus*) has been scientifically clocked at 43.4 m.p.h. in a 20-second dash. The four-winged flying fish (*Cypselurus heterururs*) may also exceed 40 m.p.h. during its rapid rush to the surface before take-off (the average speed in the air is about 35 m.p.h.). Record flights of 90 seconds, 36 feet in altitude and 3,640 feet in length have been recorded in the tropical Atlantic.

Longest-Lived. Aquaria are of too recent origin to be able to establish with certainty which species of fish can fairly be regarded as the longest-lived. Early indications are that it is the lake sturgeon (*Acipenser fulvescens*) of North America. In one study of the growth rings (annuli) of 966 specimens caught in the Lake Winnebago, Wisconsin region between 1951 and 1954, the oldest sturgeon was found to be a male, 6 feet 7 inches long, which gave a reading of 82 years and was still growing. In July, 1974, a figure of 228 years was attributed by growth ring count to a female Koi fish, a form of fancy carp named "Hanako" living in a pond in Higashi Shirakawa, Gifu Prefecture, Japan, but the greatest authoritatively accepted age for this species is "more than 50 years."

The death of an 88-year-old female European eel (*Anguilla anguilla*) named "Putte" in the aquarium at Halsingborn Museum, Sweden was reported in 1948. She was allegedly born in the Sargasso Sea in 1860, and was caught in a river as a 3-year-old elver (young eel).

Oldest Goldfish. The exhibition life of a goldfish (*Carassius auratus*) is normally about 17 years, but much greater ages have been reliably reported. A specimen belonging to Mr. H. S. Taylor of Lincolnshire, England was probably 36 years old when it died on February 27, 1978. There have been reports of goldfish living for over 40 years in China.

Shortest-Lived. The shortest-lived fishes are probably certain species of the sub-order Cyprinodontei (killifish) found in Africa and South America which normally live about 8 months in the wild.

Deepest. The greatest depth from which a fish has been recovered is 27,230 feet in the Puerto Rico Trough (27,488 feet) in the Atlantic by Dr. Gilbert L. Voss of the U.S. research vessel *John Elliott*. The fish, taken in April, 1970, was a 6½-inch-long *Bassogigas profundissimus* and was only the fifth such brotulid ever caught. Dr. Jacques Piccard and Lieutenant Don Walsh, U.S. Navy, reported they saw a sole-like fish about 1 foot long (tentatively identified as *Chascanopsetta lugubris*) from the bathyscaphe *Trieste* at a depth of 35,802 feet in the Challenger Deep (Marianas Trench) in the western Pacific on January 24, 1960. This sighting, however, has been questioned by some authorities, who still regard the brotulids of the genus *Bassogigas* as the deepest-living vertebrates.

Most Venomous. The most venomous fish in the world are the stonefish (family Synanceidae) of the tropical waters of the Indo-Pacific. Direct contact with the spines of their fins, which contain a strong neurotoxic poison, often proves fatal.

Most and Least Eggs. The ocean sunfish (*Mola mola*) produces up to 300,000,000 eggs, each of them measuring about 0.05 inches in diameter. The egg yield of the tooth carp *Jordanella floridae* of Florida is only about 20 over a period of several days.

Most Electric. The most powerful electric fish is the electric eel (*Electrophorus electricus*), which is found in the rivers of Brazil, Colom-

HEAVIEST STARFISH: The appropriately named Rhinoceros starfish can weigh up to 13 lbs.

bia, Venezuela and Peru. An average-sized specimen can discharge 400 volts at 1 ampere, but measurements up to 650 volts have been recorded.

6. Starfishes (Asteroidea)

Largest. The largest of the 1,600 known species of starfish in terms of total arm span is the very fragile brisingid *Midgardia xandaros*. A specimen collected by the Texas A & M University research vessel *Alaminos* in the southern part of the Gulf of Mexico in the late summer of 1968 measured 54.33 inches from tip to tip but the diameter of its disc was only 1.02 inches. Its dry weight was only 2.46 ounces. The heaviest species of starfish is the five-armed *Thromidia catalai* of the western Pacific. One specimen, collected off Ilot Amedee, New Caledonia, on September 14, 1969, and later deposited in the Noumea Aquarium, weighed an estimated 13.2 lbs., with a total arm span of 24.8 inches.

Smallest. The smallest known starfish is *Marginaster capreensis*, found deep in the Mediterranean, which is not known to exceed a diameter of 0.78 inches.

Deepest. The greatest depth from which a starfish has been recovered is 24,881 feet for a specimen of *Porcellanaster ivanovi*, collected by the Russian research ship *Vityaz* in the Marianas Trench, in the Pacific in 1962.

7. Arachnids (Arachnida)

Spiders (Order Araneae)

Largest. The world's largest known spider is the South American "bird-eating" spider (*Theraphosa blondi*). A male specimen with a body 3½ inches long and a leg span of 10 inches, when fully extended, was collected in April, 1925, at Montagne la Gabrielle, French Guiana. It weighed nearly 2 ounces.

The heaviest spider ever recorded was a female "tarantula" of the long-haired species, *Lasiodora klugi*, collected at Manaos, Brazil, in 1945. It measured 9½ inches across the legs and weighed almost 3 ounces.

Smallest. The smallest known spider in the world is *Patu marplesi* (family Symphytognathidae) of Western Samoa. The type specimen (a male found in moss at *c.* 2,000-foot altitude near Malolelei, Upolu, in January, 1956) measures 0.016 inches overall—half the size of a printed period (.).

Largest and Smallest Webs. The largest webs are the aerial ones spun by the tropical orb weavers of the genus *Nephila*, which have been measured up to 18 feet 9¾ inches in circumference.

The smallest webs are spun by spiders like *Glyphesis cottonae*, etc. and are about the size of a small postage stamp.

Most Venomous. The most venomous spider in the world is probably *Latrodectus mactans* of the Americas, which is better known as the "black widow." Females of this species, measuring up to 2½ inches overall, have a bite capable of killing a human being, but deaths are rare. The funnel web spider (*Atrax robustus*) of Australia, the jockey spider (*Latrodectus hasseltii*) of Australia and New Zealand, the button spider (*Latrodectus indistinctus*) of South Africa, the podadora (*Glyptocranium gasteracanthoides*) of Argentina and the brown recluse spider (*Loxosceles reclusa*) of the central and southern United States have been credited with fatalities.

Rarest. The most elusive of all spiders are the primitive atypical tarantulas of the genus *Liphistius*, which are found in Southeast Asia.

Fastest. The highest speed measured for a spider on a level surface is 1.73 feet per second (1.17 m.p.h.) in the case of a specimen of *Tegenaria atrica*. This is 33 times its body length per second (compare with the human record of $5\frac{1}{2}$ times its body length per second).

Longest-Lived. The longest-lived of all spiders are the primitive *Mygalomorphae* (tarantulas and allied species). One mature female tarantula, collected at Mazatlan, Mexico, in 1935 and estimated to be 12 years old at the time, was kept in a laboratory for 16 years, making a total of 28 years.

Largest Tick. The largest known tick is an engorged female *Amblyomma varium* from a Venezuelan sloth.

Smallest Tick. The smallest is a male *Ixodes soricis* from a British Columbian shrew.

8. Crustaceans *(Crustacea)*

(Crabs, lobsters, shrimps, prawns, crayfish, barnacles, water fleas, fish lice, wood lice, sand hoppers and krill, etc.)

Largest. The largest of all crustaceans (although not the heaviest) is the giant spider crab (*Macrocheira kaempferi*), also called the stilt crab, which is found in deep waters off the southeastern coast of

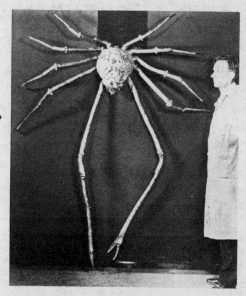

LARGEST CRAB: The Japanese spider crab has legs which can span over 12 feet.

Japan. Mature specimens usually have a 12–14-inch-wide body and a claw span of 8–9 feet, but unconfirmed measurements up to 19 feet have been reported. A specimen with a claw span of 12 feet 1½ inches weighed 41 lbs.

The largest species of lobster, and the heaviest of all crustaceans, is the American or North Atlantic lobster (*Homarus americanus*). The largest lobster, a specimen weighing 44 lbs. 6 oz., measuring 3 feet 6 inches from the end of the tail-fan to the tip of the largest claw, was caught off Nova Scotia, Canada, on February 11, 1977. It was later sold to Steve Karathanos, owner of a Bayville, New York restaurant.

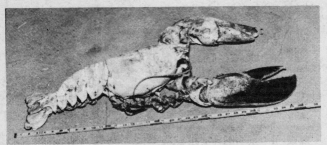

LARGEST LOBSTER: This mammoth 44-lb. crustacean shrank to 3 feet long when cooked.

Smallest. The smallest known crustaceans are water fleas of the genus *Alonella*, which may measure less than 1/100th of an inch long. They are widely distributed.

The smallest known lobster is the cape lobster (*Homarus capensis*) of South Africa which measures 3.9–4.7 inches in total length.

The smallest crabs in the world are the aptly named pea crabs (family Pinnotheridae). Some species have a shell diameter of only 0.25 in., including *Pinnotheres pisum* which is found in British waters.

Longest-Lived. The longest-lived of all crustaceans is the American lobster (*Homarus americanus*). Very large specimens may be as much as 50 years old.

Deepest. The greatest depth from which a crustacean has been recovered is 32,119 feet for an amphipod (order Amphipoda) collected by the Galathea Deep Sea Expedition in the Philippine Trench in 1951. The marine crab *Ethusina abyssicola* has been taken at a depth of 14,000 feet. Amphipods have also been collected in the Ecuadorean Andes at a height of 13,300 feet.

9. Insects *(Insecta)*

Heaviest. The heaviest insects in the world are the Goliath beetles (family Scarabaeidae) of equatorial Africa. The largest member of the group is *Goliathus goliathus*. In one group of fully-grown males the weight ranged from 2.5 to 3.5 oz.

BIGGEST BUG: Specimens of the huge Goliath beetle have been found weighing nearly a quarter pound. The example at right is shown alongside a common ladybug.

Longest. The longest insect in the world is the tropical stick-insect *Pharnacia serratipes*, females of which have been measured up to 12.99 inches in body length. The longest beetle known (excluding antennae) is the Hercules beetle (*Dynastes hercules*) of Central and South America, which has been measured up to 7.08 inches, but over half of this length is accounted for by the "prong" from the thorax. The longhorn beetle *Batocera wallacei* of New Guinea has been measured up to 10.5 inches, but 7.5 inches of this was antenna.

Smallest. The smallest insects recorded so far are the "hairy-winged" beetles of the family Ptiliidae (= Trichopterygidae) and the "battledore-wing fairy flies" (parasitic wasps) of the family Myrmaridae. They measure only 0.008 of an inch in length, and the fairy flies have a wing span of only 0.04 of an inch. This makes them smaller than some of the protozoa (single-celled animals).

The male bloodsucking banded louse (*Enderleinellus zonatus*), ungorged, and the parasitic wasp *Caraphractus cinctus* may each weigh as little as 0.005 of a milligram, or 1/567,000th of an ounce. The eggs of the latter each weigh 0.0002 of a milligram, or 1/141,750,000th of an ounce.

Commonest. The most numerous of all insects are the springtails (order Collembola), which have a very wide geographical range. It has been calculated that the top 9 inches of soil in one acre of grass-land contains 230,000,000 springtails or more than 5,000 per square foot.

Fastest-Flying. Experiments have proved that a widely pub-licized claim by an American entomologist in 1926 that the deer bot-fly (*Cephenemyia pratti*) could attain a speed of 818 m.p.h. was wildly exaggerated. If true, it would have generated a supersonic "pop." Acceptable modern experiments have now established that the highest maintainable air speed of any insect, including the deer bot-fly, is 24 m.p.h., rising to a maximum of 36 m.p.h. for short bursts. A relay of bees (maximum speed 11 m.p.h.) would use only a gallon of nectar in cruising 4,000,000 miles at 7 m.p.h.

Longest-Lived. The longest-lived insects are queen termites (order Isoptera), which have been known to lay eggs for up to 50 years.

Loudest. The loudest of all insects is the male cicada (family Cicadidae). At 7,400 pulses per minute its tymbal (sound) organs produce a noise (officially described by the U.S. Department of Agriculture as "Tsh-ee-EEEE-e-ou") detectable over a quarter of a mile distance.

Southernmost. The farthest south at which any insect has been found is 77°S. (900 miles from the South Pole) in the case of a spring-tail (order Collembola).

Largest Locust Swarm. The greatest swarm of desert locusts (*Schistocera gregaria*) ever recorded was one covering an estimated 2,000 square miles, observed crossing the Red Sea in 1889. Such a swarm must have contained about 250,000,000,000 insects weighing about 550,000 tons.

Fastest Wing Beat. The fastest wing beat of any insect under natural conditions is 62,760 a minute by a tiny midge of the genus *Forcipomyia*. In experiments with truncated wings at a temperature of 98.6°F., the rate increased to 133,080 beats per minute. The muscular contraction-expansion cycle in 0.00045 or 1/2,218th of a second represents the fastest muscle movement ever measured.

Slowest Wing Beat. The slowest wing beat of any insect is 300 a minute by the swallowtail butterfly (*Papilio machaon*). Most butter-flies beat their wings at a rate of 460 to 636 a minute.

Largest Ant. The largest ant in the world is the Ponerine ant (*Dinoponera gigantea*) of Brazil. Workers of this species have been measured up to 1.31 inches in length. Workers of the rare bull ant (*Myrmecia brevinoda* or *M. gigas*) of Queensland and northern New South Wales, Australia, have been measured up to 1.44 inches long. Bull ants have longer mandibles than Ponerine ants, and so are less bulky.

Smallest Ant. The smallest is the thief ant (*Solenopsis fugax*), whose workers measure 0.059–0.18 of an inch.

Honey from a Hive. The greatest amount of wild honey ever extracted from a single hive is 404 lbs., recorded by Ormond R. Aebi of Santa Cruz, California, on August 29, 1974.

MAMMOTH MOTH: This female owlet moth reputedly had a wing expanse of over 14 inches, but the specimen was somehow mislaid.

Largest Grasshopper. The bush-cricket with the largest wing span is the New Guinean grasshopper *Siliquofera grandis* with some females measuring more than 10 inches. The *Pseudophyllanax imperialis*, found on the island of New Caledonia, in the southwestern Pacific Ocean, has antennae measuring up to 8 inches.

Largest Dragonfly. The largest dragonfly in the world is *Megaloprepes ceruleata* of Central and South America, which has been measured up to 7.52 inches across the wings and 4.72 inches in body length.

Largest Flea. The largest known flea is *Hystrichopsylla schefferi schefferi*, which was described from a single specimen taken from the nest of a mountain beaver (*Aplondontia rufa*) at Puyallup, Washington, in 1913. Females measure up to 0.31 inches in length, which is the diameter of a pencil.

Flea Jumps. The champion jumper among fleas is the common flea (*Pulex irritans*). In one American experiment carried out in 1910 a specimen allowed to leap at will performed a long jump of 13 inches and a high jump of 7¾ inches. In jumping 130 times its own height a flea subjects itself to a force of 200 g. Siphonapterologists recognize about 1,830 varieties.

Butterflies and Moths (Order Lepidoptera)

Largest. The largest known butterfly is the Queen Alexandra birdwing (*Ornithoptera alexandrae*) of New Guinea. Females may have a wing span exceeding 11.02 inches and weigh over 0.176 oz.

The largest moth in the world (though not the heaviest) is the Hercules emperor moth (*Coscinoscera hercules*) of tropical Australia and New Guinea. A wing area of up to 40.8 inches and a wing span of 11 inches have been recorded. In 1948 an unconfirmed measurement of 14.17 inches was reported for a female captured near the post office at the coastal town of Innisfail, Queensland, Australia. The rare owlet moth (*Thysania agrippina*) of Brazil has been measured up to 11.81 inches in wing span, and the Philippine atlas moth (*Attacus crameri caesar*) of Southeast Asia up to 11.02 inches, but both these species are lighter than *C. hercules*.

Smallest. The smallest of the estimated 140,000 known species of Lepidoptera are the moth *Johanssonia acetosae* (*Stainton*), found in Great Britain, and *Stigmella ridiculosa* from the Canary Islands, which have a wing span of 0.08 of an inch and a similar body length. The smallest known butterfly is the dwarf blue (*Brephidium barberae*) from South Africa. It is 0.55 of an inch from wing tip to wing tip.

Rarest. The rarest of all butterflies (and the most valuable) is the giant birdwing *Troides allottei*, which is found only on Bougainville in the Solomon Islands. A specimen was sold for $1,800 at an auction in Paris, on October 24, 1966.

Fastest. The highest speeds recorded for Lepidoptera are: for moths, 34.7 m.p.h. by the hawk-head moth (family Sphingidae), and for butterflies, 17 m.p.h. by the great monarch butterfly (*Danaus plexippus*) in 1966.

Most Acute Sense of Smell. The most acute sense of smell exhibited in nature is that of the male emperor moth (*Eudia pavonia*), which, according to German experiments in 1961, can detect the sex attractant of the virgin female at the almost unbelievable range of 6.8 miles upwind. This scent has been identified as one of the higher alcohols ($C_{16}H_{29}OH$) of which the female carries less than 0.0001 of a milligram.

10. Centipedes *(Chilopoda)*

Longest. The longest recorded species of centipede is a large variant of the widely distributed *Scolopendra morsitans*, found on the Andaman Islands, Bay of Bengal. Specimens have been measured up to 13 inches in length and 1½ inches in breadth.

Shortest. The shortest recorded centipede is an unidentified species which measures only 0.19 of an inch.

Most Legs. The centipede with the greatest number of legs is *Himantarum gabrielis* of southern Europe which has 171–177 pairs when adult.

Fastest. The fastest centipede is probably *Scutigera coleoptrata* of southern Europe which can travel at a rate of 19.68 inches a second or 1.1 m.p.h.

11. Millipedes *(Diplopoda)*

Longest. The longest species of millipede known are the *Graphidostreptus gigas* of Africa and *Scaphistostreptus seychellarum* of the Seychelles Islands in the Indian Ocean, both of which have been measured up to 11.02 inches in length and 0.78 of an inch in diameter.

Shortest. The shortest millipede in the world is the British species *Polyxenus lagurus*, which measures 0.082–0.15 of an inch in length.

Most Legs. The greatest number of legs reported for a millipede is 355 pairs (710 legs) for an unidentified South African species.

12. Segmented Worms *(Annelida* or *Annulata)*

Longest Earthworm. The longest known species of giant earthworm is *Microchaetus rappi* (= *M. microchaetus*) of South Africa. An average-sized specimen measures 4 feet 6 inches in length (25½ inches when contracted), but much larger examples have been reliably reported. In *c.* 1937 a giant earthworm measuring 22 feet in length when naturally extended and 0.78 inches in diameter was collected in the Transvaal, and in November, 1967, another specimen measuring 11 feet in length and 21 feet when naturally extended was found reaching over the national road (width 19 feet 8½ inches) near Debe Nek, eastern Cape Province, South Africa.

Shortest. The shortest segmented worm known is *Chaetogaster annandalei*, which measures less than 0.019 of an inch in length.

LONGEST EARTHWORM: This species measures 4 feet in length, 7 feet when naturally extended.

13. Mollusks *(Mollusca)*

(Squids, octopuses, snails, shellfish, etc.)

Largest. The heaviest of all invertebrate animals is the Atlantic giant squid (*Architeuthis sp.*). The largest specimen ever recorded was one measuring 55 feet in total length (head and body 20 feet, tentacles 35 feet), captured on November 2, 1878, after it had run aground in Thimble Tickle Bay, Newfoundland. Its eyes were 9 inches in diameter. The total weight was estimated to be 4,480 lbs.

The rare Pacific giant squid *Architeuthis longimanus* is much less bulky, but the longest recorded specimen was one measuring 57 feet overall, with a head and body length of 8 feet and tentacles of 49 feet, found in Lyall Bay, New Zealand, in October, 1887.

Largest Octopus. In November, 1896, the remains of an unknown marine animal weighing an estimated 6–7 tons were found on a beach near St. Augustine, Florida. Tissue samples were later sent to the U.S. National Museum in Washington, D.C., and in 1970 they were *positively* identified as belonging to a giant form of octopus. It is estimated that this creature had a tentacular span of 200 feet.

On February 18, 1973, Donald E. Hagen, a skindiver, caught a common Pacific octopus in Lower Hood Canal, Puget Sound, Washington, which had a radial spread of 25 feet 7 inches and weighed 118 lbs. 10 oz. The octopus was seized at a depth of 60 feet and then "wrestled" to the surface single-handed.

Most Ancient. The longest existing living creature is *Neopilina galatheae*, a deep-sea worm-snail which had been believed extinct for about 320,000,000 years, but which was found at a depth of 11,400 feet off Costa Rica by the Danish research vessel *Galathea* in 1952. Fossils found in New York State, in Newfoundland, and in Sweden show that this mollusk was also living about 500,000,000 years ago.

Longest-Lived. The longest-lived mollusk is probably the deep-sea clam (*Tindaria callistiformis*) which lives an estimated 100 years. The giant clam (*Tridacna derasa*) lives about 30 years.

RAREST SHELL: This is the only surviving example of *Tibia serrata*, the world's rarest shell.

Shells

Largest. The largest of all existing bivalve shells is the marine giant clam (*Tridacna gigas*), found on the Indo-Pacific coral reefs. A specimen measuring 43 inches by 29 inches and weighing 579½ lbs. was collected from the Great Barrier Reef in 1917, and is now preserved in the American Museum of Natural History, New York City. Another lighter specimen was measured at 53.9 inches overall.

Smallest. Probably the smallest bivalve shell in the world is the coin shell (*Neolepton sykesi*), known only from a few specimens collected off Guernsey, Channel Islands and west Ireland, which measures 0.047 inches long.

Rarest. A second example of the species *Tibia serrata* (Perry), first found in 1811 and believed lost, was reported in August, 1977, from Bandar Abbas, Iran, by Franco Perantoni of Italy. It is gray-cream and golden-yellow and 5.1 inches in length.

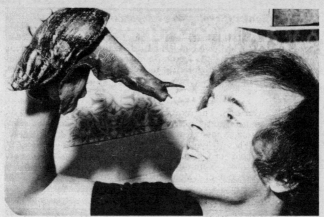

LARGEST SNAIL: This gigantic land snail measures 15½ inches long.

Gastropods

Largest. The largest gastropod is the trumpet or Baler conch (*Syrinx aruanus*) of Australia. One huge specimen collected at Bunbury, Western Australia, in 1974 and now owned by Morton Hahn· of Randolph, New Jersey, weighed 35 lbs. when alive. Its shell is 28.1 inches long and has a maximum girth of 38 inches.

The largest known land gastropod is the African giant snail (*Achatina sp.*). A huge specimen which measured 15½ inches from snout to tail (shell length 10¾ inches) and weighed 2 lbs. in December, 1978, was collected by Christopher Hudson of Hove, East Sussex, England in June, 1976, in Sierra Leone. He named the snail "Gee-Geronimo." Shell lengths of up to 14 inches have been reliably reported in Sierra Leone.

Speed. The fastest-moving species of land snail is probably the common garden snail (*Helix aspersa*).

A snail's pace varies from as slow as 0.00036 m.p.h., or 23 inches per hour, up to 0.0313 m.p.h. (or 55 yards per hour) for the common garden snail (*Helix aspersa*). Tests were carried out in the United States. The snail-racing equivalent of the 4-minute mile is 24 inches in 3 minutes, which would result in a 7,920-minute or 5½-day mile.

14. Ribbon Worms *(Nemertina or Rhynchopods)*

Longest Worm. The longest of the 550 recorded species of ribbon worms, also called nemertines (or nemerteans), is the "boot-lace worm" (*Lineus longissimus*), a highly elastic worm found in the shallow waters of the North Sea. A specimen washed ashore at St. Andrews, Fife, Scotland, in 1864, after a severe storm, measured more than 180 feet in length, making it easily the longest recorded worm of any variety.

15. Jellyfishes *(Scyphozoa* or *Scyphomedusia)*

Largest and Smallest. The longest jellyfish ever recorded is *Cyanea arctica.* One specimen washed up on the coast of Massachusetts, *c.* 1865, had a bell 7½ feet in diameter and tentacles measuring 120 feet, thus giving a theoretical tentacular span of some 245 feet.

Some true jellyfishes have a bell diameter of less than 0.78 of an inch.

Most Venomous. The most venomous are the box jellies of the genera *Chiropsalmus* and *Chironex* of the Indo-Pacific region, which carry a neurotoxic venom similar in strength to that found in the Asiatic cobra. These jellyfish have caused the deaths of at least 60 people off the coast of Queensland, Australia, in the past 25 years. Victims die within 1–3 minutes. A most effective defense is panty hose, outsize versions of which are now worn by Queensland life savers at surf carnivals.

16. Sponges *(Parazoa, Porifera* or *Spongida)*

Largest and Smallest. The largest sponge is the barrel-shaped loggerhead *(Spheciospongia vesparium),* found off the islands of the West Indies and off Florida, measuring 3½ feet high and 3 feet in diameter. Neptune's cup or goblet *(Poterion patera)* of Indonesia stands up to 4 feet in height, but it is a less bulky animal. In 1909, a wool sponge *(Hippospongia canaliculatta)* measuring 6 feet in circumference was collected off the Bahama Islands. When first taken from the water it weighed between 80 and 90 lbs., but after it had been dried and relieved of all excrescences it scaled 12 lbs. (This sponge is now preserved in the Smithsonian Institution, Washington, D.C.)

The smallest known sponge is the widely distributed *Leucosolenia blanca,* which measures 0.11 of an inch in height when fully grown.

Deepest. Sponges have been taken from depths of up to 18,500 feet.

17. Extinct Animals

Largest. The first dinosaur to be scientifically described was *Megalosaurus* ("large lizard"), a 20-foot-long bipedal theropod, in 1824. A lower jaw and other bones of this animal had been discovered before 1818 in a slate quarry at Stonesfield, near Woodstock, Oxfordshire, England. It stalked across southern England about 130,000,000 years ago. The word "dinosaur" ("fearfully great lizard") was not used for such reptiles until 1841. The longest recorded dinosaur was *Diplodocus* ("double beam"), an attenuated sauropod which ranged over western North America about 150,000,000 years ago. A composite skeleton of three individuals excavated near Split Mountain, Utah, and mounted in the Carnegie Museum of the Natural Sciences, Pittsburgh, measures 87½ feet in length (neck 22 feet, body 15 feet, tail 50½ feet) and stands 11 feet 9 inches at the pelvis (the highest point on the body). This animal weighed an estimated 11.63 tons in life.

LONGEST DINOSAUR?: Researchers believe that this 8-foot-long scapula, shown alongside its discoverer, Dr. James Jensen, may have belonged to a sauropod 110 feet long.

The heaviest prehistoric animal described scientifically so far has been the swamp-dwelling *Brachiosaurus brancai* ("arm lizard") which lived from 135,000,000 to 165,000,000 years ago. Its remains have been found in East Africa, Colorado, Oklahoma and Utah and Europe. A complete skeleton excavated near Tendaguru Hill, southern Tanganyika (Tanzania) in 1909 and mounted in the Museum für Naturkunde in East Berlin, Germany, measures 74 feet 6 inches in total length and 21 feet at the shoulder. This reptile weighed a computed 87.65 tons in life, but isolated bones have since been discovered in East Africa which indicate that some specimens may have weighed as much as 140 tons.

In the summer of 1972, the remains of another enormous sauropod, new to science, were discovered in a flood-plain bonejam in Colorado, by an expedition from Brigham Young University, Provo, Utah. Excavations are still continuing, but a study of the incomplete series of cervical vertebrae indicates that this dinosaur must have had a neck length of about 39 feet (compared with 22 feet for *Diplodocus*). If the rest of "Supersaurus" (as it has been nicknamed) was built similarly to the *Brachiosaurus*, the overall length would be approximately 130 feet, the shoulder height 37 feet, and the raised head measurement 75 feet. Its weight would have been at least 280 tons, making it the largest animal that has ever existed.

Largest Predator. The largest of the carnosaurs (family Megalosauridae) was probably *Tyrannosaurus rex*, which lived about 75,000,000 years ago in what are now Montana and Wyoming. No complete skeleton has ever been discovered, but composite remains indicate that it measured up to 35 feet in overall length, had a bipedal height of 18½ feet, and weighed a calculated 8 tons. In a recent reinterpretation of the *Tyrannosaurus* remains, 12 feet was chopped off the tail length to produce a more symmetrical animal. Its 4-foot-long skull contained serrated teeth up to 6 inches long.

The body of a huge *Allosaurus*, with a body much more massive in proportion to its height than *Tyrannosaurus*, was excavated near

Kenton, Oklahoma, in 1934. This carnosaur had a bipedal height of 16 feet and measured 42 feet in overall length.

Longest Tusks. The longest tusks of any prehistoric animal were those of the straight-tusked elephant *Hesperoloxodon antiquus germanicus*, which lived in what is now northern Germany about 2,000,000 years ago. The average length in adult bulls was 16 feet 4¾ inches. A single tusk of a woolly mammoth (*Mammonteus primigenius*) preserved in the Franzens Museum at Brno, Czechoslovakia, measures 16 feet 5½ inches along the outside curve. In *c.* August, 1933, a single tusk of an Imperial mammoth (*Archidiskodon imperator*) measuring 16+ feet (anterior end missing) was unearthed near Post, Texas. In 1934, this tusk was presented to the American Museum of Natural History in New York City.

Heaviest Tusks. The heaviest fossil tusk on record is one weighing 330 lbs., with a girth of 35 inches, now preserved in the Museo Civico di Storia Naturale, Milan, Italy. The specimen (in two pieces) measures 11 feet 9 inches in length.

The heaviest recorded mammoth tusks are a pair in the University of Nebraska Museum, Lincoln, Nebraska, which have a combined weight of 498 lbs. and measure 13 feet 9 inches and 13 feet 7 inches respectively. They were found near Campbell, Nebraska, in April, 1915.

Longest Antlers. The prehistoric giant deer (*Megaceros giganteus*), which lived in northern Europe and northern Asia as recently as 50,000 B.C., stood 7 feet at the shoulder and had the longest antlers of any known animal. One specimen recovered from an Irish bog had greatly palmated antlers measuring 14 feet across.

Most Brainless. The *Stegosaurus* ("plated reptile"), which measured up to 30 feet in length, 8 feet in height at the hips and weighed up to 2 tons, had a walnut-sized brain weighing only 2½ ounces. It represented 0.004 of one per cent of its body weight, compared with 0.074 of one per cent for an elephant and 1.88 per cent for a human. It roamed widely across the Northern Hemisphere about 150,000,000 years ago, trying to remember where it had been.

Largest Mammal. The largest prehistoric land mammal was *Baluchitherium* (= *Indricotherium, Paraceratherium, Aceratherium, Thaumastotherium, Aralotherium* and *Benaratherium*), a long-necked hornless rhinoceros which lived in Europe and central western Asia between 20,000,000 and 40,000,000 years ago. It stood up to 17 feet 9 inches to the top of the shoulder hump (27 feet to the crown of its raised head), measured 35–37 feet in length and weighed nearly 22 tons. The bones of this gigantic browser were first discovered in 1907–08 in the Bugti Hills in east Baluchistan, Pakistan.

The largest known prehistoric marine mammal was *Basilosaurus* (= *Zeuglodon*) of 50,000,000 years ago. A specimen from Alabama measured 70 feet and weighed an estimated 30 tons.

Largest Flying Creature. The largest flying creature was a winged reptile (not yet named) of the order Pterosauria which glided over what is now Texas about 70,000,000 years ago. Partial remains (four wings, a neck, hind legs, and mandibles) of three specimens recently discovered in Big Bend National Park, Texas, indicate that this pterosaur must have had a wing span of at least 36 feet and that the maximum spread may have been as great as 69 feet. *Pteranodon ingens*, the previous title-holder, had a maximum expanse of 27 feet.

Largest Mammoth. The tallest extinct elephant was the Steppe mammoth *Paraelephas* (= *Mammuthus*) *trogontherii* which lived 1 million years ago in what is now Central Europe. A fragmentary skeleton found in Mosbach, West Germany, indicates a shoulder height of 14¾ feet.

Largest Dinosaur Eggs. The largest dinosaur eggs discovered were those of a *Hypselosaurus priscus* found in October, 1961, in the valley of the Durance, near Aix-en-Provence, in southern France. The eggs of this 30-foot-long sauropod, believed to be 80,000,000 years old, would have had, uncrushed, a length of 12 inches and a diameter of 10 inches.

Largest Bird. The largest prehistoric bird was *Dromornis stirtoni*, a huge emu-like creature which lived in central Australia about 10–11 million years ago. Fossil leg bones found near Alice Springs in 1974 indicate that the bird must have stood 9–10 feet in height and weighed at least 1,100 lbs. The flightless moa *Dinornis giganteus* of North Island, New Zealand, was taller, attaining a height of over 13 feet, but probably only weighed about 500 lbs.

The largest prehistoric bird actually to fly was probably the condor-like *Teratornis incredibilis*, which lived in North America about 100,000,000 years ago. Fossil remains of one of this species, discovered in Smith Creek Cave, Nevada, in 1952, indicate a wing span of 16 feet 4¾ inches, and the bird must have weighed nearly 50 lbs. Another gigantic flying bird named *Osteodontornis orri*, which lived in what is now California, about 20,000,000 years ago, had a wing span of 16 feet and was probably even heavier. It was related to the pelicans and storks. The albatross-like *Gigantornis eaglesomei* has been credited with a wing span of 20 feet on the evidence of a single fossilized breastbone. It flew over what is now Nigeria between 34,000,000 and 58,000,000 years ago.

A wing span measurement of 16 feet 4¾ inches has also been reported for another flying bird named *Ornithodesmus latidens*, which flew over what is now Hampshire and the Isle of Wight, England, about 90,000,000 years ago.

Largest Marine Reptile. The largest marine reptile ever recorded was the short-necked pliosaur *Kronosaurus queenslandicus*, which swam in the seas around what is now Australia about 100,000,000 years ago. It measured up to 55 feet in length, with a skull 11½ feet long. *Stretosaurus macromerus*, another short-necked pliosaur, was of comparable size. A mandible found in Cumnor, Oxfordshire, England, must have belonged to a reptile measuring at least 50 feet in length.

Largest Crocodile. The largest known crocodile was *Deinosuchus riograndensis*, which lived in the lakes and swamps of what is now Texas about 75,000,000 years ago. Fragmentary remains discovered in Big Bend National Park, Texas, indicate it must have measured at least 50 feet in total length. The less bulky gavial *Rhamphosuchus*, which lived in northern India about 7,000,000 years ago, also reached a length of 50 feet.

Largest Chelonians. The largest prehistoric chelonian was the possibly marine pelomedusid turtle *Stupendemys geographicus*, which lived about 80,000,000 years ago. Fossil remains discovered by a Harvard University paleontological expedition in northern Venezuela in 1972 indicate that this turtle had a carapace (shell) measuring 7½–8 feet in mid-line length and probably at least 12 feet in overall length.

The largest prehistoric tortoise was probably *Geochelone* (= *Colossochelys*) *atlas*, which lived in what is now northern India, Burma, Java, the Celebes and Timor between 1,000,000 and 2,500,000 years ago. An almost complete skeleton with a carapace 5 feet 5 inches long (7 feet 4 inches over the curve) and 2 feet 11 inches high was discovered in 1923 near Chandigarh in the Siwalik Hills, India. This animal had an overall length of 8 feet and is computed to have weighed about 2,100 lbs. when it was alive. Fossil remains of similarly sized tortoises have been found recently in Florida and Texas.

Largest Fish. No prehistoric fish has yet been discovered that is larger than living species. The belief that the great shark *Carcharodon megalodon*, which abounded in Miocene seas some 15,000,000 years ago, measured 80 feet in length (based on ratios from fossil teeth) has now been shown to be in error. The modern estimate is that this shark did not exceed 43 feet.

LARGEST CHELONIAN: A 6-foot-2-inch man stands beside the shell of the largest known prehistoric turtle.

JAWS OF THE LARGEST PREHISTORIC FISH: This shark, which lived about 15,000,000 years ago, must have been 43 feet long.

Earliest Animals by Type

The earliest known primates originated about 70,000,000 years ago and were similar in form to the tarsier of Indonesia and the lemur of Madagascar. The earliest known ape was *Aegyptopithecus zeuxis* of 28,000,000 years ago, whose remains were found in 1966 in El Faiyum, Egypt. The earliest known bird was the glider *Archaeopteryx* of about 150,000,000 years ago. The earliest known mammal was a shrew-like animal between 1 and 2 inches long, whose fossilized remains, estimated to be 190,000,000 years old, were found at Thabaea-Litau, Lesotho (formerly called Basutoland), in December, 1966. The earliest known reptiles were *Hylonomus, Archerpeton, Romericus* and *Protoclepsybrops*, which all lived in Nova Scotia, Canada, about 290,000,000 years ago. The earliest amphibian and the earliest known four-legged creature was *Ichthyostega*, measuring 4 feet long, which lived in Greenland about 350,000,000 years ago. The earliest spider, *Palaeostenzia crassipes*, and the earliest insect, *Rhyniella procursor*, a springtail, occur in a fossil peat of Middle Devonian age (about 370,000,000 years old) in Tayside, Scotland. The earliest vertebrates were *anatolepis*, fish scales of which were found in Crook County, Wyoming, dating to 510,000,000 years ago. The most archaic living mollusk is *Neopilina galatheae*, found in 1952 off Costa Rica, belonging to a group which has survived almost unchanged for 510,000,000 years. The earliest known crustacean was the 12-legged shelled *Karagassiema*, measuring 2 feet long, found in pre-Cambrian rock in the eastern Sayan Mountains of Siberia, U.S.S.R. This animal lived about 650,000,000 years ago.

Longest Snake. The longest prehistoric snake was the python-like *Gigantophis garstini*, which inhabited what is now Egypt about 50,000,000 years ago. Parts of a spinal column and a small piece of jaw discovered at El Faiyum indicate a length of about 33 feet, which is comparable with the longest constrictors living today.

Largest Amphibian. The largest amphibian ever recorded was the gavial-like *Prinosuchus plummeri* which lived 230,000,000 years ago. In 1972 the fragmented remains of a specimen measuring an estimated 29.5 feet in life were discovered in northern Brazil.

Largest Arachnid. The largest arachnid ever recorded was *Pterygotus buffaloensis*, a sea scorpion (eurypterid) which lived about 400,000,000 years ago. It grew to a length of 9 feet.

Largest Insect. The largest prehistoric insect was *Meganeura monyi*, a dragonfly that lived about 280,000,000 years ago. Fossil remains (impression of wings) discovered at Commentry, France, indicate that it had a wing span reaching 27½ inches.

Largest Shelled Mollusk. The Cretaceous fossil ammonite (*Pachydiscus seppenradensis*) of about 75,000,000 years ago, had a shell measuring up to 8 feet 5 inches in diameter.

Most Southerly. The most southerly creature yet found is a freshwater salamander-like amphibian *Labyrinthodont*, represented by a 2½-inch piece of jawbone found near Beardmore Glacier, Antarctica, 325 miles from the South Pole, which dates from the early Jurassic period of 200,000,000 years ago. This discovery was made in December, 1967.

PLANT KINGDOM (*PLANTAE*)

Earliest Flower. The oldest fossil of a flowering plant with palm-like imprints was found in Colorado in 1953 and dated about 65,000,000 years old.

Largest Forest. The largest afforested areas are the vast coniferous forests of the northern U.S.S.R., lying mainly between latitude 55°N. and the Arctic Circle. The total wooded areas amount to 2,700,000,000 acres (25 per cent of the world's forests), of which 38 per cent is Siberian larch. The U.S.S.R. is 34 per cent afforested.

Plant Life

Rarest. Plants thought to be extinct are rediscovered each year and there are thus many plants of which specimens are known in but a single locality. The small pink blossoms of *Presidio manzanita* survive in a single specimen reported in June, 1978, at an undisclosed site in California.

Northernmost. The yellow poppy (*Papaver radicatum*) and the Arctic willow (*Salix arctica*) survive, the latter in an extremely stunted form, on the northernmost land (83°N.).

Southernmost. The most southerly plant life recorded is seven species of lichen found in 1933–34 by the second expedition of Rear Admiral Richard E. Byrd, U.S. Navy, in latitude 86° 03′ S. in the Queen Maud Mountains, Antarctica. The southernmost recorded flowering plant is the carnation (*Colobanthus crassifolius*), which was found in latitude 67° 15′ S. on Jenny Island, Margaret Bay, Graham Land (Palmer Peninsula), Antarctica.

SMALLEST FLOWERING
PLANT: The metal object
shown with the newly
discovered *Pilea microphylla*
is the point of a needle (see
page 120).

Highest Altitude. The *Stellaria decumbens* is the flowering plant found at the highest verified altitude—20,130 feet up in the Himalayas. A claimed height of 23,000 feet in the Himalayas for *Christolea crassifolia* remains unconfirmed.

A non-flowering plant of *Androsace microphylla* was recorded by A. Zimmermann at 20,333 feet on the 1952 Swiss Everest expedition.

Deepest and Densest Roots. The greatest reported depth to which roots have penetrated is a calculated 400 feet in the case of a wild fig tree at Echo Caves, near Ohrigstad, East Transvaal, South Africa. A single winter rye plant (*Secale cereale*) has been shown to produce 387 miles of roots in 1.83 cubic feet of earth.

Largest Blooms. The mottled orange-brown and white parasitic stinking corpse lily (*Rafflesia arnoldi*) has the largest of all blooms. These attach themselves to the cissus vines of the jungle in southeast Asia. They measure up to 3 feet across and ¾ of an inch thick, and attain a weight of 15 lbs.

The largest known inflorescence is that of *Puya raimondii*, a rare Bolivian plant with an erect panicle (diameter 8 feet) which emerges to a height of 35 feet. Each of these bears up to 8,000 white blooms. In 1974, the flower-spike of an agave in Berkeley, California, was measured to be 52 feet long. (See also Slowest-Flowering Plant.)

The world's largest blossoming plant is the giant Chinese wisteria at Sierra Madre, California. It was planted in 1892 and now has branches 500 feet long. It covers nearly an acre, weighs 252 tons and has an estimated 1,500,000 blossoms during its blossoming period of five weeks, when up to 30,000 people pay admission to visit. In November, 1974, it was reported that a passion plant, owned by Dennis and Patti Carlson of Blaine, Minnesota, and fed with a hormone, had grown to a length of 600 feet.

Smallest Flowering Plant. Many formerly unsuspected minute flowers have been discovered since 1972 by Mr. and Mrs. Robert Gilbreath of California. The smallest is the *Pilea microphylla* of western India, measuring $\frac{1}{72}$ of an inch in diameter.

Rarest Flower. The $20,000 prize offered by the Burpee Co. in 1924 for producing the first all-white marigold was won in 1945 by Alice Vonk of Sully, Iowa.

Fastest Growth. The case of a *Liliacea hesperogucca whipplei* growing 12 feet in 14 days was reported from Treco Abbey, Isles of Scilly, England, in July, 1978.

Slowest-Flowering Plant. The slowest-flowering of all plants is the rare *Puya raimondii*, the largest of all herbs, discovered in Bolivia in 1870. The panicle emerges after about 150 years of the plant's life. It then dies. (See also above under Largest Blooms.)

Some agaves, erroneously called century plants, first flower after 40 years.

Largest Leaves. The largest leaves of any plant belong to the raffia palm (*Raphia ruffia*) of the Mascarene Islands, in the Indian Ocean, and the Amazonian bamboo palm (*R. toedigera*) of South America, whose leaf blades may measure up to 65 feet in length with petioles up to 13 feet.

The largest undivided leaf is that of *Alocasia macrorrhiza*, found in Sabah, East Malaysia. One found in 1966 measured 9 feet 11 inches long and 6 feet 3½ inches wide, and had an area of 34.2 square feet on one side.

Most and Least Nutritive Fruit. An analysis of the 38 commonly eaten raw (as opposed to dried) fruits shows that the one with the highest calorific value is the avocado (*Persea americana*) with 741 calories per edible lb. That with the lowest value is cucumber with 73 calories per lb. Avocados probably originated in Central and South America and also contain vitamins A, C, and E and 2.2 per cent protein.

Largest Melons. A watermelon weighing 197 lbs. was reported by Grace's Gardens, Hackettstown, New Jersey, in 1975. The grower was Ed Weeks of Tarboro, North Carolina. His longest watermelon to date measured 48 inches.

Mr. Weeks also lays claim to the record for largest cantaloupe with a 39-lb. giant grown in 1977.

Largest Pineapple. A pineapple weighing 17 lbs. was picked by H. Retief in Malindi, Kenya, in December, 1978.

Largest Cabbage. In 1865, William Collingwood of The Stalwell, County Durham, England, grew a red cabbage with a circumference of 259 inches. It reputedly weighed 123 lbs.

Largest Carrot. A carrot weighing 11 lbs. was grown by Bob McEwan of Beeac, Victoria, Australia, in September, 1967.

Largest Sweet Potato. A 22½-lb. specimen grown by George Wynn of Gibsonton, Florida in 1977 was reported by Grace's Gardens.

MELON KING: Ed Weeks of Tarboro, North Carolina, proudly displays the longest watermelon ever grown, 48 inches from end to end.

Largest Lemon. Mrs. D. G. Knutzen of Whittier, California, reported in January, 1977, a lemon with a circumference of $28\frac{3}{4}$ inches, weighing 6 lbs. 4 oz.

Largest Orange. The heaviest orange is one weighing 3 lbs. 11 oz. grown by Shane and Shawn Calendine of Tucson, Arizona, in 1977.

Largest Squash. A squash weighing 513 lbs. was grown by Harold Fulp, Jr., at Ninevah, Indiana, in 1977.

LARGEST SQUASH: The Fulp family of Ninevah, Indiana, display their 513-lb. Hungarian Mammoth squash.

Largest Sugar Beet. A 45.5-lb. sugar beet was grown by the Bob Meyer Farms in Brawley, California, in 1974.

Largest Peanut. Ed Weeks of Tarboro, North Carolina, grew a peanut 3½ inches long in 1978, as reported by Grace's Gardens.

Longest Pepper. A NuMex Big Jim pepper 13½ inches long, grown by June Rutherford of Hatch, New Mexico, in 1975, was reported by Grace's Gardens.

Largest Pepper Plant. A sweet pepper plant owned by Ralph Savarese of Pascagoula, Mississippi, grew to be 56 inches tall, yielding 53 peppers, in 1978, as reported by Grace's Gardens.

Largest Mushroom. A common mushroom with a 75 inch circumference was found near the Lualaba River, Zaïre, in 1920. A mushroom weighing 18 lbs. 10 oz. was reported from Whidbey Island, Washington, in September, 1968.

Largest Radish. Radishes weighing 25 lbs. have been grown by Glen Tucker of Stanbury, South Australia, in August, 1974, and by Herbert Breslow of Ruskin, Florida, in 1977.

Largest Tomato. Grace's Gardens, Hackettstown, New Jersey, reported a 6-lb.-8-oz. tomato grown by Clarence Dailey of Monona, Wisconsin, in August, 1976.

Largest Tomato Plant. A 21-foot 3½-inch plant was grown by David Vibert in Wyckoff, New Jersey, in July, 1976.

Cherry Tomato Yield. A cherry tomato plant owned by James Grohman of Temple, Pennsylvania, produced 107 tomatoes in 1978.

Largest Cucumber. A 13-lb. example was grown by George J. Kucera of Mexia, Texas, in July, 1978. A Vietnamese variety 6 feet long was reported by L. Szabo of Debrecen, Hungary in September, 1976.

Longest Gourd. Grace's Gardens, Hackettstown, New Jersey, reported a Snake longissima gourd 80¼ inches long grown by Dr. Leslie Miller of Columbus, Ohio, in 1976.

Largest Okra Stalk. An okra stalk 17 feet tall grown in 1979 by P. C. Cain of Kosciusko, Mississippi, was reported by Grace's Gardens.

Largest Kohlrabi. John Hritz grew an 11½-inch tall, 4-lb. kohlrabi in Brownsville, Pennsylvania, in 1978.

Largest Poinsettia Tree. Frank Trojanowski and his students in Trumbull, Connecticut, grew a 7-foot-6-inch-tall poinsettia tree in 1978, as reported by Grace's Gardens.

Largest Dahlia. A 9-foot-10¾-inch dahlia was grown by H. W. Deem of Victoria, Australia, in 1977.

Largest Rose Tree. A "Lady Banks" rose tree at Tombstone, Arizona, has a trunk 40 inches thick, stands 9 feet high and covers an area of 5,380 square feet, supported by 68 posts and several thousand feet of iron piping. This enables 150 people to be seated under the arbor. The original cutting came from Scotland in 1884.

Largest Rhododendron. The largest species of rhododendron is the scarlet *Rhododendron arboreum*, examples of which reach a height of 60 feet at Mangalbaré, Nepal. The cross section of the trunk of a *Rhododendron giganteum*, from Yunnan, China, reputedly 90 feet high, is preserved at Inverewe Garden, Highland, Scotland.

Largest Philodendron. A philodendron 300 feet long now grows in the La Carreta Restaurant in San Jacinto, California.

Largest Aspidistra. The aspidistra (*Aspidistra elatior*) was introduced as a parlor palm to Britain from Japan and China in 1822. The biggest aspidistra in the world is one $51\frac{3}{4}$ inches tall, grown by Cliff W. Evans at Kiora, Moruya, New South Wales, Australia, and measured in December, 1977.

Largest Vine. The largest recorded grape vine was one planted in 1842 at Carpinteria, California. By 1900 it was yielding more than 9 tons of grapes in some years, and averaging 7 tons per year. It died in 1920.

The most northerly vineyard is located in Sabile, Latvia, U.S.S.R., just north of latitude 57°N. The Coonawarra vineyard in South Australia (latitude 37° 20′ S.) is the world's most southerly.

Tallest Hedge. The world's tallest hedge is the Meikleour beech hedge in Perthshire, Scotland. It was planted in 1746 and has now attained a trimmed height of 85 feet. It is 600 yards long, and some of its trees now exceed 100 feet.

The tallest yew hedge in the world is in Earl Bathurst's Park, Gloucestershire, England. It was planted in 1720, runs for 170 yards, reaches 36 feet in height and 15 feet in thickness, and takes 20 man-days to trim.

The tallest box hedge, 35 feet in height, is at Birr Castle, Offaly, Ireland, and dates from the 18th century.

Largest Cactus. The largest of all cacti is the saguaro (*Cereus giganteus* or *Carnegiea gigantea*), found in Arizona, southeastern California, and Sonora, Mexico. The green fluted column is surmounted by candelabra-like branches rising to a height of 52 feet $5\frac{3}{4}$ inches in the case of a specimen measured on the boundary of the Saguaro National Monument, Arizona. They have waxy white blooms which are followed by edible crimson fruit. An armless cactus 78 feet in height was measured in April, 1978, by Hube Yates in Cave Creek, Arizona.

Worst Weeds. The most intransigent weed is the mat-forming water weed *Salvinia auriculata*, found in Africa. It was detected on the filling of Kariba Lake, in May, 1959, and within 11 months had choked an area of 77 sq. miles, rising by 1963 to 387 sq. miles. The world's worst land weeds are regarded as purple nut sedge, Bermuda grass, barnyard grass, junglerice, goose grass, Johnson grass, Guinea grass, cogon grass and lantana.

LARGEST WREATH: The centerpiece of the big Christmas 1977 celebration was this 39-foot diameter wreath in Morrisville, Pennsylvania.

Longest Seaweed. Claims made that seaweed off Tierra del Fuego, South America, grows to 600 and even 1,000 feet in length have gained currency. More recent and more reliable records indicate that the longest species of seaweed is the Pacific giant kelp (*Macrocystis pyrifera*), which does not exceed 196 feet in length. It can grow 17¾ inches in a day. The Japanese seaweed *Sargassum muticum* introduced *c.* 1970 can grow to 30 feet.

Tallest Hollyhock. The tallest reported hollyhock (*Althaea rosea*) is one of 19 feet 7 inches grown by G. Palmer of Surrey, England, in 1978.

Most-Spreading. The greatest area covered by a single clonal growth is that of the wild box huckleberry (*Gaylussacia brachyera*), a mat-forming evergreen shrub first reported in 1796. A colony covering 8 acres was discovered in 1845 near New Bloomfield, Pennsylvania. Another colony, covering about 100 acres, was "discovered" on July 18, 1920, near the Juniata River in Pennsylvania. It has been estimated that this colony began 13,000 years ago.

Fourteen-Leafed Clover. A fourteen-leafed white clover (*Trifolium repens*) was found by Randy Farland near Sioux Falls, South Dakota, on June 16, 1975.

Largest Wreath. The largest wreath was constructed by Joe Marrazzo and James Piscopo in Morrisville, Pennsylvania, in December, 1977. It weighed 2,687 lbs. and measured 39 feet in diameter.

Trees

Oldest. The oldest recorded tree is a bristlecone pine (*Pinus longaeva*) designated WPN-114, which grew at 10,750 feet above sea level on the northeast face of Wheeler Peak (13,063 feet) in eastern California. During studies in 1963 and 1964 it was found to be about 4,900 years old, but was cut down with a chain saw. The oldest known *living* tree is the bristlecone pine named *Methuselah*, growing at 10,000 feet on the California side of the White Mountains, with a confirmed age of 4,600 years. In March, 1974, it was reported that this tree produced 48 live seedlings. Dendrochronologists estimate the *potential* life span of a bristlecone pine at nearly 5,500 years, but that of a "big tree" at perhaps 6,000 years.

Earliest. The earliest species of tree still surviving is the maidenhair tree (*Ginkgo biloba*) of China, which first appeared about 160,000,000 years ago, during the Jurassic era. It was "re-discovered" by Kaempfer (Netherlands) in 1690, and reached England *c.* 1754. It has been grown in Japan since *c.* 1100 where it was known as *ginkyo* (silver apricot) and is now known as *icho*. (See photograph on page 127). A report in March, 1976, stated that some enormous specimens of Japanese cedar (*Cryptomeria japonica*) had been dated by carbon-14 to 5200 B.C.

Largest Living Thing. The most massive living thing on earth is a California "big tree" (*Sequoiadendron giganteum*) named the "General Sherman," standing 272 feet 4 inches tall, in Sequoia National Park, California. It has a true girth of 79.1 feet (at 5 feet above the ground). The "General Sherman" has been estimated to contain the equivalent of 600,120 board feet of timber, sufficient to

OLDEST LIVING THING: Bristlecone pines in California have been found to exist since the 3rd millennium B.C.

make 5,000,000,000 matches. The foliage is blue-green, and the red-brown tan bark may be up to 24 inches thick in parts. In 1968, the official published figure for its estimated weight was 2,145 tons.

The seed of a "big tree" weighs only 1/6,000th of an ounce. Its growth to maturity may therefore represent an increase in weight of over 250,000,000,000 fold.

Tallest. The tallest known species of tree is the coast redwood (*Sequoia sempervirens*), growing indigenously near the coastline in California north of Monterey to Oregon. The tallest measured example is the Howard Libbey Tree in Redwood Creek Grove, Humboldt County, California, announced at 367.8 feet in 1963 but discovered to have an apparently dead top and re-estimated at 366.2 feet in 1970. It has a girth of 44 feet. The nearby tree announced to a Senate Committee by Dr. Rudolf W. Becking on June 18, 1966, to be 385 feet, proved on re-measurement to be no more than 311.3 feet tall. A coast redwood of 367 feet 8 inches, felled in 1873 near Guerneville, California, was almost exactly the same height as the Howard Libbey redwood as originally measured.

The tallest non-sequoia is a Douglas fir at Quinault Lake Park, Washington, of *c.* 310 feet. The tallest broadleaf tree in the world is a *Eucalyptus regnans* measured in Western Australia at 338 feet.

The identity of the tallest tree of all time has never been satisfactorily resolved. A claim as high as 525 feet has been made (subsequently reduced on re-measurement, in May, 1889, to 220 feet). Currently, the accepted view is that the maximum height recorded by a qualified surveyor was 375 feet for the Cornthwaite Tree (*Eucalyptus regnans*) in Thorpdale, Gippsland, Victoria, Australia, measured in 1880. The claim that a Douglas fir (*Pseudotsuga taxifolia*) felled by George Carey in 1895 in British Columbia had a height of 417 feet and a 77-foot circumference has been called into question, though not necessarily invalidated, by a falsified photograph. The tallest Douglas fir now known is the one mentioned above of *c.* 310 feet.

Tallest Christmas Tree. The world's tallest cut Christmas tree was a 221-foot Douglas fir erected at Northgate Shopping Center, Seattle, Washington, in December, 1950.

Greatest Girth. The Santa Maria del Tule tree, in the state of Oaxaca, in Mexico, is a Montezuma cypress (*Taxodium mucronatum*) with a girth of 112–113 feet at a height of 5 feet above the ground in 1949.

A figure of 167 feet in circumference was reported for the European chestnut (*Castanea sativa*) known as the "Tree of the 100 Horses" on the edge of Mount Etna, Sicily, Italy, in 1972.

Remotest. The tree most distant from any other is believed to be one at an oasis in the Ténéré Desert, Niger Republic. There were no other trees within 31 miles. In February, 1960, it survived being rammed by a truck driven by a Frenchman. The tree was transplanted and is now in the Museum of Niamey, Niger.

Fastest-Growing. Discounting bamboo, which is not botanically classified as a tree, but as woody grass, the fastest rate of growth

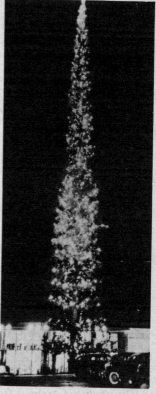

LONG-SURVIVING TREE SPECIES (above): The maidenhair tree first appeared about 160,000,000 years ago. **TALLEST CHRISTMAS TREE** (right): Measuring 221 feet, this Douglas fir was erected at a shopping center in Seattle, Washington, in 1950.

recorded is 35 feet 3 inches in 13 months by an *Albizzia falcata* planted on June 17, 1974, in Sabah, Malaysia. The youngest recorded age for a tree to reach 100 feet is 7 years for a *Eucalyptus regnans* in Rhodesia.

Slowest-Growing. The speed of growth of trees depends largely upon conditions, although some species, such as box and yew, are always slow-growing. The extreme is represented by a specimen of Sitka spruce which required 98 years to grow to 11 inches tall, with a diameter of less than one inch, on the Arctic tree-line. The growing of miniature trees or *bonsai* is an Oriental cult mentioned as early as c. 1320.

Most Leaves. Little work has been done on the laborious task of establishing which species of tree has the most leaves. A large oak has perhaps 250,000, but a cypress may have some 45-50 million leaf scales.

Most Expensive. The highest price ever paid for a tree is $51,000 for a single Starkspur golden delicious apple tree from near Yakima, Washington, bought by a nursery in Missouri in 1959.

Largest Petrified. A California "big tree" (*Sequoiadendron giganteum*) near Coaldale, Nevada, measuring 295 feet tall is the largest known petrified tree.

Wood

Heaviest. The heaviest of all woods is black ironwood (*Olea laurifolia*), also called South African ironwood, with a specific gravity of up to 1.49, and weighing up to 93 lbs. per cubic foot.

Lightest. The lightest wood is *Aeschynomene hispida*, found in Cuba, which has a specific gravity of 0.044 and a weight of only $2\frac{3}{4}$ lbs. per cubic foot. The wood of the balsa tree (*Ochroma pyramidale*) is of very variable density—between $2\frac{1}{2}$ and 24 lbs. per cubic foot. The density of cork is 15 lbs. per cubic foot.

Seeds

Largest. The largest seed in the world is that of the double coconut or Coco de Mer (*Lodoicea seychellarum*), the single-seeded fruit of which may weigh 40 lbs. This grows only in the Seychelles Islands, in the Indian Ocean.

Smallest. The smallest seeds are those of epiphytic orchids, at 35,000,000 to the ounce (*cf.* grass pollens at up to 6,000,000,000 grains per ounce). A single plant of the American ragweed can generate 8,000,000,000 pollen grains in five hours.

Most Durable. The most durable of all seeds are those of the Arctic lupin (*Lupinus arcticus*) found in frozen silt at Miller Creek in the Yukon, Canada, in July, 1954. They were germinated in 1966 and dated by the radio-carbon method to at least 8,000 B.C. and more probably to 13,000 B.C.

Mosses

The smallest of mosses is the pygmy moss (*Ephemerum*), and the longest is the brook moss (*Fontinalis*), which forms streamers up to 3 feet long in flowing water.

Bamboo

Tallest. The tallest recorded bamboo was a thorny bamboo culm (*Bambusa arundinacea*) felled at Pattazhi, Travancore, India, in November, 1904, which measured $121\frac{1}{2}$ feet.

Fastest-Growing. Some species of the 45 genera of bamboo have attained growth rates of up to 36 inches per day (0.00002 m.p.h.), on their way to reaching a height of 100 feet in less than three months.

Ferns

Largest. The largest of all the more than 6,000 species of fern is the tree-fern (*Alsophila excelsa*) of Norfolk Island, in the South Pacific, which attains a height of up to 60 feet.

LARGEST SEED:
The Coco de Mer
seed may weigh
40 lbs. It grows only
in the Seychelles
Islands in the
Indian Ocean.

Smallest. The world's smallest ferns are *Hecistopteris pumila*, found in Central America, and *Azolla caroliniana*, which is native to the U.S.

Grasses

Commonest. The world's commonest grass is *Cynodon ductylon* or Bermuda grass.

Fastest Growing. The "Callie" hybrid, selected in 1966, grows as much as 6 inches a day and stolons reach 18 feet in length.

Orchids

Largest. The largest of all orchids is *Grammatvphyllum speciosum*, native to Malaysia. Specimens up to 25 feet high have been recorded.

The largest orchid flower is that of *Phragmipedium caudatum*, found in tropical areas of America. Its petals are up to 18 inches long, giving it a maximum outstretched diameter of 3 feet. The flower is, however, much less bulky than that of the stinking corpse lily (see Largest Blooms, p. 119).

Tallest. The tallest free-standing orchid is *Grammatophyllum speciosum* (see above). *Galeola foliata* may attain 45 feet on decaying rainforest trees in Queensland, Australia.

Smallest. The smallest orchid is *Bulbophyllum minutissimum,* found in Australia. Claims have also been made for *Notylia norae,* found in Venezuela. The smallest orchid flowers are less than 0.04 inches long, borne by *Stella graminea.*

Highest-Priced. The highest price ever paid for an orchid is £1,207.50 (then $6,000), paid by Baron Schröder to Sanders of St. Albans for an *Odontoglossum crispum* (variety *pittianum*) at an auction by Protheroe & Morris of Bow Lane, London, England, on March 22, 1906. A cymbidium orchid called "Rosanna Pinkie" was sold in the United States for $4,500 in 1952.

KINGDOM PROTISTA

Protista. Protista were first discovered in 1676 by Anton van Leeuwenhoek (1632–1723), a Dutch microscopist. Among Protista, characteristics common to both plants and animals are exhibited. The more plant-like are termed Protophyta (protophytes), including unicellular algae, and the more animal-like are placed in the phylum Protozoa (protozoans) which includes amoebas and flagellates.

Largest. The largest protozoans which are known to have existed were the now extinct Nummulites, which each had a diameter of 0.95 of an inch. The largest existing protozoan is *Pelomyxa palustris*, which may attain a length of up to 0.6 of an inch. The smallest of all protophytes is *Micromonas pusilla*, with a diameter of less than 2 microns or micrometers (2×10^{-6} m.) or 0.00008 of an inch.

Fastest-Moving. The protozoan *Monas stigmatica* has been measured to move a distance equivalent to 40 times its own length in a second. No human can cover even seven times his own length in a second.

Fastest Reproduction. The protozoan *Glaucoma*, which reproduces by binary fission, divides as frequently as every three hours. Thus in the course of a day it could become a "six greats grandparent" and the progenitor of 510 descendants.

KINGDOM FUNGI

Fungi. Fungi were once classified in the subkingdom Protophyta of the Kingdom Protista, but are now considered a separate Kingdom.

Largest. The largest recorded specimen of the giant puff ball (*Lycoperdon gigantea*) was one 62 inches in diameter and 18 inches high found at Mellor, Derbyshire, England, in 1971. A flatter specimen 64 inches in diameter was recorded in New York State in 1877. A 721-lb. example of the edible mushroom *Polyporus frondosus* was reported by Joseph Opple near Solon, Ohio, in September, 1976.

Largest Tree Fungus. The largest officially recorded tree fungus was a specimen of *Oxyporus* (*Fomes*) *nobilissimus*, measuring 56 inches by 37 inches and weighing at least 300 lbs., found by J. Hisey in Washington State in 1946.

Most Poisonous Toadstool. The yellowish-olive death cup (*Amanita phalloides*) is regarded as the world's most poisonous fungus. From 6 to 15 hours after tasting, the effects are vomiting, delirium, collapse and death. Among its victims was Cardinal Giulio de' Medici, Pope Clement VII (1478–1534).

KINGDOM PROCARYOTA

Earliest Life Form. Spherical microfossils, unicellular and physically similar to the blue-green algae *Aphanocapsa*, were reported by Dr. Elso S. Barghoorn of Harvard University and Dr. Andrew H.

Knoll in October, 1977. Discovered in chert (flintlike rock) datable to 3,400,000,000 years ago located 12 miles southwest of Barbertown, South Africa, their average diameter is 2.5 microns. There is some evidence that life forms were first existent even 500 million years earlier.

Bacteria

Largest. The largest of the bacteria is the sulphur bacterium *Beggiatoa mirabilis,* which is from 16 to 45 microns in width and which may form filaments several millimeters long. Anton van Leeuwenhoek (1632–1723) was the first to observe bacteria, in 1675.

Smallest. The smallest of all free-living organisms are the pleuro-pneumonia-like organisms (P.P.L.O.) of the *Mycoplasma.* One of these, *Mycoplasma laidlawii,* first discovered in sewage in 1936, has a diameter during the early part of its life of only 100 millimicrons, or 0.000004 of an inch. Examples of the strain known as H.39 have a maximum diameter of 300 millimicrons and weigh an estimated 1.0×10^{-16} of a gram. A blue whale would weigh 1.77×10^{23} or 177,000 quintillion times as much.

Highest. In April, 1967, the U.S. National Aeronautics and Space Administration reported that bacteria had been discovered at an altitude of 135,000 feet (more than $25\frac{1}{2}$ miles).

Longest-Lived. The oldest deposits from which living bacteria are claimed to have been extracted are salt layers near Irkutsk, U.S.S.R., dating from about 600,000,000 years ago. The discovery of their survival was made on February 26, 1962, by Dr. H. J. Dombrowski of Freiburg University, West Germany, but it is not accepted internationally.

The U.S. Dry Valley Drilling Project in Antarctica claimed resuscitated rod-shaped bacteria from caves up to a million years old.

Toughest. The bacterium *Micrococcus radiodurans* can withstand atomic radiation 10,000 times greater than radiation that is fatal to the average man (i.e. 6,500,000 röntgens).

Viruses

Largest. The largest true viruses are the brick-shaped pox viruses (e.g. smallpox, vaccinia, orf, etc.), measuring *c.* 250×300 nanometers (1 nanometer equals .000000001 of a meter). Viruses were discovered in 1892 by Dmitriy Ivanovsky (1864–1920).

Smallest. Of more than 1,000 identified viruses, the smallest is the sheep scrapie virus with a diameter of 14 nanometers or 14 millionths of a millimeter. Some 40 times smaller still is the nanovariant WS1 RNA, with a length of 91 nucleotides, described by Dr. Walter Schaffner of the University of Zurich in 1977.

Parks, Zoos, Aquaria and Oceanaria

Largest Park. The world's largest park is the Wood Buffalo National Park in Alberta, Canada (established 1922), which has an area of 11,172,000 acres (17,560 square miles).

Largest Zoo. It has been estimated that throughout the world there are some 500 zoos with an estimated annual attendance of 330,000,000. The largest zoological preserve in the world is the Etosha Reserve, Namibia (South-West Africa), with an area which has grown since 1907 to 38,427 square miles. (It is thus larger than Ireland.)

Oldest. The oldest known zoo is that at Schönbrunn, Vienna, Austria, built in 1752 by the Holy Roman Emperor Francis I for his wife Maria Theresa. The oldest privately owned zoo in the world is that of the Zoological Society of London, founded in 1826. Its collection is housed partly in Regent's Park, London (36 acres), and partly at Whipsnade Park, Bedfordshire (541 acres, opened 1931). At the stocktaking on January 1, 1979, it was found to house 11,035 specimens—2,102 mammals, 2,118 birds, 657 reptiles and amphibians, an estimated 2,920 fish, and an estimated total of 3,238 invertebrates. Locusts, bees and ants are excluded from this figure.

The earliest known collection of animals (not a public zoo) was that set up by Shulgi, a 3rd dynasty ruler of Ur in 2094–2407 B.C. at Puzurish in southeast Iraq.

Largest Aquarium. The world's largest is the John G. Shedd Aquarium, 12th Street and Lake Shore Drive, Chicago, completed in November, 1929, at a cost of $3,250,000. The total capacity of its display tanks is 450,000 gallons, with reservoir tanks holding 2,000,000 gallons. Exhibited are 5,500 specimens from 350 species. Most of these specimens are collected by the Aquarium collecting boat based in Miami, Florida, and are shipped by air to Chicago. The record attendances are 78,658 in a day on May 21, 1931, and 4,689,730 visitors in the single year of 1931.

Earliest Oceanarium. The world's first oceanarium is Marineland of Florida, opened in 1938 at a site 18 miles south of St. Augustine. Up to 7,000,000 gallons of sea water are pumped daily through two major tanks, one rectangular (100 feet long by 40 feet wide by 18 feet deep) containing 450,000 gallons and one circular (233 feet in circumference and 12 feet deep) containing 400,000 gallons. The tanks are seascaped, including coral reefs and even a shipwreck.

Largest Oceanarium. The largest salt water tank in the world is that at Hanna-Barbera's Marineland, located on the Palos Verdes Peninsula, California. It is 251½ feet in circumference and 22 feet deep, with a capacity of 640,000 gallons. The total capacity of the whole oceanarium is 2,500,000 gallons.

Chapter Three

THE NATURAL WORLD

1. Natural Phenomena

EARTHQUAKES

It is estimated that each year there are some 500,000 detectable seismic or micro-seismic disturbances of which 100,000 can be felt and 1,000 cause damage. (Note: Seismologists record all earthquake dates with the year first, based *not* on local time but on Greenwich Mean Time.)

Greatest. Using the new Seismic moment magnitudes (defined in 1977), the world's strongest assessable earthquake has been the cataclysmic Lebu shock, south of Concepción, Chile, on 1960 May 22, assessed at 9.5.

Worst. The greatest loss of life occurred in the earthquake in the Shensi, Shansi and Honan provinces of China, of 1556 February 2 (New Style) (January 23 Old Style), when an estimated 830,000 people were killed. The highest death toll in modern times has been in the Tangshan earthquake (magnitude 8.2) in eastern China on 1976 July 27 (local time was 3:00 a.m. on July 28). A first figure published on January 4, 1977 revealed 655,237 killed, later adjusted to 750,000. The greatest material damage was in the earthquake on the Kwanto plain, Japan, at 11:58 a.m. of 1923 September 1 (magnitude 8.2, epicenter in Latitude 35°15′N., Longitude 139° 30′E.). In Sagami Bay, the sea bottom in one area sank 1,310 feet. The official total of persons killed and missing in this earthquake, called the *Shinsai* or Great 'Quake, and the resultant fires was 142,807. In Tokyo and Yokohama 575,000 dwellings were destroyed. The cost of the damage was estimated at $2,800,000,000.

VOLCANOES

The total number of known active volcanoes in the world is 455 with an estimated 80 more that are submarine. The greatest concentration is in Indonesia, where 77 of its 167 volcanoes have erupted within historic times. The name "volcano" was first applied to the now dormant Vulcano Island in the Aeolian group in the Mediterranean, and that name derives from Vulcan, Roman god of destructive fire.

Greatest Eruption. The total volume of matter discharged in the eruption of Tambora, a volcano on the island of Sumbawa, in

Indonesia, April 5–7, 1815, has been estimated as 36.4 cubic miles. The energy of this eruption was 8.4×10^{26} ergs. The volcano lost about 4,100 feet in height and a crater 7 miles in diameter was formed. This compares with a probable 15 cubic miles ejected by Santorini and 4.3 cubic miles ejected by Krakatoa (see below). The internal pressure causing the Tambora eruption has been estimated at 46,500,000 lbs. per square inch.

Greatest Explosion. The greatest explosion (possibly since Santorini in the Aegean Sea *c.* 1470 B.C.) occurred *c.* 10:00 a.m. (local time), or 3:00 a.m. G.M.T., on August 27, 1883, with an eruption of Krakatoa, an island (then 18 square miles) in the Sunda Strait between Sumatra and Java, in Indonesia. A total of 163 villages were wiped out, and 36,380 people killed by the wave it caused. Rocks were thrown to a height of 34 miles and dust fell 10 days later at a distance of 3,313 miles. The explosion was recorded four hours later on the island of Rodrigues, 2,968 miles away, as "the roar of heavy guns" and was heard over 1/13th part of the surface of the globe. This explosion has been estimated to have had about 26 times the power of the greatest H-bomb test detonation, but was still only a fifth of the size of the Santorini cataclysm.

Highest—Extinct. The highest extinct volcano in the world is Cerro Aconcagua (Stone Sentinel), 22,834 feet high, on the Argentine side of the Andes. It was first climbed on January 14, 1897 by Mathias Zurbriggen, and was the highest mountain climbed anywhere until June 12, 1907.

Highest—Dormant. The highest dormant volcano is Volcán Llullaillaco (22,057 feet), on the frontier between Chile and Argentina.

Highest—Active. The highest volcano regarded as active is Volcán Antofalla (21,162 feet) in Argentina, though a more definite claim is made for Volcán Guayatiri or Guallatiri (19,882 feet), in Chile, which erupted in 1959.

HIGHEST EXTINCT VOLCANO: Cerro Aconcagua, with a height of 22,834 feet, is the tallest mountain in the western hemisphere.

MOST NORTHERN VOLCANO: Beeren Berg (7,470 feet) sits on Jan Mayen Island in the Greenland Sea.

Northernmost. The northernmost volcano is Beeren Berg (7,470 feet) on the island of Jan Mayen (71°05′N.) in the Greenland Sea. The island was possibly discovered by Henry Hudson in 1607 or 1608, but definitely visited by Jan Jacobsz May (Netherlands) in 1614. It was annexed by Norway on May 8, 1929. It erupted on September 20, 1970, and the island's 39 male inhabitants had to be evacuated.

The Ostenso seamount (5,825 feet) (Lat. 85°10′N., Long. 133°W.), 346 miles from the North Pole, was volcanic.

Southernmost. The most southerly known active volcano is Mount Erebus (12,450 feet) on Ross Island (77°35′S.), in Antarctica It was discovered on January 28, 1841, by the expedition of Captain (later Rear-Admiral Sir) James Clark Ross (1800–62) of the British Royal Navy, and first climbed at 10 a.m. on March 10, 1908, by a British party of five, led by Professor (later Lieut.-Col. Sir) Tannatt William Edgeworth David (1858–1934).

Longest Lava Flow. The longest lava flow, known as *pahoehoe* (twisted cord-like solidifications), is that from the eruption of Laki in southeast Iceland, which flowed $40\frac{1}{2}$–$43\frac{1}{2}$ miles. The largest known prehistoric flow is the Roza basalt flow in North America, *c.* 15,000,000 years ago, which had an unsurpassed length (300 miles), area (15,400 square miles) and volume (300 cubic miles).

Largest Crater. The world's largest *caldera* or volcano crater is that of Mt. Aso (5,223 feet) in Kyushu, Japan, which measures 17 miles north to south, 10 miles east to west and 71 miles in circumference.

GEYSERS

Tallest. The Waimangu geyser, in New Zealand, erupted to a height in excess of 1,500 feet in 1904, but has not been active since it erupted violently at 6:20 a.m. on April 1, 1917, killing 4 people. The name is the Maori word for "black water."

ICELANDIC "GUSHER": The English word "geyser" comes from the "Geysir" in Iceland, which erupts up to 180 feet in the air.

Currently the world's tallest active geyser is the U.S. National Park Service Steamboat Geyser, in Yellowstone National Park, Wyoming, which erupted at intervals ranging from 5 days to 10 months between 1962 and 1969 to a height of 250–380 feet. The *Geysir* ("gusher") near Mt. Hekla in south-central Iceland, from which all others have been named, spurts, on occasion, to 180 feet, while the adjacent Strokkur, reactivated by drilling in 1963, spurts at 10 to 15 minute intervals.

Greatest Discharge. The greatest measured water discharge from a geyser is 990,000 gallons by the Giant Geyser in Yellowstone National Park, Wyoming.

2. Structure and Dimensions

The earth is not a true sphere, but flattened at the poles and hence an ellipsoid. The polar diameter of the earth (7,899.809 miles) is 26.576 miles less than the equatorial diameter (7,926.385 miles). The earth also has a slight ellipticity of the equator since its long axis (about Longitude 37° W.) is 174 yards greater than the short axis. The greatest departures from the reference ellipsoid are a protuberance of 244 feet in the area of Papua, New Guinea, and a depression of 354 feet south of Sri Lanka (Ceylon) in the Indian Ocean.

The greatest circumference of the earth, at the equator, is 24,901.47 miles, compared with 24,859.75 miles at the meridian. The area of the surface is estimated to be 196,937,600 square miles. The period of axial rotation, *i.e.* the true sidereal day, is 23 hours 56 minutes 4.0996 seconds, mean time.

OLD ROCKS: These metamorphosed and highly deformed igneous rocks, called the Amitsoq gneiss, are up to 3,750,000,000 years old.

Earth's Structure

The mass of the earth is 6,585,600,000,000,000,000,000 tons and its density is 5.515 times that of water. The volume is an estimated 259,875,620,000 cubic miles. The earth picks up cosmic dust but estimates vary widely with 30,000 metric tons a day being the upper limit. Modern theory is that the earth has an outer shell or lithosphere about 25 miles thick, then an outer and inner rock layer or mantle extending 1,800 miles deep, beneath which there is an iron-nickel core at an estimated temperature of 3,700°C. and at a pressure of 22,000 metric tons per square inch or 3,400 kilobars. If the iron-nickel core theory is correct, iron must be by far the most abundant element.

Rocks

The age of the earth is generally considered to be within the range 4,600 $\pm$ 100 million years, by analogy with directly measured ages of meteorites and of the moon. However, no rocks of this great age have yet been found on the earth, since geological processes have presumably destroyed the earliest record.

Oldest. The greatest reported age for any scientifically dated rock is 3,800 $\pm$ 100 million years for granite gneiss rock found near Granite Falls in the Minnesota River valley, as measured by the lead-isotope and rubidium-uranium methods by the U.S. Geological Survey, and announced on January 26, 1975. These metamorphic samples compare with the Amitsoq gneiss from Godthaab, Greenland, which is unreservedly accepted to be between 3,700 and 3,750 million years old.

Largest. The largest exposed rocky outcrop is the 1,237-foot-high Mount Augustus (3,627 feet above sea level), discovered on June 3, 1858, about 200 miles east of Carnarvon, Western Australia. It is an up-faulted monoclinal gritty conglomerate 5 miles long and 2 miles across and thus twice the size of the celebrated monolithic arkose Ayer's Rock (1,100 feet), 250 miles southwest of Alice Springs, in Northern Territory, Australia.

OCEANS

Largest. The area of the earth covered by the sea is estimated to be 139,670,000 square miles, or 70.92 per cent of the total surface. The mean depth of the hydrosphere was at one time estimated to be 12,450 feet, but recent surveys suggest a lower estimate, closer to 11,660 feet. The total weight of the water is estimated as 1.45×10^{18} tons, or 0.022 per cent of the earth's total weight. The volume of the oceans is estimated to be 308,400,000 cubic miles, compared with only 8,400,000 cubic miles of fresh water.

The largest ocean in the world is the Pacific. Excluding adjacent seas, it represents 45.8 per cent of the world's oceans and is about 63,800,000 square miles in area. From Guayaquil, Ecuador, on the east, to Bangkok, Thailand, on the west, the Pacific could be said to stretch 10,905 miles in a straight navigable line.

Longest Voyage. The longest possible great circle sea voyage is one of 19,860 miles from a point 150 miles west of Karachi, Pakistan, to a point 200 miles north of Uka, Kamchatka, U.S.S.R., *via* the Mozambique Channel, Drake Passage, and Bering Sea.

Most Southerly. The most southerly point in the oceans is 85°34′S., 154°W., at the snout of the Robert Scott Glacier, 305 miles from the South Pole, in the Pacific sector of Antarctica.

Deepest. The deepest part of the ocean was first discovered in 1951 by the British survey ship *Challenger* in the Marianas Trench in the Pacific Ocean. The depth was measured by sounding and by echo-sounder and published as 5,960 fathoms (35,760 feet). Subsequent visits to the Challenger Deep have resulted in claims by echo-sounder only, culminating in one of 36,198 feet by the U.S.S.R.'s research ship *Vityaz* in March, 1959. On January 23, 1960, the U.S. Navy bathyscaphe *Trieste* descended to 35,820 feet. A metal object, say a pound-ball of steel, dropped into water above this trench would take nearly 63 minutes to fall to the sea bed 6.85 miles below.

The average depth of the Pacific Ocean is 14,000 feet.

Remotest Spot

The world's most distant point from land is a spot in the South Pacific, approximately 48°30′S., 125°30′W., which is about 1,660 miles from the nearest points of land, namely Pitcairn Island, Ducie Island and Cape Dart, Antarctica. Centered on this spot, therefore, is a circle of water with an area of about 8,657,000 square miles— about 7,000 square miles larger than the U.S.S.R., the world's largest country (see Chapter 10).

Sea Temperature

The temperature of the water at the surface of the sea varies from —2°C. (28.5°F.) in the White Sea to 35.6°C. (96°F.) in the shallow areas of the Persian Gulf in summer. A freak geothermal temperature

of 56°C. (132.8°F.) was recorded in February, 1965, by the survey
ship *Atlantis II*, near the bottom of Discovery Deep (7,200 feet) in the
Red Sea. The normal sea temperature in the area is 22°C. (71.6°F.).
Ice-focussed solar rays have been known to heat lake water to
nearly 26.8°C. (80°F.).

Largest Sea

The largest of the world's seas (as opposed to oceans) is the South
China Sea, with an area of 1,148,500 square miles. The Malayan
Sea comprising the waters between the Indian Ocean and the South
Pacific, south of the Chinese mainland, covering 3,144,000 square
miles, is not now an entity accepted by the International Hydro-
graphic Bureau.

Largest Gulf

The largest gulf in the world is the Gulf of Mexico, with a shoreline
of 3,100 miles from Cape Sable, Florida, to Cabo Catoche, Mexico.
Its area is 580,000 square miles.

Largest Bay

The largest bay in the world is Hudson Bay in northern Canada
with a shoreline of 7,623 miles and an area of 317,500 square miles.

Highest Sea-Mountain

The highest known submarine mountain is one discovered in 1953
near the Tonga Trench between Samoa and New Zealand. It rises
28,500 feet from the sea bed, with its summit 1,200 feet below the
surface.

Highest Wave

The highest officially recorded sea wave was measured from the
U.S.S. *Ramapo* proceeding from Manila, Philippines, to San Diego,
California, on the night of February 6–7, 1933, during a 68-knot
(78.3 m.p.h.) hurricane. The wave was computed to be 112 feet from
trough to crest.

The highest instrumentally measured wave was one calculated to
be exactly 86 feet high, recorded by the British ship *Weather Reporter*
in the North Atlantic on December 30, 1972 in Lat. 59°N., Long.
19°W.

It has been calculated on the statistics of the Stationary Random
Theory that one wave in more than 300,000 may exceed the average
by a factor of 4.

On July 9, 1958, a landslip caused a wave to wash 1,740 feet high
along the fjord-like shore of Lituya Bay, Alaska.

"Tidal" Wave. The highest recorded seismic sea wave, or
tsunami, was one of an estimated 278 feet, which appeared off
Ishigaki Island, Ryukyu Chain, on April 24, 1971. It tossed an 850-
ton block of coral more than 1.3 miles. *Tsunami* (a Japanese word
which is singular and plural) have been observed to travel at 490
m.p.h. Between 479 B.C. and 1977 there were at least 500 instances
of *tsunami*, of which 270 were destructive.

Greatest Tides. The greatest tides in the world occur in the Bay
of Fundy, which separates Nova Scotia from Maine and the Cana-

dian province of New Brunswick. Burncoat Head in the Minas Basin, Nova Scotia, has the greatest mean spring range with 47.5 feet, and an extreme range of 53.5 feet.

Extreme tides are due to lunar and solar gravitational forces affected by their perigee, perihelion, and conjunctions. Barometric and wind effects can superimpose an added "surge" element. Coastal and sea-floor configurations can accentuate these forces.

Greatest Current. The greatest current in the oceans of the world is the Antarctic Circumpolar Current or West Wind Drift Current, which was measured in 1969 in the Drake Passage between South America and Antarctica, to be flowing at a rate of 9,500,000,000 cubic feet per second—nearly three times that of the Gulf Stream. Its width ranges from 185 to 1,240 miles and has a surface flow rate of ¾ of a knot.

Strongest Current. The world's strongest currents are the Nakwakto Rapids, Slingsby Channel, British Columbia, Canada (Lat. 51°05′N., Long. 127°30′W.) where the flow rate may reach 16.0 knots (18.4 m.p.h.).

Icebergs

Largest. The largest iceberg on record was an Antarctic tabular iceberg of over 12,000 square miles (208 miles long and 60 miles wide) sighted 150 miles west of Scott Island, in the South Pacific Ocean, by the U.S.S. *Glacier* on November 12, 1956. This iceberg was thus larger than Belgium.

The 200-foot-thick Arctic ice island T.1 (140 square miles), discovered in 1946, took 17 years to be plotted.

Most Southerly Arctic. The most southerly Arctic iceberg was sighted in the Atlantic by a U.S.N. weather patrol at Lat. 28°44′N., Long. 48°42′W., in April, 1935.

Most Northerly Antarctic. The most northerly Antarctic iceberg was a remnant sighted in the Atlantic by the ship *Dochra* at Lat. 26°30′S., Long. 25°40′W., on April 30, 1894.

Tallest. The tallest iceberg measured was one of 550 feet reported off western Greenland by the U.S.C.G. icebreaker *East Wind* in 1958.

Straits

Longest. The longest straits in the world are the Tatarskiy Proliv or Tartar Straits between Sakhalin Island and the U.S.S.R. mainland, running 497 miles from the Sea of Japan to Sakhalinsky Zaliv. This distance is marginally longer than the Malacca Straits, which extend 485 miles.

Broadest. The broadest named straits are the Davis Straits between Greenland and Baffin Island, which at one point narrow to 210 miles. The Drake Passage between the Diego Ramírez Islands, Chile, and the South Shetland Islands, is 710 miles across.

Narrowest. The narrowest navigable straits are those between the Aegean island of Euboea and the mainland of Greece. The gap is

TALLEST ICEBERG: This 550-foot-tall giant was sighted off Melville Light, Greenland.

only 45 yards wide at Khalkis. The Seil Sound, Strathclyde, Scotland, narrows to a point only 20 feet wide where a bridge joins the island of Seil to the mainland and is thus said to span the Atlantic.

LAND

There is satisfactory evidence that at one time the earth's land surface comprised a single primeval continent of 80,000,000 square miles, now termed Pangaea, and that this split about 190,000,000 years ago, during the Jurassic period, into two super-continents, termed Laurasia (Eurasia, Greenland and North America) and Gondwanaland (comprising Africa, Arabia, India, South America, Oceania and Antarctica), named after Gondwana, India, which itself split 120,000,000 years ago. The South Pole was apparently in the area of the Sahara as recently as the Ordovician period of *c*. 450 million years ago.

Largest and Smallest Continents. Only 29.08 per cent, or an estimated 57,270,000 square miles, of the earth's surface is land, with a mean height of 2,480 feet above sea level. The Eurasian land mass is the largest with an area (including islands) of 21,053,000 square miles.

The smallest is the Australian mainland, with an area of about 2,940,000 square miles, which, together with Tasmania, New Zealand, New Guinea and the Pacific Islands, is described as Oceania. The total area of Oceania is about 3,450,000 square miles, including West Irian (formerly West New Guinea) which is politically in Asia.

Remotest Land. There is an unpinpointed spot in the Dzoosotoyn Elisen (desert), northern Sinkiang, China, that is more than 1,500 miles from the open sea in any direction. The nearest large town to this point is Wulumuchi (Urumchi) to its south.

Peninsula. The world's largest peninsula is Arabia, with an area of about 1,250,000 square miles.

Islands

Largest. Discounting Australia, which is usually regarded as a continental land mass, the largest island in the world is Greenland (Kingdom of Denmark), with an area of about 840,000 square miles. There is some evidence that Greenland is in fact several islands overlaid by an ice-cap in which case it would have an area of 650,000 square miles.

The largest island surrounded by fresh water is the Ilha de Marajó (13,500 square miles), in the mouth of the Amazon River, Brazil. The largest island in a lake is Manitoulin Island (1,068 square miles) in the Canadian (Ontario) section of Lake Huron. The largest inland island (*i.e.* land surrounded by rivers) is Ilha do Bananal, Brazil.

Remotest. The remotest island in the world is Bouvet Øya (formerly Liverpool Island), discovered in the South Atlantic by J. B. C. Bouvet de Lozier on January 1, 1739, and first landed on by Capt. George Norris on December 16, 1825. Its position is 54°26'S., 3°24'E. This uninhabited Norwegian dependency is about 1,050 miles from the nearest land—the uninhabited Queen Maud Land coast of eastern Antarctica.

The remotest inhabited island in the world is Tristan da Cunha, discovered in the South Atlantic by Tristão da Cunha, a Portuguese admiral, in March, 1506. It has an area of 38 square miles (habitable area 12 square miles) and was annexed by the United Kingdom on August 14, 1816. After evacuation in 1961 (due to volcanic activity), 198 islanders returned in November, 1963. The nearest inhabited land is the island of St. Helena, 1,320 miles to the northeast. The nearest continent, Africa, is 1,700 miles away.

Largest Atoll. The largest atoll in the world is Kwajalein in the Marshall Islands, in the central Pacific Ocean. Its slender 176-mile-long coral reef encloses a lagoon of 1,100 square miles.

The atoll with the largest land area is Christmas Atoll, in the Line Islands, in the central Pacific Ocean. It has an area of 184 square miles. Its two principal settlements, London and Paris, are 4 miles apart.

Highest Rock Pinnacle. The world's highest rock pinnacle is Ball's Pyramid near Lord Howe Island in the Pacific, which is 1,843 feet high, but has a base axis of only 218 yards. It was first scaled in 1965.

Longest Reef. The longest reef in the world is the Great Barrier Reef off Queensland, northeastern Australia, which is 1,260 statute miles in length. Between 1959 and 1971 a large section between

HIGHEST MOUNTAIN:
A team of Chinese scientists braves the intense cold and steep slopes of Mount Everest in a 1975 expedition.

Cooktown and Townsville was destroyed by the proliferation of the Crown of Thorns starfish (*Acanthaster planci*).

Greatest Archipelago. The world's greatest archipelago is the 3,500-mile-long crescent of over 13,000 islands which forms Indonesia.

Northernmost Land. The most northerly land is Kaffeklubben Øyen off the northeast of Greenland, 440 miles from the North Pole, discovered by Dr. Lange Koch in 1921, but determined only in June, 1969 to be in latitude 83° 40′ 6″. The name means "Coffee-Club Island."

Southernmost Land. The South Pole, unlike the North Pole, is on land. The Amundsen-Scott South Polar station was built there at an altitude of 9,370 feet in 1957. It is drifting bodily with the ice cap 27 to 30 feet per annum in the direction 43° W. and was replaced by a new structure in 1975.

Mountains

Highest. An eastern Himalayan peak of 29,028 feet above sea level on the Tibet-Nepal border (in an area first designated Chu-mu-lang-ma on a map of 1717) was discovered to be the world's highest mountain in 1852 by the Survey Department of the Government of India, from theodolite readings taken in 1849 and 1850. In 1860 its height was computed to be 29,002 feet. On July 25, 1973, the Chinese announced a height of 8,848.1 meters or 29,029 feet 3 inches. In practice the altitude can only be justified as 29,028 ± 25 feet. The 5½-mile-high peak was named Mount Everest after Sir George Everest (1790–1866), formerly Surveyor-General of India. After a total loss of 11 lives since the first reconnaissance in 1921, Everest was finally conquered at 11:30 a.m. on May 29, 1953. (For details of ascents, see under Mountaineering in Chapter 12.)

The mountain whose summit is farthest from the earth's center is the Andean peak of Chimborazo (20,561 feet), 98 miles south of the equator in Ecuador. Its summit is 7,057 feet further from the earth's center than the summit of Mt. Everest. The highest mountain on the equator is Volcán Cayambe (19,285 feet), Ecuador, at Longitude 77° 58' W.

The highest insular mountain in the world is the unsurveyed Ngga Pula, formerly Mount Sukarno, formerly Carstensz Pyramide, in Irian Jaya, Indonesia, formerly Netherlands New Guinea. According to cross-checked altimeter estimates, it is 16,500 feet high.

Highest Unclimbed. The highest separate unclimbed mountain in the world is now only the 31st highest—Zemu Gap Peak (25,526 feet) in the Sikkim Himalayas.

Largest. The world's tallest mountain measured from its submarine base (3,280 fathoms) in the Hawaiian Trough to peak is Mauna Kea (Mountain White) on the island of Hawaii, with a combined height of 33,476 feet, of which 13,796 feet are above sea level. Another mountain whose dimensions, but not height, exceed those of Mount Everest is the Hawaiian peak of Mauna Loa (Mountain Long) at 13,680 feet. The axes of its elliptical base, 16,322 feet below sea level, have been estimated at 74 miles and 53 miles. It should be noted that Cerro Aconcagua (22,834 feet) is more than 38,800 feet above the 16,000-foot-deep Pacific abyssal plain or 42,834 feet above the Peru-Chile Trench, which is 180 miles distant in the South Pacific.

Greatest Ranges. The world's greatest land mountain range is the Himalaya-Karakoram, which contains 96 of the world's 109 peaks of over 24,000 feet. The greatest of all mountain ranges is, however, the submarine Indian-East Pacific Oceans Cordillera, extending 19,200 miles from the Gulf of Aden to the Gulf of California by way of the seabed between Australia and Antarctica, with an average height of 8,000 feet above the base ocean depth.

Longest Line of Sight. Alaska's Mt. McKinley (20,320 feet) has been sighted from Mt. Sanford (16,237 feet) 230 miles away.

Greatest Plateau. The most extensive high plateau in the world is the Tibetan Plateau in Central Asia. The average altitude is 16,000 feet and the area is 77,000 square miles.

Sheerest Wall. The 3,200-foot-wide northwest face of Half Dome, Yosemite, California, is 2,200 feet high, but nowhere departs more than 7 degrees from the vertical. It was first climbed (Class VI) in 5 days in July, 1957, by Royal Robbins, Jerry Gallwas, and Mike Sherrick.

Highest Halites. Along the northern shores of the Gulf of Mexico for 725 miles there exist 330 subterranean "mountains" of salt, some of which rise more than 60,000 feet from bedrock and appear as the low salt domes first discovered in 1862.

Sand Dunes. The world's highest measured sand dunes are those in the Saharan sand sea of Isaouane-n-Tifernine of east central Algeria at Lat. 26° 42' N., Long. 6° 43' E. They have a wave-length of nearly 3 miles and attain a height of 1,410 feet.

GREATEST PLATEAU: Horses on the extensive Tibetan plateau in China.

Depressions

Deepest. The deepest depression so far discovered is beneath the Hollick-Kenyon Plateau in Marie Byrd Land, Antarctica, where, at a point 5,900 feet above sea level, the ice depth is 14,000 feet, hence indicating a bedrock depression 8,100 feet below sea level.

The deepest exposed depression on land is the shore surrounding the Dead Sea, 1,291 feet below sea level. The deepest point on the bed of the lake is 2,600 feet below the Mediterranean. The deepest part of the bed of Lake Baykal in Siberia, U.S.S.R., is 4,872 feet below sea level.

The greatest submarine depression is a large area of the floor of the northwest Pacific which has an average depth of 15,000 feet.

Largest. The largest exposed depression in the world is the Caspian Sea basin in the Azerbaydzhani, Russian, Kazakh, and Turkmen republics of the U.S.S.R. and northern Iran (Persia). It is more than 200,000 square miles, of which 143,550 square miles is lake area. The preponderant land area of the depression is the Prikaspiyskaya Nizmennost', lying around the northern third of the lake and stretching inland for a distance of up to 280 miles.

Rivers

Longest. The two longest rivers in the world are the Amazon (*Amazonas*), flowing into the South Atlantic, and the Nile (*Bahr-el-Nil*) flowing into the Mediterranean. Which is the longer is more a matter of definition than of measurement.

The true source of the Amazon was discovered in 1953 to be a stream named Huarco, rising near the summit of Cerro Huagra (17,188 ft.) in Peru. This stream progressively becomes the Toro, then the Santiago, then the Apurímac, which in turn is known as the Ene, and then the Tambo before its confluence with the Amazon prime tributary, the Ucayali. The length of the Amazon from this source to the South Atlantic *via* the Canal do Norte was measured in 1969 to be 4,007 miles (usually quoted to the rounded-off figure of 4,000 miles).

If, however, a vessel navigating downriver turns to the south of Ilha de Marajó through the straits of Breves and Boiuci into the Pará, the total length of the waterway becomes 4,195 miles. The Pará is not, however, a tributary of the Amazon, being hydrologically part of the basin of the Tocantins.

The length of the Nile waterway, as surveyed by M. Devroey (Belgium) before the loss of a few miles of meanders due to the formation of Lake Nasser, behind the Aswan High Dam, was 4,145 miles. This course is the hydrologically acceptable one from the source in Burundi of the Luvironza branch of the Kagera feeder of the Victoria Nyanza *via* the White Nile (*Bahr-el-Jebel*) to the delta.

Shortest River. The world's shortest named river is the D River, Lincoln City, Oregon, which connects Devil's Lake to the Pacific Ocean and is 440 feet long at low tide.

Greatest Flow. The greatest flow of any river in the world is that of the Amazon, which discharges an average of 4,200,000 cubic feet of water per second into the Atlantic Ocean, rising to more than 7,000,000 "cusecs" in full flood. The lowest 900 miles of the Amazon average 300 feet in depth.

Largest Basin. The largest river basin in the world is that drained by the Amazon (4,007 miles). It covers about 2,720,000 square miles. It has about 15,000 tributaries and sub-tributaries, of which four are more than 1,000 miles long.

Longest Tributary and Sub-Tributary. The longest of all tributaries is the Madeira (part of the Amazon) with a length of 2,100 miles, which is surpassed by only 14 rivers in the whole world. The longest sub-tributary is the Pilcomayo (1,000 miles long) in South America. It is a tributary of the Paraguay (1,500 miles long), which is itself a tributary of the Paraná (2,500 miles).

Submarine River. In 1952, a submarine river 250 miles wide, known as the Cromwell Current, was discovered flowing eastward 300 feet below the surface of the Pacific for 3,500 miles along the equator. Its volume is 1,000 times that of the Mississippi.

Subterranean River. In August, 1958, a crypto-river was tracked by radio-isotopes flowing under the Nile, with a mean annual flow six times greater—500 billion cubic meters (20 trillion cubic feet).

Longest Estuary. The world's longest estuary is that of the often-frozen Ob', in the northern U.S.S.R., at 550 miles. It is up to 50 miles wide.

Largest Delta. The world's largest delta is that created by the Ganga (Ganges) and Brahmaputra in Bangladesh (formerly East

Pakistan) and West Bengal, India. It covers an area of 30,000 square miles.

Greatest River Bores. The bore on the Ch'ient'ang'kian (Hang-chou-fe) in eastern China is the most remarkable in the world. At spring tides, the wave attains a height of up to 25 feet and a speed of 13 knots. It is heard advancing at a range of 14 miles. The bore on the Hooghly branch of the Ganges travels for 70 miles at more than 15 knots. The annual downstream flood wave on the Mekong River of Southeast Asia sometimes reaches a height of 46 feet. The greatest volume of any bore is that of the Canal do Norte (10 miles wide) in the mouth of the Amazon.

Fastest Rapids. The fastest rapids which have ever been navigated are the Lava Falls on the Colorado River. At times of flood these attain a speed of 30 m.p.h. with waves boiling up to 12 feet high.

Lakes and Inland Seas

Largest. The largest inland sea or lake in the world is the Kaspiskoye More (Caspian Sea) in southern U.S.S.R. and Iran (Persia). It is 760 miles long and its total area is 143,550 square miles. Of the total area, 55,280 square miles (38.6 per cent) are in Iran, where the lake is named the Darya-ye-Khazar. Its maximum depth is 3,215 feet and its surface is 92 feet below sea level. Since 1930 it has diminished 15,000 square miles in area with a fall of 62 feet, while the shoreline has retreated more than 10 miles in some places. The U.S.S.R. government plans to reverse the flow of the upper Pechora River from flowing north to the Barents Sea by blasting a 70-mile-long canal with nuclear explosives into the south-flowing Kolva River so that *via* the Kama and Volga rivers the Caspian will be replenished.

The fresh-water lake with the greatest surface area is Lake Superior, one of the Great Lakes. The total area is about 31,800 square miles, of which 20,700 square miles are in the U.S. and 11,100 square miles in Ontario, Canada. It is 600 feet above sea level. The fresh-water lake with the greatest volume is Baykal (see Deepest, below) with an estimated volume of 5,520 cubic miles.

Deepest. The deepest lake in the world is Ozero (Lake) Baykal in central Siberia, U.S.S.R. It is 385 miles long and between 20 and 46 miles wide. In 1957, the lake's Olkhon Crevice was measured to be 6,365 feet deep and hence 4,872 feet below sea level.

Largest Lagoon. The largest lagoon in the world is Lagoa dos Patos in southernmost Brazil. It is 158 miles long and extends over 4,110 square miles.

Lake in a Lake. The largest lake in a lake is Manitou Lake (41.09 square miles) on the world's largest lake island Manitoulin Island (1,068 square miles), in the Canadian part of Lake Huron. It contains a number of islands itself.

Underground. Reputedly the world's largest underground lake is the Lost Sea, which lies 300 feet underground in the Craighead Caverns, Sweetwater, Tennessee. Discovered in 1905, it covers an area of 4½ acres.

Highest. The highest steam-navigated lake in the world is Lago Titicaca (maximum depth 1,214 feet), with an area of about 3,200 square miles (1,850 square miles in Peru, 1,350 square miles in Bolivia), in South America. It is 130 miles long and is situated at 12,506 feet above sea level.

There is an unnamed glacial lake near Mt. Everest at 19,300 feet. Tibet's largest lake, Nam Tso (722 square miles), lies at an elevation of 15,060 feet.

Waterfalls

Highest. The highest waterfall (as opposed to a vaporized "Bridal Veil") in the world is the Salto Angel (Angel Falls), in Venezuela, on a branch of the Carrao River, an upper tributary of the Caroní, with a total drop of 3,212 feet and the longest single drop 2,648 feet. It was re-discovered in 1935 by a U.S. pilot named Jimmy Angel (died December 8, 1956), who crashed nearby on October 9, 1937. The falls, known by the Indians as Cherun-Meru, were first reported by Ernesto Sanchez La Cruz in 1910.

HIGHEST WATERFALLS—BY COUNTRIES

Country	Drop in feet	Name and Location
Venezuela	3,212	Angel Falls, Carrao River
South Africa	3,110	Tugela, Natal
Norway	2,625	Utigardsfossen
United States	2,425	Yosemite, California
New Zealand	1,904	Sutherland Falls, River Arthur
Guyana	1,600	King George VI, Utshi
Australia	1,580	Wollomombi, N.S.W.
Tanzania-Zambia	1,400	Kalambo
France	1,384	Gavarnie, Gave de Pau
Brazil	1,325	Glass Fall, Iguazi
Austria	1,280	Krimmler Fälle
Congo (Zaïre)	1,259	Lofoi
Canada	1,248	Takkakaw, Yoho River, B.C.
Italy	1,033	Serio, Lombardy
Switzerland	978	Staubbach

HIGHEST NAVIGABLE LAKE: Lake Titicaca, which separates Peru and Bolivia, is 12,506 feet above sea level.

HIGHEST WATERFALL: Angel Falls in Venezuela has a single drop of 2,648 feet, and a total fall of 3,212 feet. Note the airplane passing in front of the Falls.

Greatest. On the basis of the average annual flow, the greatest waterfall in the world is the Guairá (374 feet high), known also as the Salto dos Sete Quedas, on the Alto Paraná River between Brazil and Paraguay. Although attaining an average height of only 110 feet, its estimated annual average flow over the lip (5,300 yards wide) is 470,000 cubic feet per second. It has a peak flow of 1,750,000 cubic feet per second. The seven cataracts of Boyoma (formerly Stanley) Falls in the Congo (Zaïre) have an average annual flow of 600,000 cubic feet per second.

It has been calculated that, when some 5,500,000 years ago the Mediterranean basins began to be filled from the Atlantic through the Straits of Gibraltar, a waterfall 26 times greater than the Guairá and perhaps 2,625 feet high was formed.

Widest. The widest waterfalls in the world are Khône Falls (50 to 70 feet high) in Laos, with a width of 6.7 miles and a flood flow of 1,500,000 cubic feet per second.

Natural Phenomena

Longest Fjords. The world's longest "fjord" is the Nordvest Fjord arm of the Scoresby Sund in eastern Greenland, which extends inland 195 miles from the sea. The longest of Norwegian fjords is the Sogne Fjord, which extends 113.7 miles inland from Sygnefest to the head of the Lusterfjord arm at Skjolden. It averages barely 3 miles in width and has a deepest point of 4,085 feet. If measured from Huglo along the Bømlafjord to the head of the Sørfjord arm at Odda, the Hardangerfjorden can also be said to extend 113.7 miles. The longest Danish fjord is Limfjorden (100 miles long).

Longest Glaciers. It is estimated that 6,020,000 square miles, or about 10.4 per cent of the earth's land surface, is permanently glaciated. The world's longest known glacier is the Lambert Glacier, discovered by an Australian aircraft crew in Australian Antarctic Territory in 1956–57. It is up to 40 miles wide and, with its upper section known as the Mellor Glacier, it measures at least 250 miles in length. With the Fisher Glacier limb, the Lambert forms a continuous ice passage about 320 miles long. The longest Himalayan glacier is the Siachen (47 miles) in the Karakoram range, though the Hispar and Biafo combine to form an ice passage 76 miles long.

Fastest-Moving Glacier. The fastest-moving glacier is the Quarayaq in Greenland which flows 65–80 feet per day.

Greatest Avalanches. The greatest avalanches, though rarely observed, occur in the Himalayas, but no estimate of their volume has been published. It was estimated that 3,500,000 cubic meters (120,000,000 cubic feet) of snow fell in an avalanche in the Italian Alps in 1885. (See also Disasters.)

Natural Bridge. The longest natural bridge in the world is the Landscape Arch in the Arches National Park 25 miles north of Moab, Utah. This natural sandstone arch spans 291 feet and is set about 100 feet above the canyon floor. In one place erosion has narrowed its section to 6 feet.

Larger in mass, however, is the Rainbow Bridge, Utah, discovered on August 14, 1909, with a span of 278 feet but over 22 feet wide.

LONGEST NATURAL BRIDGE: This natural arch near Moab, Utah, spans 291 feet. Its size can be judged by the man near the left side.

LARGEST CAVERN: Visitors are dwarfed in the Big Room at Carlsbad, where the ceiling height reaches 255 feet.

The highest natural arch is the sandstone arch 25 miles west-northwest of K'ashih, Sinkiang, China, estimated in 1947 to be nearly 1,000 feet tall, with a span of about 150 feet.

Largest Desert. Nearly an eighth of the world's land surface is arid with an annual rainfall of less than 9.8 inches. The Sahara Desert in North Africa is the largest in the world. At·its greatest length, it is 3,200 miles from east to west. From north to south it is between 800 and 1,400 miles. The area covered by the desert is about 3,250,000 square miles. The land level varies from 436 feet below sea level in the Qattara Depression, Egypt, to the mountain Emi Koussi (11,204 feet) in Chad. The diurnal temperature range in the western Sahara may be more than 80°F.

Largest Swamp. The world's largest tract of swamp is in the basin of the Pripet or Pripyat River—a tributary of the Dnieper in the U.S.S.R. These swamps cover an estimated area of 18,125 square miles.

Caves

Longest. The most extensive cave system in the world is that under the Mammoth Cave National Park, Kentucky, first discovered in 1799. On September 9, 1972, an exploration group led by Dr. John P. Wilcox completed a connection, pioneered by Mrs. Patricia Crowther, on August 30, between the Flint Ridge Cave system and the Mammoth Cave system, so making a combined system with a total mapped passageway length of 190.3 miles.

Largest Cavern. The Big Room of Carlsbad Caverns, New Mexico, covers 14 acres with a ceiling height ranging from 80 to 255 feet. The longest axis is 1,800 feet.

DEEPEST CAVES BY COUNTRIES

These depths are subject to continuous revisions.

Feet below entrance	Cave and mountain range	Country
4,370	Gouffre de la Pierre Saint-Martin, Pyrenees	France/Spain
4,258	Gouffre Jean Bernard	France
3,563	Schneeloch, Salzburg	Austria
3,510	Sima G.E.S.M., Málaga	Spain
3,163	Kievskaya, Pamir	U.S.S.R.
3,118	Antro di Corchia	Italy
2,953	Sistema Purificacion	Mexico
2,716	Hölloch, Muotathal, Schwyz	Switzerland
2,569	Jaskini Snieznej, Tatras	Poland
2,464	Ghar Parau, Zagros Mountains	Iran
2,296	Kef Toghobeit	Morocco
2,245	Poloska Jama	Yugoslavia
1,170	Neffs Canyon Cave, Utah	U.S.

Tallest Stalagmite. The tallest known stalagmite in the world is La Grande Stalagmite in the Aven Armand cave, Lozère, France, which has attained a height of 98 feet from the cave floor. It was found in September, 1897.

The tallest cave column is the 106-foot-tall Bicentennial Column in Ogle Cave in Carlsbad Cavern National Park, New Mexico.

LARGEST GORGE: The Grand Canyon stretches across 217 miles in northern Arizona.

Longest Stalactite. The longest known stalactite in the world is a wall-supported column extending 195 feet from roof to floor in the Cueva de Nerja, near Málaga, Spain. The rather low tensile strength of calcite (calcium carbonate) precludes very long free-hanging stalactites, but one of 38 feet exists in the Poll an Ionain cave in County Clare, Ireland.

Gorges

Largest. The largest land gorge in the world is the Grand Canyon on the Colorado River in north-central Arizona. It extends from Marble Gorge to the Grand Wash Cliffs, over a distance of 217 miles. It varies in width from 4 to 13 miles and is up to 7,000 feet deep.

The submarine Labrador basin canyon is *c.* 2,150 miles long.

Deepest. The deepest canyon in low relief territory is Hell's Canyon, dividing Oregon and Idaho. It plunges 7,900 feet from the Devil Mountain down to the Snake River. A stretch of the Kali River in central Nepal flows 18,000 feet below its flanking summits of the Dhaulagiri and Annapurna groups. The deepest submarine canyon yet discovered is one 25 miles south of Esperance, Western Australia, which is 6,000 feet deep and 20 miles wide.

Sea Cliffs

The highest sea cliffs yet pinpointed anywhere in the world are those on the north coast of east Molokai, Hawaii, near Umilehi Point, which descend 3,300 feet to the sea at an average gradient of more than 55°.

3. Weather

The meteorological records given below necessarily relate largely to the last 130 to 150 years, since data before that time are both sparse and unreliable. Reliable registering thermometers were introduced as recently as *c.* 1820.

The longest continuous observations have been maintained at the Radcliffe Observatory, Oxford, England, since 1815.

Upper Atmosphere

A jet stream moving at 408 m.p.h. at 154,200 feet (29.2 miles) was recorded by Skua rocket above South Uist, Outer Hebrides, Scotland, on December 13, 1967.

Atmospheric Temperature

The lowest temperature ever recorded in the atmosphere is −225.4°F. at an altitude of about 50 to 60 miles, during noctilucent cloud research above Kronogård, Sweden, from July 27 to August 7, 1963.

Most Equable Temperature

The location with the most equable recorded temperature over a short period is Garapan, on Saipan, in the Mariana Islands, Pacific

Ocean. During the nine years from 1927 to 1935, inclusive, the lowest temperature recorded was 67.3°F. on January 30, 1934, and the highest was 88.5°F. on September 9, 1931, giving an extreme range of 21.2 degrees F. Between 1911 and 1966 the Brazilian off-shore island of Fernando de Noronha had a minimum temperature of 65.5°F. on November 17, 1913, and a maximum of 89.6° F. on March 2, 1965, an extreme range of 24.1 degrees F.

COLDEST PLACE: Soviet researchers chose this Antarctic "inaccessibility station," where the thermometer averages 72° below zero, to conduct experiments.

Greatest Temperature Ranges

The world's extremes of temperature have been noted progressively thus:

World's Highest Shade Temperatures

127.4°F.	Ouargla, Algeria	Aug. 27, 1884
130°F.	Amos and Mammoth Tank, California	Aug. 17, 1885
134°F.	Death Valley, California	July 10, 1913
136.4°F.	Al 'Aziziyah (el-Azizia), Libya*	Sept. 13, 1922†‡

World's Lowest Screen Temperatures

— 73°F.	Floeberg Bay, Ellesmere Island, Canada	1852
— 90.4°F.	Verkhoyansk, Siberia, U.S.S.R.	Jan. 3, 1885
— 90.4°F.	Verkhoyansk, Siberia, U.S.S.R.	Feb. 5 & 7, 1892
— 90.4°F.	Oymyakon, Siberia, U.S.S.R.	Feb. 6, 1933
—100.4°F.	South Pole, Antarctica	May 11, 1957
—102.1°F.	South Pole, Antarctica	Sept. 17, 1957
—109.1°F.	Sovietskaya, Antarctica	May 2, 1958
—113.3°F.	Vostok, Antarctica	June 15, 1958
—114.1°F.	Sovietskaya, Antarctica	June 19, 1958
—117.4°F.	Sovietskaya, Antarctica	June 25, 1958
—122.4°F.	Vostok, Antarctica	Aug. 7–8, 1958
—124.1°F.	Sovietskaya, Antarctica	Aug. 9, 1958
—125.3°F.	Vostok, Antarctica	Aug. 25, 1958
—126.9°F.	Vostok, Antarctica	Aug. 24, 1960

* Obtained by the National Geographical Society but not officially recognized by the Libyan Ministry of Communications.

† A reading of 140°F. at Delta, Mexico, in August, 1953, is not now accepted because of over-exposure to roof radiation. The official Mexican record of 136.4°F. at San Luis, Sonora, on August 11, 1933, is not internationally accepted.

‡ A freak heat flash reported from Coimbra, Portugal, in September, 1933, said to have caused the temperature to rise to 70°C. (158°F.) for 120 seconds, is apocryphal.

The greatest temperature variation recorded in a day is 100°F. (a fall from 44°F. to −56°F.) at Browning, Montana, on January 23–24, 1916. The most freakish rise was 49°F. in 2 minutes at Spearfish, South Dakota, from −4°F. at 7:30 a.m. to 45°F. at 7:32 a.m. on January 22, 1943.

The greatest recorded temperature ranges in the world are around the Siberian "cold pole" in the eastern U.S.S.R. Verkhoyansk (67°33′N., 133°23′E.) has ranged 192°F. from −94°F. (unofficial) to 98°F.

Deepest Permafrost

The greatest recorded depth of permafrost is 4,920 feet, reported in April, 1968, in the basin of the Lena River, Siberia, U.S.S.R.

Humidity and Discomfort

Human discomfort depends not merely on temperature but on the combination of temperature, humidity, radiation and wind speed. The U.S. Weather Service uses a Temperature-Humidity Index, which equals two-fifths of the sum of the dry and wet bulb thermometer readings plus 15. When the THI in still air reaches 75, at least half of the people will be uncomfortable while at 79 few, if any, will be comfortable. A THI reading of 98.2 has been recorded twice in Death Valley, California—on July 27, 1966 (119°F., 31 per cent humidity) and on August 12, 1970 (117°F., 37 per cent humidity). A person driving at 45 m.p.h. in a car without a windshield in a temperature of –45°F. would, by the chill factor, experience the equivalent of –125°F., which is within 2°F. of the world record.

Most Intense Rainfall

Difficulties attend rainfall readings for very short periods but the figure of 1.50 inches in one minute at Barst, Guadeloupe, on November 26, 1970, is regarded as the most intense recorded in modern times. The cloudburst of "near two foot . . . in less than a quarter of half an hour" at Oxford, England, on the afternoon of May 31 (Old Style), 1682, is regarded as unacademically recorded.

Cloud Extremes

The highest standard cloud form is cirrus, averaging 27,000 feet and above, but the rare nacreous or mother-of-pearl formation sometimes reaches nearly 80,000 feet. The lowest is stratus, below 3,500 feet. The cloud form with the greatest vertical range is cumulonimbus, which has been observed to reach a height of nearly 68,000 feet in the tropics.

Mirage

The largest mirage on record was that sighted in the Arctic at 83° N., 103° W. by Donald B. MacMillan in 1913. This type of mirage, known as the Fata Morgana, appeared as the same "hills, valleys, snow-capped peaks extending through at least 120 degrees of the horizon" that Peary had named Crocker Land 6 years earlier.

On July 17, 1939, a mirage of Snaefellsjokull glacier (4,715 feet) on Iceland was seen from the sea when 335–350 miles distant.

Lightning

The visible length of lightning strokes varies greatly. In mountainous regions, when clouds are very low, the flash may be less than 300 feet long. In flat country with very high clouds, a cloud-to-earth flash sometimes measures four miles, though in extreme cases such flashes have been measured at 20 miles. The intensely bright central core of the lightning channel is extremely narrow. Some authorities suggest that its diameter is as little as half an inch. This core is surrounded by a "corona envelope" (glow discharge) which may measure 10 to 20 feet in diameter.

The speed of a lightning discharge varies from 100 to 1,000 miles per second for the downward leader track, and reaches up to 87,000 miles per second (nearly half the speed of light) for the powerful return stroke.

Every few million strokes there is a giant discharge, in which the cloud-to-earth and the return lightning strokes flash from the top of the thunder clouds. In these "positive giants" energy of up to 3 billion joules (3×10^{16} ergs) is sometimes recorded. The temperature reaches about 30,000° C. (54,000° F.), which is more than five times greater than that of the surface of the sun. A theory that lightning was triggered by cosmic rays was published in 1977.

Waterspouts

The highest waterspout of which there is reliable record was one observed on May 16, 1898, off Eden, New South Wales, Australia. A theodolite reading from the shore gave its height as 5,014 feet. It was about 10 feet in diameter.

WEATHER RECORDS

Highest Shade Temperature: 136.4°F., Al 'Aziziyah, Libya, September 13, 1922.

Lowest Screen Temperature: —126.9°F., Vostok, Antarctica (11,500 feet above sea level), August 24, 1960[1].

Hottest Place (Annual mean):[6] Dallol, Ethiopia, 94°F., 1960–66.

Coldest Place (Annual mean): Pole of Cold (78°S., 96°E.), Antarctica, —72°F. (16 deg. F. lower than Pole).

Greatest Rainfall (24 hours): 73.62 in., Cilaos, La Réunion, Indian Ocean, March 15–16, 1952[2].

(Calendar month): 366.14 in., Cherrapunji, Meghalaya, India, July, 1861.

(12 months): 1,041.78 in., Cherrapunji, Meghalaya, August 1, 1860 to July 31, 1861.

Greatest Snowfall (24 hours): 76 in., Silver Lake, Colorado, April 14–15, 1921[3].

(12 months): 1,224.5 in., Paradise, Mt. Rainier, Washington, February 19, 1971–February 18, 1972.

HOTTEST PLACE: Dallol, Ethiopia, averaged 94° over a 6-year period.

Maximum Sunshine (Year):   97%+ (over 4,300 hours), eastern Sahara.
768 days, February 9, 1967–March 17, 1969, St. Petersburg, Florida.

Minimum Sunshine: Nil at North Pole—for winter stretches of 186 days.

Barometric Pressure (Highest): 1,083.8 mb. (32 in.), Agata, Siberia, U.S.S.R., December 31, 1968.

(Lowest): 877 mb. (25.90 in.), about 600 miles northwest of Guam, Pacific Ocean, September 24, 1958[9].

Highest Surface Wind-speed:[4] 231 m.p.h., Mt. Washington (6,288 ft.), New Hampshire, April 12, 1934.

Thunder Days (Year):[5] 322 days, Bogor (formerly Buitenzorg), Java, Indonesia (average, 1916–19).

Wettest Place (Annual mean): Mt. Waialeale (5,148 ft.), Kauai, Hawaii, 451 in. (average, 1920–72).[10]

Driest Place (Annual mean): Calama, in the Desierto de Atacama, Chile. None.

Longest Drought: *c.* 400 years to 1971, Desierto de Atacama, Chile.

Most Rainy Days (Year): Mt. Waialeale, Kauai, Hawaii, up to 350 days per year.

WINDIEST PLACE: Gales reach 200 m.p.h. at Commonwealth Bay, Antarctica.

Largest Hailstones:[7]	1.67 lbs. (7½ in. diameter, 17½ in. circumference), Coffeyville, Kansas, September 3, 1970.
Longest Sea Level Fogs (Visibility less than 1,000 yards):	Fogs persist for weeks on the Grand Banks, Newfoundland, Canada, and the average is more than 120 days per year[8].
Windiest Place:	The Commonwealth Bay, George V Coast, Antarctica, where gales reach 200 m.p.h.

---

[1] The coldest permanently inhabited place is the Siberian village of Oymyakon (63°16′N., 143°15′E.), in the U.S.S.R., where the temperature reached −96°F. in 1964.

[2] This is equal to 8,327.2 tons of rain per acre. Elevation 3,937 feet.

[3] The record for a single snowstorm is 189 inches at Mount Shasta Ski Bowl, California. The greatest depth of snow on the ground was 25 feet 5 inches at Paradise, Mt. Rainier, Washington, on April 17, 1972.

[4] The highest speed yet measured in a tornado is 280 m.p.h. at Wichita Falls, Texas, on April 2, 1958.

[5] Between Lat. 35°N. and 35°S. there are 3,200 thunderstorms in each 12-hour night, some of which can be heard at a range of 18 miles.

[6] In Death Valley, California, maximum temperatures of over 120°F. were recorded on 43 consecutive days—July 6 to August 17, 1917. At Marble Bar, Western Australia (maximum 121°F.), 160 consecutive days with maximum temperatures of over 100°F. were recorded—October 31, 1923 to April 7, 1924. At Wyndham, Western Australia, the temperature reached 90°F. or more on 333 days in 1946.

[7] Much heavier hailstones are sometimes reported. These are usually not single but coalesced hailstones. An ice block of 35–70 oz. was reported at Withington, Manchester, England, on April 2, 1973.

[8] Lower visibilities occur at higher altitudes, Ben Nevis is reputedly in cloud 300 days per year.

[9] The U.S.S. *Repose*, a hospital ship, recorded 856 mb. (25.55 in.) in the eye of a typhoon at 25°35′N., 128°20′E. off Okinawa, Japan, on September 16, 1954.

[10] In 1948 rainfall was 621 inches.

Chapter Four

THE UNIVERSE AND SPACE

LIGHT-YEAR—that distance traveled by light (speed 186,282.397 miles per second, or 670,616,629.4 m.p.h., *in vacuo*) in one tropical (or solar) year (365.24219878 mean solar days at January 0, 12 hours Ephemeris time in 1900 A.D.) and is 5,878,499,814,000 miles. The unit was first used in March, 1888.

MAGNITUDE—a measure of stellar brightness such that the light of a star of any magnitude bears a ratio of 2.511886 to that of a star of the next magnitude. Thus a fifth magnitude star is 2.511886 times as bright, while one of the first magnitude is exactly 100 (or 2.511886^5) times as bright, as a sixth magnitude star. In the case of such exceptionally bright bodies as Sirius, Venus, the moon (magnitude −11.2) or the sun (magnitude −26.7), the magnitude is expressed as a minus quantity.

PROPER MOTION—that component of a star's motion in space which, at right angles to the line of sight, constitutes an apparent change of position of the star in the celestial sphere.

The universe is the entirety of space, matter and antimatter. An appreciation of its magnitude is best grasped by working outward from the earth, through the solar system and our own Milky Way galaxy, to the remotest extra-galactic nebulae and quasars.

Meteoroids

Meteor Shower

Meteoroids are mostly of cometary or asteroidal origin. A meteor is the light phenomenon caused by entry of a meteoroid into earth's atmosphere. The greatest meteor "shower" on record occurred on the night of November 16–17, 1966, when the Leonid meteors (which recur every 33¼ years) were visible over North America. It was calculated that meteors passed over Arizona at a rate of 2,300 per minute for a period of 20 minutes from 5 a.m. on November 17, 1966.

Meteorites

Oldest. It was reported in August, 1978, that dust grains in the Murchison meteorite which fell in Australia in September, 1969, predate the formation of the solar system.

Largest. When a meteoroid penetrates to the earth's surface, the remnant is described as a meteorite. This occurs about 150 times per year over the whole land surface of the earth. The largest known meteorite is one found in 1920 at Hoba West, near Grootfontein in southwest Africa. This is a block of about 9 feet long by 8 feet broad, weighing 132,000 lbs.

The largest meteorite exhibited by any museum is the "Tent" meteorite, weighing 68,085 lbs., found in 1897 near Cape York, on the west coast of Greenland, by the expedition of Commander (later Rear-Admiral) Robert Edwin Peary (1856–1920). It was known to the Eskimos as the Abnighito and is now exhibited in the Hayden Planetarium in New York City.

The largest piece of stony meteorite recovered is a piece of 3,902 lbs. which was part of a shower which struck Kirin, Kaoshan Province, China, on March 8, 1976. The oldest dated meteorites are from the Allende fall over Chihuahua, Mexico, on February 8, 1969.

There was a mysterious explosion of $12\frac{1}{2}$ megatons at Lat. 60° 55′ N., Long. 101° 57′ E., in the basin of the Podkamennaya Tunguska River, 40 miles north of Vanavar, in Siberia, U.S.S.R. at 00 hrs. 17 min. 11 sec. U.T. on June 30, 1908. The cause was variously attributed to a meteorite (1927), a comet (1930), a nuclear explosion (1961) and to antimatter (1965). This devastated an area of about 1,500 square miles, and the shock was felt more than 600 miles away. The comet theory is now favored.

Largest Craters. A crater 150 miles across and a half mile deep has been postulated in Wilkes Land, Antarctica, since 1962. It would have been caused by a 14,560,000,000-ton meteorite striking at 44,000 m.p.h. In December, 1970, U.S.S.R. scientists reported an astrobleme in the basin of the Popigai River with a 60-mile diameter and a maximum depth of 1,300 feet. There is a possible crater-like formation 275 miles in diameter on the eastern shore of Hudson Bay, where the Nastapoka Islands are just off the coast.

Evidence was published in 1963 discounting a meteoric origin for the crypto-volcanic Vredefort Ring (diameter 26 miles) to the southwest of Johannesburg, South Africa, but this claim has now been reasserted.

LARGEST METEORITE: The Hayden Planetarium in New York City displays the "Tent" meteorite, weighing over 34 tons.

LARGEST PROVEN CRATER: Meteor Crater in northern Arizona was gouged out in about 25,000 B.C. It is 575 feet deep, almost a mile wide.

The largest proven crater is called Barringer Crater or Meteor Crater, formerly called Coon Butte, discovered in 1891 near Winslow, northern Arizona. It is 4,150 feet in diameter and now about 575 feet deep, with a parapet rising 130 to 155 feet above the surrounding plain. It has been estimated that an iron-nickel mass with a diameter of 200 to 260 feet, and weighing about 2,240,000 tons, gouged this crater in *c.* 25,000 B.C.

The New Quebec (formerly the Chubb) "Crater," first sighted on June 20, 1943, in northern Ungava, Canada, is 1,325 feet deep and measures 6.8 miles around its rim.

Fireball. The brightest fireball ever recorded photographically was one observed over Sumava, Czechoslovakia, on December 4, 1974, by Dr. Zdeněk Ceplecha, which had a momentary magnitude of —22, or 10,000 times brighter than a full moon.

Tektites. The largest tektite of which details have been published was one of 7.04 lbs. found in 1932 at Muong Nong, Saravane Province, Laos, and now in the Paris Museum.

Aurorae

Most Frequent. Polar lights, known since 1560 as Aurora Borealis or Northern Lights in the northern hemisphere and since 1773 as Aurora Australis in the southern hemisphere, are caused by electrical solar discharges in the upper atmosphere and occur most frequently in high latitudes. Aurorae are visible at some time on *every* clear dark night in the polar areas within 20 degrees latitude of the magnetic poles.

Lowest Latitudes. Reliable figures exist only from 1952. Extreme cases of displays in very low latitudes were those reported at Cuzco, Peru (August 2, 1744); Honolulu, Hawaii (September 1, 1859); and, questionably, Singapore (September 25, 1909).

Altitude. The extreme height of aurorae has been measured at 620 miles, while the lowest may descend to 45 miles.

FAR SIDE OF THE MOON: Seen here in a NASA photograph, the hidden side of the moon was first glimpsed by a Soviet space probe in 1959.

The Moon

The earth's closest neighbor in space and only natural satellite is the moon, at a mean distance of 238,855 statute miles center to center or 233,812 miles surface to surface. Its closest approach (perigee) and most extreme distance away (apogee) measured surface to surface are 216,420 and 247,667 miles respectively. It has a diameter of 2,159.3 miles and has a mass of 7.23×10^{19} long tons with a mean density of 3.34. The average orbital speed is 2,287 m.p.h.

The first direct hit on the moon was achieved at 2 minutes 24 seconds after midnight (Moscow time) on September 14, 1959, by the Soviet space probe *Lunik II* near the *Mare Serenitatis*. The first photographic images of the hidden side were collected by the U.S.S.R.'s *Lunik III* from 6:30 a.m. on October 7, 1959, from a range of up to 43,750 miles, and transmitted to the earth from a distance of 292,000 miles. The first "soft" landing was made by the U.S.S.R.'s *Luna IX*, launched at about 11 a.m. G.M.T. on January 31, 1966. It landed in the area of the Ocean of Storms (*Oceanus Procellarum*) at 18 hours 45 minutes 30 seconds G.M.T. on February 3, 1966.

"Blue Moon." Owing to sulphur particles in the upper atmosphere from a forest fire covering 250,000 acres between Mile 103 and Mile 119 on the Alaska Highway in northern British Columbia, Canada, the moon took on a bluish color, as seen from Great Britain, on the night of September 26, 1950. The moon appeared green after the Krakatoa eruption of August 27, 1883 (see Volcanoes) and in Stockholm for 3 minutes on January 17, 1884.

Crater

Largest. Only 59 per cent of the moon's surface is directly visible from the earth because it is in "captured rotation," *i.e.* the period of rotation is equal to the period of orbit. The largest wholly visible crater is the walled plain Bailly, toward the moon's South Pole, which is 183 miles across, with walls rising to 14,000 feet. Partly on the averted side the Orientale Basin measures more than 600 miles in diameter.

Deepest. The deepest crater is the moon's Newton crater, with a floor estimated to be between 23,000 and 29,000 feet below its rim and 14,000 feet below the level of the plain outside. The brightest directly visible spot on the moon is *Aristarchus*.

Highest Mountains

As there is no water on the moon, the heights of mountains can be measured only in relation to a reference sphere with a radius of 1,079.943 miles. Thus the greatest elevation attained by any of the 12 U.S. astronauts has been 25,688 feet, on the Descartes Highlands, by Capt. John Walter Young, U.S.N., and Major Charles M. Duke, Jr., on April 27, 1972.

Temperature Extremes

When the sun is overhead, the temperature on the lunar equator reaches 243°F. (31°F. above the boiling point of water). By sunset the temperature is 58°F., but after nightfall it sinks to −261°F.

Moon Samples

The age attributed to the oldest of the moon material brought back to earth by the *Apollo* crews has been soil-dated to 4,720,000,000 years.

LUNAR SURFACE: This photo of the rock-strewn moon landscape was taken by the *Apollo XVI* astronauts. The oldest moon rocks analyzed have been 4,720,000,000 years old.

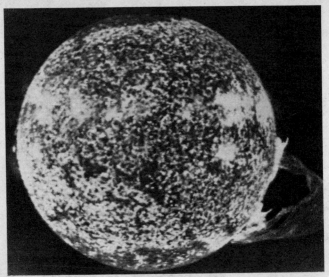

SOLAR ERUPTION: The most spectacular solar flare ever recorded, spanning more than 365,000 miles, was photographed during the final Skylab mission.

The Sun
Distance Extremes

The earth's 66,620 m.p.h. orbit of 584,017,800 miles around the sun is elliptical, hence our distance from the sun varies. The orbital speed varies between 65,520 m.p.h. (minimum) and 67,750 m.p.h. The average distance of the sun is 1.000000230 astronomical units or 92,955,829 miles. The closest approach (perihelion) is 91,402,000 miles, and the farthest departure (aphelion) is 94,510,000 miles. The solar system is revolving around the center of the Milky Way once in each 225 million years at a speed of 481,000 m.p.h. and has a velocity of 42,500 m.p.h. relative to stars in our immediate region such as Vega, toward which it is moving.

Temperature and Dimensions

The sun has an internal temperature of about 16,000,000°K., a core pressure of 560,000,000 tons per square inch and uses up nearly 4,500,000 tons of hydrogen per second, thus providing a luminosity of 3×10^{27} candlepower, or 1,500,000 candlepower per square inch. The sun has the stellar classification of a "yellow dwarf" and, although its density is only 1.407 times that of water, its mass is 332,946 times as much as that of the earth. It has a mean diameter of 865,270 miles. The sun with a mass of $2,096 \times 10^{27}$ tons represents more than 99 per cent of the total mass of the solar system. (K. stands for the Kelvin absolute scale of temperatures.)

Sunspots

Largest. To be visible to the *protected* naked eye, a sunspot must cover about one two-thousandth part of the sun's hemisphere and thus have an area of about 500,000,000 square miles. The largest recorded sunspot occurred in the sun's southern hemisphere on April 8, 1947. Its area was about 7 billion square miles, with an extreme longitude of 187,000 miles and an extreme latitude of 90,000 miles. Sunspots appear darker because they are more than 1,500°C. cooler than the rest of the sun's surface temperature of 5,525°C. The largest observed solar prominence was one protruding 365,000 miles, observed from Skylab in 1973.

Most Frequent. In October, 1957, a smoothed sunspot count showed 263, the highest recorded index since records started in 1755 (*cf.* previous record of 239 in May, 1778). In 1943 a sunspot lasted for 200 days from June to December.

LONGEST ECLIPSE: This solar eclipse on June 20, 1955, lasted a record 7 minutes 8 seconds as viewed from the Philippines.

Eclipses

Earliest Recorded. The earliest extrapolated eclipses that have been identified are 1361 B.C. (lunar) and October, 2136 B.C. (solar). For the Middle East only, lunar eclipses have been extrapolated to 3450 B.C. and solar ones to 4200 B.C.

Longest Duration. The maximum possible duration of an eclipse of the sun is 7 minutes 31 seconds. The longest actually *measured* was on June 20, 1955 (7 minutes 8 seconds), seen from the Philippines. That of July 16, 2186, in the mid-Atlantic should last 7 minutes 29 seconds. This will be the longest for 1,469 years. Durations can be extended by observers being airborne, as on June 30, 1973, when an eclipse was "extended" to 72 minutes for observers aboard a *Concorde* jet. An annular eclipse may last for 12 minutes 24 seconds. The longest totality of any lunar eclipse is 104 minutes. This has occurred many times.

Most and Least Frequent. The highest number of eclipses possible in a year is seven, as in 1935, when there were five solar and two lunar eclipses; or four solar and three lunar eclipses, as will occur in 1982. The lowest possible number in a year is two, both of which must be solar, as in 1944 and 1969.

Comets

Earliest Recorded. The earliest records of comets date from the 7th century B.C. The speeds of the estimated 2,000,000 comets vary from 700 m.p.h. in outer space to 1,250,000 m.p.h. when near the sun.

The successive appearances of Halley's Comet have been traced back to 467 B.C. It was first depicted in the Nuremberg Chronicle of 684 A.D. The first prediction of its return by Edmund Halley (1656–1742) proved true on Christmas Day, 1758, 16 years after his death. Its next perihelion should be at 9:30 p.m. Greenwich Mean Time on February 9, 1986, exactly 75.81 years after the last, which was on April 19, 1910. A sighting may occur in December, 1984.

Closest Approach. On July 1, 1770, Lexell's Comet, traveling at a speed of 23.9 miles per second (relative to the sun), came within 745,000 miles of the earth. However, the earth is believed to have passed through the tail of Halley's Comet, most recently on May 19, 1910.

Largest

Comets are so tenuous that it has been estimated that even the head of one rarely contains solid matter greater than 0.6 mile in diameter. The tails, as in the case of the Great Comet of 1843, may trail for 205,000,000 miles. The head of Holmes Comet of 1892 once measured 1,500,000 miles in diameter.

Comet Bennett which appeared in January, 1970, was found to be enveloped in a hydrogen cloud measuring some 8,000,000 miles long.

HALLEY'S COMET: Edmund Halley correctly predicted that the comet which bears his name would return on Christmas Day, 1758. Its first known appearance was in 467 B.C.

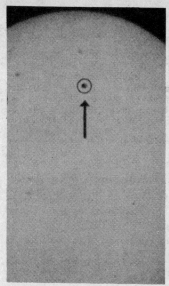

FASTEST PLANET (left): Mercury orbits the sun at over 100,000 m.p.h. **MARTIAN SURFACE (top):** The existence of craters on Mars was proven in 1965. This view, taken by *Mariner IX*, shows the landscape in the Argyre Dorsum.

Period

Shortest. Of all the recorded periodic comets (these are members of the solar system), the one which most frequently returns is Encke's Comet, first identified in 1786. Its period of 1,206 days (3.3 years) is the shortest established. Not one of its 51 returns (to the end of 1977) has been missed by astronomers. Now increasingly faint, it is expected to "die" by February, 1994. The most frequently observed comets are Schwassmann-Wachmann I, Kopff and Oterma, which can be observed every year between Mars and Jupiter.

Longest. The path of Delavan's Comet of 1914 has not been accurately determined but it is not expected to return for perhaps 24,000,000 years.

Planets

Planets (including the earth) are bodies within the solar system which revolve around the sun in definite orbits.

Largest. Jupiter, with an equatorial diameter of 88,780 miles and a polar diameter of 82,980 miles, is the largest of the nine major planets, with a mass 317.83 times and a volume 1,318 times that of the earth. It also has the shortest period of rotation, with a "day" of only 9 hours 50 minutes 30.003 seconds in its equatorial zone.

Fastest. Mercury, which orbits the sun at an average distance of 35,983,100 miles, has a period of revolution of 87.9686 days, so giving the highest average speed in orbit of 107,030 m.p.h.

Hottest. A surface temperature of *c.* 896°F. has been estimated from measurements made from Venus by the U.S.S.R. probes *Venera 7* and *Venera 8* in 1970 and 1972.

Smallest and Coldest. The coldest planet is Pluto, which has an estimated surface temperature of —360°F. (100°F. above absolute zero). Its mean distance from the sun is 3,674,488,000 miles and its period of revolution is 248.54 years. Its diameter is about 1,880 miles and it has a mass about .2 per cent that of the earth. Pluto was first recorded by Clyde William Tombaugh (born February 4, 1906) at Lowell Observatory, Flagstaff, Arizona, on February 18, 1930, from photographs taken on January 23 and 29, and announced on March 13. Because of its orbital eccentricity, Pluto will have moved closer to the sun than Neptune between January 23, 1979, and March 15, 1999.

Nearest. The fellow planet closest to the earth is Venus, which is, at times, about 25,700,000 miles inside the earth's orbit, compared with Mars' closest approach of 34,600,000 miles outside the earth's orbit. Mars, known since 1965 to be cratered, has temperatures ranging from 85°F. to —190°F.

Surface Features. By far the highest and most spectacular is Olympus Mons (formerly Nix Olympica) in the Tharsis region of Mars, with a diameter of 310–370 miles and a height of 75,450–95,150 feet above the surrounding plain.

Brightest and Faintest. Viewed from the earth, by far the brightest of the five planets visible to the naked eye is Venus, with a maximum magnitude of —4.4. The faintest is Pluto, with a magnitude of 14. Uranus at magnitude 5.7 is only marginally visible.

Densest and Least Dense. Earth is the densest planet with an average figure of 5.515 times that of water, while Saturn has an average density only about one-eighth of this value or 0.705 times that of water.

Longest "Day." The planet with the longest period of rotation is Venus, which spins on its axis once every 243.16 days, so its "day" is longer than its "year" (224.7007 days). The shortest "day" is that of Jupiter (see Largest Planet).

Conjunctions. The most dramatic recorded conjunction (coming together) of the other seven principal members of the solar system (sun, moon, Mercury, Venus, Mars, Jupiter and Saturn) occurred on February 5, 1962, when 16° covered all seven during an eclipse. It is possible that the seven-fold conjunction of September, 1186, spanned only 12°. The next notable conjunction will take place on May 5, 2000.

Satellites

Most. Of the nine major planets, all but Venus and Mercury have known natural satellites. The planet with the most is Jupiter, with four large and nine small moons. The earth and Pluto are the only planets with a single satellite. The distance of the solar system's

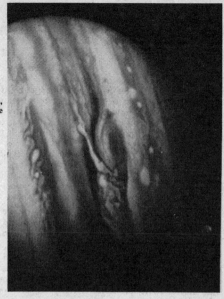

THE MOONS OF JUPITER: Jupiter has a total of 13 natural satellites, including the heaviest satellite in the Solar System, *Ganymede*, shown in this photo at the lower right.

known satellites from their parent planets varies from the 5,827 miles of *Phobos* from the center of Mars to the 14,730,000 miles of Jupiter's outer satellite *Sinope* (Jupiter IX). The solar system has a total of 33 satellites, excluding Saturn's unproven Xth and XIth and Jupiter's unproven XIVth moons, but including Pluto's probable moon *Charon*, announced in July, 1978.

Largest and Smallest. The largest satellite is the sixth moon of Saturn, *Titan*, with a diameter of 3,400 miles and a possible atmospheric thickness of 90 miles. The heaviest satellite is *Ganymede* (Jupiter III) with a diameter of 3,275 miles and a mass 2.02 times that of our moon, but it is possible that the large satellite of Neptune, *Triton*, is larger than *Titan* and heavier than *Ganymede*.

The smallest satellite is Jupiter XIII, with a diameter of only 5 miles.

Largest Asteroids. In the belt which lies between Mars and Jupiter, there are some 45,000 (only 2,042 numbered as of October, 1977) minor planets or asteroids which are, for the most part, too small to yield to diameter measurement. The largest and first discovered (by Piazzi at Palermo, Sicily, on January 1, 1801) of these is *Ceres*, with a diameter of 623 miles. The only one visible to the naked eye is *Vesta* (diameter 334 miles), discovered on March 29, 1807, by Dr. Heinrich Wilhelm Olbers, a German amateur astronomer. The closest measured approach to the earth by an asteroid was 485,000 miles, in the case of *Hermes* on October 30, 1937.

The most distant detected is Object Kowal found between Saturn and Uranus on October 18–19, 1977, by Charles Kowal from the Hale Observatory, California, and tentatively named *Chiron*.

Stars

Largest and Most Massive. Betelgeux (at top left in the constellation Orion) has a diameter of more than 250,000,000 miles, and in 1978 was found to be surrounded by a tenuous "shell" of potassium of over 1 trillion miles (11,000 astronomical units). The light from Betelgeux which reaches the earth today left the star in 1460 A.D.

The diameter of IRS 5 is believed to be 9,500,000,000 miles.

The fainter component of Plaskett's Star, discovered by J. S. Plaskett from the Dominion Astrophysical Observatory, Victoria, British Columbia, Canada, in 1922, is the most massive star known, with a mass *c.* 55 times that of the sun.

Smallest. The least massive stars known are the two components of the binary star *Wolf 424*, a faint star in the constellation Virgo. Each of the two stars has only 0.06 solar masses.

Farthest. The solar system, with its sun, nine principal planets, 33 satellites, asteroids and comets, was discovered in 1921 to be about 32,000 light-years from the center of the lens-shaped Milky Way galaxy (diameter 100,000 light-years) of about 100 billion stars. The most distant star in our galaxy is therefore about 80,000 light-years distant.

Nearest. Excepting the special case of our own sun, the nearest star is the very faint *Proxima Centauri*, which is 4.28 light-years (25,200,000,000,000 miles) away. The nearest star visible to the naked eye is the southern hemisphere star *Alpha Centauri*, or *Rigel Kentaurus* (4.38 light-years), with a magnitude of —0.29. By 11,800 A.D., the nearest star will be Barnard's Star (see *Stellar Planets*, page 171) at a distance of 3.75 light-years.

Brightest. Sirius A (*Alpha Canis Majoris*), also known as the Dog Star, is apparently the brightest star of the 5,776 stars visible in the heavens, with an apparent magnitude of —1.46. It is in the constellation *Canis Major* and is visible in the winter months of the northern hemisphere, being due south at midnight on the last day of the year. The Sirius system is 8.64 light-years distant and has a luminosity 26 times as much as that of the sun. It has a diameter of 1,450,000 miles and a mass of 4,704,000,000,000,000,000,000,000,000 tons.

Most and Least Luminous. If all stars could be viewed at the same distance, the most luminous would be the apparently faint variable *S. Doradûs*, in the Greater Magellanic Cloud (*Nebecula Major*), which can be nearly a million times brighter than the sun, and has an absolute magnitude of —8.9. The variable η *Carinae* in *c.* 1840 was perhaps 4 million times more luminous than the sun. The faintest star detected visually is a very red star, known as LP 425–140, which is 23.5 light-years distant, with about one-millionth of the sun's brightness.

Longest Name. The longest name for any star is *Shurnarkabtisha-shutu*, which is Arabic for "under the southern horn of the bull."

Constellations

The largest of the 89 constellations is *Hydra* (the Sea Serpent) which covers 1,302.844 square degrees or 6.3 per cent of the hemisphere and contains at least 68 stars visible to the naked eye (to 5.5 mag.). The constellation *Centaurus* (Centaur), ranking ninth in area, embraces, however, at least 94 such stars. The smallest constellation is *Crux Australis* (Southern Cross) with an area of 68.477 square degrees compared with the 41,252.96 square degrees of the whole sky.

Brightest Super-Nova

Super-novae, or temporary "stars" which flare and then fade, occur perhaps five times in 1,000 years in our galaxy. The brightest "star" ever seen by historic man is believed to be the super-nova in April, 1006 near Lupus β which flared for 2 years and attained a magnitude of —9 to —10. It is now believed to be the radio source G.327.6 + 14.5, nearly 3,000 light-years distant.

Stellar Planets. Planetary companions, with a mass of less than 7 per cent of their parent star, have been reported for 61 *Cygni* (1942), *Lalande 21185* (1960), *Krüger 60, Ci 2354, BD + 20° 2465* and one of the two components of 70 *Ophiuchi*.

A planet with 6 times the mass of Jupiter, 750 million miles from *Epsilon Eridani* (see below), was reported by Peter van de Kamp in January, 1973.

In August, 1975, van de Kamp reported that Barnard's Star (Munich 15040) possibly had two planets equivalent in mass to Jupiter and Saturn.

Listening operations ("Project Ozma") on *Tau Ceti* and *Epsilon Eridani* were maintained from April 4, 1960 to March, 1961, using an 85-foot radio telescope at Deer Creek Valley, Green Bank, West Virginia. The apparatus was probably insufficiently sensitive for any signal from a distance of 10.7 light-years to be received. Monitoring has been conducted from Gorkiy, U.S.S.R., since 1969.

Black Holes

The first tentative identification of a Black Hole was announced in December, 1972, in the binary-star X-ray source Cygnus X-1. This is a small, dark companion of some 10 solar masses, from which the escape velocity tends to c (the velocity of light). The critical size has been estimated to be as low as a diameter of 3.67 miles. In early 1978 supermassive Black Holes were suggested with a mass of 100 million suns—2 $\times$ 10^{35} metric tons.

The Universe

Outside the Milky Way galaxy, which possibly moves around the center of the local super-cluster of 2,500 neighboring galaxies at a speed of 1,350,000 m.p.h., there exist 10 billion other galaxies.

MOST POWERFUL ROCKET:
The *Saturn V*, capable of lifting an 82-ton payload, stands over 360 feet tall. Its enormous size can be judged in comparison to the man standing (circled) at right.

These range in size up to the largest known object in the universe, the radio galaxy 3C-236 in Leo Minor, announced from Westerbork Synthesis Radio Telescope, Netherlands, in August, 1974, which is 18,600,000 light-years across. In October, 1976, it was suggested that 3C-123 may have a diameter of 120,000,000 light-years.

Farthest Visible Object. The remotest heavenly body clearly visible to the naked eye is the Great Galaxy in *Andromeda* (Mag. 3.47) known as Messier 31. This is a rotating nebula of spiral form, and its distance from the earth is about 2,200,000 light-years, or about 13,000,000,000,000,000,000 miles.

It is just possible, however, that, under ideal seeing conditions, Messier 33, the Spiral in Triangulum (Mag. 5.79), can be glimpsed by the naked eye of keen-sighted people at a distance of 2,300,000 light-years.

"Quasars"

In November, 1962, the existence of quasi-stellar radio sources ("quasars" or QSO's) was established. No satisfactory model has yet been constructed to account for the immensely high luminosity of bodies apparently so distant and of such small diameter. In April, 1975, it was announced that 3C-279 had a measured luminosity of 2.75×10^{14} times that of the sun.

"Pulsars"

The earliest observation of a pulsating radio source or "pulsar" CP 1919 by Dr. Jocelyn Bell Burnell was announced from the Mullard Radio Astronomy Observatory, Cambridgeshire, England, on February 29, 1968. The 100th was announced from Jodrell Bank,

England, in June, 1973. The fastest so far discovered is NP 0532 in the Crab Nebula with a pulse period of 33 milliseconds. It is now accepted that pulsars are rotating neutron stars with an inner core density of 74,400,000,000 metric tons per cubic inch.

Remotest Object

The interpretation of very large red-shifts exhibited by quasars is controversial. The remotest galaxy, with a record red shift value of $Z = 3.53$, is Quasar OQ172, interpreted in August, 1978, as between 13.5 and 15.5 billion light years. The 3° background radiation discovered in 1965 by Penzias and Wilson appears to be moving at a velocity of 99.9998 per cent of the speed of light.

Age of the Universe

In November, 1976, a newly published value of Hubble's constant indicated that the age of the universe lay between 17.5 and 21.3 billion years. In August, 1978, however, the parameters were reassessed at between 13.5 and 15.5 billion years.

Rocketry and Missiles

Earliest Uses

War rockets, propelled by a charcoal-saltpeter-sulphur gunpowder, were described by Tsen Kung Liang of China in 1042. These early rockets became known in Europe by 1258.

The first launching of a liquid-fueled rocket (patented July 14, 1914) was by Dr. Robert Hutchings Goddard (1882–1945) (U.S.) at Auburn, Massachusetts, on March 16, 1926, when his rocket reached an altitude of 41 feet and traveled a distance of 184 feet. The U.S.S.R.'s earliest rocket was the semi-liquid fueled GIRD-IX tested on August 17, 1933.

Longest Ranges

On March 16, 1962, Nikita Khrushchev, then Prime Minister of the U.S.S.R., claimed in Moscow that the U.S.S.R. possessed a "global rocket" with a range of 19,000 miles (more than half the earth's circumference), capable of hitting any target in the world from either direction.

Most Powerful

It has been suggested that the U.S.S.R. lunar booster which blew up at Tyura Tam in the summer (July ?) of 1969 had a thrust of 10,000,000 to 14,000,000 lbs. There is some evidence of a launch of a U.S.S.R. "G" class lunar booster, larger than *Saturn V*, on May 11, 1973.

The most powerful rocket that has been publicized is the *Saturn V*, used for the Project Apollo and Skylab programs, on which development began in January, 1962, at the John F. Kennedy Space Center, Merritt Island, Florida. The rocket is 363 feet 8 inches tall, with a payload of over 82 tons in the case of *Skylab 1*, and gulps 15 tons of propellant per second for $2\frac{1}{2}$ minutes. Stage I (S-IC) is 138 feet tall and powered by 5 Rocketdyne F-1 engines, using liquid oxygen (LOX) and kerosene, each delivering 1,514,000 lbs. thrust. Stage II (S-II) is powered by 5 LOX and liquid hydrogen Rocketdyne J-2 engines with a total thrust of 1,141,453 lbs., while Stage III (designated S-IVB) is powered by a single 228,290-lb.-thrust J-2 engine. The whole assembly generates 175,600,000 h.p. and weighs up to 7,600,000 lbs. when fully loaded, as in the case of *Apollo XVII*. *Saturn V* was first launched on November 9, 1967, from Cape Canaveral (then Kennedy), Florida.

PROGRESSIVE ROCKET ALTITUDE RECORDS:

Height in miles	Rocket	Place	Launch Date
0.71 (3,762 ft.)	A 3-inch rocket	near London, England	April, 1750
1.24 (6,460 ft.)	Rheinhold Tiling[1] (Germany) solid fuel rocket	Osnabrück, Germany	April, 1931
3.1	OR-2 liquid-fuel rocket (U.S.S.R.)	U.S.S.R.	Nov. 25, 1933
8.1	U.S.S.R. "Stratosphere" rocket	U.S.S.R.	1935
52.46	A.4 rocket (Germany)	Peenemünde, Germany	Oct. 3, 1942
c. 85	A.4 rocket (Germany)	Heidelager, Poland ...	early 1944
118	A.4 rocket (Germany)	Heidelager, Poland ...	mid-1944
244	V-2/W.A.C. Corporal (2-stage Bumper), No. 5 (U.S.)	White Sands, N.M. ...	Feb. 24, 1949
318	GFR (B-5-B) (U.S.S.R.) ......?	Tyura Tam, U.S.S.R.	1950–52
682	Jupiter C (U.S.)	Cape Canaveral, Fla....	Sept. 20, 1956
>800	I.C.B.M. test flight (U.S.S.R.)	Tyura Tam/Baikonur, U.S.S.R.................	Aug. 1957
>2,700	Farside (4 stage) (U.S.)	Eniwetok Atoll	Oct. 20, 1957
70,700	Pioneer I-B Lunar Probe (U.S.)	Cape Canaveral, Fla.	Oct. 11, 1958
215,300,000*	Luna I (U.S.S.R.)	Tyura Tam, U.S.S.R................	Jan. 2, 1959
242,000,000*	Mars I (U.S.S.R.)	U.S.S.R.	Nov. 1, 1962
1,446,403,000[2]	Pioneer 10 (U.S.)	Cape Canaveral, Fla.	Mar. 2, 1972

* Apogee in solar orbit.

[1] There is some evidence that Tiling may shortly after have reached 31,000 ft. (5.90 miles) with a solid-fuel rocket at Wangerooge, East Friesian Islands, West Germany.

[2] Distance by July 1, 1978. A distance of 3,600,000,000 miles will be reached by 1987 on its way to crossing the orbit of Pluto and leaving the solar system's gravitational field. Pioneer 11 will fly by Saturn on or about September 1, 1979, traveling 108,000 m.p.h., and then chase Pioneer 10, leaving the solar system for deep space. Mariner 11 (launched August 20, 1977) and Mariner 12 (September 1, 1977) comprise the Jupiter-Saturn Mission. On August 27, 1981, it may prove possible to re-target Mariner 11 to approach Uranus (January 31, 1986) and even Neptune (September, 1989).

Highest Velocity

The first space vehicle to achieve the third cosmic velocity sufficient to break out of the solar system was *Pioneer 10*. The Atlas SLV-3C launcher with a modified Centaur D second stage and a Thiokol Te-364-4 third stage left the earth at an unprecedented 32,114 m.p.h. on March 2, 1972. The highest recorded velocity of any space vehicle has been 149,125 m.p.h. in the case of the U.S.-German solar probe *Helios B* launched on January 15, 1976.

Ion Rockets

Speeds of up to 100,000 m.p.h. are envisaged for rockets powered by an ion discharge. An ion thruster has been maintained for 9,715 hours (404 days 19 hours) at the Lewis Research Center in Cleveland, Ohio. Ion rockets were first used in flight by NASA's SERT I rocket, launched on July 20, 1964.

Space Flight

The dynamics of artificial satellites were first propounded by Sir Isaac Newton (1642–1727) in his *Philosophiae Naturalis Principia Mathematica* ("Mathematical Principles of Natural Philosophy"), begun in March, 1686, and first published in the summer of 1687. The first artificial satellite was successfully put into orbit at an altitude of 142/588 miles and a velocity of more than 17,750 m.p.h. from Tyura Tam, a site located 170 miles east of the Aral Sea, on the night of October 4, 1957. This spherical satellite, *Sputnik* ("Fellow Traveler") *1*, officially designated "Satellite 1957 Alpha 2," weighed 184.3 lbs., with a diameter of 22.8 inches, and its lifetime is believed to have been 92 days, ending on January 4, 1958. It was designed under the direction of Dr. Sergey Pavlovich Korolyov (1907–66).

By January, 1978, it was estimated that there were 4,470 discrete pieces of hardware in earth orbit. By October, 1977, it was estimated that 40 per cent of all launches were from Plesetsk, U.S.S.R.

Largest Space Object

The heaviest object orbited is the *Apollo 15* (spacecraft plus third stage) which, prior to translunar injection in parking orbit, weighed 155.9 tons. The 442-lb. U.S. R.A.E. (radio astronomy explorer) B, or Explorer 49, launched on June 10, 1973, has, however, antennae 1,500 feet from tip to tip.

Earliest Successful Manned Satellites

The first successful manned space flight began at 9:07 a.m. (Moscow time), or 6:07 a.m. G.M.T., on April 12, 1961. Flight Major (later Colonel) Yuriy Alekseyevich Gagarin (born March 9, 1934) completed a single orbit of the earth in 89.34 minutes in the U.S.S.R.'s space vehicle *Vostok* ("East") *1* (10,416 lbs.). The take-off was from Tyura Tam in Kazakhstan, and the landing was 108 minutes later near the village of Smelovka, in the Saratov region of the U.S.S.R. The maximum speed was 17,560 m.p.h. and the maximum altitude 203.2 miles in a flight of 25,394.5 miles. Major Gagarin, invested a Hero of the Soviet Union and awarded the Order of Lenin and the Gold Star Medal, was killed in a jet plane crash near Moscow on March 27, 1968.

First Fatality in Space Flight

Col. Vladimir Mikhailovich Komarov (born March 16, 1927) was launched in *Soyuz* ("Sunrise") *1* at 00:35 a.m. G.M.T. on April 23, 1967. The spacecraft was in orbit for about $25\frac{1}{2}$ hours before crashing on the final descent after parachute failure. Komarov was thus the first man indisputably known to have died during space flight.

Rocketry and Space Records

	Earth Orbits	Moon Orbits	Solar Orbits
Earliest Satellite	Sputnik I, October 4, 1957	Luna X, March 31, 1966	Luna I, January 2, 1959
Earliest Planetary Contact	Sputnik I rocket—burnt out December 1, 1957	Luna II hit moon, September 13, 1959	Venus III hit Venus, March 1, 1966
Earliest Planetary Touchdown	Discoverer XIII capsule, landed August 11, 1960	Luna IX soft landed on moon February 3, 1966	Venus VII soft landed on Venus, December 15, 1970
Earliest Rendezvous, Docking	Gemini 8 and Agena 8, March 16, 1966	Apollo X and LM 4 docked May 23, 1969	None
Earliest Crew Exchange	Soyuz IV and V, January 16, 1969	Apollo X and LM 4, May 22, 1969	None
Heaviest Satellite	99.87 tons, Skylab, May 14, 1973	33.98 tons, Apollo XV, July 29, 1971	15.23 tons, Apollo X rocket, May 18, 1969
Lightest Satellite	1.47 lbs. each, Tetrahedron Research Satellites (TRS) 2 and 3, May 9, 1963	150 lbs., Interplanetary Monitoring Probe IMP 6, July 19, 1967	13 lbs., Pioneer IV, March 3, 1959
Longest First Orbit	42 days, Apollo XII rocket, November 14, 1969	720 minutes, Lunar Orbiter 4, May 4, 1967	636 days, Mariner 6 (Mars Probe), February 25, 1969
Shortest First Orbit	86 min. 30.6 sec., Cosmos 169 rocket, July 17, 1967	114 min., LM 9 ascent stage (Apollo XVI, August 2, 1971	195 days, Mariner 5 (Venus Probe), June 14, 1967
Longest Expected Lifetime	>1 million years, Vela 12, April 8, 1970	Unlimited, IMP 6 (see above), July 19, 1967	All unlimited
Nearest First Perigee, Pericynthion or Perihelion	63 miles, Cosmos 169 rocket, July 17, 1967	10 miles, LM 6 ascent stage (Apollo XII, November 20, 1969	50,700 miles, Apollo IX rocket, March 3, 1969
Furthest First Apogee, Apocynthion or Aphelion	535,522 miles, Apollo XII rocket, November 14, 1969	4,900 miles, IMP 6 (see above), July 19, 1967	162,900,000 miles, Mariner 6 (Mars Probe), February 25, 1969

The highest and lowest speeds in solar orbit are by Apollo IX rocket and Mariner 6 (see above), respectively.

NOTE:—The artificial satellite with the largest dimension is the spider-like U.S. RAE (Radio-astronomy explorer), launched into lunar orbit in June, 1973, which has antennae measuring 1,500 feet from tip to tip. Echo I and II were the brightest artificial satellites (their magnitudes were about −1), and it has been claimed that Echo I became the man-made object seen by more people than any other. Its lifetime was 93 months from August 12, 1960 until it burned up in May, 1968.

LONGEST IN SPACE: The most well-traveled humans of all time, Col. Vladimir Kovalyonok and Aleksandr Ivanchenkov, spent nearly 20 weeks in space.

Oldest and Youngest Astronauts

The oldest of the 87 people in space has been Donald Kent ("Deke") Slayton (born Sparta, Wisconsin, March 1, 1924) who was aged 51 years 146 days when launched on the *Apollo-Soyuz* mission on July 24, 1975. The youngest was Major (later Col.) Gherman Stepanovich Titov (born September 11, 1935) who was 25 years 329 days old when he was launched in *Vostok II* on August 6, 1961.

First Woman in Space

The first woman to orbit the earth was Jr. Lt. (now Lt.-Col.) Valentina Vladimirovna Tereshkova (born March 6, 1937), who was launched in *Vostok VI* from Tyura Tam, U.S.S.R., at 9:30 a.m. G.M.T. on June 16, 1963, and landed at 8:16 a.m. on June 19, after a flight of 2 days 22 hours 42 minutes, during which she completed over 48 orbits (1,225,000 miles) and came to within 3 miles of *Vostok V.* Her mission was variously reported to be punctuated with pleas to be brought back due to giddiness, or to be extended because of her excellent performance. She had formerly been a textile worker.

First "Walk" in Space

The earliest undoubted instance of an astronaut floating free outside a space vehicle was by Astronaut Edward H. White II, for 21 minutes over Hawaii to the U.S. Atlantic coast on June 3, 1965, from *Gemini IV.* Evidence for the earlier claim of Lt.-Col. Aleksey A. Leonov from *Voshkod 2* on March 18, 1965, is not internationally accepted.

Longest Manned Space Flight

The longest time spent in the weightlessness of space has been 139 days 14 hours 47 minutes by Col. Vladimir Kovalyonok (b. 1942) and Aleksandr Sergeyevich Ivanchenkov (b. 1940), who were launched at 11:17 p.m. Moscow time on June 15, 1978, from the Baikonur Cosmodrome, to join *Salyut 6,* and landed 112 miles southeast of Dzhezkazgan, Kazakhstan, at 2:05 p.m. on November 2, 1978. During this time they became the most traveled humans of all time, with a mileage of more than 56 million miles. It was reported that on their return to Earth's gravity they had difficulty in relearning to walk and in picking up cups of tea. In addition, in the mornings they tried to "swim" out of bed.

Splashdown Record

The most accurate recovery from space was the splashdown of *Gemini IX* on June 6, 1966, only 769 yards from the U.S.S. *Wasp* in the western Atlantic.

Extra-Terrestrial Vehicles

The first wheeled vehicle landed on the moon was the Soviet *Lunokhod I* which began its earth-controlled travels on November 17, 1970. It moved a total of 6.54 miles on gradients up to 30 degrees in the Mare Imbrium and did not become non-functioning until October 4, 1971.

The lunar speed and distance record was set by the *Apollo XVI* Rover with 11.2 m.p.h. and 22.4 miles.

Duration Record on the Moon

The crew of *Apollo XVII*'s lunar exploration module *Challenger*, Capt. Eugene Andrew Cernan, U.S.N., and Dr. Harrison H. "Jack" Schmitt, were on the lunar surface for 74 hours 59½ minutes from December 7 to 12, 1972. They collected a record 253 lbs. of rock and soil during their 22-hour-5-minute "extra-vehicular activity." Schmitt was the 12th and last man on the moon.

Most Expensive Project

The total cost of the U.S. manned space program up to and including the lunar mission of *Apollo XVII* has been estimated at $25,541,400,000. The cost of the U.S.S.R. space program from 1958 to September, 1973, has been estimated, however, at $45,000,000,000.

Closest Approach to the Sun

The research spacecraft *Helios B* approached within 27,000,000 miles of the sun on April 16, 1976. It was carrying both U.S. and West German instrumentation.

Chapter Five

THE SCIENTIFIC WORLD

Elements

All known matter in the solar system is made up of chemical elements. The total of naturally occurring elements so far detected is 94, comprising, at ordinary temperature, two liquids, 11 gases and 81 solids. The so-called "fourth state" of matter is plasma, when negatively charged electrons and positively charged ions are in flux.

Lightest and Heaviest Sub-Nuclear Particles

By January, 1979, the existence of 23 "stable particles, 37 meson resonance triplets and 56 baryon resonance multiplets" was accepted, representing the possible eventual discovery of 221 particles and an equal number of anti-particles. Of $SU(3)$ particles, the one with the highest mass is the omega minus, announced on February 24, 1964, from the Brookhaven National Laboratory, near Upton, Long Island, N.Y. It has a mass state of 1672.2 ± 0.4 Mev and a lifetime of 1.1×10^{-10} seconds. Sub-atomic concepts require that the masses of the graviton, photon, and neutrino should all be zero. Based on the sensitivities of various cosmological theories, upper limits for the masses of these particles are 7.6×10^{-67}g. for the graviton; 3.0×10^{-53}g. for the photon and 1.4×10^{-32}g. for the neutrino (*cf.* 9.10953×10^{-28}g. for the mass of an electron).

Most and Least Stable Particles

The proton was measured in 1974 to be stable against decay for a lifetime in excess of 2×10^{30} years.

The least stable or shortest-lived nuclear particles discovered are the rho prime meson (definite proof of existence announced on January 29, 1973), and the four baryon resonances N (2650), N (3030), Δ (2850), and Δ (3230), all lasting 1.6×10^{-24} second.

Newest Particles

After 41 months of experimentation, the tau lepton (symbol T−) was confirmed by Prof. Martin Perl at the Stanford Linear Accelerator Center in California in December, 1978.

Fastest Particles

A search for the existence of super-luminary particles, named tachyons (symbol T+ and T−), with a speed *in vacuo* greater than *c.* the speed of light, was instituted in 1968 by Dr. T. Alvager and Dr. M. Kriesler of Princeton University. Such particles would create the conceptual difficulty of disappearing before they exist.

The 107 Elements

There are 94 known naturally occurring elements comprising at ordinary temperatures two liquids, 11 gases and 81 solids, of which 72 are metallic. To date, a further 13 transuranic elements (Elements 95 to 107) have been claimed, of which 9 are undisputed.

Commonest (lithosphere)
  46.60 per cent by weight

Commonest (atmosphere)
  78.09 per cent by volume

Commonest (extra-terrestrial)
  90 per cent of all matter

Rarest (of the 94)
  1/100th oz. in earth's crust

Lightest
  0.005612 lb. per cubic foot

Lightest (Metal)
  33.30 lb. per cubic foot

Densest
  1,410 lb. per cubic foot

Heaviest (Gas)
  0.6299 lb. per cubic foot

Newest[1]
  Element 107,
  highest atomic number

Purest
  2 parts in 10^{15} (1978)

Hardest
  Diamond Allotrope, Knoop value 8,400

Most Expensive
  Sold in 1968 for $1000 per μg.

Most Stable[2]
  Half-life of 2.51×10^{21} years (1974)

Oxygen (O)
  Discovered by Scheele (Germany-Sweden), 1771

Nitrogen (N)
  Discovered by Priestley (G.B.) *et al.*, 1772

Hydrogen (H)
  Discovered by Cavendish (G.B.), 1776

Astatine (At)
  Discovered by Corson (U.S.) *et al.*, 1940

Hydrogen (H)
  Discovered by Cavendish (G.B.), 1776

Lithium (Li)
  Discovered by Arfvedson (Sweden), 1817

Osmium (Os)
  Discovered by Tennant (G.B.), 1804

Radon (Rn)
  Discovered by Dorn (Germany), 1900

Unnilseptium (Uns)
  Discovered by Oganesyan (U.S.S.R.) *et al.*

Helium (He)
  Discovered by Ramsay (G.B.), 1895

Carbon (C)
  Prehistoric

Californium (Cf)
  Discovered by Seaborg (U.S.) *et al.*, 1950

Tellurium (Te 130)
  Discovered by von Reichenstein (Austro-Hungary), 1782

---

[1] "Unnilseptium" is provisional I.U.P.A.C. name. Evidence alleging the existence of Elements 116, 124, and 126, published on June 17, 1976, was subsequently declared to have been misconceived. Unnilhexium (Unh), or Element 106, was identified by Ghiorso (U.S.) *et al.* on September 9, 1974.

[2] Double beta decay estimate. Alpha particle record is Lead-204 at 1.4×10^{17} years (1958) and Beta particle record is Cadmium 113 at 9×10^{15} years (Greth, Gangadharan and Wolke, 1969).

Least Stable
Half-life of 4.4×10^{-22} seconds

Lithium (isotope 5) (Li 5)
Discovered by Arfvedson
(Sweden), 1817

Most Isotopes
34

Cesium (Cs)
Discovered by Bunsen &
Kirchhoff (Germany), 1860

Least Isotopes
3 (confirmed)

Hydrogen (H)
Discovered by Cavendish
(G.B.), 1776

Most Ductile
1 oz. drawn to 43 miles

Gold (Au)
ante 3000 B.C.

Highest Ductility in Tension

Lead-Tin (1:1)

Highest Tensile Strength
3.91×10^{6} lb. force per square
inch

Boron (B)
Discovered by Gay-Lussac
(France) *et al.*, 1808

Lowest Melting/Boiling Points
−271.72°C. under pressure of
26 atmospheres and
−268.926°C.

Helium (He)
Discovered by Ramsay (G.B.),
1895

Highest Melting/Boiling Points
3,422°C. and 5,730°C.

Tungsten (W)
Discovered by J. J. & F.
d'Elhuyar (Spain), 1783

Lowest Expansion (negative)
-5.8×10^{-5} cm. per cm. per
degree C. between 450°-480°C.
(Delta prime allotrope,
discovered 1953)

Plutonium (Pu)
Discovered by Seaborg (U.S.)
et al., 1940

Lowest Expansion (positive)
1.0×10^{-6} cm. per cm. per
degree C. (at 20°C.)

Carbon (diamond) (C)
Prehistoric

Highest Expansion (metal)
9.7×10^{-5} cm. per cm. per
degree C. (at 20°C.)

Cesium (Cs)
Discovered by Bunsen &
Kirchhoff (Germany), 1860

Highest Expansion (gas)
108×10^{3} cm. per cm. per
degree C. (at −210°C.)
(Beta allotrope discovered
1916)

Nitrogen (N)
Discovered by Priestley
(G.B.) *et al.*, 1772

Most Poisonous
1 μg. or microgram (1 thirty-
millionth of an oz.) inhaled or
swallowed will cause cancer.
With a half-life of 23,640
years, toxicity is retained for a
thousand centuries.

Plutonium (Pu)
Discovered by Seaborg (U.S.)
et al., 1940

Chemical Compounds

It has been estimated that there are more than 4,040,000 described
chemical compounds, of which 63,000 are now in common use.

Most Refractory
Tantalum Carbide ($TaCo_{0.88}$)   Melts at 4,010° ± 75°C.

Most Refractory (plastics) Modified Polymides	482°C. for short periods
Lowest Expansion Invar metal (Ni-Fe alloy with C and Mn)	1.3×10^{-7} cm. per cm. per degree C. (at 20°C.)
Highest Tensile Strength Sapphire whisker Al_2O_3	6×10^6 lb. force per square inch
Highest Tensile Strength (plastics) Polyvinyl alcoholic fibers	1.4×10^5 lb. force per square inch
Most Magnetic Cobalt-copper-samarium Co_3Cu_2Sm	10,500 oersted coercive force
Least Magnetic Alloy Copper nickel alloy CuNi	963 parts Cu to 37 parts Ni
Most Pungent Vanillaldehyde	Detectable at 2×10^{-8} milligram per liter of air
Sweetest 1n-propoxy-2-amino-4-nitro-benzene	$5,600 \times$ as sweet as 1 per cent sucrose
Bitterest Bitrex or Benzyl diethyl ammonium benzoate	$200 \times$ as bitter as quinine sulphate
Most Acidic[1] Perchloric acid ($HClO_4$)	pH value of normal solution tends to zero
Most Alkaline Caustic soda (NaOH) and potash (KOH) and tetra-methylammonium hydroxide ($N[CH_3]_4OH$)	pH value of normal solution is 14
Highest Specific Impulse Hydrogen with liquid fluorine	447 lb. force per second per lb.
Most Poisonous Thiopentone (a barbiturate)	Intracardiac injection will kill in 1 to 2 seconds

[1]The most powerful acid assessed on its power as a hydrogen-ion donor is a solution of antimony pentafluoride in fluorosulphonic acid ($SbF_5 + FSO_3H$).

Finest Powder

Particulate matter of 25 to 40 Å was reportedly produced by an electron beam evaporation process at the Atomic Energy Establishment, Harwell, England, in October, 1972. The paper was published by Dr. P. RamaKrishnan.

Most Absorbent Substance

The U.S. Department of Agriculture Research Service announced on August 18, 1974, that "H-span" or Super Slurper, composed of one half starch derivative and one fourth each of acrylamide and acrylic acid, can, when treated with iron, retain water 1,300 times its own weight.

Smelliest Substance

The most evil-smelling substance, of the 17,000 smells so far classified, must be a matter of opinion, but ethyl mercaptan (C_2H_5SH) and butyl seleno-mercaptan (C_4H_9SeH) are powerful claimants, each with a smell reminiscent of a combination of rotting cabbage, garlic, onions and sewer gas.

Most Expensive Perfume

The retail prices of the most expensive perfumes tend to be fixed at public relations rather than economic levels. The most expensive ingredient in perfume is pure French middle note jasmine essence at £2,900 ($6,960) per kilogram or £82.20 ($197) per ounce.

Most Powerful Fuel

The greatest specific impulse of any rocket-propulsion fuel combination is 447 lbs./f./sec. per lb. produced by liquid fluorine and hydrogen. This compares with a figure of 300 for liquid oxygen and kerosene.

Most Potent Poison

The rickettsial disease, Q-fever, can be instituted by a *single* organism but is only fatal in 1 in 1,000 cases. About 10 organisms of *Francisella tularenesis* (formerly known as *Pasteurella tularenesis*) can institute tularemia, variously called alkali disease, Francis disease or deerfly fever, and this is fatal in upwards of 10 cases in 1,000.

Most Powerful Nerve Gas

In the early 1950's, substances known as V-agents, notably VX, 300 times more toxic than phosgene ($COCl_2$) used in World War I, were developed at the Chemical Defence Experimental Establishment, Porton Down, Wiltshire, England, which are lethal at 1 milligram per man. Patents were applied for in 1962 and published in February, 1974.

Drugs

Most Powerful. The most powerful commonly available drug is d-Lysergic Acid Diethylamide tartrate (LSD–25, $C_{20}H_{25}N_3O$) first produced in 1938 for common cold research and as a hallucinogen by Dr. Albert Hoffmann (Swiss), on April 16–19, 1943.

The most potent analgesic drug is Etorphine or M-99, announced in June, 1963, by Dr. K. W. Bentley (b. 1923) and D. G. Hardy of Reckitt & Sons Ltd. in Hull, Yorkshire, England. The drug has almost 10,000 times the potency of morphine.

Most Prescribed. The benzodiazepine group tranquilizing drug Valium, discovered by Hoffmann–La Roche, is the world's most widely used drug.

Drink

Most Alcoholic

The strength of liquor is gauged by degrees proof. In the U.S., proof spirit is that mixture of ethyl alcohol (C_2H_5OH) and water which contains one half its volume of alcohol of a specific gravity of 0.7939 at 60°F., referred to water at 60°F. as unity. Pure or absolute alcohol is thus 200 proof. A "hangover" is due to toxic congenerics such as amyl alcohol ($C_5H_{11}OH$).

During independence (1918–1940) the Estonian Liquor Monopoly marketed 196 proof potato alcohol. In 31 U.S. states *Everclear* (190 proof) is marketed by the American Distilling Co., "primarily as a base for homemade cordials."

Beer

Strongest Beer. The world's strongest and most expensive beer is EKU Kulminator Urtyp Hell from Kulmbach, West Germany, which retails for up to $1.70 for a ½-pint bottle. It is 13.2 per cent alcohol by volume at 20°C. with an original gravity of 1117.6°.

Weakest Beer. The weakest liquid ever marketed as beer was a sweet ersatz beer which was brewed in Germany by Sunner, Colne-Kalk, in 1918. It had an original gravity of 1000.96°, with less than 0.2 per cent alcohol.

Liqueurs

The most expensive liqueur in France is *Eau de vie de poire avec poire*, sold for 100 francs ($22.50) a bottle at Fauchon in Paris.

The most expensive bottle of spirits sold was a magnum of *Grande Fine Champagne Cognac*, 1811 which was auctioned at Christie's of London on November 30, 1978, for £780 ($1,560). *Cognac Coutier* (50 years old) retails for 1200 francs ($270) a bottle at Fauchon in Paris.

Wine

Oldest Vintage. The oldest datable wine has been an amphora salvaged and drunk by Capt. James Cousteau from the wreck of a Greek trader sunk in the Mediterranean *c.* 230 B.C. Wine jars recovered from the Pompeii eruption of A.D. 79 were found labelled VESUVINUM—the oldest known trade mark.

Most Expensive. The highest price ever paid for a bottle of wine of any size is $18,000 for a jeroboam (equivalent to 4 bottles) of 1864 Château Lafite claret purchased at Heublein Incorporated's 10th Annual Auction in Atlanta, Georgia, on May 25, 1978, by John A. Grisanti, 49, proprietor of Grisanti's Restaurant in Memphis, Tennessee.

Greatest Wine Auction

The largest single sale of wine was conducted by Christie's of King Street, St. James, London, on July 10–11, 1974 at Quaglino's Ballroom, London, when 2,325 lots containing 432,000 bottles realized £962,190 (then $2,309,256).

Greatest Wine Tasting

The largest wine tasting ever was held for 1,737 people at Nederburg, South Africa, on March 4, 1978, with 15 openers, 93 pourers and 2,012 bottles of wine.

Largest Bottles

The largest bottles normally used in the wine and spirit trade are the jeroboam (equal to 4 bottles of champagne or, rarely, of brandy, and from 5 to 6½ bottles of claret, depending on whether the bottle was blown or molded) and the double magnum (equal, since *c.* 1934, to 4 bottles of claret or, more rarely, red burgundy). A complete set of Monopole champagne bottles would consist of the ¼ bottle, ½ bottle, bottle, magnum, Jeroboam, Rehoboam, Methuselah, Salmanazar, Balthazar and the Nebuchadnezzar, which has a capacity of 16 liters (33.8 pints), and is equivalent to 20 bottles.

In May, 1958, a 5-foot-tall sherry bottle with a capacity of 20½ Imperial gallons (24.6 U.S. gallons) was blown in Stoke-on-Trent, Staffordshire, England. This bottle, with the capacity of 131 normal bottles, was named an "Adelaide."

Smallest Bottles

The smallest bottles of liquor sold are the 24 minim bottles of Scotch whisky marketed by the Cumbrae Supply Co. of Scotland. They contain $\frac{1}{20}$ of a fluid ounce and retailed in 1979 for the equivalent of 64 cents (which includes the match box in which it is packaged).

Champagne Cork Flight

The longest distance for a champagne cork to fly from an untreated and unheated bottle 4 feet from level ground is 102 feet 11 inches by Gary P. Mahan at La Habra Heights, California, on August 2, 1975.

Miniature Bottles

The largest reported collection of unduplicated miniature bottles is one of 2,125 as of April 30, 1979, owned by B. A. Everest of Tunbridge Wells, Kent, England.

Gems

Most Precious. From 1955, the value of rubies rose, due to a drying up of supplies from Ceylon and Burma. A flawless natural ruby of good color was carat for carat more valuable than emerald, diamond or sapphire and, in the case of a 6-carat ruby, brought $30,000. The ability to produce very large corundum prisms of 12 inches or over in length in the laboratory for use in lasers seems to have little bearing on the market for natural gems.

Largest. The largest recorded stone of gem quality was a 520,000-carat (229-lb.) aquamarine ($Al_2Be_3[Si_6O_{18}]$) found near Marambaia, Brazil, in 1910. It yielded over 200,000 carats of gem quality cut stones.

Rarest. Only four stones are known of the pale mauve gem Taaffeite ($Be_4Mg_4Al_{15}O_{32}$), first discovered in Dublin, Ireland, in November, 1945. The largest known example weighs 0.84 of a carat.

Hardest. The hardest of all gems, and the hardest known naturally occurring substance, is diamond, which is, chemically, pure carbon. Diamond is 90 times as hard as the next hardest mineral, corundum (Al_2O_3), and those from Borneo, in Indonesia, and New South Wales, Australia, have a particular reputation for hardness. Hardnesses are compared on Mohs' scale, on which talc is 1, a fingernail is 2½, window glass 5, topaz 8, corundum 9, and diamond

Precious Stone Records

	Largest	Largest Cut Stone	Other Records
Diamond (pure crystallized carbon)	3,106 metric carats (over 1¼ lbs.) —*The Cullinan*, found by Capt. M. F. Wells, Jan. 26, 1905, in the Premier Mine, Pretoria, South Africa.	530.2 metric carats. Cleaved from *The Cullinan* in 1908 in Amsterdam by Jak Asscher and polished by Henri Koe. Known as *The Star of Africa* No. 1 and now in the British Royal Sceptre. In December, 1977, top blue-white 5-carat gems were quoted at $64,000 to $128,000.	Diamond is the *hardest* known naturally occurring substance, being 90 times as hard as the next hardest mineral, corundum (Al_2O_3). The peak hardness value on the Knoop scale is 8,400 compared with an average diamond of 7,000. The rarest colors for diamond are blue (record—44.4 carat *Hope* diamond) and pink (record—24 carat presented by Dr. John Thoburn Williamson to H.M. The Queen of the U.K. in 1958). The 137.02-carat Premier Rose diamond was bought by Goldberg-Weiss in December, 1978, for a reputed $11,500,000. The 353.9-carat uncut stone was found in the Premier Mine in April, 1978, and auctioned by De Beers for $5,170,000 in May to a Mouw-Goldberg-Weiss syndicate. The record auction price for a diamond ring is £413,173 ($766,660), amounting to $37,289 per carat, for a 20.56-carat pear-shaped flawless "D" diamond at Sotheby's, Zurich, on November 22, 1978.
Emerald (green beryl) [$Be_3Al_2(SiO_3)_6$]	125-lb. crystal (up to 15½ inches long and 9¾ inches in diameter) from a Ural, U.S.S.R. mine.	2,680-carat unguent jar carved by Dionysio Miseroni in the 17th century owned by the Austrian Government. 1,350 carats of *gem* quality, the *Devonshire* stone from Muso, Colombia.	A necklace of eight major emeralds and one pendant emerald of 75.63 carats with diamonds was sold by Sotheby's in Zurich, Switzerland, on November 24, 1971 for £436,550 (then $1,090,000). The Swiss customs at Geneva confirmed the existence of a hexagonal emerald of about 20,000 carats, thus possibly worth more than $100,000,000.
Sapphire (blue corundum) (Al_2O_3)	2,302-carat stone found at Anakie, Queensland, Australia, in c. 1935, now a 1,318-carat head of President Abraham Lincoln (1809–65).	1,444-carat black star stone carved from a 2,097-carat stone in 1953–55 into a bust of General Dwight David Eisenhower (1890–1969).	*Note:* Both the sapphire busts are in the custody of the Kazanjian Foundation of Los Angeles.
Ruby (red corundum) (Al_2O_3)	3,421-carat broken stone reported found in July, 1961 (largest piece 750 carats).	1,184-carat natural gem stone of Burmese origin.	Since 1955 rubies have been the world's most precious gem stone attaining a price of up to $10,000 per carat by 1969. The largest star ruby is the 138.72-carat Rosser Reeves stone on display at the Smithsonian Institution in Washington, D.C.

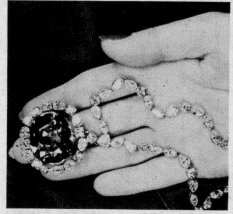

LARGEST BLUE DIAMOND: The 44.4-carat Hope diamond (left), on exhibit at the Smithsonian Institution, carries a legendary curse. **LARGEST DIAMOND** (right): The Star of Africa No. 1 in the British Royal Sceptre was cut, with 74 facets, from the 1¼-pound Cullinan diamond.

10. Diamonds average 7,000 on the Knoop scale, with a peak value of 8,400. This index represents a micro-indentation index based on kilograms per one hundredth of a square millimeter $(kg/(mm^2)^{-2})$.

Densest Gem Mineral. The densest of all gem minerals is stibiotantalite $[(SbO)_2 (Ta,Nb)_2 O_6]$, a rare brownish-yellow mineral found in San Diego County, California, with a density of 7.46 grams per c.c. The alloy platiniridium has a density of more than 22.0.

GIANT JADE: Karl Ebner stands beside the record jade boulder he discovered.

Records for Other Precious Materials

	Largest	Where Found	Notes on Present Location, etc.
Pearl (Molluscan concretion)	14 lbs. 1 oz., 9¼ in. long by 5¼ in. in diameter—*Pearl of Lao-tze*	At Palawan, Philippines, May 7, 1934, in shell of giant clam.	In a San Francisco bank vault. It is the property since 1936 of Wilburn Dowell Cobb and was valued at $4,080,000 in July, 1971.
Opal ($SiO_2 . NH_2O$)	34,215 carats (yellow-orange)	Andamooka, South Australia, Jan., 1970.	The Andamooka specimen, weighing 220 troy oz., was unearthed by a bulldozer.
	Gem stone: 17,700 carats (*Olympic Australis*)	Coober Pedy, South Australia, Aug., 1956.	
Crystal (SiO_2)	280 tons (beryl)	Malakialina, Madagascar, 1964.	Measures 59 feet long with a volume of 226 cubic yards.
Topaz [$Al_2(F, OH)_2 SiO_4$]	Ball: 106¾ lbs., 12¼ in. diameter, the *Warner* sphere	Burma (originally a 1,000-lb. piece).	Smithsonian Institution Museum (U.S. National Museum) in Washington, D.C.
	"Brazilian Princess," 21,327 carats, 221 facets (light blue)	Brazil.	Exhibited by Smithsonian Institution, November, 1978. Valued at $1,066,350, or $50 a carat.
Amber (coniferous fossil resin)	33 lbs. 10 oz.	Reputedly from Burma, acquired in 1860.	Bought by John Charles Bowring (d. 1893) for £300 in Canton. China. Natural History Museum, London, since 1940.
Turquoise [$CuAl_6(PO_4)_4 (OH)_8 4H_2O$]	218 lbs.	Riverside County, California, January 17, 1975.	Found by Chester Jastromb and Kenneth Casper. Original weight was probably c. 250 lbs.
Jade [$NaAl(Si_2O_6)$]	Boulder of 63,307 lbs.	Watson Lake, British Columbia, Canada, 1977.	Found by Karl Ebner. Jadeite can be virtually any color. The less precious nephrite is [$Ca_2 (Mg, Fe)_5 (OH)_2 (Si_4 O_{11})_2$].
Marble (Metamorphosed $CaCO_3$)	100.8 tons (single slab)	Quarried at Yule, Colorado.	A piece of over 50 tons was dressed from this slab for the coping stone o the Tomb of the Unknown Soldier in Arlington National Cemetery, Virginia.
Nuggets—Gold (Au)	7,560 oz. (472¼ lbs.) (reef gold) *Holtermann Nugget*	Beyers & Holtermann Star of Hope Gold Mining Co., Hill End, N.S.W., Australia, Oct. 19, 1872.	The purest large nugget was the *Welcome Stranger*, found at Mollagul Victoria, Australia, which yielded 2,248 troy oz. of pure gold from 2,280½ oz.
Silver (Ag)	2,750 lbs. troy	Sonora, Mexico.	Appropriated by the Spanish Government before 1821.

Telescopes

Earliest. Although there is evidence that early Arabian scientists understood something of the magnifying power of lenses, the first use of lenses to form a telescope has been attributed to Roger Bacon (*c.* 1214–92) in England. The prototype of modern refracting telescopes was completed by Johannes Lippershey for the Netherlands government on October 2, 1608.

Largest Reflector. The largest telescope in the world is the 236.2-inch telescope sited on Mount Semirodriki, near Zelenchukskaya in the Caucasus Mountains, U.S.S.R., at an altitude of 6,830 feet. Work on the mirror, weighing 78 tons, was not completed until the summer of 1974. Regular observations were begun on February 7, 1976, after 16 years' work. The weight of the 138-foot-high assembly is 946 tons. Being the most powerful of all telescopes, its range, which includes the location of objects down to the 25th magnitude, represents the limits of the observable universe. Its light-gathering power would enable it to detect the light from a candle at a distance of 15,000 miles.

Largest Refractor. The largest refracting (*i.e.* magnification by lenses) telescope in the world is the 62-foot-long, 40-inch telescope completed in 1897 at the Yerkes Observatory, Williams Bay, Wisconsin, and belonging to the University of Chicago. In 1900, a 49.2-inch refractor 180 feet in length was built for the Paris Exposition, but its optical performance was too poor to justify attempts to use it.

Solar

The world's largest solar telescope is the 480-foot-long McMath telescope at Kitt Peak National Observatory near Tucson, Arizona.

LARGEST SOLAR TELESCOPE: The McMath solar telescope is located atop a 6,800-foot mountain on the Papago Indian Reservation in Arizona.

It has a focal length of 300 feet and an 80-inch heliostat mirror. It was completed in 1962 and produces an image measuring 33 inches in diameter.

Earliest Observatory

The oldest astronomical observatory building in the world is the Chomsong-dae in Kyongju, South Korea, which was built in 632 A.D.

Highest Observatory

The highest-altitude observatory in the world is the University of Denver's High Altitude Observatory at an altitude of 14,100 feet, opened in 1973, on Mount Evans, Colorado. The principal instrument is a 24-inch Ealing Beck reflecting telescope.

Radio-Telescopes

Largest. The first $3,000,000 installment for the building of the world's largest and most sensitive radio-telescope was included by the National Science Foundation in its federal budget for the fiscal year 1973. The instrument termed the VLA (Very Large Array) will be Y-shaped with each arm 13 miles long with 27 mobile antennae (each 82 feet in diameter) on rails. The site selected is 50 miles west of Socorro in the Plains of San Augustin, New Mexico, and the completion date will be in January, 1981 at an estimated total cost of $78,000,000.

Largest Steerable Dish. Radio waves of extraterrestrial origin were first detected by Karl Jansky of Bell Telephone Laboratories, Holmdel, New Jersey, using a 100-foot-long rotatable shortwave antenna in 1932. The world's largest trainable dish-type radio-telescope is the 328-foot-diameter, 3,360-ton assembly at the Max Planck Institute for Radio Astronomy of Bonn in the Effelsberger Valley, West Germany; it became operative in May, 1971. The cost of the installation, begun in November, 1967, was DM36,920,000 ($14,760,000).

The world's largest dish-type radio-telescope is the partially-steerable ionospheric assembly built over a natural bowl at Arecibo, Puerto Rico, completed in November, 1963, at a cost of about $9,000,000. It has a diameter of 1,000 feet and the dish covers 18½ acres. Its sensitivity was raised by a factor of 1,000 and its range to the edge of the observable universe at some 15 billion light-years by the fitting of new aluminum plates at a cost of $8,800,000. Re-dedication was on November 16, 1974.

The RATAN-600 radio-telescope being built in the northern Caucasus, U.S.S.R., will have mirror dishes on a 1,968.5-foot perimeter.

Planetaria

The ancestor of the planetarium is the rotatable Gottorp Globe, built by Andreas Busch in Denmark between 1654 and 1664 to the orders of Olearius, court mathematician to Duke Frederick III of Holstein. It is 34.6 feet in circumference, weighs 4 tons and is now preserved in Leningrad, U.S.S.R. The stars were painted on the inside.

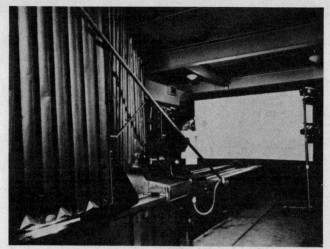

LARGEST CAMERA: This 30¼-ton Rolls-Royce camera is almost 9 feet high, more than 8 feet wide and 35 feet long.

The earliest optical installation was not until 1923 in the Deutsches Museum, Munich, by Zeiss of Jena, Germany.

The world's largest planetarium, with a diameter of 82½ feet, is in Moscow, U.S.S.R.

Photography

Cameras

Earliest. The earliest photograph was taken in the summer of 1826 by Joseph Nicéphore Niepce (1765–1833), a French physician and scientist. It showed the courtyard of his country house at Gras, near St. Loup-de-Varennes. It probably took eight hours to expose and was taken on a bitumen-coated polished pewter plate measuring 7¾ inches by 6½ inches.

One of the earliest photographs taken was one of a diamond-paned window in Lacock Abbey, Wiltshire, England, taken in 1835 by William Henry Fox Talbot (1800–1877), the inventor of the negative-positive process.

Largest. The largest camera ever built is the 30¼-ton Rolls-Royce camera built for Product Support (Graphics) Ltd. of Derby, England, completed in 1959. It measures 8 feet 10 inches high, 8 feet 3 inches wide and 35 feet long. The lens is a 63″ f/15 Cooke Apochromatic. Its value after improvements in 1971 was in excess of $240,000.

Smallest. Apart from cameras built for intra-cardiac surgery and espionage, the smallest camera that has been marketed is the circular

Japanese "Petal" camera with a diameter of 1.14 inches and a thickness of 0.65 of an inch. It has a focal length of 0.47 inch. The BBC-TV program *Record Breakers* showed prints from this camera on December 3, 1974.

Most Expensive. The most expensive complete range of camera equipment is that of Nikon of Tokyo, Japan, who marketed a range of 19 cameras with 62 lenses and 366 accessories in 1979. The total cost of the range would exceed $110,000. A Thomas Sutton wet-plate camera, *c.* 1865, was sold at auction at Sotheby's for $26,400 on March 8, 1974.

FASTEST CAMERA: The Imacon 600 can take up to 600,000,000 pictures in one second.

Fastest. In 1972, Prof. Basor of the U.S.S.R. Academy of Sciences published a paper describing an experimental camera with a time resolution of 5×10^{-13} of a second or $\frac{1}{2}$ a picosecond. The fastest production camera in the world is the Imacon 600 manufactured by John Hadland (P.I.) Ltd. of Bovingdon, Hertfordshire, England, which is capable of 600 million pictures per second, with the maximum framing rate 600 million frames per second. Uses include laser, ballistic, detonic, plasma and corona research.

First Aerial Photography. The world's earliest aerial photograph was taken in 1858 by Gaspard Félix Tournachon (1820–1910), *alias* Nadar, from a balloon near Villacoublay, on the outskirts of Paris, France.

Numeration

In dealing with large numbers, scientists use the notation of 10 raised to various powers, to eliminate a profusion of zeros. For example, 19,160,000,000,000 miles would be written 1.916×10^{13} miles. Similarly, a very small number, for example, 0.0000154324 of a gram, would be written 1.54324×10^{-5} gram (g.). Of the prefixes used before numbers the smallest is "atto-," from the Danish *atten* for 18, indicating a million million millionth part (10^{-18}) of the unit, and the highest is "exa-" (Greek, *hexa*=six), indicating a quintillion (10^{18}) fold.

Numbers

Prime Numbers. A prime number is any positive integer (excluding 1) having no integral factors other than itself and unity, *e.g.* 2, 3, 5, 7, or 11. The lowest prime number is 2. The highest known prime number is $2^{21701} -1 \cdot$ (a number of 6,533 digits), discovered after months of trials by computer by Laura Nickel, 18, and Curt Noll, 18, on October 30, 1978, at California State University.

Perfect Numbers. A number is said to be perfect if it is equal to the sum of its divisors other than itself, *e.g.* $1+2+4+7+14=28$. The lowest perfect number is 6 $(1+2+3)$. The highest known, and the 25th so far discovered, is $(2^{21701}-1) \times 2^{21700}$. It is a consequence of the highest known prime.

Highest. The highest lexicographically accepted named number in the system of successive powers of ten is the centillion, which is 1 followed by 303 zeros, or 10^{303} in the U.S. system. The highest named number outside the decimal notation is the Buddhist *asankhyeya*, which is equal to 10^{140} or 100 quinto-quadragintillions.

The number 10^{100} (10 duotrigintillion) is designated a Googol, a term devised by Dr. Edward Kasner of the U.S. (d. 1955). Ten raised to the power of a Googol is described as a Googolplex. Some conception of the magnitude of such numbers can be gained when it is said that the number of atoms in some models of the observable universe probably does not exceed 10^{85}.

The highest number ever used in a mathematical proof is a bounding value published in 1977 and known as Graham's number. It concerns bichromatic hypercubes and is inexpressible without the special "arrow" notation, devised by Knuth in 1976, extended to 64 layers.

Most Primitive. The most unnumerate people are the Nambiquara of the northwest Mato Grosso section of Brazil who lack any system of numbers. They do, however, have a verb which means "they are two alike."

Earliest Measures. The earliest known measure of weight is the *beqa* of the Amratian period of Egyptian civilization *c.* 3800 B.C. found at Naqada, Egypt. The weights are cylindrical with rounded ends from 188.7 to 211.2 grams (6.65–7.45 oz.). The unit of length used by the megalithic tomb-builders in Britain *c.* 2200 B.C. appears to have been 2.72 ± 0.003 feet.

Smallest Units

The shortest unit of length is the atto-meter, which is 1.0×10^{-16} of a centimeter. The smallest unit of area is a "shed," used in sub-atomic physics and first mentioned in 1956. It is 1.0×10^{-48} of a square centimeter. A "barn" is equal to 10^{24} "sheds." The interaction of a neutrino with electrons was reported in 1976 to occur over the area of 1.0×10^{45} of a square centimeter.

Most Accurate Version of "Pi." The greatest number of decimal places to which *pi* (π) has been calculated is 1,000,000 by the French mathematicians Jean Guilloud and Mlle. Martine Bouyer, achieved on May 24, 1973, on a CDC 7600 computer, but not verified until September 3, 1973. The published value to a million places was 3.141592653589793 . . . (omitting the next 999,975 places) . . . 5779458151. This has been described as the world's most boring 400-page book.

In 1897, the General Assembly of Indiana enacted in House Bill No. 246 that *pi* was *de jure* 4, for the most inaccurate version.

Square Root of Two. The greatest accuracy was an enumeration to 1,000,082 places by Jacques Dutka of Columbia University, New York City, announced in October, 1971, after a $47\frac{1}{2}$-hour run on a computer.

Longest Slide Rule

The world's longest slide rule is one 320 feet 11.1 inches in length completed in March, 1979, by students of Alvirne High School, Hudson, New Hampshire.

Time Measure

Longest. The longest measure of time is the *kalpa* in Hindu chronology. It is equivalent to 4,320 million years. In astronomy a cosmic year is the period of rotation of the sun around the center of the Milky Way galaxy, *i.e.* about 225,000,000 years. In the Late Cretaceous Period of *c.* 85 million years ago, the earth rotated faster so resulting in 370.3 days per year, while in Cambrian times, some 600 million years ago, there is evidence that the year contained 425 days.

Shortest. Owing to variations in the length of a day, which is estimated to be increasing irregularly at the average rate of about 2 milliseconds per century, due to the moon's tidal drag, the second has been redefined. Instead of being 1/86,400th part of a mean solar day, it is now reckoned as 1/31,556,925.9747th part of the solar (or tropical) year at 1900 A.D., January 0 at 12 hours, Ephemeris time. In 1958 the second of Ephemeris time was computed to be equivalent to $9,192,631,770 \pm 20$ cycles of the radiation corresponding to the transition of a cesium 133 atom when unperturbed by exterior fields. The greatest diurnal change recorded has been 10 milliseconds on August 8, 1972, due to the most violent solar storm recorded in 370 years of observation. The shortest blip of light is one of 0.2 of a picosecond (0.2×10^{-12} of a second) produced by the Center of Laser Studies, University of Southern California, in August, 1978. Light travels 0.0023 of an inch in that period of time.

Physical Extremes (Terrestrial)

Temperatures

Highest. The highest man-made temperatures yet attained are those produced in the center of a thermonuclear fusion bomb, which are of the order of 300,000,000° to 400,000,000°C. Of controllable temperatures, the highest effective laboratory figure reported is 50,000,000°C. for 2/100ths of a second, by Prof. Lev A. Artsimovich at Tokamuk, U.S.S.R., in 1969. At very low particle densities, even higher figures are obtainable. Prior to 1963, a figure of 3,000 million °C. was reportedly achieved in the U.S.S.R. with Ogra injection-mirror equipment.

Lowest. The lowest temperature reached is 5×10^{-7} degree Kelvin, achieved by Professor A. Abragam (b. 1914) in collaboration with M. Chapellier, M. Goldman, and Vu Hoang Chau at the Centre d'Etudes Nucléaires, Saclay, France, in 1969. Absolute or thermodynamic temperatures are defined in terms of ratios rather than as differences reckoned from the unattainable absolute zero, which on the Kelvin scale is −273.15°C. or −459.67°F. Thus the lowest temperature ever attained is 1 in 5.46×10^8 of the melting point of ice (0°C. or 273.15°K. or 32°F.).

The lowest equilibrium temperature ever attained is 0.0003°K. by nuclear refrigeration in a 3-lb. copper specimen by Prof. Olli V. Lounasmaa (born 1920) and his team at the Helsinki University of Technology, Otaniemi, Finland, on April 17, 1974.

Highest Pressures

The highest sustained laboratory pressures yet reported are of 1.7 megabars (12,300 tons force per square inch) achieved in the giant hydraulic diamond-faced press at the Carnegie Institution's Geophysical Laboratory in Washington, D.C., reported in June, 1978. Using dynamic methods and impact speeds of up to 18,000 m.p.h., momentary pressures of 75,000,000 atmospheres (548,000 tons per square inch) were reported from the U.S. in 1958.

Highest Vacuum

The highest or "hardest" vacuums obtained in scientific research are of the order of 10^{-14} torr, achieved at the I.B.M. Thomas J. Watson Research Center, Yorktown Heights, New York, in October, 1976, in a cryogenic system with temperatures down to −269°C. (−452°F.). This is equivalent to depopulating baseball-sized molecules from 1 yard apart to 50 miles apart. This compares with an estimated pressure in interstellar space of 1.0×10^{-19} of an atmosphere. At sea level there are 3×10^{19} molecules per cubic centimeter in the atmosphere, but in interstellar space there are probably less than 10 per c.c.

Fastest Centrifuge

The highest man-made rotary speed ever achieved and the fastest speed of any earth-bound object is 4,500 m.p.h. by a swirling tapered 6-inch carbon fiber rod in a vacuum at Birmingham University, England, reported on January 24, 1975.

Highest Note

The highest note yet attained is one of 60,000 megahertz (60 GHz) (60,000,000,000 vibrations per second), generated by a "laser" beam striking a sapphire crystal at the Massachusetts Institute of Technology, Cambridge, Massachusetts, in September, 1964.

Highest Frequency

It was announced in July, 1977, that K. M. Evenson, D. A. Jenkins and F. R. Peterson of the U.S. National Bureau of Standards, Boulder, Colorado, had attained a frequency of 1.97×10^{14} Hz, or 197 terahertz with a helium-neon laser emission.

Loudest Noise

The loudest noise created in a laboratory is 210 decibels or 400,000 acoustic watts reported by NASA in October, 1965. The noise came from a 48-foot steel and concrete horn at Huntsville, Alabama. Holes can be bored in solid material by this means.

Quietest Place

The "dead room," measuring 35 feet by 28 feet, in the Bell Telephone System Laboratory at Murray Hill, New Jersey, is the most anechoic room in the world, eliminating 99.98 per cent of reflected sound.

Finest Balance

The most accurate balance in the world is the Sartorius Model 4108, manufactured in Göttingen, West Germany, which can weigh objects of up to 0.5 grams (about .018 oz.) to an accuracy of 0.01 μg or 0.00000001 g., which is equivalent to little more than one-sixtieth of the weight of ink on this period dot (.).

Lowest Viscosity

The California Institute of Technology announced on December 1, 1957, that there was no measurable viscosity, *i.e.* perfect flow, in liquid helium II, which exists only at temperatures close to absolute zero (−273.15°C. or −459.67°F.).

Lowest Friction

The lowest coefficient of static and dynamic friction of any solid is 0.02, in the case of polytetrafluoroethylene ($(C_2F_4)n$), called P.T.F.E. —equivalent to wet ice on wet ice. It was first manufactured in quantity by E. I. du Pont de Nemours & Co. Inc. in 1943, and is marketed as Teflon.

In the centrifuge at the University of Virginia a 30-lb. rotor magnetically supported has been spun at 1,000 revolutions per second in a vacuum of 10^{-6} mm. of mercury pressure. It loses only one revolution per second per day, thus spinning for years.

Longest Siphon

The longest siphon ever constructed was one with a pull of 35.1 feet, built on No. 2 Chimney, Ringsend Power Station, Dublin City, Ireland, on July 16, 1964 by A. G. Kelly. The discovery that water can be siphoned through a greater height than the barometric pressure column has been patented.

Most Powerful Electric Current

The most powerful electric current generated is that from the Zeus capacitor at the Los Alamos Scientific Laboratory, New Mexico. If fired simultaneously the 4,032 capacitors would produce

SOUNDS OF SILENCE: This room in the Bell Telephone System Laboratory absorbs sound so completely you couldn't hear a pin drop.

for a few microseconds twice as much current as that generated elsewhere on earth.

Strongest and Weakest Magnetic Fields

The strongest magnetic field strength achieved has been one of 301 kilogauss at the Francis Bitter National Magnet Laboratory at M.I.T., Cambridge, Massachusetts, announced in July, 1977. The outer magnet is of superconducting niobium-titanium.

The weakest magnetic field measured is one of 8×10^{-11} gauss in the heavily shielded room at the Francis Bitter National Magnet Laboratory, at M.I.T., Cambridge, Massachusetts. It is used for research by Dr. David Cohen into the very weak magnetic fields generated in the heart and brain.

Heaviest Magnet

The heaviest magnet in the world is one measuring 196 feet in diameter, with a weight of 40,000 tons, for the 10 GeV synchrophasotron in the Joint Institute for Nuclear Research at Dubna, near Moscow, U.S.S.R. Intermagnetics General Corporation announced in 1975 plans for a 180 kG vanadium-gallium magnet.

Most Powerful Microscope

The world's most powerful microscope was announced by Dr. Lawrence Bartell and Charles Ritz of the University of Michigan in July, 1974, with an image magnification of 260 million fold. It uses an optical laser to decode holograms produced with 40 Kev radiation and has produced photographs of electron clouds of atoms of neon and argon.

Finest Cut

Biological specimens embedded in epoxy resin can be sectioned by a glass knife microtome under ideal conditions to a thickness of 1/875,000th of an inch or 2.9×10^{-5} mm.

Sharpest Objects

The University of California Medical Center, San Francisco, announced in July, 1974, the ultimate in sharpness—glass electrodes more than 200 times slimmer than a diamond phonograph stylus. These can be used for exploring the cells in the eye. The points are 0.05 µm.

Most Powerful Particle Accelerator

The 1.24-mile diameter proton synchrotron at the Fermi National Accelerator Laboratory at Batavia, Illinois, is the highest-energy "atom-smasher" in the world. An energy of 500 billion (5×10^{11}) electron volts was attained by June, 1976. Plans to double the energy to nearly 1 Tera electron volts have begun. This will involve constructing 1,000 superconducting magnets maintained at a temperature of —452°F. by means of an 830-gallon per hour helium liquefying plant.

The $76,800,000 CERN intersecting storage rings (ISR) project near Geneva, Switzerland, started on January 27, 1971, using two 28 GeV proton beams and is designed to yield the equivalent of 1,700 GeV or 1.7 TeV (1.7 million million electron volts) in its center of mass experiments.

Wind Tunnels

The world's largest wind tunnel is a low-speed tunnel with a closed test section measuring 40 feet by 80 feet, built in 1944, at Ames Research Center, Moffett Field, California. The tunnel encloses 900 tons of air and cost approximately $7,000,000. The maximum volume of air that can be moved is 60,000,000 cubic feet per minute. On July 30, 1974, NASA announced an intention to increase it in size to 80 by 120 feet for 345-m.p.h. speeds with a 135,000-h.p. system.

The most powerful is the 216,000-h.p. installation at the Arnold Engineering Test Center at Tullahoma, Tennessee. The highest Mach number attained with air is Mach 27 at the plant of the Boeing Company, Seattle, Washington. For periods of microseconds, shock Mach numbers of the order of 30 (22,830 m.p.h.) have been attained in impulse tubes at Cornell University, Ithaca, N.Y.

Largest Bubble Chamber

The largest bubble chamber in the world is the $7,000,000 installation completed in October, 1973, at Batavia, Illinois (see *Most Powerful Particle Accelerator*). It is 15 feet in diameter and contains 7,259 gallons of liquid hydrogen at a temperature of —247°C. (—412.6°F.) with a superconducting magnet of 30,000 gauss.

Shortest Wavelength

On April 15, 1974, I.B.M. researchers E. Spillar and A. Segmüller announced that X-rays with a wavelength of only 4.6×10^{18} Hz

(390 millionths of an inch) had been harnessed in a device which may become a "light pipe" to guide X-rays to required locations.

Longest-Lived Electric Battery

A battery kept in the Clarendon Laboratory, University of Oxford, England, has been causing a suspended bob to be electrostatically attracted a few times a second alternately by two small bells since 1840 when it was made by the London firm of scientific apparatus makers, Watkins and Hill. It produces about 2 kV at 10^{-8}A and is an example of the so-called "dry column" associated with the names of Marechaux, de Luc, Behrens and Zamboni. The only known use of this form of battery in this century was for an infra-red viewer in the 1939–45 war.

Most Durable Light

The electric light *bulb* was demonstrated in 1860, by Heinrich (later Henry) Goebel (1818–93) of Springe, Germany in New York and first perfected to a commercial success by Thomas A. Edison in Menlo Park, New Jersey, on October 21, 1879. The average bulb lasts for 750 to 1,000 hours. There is some evidence that a carbon filament bulb burning in the Fire Department, Livermore, south Alameda County, California, has been burning since 1901.

Fastest Switch

An electric device that can be switched in less than one 10 billionth of a second (10^{-10} sec.) was announced on January 18, 1973. It utilizes the prediction of the British physicist Brian Josephson (b. 1940) in 1962 that ultra-thin insulators can be made superconductive.

Smallest Hole

Inco Nickel Company was reported to have produced a hole with a diameter of a ten millionth of an inch (0.000004 mm.), or one thousand times smaller than the width of a human hair.

Brightest Light

The brightest steady artificial light sources are "laser" beams, with an intensity exceeding the sun's 1,500,000 candles per square inch by a factor of well in excess of 1,000. Of continuously burning sources, the most powerful is a 200-kilowatt high pressure xenon arc lamp of 600,000 candle-power, reported from the U.S.S.R. in 1965.

In May, 1969, the U.S.S.R. Academy of Sciences announced blast waves traveling through a luminous plasma of inert gases heated to 90,000 K. The flare-up for up to 3 microseconds shone at 50,000 times the brightness of the sun, *viz.* 75 billion candles per square inch.

The synchrotron radiation emitted through a 4 inch by $\frac{1}{2}$ inch slit in the SPEAR high energy physics plant at the end of the 2-mile-long Stanford Linear Accelerator, California, has been described as the world's most powerful light beam.

The most powerful searchlight ever developed was one produced during the 1939–45 war by the General Electric Company Ltd. at the Hirst Research Centre in Wembley, Greater London, England. It had a consumption of 600 kilowatts and gave an arc luminance of 300,000 candles per square inch and a maximum beam intensity of 2,700,000,000 candles from its parabolic mirror (diameter 10 feet).

"Laser" Beams

The first illumination of another celestial body was achieved on May 9, 1962, when a beam of light was successfully reflected from the moon by the use of an optical "maser" (microwave amplification by stimulated emission of radiation) or "laser" (light amplification by stimulated emission of radiation) attached to a 48-inch telescope at the Massachusetts Institute of Technology, Cambridge, Massachusetts. The spot was estimated to be 4 miles in diameter on the moon. A "maser" beam is focused into a liquid nitrogen-cooled ruby crystal. Its chromium atoms are excited into a high-energy state in which they emit a red light which is allowed to escape only in the direction desired. The maser was devised in 1958 by Dr. Charles Hard Townes (born 1915) of Bell Telephone Laboratories. Such a flash for 1/5,000th of a second can bore a hole through a diamond by vaporization at 10,000°C., produced by 2×10^{23} photons.

The "Shiva" laser was reported at the Lawrence Livermore Laboratory, California, to be concentrating 2.6×10^{13} watts into a pinhead-sized target for 9.5×10^{-11} of a second in a test on May 18, 1978.

Computers

The modern computer was made possible by the invention of the paint-contact transistor by John Bardeen and Walter Brattain, announced in July, 1948, and the junction transistor by R. L. Wallace, Morgan Sparks and Dr. William Shockley in early 1951.

Most Powerful and Fastest Computer

The world's most powerful and fastest computer is the CRAY-1, designed by Seymour R. Cray of Cray Research, Inc., Minneapolis, Minnesota. The clock period is 12.5 nanoseconds and memory ranges up to 1,048,576 64-bit words, resulting in a capacity of 8,388,608 bytes of main memory. It attains speeds of 200,000,000 floating point operations per second. With 32 CRAY DD-19 disk storage units, it has a storage capacity of 7.7568×10^{10} bits. Floating decimal points may vary between 10^{-2500} to 10^{2500}. The cost of a mid-range system is $6,500,000.

Chapter Six

THE ARTS AND ENTERTAINMENT

Painting

Earliest Art

Pieces of ochre with ground facets found at Lake Mungo, N.S.W., Australia, reported in 1973 to be dated *ante* 30,000 B.C. *may* have been used as cave art pigments. If confirmed, these would antedate the cave art from the Aurignacian II period (*c.* 25,000 B.C.) found at La Ferrassie in the Périgord, France.

Largest

Panorama of the Mississippi, completed by John Banvard (1815–91) in 1846, showing the river scene for 1,200 miles in a strip probably 5,000 feet long and 12 feet wide, was the largest painting in the world, with an area of more than 1.3 acres. The painting is believed to have been destroyed when the rolls of canvas, stored in a barn at Cold Spring Harbor, Long Island, New York, caught fire shortly before Banvard's death on May 16, 1891.

The largest painting now in existence is probably *The Battle of Gettysburg*, completed in 1883, after 2½ years of work, by Paul Philippoteaux (France) and 16 assistants. The painting is 410 feet long, 70 feet high and weighs 11,792 lbs. It depicts the climax of the Battle of Gettysburg, in south-central Pennsylvania, on July 3, 1863. In 1964, the painting was bought by Joe King of Winston-Salem, North Carolina, after being stored by E. W. McConnell in a Chicago warehouse since 1933.

The largest "Old Master" is *Il Paradiso*, painted between 1587 and 1590 by Jacopo Robusti, *alias* Tintoretto (1518–94), and his son Domenico on Wall "E" of the Sala del Maggior Consiglio in the Palazzo Ducale (Doge's Palace) in Venice, Italy. The work is 72 feet 2 inches long and 22 feet 11½ inches high and contains more than 100 human figures.

Smallest

The smallest reported painting in the world is *My Small Country–Holland* executed by Gert Twigt in January, 1979, within a circle with a diameter of 6/1000th of an inch.

The finest standard brush sold is the 000 in Series 7 by Winsor and Newton, known as the "triple goose." It is made of 150–200 Kolinsky sable hairs weighing 0.000529 oz.

Most Valuable

The portrait of "Mona Lisa" (*La Gioconda*) by Leonardo da Vinci (1452–1519) in the Louvre, Paris, was assessed for insurance purposes at $100,000,000 for its move for exhibition in Washington,

D.C., and New York City, from December 14, 1962, to March 12, 1963. However, insurance was not concluded because the cost of the closest security precautions was less than that of the premiums. It was painted in c. 1503–07 and measures 30.5 × 20.9 inches. It is believed to portray Mona (short for Madonna) Lisa Gherardini, the wife of Francesco del Giocondo of Florence. The husband is said to have disliked it and refused to pay for it. Francis I, King of France, bought the painting for his bathroom for 4,000 gold florins or 492 ounces of gold (now equivalent to $60,000) in 1517.

Highest Price

Auction Price. The highest price ever bid in a public auction was $5,544,000 for a portrait by Diego Velázquez, of his mulatto assistant and servant, called variously *Portrait of Juan de Pareja* and *The Slave of Velázquez*, painted in Rome in 1649, and sold on November 27, 1970, at Christie's salesrooms, London, to the Wildenstein Gallery of New York. When the same painting was sold at Christie's at auction in 1801, it went for 39 guineas (about $200). It remained in the possession of the Earls of Radnor from 1811 until 1970.

The highest price ever paid for a painting by a woman is $150,000 at Parke Bernet's salesrooms in New York on March 3, 1971, for *Summertime* by Mary Cassatt (U.S.) (1844–1926). She worked mainly in Paris.

HIGHEST PRICED PAINTINGS—PROGRESSIVE RECORDS

Price	Painter, title, sold by and sold to	Date
$32,500	Correggio's *The Magdalen, Reading* (in fact spurious) to Elector Friedrich Augustus II of Saxony.	1746
$42,500	Raphael's *The Sistine Madonna* to Elector Friedrich Augustus II of Saxony.	1759
$80,000	Van Eyck's *Adoration of the Lamb*, 6 outer panels of Ghent altarpiece by Edward Solby to the Government of Prussia.	1821
$123,000*	Murillo's *The Immaculate Conception* by estate of Marshall Soult to the Louvre (against Czar Nicholas I) in Paris.	1852
$350,000	Raphael's *Ansidei Madonna* by the 8th Duke of Marlborough to the National Gallery, London.	1885
$500,000	Raphael's *The Colonna Altarpiece* by Sedelmeyer to J. Pierpont Morgan.	1901
$514,400	Van Dyck's *Elena Grimaldi-Cattaneo* (portrait) by Knoedler to Peter Widener (1834–1915).	1906
$514,400	Rembrandt's *The Mill* by 6th Marquess of Lansdowne to Peter Widener.	1911
$582,500	Raphael's smaller *Panshanger Madonna* by Joseph (later Baron) Duveen (1869–1939) to Peter Widener.	1913
$1,572,000	Leonardo da Vinci's *Benois Madonna* to Czar Nicholas II in Paris.	1914
$2,300,000*	Rembrandt's *Aristotle Contemplating Bust of Homer* by Mr./Mrs. Alfred Erickson to New York Metropolitan Museum of Art.	1961
$5,000,000– $6,000,000	Leonardo da Vinci's *Ginevra de' Benci* by Prince Franz Josef II of Liechtenstein to National Gallery, Washington.	1967
$5,544,000*	Velázquez's *Portrait of Juan de Pareja*, sometimes known as *The Slave of Velázquez* by the Earl of Radnor (U.K.) to Wildenstein Gallery, New York.	1970

* indicates price at auction, otherwise prices were by private treaty.

Miniature Portrait. The highest price ever paid for a portrait miniature is $169,260 by an anonymous buyer at a sale held by Christie's, London, on June 8, 1971, for a miniature of Frances Howard, Countess of Essex and Somerset, by Isaac Oliver (c. 1556–1617), painted c. 1605. This miniature, sent for auction by Lord Derby, measured 5⅛ inches in diameter.

HIGHEST AUCTION PRICE FOR MODERN PAINTING: *Le Jeune Marin I* by Matisse brought $1,576,800 at a London auction on July 3, 1979.

Modern Painting. The highest price paid for a modern painting is $2,000,000 paid by the Australian National Gallery in Canberra for *Blue Poles* by Jackson Pollock (U.S.) (1912–56) on September 21, 1973. This is also the highest price ever paid for any American painting.

Henry Matisse's 1906 painting *Le Jeune Marin I* (The Young Sailor) was sold at Christie's, London, for $1,576,800 on July 3, 1979, to set an auction price record for a 20th century painting.

Living Artist. The highest price paid for paintings in the lifetime of the artist is $1,950,000 paid for the two canvases *Two Brothers* (1905) and *Seated Harlequin* (1922) by Pablo Diego José Francisco de Paula Juan Nepomuceno Crispin Crispiano de la Santisima Trinidad Ruiz y Picasso (1881–1973), born in Spain. This was paid by the Basle City government to the Staechelin Foundation to enable the Basle Museum of Arts to retain the painting after an offer of $2,560,000 had been received from the U.S. in December, 1967.

Most Prolific Painter. Picasso was the most prolific of all painters. In a career that lasted 78 years, it has been estimated that he produced about 13,500 paintings or designs, 100,000 prints or engravings, 34,000 book illustrations, and 300 sculptures or ceramics. His lifetime work has been valued at $1 billion.

Most Prolific Portrait Painter. John A. Wismont, Jr. (born New York City, September 20, 1941), formerly of Disneyland, Anaheim, California, had painted 45,423 watercolor paintings in his career through 1978, including 9,853 in 1976.

Most Repetitious Painter. Antonio Bin of Paris has painted the *Mona Lisa* on some 300 occasions. These copies sell for up to $1,700 each.

Drawing. The highest price ever attached to any drawing was £804,361 ($2,252,210) for the cartoon *The Virgin and Child with St.*

John the Baptist and St. Anne, measuring 54⅛ inches by 39¼ inches, drawn in Milan, probably in 1499–1500, by Leonardo da Vinci (1452–1519) of Italy. The National Gallery (London) retained possession in 1962, after three U.S. bids of over $4,000,000 were reputedly made for the cartoon.

Largest Mosaic

The world's largest mosaic is on the walls of the central library of the Universidad Nacional Autónoma de México, Mexico City. There are four walls; the two largest measuring 12,949 square feet each represent the pre-Hispanic past.

Murals

Earliest. The earliest known murals on man-made walls are those at Çatal Hüyük in southern Anatolia, Turkey, dating from *c.* 5850 B.C.

Largest. The largest logo and mural painting in the world is the American Revolution Bicentennial symbol on the curved roof of the Arizona Veterans Memorial Coliseum, Phoenix, Arizona. It occupies 110,000 square feet, or more than 2½ acres. It was to be painted over in 1977. After being outlined with the aid of a computer, it took 45 man-days, under the supervision of its designer John M. Glitsos, to apply the necessary 870 gallons of patriotic red, white and blue paint on August 18–26, 1973.

A ground mural, measuring 1,400 feet long by 100 feet wide, named *Yellow Brick Road—Leisure Time,* painted on a disused runway near the Tamiami Stadium, South Dade, Florida, was completed on March 18, 1976.

Largest Cartoon

The largest cartoon ever exhibited was one covering five stories (50 feet by 150 feet) of a University of Arizona building, drawn by Peter A. Kesling for Mom 'n' Dad's Day, 1954.

Museums

Oldest. The oldest museum in the world is the Ashmolean Museum in Oxford, England, built in 1679.

Largest. The largest museum in the world is the American Museum of Natural History between 77th and 81st Streets on Central Park West, New York City. Founded in 1874, it comprises 19 interconnected buildings with 23 acres of floor space.

Largest Gallery

The world's largest art gallery is the Winter Palace and the neighboring Hermitage in Leningrad, U.S.S.R. One has to walk 15 miles to visit each of the 322 galleries, which house nearly 3,000,000 works of art and archeological remains.

The world's largest modern art museum is the Georges Pompidou National Center for Art and Culture in Paris, with a floor space of 183,000 square feet.

Upside Down Duration Record

The longest period of time for which a modern drawing has hung upside down in a public gallery unnoticed is 47 days. This occurred to *Le Bateau*, by Henri Émile Benoît Matisse (1869–1954) of France, in the Museum of Modern Art, New York City, between October 18 and December 4, 1961. In this time 116,000 people had passed through the gallery.

Sculptures

Earliest. The earliest known examples of sculpture are the so-called Venus figurines from Aurignacian sites, dating to *c*. 25,000–22,000 B.C., *e.g.* the famous Venus of Willendorf from Austria and the Venus of Brassempouy (Landes, France). A piece of ox rib found in 1973 at Pech de l'Aze, Dordogne, France, in an early Middle Paleolithic layer of the Riss glaciation *c*. 105,000 B.C. appears to have several intentionally engraved lines on one side.

Largest. The world's largest sculptures are the mounted figures of Jefferson Davis (1808–89), Gen. Robert Edward Lee (1807–70) and Gen. Thomas Jonathan ("Stonewall") Jackson (1824–63), covering 1.33 acres on the face of Stone Mountain, near Atlanta, Georgia. They are 90 feet high. Roy Faulkner was on the mountain face for 8 years 174 days with a thermo-jet torch, working with the sculptor Walker Kirtland Hancock and other helpers from September 12, 1963 to March 3, 1972.

When completed the world's largest sculpture will be that of the Indian chief Tashunca-Uitco, known as Crazy Horse, of the Oglala tribe of the Dakota or Nadowessioux (Sioux) group. He is believed to have been born in about 1849, and he died at Fort Robinson, Nebraska, on September 5, 1877. The sculpture was begun on June

3, 1948, near Mount Rushmore, South Dakota. A projected 561 feet high and 641 feet long, it has required blasting 6,500,000 tons of stone and is the life work of one man, Korczak Ziolkowski. It is estimated that the work will take several more years.

Most Expensive. The highest price ever paid for a sculpture is $3,900,000 paid by private treaty in London in early 1977 by J. Paul Getty's Museum in California for the 4th-century B.C. bronze statue of a youth attributed to the school of Lysippus. It was found by fishermen on the seabed off Fano, Italy in 1963. The $46-million museum with 38 galleries, opened in Malibu in January 1974, is the world's most heavily endowed museum with $1,400,000,000. (See photos, page F.)

The highest price paid for the work of a living sculptor is $260,000 given at Sotheby Parke Bernet Galleries, New York, on March 1, 1972, by Fischer Fine Arts of London, England, for the 75-inch wooden carving *Reclining Figure* by Henry Moore (born Castleford, West Yorkshire, England, July 30, 1898), sold by Cranbrook Academy, Bloomfield Hills, Michigan.

Ground Figures. In the Nazca Desert, south of Lima, Peru, there are straight lines (one more than 7 miles long), geometric shapes and plants and animals drawn on the ground by still unknown persons between 100 B.C. and 700 A.D. for an uncertain but probably religious or astronomical purpose. They were first detected from the air *c.* 1928.

Hill Figures. In August, 1968, a 330-foot-tall figure was found on a hill above Tarapacá, Chile.

Largest Mobile

The most massive recorded mobile is *Quest* by Jerome Kirk, installed at TRW Inc., Redondo Beach, California, in September, 1968. It is a 32-foot-long pivotal mobile weighing 5.98 tons. The term "mobile" was coined to contrast with "stabile" sculpture by Marcel Duchamp (1887–1968) in 1932.

Language

Earliest. Anthropologists have evidence that the truncated pharynx of Neanderthal man precluded his speaking anything akin to a modern language any more than an ape or a modern baby. Cro-Magnon man of 40,000 B.C. had however developed an efficient vocal tract. Clay tablets of the neolithic Danubian culture discovered in December, 1966, at Tartaria, Moros River, Rumania have been dated to the fifth or fourth millennium B.C. The tablets bear symbols of bows and arrows, gates and combs. Writing tablets bearing an early form of the Elamite language dating from 3,500 B.C. were found in southeastern Iran in 1970. Tokens or tallies from Tepe Asiab and Ganji-I-Dareh Tepe in Iran have however been dated to 8,500 B.C.

Oldest. The written language with the longest continuous history is Egyptian from the earliest hieroglyphic inscriptions on the palette

LARGEST MOBILE: This 6-ton sculpture in California, composed of 7 triangular metal "wings," required 6 men and a 25-ton crane to install it.

of Narmer, dated to *c.* 3100 B.C., to Coptic used in churches at the present day, more than 5,000 years later. Hieroglyphs were used until 394 A.D., and thus may be overtaken by Chinese characters as the most durable script in the 21st century.

Oldest Words in English. Some as yet unpublished research indicates some words of a pre-Indo-European substrate survive in English, including apple (apal), bad (bad), gold (gol), and tin (tin).

Commonest. The language spoken by more people than any other is Northern Chinese, or Mandarin, by an estimated 68 per cent of the Chinese population (575,000,000 people) in 1975.

OLDEST WRITTEN LANGUAGE: This ancient Egyptian palette commemorating the victories of King Narmer is over 5,000 years old.

The so-called national language (*Guoyu*) is a standardized form of Northern Chinese (*Beifanghua*) as spoken in the Peking area. This was alphabetized into *zhuyin fuhao* of 37 letters in 1918. In 1958, the *pinyin* system, which is a phonetic pronunciation guide, was introduced.

The next most commonly spoken language and the most widespread is English, with an estimated 360,000,000 speakers in mid-1975. English is spoken by 10 per cent or more of the population in 34 sovereign countries. Today's world total of languages and dialects still spoken is about 5,000 of which some 845 come from India.

Rarest. There are believed to be 20 or more languages, including 6 North American Indian languages, in which no one can converse, because there is only one speaker left alive. Eyak is still spoken in southeast Alaska by two aged sisters if they meet.

Most Complex. The following extremes of complexity have been noted: Chippewa, the North American Indian language of Minnesota, has the most verb forms with up to 6,000; Tillamook, the North American Indian language of Oregon, has the most prefixes with 30; Tabassaran, a language in Daghestan, U.S.S.R., uses the most noun cases with 35; the Eskimo language uses 63 forms of the present tense and simple nouns have as many as 252 inflections.

In Chinese, the 40-volume *Chung-wen Ta Tz'u-tien* Dictionary lists 49.905 characters. The fourth tone of "i" has 84 meanings, varying as widely as "dress," "hiccough" and "licentious." The written language provides 92 different characters for "i⁴." The most complex written character in Chinese is that representing *xie* which has 64 strokes and means "talkative." The most complex in current use is *yu*, which consists of 32 strokes and means to urge or implore.

Rarest and Commonest Sounds. The rarest speech sound is probably the sound written ř in Czech which occurs in very few languages and is the last sound mastered by Czech children. In the southern Bushman language !xo, there is a click, articulated with both lips, which is written ☉ . The *l* sound in the Arabic word *Allah*, in some contexts, is pronounced uniquely in that language. The commonest sound is the vowel *a* (as in the English "father"); no language is known to be without it.

Most and Least Irregular Verbs. Esperanto was first published by Dr. Ludwig Zamenhof (1859–1917), of Warsaw, in 1887 without irregular verbs. It is now estimated from textbook sales to have a million speakers. Swahili has a strict 6-class pattern of verbs and no verbs which are irregular to this pattern. According to more daunting grammars published in West Germany, English has 194 irregular verbs, though there are arguably 214.

Largest Vocabulary. The English language contains about 490,000 words, plus another 300,000 technical terms, the most in any language, but it is doubtful if any individual uses more than 60,000.

Literature, Smallest. Of written languages, that with the smallest literature is Kamassian. The only surviving fragment from these Samoyed people near Lake Baykal, U.S.S.R., is a 24-line lament translated in *The Elek Book of Oriental Verse*.

Greatest Linguist

If the yardstick of ability to speak with fluency and reasonable accuracy is adhered to, it is doubtful whether any human could maintain fluency in more than 20–25 languages concurrently or achieve fluency in more than 40 in a lifetime. The most multilingual living person in the world is Georges Henri Schmidt (b. Strasbourg, France, December 28, 1914), who served as Chief of the U.N. Terminology Section in 1965–71. In the 1975 edition of *Who's Who in the United Nations* he listed "only" 19 languages because he was then unable to find the time to "revive" his former fluency in 12 others. Historically, the greatest linguists have been proclaimed as Cardinal Mezzofanti (fluent in 26 or 27), Professor Rask (1787–1832), Sir John Bowering (1792–1872) and Dr. Harold Williams of New Zealand (1876–1928), who was fluent in 28 languages.

Alphabets

Oldest. The development of the use of an alphabet in place of pictograms occurred in the Sinaitic world between 1700 and 1500 B.C. This western Semitic language developed the consonantal system based on phonetic and syllabic principles.

Longest and Shortest. The language with most letters is Cambodian with 72 (including useless ones). Rotokas, spoken in the center of Bougainville Island in the South Pacific, has least with 11 (just a, b, e, g, i, k, o, p, ř, t and u). Amharic has 231 formations from 33 basic syllabic forms, each of which has seven modifications, so this Ethiopian language cannot be described as alphabetic.

Most and Least Consonants and Vowels. The language with most consonantal sounds is the Caucasian language Ubyx, with 80 and that with the least is Rotokas (see above) with only 6 consonants. The language with the most vowels is Sedang, a central Vietnamese language with 55 distinguishable vowel sounds. The language with the least (2 vowels) is the Caucasian language Abkhazian. The Hawaiian word for "certified" has 8 consecutive vowels—hooiaioia. The English record is 6 in the musical term *euouae*. The Estonian word jäääärne, meaning "the edge of the ice," has the same vowel four consecutive times. Voiauai, a language in the Pará state in Brazil, consists solely of 7 vowels. The English word "latch-string" has 6 consecutive consonants.

Oldest and Youngest Letters. The oldest letter is "O," unchanged in shape since its adoption in the Phoenician alphabet *c.* 1300 B.C. The newest letters in the English alphabet are "j" and "v," which are of post-Shakespearean use, *c.* 1630. There are now some 65 alphabets in use.

Largest Letter. The largest permanent letters in the world are the giant 600-foot letters spelling READYMIX on the ground in the Nullarbor near East Balladonia, Western Australia. This was constructed in December, 1971.

In sky-writing (normally at *c.* 8,000 feet) a 7-letter word may stretch for 6 miles in length and can be read from 50 miles. The world's earliest example was over Epsom racecourse, England, on May 30, 1922, when Cyril Turner "spelt out" "London Daily Mail" from an S.E.5A biplane.

Longest Words

World. The longest word ever to appear in literature occurs in *The Ecclesiazusae*, a comedy by Aristophanes (448–380 B.C.). In the Greek it is 170 letters long but transliterates into 182 letters in English, thus: lopadotemachoselachogaleokranioleipsanodrimhypo-trimmatosilphioparaomelitokatakechymenokichlepikossyphophatto-peristeralektryonoptekephalliokigklopeleiolagoiosiraiobaphetragano-pterygon. The term describes a fricassee of 17 sweet and sour ingredients, including mullet, brains, honey, vinegar, pickles, marrow (the vegetable) and ouzo (a Greek drink laced with anisette).

English. The longest word in the Oxford English Dictionary is floccipaucinihilipilification (alternatively spelt in hyphenated form with "n" in seventh place), with 29 letters, meaning "the action of estimating as worthless," first used in 1741, and later by Sir Walter Scott (1771–1832). Webster's Third International Dictionary lists among its 450,000 entries pneumonoultramicroscopicsilicovolcanoconiosis (45 letters), the name of a miner's lung disease.

The nonce word used by Dr. Edward Strother (1675–1737) to describe the spa waters at Bristol was aequeosalinocalcalinoceraceoaluminosocupreovitriolic (52 letters).

The longest regularly formed English word is praetertranssubstantiationalistically (37 letters), used by Mark McShane in his novel *Untimely Ripped*, published in 1963. The medical term hepaticocholangiocholecystenterostomies (39 letters) refers to the surgical creations of new communications between gall bladders and hepatic ducts and between intestines and gall bladders. The longest in common use are disproportionableness and incomprehensibilities (21 letters) and interdenominationalism (22 letters).

Longest Chemical Name. The longest chemical term is that describing Bovine NADP-specific glutamate dehydrogenase, which contains 500 amino acids and a resultant name of some 3,600 letters.

Longest Palindromic Words. The longest known palindromic word (same spelling backwards as forwards) is *saippuakivikauppias* (19 letters), the Finnish word for a dealer in lye. The longest in the English language is *redivider* (nine letters), while another nine-letter word, *Malayalam*, is a proper noun given to the language of the Malayali people in Kerala, southern India. The nine-letter word *ROTAVATOR* is a registered trademark belonging to Howard Machinery Ltd., of England. The contrived chemical term *detartrated* has 11 letters. In American English the word *releveler* is also a nine-letter palindrome, though in England the word is spelled *releveller* and hence is not palindromic.

Some baptismal fonts in Greece and Turkey bear the circular 25-letter inscription NIΨON ANOMHMATA MH MONAN OΨIN meaning "wash (my) sins not only (my) face."

The longest palindromic composition devised is one of 11,125 words completed by Jeff Grant of Hastings, New Zealand, in January, 1979. It begins, "No elate man I meet sees a bed . . ." and hence predictably ends ". . . Debase esteem in a metal eon."

Commonest Words. In written English, the most frequently used words are in order: the, of, and, to, a, in, that, is, I, it, for *and* as. The most used in conversation is I. The commonest letter is "e" and the commonest initial letter is "T."

Most Meanings. The most overworked word in English is the word "set" which has 58 noun uses, 126 verbal uses and 10 as a participial adjective.

Most Homophones. The most homophonous sounds in English are *air* and *sol* which, according to the researches of Dora Newhouse of Los Angeles, both have 38 homophones. The homophone with the most variant spellings is *air*, with aire, are, ayr, e'er, eir, ere, err, erre, eyre, heir, eire, eyr *and* ore.

Most Accents. The word with most accents is the French word *hétérogénéité*, meaning heterogeneity. An atoll in the Pacific Ocean 320 miles east southeast of Tahiti is named Héréhérétué. Accents were introduced into French during the reign of Louis XIII (1601–43).

Shortest Holoalphabetic Sentence. A contrived headline describing the reaction of despicable vandals from the valley thwarted by finding a block of quartz with carvings (already) upon it—"Quartz glyph job vex'd cwm finks"—represents the ultimate in containing all (but only) 26 letters. This was devised by Jeff Grant of Hastings, New Zealand.

Worst Tongue-Twisters. The most difficult tongue-twister is deemed by Ken Parkin of Teesside to be "The sixth sick sheik's sixth sheep's sick"—especially when spoken quickly.

Perhaps more difficult is the Xhosa (from Transkei, South Africa) for "The skunk rolled down and ruptured its larynx": "Iqaqa laziqikaqika kwaze kwaqhawaka uqhoqhoqha." The last word contains three "clicks." A European rival is the vowelless *Strch prst skrz krk*, the Czech for "stick a finger in the throat."

Longest Abbreviation. The longest known abbreviation is S.K.O.M.K.H.P.K.J.C.D.P.W.B., the initials of the Sharikat Kerjasama Orang-orang Melayu Kerajaan Hilir Perak Kerana Jimat Cermat Dan Pinjaman Wang Berhad. This is the Malay name for the Lower Perak Malay Government Servants' Co-operative Thrift and Loan Society Limited, in Teluk Anson, Perak, West Malaysia (formerly called Malaya). The abbreviation for this abbreviation is Skomk.

The 55-letter full name of Los Angeles (El Pueblo de Nuestra Señora la Reina de los Angeles de Porciuncula) is abbreviated to L.A., or 3.63 per cent of its length.

Longest Acronym. The longest acronym is NIIOMTPIABO-PARMBETZHELBETRABSBOMONIMONIMONKONOTDTE-KHSTROMONT with 56 letters (54 in Cyrillic) in the *Concise*

Dictionary of Soviet Terminology meaning: The laboratory for stuttering, reinforcement, concrete and ferro-concrete operations for composite-monolithic and monolithic constructions of the Department of the Technology of Building—assembly operations of the Scientific Research Institute of the Organization for building mechanization and technical aid of the Academy of Building and Architecture of the U.S.S.R.

Longest Anagrams. The longest non-scientific English words which can form anagrams are the 17-letter transpositions "misrepresentation" and "representationism." The longest scientific transposals are cholecystoduodenostomy/duodenocholecystostomy and hydropneumopericardium/pneumohydropericardium, each of 22 letters.

Longest Sentence. A sentence of 1,300 words appears in *Absalom, Absalom!* by William Faulkner, and one of 3,153 words with 86 semicolons and 390 commas occurs in the *History of the Church of God* by Sylvester Hassell of Wilson, North Carolina, *c.* 1884. Some authors such as James Joyce (1882–1941) eschew punctuation altogether. The first 40,000 words of the *Gates of Paradise* by George Andrzeyevski (Panther) appear to lack any punctuation.

The longest sentence recorded ever to have gotten past the editor of a major newspaper is one of 1,030 words in the TV column by Clarence G. Peterson, which appeared in the August 19, 1970 edition of the *Chicago Tribune*.

The Report of the President of Columbia University, 1942–43, contained a sentence of 4,284 words.

Place Names

Longest. The official name for Bangkok, capital of Thailand, is Krungtep Mahanakhon. The full name is however: Krungthep Mahanakhon Bovorn Ratanakosin Mahintharayutthaya Mahadilokpop Noparatratchathani Burirom Udomratchanivetmahasathan Amornpiman Avatarnsathit Sakkathattiyavisnukarmprasit (167 letters) which, in the most scholarly transliteration, emerges with 175 letters.

The longest name now in use is Taumatawhakatangihangakoauauotamatea(turipukakapikimaungahoronuku)pokaiwhenuakitanatahu, the unofficial 85-letter version of the name of a hill (1,002 feet above sea level) in the Southern Hawke's Bay district of North Island, New Zealand. This Maori name means "the hill whereon was played the flute of Tamatea, circumnavigator of lands, for his lady love." The official version has 57 letters (1 to 36 and 65 to 85).

Ijouaououene, Morocco, has 8 consecutive vowels.

Shortest. The shortest place names in the world are the French village of Y (population 143), so named since 1241, the Danish village Å on the island Fyn, the Norwegian village of Å (pronounced "Aw"), the Swedish place Å in Vikholandet, U in the Caroline Islands of the Pacific, and the Japanese town of Sosei which is alternatively called Aioi or O-o or even O. There was once a 6 in West Virginia. Today in the U.S., there are seven two-lettered place names, including Ed and Uz, both in Kentucky.

HIS NAME UP IN LIGHTS: Mr. Wolfe + 585, Senior, of Philadelphia watches as a New York City electrical sign misspells his 590-letter surname.

Personal Names

Earliest. The earliest personal name which has survived is possibly N'armer, the earliest Egyptian pharaoh, which dates from *c.* 3050 B.C.

Longest. The longest name used by anyone is Adolph Blaine Charles David Earl Frederick Gerald Hubert Irvin John Kenneth Lloyd Martin Nero Oliver Paul Quincy Randolph Sherman Thomas Uncas Victor William Xerxes Yancy Zeus Wolfeschlegelsteinhausenbergerdorffvoralternwarengewissenhaftschaferswessenschafewarenwohlgepflegeundsorgfaltigkeitbeschutzenvonangreifendurchihrraubgierigfeindewelchevoralternzwolftausendjahresvorandieerscheinenwanderersteerdemenschderraumschiffgebrauchlichtalsseinursprungvonkraftgestartseinlangefahrthinzwischensternartigraumaufdersuchenachdiesternwelchegehabtbewohnbarplanetenkreisedrehensichundwohinderneurassevonverstandigmenschlichkeitkonntefortpflanzenundsicherfreuenanlebenslanglichfreudeundruhemitnichteinfurchtvorangreifenvonandererintelligentgeschopfsvonhinzwischensternartigraum, Senior, who was born at Bergedorf, near Hamburg, Germany, on February 29, 1904. On printed forms, he uses only his eighth and second Christian names and the first 35 letters of his surname. He lives in Philadelphia, and has recently shortened his surname to Wolfe+585, Senior.

The longest Christian or given name on record is Napua-mohalaonaona - a - me - ka - wehiwehi - o - na - kuahiwi - a - me - na - awawa - kehoomaka-ke-hoaala-ke-ea-o-na-aina-nani-akea-o-hawaii-i-ka-wanaao (102 letters), in the case of Miss Dawne E. Lee of Honolulu, so named in February, 1967. The name means "the abundant, beautiful blossoms of the mountains and valleys begin to fill the air with their fragrance throughout the length and breadth of Hawaii."

Shortest. The single-letter surname O, of which 28 examples appear in Belgian telephone directories, besides being the commonest single-letter name, is the one obviously causing the most distress to those concerned with the prevention of cruelty to computers. There are two one-letter Burmese names: E (calm), pronounced "aye," and U (egg), pronounced "oo." U used before the name means "uncle."

Most Christian Names. The great-great-grandson of Carlos III of Spain, Don Alfonso de Borbón y Borbón (1866–1934), had 89 Christian names, of which several were lengthened by hyphenation.

Mr. Brian Brown of Wolverhampton, England, in February, 1974, had his daughter christened Maria Sullivan Corbett Fitzsimmons Jeffries Hart Burns Johnson Willard Dempsey Tunney Schmeling Sharkey Carnera Baer Braddock Louis Charles Walcott Marciano Patterson Johansson Liston Clay Frazier Foreman Brown. He added, "I hope she will marry a boxer."

Most Versions. Mr. R. B. McAtee of Arlington, Virginia, has collected 334 versions of the spelling of his family name since 1902. The Zulu ruler Mzilikazi (b. *c.* 1795) had his name chronicled in 325 spellings, according to researches by Dr. R. Kent Rasmussen.

Commonest. The commonest family name in the world is the Chinese name Chang which is borne, according to estimates, by between 9.7 per cent and 12.1 per cent of the Chinese population, so indicating even on the lower estimate that there are at least some 75,000,000 Changs—more than the entire population of all but 7 of the 159 other sovereign countries of the world.

The commonest surname in the English-speaking world is Smith. There are 659,050 nationally insured Smiths in Great Britain, of whom 10,102 are plain John Smith, and another 19,502 are John plus one or more given-name Smiths. Including uninsured persons, there are over 800,000 Smiths in England and Wales alone. There were an estimated 2,382,509 Smiths in the United States in 1973.

There are, however, estimated to be 1,600,000 persons in Britain with M', Mc or Mac (Gaelic "son of") as part of their surnames. The commonest of these is Macdonald which accounts for about 55,000 of the Scottish population.

Most Contrived Name. In the United States, the determination to derive commercial or other benefit from being the last listing in the local telephone book has resulted in self-given names starting with six z's—for example, Mr. Vladimir Zzzzzzabakov of the San Francisco book. Last in the book for Madison, Wisconsin, however, is Mr. Hero Zzyzzx (pronounced Ziz-icks) whose name, he claims, is for real.

The Written Word

Texts and Books

Oldest. The oldest known written text is the pictographic expression of Sumerian speech, dating from *c.* 3500 B.C. The Samarian papyri, written in Aramaic, found 8½ miles north of Jericho, are dated 375–335 B.C.

Oldest Printed. The oldest surviving printed work is a Korean scroll or *sutra*, printed from wooden blocks found in the foundations of the Pulguk Sa pagoda, Kyongju, Korea, on October 14, 1966. It has been dated no later than 704 A.D. It was claimed in November, 1973, that a 28-page book of Tang dynasty poems at Yonsei University, Korea, was printed from metal type *c.* 1160.

Oldest Mechanically Printed. It is generally accepted that the earliest mechanically printed full-length book was a "42-line" Gutenberg Bible, printed at Mainz, Germany, *c.* 1454 by Johann Henne zum Gensfleisch zur Laden, called "zu Gutenberg" (*c.* 1398–*c.* 1468). Recent work on watermarks published in 1967 indicates a copy of a surviving printed "Donatus" Latin grammar was made from paper made in *c.* 1450. The earliest exactly dated printed work is the Psalter completed on August 14, 1457, by Johann Fust (*c.* 1400–1466) and Peter Schöffer (1425–1502), who had been Gutenberg's chief assistant. The earliest printing by William Caxton, though undated, would appear to be *The Recuyel of the Historyes of Troye* in late 1473 to spring 1474.

Manuscripts. The highest price ever paid is £280,000 (then $490,000) paid at Christie's, London, on November 17, 1976, for a single leaf of *The Death of Zahhak* from the 258-page Persian *Shahnamel*, commissioned by Shah Ismai'l in 1522 and sold by Arthur J. Houghton of New York. The splitting of this manuscript has been greatly criticized. It has been estimated that the total value of this manuscript, acquired by Mr. Houghton in 1959, may be as high as $60 million.

Largest Publication. The largest publication in the world is the 1,112-volume set of *British Parliamentary Papers* of 1800–1900 published by the Irish University Press in 1968–1972. A complete set weighs 3.64 tons, costs $65,000 and would take 6 years to read at 10 hours per day. The binding of the edition involved the death of 34,000 Indian goats and $39,000 worth of gold ingots. The total print run was 500 sets.

Smallest. The smallest marketed bound printed book with cursive material is one of 15 pages measuring $\frac{1}{12} \times \frac{1}{12} \times \frac{1}{32}$ of an inch comprising *Three Blind Mice* and produced by Glenniffer Press of Paisley, Scotland, in 1978.

Most Expensive Book. The highest price ever paid for a printed book is $2,400,000 for one of the only 21 known complete copies of the Gutenberg Bible, printed in Mainz, (West) Germany, in *c.* 1454. It was bought from the Carl and Lily Pforzheimer Foundation by Texas University in a sale arranged by Quaritch of London in New York on June 9, 1978.

Highest-Priced Printed Document. The highest price ever paid for a broadsheet was $404,000 for one of the 16 known copies of *The Declaration of Independence*, printed in Philadelphia in 1776 by Samuel T. Freeman & Co., and sold to a Texan in May, 1969.

Highest-Priced Atlas. The highest price paid for an atlas is $697,000 for a 16th century Mercator atlas of Europe sold at Sotheby's, London, on March 13, 1979.

Longest Novel. The longest important novel ever published is *Les hommes de bonne volonté* by Louis Henri Jean Farigoule (born August 26, 1885), *alias* Jules Romains, of France, in 27 volumes in 1932–46. The English version, *Men of Good Will*, was published in 14 volumes in 1933–46 as a "novel-cycle." The 4,959-page edition published by Peter Davies Ltd. has an estimated 2,070,000 words, excluding a 100-page index. The novel *Tokuga-Wa Ieyasu* by Sohachi Yamaoka has been serialized in Japanese daily newspapers since 1951. Now completed, it will require nearly 40 volumes in book form.

Encyclopaediae

Earliest. The earliest known encyclopaedia was compiled in Athens by Speusippus (*post* 408–*c.* 338 B.C.) in *c.* 370 B.C. He was a nephew of Plato.

Most Comprehensive. The most comprehensive present-day encyclopaedia is the *Encyclopaedia Britannica*, first published in Edinburgh, Scotland, in December, 1768. A group of booksellers in the U.S. acquired reprint rights in 1898 and complete ownership in 1899. In 1943, the *Britannica* was given to the University of Chicago. The current 30-volume 15th edition contains 33,141 pages and 43,000,000 words from 4,277 contributors. It is now edited in Chicago and in London.

Largest. The largest encyclopaedia ever compiled was the *Great Standard Encyclopaedia* of Yung-lo ta tien of 22,937 manuscript books (370 still survive), written by 2,000 Chinese scholars in 1403–08.

Longest Index

The Ninth Collective Index of *Chemical Abstracts*, completed on August 23, 1978, contains 20,550,000 entries in 95,882 pages in 57 volumes, and weighs 251 lbs.

Largest Dictionary

The largest dictionary now published is the 12-volume Royal quarto *The Oxford English Dictionary* of 15,487 pages published between 1884 and 1928 with a first supplement of 963 pages in 1933 and a further 4-volume supplement, edited by R. W. Burchfield, in which the third and fourth volumes, covering O-S and T-Z have yet to appear. The work contains 414,825 word listings, 1,827,306 illustrative quotations and reputedly 227,779,589 letters and figures, 63.8 times more than the Bible.

Bible

Oldest. Biblical texts in Hebrew are known to have become stabilized as early as 70 A.D. The oldest leather and papyrus Dead Sea Scrolls date from *c.* 250 B.C. The oldest known Bible is the *Codex Vaticanus*, written in Greek *ante*-350 A.D., and preserved in the Vatican Museum, Rome.

The earliest complete Bible printed in English was edited by Miles Coverdale (*c.* 1488–1569), while living in Antwerp, and printed in

HIGHEST-PRICED ATLAS: This engraving, depicting geographer Gerhardus Mercator, appears in the most expensive atlas ever sold.

1535. The New Testament in English, had, however, been printed by William Tyndale in Cologne and in Worms, Germany, in 1525.

Longest and Shortest Books. The longest book in the Authorized Version (King James) of the Bible is the Book of Psalms, while the longest book, including prose, is the Book of the Prophet Isaiah, with 66 chapters. The shortest is the Third Epistle of John, with 294 words in 14 verses. The Second Epistle of John has only 13 verses but 298 words.

Longest Psalm, Verse, Sentence and Name. Of the 150 Psalms, the longest is the 119th, with 176 verses, and the shortest is the 117th, with two verses. The shortest verse in the English Authorized Version of the Bible is verse 35 of Chapter XI of the Gospel according to St. John, consisting of the two words "Jesus wept." The longest is verse 9 of Chapter VIII of the Book of Esther, which extends to a 90-word description of the Persian empire. The total number of letters in the Bible is 3,566,480. The total number of words depends on the method of counting hyphenated words, but is usually given as between 773,692 and 773,746.

The word "and" appears 46,227 times, according to Colin McKay Wilson (U.K.) of the Salvation Army.

The longest personal name is Maher-shalal-hash-baz, the symbolic name of the second son of Isaiah (Isaiah, Chapter VIII, verses 1 and 3). Longer by 2 letters is the title in the caption of Psalm 22, in Hebrew, sometimes rendered Al-'Ayyeleth Hash-Shahar (20 letters).

Most Prolific Writers

The most prolific writer for whom a word count has been published was Charles Hamilton, *alias* Frank Richards (1875–1961), the

OLDEST AND YOUNGEST AUTHOR-ESSES: Mrs. Alice Pollock had her latest book published in 1971 when she was more than 102 years old. Dorothy Straight, of Washington, D.C., had her first book published at the age of 4.

Englishman who created Billy Bunter. At the height of his career in 1908 he wrote the whole of the boys' comics *Gem* (founded 1907) and *Magnet* (1908–1940) and most of two others, totaling 80,000 words a week. His lifetime output has been put at 100,000,000 words. He enjoyed the advantages of electric light rather than candlelight, and of being unmarried.

The champion of the goose-quill era was Józef Ignacy Kraszewski (1812–1887) of Poland, who produced more than 600 volumes of novels and historical works.

The greatest number of novels published by any author is 904 by Kathleen Lindsay (Mrs. Mary Faulkner) (1903–1973) of Somerset West, Cape Province, South Africa. She wrote under six pen names, two of them masculine. The most prolific living novelist is Lauran Paine of California, who has had some 850 works published under 70 pen names.

From 1932 to 1973, the British novelist John Creasey (1908–73) wrote under his own name and 13 *aliases*, 564 books totaling more than 40,000,000 words. Previously, he had received a probable record 743 rejection slips.

Enid Mary Blyton (Mrs. Darrell Waters) (1898–1968) (U.K.), completed 600 titles of children's stories, many of them brief, with 59 in the single year 1955. They have been translated into a record 128 languages.

Oldest Authoress

The oldest authoress in the world was Mrs. Alice Pollock (*née* Wykeham-Martin) (1868–1971) of Haslemere, Surrey, England, whose book *Portrait of My Victorian Youth* (Johnson Publications) was published in March, 1971, when she was aged 102 years 8 months.

Youngest Author

The youngest recorded commercially published author is Dorothy Straight (born May 25, 1958) of Washington, D.C., who wrote *How the World Began* in 1962, aged 4. It was published in August, 1964, by Pantheon Books, New York.

Highest-Paid Writer

In 1958, a Mrs. Deborah Schneider of Minneapolis, Minnesota, wrote 25 words to complete a sentence in a competition for the best blurb for Plymouth cars. She won from about 1,400,000 entrants the prize of $500 every month for life. On normal life expectations she would collect $12,000 per word. No known anthology includes Mrs. Schneider's deathless prose.

By way of comparison, a modern author of a highly successful 100,000-word filmed novel might expect to earn up to $17.50 per word.

Top-Selling Author

The all-time sales estimate of books by Erle Stanley Gardner (1889–1970) (U.S.) to January 1, 1979, is 310,910.603 copies in 23 languages. The top selling woman writer has been Dame Agatha Christie (*née* Agatha Mary Clarissa Miller), later Lady Mallowan (formerly Mrs. Archibald Christie) (1890–1976). Her 87 crime novels have sold an estimated 300,000,000 copies in 103 languages. *Sleeping Murder* was published posthumously in 1977.

Currently the top-selling authoress is Barbara Cartland (Mrs. McCorquodale) with global sales exceeding 100,000,000 for 242 novels in 18 languages.

On March 13, 1953, it was announced that 672,058,000 copies of the works of Marshal Iosif Vissarionovich Dzhugashvili, *alias* Stalin (1879–1953), had been sold or distributed in 101 languages.

Most Rejections

The greatest recorded number of publishers' rejections for a manuscript is 109 for the 130,000-word manuscript "World Government Crusade" by Gilbert Young (born 1906) since 1958. His public meeting in Bath, England, in support of his parliamentary candidacy as a World Government Candidate, however, drew a crowd of one.

Highest Printings

The world's most widely distributed book is the Bible, portions of which have been translated into 1,659 languages. This compares with 222 languages for Lenin. It has been estimated that between 1815 and 1975 some 2,500,000,000 Bibles were printed, of which 1,500,000,000 were handled by Bible Societies. The total distribution of complete Bibles by the United Bible Societies (covering 150 countries) in the year 1978 was 9,280,222.

It has been reported that 800,000,000 copies of the red-covered booklet *Quotations from the Works of Mao Tse-tung* were sold or distributed between June, 1966, when possession became virtually mandatory in China, up to September, 1971, when their promoter, Marshal Lin Piao, was killed.

The total disposal through non-commercial channels by Jehovah's Witnesses of the 190-page hardbound book *The Truth That Leads to Eternal Life*, published by the Watchtower Bible and Tract Society of Brooklyn, New York, on May 8, 1968, reached 90,000,000 in 112 languages by January, 1, 1979.

Some 75,000,000 copies of *The American Spelling Book* by Noah Webster were distributed with Federal funds.

Best Sellers

The world's all-time best selling book is the annual reference work *The World Almanac & Book of Facts*, first published in 1868, and currently edited by George E. Delury. Its cumulative sale to October, 1978, is estimated at 38,000,000 copies, increasing by 1,100,000 each year.

The authors who have written the fastest selling title are Norris Dewar McWhirter (born August 12, 1925) and his twin brother Alan Ross McWhirter (killed November 27, 1975), editors and compilers of the *Guinness Book of World Records*, first published from 107 Fleet Street, London, England, in October, 1955. In May, 1979, global sales in 19 languages had reached over 38,000,000 copies.

Slowest Seller. The accolade for the world's slowest-selling book (known in publishing as slooow-sellers) probably belongs to David Wilkins' Translation of the New Testament from Coptic into Latin, published by Oxford University Press in 1716 in 500 copies. Selling an average of one each 139 days it was in print for 191 years.

Fiction. The novel with the highest sales has been *Valley of the Dolls* (first published in March, 1966) by Jacqueline Susann (1921–1974) with a worldwide total of 21,472,000 copies by May 1, 1979. Within the first six months after paperback publication by Bantam Books in 1967, some 6,800,000 copies were sold.

Longest Literary Gestation

The standard German dictionary *Deutsches Wörterbuch*, begun by the brothers Grimm in 1854, was finished in 1971. *Acta Sanctorum*, begun by Jean Bolland in 1643, arranged according to saints' days, reached the month of November in 1925, and an introduction for December was published in 1940.

Post Cards. The top-selling post card of all time was said to be a drawing by Donald McGill (1875–1962) with the caption: He: "How do you like Kipling?" She: "I don't know, you naughty boy, I've never kippled." It sold about 6,000,000. Between 1904 and his death McGill sold more than 350,000,000 cards to users and deltiologists (picture post card collectors).

The world's first post cards were issued in Vienna on October 1, 1869. Pin-up girls came into vogue in 1914 having been pioneered in 1900 by Raphaël Kirchner (1876–1917). The most expensive on record were ones made in ivory for an Indian prince which involved the killing of 60 elephants.

" Do you like Kipling ? "
" I don't know, you naughty boy,
I've never kippled ! "

Poetry

Poets Laureate. The earliest official Poet Laureate was John Dryden (1631–1700), appointed in April, 1668. It is recorded that Henry I (1100–1135) had a King's versifier named Wale. The youngest Poet Laureate was Laurence Eusden (1688–1730), who received the bays on December 24, 1718, at the age of 30 years and 3 months. The greatest age at which a poet has succeeded is 73 in the case of William Wordsworth (1770–1850) on April 6, 1843. The longest-lived Laureate was John Masefield, O.M., who died on May 12, 1967, aged 88 years 345 days. The longest which any poet has worn the laurel is 41 years 322 days, in the case of Alfred (later the 1st Lord) Tennyson (1809–92), who was appointed on November 19, 1850, and died in office on October 6, 1892.

Longest Poem. The lengthiest poem ever published has been the Kirghiz folk epic *Manas*, which appeared in printed form in 1958, but which has never been translated into English. It runs to "more than 500,000 lines." Short translated passages appear in *The Elek Book of Oriental Verse*.

The longest poem ever written in the English language appears to be one on the life of King Alfred by John Fitchett (1766–1838) of Liverpool, England, which ran to 129,807 lines and took 40 years to write. His editor, Robert Riscoe, added the concluding 2,585 lines.

Shortest Poem. The shortest poem in the *Oxford Dictionary of Quotations* is *On the Antiquity of Microbes* and consists of the 3 words: "Adam, Had 'em."

Largest Publishers

The largest publisher in the world is the U.S. Government Printing Office in Washington, D.C., founded in 1860. The Superintendent of Documents Division dispatches items worth more than $44 million every year. The inventory is numbered at 24,500 titles in print.

Fastest Publishing

The shortest interval between the receipt of a manuscript and the publication of a book is 66½ hours, in the case of *The Pope's Journey to the United States—the Historic Record*, a paperback of 160 pages, costing 75 cents, written by 51 editors of the strike-bound *New York Times* and published by Bantam Books, Inc. of New York City. It was printed by the W. F. Hall Printing Co. of Chicago. The first article reached the publishers at 1:30 p.m. on October 4, 1965, and completed copies came off the printers' presses at 8:00 a.m. on October 7, 1965.

Largest Printers

The largest printers in the world are R. R. Donnelley & Co. of Chicago. The company, founded in 1864, has plants in 13 main centers, and has turned out $667,000,000 worth of work per year. More than 67,000 tons of inks and 1,100,000 tons of paper and board are consumed every year.

Largest Print Order

The initial print order for the 50th Automobile Association (England) Members' Handbook (1978–1979) was 4,500,000 copies. The total print run since 1908 has been 72,400,000.

Longest-Lived Comic Strip

The most durable newspaper comic strip has been the Katzen-jammer Kids (Hans and Fritz) created by Rudolph Dirks, first published in the *New York Journal* on December 12, 1897, and carried on by his son, John.

The earliest strip was *The Yellow Kid* which first appeared in the *New York Journal* on October 18, 1896. The most widely syndicated is *Blondie*, which appears in 1,800 newspapers in 58 countries, and in 33 languages.

Most Syndicated Cartoonist

Ranan R. Lurie (b. May 26, 1932) is the most widely syndicated cartoonist in the world. His work is published in 45 countries.

Autographs

Earliest. The earliest English sovereign whose handwriting is known to have survived is Edward III (1327–1377). The earliest full signature to have survived is that of Richard II (dated July 26, 1386). The Magna Carta does not bear even the mark of King John (reigned 1199–1216), but carries only his seal. An attested cross of King Canute (1016–1035) has survived.

Most Expensive Autographs. The highest price ever paid on the open market for a single letter is $51,000, paid in 1927 for a letter written by Button Gwinnett (1732–77), one of the three men from Georgia to sign the Declaration of Independence on July 4, 1776.

An expense account by Paul Revere, dated January 3, 1774 and signed by John Hancock, was auctioned for $70,000 at Sotheby Parke Bernet on April 26, 1978.

The highest price paid for a signed autograph letter of a living person is $6,250 for a letter from ex-President Richard M. Nixon to a Brigadier, dated December 14, 1971.

Letters

Longest. The longest personal letter based on word count is one of 1,113,747 words written in 8 months ending in May, 1976, by Jacqueline Jones of Lindale, Texas, to her sister Mrs. Jean Stewart of Springfield, Maine.

To the Editor. The longest recorded letter to an editor was one of 13,000 words (a third of a modern novel) written to the editor of the *Fishing Gazette* by A.R.I.E.L. and published in 7-point type spread over two issues in 1884.

The shortest literary correspondence on record was that between Victor Marie Hugo (1802–85) and his publisher, Hurst and Blackett, in 1862. The author was on holiday and anxious to know how his new novel *Les Misérables* was selling. He wrote "?". The reply was "!".

Pen Pals. The longest sustained correspondence on record is one of 72 years between Mrs. E. Darlington of Marple, Cheshire, England and Mrs. Gertrude Walker of Hawthorn, South Australia, which started on January 5, 1906.

Most Personal Mail. The highest confirmed count of letters received by any private citizen in a year is 900,000, by baseball star Henry Aaron, reported by the U.S. Postal Department in June, 1974, the year that he surpassed Babe Ruth's career home run record.

Longest Diary

No collated records exist, but the diary of T. C. Baskerville of Charlton-cum-Hardy, Manchester, England, maintained since 1939, comprises an estimated 3,390,000 words.

Crossword Puzzles

The earliest crossword was one with 32 clues invented by Arthur Wynne (born Liverpool, England) and published in the *New York World* on December 21, 1913.

Largest. The largest crossword ever published was one with 5,585 clues across and 5,358 clues down, compiled by Marvin Ryder of Aylmer, Ontario, Canada, and published by the Courier Press of Wallaceburg, Ontario, on March 28, 1979. It covers an area of 18.28 square feet.

The largest crosswords regularly published are "Mammoth" crosswords based on grids of 73 by 73 (5,329 total) squares with up to 828 clues by First Features Ltd., Hastings, England, since May 1, 1970.

The longest word included in a crossword puzzle has been Arrondissementsschoolopziener—a country school inspector (29 letters).

Fastest Solution. The fastest recorded time for completing *The Times* (London) crossword under test conditions is 3 minutes 45.0 seconds by Roy Dean, 43, of Bromley, Greater London, in the BBC "Today" radio studio on December 19, 1970.

FIRST CHRISTMAS CARD: The tradition of sending Christmas cards began in 1843, when J. C. Horsley sent this one to his friend Henry Cole.

Slowest. In May, 1966, *The Times* of London received an announcement from a Fijian woman that she had just succeeded in completing their crossword No. 673 in the issue of April 4, 1932.

Oldest Map

The oldest known map of any kind is a clay tablet depicting the Euphrates River flowing through northern Mesopotamia (Iraq), dated *c.* 3800 B.C.

The earliest printed map in the world dates from Isodore of Sevillés *Etymologiarum* of 1472.

Birthday Cards

The most parsimonious recorded use of a birthday card is that between Mrs. Amelia Finch (b. April 18, 1912) of Lakehurst, New Jersey, and Mr. Paul E. Warburgh (b. February 1, 1902) of Huntington, New York, who have exchanged the same birthday card since February 1, 1927.

Christmas Cards

The first Christmas card was designed by J. C. Horsley in London in 1843. It was suggested by, and sent to, the artist's friend, Henry Cole. The Cole-Horsley cards sold for one shilling.

The greatest number of personal Christmas cards sent out is believed to be 62,824 by Werner Erhard of San Francisco, California, in December, 1975.

Libraries

Earliest. The earliest public library is believed to be the library in Kirwall, Orkney Islands, Scotland, founded in 1683.

OLDEST MAN EVER: On June 29, 1979, Shigechiyo Izumi of Japan became the first human being ever reliably reported to reach his 114th birthday. According to a close relative, "He wakes up at 7 in the morning, takes the dog for a walk, meets newlyweds who come to see him every day, and drinks about a half-pint of spirits every night before he goes to sleep at 8."

A GOOD HOT MEAL:
Mrs. Jean Chapman of
England snuffed out a
record 1,921 flaming
torches in her mouth, one
after the other, in a
two-hour fiery feast.

PRETTY AS A PICTURE:
The profusely illustrated
Mrs. Rusty Skuse has been
decorated by her
tattoo-artist husband until
only 15 per cent of her body
is free of embellishment.

B

FARTHEST FROM THE EARTH'S CORE: The summit of Mount Chimborazo in Ecuador is 20,561 feet above sea level, less than the height of Everest, but its equatorial position places the peak farther away from the center of the earth than any other mountaintop.

FAT CAT: Norris McWhirter, editor of the "Guinness Book," holds the peak example of purring poundage, "Tiger," who consistently weighs 42-43 lbs. (Photo courtesy of BBC-TV "Record Breakers")

C

"WHITE LIGHTNING": The single and two-man records for human-powered speed were set in this streamlined vehicle. It just missed breaking the 55 m.p.h. speed limit in its recordbreaking two-man run on May 7, 1978, at Ontario Speedway, California.

LONGEST CAR: This specially "extended" 1976 Fleetwood Cadillac measures 29 feet 6 inches long. Built for Joel D. Nelson of Bakersfield, California, it was unveiled in April, 1979, on the "Guinness Spectacular" ABC-TV program. (Photo by Franklin Berger)

D

Largest. The largest library in the world is the Library of Congress (founded on April 24, 1800), on Capitol Hill, Washington, D.C. By 1978, it contained 74,387,000 items, including 18,638,633 books and pamphlets. The buildings contain 35 acres of floor space and 50 miles of book shelves. The James Madison Memorial Extension, begun in 1971, is due for completion in 1980.

The tallest library is the University of Massachusetts Library, Amherst, Mass., with 28 stories and a height of 296 feet 4 inches, opened in May, 1973.

The largest non-statutory library in the world is the New York Public Library (founded 1895) on Fifth Avenue, New York City, with a floor area of 525,276 square feet and 80 miles of shelving. Including 83 branch libraries, its collection embraces 8,605,610 volumes, 10,683,105 manuscripts, and 317,183 maps.

Overdue Books. The most overdue book taken out by a known borrower was a book on febrile diseases (London, 1805, by Dr. J. Currie) checked out in 1823 from the University of Cincinnati Medical Library and reported returned on December 7, 1968, by the borrower's great-grandson Richard Dodd. The fine was calculated as $2,264, but waived.

Newspapers

Most. The U.S. had 1,756 English-language daily newspapers on October 1, 1978. They had a combined net paid circulation of 62,200,000 copies per day as of September 30, 1978. The peak year for U.S. newspapers was 1910, when there were 2,202. The leading newspaper readers in the world are the people of Sweden, where 564 newspapers were sold for each 1,000 of the population.

Oldest. The oldest existing newspaper in the world is the Swedish official journal *Post och Inrikes Tidningar*, founded in 1645. It is published by the Royal Swedish Academy of Letters. The oldest existing commercial newspaper is the *Haarlems Dagblad/Oprechte Haarlemsche Courant*, published in Haarlem, in the Netherlands. The *Courant* was first issued as the *Weeckelycke Courante van Europa* on January 8, 1656, and a copy of issue No. 1 survives.

Largest. The most massive single issue of a newspaper was *The New York Times* of Sunday, October 17, 1965. It comprised 15 sections with a total of 946 pages, including about 1,200,000 lines of advertising. Each copy weighed 7½ lbs. and sold for 50 cents locally.

The largest page size ever used has been 51 inches by 35 inches for *The Constellation*, printed in 1859 by George Roberts as part of the Fourth of July celebrations in New York City.

The smallest recorded page size has been 3 inches by 3¾ inches, as used in the *Daily Banner* of Roseburg, Oregon (25 cents per month), issues of which, dated February 1 and 2, 1876, survive.

Highest Circulation. The first newspaper to achieve a circulation of 1,000,000 was *Le Petit Journal*, published in Paris, which reached this figure in 1886, when selling at 5 centimes (fractionally more than one cent) per copy.

The highest circulation for any newspaper is that for the *Yomiuri Shimbun* (founded 1874) of Japan with a figure which attained more than 13,029,424 copies in April, 1979. This, however, has been achieved by totaling the figures for editions published in various centers with a morning figure of 8,190,598 and an evening figure of 4,838,826.

The highest circulation of any evening newspaper is that of the *Evening News*, established in London in 1881. The latest figure is 537,784 copies per issue (average for March, 1979), with an average readership of 1,396,000 (July–December, 1978).

Most Read. The newspaper which achieves the closest to a saturation circulation is *The Sunday Post*, established in Glasgow, Scotland, in 1914. In 1978, its total estimated readership of 2,909,000 represented more than 74 per cent of Scotland's entire population aged 15 and over.

Periodicals

Largest Circulation. The largest circulation of any weekly periodical is that of *TV Guide*, which, in 1974, became the first magazine in history to sell a billion copies in a year. The weekly average for July to December, 1978, was 19,495,113.

In its 39 international editions the *Reader's Digest* (established February, 1922) circulates 29,701,000 copies monthly, in 15 languages, including a U.S. edition of more than 17,750,000 copies.

Parade, the syndicated Sunday newspaper color magazine supplement, is distributed with 128 newspapers every Sunday, yielding a circulation of 21,195,624 as of May, 1979.

Oldest. The oldest continuing periodical in the world is the *Philosophical Transactions of the Royal Society*, which first appeared on March 6, 1665.

Old Moore's Almanack has been published annually since 1697, when it first appeared as a broadsheet by Dr. Francis Moore (1657–1715) of Southwark, London, England, to advertise his "physiks." The annual sale certified by its publishers, W. Foulsham & Co. Ltd., Slough, England, is 1,096,000 copies, and its aggregate sale is estimated to be in excess of 107,000,000.

Advertising Rates. The highest price ever for a single page of advertising has been $142,600 for a four-color back cover of *Parade* (circulation 21 million per week) in May, 1979.

The advertising revenue from the October, 1978 edition of *Reader's Digest* was $10,393,200.

The highest expenditure ever incurred on a single advertisement in a periodical is $5,200,000 by Gulf and Western Industries for insertions in the February 5, 1979 *Time* magazine (U.S. and selected overseas editions).

The world's highest newspaper advertising rate is 25,704,000 yen ($106,000) for a full page in the morning edition and 20,491,800 yen ($85,000) for the evening edition of the *Asahi Shimbun* of Tokyo (April, 1978).

Music

Instruments

Oldest. The world's oldest surviving musical notation is a heptonic scale deciphered from a clay tablet by Dr. Duchesne-Guillemin in 1966–67. The tablet has been dated to *c.* 1800 B.C. and was found at a site in Nippur, Sumer, now Iraq. Also dated *c.* 1800 B.C. is an Assyrian love song to a Ugarit god, reconstructed for an 11-string lyre from a tablet of notation and lyric at the University of California, Berkeley, on March 6, 1974. Musical history is, however, able to be traced back to the 3rd millennium B.C., when the yellow bell (*huang chung*) had a recognized standard musical tone in Chinese temple music. Whistles and flutes made from perforated phalange bones have been found at Upper Paleolithic sites of the Aurignacian Period (*c.* 25,000–22,000 B.C.), *e.g.* at Istallóskö, Hungary, and in Molodova, U.S.S.R.

Earliest Piano. The earliest pianoforte in existence is one built in Florence, Italy, in 1720, by Bartolommeo Cristofori (1655–1731) of Padua, and now preserved in the Metropolitan Museum of Art, New York.

Grandest Piano. The grandest grand piano was one of 1¼ tons, 11 feet 8 inches long, made by Chas. H. Challen & Son Ltd. of London in 1935. The longest bass string measured 9 feet 11 inches and the tensile stress on the 726-lb. frame was 33.6 tons.

Organs. The largest and loudest musical instrument ever constructed is the Auditorium Organ in Atlantic City, New Jersey. Completed in 1930, this heroic instrument has two consoles (one with seven manuals and another movable one with five), 1,477 stop controls and 33,112 pipes ranging in tone from $\frac{3}{16}$ of an inch to the 64-foot tone. It is powered with blower motors of 365 horse-power, cost $500,000 and has the volume of 25 brass bands, with a range of seven octaves. It is now only partially functional.

The world's largest church organ is that in Passau Cathedral, Germany. It was completed in 1928 by D. F. Steinmeyer & Co. It has 16,000 pipes and five manuals.

The world's only five-manual electric organ was installed in Carnegie Hall, New York City, in September, 1974.

The grand organ at John Wanamaker's department store in Philadelphia, installed in 1911, was enlarged until by 1930 it had six manuals and 30,067 pipes including a 64-foot tone Gravissima.

The loudest organ stop in the world is the Ophicleide stop of the Grand Great in the Solo Organ in the Atlantic City Auditorium (see above). It is operated by a pressure of 100 inches of water (3½ lbs. per square inch) and has a pure trumpet note of earsplitting volume, more than six times the volume of the loudest locomotive whistles.

Most Durable Organist. The longest recorded career as an organist is 81 years in the case of Charles Bridgeman (1779–1873) of All Saints Parish Church, Hertford, England, who was appointed in 1792, and who was still playing in 1873. The year in which he reached his crescendo was not recorded.

Stringed Instruments. The largest moveable stringed instrument ever constructed was a pantaleon with 270 strings stretched over 50 square feet, used by George Noel in 1767.

Largest Guitar. The largest, loudest guitar in the world is an electric guitar 9 feet 10 inches tall, weighing 380 lbs., built by the Odessey Guitar Company of Vancouver, British Columbia, Canada.

The most expensive standard-sized guitar is the German chittara battente, built by Jacob Stadler (dated 1624), which sold for £10,500 ($25,200) at Christie's, London, on June 12, 1974.

Largest Double Bass. The largest double bass ever constructed was 14 feet tall, built in 1924 in Ironia, New Jersey, by Arthur K. Ferris, allegedly on orders from the Archangel Gabriel. It weighed 1,300 lbs. with a sound box 8 feet across, and had leather strings totaling 104 feet. Its low notes could be felt rather than heard.

Most Valuable Violin. The highest price ever paid at auction for a violin is $297,250 for one of the "Hubermann" *ex* Kreisler Stradivari dated 1733 at Sotheby's, London, on May 3, 1979. Some 700 of the 1,116 violins by Stradivarius (1644–1737) have survived. His inlaid "Hellier" violin was sold by private treaty in the U.S. in March, 1979, for a reported $400,000.

Underwater Violinist. The only violinist to surmount the problems of playing the violin under water has been Mark Gottlieb. Submerged in the Evergreen State College swimming pool in Olympia, Washington, in March, 1975, he gave his first submarine rendition of Handel's "Water Music." He is still working on the problems of bow speed and *détaché*. He joined with his sister, Karen, on the organ to perform the world's first underwater duet, a stirring rendition of "The Blue Danube," for the "Guinness Spectacular" TV Show on ABC television in May, 1979.

LARGEST GUITAR (left): This electrical guitar measures 9 feet 10 inches tall. SMALLEST VIOLIN: (right): This fully functional violin is only 2 inches long. It was made by Morris Samskin of Brooklyn, New York.

Most Durable Fiddler. Otto E. Funk, 62, walked 4,165 miles from New York City to San Francisco, playing his Hopf violin every step of the way westward. He arrived on June 16, 1929, after 183 days on the road. Rolland S. Tapley retired as a violinist from the Boston Symphony Orchestra after playing for a reputedly unrivaled 58 years from February, 1920, to August 27, 1978.

Brass Instruments. The largest recorded brass instrument is a tuba standing 7½ feet tall, with 39 feet of tubing and a bell 3 feet 4 inches across. This contrabass tuba was constructed for a world tour by the band of John Philip Sousa (1854–1932), the "march king," c. 1896–98, and is still in use. This instrument is now owned by a circus promoter in South Africa.

Longest Alphorn. The longest alphorn is 43 feet 11½ inches long, built from a spruce log by Herr Stocker in Switzerland in 1976. It weighs 70½ lbs and was seen on the 1977 BBC-TV *Christmas Record Breaker Show*.

Largest Drum. The largest drum in the world is the Disneyland Big Bass Drum with a diameter of 10 feet 6 inches and a weight of 450 lbs. It was built in 1961 by Remo, Inc., of North Hollywood, California, and is mounted on wheels and towed by a tractor.

Easiest and Most Difficult Instruments. The American Music Conference announced in September, 1977, that the easiest instrument is the ukelele and the most difficult are the French horn and the oboe. The latter has been described as "the ill woodwind that no one blows good."

Most Players for an Instrument. The greatest number of musicians required to operate a single instrument was the six required to play the gigantic orchestrion, known as the Apollonican, a stringed instrument built in 1816 and played until 1840.

Orchestras

Most. The greatest number of professional orchestras maintained in one country is 94 in West Germany. The total number of symphony orchestras in the U.S., including "community" orchestras, was estimated to be in excess of 1,470, including 31 major and 106 metropolitan orchestras, as of June, 1979. The American Symphony Orchestra League lists 29 regional, 76 urban, 146 chamber, 804 community, and 278 college, university and conservatory orchestras in this total of U.S. ensembles.

Largest. The most massive orchestra ever assembled was one of 20,100 at the Ullevaal Stadium, Oslo, on June 28, 1964, made up of Norges Musikkorps Forbund bands from all over Norway.

On June 17, 1872, Johann Strauss the Younger (1825–99) conducted an orchestra of 987, supported by a choir of 20,000, at the World Peace Jubilee in Boston, Massachusetts. The number of first violinists was more than 400.

Largest Marching Band. The largest on record was one of 1,976 musicians and 54 drill majors, flag bearers and directors who marched 2 miles down Pennsylvania Avenue, Washington, D.C., in President Nixon's Second Inaugural Parade, January 20, 1973.

Greatest Classical Attendance. The greatest attendance at any classical concert was an estimated 400,000 for a presentation by the Boston Pops Orchestra, conducted by Arthur Fiedler (b. December 17, 1894, d. July 10, 1979) at the Hatch Memorial Shell, Boston, Massachusetts, on July 4, 1977. At the 1978 concert the 83-year-old conductor was presented with a testimonial bearing a record 500,000 signatures.

Pop Festival Attendance. The greatest claimed attendance was 600,000 for a rock festival at Watkins Glen, New York, on July 29, 1973. Of those attending, about 150,000 actually paid for admission. There were 12 "sound towers."

The highest recorded paid attendance for a single pop recording group in concert is 76,229 for an appearance by the British group Led Zeppelin, at the Silver Dome, Pontiac, Michigan, on April 30, 1977. The gross for this performance was a record $792,361.

Highest and Lowest Notes. The extremes of orchestral instruments (excluding the organ) range between a handbell tuned to g′′′′′ or 6,272 cycles per second, and the sub-contrabass clarinet, which can reach C,, or 16.4 cycles per second. The highest note on a standard pianoforte is C′′′′′, 4,186 cycles per second, which is also the violinist's limit. In 1873, a sub double bassoon able to reach B,,,♯ or 14.6 cycles per second was constructed, but no surviving specimen is known. The extremes for the organ are g′′′′′′ (the sixth G above middle C) (12,544 cycles per sec.) and C,,, (8.12 cycles per sec.) obtainable from ¾-inch and 64-foot pipes, respectively.

Composers

Most Prolific. The most prolific composer of all time was probably Georg Philipp Telemann (1681–1767) of Germany. He composed 12 complete sets of services (one cantata every Sunday) for a year, 78 services for special occasions, 40 operas, 600 to 700 orchestral suites, 44 Passions, plus concertos and chamber music.

The most prolific symphonist was Johann Melchior Molter (*c.* 1695–1765) of Germany, who wrote 165. Joseph Haydn (1732–1809) of Austria wrote 104 numbered symphonies, some of which are regularly played today.

Most Rapid. Among classical composers the most rapid was Wolfgang Amadeus Mozart (1756–91) of Austria, who wrote 1,000 operas, operettas, symphonies, violin sonatas, divertimenti, serenades, motets, concertos for piano and many other instruments, string quartets, other chamber music, masses and litanies, of which only 70 were published before he died, aged 35. His opera *The Clemency of Titus* (1791) was written in 18 days and three symphonic master-pieces, *Symphony No. 39 in E flat major, Symphony in G minor* and the *"Jupiter" Symphony in C*, were reputedly written in the space of 42 days in 1788. His overture to *Don Giovanni* was written in full score at one sitting in Prague in 1787 and finished on the day of its opening performance.

National Anthems

The oldest national anthem is the *Kimigayo* of Japan, in which the words date from the 9th century. The anthem of Greece constitutes the first four verses of the Solomos poem, which has 158 verses. The shortest anthems are those of Japan, Jordan and San Marino, each with only four lines. Of the 23 wordless national anthems, the oldest is that of Spain, dating from 1770.

Longest Rendering

"God Save the King" was played non-stop 16 or 17 times by a German military band on the platform of Rathenau Railway Station, Brandenburg, on the morning of February 9, 1909. The reason was that King Edward VII was struggling inside the train to get into his German Field-Marshal uniform before he could emerge.

Longest Symphony

The longest of all single classical symphonies is the orchestral Symphony No. 3 in D minor by Gustav Mahler (1860–1911) of Austria. This work, composed in 1896, requires a contralto, a women's and a boys' choir, in addition to a full orchestra. A full performance requires 1 hour 34 minutes, of which the first movement alone takes 45 minutes.

The Symphony No. 2 (the Gothic, now renumbered as No. 1), composed in 1919–22 by Havergal Brian (1876–1972) was played by over 800 performers (4 brass bands) in the Victoria Hall, Hanley, Staffordshire, England, on May 21, 1978, conducted by Trevor Stokes. Havergal Brian wrote an even vaster work based on Shelley's *Prometheus Unbound* lasting 4 hours 11 minutes but the full score has been missing since 1961.

The symphony *Victory at Sea* written by Richard Rodgers and arranged by Robert Russell Bennett for NBC-TV in 1952 took 13 hours to perform.

Longest Piano Composition

The longest non-repetitious piece for piano ever composed was the Opus Clavicembalisticum by Kaikhosru Shapurji Sorabji (born

1892). The composer himself gave it its only public performance on December 1, 1930, in Glasgow, Scotland. The work is in 12 movements with a theme and 44 variations and a passacaglia with 81 and a playing time of 2¾ hours.

Longest Silence

The most protracted silence in modern sheet music is one entitled *4 minutes 33 seconds* in a totally silent *opus* by John Cage (U.S.). Commenting on this trend among young composers, Igor Fyodorovich Stravinsky (1882–1971) said that he now looked forward to their subsequent compositions being "works of major length."

Highest-Paid Musicians

Pianist. The highest-paid classical concert pianist was Ignace Jan Paderewski (1860–1941), Prime Minister of Poland in 1919–21, who accumulated a fortune estimated at $5,000,000, of which $500,000 was earned in a single season in 1922–23. The *nouveau riche* wife of a U.S. industrialist once required him to play behind a curtain.

Liberace (b. May 16, 1917, West Allis, Wisconsin) earns more than $2,000,000 for each 26-week season with a peak of $138,000 for a single night's performance at Madison Square Garden, New York City, in 1954. His real name is Wladziu Valentino Liberace.

Violinist. The Austrian-born Fritz Kreisler (1875–1962) is reputed to have received more than $3,000,000 during his career.

Singers. Of great fortunes earned by singers, the highest on record are those of Enrico Caruso (1873–1921), the Italian tenor, whose estate was about $9,000,000, and the Italian-Spanish coloratura soprano Amelita Galli-Curci (1889–1963), who received about $3,000,000. In 1850, up to $653 was paid for a single seat at the concerts given in the U.S. by Johanna ("Jenny") Maria Lind (1820–87), later Mrs. Otto Goldschmidt, the "Swedish Nightingale." She had a range of nearly three octaves, of which the middle register is still regarded as unrivaled.

The tenor "Count" John Francis McCormack (1884–1945) of Ireland gave up to 10 capacity-filled concerts in a single season in New York City's Carnegie Hall.

While no agreement exists as to the identity of history's greatest singer, there is unanimity on the worst. The excursions of the soprano Florence Foster Jenkins (1868–1944) into lieder and even high coloratura culminated on October 25, 1944, in her sell-out concert at Carnegie Hall, New York. The diva's (already high) high F was said to have been made higher in 1943 by a crash in a taxi. It is one of the tragedies of musicology that Madame Jenkins' *Clavelitos*, accompanied by Cosme McMoon, was never recorded for posterity. Eight of her other "renderings" were, however.

Opera

Longest. The longest of commonly performed operas is *Die Meistersinger von Nürnberg* by Wilhelm Richard Wagner (1813–83) of Germany. A normal uncut performance of this opera as performed by the Sadler's Wells company between August 24 and September 19, 1968, entailed 5 hours 15 minutes of music. *The Heretics* by Gabriel von Wayditch, a Hungarian-American, is orchestrated for 110 pieces and lasts 8½ hours.

Shortest. The shortest opera written was *The Deliverance of Theseus* by Darius Milhaud (born September, 1892), first performed in 1928, which lasts for 7 minutes 27 seconds.

Aria. The longest single aria, in the sense of an operatic solo, is Brünnhilde's immolation scene in Wagner's *Götterdämmerung*. A well-known recording has been precisely timed at 14 minutes 46 seconds.

Opera House—Largest. The largest opera house in the world is the Metropolitan Opera House, Lincoln Center, New York City, completed in September, 1966, at a cost of $45,700,000. It has a capacity of 3,800 seats in an auditorium 451 feet deep. The stage is 234 feet in width and 146 feet deep. The tallest opera house is one housed in a 42-story building on Wacker Drive in Chicago.

Opera Houses—Most Tiers. The Teatro della Scala (La Scala) in Milan, Italy, shares with the Bolshoi Theatre in Moscow, U.S.S.R., the distinction of having the greatest number of tiers. Each has six, with the topmost being nicknamed the *Galiorka* by Russians.

Opera Singers—Youngest and Oldest. The youngest opera singer in the world has been Jeanette Gloria (Ginetta) La Bianca, born in Buffalo, New York, on May 12, 1934, who made her official debut as Rosina in *The Barber of Seville* at the Teatro dell'Opera, Rome, on May 8, 1950, aged 15 years 361 days, but who appeared as Gilda in *Rigoletto* at Velletri, Italy, 45 days earlier. Miss La Bianca was taught by Lucia Carlino and managed by Angelo Carlino.

The tenor Giovanni Martinelli sang Emperor Altoum in *Turandot* in Seattle, Washington, on February 4, 1967, when aged 81.

Bells

Oldest. The oldest bell is reputed to be that found in the Babylonian Palace of Nimrod in 1849 by Mr. (later Sir) Austen Henry Layard (1817–94). It dates from *c.* 1000 B.C.

Largest Carillon. The largest carillon in the world is the Laura Spelman Rockefeller Memorial carillon in Riverside Church, New York City. It has 74 bells weighing 112 tons. The bourdon weighs 40,900 lbs. and is 10 feet 2 inches in diameter.

Heaviest. The heaviest bell in the world is the Tsar Kolokol, cast on November 25, 1735 in Moscow, U.S.S.R. It weighs 216 tons, measures 19 feet 4¼ inches in diameter, is 19 feet 3 inches high, and its greatest thickness is 24 inches. The bell is cracked, and a fragment, weighing about 12 tons, is broken from it. The bell has stood on a platform in the Kremlin, in Moscow, since 1836.

The heaviest bell in use is the Mingun bell, weighing 101.4 tons,

LARGEST BELL: The Tsar Kolokol bell, weighing 216 tons, has stood in the Kremlin, Moscow, since 1836.

in Mandalay, Burma, which is struck by a teak boom from the outside. It has a diameter of 16 feet 8½ inches at the lip.

The heaviest swinging bell in the world is the Petersglocke in Cologne Cathedral, Germany, which was cast in 1923. It has a diameter of 11 feet 1¾ inches and weighs 28.4 tons.

Bell Ringing. Eight bells have been rung to their full "extent" (a complete "Bob Major" of 40,320 changes) only once without relays. This took place in a bell foundry at Loughborough, Leicestershire, England, beginning at 6:52 a.m. on July 27, 1963, and ending at 12:50 a.m. on July 28, after 17 hours 58 minutes. The peal was composed by Kenneth Lewis of Altrincham, Cheshire, and the eight ringers were conducted by Robert B. Smith, aged 25, of Marple, Cheshire. Theoretically it would take 37 years 355 days to ring 12 bells (maximus) to their full extent of 479,001,600 changes.

The greatest number of peals (minimum of 5,040 changes, all on tower bells) rung in a year is 209 by Mark William Marshall of Ashford, Kent, England, in 1973. The late George E. Fearn rang 2,666 peals from 1928 to May, 1974.

Matthew Lakin (1801–1899) was a regular bell-ringer at Tetney Church near Grimsby, England, for 84 years.

Song

Oldest. The oldest is the *shaduf* chant, which has been sung since time immemorial by irrigation workers on the man-powered pivot-rod bucket raisers of the Nile water mills (or *saqiyas*) in Egypt. The English song *Sumer is icumen in* dates from *c.* 1240.

Top Songs of All Time. The most frequently sung songs in English are *Happy Birthday to You* (based on the original *Good Morning to All*, by Mildred and Patty S. Hill of New York, published in 1935 and in copyright until 2010); *For He's a Jolly Good Fellow* (originally the French *Malbrouk*), known at least as early as 1781, and *Auld Lang Syne* (originally the Strathspey *I fee'd a Lad at Michaelmas*, some words of which were written by Robert Burns (1759–96). *Happy Birthday* was sung in space by the Apollo IX astronauts on March 8, 1969.

Top Selling Sheet Music. Sales of three non-copyright pieces are known to have exceeded 20,000,000, namely *The Old Folks at Home* by Stephen Foster (1855), *Listen to the Mocking Bird* (1855) and *The Blue Danube* (1867). Of copyright material, the two top-sellers are *Let Me Call You Sweetheart* (1910, by Whitson and Friedman) and *Till We Meet Again* (1918, by Egan and Whiting), each with some 6,000,000 by 1967. Other huge sellers have been *St. Louis Blues, Stardust* and *Tea for Two.*

Most Successful Song Writer. In terms of sales of single records, the most successful of all song writers has been Paul McCartney (formerly of the Beatles and now of Wings). Between 1962 and January 1, 1978, he wrote jointly or solo 43 songs which sold 1,000,000 or more records.

Hymns

Earliest. There are more than 950,000 Christian hymns in existence. The earliest exactly datable hymn is the Heyr Rimna Smiour (Hear, the maker of heaven) from 1208 by the Icelandic bard and chieftain Kolbeinn Tumason (1173–1208). Hymn 91 in the Methodist School hymnal is attributed to Clement of Alexandria (170–220 A.D.).

Longest and Shortest. The longest hymn is "Hora novissima tempora pessima sunt; vigilemus" by Bernard of Cluny (12th century), which runs to 2,966 lines. In English the longest is "The Sands of Time are Sinking" by Mrs. Anne Ross Cousin, *née* Cundell (1824–1906), which is in full 152 lines, though only 32 lines in the Methodist Hymn Book. The shortest hymn is the single verse in Long Metre "Be Present at our Table, Lord," anonymous but attributed to "J. Leland."

Most Prolific Hymnists. Mrs. Frances Jane Van Alstyne, *née* Crosby (U.S.) (1820–1915), wrote more than 8,500 hymns although she had been blinded at the age of 6 weeks. She is reputed to have knocked off one hymn in 15 minutes. Charles Wesley (1707–88) wrote about 6,000 hymns. In the seventh (1950) edition of *Hymns Ancient and Modern* the works of John Mason Neale (1818–66) appear 56 times.

Theatre

Origins. Theatre as we know it has its origins in Greek drama performed in honor of a god, usually Dionysus. The earliest amphitheatres date from the 5th century B.C. The largest of all known is one at Megalopolis in central Greece, where the auditorium reached a height of 75 feet and had a capacity of 17,000. The first stone-built theatre in Rome (erected in 55 B.C.) could accommodate 40,000 spectators.

Oldest. The oldest indoor theatre in the world is the Teatro Olimpico in Vicenza, Italy. Designed in the Roman style by Andrea di Pietro, *alias* Palladio (1508–80), it was begun three months before his death and finished in 1582 by his pupil Vincenzo Scamozzi (1552-1616). It is preserved today in its original form.

Largest. The largest building used for theatre is the National People's Congress Building (*Ren min da hui tang*) on the west side of Tian an men Square, Peking, China. It was completed in 1959 and covers an area of 12.9 acres. The theatre seats 10,000 and is only occasionally used as such, as in 1964 for the play "The East Is Red."

The highest capacity purpose-built theatre is the Perth Entertainment Centre in Western Australia, completed at a cost in Australian dollars of $8.3 million in November, 1976, with a capacity of 8,003 seats. The stage area is 12,000 square feet.

Smallest. The smallest regularly operated professional theatre is the Mull Little Theatre, near Dervaig, Isle of Mull, Scotland, with a capacity of 36 seats.

Largest Amphitheatre. The largest amphitheatre ever built is the Flavian amphitheatre or Colosseum of Rome, Italy, completed in 80 A.D. Covering 5 acres and with a capacity of 87,000, it has a maximum length of 612 feet and maximum width of 515 feet.

Longest Runs

The longest continuous run of any show is of *The Mousetrap* by Agatha Christie (Lady Mallowan) (1890–1976). This thriller opened at the Ambassadors Theatre (capacity 453), London, on November 25, 1952, and moved after 8,862 performances "down the road" to St. Martin's Theatre, London, on March 25, 1974. The Silver Jubilee performance on November 25, 1977, was No. 10,390, and the 11,000th was on May 9, 1979.

The greatest number of performances of any theatrical presentation is 43,310 (to April 27, 1979) in the case of *The Golden Horseshoe Revue*— a 45-minute show staged at Disneyland Park, Anaheim, California. The show was first put on July 17, 1955. The three main performers, Fulton Burley, Wally Baag and Betty Taylor, play as many as five houses a day.

The Broadway record is 3,242 performances by *Fiddler on the Roof*, which, in its first run, opened on September 22, 1964, and closed on July 3, 1972. Paul Lipson played Tevye 1,811 times during which he had ten "wives" and 58 "daughters." The world gross earnings reached $64,300,000 on an original investment of $375,000.

The off-Broadway musical show *The Fantasticks* by Tom Jones and Harvey Schmidt achieved its 7,999th performance as it entered its 20th year at the Sullivan Street Playhouse, Greenwich Village, New York City, on May 3, 1979. It has been played in a record 3,788 productions in 55 countries.

One-Man Show. The longest run of one-man shows is 849 by Victor Borge in his *Comedy in Music* from October 2, 1953, to January 21, 1956, at the Golden Theater, New York City.

LONGEST RUNS: Victor Borge (above) played **849 performances** of his one-man show on Broadway. The Shakespearean actor and the cockney Indian (right) appear in "The Fantasticks," which continues to run in New York after **8,000 performances.**

The world aggregate record for one-man shows is 1,700 performances of *Brief Lives* by Roy Dotrice (born Guernsey, England, May 5, 1923) including 400 straight at the Mayfair Theatre, London, ending on July 20, 1974. He was on stage for more than 2½ hours per performance of this 17th century monologue, and required 3 hours for makeup and 1 hour for removal, thus aggregating 40 weeks in the chair as well.

Shortest Runs. The shortest run on record was that of *The Intimate Revue* at the Duchess Theatre, London, on March 11, 1930. Anything which could go wrong did. With scene changes taking up to 20 minutes apiece, the management scrapped seven scenes to get the finale on before midnight. The run was described as "half a performance." In a number of Broadway productions, the opening and closing nights have coincided.

Of the many Broadway and off-Broadway shows for which the opening and closing nights coincided, the most costly was *Kelly*, a musical costing $700,000 which suffered its double ceremony on February 6, 1965.

Youngest Broadway Producer. Margo Feiden (Margo Eden) (b. New York, December 2, 1944) produced the musical *Peter Pan*, which opened on April 3, 1961, when she was 16 years 5 months old. She wrote *Out Brief Candle*, which opened on August 18, 1962. She is now a leading art dealer.

MAN OF 1,000 DISGUISES: Jan Leighton of New York City has played over 1,259 historical roles on television, on the stage and for advertising. Left to right are Leighton as (top row) Sherlock Holmes, Popeye, Groucho Marx; (bottom row) Albert Einstein, Napoleon and Leighton himself, undisguised.

Longest Play. The longest recorded theatrical production has been *The Warp* by Neil Oram, directed by Ken Campbell, a 10-part play cycle played at the Institute of Contemporary Art, the Mall, London, January 18–20, 1979. Russell Denton was on stage for all but 5 minutes of the 18 hours 5 minutes. The three intermissions totaled 3 hours 10 minutes.

Most Durable Actor. Richard Hearne (born in Norwich, England, on January 30, 1909) played a baby at the age of 6 weeks and performed continuously through childhood in circus, pantomime and musical comedy. On Christmas 1977, he was in *Cinderella* at the London Palladium.

Most Durable Leading Actress. Dame Anna Neagle (born October 20, 1904) played the lead in *Charlie Girl* at the Adelphi Theatre, London, England, for 2,062 of 2,202 performances between December 15, 1965, and March 27, 1971. She played the same rôle a further 327 times in 327 performances in Australasia.

Most Roles. The greatest recorded number of theatrical, film and television rôles is 1,259 from 1951 to May, 1979 by Jan Leighton (U.S.).

Shakespeare. The first all-amateur company to have staged all 37 of Shakespeare's plays was The Southsea Shakespeare Actors, Hampshire, England, when in October, 1966, they presented *Cymbeline*. The amateur director throughout was K. Edmonds Gateloy, M.B.E. Ten members of the Royal Holloway College, Englefield Green, Surrey, England, completed a dramatic reading of all 37 plays, 154 sonnets and five narrative poems in 37 hours 22 minutes on April 15–16, 1977. The longest is *Hamlet*, with 4,042 lines and 29,551 words, 1,242 words longer than *Richard III*. Of Shakespeare's 1,277 speaking parts, the longest is *Hamlet* with 11,610 words.

Cabaret. The highest night-club fee in history was $100,000 collected by Liza Minnelli (born March 12, 1946) for the New Year's Eve show at The Colonie Hill Club, Long Island, New York, on January 1, 1975. Patrons paid $150 per seat. Don Tai Loy Ho (b. August 13, 1930, Oahu, Hawaii) has played the Polynesian Palace in the Reef Towers Hotel, Honolulu, since September, 1970. In 4,000 performances to January, 1979, he is estimated to have kissed over 250,000 grandmothers.

Longest Chorus Line. The world's longest permanent chorus line is formed by the Rockettes in the Radio City Music Hall, New York City, which opened in December, 1932. The 36 girls dance precision routines across the 144-foot-wide stage. There are 10 reserves for vacations and other absences.

Ice Shows. Holiday on Ice Productions Inc., founded by Morris Chalfen in 1945, stages the world's most costly live entertainment with its seven productions playing simultaneously in several of 75 countries drawing 20,000,000 spectators paying $40,000,000 in a year. The total number of skaters and other personnel exceeds 900.

LONGEST-RUNNING CABARET ACT: Don Ho has played over 4,000 performances since 1970 in the Reef Towers Hotel in Honolulu.

Shortest Criticism. The shortest dramatic criticism in theatrical history was that attributed to Wolcott Gibbs (1902–58), writing about the farce *Wham!*. He wrote the single word "Ouch!"

Most Ardent Theatregoer. The highest recorded number of paid theatre attendances is 3,325 shows in 26 years from March 28, 1953 to March 28, 1979, by John Iles of Salisbury, Wiltshire, England. He estimates that he has traveled 136,361 miles and seen 137,829 performers, spending 8,556 hours (over 50 weeks) inside theatres.

It has been estimated by the press that H. Howard Hughes (born 1904) of Fort Worth, Texas, had seen 4,160 shows in the period 1956–1976.

Edward Sutro (1900–1978) in England saw 3,000 first-night productions from 1916 to 1956, and possibly more than 5,000 in his 60 years of theatre-going.

Professional Wrestling. The highest-paid professional wrestler is reputedly Lars Anderson, who has a $2.3 million 3-year contract with the Universal Wrestling Alliance in Georgia. Lou Thesz (still active) has won 7 of the world's many "world" titles. "Fabulous" Moolah has won major U.S. women's alliance titles every year since 1956. The heaviest wrestler ever has been William J. Cobb of Macon, Georgia (b. 1926), who was billed in 1962 as the 802-lb. "Happy" Humphrey. Ed "Strangler" Lewis (1890–1966), *né* Robert H. Friedrich, fought 6,200 bouts in 44 years, losing only 33 matches. He won world titles in 1921, 1922, 1928 and 1931–32.

Radio Broadcasting

Origins. The earliest description of a radio transmission system was written by Dr. Mahlon Loomis (born New York State, 1826) on July 21, 1864, and demonstrated between two kites at Bear's Den, Loudoun County, Virginia, in October, 1866. He received U.S. Patent No. 129971, entitled Improvement in Telegraphing, on July 20, 1872.

Earliest Patent. The first patent for a system of communication by means of electro-magnetic waves, numbered No. 12039, was granted on June 2, 1896, to the Italian-Irish Marchese, Guglielmo Marconi (1874–1937). The first permanent wireless installation was at The Needles on the Isle of Wight, Hampshire, England, by Marconi's Wireless Telegraph Co., Ltd., in November, 1896.

A prior public demonstration of wireless transmission of speech was given in the town square of Murray, Kentucky, in 1892 by Nathan B. Stubblefield. He died, destitute, on March 28, 1928.

Earliest Broadcast. The first advertised broadcast was made on December 24, 1906, by Prof. Reginald Aubrey Fessenden (1868–1932) from the 420-foot mast of the National Electric Signaling Company at Brant Rock, Massachusetts. The transmission included the *Largo* by Georg Friedrich Händel (1685–1759) of Germany. Fessenden had achieved the broadcast of highly distorted speech as early as November, 1900.

Transatlantic Transmissions. The earliest transatlantic wireless signals (the letter S in Morse Code) were received by Marconi,

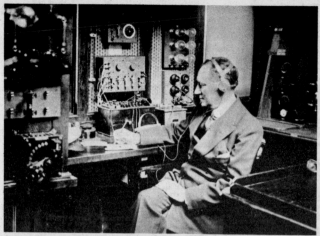

EARLIEST RADIO PATENT: Guglielmo Marconi received a patent for an electro-magnetic wave communication system on June 2, 1896.

George Stephen Kemp and Percy Paget from a 10-kilowatt station at Poldhu, Cornwall, England, at Signal Hill, St. John's, Newfoundland, Canada, at 12:30 p.m. on December 12, 1901. Human speech was first heard across the Atlantic in November, 1915, when a transmission from the U.S. Navy station at Arlington, Virginia, was received by U.S. radio-telephone engineers up in the Eiffel Tower, Paris.

Earliest Antipodal Reception. Frank Henry Alfred Walker (born November 11, 1904) on the night of November 12, 1924, received on his homemade 2-valve receiver on 75 meters at Crown Farm, Surrey, England, signals from Marconi's yacht *Electra* (call sign ICCM) which was then in Australian waters.

Earliest Radio-Microphone. The first radio-microphone, which was in essence also the first "bug," was devised by Reg Moores of Great Britain in 1947, and first used in the ice show *Aladdin* at Brighton Sports Stadium, England, in September, 1949.

Most Stations. The country with the greatest number of radio broadcasting stations is the U.S. In 1978, there were 8,608 authorized, of which 4,547 were AM and 4,061 FM.

Longest Broadcast. The longest continuous radio broadcast (excluding disc-jockeying) has been one of 336 hours by Bill Tinsley of WATN radio, Watertown, New York, March 17–31, 1979.

Highest Listener Response. The highest recorded response to a radio show occurred on November 27, 1974, when on a 5-hour talk show on WCAU, Philadelphia, Howard Sheldon, the astrologist, registered a total of 388,299 calls on the "Bill Corsair Show."

Television

Invention. The invention of television, the instantaneous viewing of distant objects, was not an act but a process of successive and inter-dependent discoveries. The first commercial cathode ray tube was introduced in 1897 by Karl Ferdinand Braun (1850–1918), but was not linked to "electric vision" until 1907 by Boris Rosing of Russia in St. Petersburg (now Leningrad). A. A. Campbell Swinton (G.B., 1863–1930) published the fundament of television transmission on June 18, 1908 in a brief letter to *Nature* entitled "Distant Electric Vision." The earliest public demonstration of television was given on January 27, 1926, by John Logie Baird (1888–1946) of Scotland, using a development of the mechanical scanning system suggested by Paul Nipkov in 1884. He had achieved the transmission of a Maltese Cross over 10 feet in Hastings, East Sussex, England, in February, 1924, and the first facial image (of William Taynton, 15) on October 30, 1925. Taynton had to be bribed with 2 shillings six-pence. A patent application for the Iconoscope (No. 2,141,059) had been filed on December 29, 1923, by Vladimir Kosma Zworykin (born in Russia in 1889, became a U.S. citizen in 1924), though not issued until December 20, 1938. The patent applied for on January 7, 1927, by Philo Taylor Farnsworth (U.S.) was, however, granted on August 26, 1930. Farnsworth succeeded with a low-definition image at 202 Green Street, Los Angeles, in November, 1927.

Alexander M. Poniatoff first demonstrated video tape recording, known as Ampex (his initials plus "ex" for excellence) in 1956.

Earliest Service. The first high-definition television broadcasting service was opened from Alexandra Palace, London, on November 2, 1936, when there were about 100 sets in the United Kingdom. A television station in Berlin, Germany, began low-definition broad-casting on March 22, 1935. The transmitter burned out in August, 1935.

Most Transmitters and Sets. In 1975, the total estimated number of television transmitters in use or under construction was 19,870 serving 363,770,000 sets (91per 1,000 people worldwide).

In the U.S., where 99 per cent of the population was reached by 1976, the number of color sets has grown from 200,000 in 1960 to 56,900,000 by October, 1978.

Most Television Viewing. In July, 1978, it was estimated that the *average* American child, by his or her 18th birthday, has watched the equivalent of 710 days (17,040 hours) of TV, seen more than 350,000 commercials and more than 15,000 TV murders. There are 571 TV sets per 1,000 people in the U.S., compared with 348 in Sweden and 315 in Britain.

Least Television Viewing. Iceland has a TV-free day on Thursday to reduce disruption of family life. Otherwise transmissions are normally limited to between 8 and 11 p.m.

Upper Volta had only one set for each 1,000 inhabitants by 1974.

Smallest Set. The world's smallest TV set is the 26-oz. Sinclair "Microvision" with overall dimensions of $6 \times 4 \times 1\frac{1}{2}$ inches and a

$128,000 WINNERS: Don Chu (left, in isolation booth) and Barbara Anne Eddy (right, with TV host Alex Trebek) have each won the $128,000 prize on a syndicated quiz show.

screen measuring 2 inches diagonally, manufactured by Sinclair Radionics Ltd. of Cambridgeshire, England. (See photo, page E.)

Transatlantic Transmission. The first transatlantic transmission by satellite was achieved at 1 a.m. on July 11, 1962, *via* the active satellite *Telstar I* from Andover, Maine, to Pleumeur Bodou, France. The picture was of Frederick R. Kappell, chairman of the American Telephone and Telegraph Company, which owned the satellite. The first "live" broadcast was made on July 23, 1962, and the first woman to appear was the *haute couturière* Ginette Spanier, directrice of Balmain, Paris, the next day. On February 9, 1928, the image of John Logie Baird and a Mrs. Howe was transmitted from Station 2KZ at Coulsdon, Surrey, England, to Station 2CVJ, Hartsdale, New York.

Greatest Audience. The greatest number of viewers for a televised event is an estimated 1,000,000,000 each for the live and recorded transmissions of the XXth Olympic Games in Munich, from August 26 to September 11, 1972, and the XXIst Games in Montreal, from July 17 to August 1, 1976.

Largest TV Prizes. The greatest amount won by an individual in TV prizes was $264,000 by Teddy Nadler on quiz programs in the United States up to September, 1958. He reportedly had to pay $155,000 in federal and state taxes, and remained unemployed thereafter.

On July 24, 1975, WABC-TV, New York City, transmitted the first televised Grand Tier draw of the State Lottery in which the winner took the grand prize of $1,000,000. This was, of course, taxable.

Don Chu of Forrest City, Arkansas, won $128,000 on the syndi-

HIGHEST-PAID TV PERFORMERS: Johnny Carson (left) now earns over $2.5 million a year for his "Tonight Show" duties. Barbara Walters (right) receives $1 million annually for her services as a newswoman.

cated quiz show "The $128,000 Question" aired on June 18, 1977. Barbara Anne Eddy of Vancouver, British Columbia, won the same amount on the show taped on February 1, 1978, and as a Canadian citizen she paid no tax on her winnings.

Largest Contract. The largest TV contract ever signed was one for $34,000,000 in a three-year no-option contract between Dean Martin (born Dino Paul Crocetti, on June 7, 1917) and NBC in 1968. Currently, television's highest-paid performer is Johnny Carson, the host of the *Tonight* show. His current five-year NBC contract reportedly calls for annual payments of some $2,500,000 for a 125-day working year, with perhaps double that in percentages on commercial fees.

The top-paid news performer is Barbara Walters, who was signed to a 5-year contract by ABC in April, 1976, for about $1,000,000 per year.

Mary Tyler Moore (born December 29, 1937), as head of her own production company, reputedly earned some $2,250,000 for the last series of episodes of the show in which she starred, which ended in 1977.

In 1977, James Coburn of Beverly Hills, California, was reputedly paid $500,000 for uttering two words on a series of Schlitz beer commercials. The words "Schlitz Light" were thus priced at a quarter of a million dollars per syllable.

Peter Falk (born September 16, 1927) was paid from $300,000 to $350,000 per single episode (six total) for his series *Columbo*, so totaling $1,950,000 in 1976.

Largest Production. The BBC production of the 37 plays of Shakespeare in 1978–1984 will cost a minimum of $14,000,000. The series was conceived by its producer, Cedric Messina.

Longest Program. The longest pre-scheduled telecast on record was one of 163 hours 18 minutes by GTV 9 of Melbourne, Australia, covering the Apollo XI moon mission July 19–26, 1969. The longest continuous TV transmission under a single director was the Avro Television Production *Open Het Dorpe* transmitted in the Netherlands November 26–27, 1962 for 23 hours 20 minutes under the direction of Theo Ordaman.

Most Durable Show. The world's most durable TV show is NBC's *Meet the Press,* first transmitted on November 6, 1947, and weekly since September 12, 1948. It was originated by Lawrence E. Spivak, who until 1975 appeared weekly as either moderator or panel member.

Greatest Sale. The greatest number of episodes of any TV program ever sold was 1,144 episodes of *Coronation Street* to CBKST, Saskatoon, Saskatchewan, Canada, by Granada Television, on May 31, 1971. This constituted 20 days 15 hours 44 minutes of continuous viewing.

Most Successful Telethons. The most successful TV appeals in the world are those transmitted in New Zealand. The telethon appeal on South Pacific TV, Auckland, in 1978 for the Arthritis and Rheumatism Foundation raised $3,002,750 from an audience of 2,550,000 people.

LARGEST TV PRODUCTION: The BBC Shakespeare series currently in production will include (clockwise from top left) *Julius Caesar, Romeo and Juliet, Richard II, Measure for Measure* and all 33 others.

Most Prolific Scriptwriter. The most prolific television writer in the world is the Rt. Hon. Lord Willis (b. January 13, 1918), who in the period 1949–79 has created 24 series, 24 stage plays, and 21 feature films. His total output since 1945 can be estimated at 15,500,000 words.

Highest TV Advertising Rates. The highest TV advertising rate was reportedly $370,000 per minute for NBC network prime time during the transmission of the Super Bowl on January 14, 1979.

Motion Pictures

Earliest. The greatest impetus in the development of cinematography came from the inventiveness of Etienne Jules Marey (1830–1903) of France in the 1870's.

The earliest demonstration of a celluloid cinematograph film on a screen was given at 44 Rue de Rennes, Paris, France, on March 22, 1895, by Auguste Marie Louis Nicolas Lumière (1862–1954) and Louis Jean Lumière (1864–1948), French brothers. The film was entitled *La Sortie des Ouvriers de l'Usine Lumière*, taken probably in August or September, 1894, outside the factory gates at Lyons. Louis Aimé Augustin Le Prince, according to evidence in *The Shell Book of Firsts*, achieved dim moving outlines on a white-washed wall at the Institute for the Deaf, Washington Heights, New York City, as early as 1885.

The earliest sound-on-film motion picture was achieved by Eugene Augustin Lauste (b. Paris, January 17, 1857) who patented his process on August 11, 1906 and produced a workable system using a string galvanometer in 1910 in London. The event is more usually attributed to Dr. Lee de Forest (1873–1961) in New York City, on March 13, 1923. The first all-talking picture was *Lights of New York*, shown at the Strand Theatre, New York City, on July 6, 1928.

Movie-Going. The people of Taiwan go to the movies more often than those of any other country in the world, with an average of 66 attendances per person per year according to the latest data. The Soviet Union claims to have the most movie theatres in the world, with 163,400 in 1974, but this includes buildings equipped with 16-mm. projectors. The U.S. has some 16,000 actual movie theatres.

Most Movie Theatre Seats. The Falkland Islands (off South America's Straits of Magellan) and the Cook Islands (in the South Pacific) have more seats per total population than any other country, with 250 for each 1,000 inhabitants. The least number are in the Central African Empire which has 8 theatres.

Oldest Theatre. The earliest structure designed and exclusively used for exhibiting projected films is believed to be one erected at the Atlanta Show, Georgia, in October, 1895, to exhibit C. F. Jenkins' phantoscope.

Largest Drive-In. The world's largest drive-in cinema is at Newington, Connecticut, with a capacity for 4,000 cars.

BIGGEST MONEY-MAKER:
Shown here are the two robot
stars of "Star Wars," the biggest
box office success in movie history.

Biggest Screen. The permanently installed cinema screen with
the largest area is one 70 feet tall by 96 feet wide, installed in the
Pictorium Theater at Marriott's Great America Entertainment
Center, Santa Clara, California, on May 16, 1978. It was made by
Harkness Screens Ltd. of Hertfordshire, England.

A temporary screen 297 feet by 33 feet was used at the 1937 Paris
Exposition.

Most Expensive Film. The most expensive film ever made is
War and Peace, the U.S.S.R. government adaptation of the masterpiece of Tolstoy directed by Sergei Bondarchuk (born 1921) over
the period 1962–67. The total cost has been stated to be more than
$96,000,000. More than 165,000 uniforms had to be made. The
re-creation of the Battle of Borodino involved 120,000 Red Army
"extras" at 3 rubles ($3.30) per month. The film runs for 6 hours
13 minutes.

The highest price ever paid for film rights is $9,500,000 announced
on January 20, 1978 by Columbia for *Annie*, the Broadway musical
based on the comic strip *Little Orphan Annie*, which opened at the
Alvin Theater in New York City on April 21, 1977.

Highest Box Office Gross. The film with the highest world
gross earnings is *Star Wars*, written and produced by Gary Kartz and
directed by George Lucas, which from May 25, 1977, to January 1,
1979, grossed $267 million worldwide.

Longest Film. The longest film ever shown is *The Human Condition*, directed in three parts by Masaki Kobayashi of Japan. It

lasts 9 hours 27 minutes, excluding breaks. It was shown in Tokyo in October, 1961, at an admission price of 250 yen (70 cents).

The longest film ever released was * * * * by Andy Warhol (born Andrew Warhola in Cleveland, Ohio, 1931), which lasted 24 hours. It proved, not surprisingly, except reportedly to its creator, a commercial failure, and was withdrawn and re-released in 90-minute form as *The Loves of Ondine*.

Highest Earnings by an Actor. The highest rate of pay in cinema history is being contested between Marlon Brando (b. April 3, 1924) for his brief part in *Superman* and Steve McQueen (b. 1930) for his role in *Tai Pan*. Each received in excess of $2,500,000, but the final amount will depend on box office percentages.

Largest Studios. The largest complex of film studios are those of Universal City, Los Angeles. The back lot contains 561 buildings. There are 34 sound stages.

Oscars. Walter (Walt) Elias Disney (1901–1966) won more "Oscars"—the awards of the Academy of Motion Picture Arts and Sciences, instituted on May 16, 1929, for 1927–28—than any other person. His total was 17 Oscars plus 12 certificates and plaques for a total of 29 awards from 1931 to 1969. The films with most awards have been *Ben Hur* (1959) with 11, followed by *Gone with the Wind* (1939) and *West Side Story* (1961), both with 10. The film with the highest number of nominations was *All About Eve* (1950) with 14. It won six.

The only performer to win three Oscars for her starring rôles has been Katharine Hepburn (born November 9, 1909), in *Morning Glory* (1933), *Guess Who's Coming to Dinner* (1967) and *The Lion in Winter* (1968). All three Oscars are on display at the Guinness World Records Exhibit Hall in New York City.

The youngest person ever to win an Oscar was Shirley Temple with her 1934 award at age 6, and the oldest is George Burns at age 80 for *The Sunshine Boys* in 1976.

Oscars are named after Oscar Pierce of Texas. When the figurines were first delivered to the executive offices of the Academy of Motion Picture Arts and Sciences, the Executive Secretary exclaimed, "Why, they look just like my uncle Oscar." And the name stuck.

Phonograph

The phonograph was first *conceived* by Charles Cros (1842–88), a French poet and scientist who described his idea in sealed papers deposited in the French Academy of Sciences on April 30, 1877. The first practical device was realized by Thomas Alva Edison (1847–1931), who gained his first patent on February 19, 1878 for a machine constructed by his mechanic, John Kruesi. It was first demonstrated on December 7, 1877.

The first practical hand-cranked, wax-coated-cylinder phonograph was manufactured in the United States by Chichester Bell and

Charles Sumner Tainter in 1886. The forerunner of the modern disc phonograph was patented in 1887 by Emile Berliner (1851–1929), a German immigrant to the U.S. Although a toy machine based on his principle was produced in Germany in 1889, the gramophone was not a serious commercial competitor to the cylinder phonograph until 1896.

Pre-recorded tapes were first marketed by Recording Associates in New York City in 1950.

The country with the greatest number of record players is the U.S. with an estimated 75,300,000 by Dec., 1976. A total of more than half a billion dollars is spent annually on 500,000 juke boxes in the U.S.

Sales in the U.S. of discs and tapes reached $2,740,000,000 in 1976, which includes sales of 273 million stereo L.P.'s, 190 million singles and 127.8 million stereo tapes.

In Sweden, disc and tape sales were a record $17.92 per head in 1976.

Oldest Record. The oldest record in the British Broadcasting Corporation's library is an Edison solid-wax cylinder, recorded in Edison's laboratory and dated June 26, 1888. The BBC library, the world's largest, contains over 750,000 records, including 5,250 with no known matrix. The library also contains a collection of early Berliner discs.

The earliest jazz record made was *Indiana* and *The Dark Town Strutters' Ball*, recorded for the Columbia label in New York City, on or about January 30, 1917, by the Original Dixieland Jazz Band, led by Dominick (Nick) James La Rocca (1889–1961). This was released on May 31, 1917. The first jazz record to be released was the O.D.J.B.'s *Livery Stable Blues* (recorded February 24), backed by *The Dixie Jazz Band One-Step* (recorded February 26), released by Victor on March 7, 1917.

Smallest Record. The smallest functional record is one 1⅜ inches in diameter of "God Save the King" of which 250 were made by HMV Record Co. in 1924.

TOP-SELLING SINGERS: Bing Crosby (left) received a platinum record in 1960 to commemorate his 200,000,000th record sale. Elvis Presley (right) earned a record 37 golden discs.

Most Successful Recording Artist. On June 9, 1960, the Hollywood Chamber of Commerce presented Harry Lillis (*alias* Bing) Crosby, Jr. (1904–1977) with a platinum disc to commemorate the alleged 200,000,000th record sold from 2,600 singles and 125 albums he had recorded. On September 15, 1970, he received a second platinum disc when Decca Records claimed a sale of 300,650,000 discs.

His first commercial recording was *I've Got the Girl* recorded on October 18, 1926 (master number W142785 (Take 3) issued on the Columbia label), and his first million-seller was *Sweet Leilani* in 1937. No detailed audit of his global lifetime sales from his royalty reports has ever been published.

Similarly no independently audited figures have been published for Elvis Aaron Presley (1935–1977). In view of Presley's 150 major hits on singles and 70 best-selling albums from 1956 and continuing after his death, it may be assumed that it was he who succeeded Crosby as the top-selling solo artist.

Most Successful Group. The singers with the greatest sales of any group were The Beatles. This group from Liverpool, England, comprised George Harrison (born February 25, 1943), John Ono (formerly John Winston) Lennon (born October 9, 1940), James Paul McCartney (born June 18, 1942) and Richard Starkey, *alias* Ringo Starr (born July 7, 1940).

The all-time Beatles sales by the end of 1978 have been estimated at 100 million singles and 100 million albums—a total unmatched by any other recording act.

Golden Discs

Earliest. The first recorded piece to sell a million copies and become a "golden disc" were performances by Enrico Caruso (born Naples, Italy, 1873 and died 1921) of the aria *Vesti la giubba* (*On with* *the Motley*) from the opera *I Pagliacci* by Ruggiero Leoncavallo (1858–1919), the earliest version of which was recorded on November 12, 1902.

The first single recording to surpass the million mark was Alma Gluck's rendition of *Carry Me Back to Old Virginny* on the Red Seal Victor label on a 12-inch single-faced (later backed) record (No. 74420).

The first literally golden disc was one sprayed by RCA Victor for presentation to Glenn Miller (1904–44) for his *Chattanooga Choo Choo* on February 10, 1942.

Most. The only *audited* measure of million-selling singles and 500,000-selling albums within the U.S. is certification by the Recording Industry Association of America (R.I.A.A.) introduced March 14, 1958. Out of the 2,390 R.I.A.A. gold-record awards made to January 1, 1979, the most have gone to The Beatles with 42 (plus one with Billy Preston) as a group. Paul McCartney has an additional 16 awards both on his own and with the group Wings.

The most awards to an individual is 38 to Elvis Presley (born at Tupelo, Mississippi, 1935, died 1977), spanning 1958 to January 1, 1979. Presley's worldwide total of million-selling singles has been authoritatively put at "approaching 80."

Most Recorded Songs. Two songs have each been recorded over 1,000 times—*Yesterday* by Paul McCartney and John Lennon, with 1,186 versions between 1965 and January 1, 1973, and *Tie a Yellow Ribbon Round the Old Oak Tree*, written by Irwin Levine and L. Russell Brown, with more than 1,000 versions recorded from 1973 to January 1, 1979.

Biggest Sellers. The greatest seller of any record to date is *White Christmas* by Irving Berlin (born Israel Bailin, at Tyumen, Russia, May 11, 1888), with 25,000,000 for the Crosby single (recorded May 29, 1942) and more than 100,000,000 in other versions.

The highest claim for any "pop" record is an unaudited 25,000,000 for *Rock Around the Clock*, copyrighted in 1953 by the late Max Friedman and James E. Myers, under the name of Jimmy De Knight, and recorded on April 12, 1954 by Bill Haley and the Comets.

Advance Sales. The greatest advance sale was 2,100,000 for *Can't Buy Me Love* by The Beatles, released in the U.S. on March 16, 1964.

Fastest Seller. The fastest-selling record of all time is *John Fitzgerald Kennedy—A Memorial Album* (Premium Albums), an L.P. recorded on November 22, 1963, the day of Mr. Kennedy's assassination, which sold 4,000,000 copies at 99 cents in six days (December 7–12, 1963), thus ironically beating the previous speed record set by the humorous L.P. *The First Family* about the Kennedys in 1962–63.

Long-Players. The best-selling album of all time is the double album (4 sides) of the soundtrack of the film *Saturday Night Fever*, with 25 million copies sold worldwide by May 1, 1979. The majority of the songs were written by the Bee Gees, comprising the three Gibb brothers, Barry Alan (born September 1, 1947) and the twins Robin and Maurice (born December 22, 1949).

The first classical long-player to sell a million was a performance featuring the pianist Harvey Lavan (Van) Cliburn, Jr. (born in Kilgore, Texas, July 12, 1934) of the *Piano Concerto No. 1* by Pyotr Ilyich Tchaikovsky (1840–93) of Russia. This recording was made in 1958 and sales reached 1,000,000 by 1961, 2,000,000 by 1965 and about 2,500,000 by January, 1970.

Best-Seller Chart Duration Record. *Billboard* first published an album chart on March 15, 1945, when the No. 1 record was *King Cole Trio* featuring Nat "King" Cole (born March 17, 1919, died February 15, 1965). *South Pacific* was No. 1 for 69 weeks (non-consecutive) from May, 1949. *Johnny's Greatest Hits* by Johnny Mathis stayed on the chart for 490 weeks (over 9 years) from April, 1958. The Beatles had the most No. 1 recordings (15) and Presley the most hit albums (75 from 1956 to May, 1979).

Singles record charts were first published by *Billboard* on July 20, 1940, when the No. 1 record was *I'll Never Smile Again* by Tommy Dorsey (born November 19, 1905, died November 26, 1956). Three discs have stayed at the top for a record 13 consecutive weeks—*Frenesi* by Artie Shaw from December, 1940; *I've Heard that Song Before* by Harry James from February, 1943; and *Goodnight Irene* by Gordon Jenkins and the Weavers from August, 1950. *I Go Crazy* by Paul Davis stayed on the chart for 40 consecutive weeks from August, 1977. The Beatles have had the most No. 1 records (20) and Elvis Presley had the most hit singles on the *Billboard Hot 100*—97 from 1956 to May, 1978.

Most Recordings. Miss Lata Mangeshker (born 1928) has reportedly recorded between 1948 and 1974 not less than 25,000 solo, duet and chorus-backed songs in 20 Indian languages. She frequently has 5 sessions in a day and has "backed" 1,800 films to 1974.

Loudest Pop Group. The amplification for *The Who* concert at Charlton Athletic Football Ground, London, England, on May 31, 1976, provided by a Tasco P.A. system, had a total power of 76,000 watts from eighty 800 W Crown D.C. 300 A amplifiers and twenty 600 W Phase Linear 200's. The readings at 50 yards from the front of the sound system were 120 decibels. Exposure to such noise levels causes P.S.H.—Permanent Shift of Hearing or partial deafness.

Chapter Seven

THE WORLD'S STRUCTURES

Earliest Structures

The earliest known human structure is a rough circle of loosely piled lava blocks found in 1960 on the lowest cultural level at the Lower Paleolithic site at Olduvai Gorge in Tanganyika (now part of Tanzania). The structure was associated with artifacts and bones and may represent a work-floor, dating to *circa* 1,750,000 B.C.

The earliest evidence of *buildings* yet discovered is that of 21 huts with hearths of pebble-lined pits and delimited by stake holes, found in October, 1965, at the Terra Amata site in Nice, France. Originally dated to 300,000 B.C., they are now thought to belong more likely to the Acheulián culture of 120,000 years ago. Excavation carried out between June 28 and July 5, 1966, revealed one hut with palisaded walls having axes of 49 and 20 feet.

The oldest free-standing structures in the world are now believed to be the megalithic temples at Mgarr and Skarba in Malta and Ggantija in Gozo, dating from *c.* 3250 B.C.

The remains of a stone tower 20 feet high built into the walls of Jericho have been excavated, and dated to 5000 B.C.

1. Buildings for Working

Largest Buildings

Commercial. The greatest ground area covered by any building in the world is that by the Ford Parts Redistribution Center, Brownstown Township, Michigan. It encloses a floor area 3,100,000 square feet or 71.16 acres. It was opened on May 20, 1971, and employs 1,400 people. The fire-control system comprises 70 miles of pipelines with 37,000 sprinklers.

The building with the largest cubic capacity in the world is the Boeing Company's main assembly plant at Everett, Washington, completed in 1968. The building, constructed for the manufacture of Boeing 747 jet airliners, has a maximum height of 115 feet and has a capacity of 200 million cubic feet.

Scientific. The most capacious scientific building in the world is the Vehicle Assembly Building (VAB) at Complex 39, the selected site for the final assembly and launching of the Apollo moon space-craft on the Saturn V rocket, at the John F. Kennedy Space Center (KSC), near Cape Canaveral (formerly Cape Kennedy), Florida. It is a steel-framed building measuring 716 feet in length, 518 feet in width and 525 feet high. The building contains four bays, each with its own door 460 feet high. Construction began in April, 1963, by the Ursum Consortium. Its floor area is 343,500 square feet (7.87 acres) and its capacity is 129,482,000 cubic feet. The building was "topped out" on April 14, 1965, at a cost of $108,700,000.

TALLEST STRUCTURES IN THE WORLD—PROGRESSIVE RECORDS

Height in feet	Structure	Location	Material	Building or Completion Dates
204	Djoser step pyramid (earliest Pyramid)	Saqqâra, Egypt	Tura limestone casing	c. 2650 B.C.
294	Pyramid of Meidum	Meidum, Egypt	Tura limestone casing	c. 2600 B.C.
c. 336	Snefru Bent pyramid	Dahshûr, Egypt	Tura limestone casing	c. 2600 B.C.
342	Snefru North Stone pyramid	Dahshûr, Egypt	Tura limestone casing	c. 2600 B.C.
480.9[1]	Great Pyramid of Cheops (Khufu)	El Gîzeh, Egypt	Tura limestone casing	c. 2580 B.C.
525[2]	Lincoln Cathedral, Central Tower	Lincoln, England	lead sheathed wood	c. 1307–1548
489[3]	St. Paul's Cathedral	London, England	lead sheathed wood	1315–1561
465	Minster of Notre Dame	Strasbourg, France	lead sheathed wood	1420–1439
502[4]	St. Pierre de Beauvais	Beauvais, France	Vosges sandstone	–1568
475	St. Nicholas Church	Hamburg, Germany	lead sheathed wood	1846–1847
485	Cologne Cathedral	Cologne, West Germany	stone and iron	1823–1876
513	Rouen Cathedral	Rouen, France	cast iron	–1880
555.9[5]	Washington Memorial	Washington, D.C.	stone	1848–1884
985.9[6]	La Tour Eiffel	Paris, France	iron	1887–1889
1,046	Chrysler Building	New York City	steel and concrete	1929–1930
1,250[7]	Empire State Building	New York City	steel and concrete	1929–1930
1,572	KWTV Television Mast	Oklahoma City	steel	Nov. 1954
1,610[8]	KSWS Television Mast	Roswell, N. Mex.	steel	Dec. 1956
1,619	WGAN Television Mast	Portland, Maine	steel	Sept. 1959
1,676	KFVS Television Mast	Cape Girardeau, Missouri	steel	June 1960
1,749	WTVM-& WRBL-TV Mast	Columbus, Georgia	steel	May 1962
1,749	WBIR-TV Mast	Knoxville, Tennessee	steel	Sept. 1963
2,063	KTHI-TV Mast	Fargo, North Dakota	steel	Nov. 1963
2,120.6	Warszawa Radio Mast	Plock, Poland	galvanized steel	July 1974

[1] Original height. With loss of pyramidion (topmost stone) height now 449 ft. 6 in.
[2] Fell in a storm.
[3] Struck by lightning and destroyed on June 4, 1561.
[4] Fell April, 1573, shortly after completion.
[5] Sinking at a rate of 5 inches per year since 1884.
[6] Original height. With addition of T.V. antenna in 1957, now 1,052 ft. 4 in.
[7] Original height. With addition of T.V. tower on May 1, 1951, now 1,472 ft. On October 11, 1972, it was revealed that the top 15 stories might be replaced by 33 to give the old champion 113 stories and a height of 1,494 feet.
[8] Fell in gale in 1960.

LARGEST OFFICE BUILDING: The Pentagon in Arlington, Virginia, covers more ground area than any other office structure in the world.

Administrative. The largest ground area covered by any office building is that of the Pentagon, in Arlington, Virginia. Built to house the U.S. Defense Department's offices, it was completed on January 15, 1943, and cost about $83,000,000. Each of the outermost sides of the Pentagon is 921 feet long and the perimeter of the building is about 1,500 yards. The five stories of the building enclose a floor area of 6,500,000 square feet. During the day 29,000 people work in the building. The telephone system of the building has more than 44,000 telephones connected by 160,000 miles of cable and its 220 staff members handle 280,000 calls a day. Two restaurants, six cafeterias and ten snack bars and a staff of 675 form the catering department of the building. The corridors measure 17 miles in length and there are 7,748 windows to be cleaned.

Office. The largest office buildings in the world are the twin towers comprising the World Trade Center in New York City, with a total of 4,370,000 square feet (100.32 acres) of rentable space in each. The taller tower is 1,350 feet high.

Tallest Buildings

The tallest office building in the world is the Sears Tower, the national headquarters of Sears Roebuck & Co. on Wacker Drive, Chicago, with 110 stories, rising to 1,454 feet and completed in 1974. Its gross area is 4,400,000 square feet (101.0 acres). It was topped out on May 4, 1973, surpassing the World Trade Center in New York in height, at 2:35 p.m. on March 6, 1973, with the first steel column reaching to the 104th story. The addition of two TV antennae brought the total height to 1,559 feet. The building's population is 16,700, served by 103 elevators and 18 escalators. It has 16,000 windows.

In Asia, where buildings must be constructed to be earthquake-proof, the tallest building is the 60-story "Sunshine 60" in Ikebukuro, Tokyo, Japan, completed in 1978 to a height of 787.4 feet.

Habitations

Greatest Altitude. The highest inhabited buildings in the world are those in the Indian-Tibetan border fort of Basisi at *c.* 19,700 feet.

A formerly occupied 3-room dwelling was discovered in April, 1961, at 21,650 feet on Cerro Llullaillaco (22,058 feet), on the Argentine-Chile border, believed to date from the late pre-Columbian period *c.* 1480. An unnamed settlement on the T'e-li-mo trail in southern Tibet is at an apparent altitude of 19,800 ft.

Northernmost. The most northerly habitation in the world is the Danish scientific station set up in 1952 in Pearyland, northern Greenland, more than 900 miles north of the Arctic Circle. The U.S.S.R. and the U.S. have maintained research stations on Arctic ice floes, which have drifted close to the North Pole. The U.S.S.R.'s "North Pole 15," which drifted 1,250 miles, passed within 1¼ miles of the North Pole in December, 1967.

The most northerly continuously inhabited place is the Canadian Department of National Defense outpost at Alert on Ellesmere Island, Northwest Territories (Lat. 82°30'N., Long. 62°W.) set up in 1950.

Southernmost. The most southerly permanent human habitation is the United States' Scott-Amundsen Base at the South Pole (see page 143), completed in 1957 and replaced in 1975.

Largest Embassy. The largest embassy in the world is the U.S.S.R. embassy on Bei Xiao Jie, Peking, China, in the north-eastern corner of the Northern walled city. The whole 45-acre area of the old Orthodox Church mission (established 1728), now known as the *Bei guan*, was handed over to the U.S.S.R. in 1949.

Industrial Structures

Largest Garage. The world's largest garage (as opposed to parking lot) is at O'Hare Airport, Chicago, with 6 levels and a capacity for 9,250 cars. It is operated by Allright Auto Parks, Inc., the world's largest parking company.

The largest private garage ever built was one for 100 cars at the Long Island, New York, mansion of William Kissam Vanderbilt (1849–1920).

The world's largest parking lot is believed to be that at the National Exhibition Centre in Birmingham, England, with a capacity of 15,000 cars.

Largest Hangars. The largest hangar is the Goodyear Airship hangar at Akron, Ohio, which measures 1,175 feet long, 325 feet

TALLEST OFFICE BUILDING: The Sears Tower dominates the Chicago skyline, standing 1,454 feet tall. Two TV antennae bring the total height to 1,559 feet.

wide and 200 feet high. It covers 364,000 square feet (8.35 acres) and has a capacity of 55,000,000 cubic feet.

The largest single fixed-wing aircraft hangar is the Lockheed-Georgia engineering test center at Marietta, Georgia, measuring 630 feet by 480 feet (6.94 acres) completed in 1967. The maintenance hangar at Frankfurt/Main Airport, West Germany, covers slightly less area but has a frontage of 902 feet. The cable-supported roof has a span of 426.5 feet.

Delta Air Lines' jet base, on a 140-acre site at Hartsfield International Airport, Atlanta, Georgia, has 36 acres under its roof.

Tallest Chimney. The world's tallest chimney is the $5,500,000 International Nickel Company's stack, 1,245 feet 8 inches tall, at Copper Cliff, Sudbury, Ontario, Canada, completed in 60 days in

1970. It was built by Canadian Kellogg Ltd. and the diameter tapers from 116.4 feet at the base to 51.8 feet at the top. It weighs 42,998 tons and became operational in 1971.

The world's most massive chimney is one of 1,148 feet at Puentes, Spain, built by M. W. Kellogg Co. It contains 20,600 cubic yards of concrete and 2,900,000 lbs. of steel and has an internal volume of 6,700,000 cubic feet.

Largest Cooling Tower. The largest cooling tower in the world is adjacent to the nuclear power plant at Uentrop, West Germany, completed in 1976, which is 590 feet tall.

Largest Sewage Works. The largest single sewage works is the West-Southwest Treatment Plant, opened in 1940 on a site of 501 acres in Chicago. It serves an area containing 2,940,000 people. It treated an average of more than 835,000,000 gallons of wastes per day in 1973. The capacity of its sedimentation and aeration tanks is 1,600,000 cubic yards.

Largest Glass Greenhouse. The largest glasshouse is one covering 7.34 acres owned by Van Heyningen Bros., at Holland Nurseries, Littlehampton, West Sussex, England.

Grain Elevator. The world's largest single-unit grain elevator is that operated by the C-G-F Grain Company at Wichita, Kansas. Consisting of a triple row of storage tanks, 123 on each side of the central loading tower or "head house," the unit is 2,717 feet long and 100 feet wide. Each tank is 120 feet high, with an inside diameter of 30 feet, giving a total storage capacity of 20,000,000 bushels of wheat. The largest collection of elevators in the world is at Thunder Bay, Ontario, Canada, on Lake Superior, with a total capacity of 103,900,000 bushels.

Wooden Buildings. The oldest extant wooden buildings in the world are those comprising the Pagoda, Chumanar Gate, and the Temple of Horyu (Horyu-ji), built at Nara, Japan, in 607 A.D. The nearby Daibutsuden, built in 1704–11, once measured 285.4 feet long, 167.3 feet wide and 153.3 feet tall. The present dimensions are 187 feet by 165.6 feet by 159.7 feet.

The world's largest timber buildings are the two U.S. Navy airship hangars built in 1942–43 at Tillamook, Oregon. Now used as a saw mill by the Louisiana-Pacific Corporation, they measure 1,000 feet long, 170 feet high at the crown and 296 feet wide at the base. They are valued at $6 million.

Air-Supported Structure. The world's largest air-supported roof is the roof of the 80,600-capacity octagonal Pontiac Silverdome Stadium, Michigan, measuring 522 feet wide and 722 feet long. The air pressure is 5 lbs. per square inch, supporting the 10-acre translucent fiberglass roofing. The structural engineers were Geiger-Berger Associates of New York City. The largest standard-size air hall is one in Lima, Ohio, which is 860 feet long, 140 feet wide and 65 feet high made by Irvin Industries of Stamford, Connecticut. (See photo, page E.)

2. Buildings for Living

Castles and Forts

Earliest. Fortifications existed in all the great early civilizations, including that of ancient Egypt from 3000 B.C. Fortified castles in the more accepted sense only existed much later. The oldest in the world is that at Gomdan, in the Yemen, which originally had 20 stories and dates from before 100 A.D.

Largest. The largest inhabited castle is the British Royal residence of Windsor Castle at New Windsor, Berkshire. It is primarily of 12th-century construction and is in the form of a waisted parallelogram, 1,890 feet by 540 feet. The total area of Dover Castle (England), however, covers 34 acres with a width of 1,100 feet and a curtain wall of 1,800 feet, or, if underground works are taken in, 2,300 feet.

The largest ancient castle in the world is Prague Castle, Czechoslovakia, originating in the 9th century. It is a very oblong irregular polygon with an axis of 1,870 feet and an average traverse diameter of 420 feet, with a surface area of 18 acres.

The walls of Babylon, north of Al Hillah, Iraq, built in 600 B.C. were up to 85 feet in thickness.

Largest Palace. The largest palace in the world is the Imperial Palace (*Gu gong*) in the center of Peking (*Bei jing*, the northern capital), China, which covers a rectangle 1,050 yards by 820 yards, an area of 177.9 acres. The outline survives from the construction of the third Ming emperor Yung-lo of 1402–24, but due to constant rearrangements most of the intramural buildings are 18th century. These consist of 5 halls and 17 palaces of which the last occupied by the last Empress was the Palace of Accumulated Elegance (*Chu xia gong*) until 1924.

The largest residential palace in the world is the Vatican Palace, in the Vatican City, an enclave in Rome, Italy. Covering an area of 13½ acres, it has 1,400 rooms, chapels and halls, of which the oldest date from the 15th century.

The world's largest moats are those which surround the Imperial Palace in Peking. From plans drawn by French sources they appear to measure 54 yards wide and have a total length of 3,600 yards. The city's moats total 23½ miles in all.

Apartments

Largest. The largest apartment building is believed to be Dolphin Square, London, covering a site of 7½ acres. The building occupies the four sides of a square enclosing gardens of about 3 acres. Dolphin Square contains 1,220 separate and self-contained flats, an underground garage for 300 cars with filling and service station, a swimming pool, 8 squash courts, a tennis court and an indoor shopping center. It cost £1,750,000 ($8,750,000) to build in 1936 but was sold to Westminster City Council for £4,500,000 ($12,600,000) in January, 1963. Its nine stories house 3,000 people.

The Hyde Park development in Sheffield, Yorkshire, England, comprises 1,322 dwellings and an estimated population of 4,675 persons. It was built between 1959 and 1966.

Tallest. The tallest block of apartments in the world is Lake Point Towers of 70 stories, 645 feet high in Chicago.

Hotels

Largest. The hotel with the most rooms in the world is the Hotel Rossiya in Moscow, U.S.S.R., with 3,200 rooms providing accommodation for 5,350 guests. It would thus require more than 8½ years to spend one night in each room. In addition, there is a 21-story "Presidential" tower in the central courtyard. The hotel employs about 3,000 people and has 93 elevators. The ballroom is reputed to be the world's largest. Muscovites are not permitted as residents while foreigners are charged 16 times more than the low rate charged to officials of the U.S.S.R. It opened in 1967.

The largest commercial hotel building in the world is the Waldorf-Astoria, on Park Avenue, between 49th and 50th Streets, New York City. It occupies a complete block of 81,337 square feet (1.87 acres) and reaches a maximum height of 625 feet 7 inches. The Waldorf-Astoria has 47 stories and 1,852 guest rooms and maintains the largest hotel radio receiving system in the world. The Waldorf can accommodate 10,000 people at one time and has a staff of 1,700. The restaurants have catered for parties up to 6,000 at a time. The coffee-makers' daily output reaches 1,000 gallons. The electricity bill is about $2,000,000 each year. The hotel has housed six heads of state simultaneously. It was opened on October 1, 1931.

Tallest. The world's tallest hotel, measured from the street level of its main entrance to the top, is the 723-foot-tall 70-story Peachtree Center Plaza Hotel in Atlanta, Georgia, opened in January, 1976. The $50,000,000, 1,100-room hotel was designed by architect John Portman, is operated by Western International Hotels, and owned

LARGEST HOUSE: Biltmore House in Asheville, North Carolina, has 250 rooms and was originally surrounded by 119,000 acres. When it was built by a Vanderbilt in the early 1890's, it cost $4,100,000, but today it is valued at $55,000,000.

by Portman Properties. The Detroit Plaza Hotel in Detroit is taller when measured from its back entrance to the top. This hotel, opened in early 1977, is 748 feet tall starting from its lower street level. Designed by the same architect as the Peachtree, it is operated also by Western International Hotels, and contains 1,400 rooms.

Most Expensive. The world's costliest hotel accommodation is the Celestial Suite on the ninth floor of the Astroworld Hotel, Houston, Texas, which is rented for $2,500 a day. This compares with the official New York City Presidential Suite in the Waldorf-Astoria at $1,200 a day.

Spas

The largest spa in the world measured by number of available hotel rooms is Vichy, Allier, France, with 14,000 rooms. Spas are named after the watering place in the Liège province of Belgium where hydropathy was developed from 1626. The highest French spa is Baréges, Hautes-Pyrénées, at 4,068 feet above sea level.

Barracks

The oldest purpose-built barracks in the world are believed to be Collins Barracks, formerly the Royal Barracks, Dublin, Ireland, completed in 1704 and still in use.

Largest House

The largest private house in the world is 250-room Biltmore House in Asheville, North Carolina. It is owned by George and William Cecil, grandsons of George Washington Vanderbilt II (1862–1914).

The house was built between 1890 and 1895 on an estate of 119,000 acres, at a cost of $4,100,000, and is now valued at $55,000,000 with 12,000 acres.

The most expensive private house ever built is The Hearst Ranch at San Simeon, California. It was built 1922–39 for William Randolph Hearst (1863–1951), at a total cost of more than $30,000,000. It has more than 100 rooms, a 104-foot-long heated swimming pool, an 83-foot-long assembly hall and a garage for 25 limousines. The house would require 60 servants to maintain it.

The highest asking price for a privately furnished house has been £3,800,000 ($6,460,000) by Ravi Tikkoo for Kenstead Hall, London, England. The buyer by private treaty on April 6, 1977, was Crown Prince Fahd of Saudi Arabia. The adjacent $1,000,000 Risinghurst was bought for servants, and the total cost of extensions and renovations had passed $16 million by November, 1978.

The world's most expensive penthouse apartment is a 4-story penthouse at the top of Galleria International on East 57th Street in New York City. With 4 main bedrooms, a 22-foot swimming pool, library, sauna and several solariums, it was on the market in March, 1976, for $3,500,000.

3. Buildings for Entertainment

Largest Circus. The world's largest permanent circus is Circus Circus, Las Vegas, Nevada, opened on October 18, 1968, at a cost of $15,000,000. It covers an area of 129,000 square feet capped by a 90-foot-high tent-shaped flexiglass roof. (See Circus Stunt records, Chapter 11.)

The largest traveling circus is the Circus Vargas in the U.S. which can accommodate 5,000 people under its Big Top.

Largest Stadiums

The world's largest stadium is the Strahov Stadium in Praha (Prague), Czechoslovakia. It was completed in 1934 and can accommodate 240,000 spectators for mass displays of up to 40,000 Sokol gymnasts.

The largest football stadium in the world is the Maracaña Municipal Stadium in Rio de Janeiro, Brazil, which has a normal capacity of 205,000, of whom 155,000 may be seated. A crowd of 199,854 was accommodated for the World Cup soccer final between Brazil and Uruguay on July 16, 1950. A dry moat, 7 feet wide and over 5 feet deep, protects players from spectators and *vice versa*. The stadium also has facilities for indoor sports, such as boxing, and these provide accommodation for an additional 32,000 spectators.

The largest covered stadium in the world is the Azteca Stadium, Mexico City, opened in 1968, which has a capacity of 107,000, of whom nearly all are under cover.

Largest One-Piece Roof. The transparent acrylic glass "tent" roof over the Munich Olympic Stadium, West Germany, measures

LARGEST COVERED CAPACITY: The Azteca Stadium in Mexico City seats 107,000, nearly all under cover.

914,940 square feet in area. It rests on a steel net supported by masts. The roof of longest span in the world is the 680-foot diameter of the Louisiana Superdome (see below). The major axis of the elliptical Texas Stadium, completed in 1971 at Irving, Texas, is, however, 784 feet 4 inches.

Largest Indoor Arena. The world's largest indoor stadium is the 13-acre $173,000,000 273-foot-tall Superdome in New Orleans, Louisiana, completed in May, 1975. Its maximum seating capacity for conventions is 97,365 or 76,791 for football. Box suites rent for $35,000, excluding the price of admission. A gondola with six 312-inch TV screens produces instant replay.

Restaurant

Highest. The highest restaurant in the world is at the Chacaltaya ski resort in Bolivia, at 17,519 feet.

Kitchen

Largest. The largest kitchen ever set up has been the Indian Government field kitchen set up in April, 1973, at Ahmadnagar, Maharashtra, in the famine area, which daily provided 1,200,000 subsistence meals.

Night Clubs

Oldest. The oldest night club (*boîte de nuit*) is "Le Bal des Anglais" at 6 Rue des Anglais, Paris 5, France. It was founded in 1843 but closed *c.* 1960.

Largest. The largest night club in the world is Gilley's Club (formerly Shelly's) built in 1955 and extended in 1971 on Spencer

LARGEST FERRIS WHEEL: The Riesenrad in Prater Park, Vienna, Austria, has a diameter of 197 feet.

Highway, Pasadena, Texas. It has a seating capacity of more than 3,000 and a total capacity of 5,500.

In the more classical sense the largest night club in the world is "The Mikado" in the Akasaka district of Tokyo, Japan, with a seating capacity of 2,000. It is "manned" by 1,250 hostesses. Binoculars are essential to an appreciation of the floor show.

Lowest. The lowest night club is the "Minus 206" in Tiberias, Israel, on the shores of the Sea of Galilee. It is 676 feet (206 meters) below sea level. An alternative candidate is "Outer Limits," opposite the Cow Palace, San Francisco, which was raided for the 151st time on August 1, 1971. It has been called both "The Most Busted Joint" and "The Slowest to Get the Message."

Largest Amusement Resort

The largest amusement resort is Disney World on 27,443 acres of Orange and Osceola Counties, 20 miles southwest of Orlando in central Florida. It was opened on October 1, 1971. This $400,000,000 investment attracted 10,700,000 visitors in its first year.

The most attended resort in the world is Disneyland, Anaheim, California, where the total number of visitors reached 175,638,309 by October 1, 1978.

Fairs

Earliest. The earliest major international fair was the Great Exhibition of 1851 in the Crystal Palace, Hyde Park, London, which in 141 days attracted 6,039,195 admissions.

Largest. The largest ever International Fair site was that for the St. Louis, Missouri, Louisiana Purchase Exposition, which covered 1,271.76 acres. It also staged the 1904 Olympic Games and drew an attendance of 19,694,855.

Record Attendance. The record attendance for any fair was 64,218,770 for Expo '70 held on an 815-acre site at Osaka, Japan, from March to September 13, 1970. It made a profit of 19,439,402,017 yen (over $45 million).

Ferris Wheel. The original Ferris Wheel, named after its constructor, George W. Ferris (1859–96), was erected in 1893 at the Midway, Chicago, at a cost of $385,000. The wheel was 250 feet in diameter, 790 feet in circumference, weighed 1,198 tons, and carried 36 cars each seating 60 people, making a total of 2,160 passengers. The structure was removed in 1904 to St. Louis, and was eventually sold as scrap for $1,800. In 1897, a Ferris Wheel with a diameter of 300 feet was erected for the Earl's Court Exhibition, London. The largest wheel now operating is the Riesenrad in Prater Park, Vienna, Austria, with a diameter of 197 feet. It was built in 1896 and carried 15,000,000 people in its first 75 years.

Largest and Fastest Roller Coaster. The maximum speeds claimed for roller coasters tend to be exaggerated for commercial reasons. The highest point on any circuit is 125 feet on the Magic Mountain "Colossus" at Valencia, California, where the record 115-foot drop produces velocities of 56 m.p.h. The dual track racing system extends over 4,631 feet and was opened in May, 1978. The top of the schuss on the "Tidal Wave" in Santa Clara, California, opened on July 8, 1977, is a claimed 140 feet high. The Fujikyu Highland Giant Coaster track in Japan is 1,566 yards long.

Longest Slide. The longest slide in the world is at Bad Tölz, West Germany. This has a length of 0.76 mile and a vertical drop of 721 ft.

Pleasure Beach

The largest pleasure beach in the world is Virginia Beach, Virginia. It has 28 miles of beach front on the Atlantic and 10 miles of estuary frontage. The area embraces 255 square miles and contains 134 hotels and motels.

Longest Pleasure Pier

The longest pleasure pier in the world is Southend Pier at Southend-on-Sea in Essex, England. It is 1.34 miles in length, and was first opened in August, 1889, with final extensions made in 1929. In 1949–50, the fair railway carried 5,750,000 passengers.

Bars

The largest beer-selling establishment in the world is the Mathäser, Bayerstrasse 5, Munich, West Germany, where the daily sale reaches 100,800 pints. It was established in 1829, was demolished in World War II, rebuilt by 1955, and now seats 5,500 people. Consumption at the Dube beer halls in the Bantu township of Soweto, Johannesburg, South Africa, may, however, be higher on some Saturdays when the average of 7,160 gallons (57,280 pints) is far exceeded.

Longest Bar. The longest bar with beer pumps was built in 1938 at the Working Men's Club, Mildura, Victoria, Australia. It has a counter 298 feet in length, served by 27 pumps. Temporary bars have been erected of greater length. The Falstaff Brewing Corp. put up a temporary bar 336 feet 5 inches in length on Wharf St., St. Louis, Missouri, on June 22, 1970.

The bar at Erickson's on Burnside Street, Portland, Oregon, in its heyday (1883–1920) ran continuously around and across the main saloon, measuring 684 feet. The chief bouncer, Edward "Spider" Johnson, had a chief assistant named "Jumbo" Reilly who weighed 320 pounds and was said to resemble "an ill-natured orangutan." Beer was 5 cents for 16 fluid ounces.

Longest Family Ownership. There are no collated records on licencees, but the "Glan-y-Afon Inn," Milwr near Holywell, North Wales, had a 418-year (1559–1977) run within a family which ended with the retirement of Mrs. Mary Evans.

Wine Cellar. The largest wine cellars in the world are at Paarl, those of the Ko-operative Wijnbouwers Vereeniging (K.W.V.), near Capetown, in the center of the wine district of South Africa. They cover an area of 25 acres and have a capacity of 36,000,000 gallons. Their largest blending vats have a capacity of 54,880 gallons, and are 17 feet high and 26 feet in diameter.

Beer Garden. The world's largest beer garden is the Augustiner Biergarten in Munich, West Germany, founded in 1901 with space for 5,200 people. It has sold as much as 2,640 gallons in a single day.

4. Towers and Masts

Tallest Structure

The tallest structure in the world is the guyed Warszawa Radio mast at Konstantynow near Gabin and Plock in Poland, which is 2,120 feet 8 inches tall, or more than four-tenths of a mile. The mast was completed on July 18, 1974, and put into operation on July 22, 1974. Work began on the tubular steel construction, with its 15 steel guy ropes, in 1970. It was designed by Jan Polak and weighs 615 tons. The mast is so high that anyone falling off the top would reach terminal velocity, and hence cease to be accelerating, before hitting the ground. It recaptured for Europe a record held in the United States since the Chrysler Building surpassed the Eiffel Tower in 1929.

Tallest Tower

The tallest self-supporting tower (as opposed to a guyed mast) in the world is the $44,000,000 CN Tower in Metro Centre, Toronto, Canada. It rises to 1,822 feet 1 inch. Excavation began on February 12, 1973, for the 145,000-ton structure of reinforced, post-tensioned concrete, and it was topped out on April 2, 1975. A 416-seat restaurant revolves in the 7-floor Sky Pod at 1,140 feet, from which the visibility extends to hills 74½ miles distant. Lightning strikes the top about 200 times (in 30 storms) each year.

The tallest tower built before the era of television masts is the Tour Eiffel (Eiffel Tower), in Paris, France, designed by Alexandre Gustave Eiffel (1832–1923) for the Paris exhibition and completed on March 31, 1889. It was 985 feet 11 inches tall, now extended by a TV antenna to 1,052 feet 4 inches, and weighs 8,091 tons. The maximum sway in high winds is 5 inches. The whole iron edifice, which has 1,792 steps, took 2 years, 2 months, and 2 days to build and cost 7,799,401 francs 31 centimes.

5. Bridges

Oldest. Arch construction was understood by the Sumerians as early as 3200 B.C., and a reference exists to a Nile bridge in 2650 B.C. The oldest surviving datable bridge in the world is the slab stone single-arch bridge over the River Meles in Smyrna (now Izmir), Turkey, which dates from *c.* 850 B.C.

Longest Suspension. The world's longest bridge span is the main span of the £67 million ($135 million) Humber Estuary Bridge in England, at 4,626 feet, due to open in June, 1980. Work began on July 27, 1972. The towers are 533 feet 1⅝ inches tall from datum and are 1⅜ inches out of parallel, to allow for the curvature of the earth. Including the Hessle and Barton side spans, the bridge stretches 1.37 miles.

The Mackinac Straits Bridge between Mackinaw City and St. Ignace, Michigan, is the longest suspension bridge in the world measured between anchorages (8,344 feet or 1.58 miles) and has an overall length, including viaducts of the bridge proper measured between abutment faces, of 19,205 feet 4 inches (3.63 miles). It was opened in November, 1957 (dedicated June 28, 1958) at a cost of $100 million and has a main span of 3,800 feet.

Work on the double-deck railroad Akashi-Kaikyo bridge linking Honshu and Shikoku, Japan, is planned to be completed in 1988. The main span will be 5,840 feet in length with an overall suspended length with side spans totaling 11,680 feet. Work began in October, 1978, and the eventual cost is expected to exceed 1 trillion yen ($4.5 billion).

Work is expected to start in 1980 on the Messina Bridge linking Sicily with the Italian mainland. The towers would be 1,000 feet high and the span exceeding 6,070 feet. The total cost has been estimated at close to $4 billion.

Longest Cantilever. The Québec Bridge (Pont de Québec) over the St. Lawrence River in Canada has the longest cantilever span of any in the world—1,800 feet between the piers and 3,239 feet overall. It carries a railway track and two roadways. Begun in 1899, it was finally opened to traffic on December 3, 1917, at a cost of Can. $22,500,000 and 87 lives.

Longest Steel Arch. The longest steel arch bridge in the world is the New River Gorge bridge near Fayetteville, West Virginia, completed in 1977, with a span of 1,700 feet.

Railroad. The longest railroad bridge in the world is the Huey P. Long Bridge, Metairie, Louisiana, with a railroad section 22,996 feet (4.35 miles) long. It was completed on December 16, 1935, with a longest span of 790 feet.

The Yangtse River Bridge completed in 1968 in Nanking, China, is the world's longest combined highway and railroad bridge. The rail deck is 4.20 miles and the road deck an additional 2.85 miles.

Floating. The longest floating bridge in the world is the Second Lake Washington Bridge in Seattle, Washington. Its total length is 12,596 feet and its floating section measures 7,518 feet (1.42 miles). It was built at a cost of $15,000,000, and completed in August, 1963.

Widest. The bridge with the widest roadway is the Crawford Street Bridge in Providence, Rhode Island, with a width of 1,147 feet.

The widest long-span bridge is the 1,650-foot-span Sydney Harbour Bridge, Australia, which is 160 feet wide. It carries two electric overhead railroad tracks, 8 lanes of roadway and a cycleway and footway. It was officially opened on March 19, 1932.

The River Roch in England is bridged for a distance of 1,460 feet where the culvert passes through the center of Rochdale, Greater Manchester, and this is sometimes claimed as a breadth.

Covered. The longest covered bridge in the world is that at Hartland, New Brunswick, Canada, measuring 1,282 feet overall, completed in 1899.

Highest. The world's highest bridge is the suspension bridge over the Royal Gorge of the Arkansas River in Colorado. It is 1,053 feet above the water level. It has a main span of 880 feet and was constructed in 6 months, ending on December 6, 1929. The highest railroad bridge in the world is at Fades, outside Clermont-Ferrand, France. It was built in 1901–09 with a span of 472 feet and is 435 feet above the River Sioule.

Longest Bridging. The world's longest bridging is the second Lake Pontchartrain Causeway, opened on March 23, 1969, joining Lewisburg and Metairie, Louisiana. Its length is 126,055 feet (23.87 miles). It was completed at a cost of $29,900,000 and is 228 feet longer than the adjoining First Causeway completed in 1956.

The longest railroad viaduct in the world is the rock-filled Great Salt Lake Railroad Trestle, carrying the Southern Pacific Railroad 11.85 miles across the Great Salt Lake, Utah. It was opened as a pile and trestle bridge on March 8, 1904, and converted to rock fill in 1955–1960.

The longest stone arch bridging in the world is the 3,810-foot-long Rockville Bridge north of Harrisburg, Pennsylvania, with 48 spans containing 219,520 tons of stone and completed in 1901.

Longest Aqueduct. The greatest of ancient aqueducts was the Aqueduct of Carthage in Tunisia, which ran 87.6 miles from the springs of Zaghouan to Djebel Djougar. It was built by the Romans during the reign of Publius Aelius Hadrianus (117–138 A.D.). By 1895, 344 arches still survived. Its original capacity has been calculated at 8,400,000 gallons per day. The triple-tiered aqueduct Pont du Gard, built in 19 A.D. near Nîmes, France, is 160 feet high. The tallest of the 14 arches of the Aguas Livres Aqueduct, built in Lisbon, Portugal, in 1784, is 213 feet 3 inches.

The world's longest aqueduct, in the modern sense of a water conduit as opposed to an irrigation canal, is the California State Water Project aqueduct, completed in 1974 to a length of 826 miles, of which 385 miles is canalized.

LONGEST BRIDGE SPANS IN THE WORLD—BY TYPE

	feet		opening
Suspension	4,626	Humber Estuary, England	1980
Cantilever	1,800	Québec Railway, Québec, Canada	1917
Steel Arch	1,700	New River Gorge, Fayetteville, W. Virginia	1977
Covered bridge	1,282	Hartland, New Brunswick, Canada	1899
Continuous truss	1,232	Astoria, Columbia River, Oregon	1966
Cable-stayed	1,500	Second Hooghly, Calcutta, India	1977
Chain suspension	1,114	Hercilio Luz, Florianopolis, Brazil	1926
Concrete arch	1,000	Gladesville, Sydney, Australia	1964
Plate and box girder	984	Rio Niterói, Rio de Janeiro, Brazil	1974

LONGEST CONTINUOUS TRUSS BRIDGE: The Astoria Bridge, over the Columbia River in Oregon, has a main span 1,232 feet long.

6. Canals

Relics of the oldest canals in the world, dated by archeologists to *c*. 4000 B.C., were discovered near Mandali, Iraq, early in 1968.

Longest. The longest canalized system in the world is the Volga-Baltic Canal opened in April, 1965. It runs 1,850 miles from Astrakhan up the Volga, *via* Kuybyshev, Gorkiy and Lake Ladoga, to Leningrad, U.S.S.R. The longest canal of the ancient world was the Grand Canal of China from Peking to Hangchow. It was begun in 540 B.C. and not completed until 1327 by which time it extended for 1,107 miles. The estimated work force *c.* 600 A.D. reached 5,000,000 on the Pien section. Having been allowed by 1950 to silt up to the point that it was in no place more than 6 feet deep, it is now, however, plied by ships of up to 2,240 tons.

The Beloye More (White Sea) Baltic Canal from Belomorsk to Povenets, in the U.S.S.R., is 141 miles long with 19 locks. It was completed with the use of forced labor in 1933 and cannot accommodate ships of more than 16 feet in draught.

The world's longest big ship canal is the Suez Canal, linking the Red and Mediterranean Seas, opened on November 16, 1869, but inoperative from June, 1967, to June, 1975. The canal was planned by the French diplomatist Ferdinand de Lesseps (1805–1894) and work began on April 25, 1859. It is 100.6 miles in length from Port Said lighthouse to Suez Roads, 197 feet wide. The work force was 8,213 men and 368 camels. The largest vessel to transit has been S.S. *British Progress*, a VLCC (Very Large Crude Carrier) of 228,569 tons dwt (length 1,081.5 feet; beam 159.7 feet at maximum draft 84 feet). This was southbound in ballast on July 5, 1976.

Busiest. The busiest big ship canal is the Panama, first transited on August 15, 1914. In 1974, there were a record 14,304 ocean-going transits. The largest liner to transit is *Queen Elizabeth 2* on March 25, 1975, for a toll of $42,077.88. The ships with the greatest beam to transit have been the *Acadia Forest* and the *Atlantic Forest*, each of 106.9 feet. The lowest toll was 36 cents for the swimmer Richard Halliburton in 1928. The fastest transit has been 3 hours 28 minutes by the destroyer U.S.S. *McDougall DD 358* in April, 1941.

Seaway. The world's longest artificial seaway is the St. Lawrence Seaway (189 miles long) along the New York State-Ontario border from Montreal to Lake Ontario, which enables 80 per cent of all ocean-going ships, and bulk carriers with a capacity of 29,000 tons, to sail 2,342 miles from the North Atlantic, up the St. Lawrence Estuary and across the Great Lakes to Duluth, Minnesota, on Lake Superior (602 feet above sea level). The project cost $470,000,000 and was opened on April 25, 1959.

Irrigation. The longest irrigation canal in the world is the Kara-kumskiy Kanal, stretching 528 miles from Haun-Khan to Ash-khabad, Turkmenistan, U.S.S.R. In September, 1971, the navigable length was reported to have reached 280 miles. The length of the $925,000,000 project will eventually reach 930 miles.

Locks

Largest. The world's largest single lock connects the Schelde with the Kanaaldok system at Zandvliet, west of Antwerp, Belgium. It is 1,640 feet long and 187 feet wide and is an entrance to an impounded sheet of water 11.2 miles long.

Deepest. The world's deepest lock is the John Day Dam lock on the Columbia River, Oregon and Washington, completed in 1963. It can raise or lower barges 113 feet and is served by a 1,100-ton gate.

Highest Lock Elevator. The world's highest lock elevator overcomes a head of 225 feet at Ronquieres on the Charleroi-Brussels Canal, Belgium. The two 236-wheeled caissons, each able to carry 1,510 tons, take 22 minutes to cover the 4,698-foot-long ramp.

Largest Cut. The Gaillard Cut (known as the "Ditch") on the Panama Canal is 270 feet deep between Gold Hill and Contractor's Hill with a bottom width of 500 feet. In one day in 1911 as many as 333 dirt trains each carrying 400 tons left this site. The total amount of earth excavated for the whole Panama Canal was 9,980,000 tons. This total will be raised by the further widening of the Gaillard Cut.

7. Dams

Earliest. The earliest dam ever built was the Sadd al-Kafara, 7 miles southeast of Helwan, Egypt. It was built in the period 2950–2750 B.C. and had a length of 348 feet and a height of 37 feet.

Most Massive. Measured by volume, the largest dam in the world is the 98-foot-high New Cornelia Tailings earthfill dam near Ajo, Arizona, with a volume of 274,026,000 cubic yards, completed in 1973 to a length of 6.74 miles.

Largest Concrete. The world's largest concrete dam, and the largest concrete structure in the world, is the Grand Coulee Dam on the Columbia River, Washington. Work on the dam was begun in 1933, it began working on March 22, 1941, and was completed in 1942, at a cost of $56,000,000. It has a crest length of 4,173 feet and is 550 feet high. It contains 10,585,000 cubic yards of concrete, and weighs about 21,600,000 tons. The hydroelectric power plant (now being extended) will have a capacity of 9,780,000 kilowatts.

LARGEST CONCRETE DAM: The Grand Coulee Dam on the Columbia River measures 550 feet tall from base to rim.

HIGHEST DAM: The Grand Dixence on the Dixence River in Valais, Switzerland, reaches a height of 935 feet.

Highest. The highest dam in the world is the Grand Dixence in Switzerland, completed in September, 1961, at a cost of $372,000,000. It is 935 feet from base to rim, 2,296 feet long and the total volume of concrete in the dam is 7,792,000 cubic yards.

The Rogunsky earthfill dam in the U.S.S.R. is expected to have a final height of 1,066 feet when completed.

The damming of the Vakh River at Tadjikistan, U.S.S.R. with the rock-fill Nourek Dam is due for completion after 19 years of work in late 1979. The final height will be 986 feet. Many microseisms have caused the rate of filling to be slowed down.

Longest. The longest river dam is the 62-foot-high Kiev dam on the Dnieper River, U.S.S.R., which was completed in 1964 to a length of 33.6 miles. In the early 17th century, an impounding dam of moderate height was built in Lake Hungtze, Kiangsu, China, to a reputed length of 62 miles.

The longest sea dam in the world is the Afsluitdijk stretching 20.195 miles across the mouth of the Zuider Zee in two sections of 1.553 miles (mainland of North Holland to the Isle of Wieringen) and 18.641 miles (Wieringen to Friesland). It has a sea-level width of 293 feet and a height of 24 feet 7 inches.

Strongest. The world's strongest structure will be the Sayano-Shusenskaya dam on the Yenisey River, U.S.S.R. Under construction, it is designed to bear a load of 20,160,000 tons from a fully-filled reservoir.

Largest Reservoir

The most voluminous man-made reservoir is Bratsk reservoir on the Angara River, U.S.S.R., with a volume of 137,214,000 acre-feet. The dam was completed in 1964.

The world's largest artificial lake measured by surface area is Lake Volta, Ghana, formed by the Akosombo dam, completed in 1965. By 1969, the lake had filled an area of 3,275 square miles with a shoreline 4,500 miles in length.

The completion in 1954 of the Owen Falls Dam near Jinja, Uganda, across the northern exit of the White Nile River from the lake Victoria Nyanza, marginally raised the level of that *natural* lake by adding 166,000,000 acre-feet, and technically turned it into a reservoir with a surface area of 17,169,920 acres (26,828 square miles).

Largest Polder

The largest of the five great polders in the old Zuider Zee, Netherlands, will be the 149,000-acre (232.8-square-mile) Markerwaard. Work on the 66-mile-long surrounding dyke was begun in 1957. The water area remaining after the erection of the 1927–32 dam (20 miles in length) is called IJssel Meer, which will have a final area of 487.5 square miles.

Largest Levees

The most massive levees ever carried out are the Mississippi levees begun in 1717 and vastly augmented by the U.S. Government after the disastrous floods of 1927. These extend for 1,732 miles along the main river from Cape Girardeau, Missouri, to the Gulf of Mexico and comprise more than 1,000,000,000 cubic yards of earthworks. Levees on the tributaries comprise an additional 2,000 miles. The 650-mile segment from Pine Bluff, Arkansas, to Venice, Louisiana, is continuous.

8. Tunnels

Longest. The world's longest tunnel of any kind is the New York City-West Delaware water supply tunnel begun in 1937 and completed in 1944. It has a diameter of 13 feet 6 inches and runs for 105 miles from the Rondout Reservoir in the Catskill Mountains into the Hillview Reservoir, on the border line of New York City and Yonkers.

Bridge-Tunnel. The world's longest bridge-tunnel system is the Chesapeake Bay Bridge-Tunnel, extending 17.65 miles from Eastern Shore of Virginia to Virginia Beach, Virginia. It cost $200,000,000, took 42 months to complete, and opened on April 15, 1964. The longest bridged section is Trestle C (4.56 miles long) and the longest tunnel is the Thimble Shoal Channel Tunnel (1.09 miles).

Canal-Tunnel. The world's longest canal-tunnel is that on the Rove Canal between the port of Marseilles, France, and the Rhône River, built in 1912–27. It is 4.53 miles long, 72 feet wide and 50 feet high, involving 2,250,000 cubic yards of excavation.

Subway. The world's longest continuous vehicular tunnel is the London Transport Board underground railway line from Morden to East Finchley, *via* Bank, in London. In use since 1939, it is 17 miles 528 yards long. The diameter of the tunnel is 12 feet and the station tunnels 22.2 feet.

Railroad. The world's longest main-line rail tunnel is the 13-mile 1,397-yard Oshimizu Tunnel on the Tokyo-Niigata Joetsu line in central Honshu, Japan, under the Tanigawa Mountain, which was holed through on January 25, 1979. The cost of the whole project will by March, 1981, reach $6.3 billion. There have been 13 fatalities in 7 years.

Sub-aqueous. The world's longest sub-aqueous railroad tunnel will be the Seikan Rail Tunnel (33.49 miles), 328 feet beneath the sea bed of the Tsugaru Strait between Tappi Saki, Honshu, and Fukushima, Hokkaido, Japan. Once due to be completed in 1979 at a cost of $552,000,000, major flooding on May 6, 1976, has put back completion beyond 1982. Tests started on the sub-aqueous section (14.5 miles) in 1963 and construction in June, 1972. The tunnel will be 787 feet below sea level.

Currently the world's longest sub-aqueous rail tunnel is the Shin Kanmon Tunnel, completed in May, 1974, which runs 11.61 miles from Honshu to Kyushu, Japan.

Road. The world's longest road tunnel is the 8.7-mile-long Arlberg Road Tunnel from St. Anton and Langen in western Austria, opened to traffic on December 9, 1978.

The largest diameter road tunnel in the world was blasted through Yerba Buena Island in San Francisco Bay. It is 76 feet wide, 58 feet high and 540 feet long. More than 35,000,000 vehicles pass through on its two decks every year.

Irrigation. The longest irrigation tunnel in the world is the 51.5-mile-long Orange-Fish Rivers Tunnel, South Africa, begun in 1967, at an estimated cost of $150,000,000. The boring was completed in April, 1973. The lining, to a minimum thickness of 9 inches, will give a completed diameter of 17 feet 6 inches. The total work force at times exceeded 5,000 men. Some of the access shafts in the eight sections descend more than 1,000 feet.

Tunneling. The record for rapid tunneling was set in 1967 in the 5-mile-long Oso Irrigation Tunnel in Colorado, when the "mole" (giant boring machine) was advanced 419 feet on the 57-square-foot tunnel face in one day.

9. Specialized Structures

Seven Wonders of the World

The Seven Wonders of the World were first designated by Antipater of Sidon in the 2nd century B.C. They included the Pyramids of Giza, built by three Fourth Dynasty Egyptian Pharaohs, Khwfw (Khufu or Cheops), Kha-f-Ra (Khafre, Khefren or Chephren) and Menkaure (Mycerinus) near El Giza (El Gizeh), southwest of El Qahira (Cairo) in Egypt. The Great Pyramid ("Horizon of Khufu") was finished *c.* 2580 B.C. Its original height was 480 feet 11 inches (now, since loss of its topmost stones and the pyramidion, reduced to 449 feet 6 inches) with a base line of 756 feet and thus covering slightly more than 13 acres. It has been estimated that a permanent work force of 4,000 required 30 years to

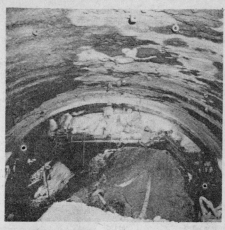

LONGEST
VEHICULAR
TUNNEL: Work
proceeds on the Seikan
Tunnel in Japan,
expected to stretch 33½
miles by completion.

LONGEST MAIN-LINE
RAILROAD TUNNEL: The
Oshimizu Tunnel in Japan
will extend over 13 miles by
March, 1981.

maneuver into position the 2,300,000 limestone blocks averaging 2¾ tons each, totaling about 7,225,000 tons and a volume of 90,700,000 cubic feet. A cost estimate published in December, 1974, indicates that today it would require 405 men working 6 years at a cost of $1,130,000,000.

Of the other six wonders, only fragments remain of the Temple of Artemis (Diana) of the Ephesians, built *c.* 350 B.C. at Ephesus, Turkey (destroyed by the Goths in 262 A.D.), and of the Tomb of King Mausolus of Caria, built at Halicarnassus, now Bodrum, Turkey, *c.* 325 B.C. No trace remains of the Hanging Gardens of Semiramis, at Babylon, Iraq (*c.* 600 B.C.); the 40-foot-tall marble, gold and ivory statue of Zeus (Jupiter) by Phidias (5th century B.C.) at Olympia, Greece (lost in a fire at Istanbul); the 117-foot-tall statue by Chares of Lindus of the figure of the god Helios (Apollo), called the Colossus of Rhodes (sculptured 292–280 B.C., destroyed by an earthquake in 224 B.C.); or the 400-foot-tall lighthouse built by Sostratus of Cnidus *c.* 270 B.C. as a pyramid-shaped tower of white marble (destroyed by an earthquake in 1375 A.D.) on the island of Pharos (Greek, *pharos*=lighthouse), off the coast of El Iskandarya (Alexandria), Egypt.

Tallest Statue. The tallest free-standing statue in the world is that of the "Motherland," an enormous female figure on Mamayev Hill, outside Volgograd, U.S.S.R., designed in 1967 by Yevgenyi Vuchetich, to commemorate victory in the Battle of Stalingrad (1942–43). The statue from its base to the tip of a sword clenched in her right hand measures 270 feet. She is constructed of prestressed concrete.

The U.S. sculptor Felix de Welton has announced a plan to reproduce the Colossus of Rhodes in a 308-foot version.

Near Bamiyan, Afghanistan, there are the remains of the recumbent Sakya Buddha, built of plastered rubble, which was "about 1,000 feet long" and is believed to date from the 3rd or 4th century A.D.

Tallest Columns

The tallest columns in the world are the thirty-six fluted pillars of Vermont marble in the colonnade of the Education Building, Albany, New York. Each one measures 90 feet tall and 6½ feet in base diameter.

The tallest load-bearing stone columns are those measuring 69 feet in the Hall of Columns of the Temple of Amun at Karnak, opposite Thebes on the Nile, the ancient capital of Upper Egypt. They were built in the 19th dynasty in the reign of Rameses II in *c.* 1270 B.C.

Tallest Totem Pole

The tallest totem pole in the world is 173 feet tall raised on June 6, 1973 at Alert Bay, British Columbia, Canada. It tells the story of the Kwakiutl and took 36 man-weeks to carve.

Tallest Barber's Pole

The world's tallest barber pole is 50 feet 3 inches high, erected on November 1, 1973, on Walker Road, Alexander, New York.

Tallest Flagpole

The tallest flagpole ever erected was outside the Oregon Building at the 1915 Panama-Pacific International Exposition in San Francisco. Trimmed from a Douglas fir, it stood 299 feet 7 inches in height. The world's tallest unsupported flagpole is a 170-foot-tall (plus 10 feet below ground) metal pole weighing 28,000 lbs., erected in 1943 at the U.S. Merchant Marine Academy in King's Point, New York. The pole, built by Kearney-National Inc., tapers from 24 inches to 5½ inches at the jack.

Pyramids

Largest. The largest pyramid, and the largest monument ever constructed, is the Quetzalcóatl at Cholula de Rivadabia, 63 miles southeast of Mexico City. It is 177 feet tall and its base covers an area of nearly 45 acres. Its total volume has been estimated at 4,300,000 cubic yards, compared with 3,360,000 cubic yards for the Pyramid of Cheops (see above). The pyramid-building era here was between the 2nd and 6th centuries A.D.

Oldest. The oldest known pyramid is the Djoser step pyramid at Saqqâra, Egypt, constructed to a height of 204 feet, originally with a Tura limestone casing, *c.* 2650 B.C. The oldest New World pyramid is that on the island of La Venta in southeastern Mexico built by the Olmec people *c.* 800 B.C. It is 100 feet tall with a base diameter of 420 feet.

Obelisks

Oldest. The longest an obelisk has remained *in situ* is that at Heliopolis, near Aswan, Egypt, erected by Senusret I *c.* 1750 B.C.

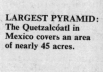

LARGEST PYRAMID: The Quetzalcóatl in Mexico covers an area of nearly 45 acres.

Largest. The largest standing obelisk in the world is that in the Piazza of St. John Lateran, Rome, erected in 1588. It came originally from the Circus Maximus (erected 357 A.D.) and before that from Heliopolis, Egypt (erected *c.* 1450 B.C.). It is 110 feet in height and weighs 504 tons.

Monuments

Tallest. The world's tallest monument is the stainless steel Gateway Arch in St. Louis, Missouri, completed on October 28, 1965, to commemorate the westward expansion after the Louisiana Purchase of 1803. It is a sweeping arch of stainless steel, spanning 630 feet and rising to a height of 630 feet, and costing $29,000,000. It was designed in 1947 by Eero Saarinen (died 1961).

The tallest monumental column in the world commemorates the battle of San Jacinto (April 21, 1836), on the bank of the San Jacinto River near Houston, Texas. General Sam Houston (1793–1863) and his force of 743 Texan troops killed 630 Mexicans (out of a total force of 1,600) and captured 700 others, with the loss of nine men killed and 30 wounded. Constructed in 1936–39, at a cost of $1,500,000, the tapering column is 570 feet tall. 47 feet square at the base, and 30 feet square at the observation tower, which is surmounted by a star weighing 220 tons. It is built of concrete, faced with buff limestone, and weighs 35,150 tons.

Largest Prehistoric. The largest megalithic prehistoric monuments in Britain are the 28½-acre earthworks and stone circles of Avebury, Wiltshire, rediscovered in 1646. The earliest calibrated date in the area of this neolithic site is *c.* 4200 B.C. The whole work is 1,200 feet in diameter with a 40-foot ditch around the perimeter and required an estimated 15 million man-hours of work. The largest trilithons exist at Stonehenge, to the south of Salisbury Plain, Wiltshire, with single sarsen blocks weighing over 50 tons and requiring over 550 men to drag them up a 9° gradient. The dating of the ditch was, in 1969, revised to 2180 B.C.$\pm$105. Whether Stonehenge was a lunar calendar, a temple, or an eclipse-predictor remains debatable.

Largest Earthworks. The largest earthworks in the world carried out prior to the mechanical era were the Linear Earth Boundaries of the Benin Empire in the Bendel state of Nigeria. These were first reported in 1900 and partially surveyed in 1967. In April, 1973, it was estimated that the total length of the earthworks was probably between 4,000 and 8,000 miles with a total of from 500,000,000 to 600,000,000 cubic yards of earth moved.

The largest artificial mound in the world is the gravel mound built as a memorial to the Seleucid King Antiochus I (reigned 69–34 B.C.). Located on the summit of Nemud Dagi, southeast of Malatya, eastern Turkey, the mound measures 197 feet tall and covers 7.5 acres.

Largest Tomb

The largest tomb in the world is that of Emperor Nintoku (died *c.* 428 A.D.) south of Osaka, Japan. It measures 1,594 feet long by 1,000 feet wide by 150 feet high.

TALLEST MONUMENT (left): The Gateway Arch at the edge of the Mississippi River in St. Louis is 630 feet high. TALLEST MONUMENTAL COLUMN (right): This 570-foot-tall column near Houston, Texas, commemorates the Battle of San Jacinto.

Ziggurat (Temple Tower)

The largest surviving ziggurat (from the verb *zaqaru*, Babylonian, to build high) is the Ziggurat of Ur (now Muqqayr, Iraq) with a base 200 feet by 150 feet built to at least three stories of which only the first and part of the second now survive to a height of 60 feet. It has been variously dated between *c.* 2050 B.C. and *c.* 2800 B.C.

Largest Dome

The world's largest dome is the Louisiana Superdome in New Orleans. It has an outside diameter of 680 feet.

The largest dome of ancient architecture is that of the Pantheon, built in Rome in 112 A.D., with a diameter of $142\frac{1}{2}$ feet.

Docks

Largest Drydock. The largest drydock in the world is that at Koyagi, Nagasaki, Japan completed in 1972. It measures 3,182 feet by 328 feet with a maximum depth of 47.6 feet.

The drydock at Port Rashid, Dubai, Persian Gulf, opened in March, 1979, measures 1,722 feet by 328 feet.

Largest Dock Gate. The world's largest dock gate is that at Nigg Bay, Cromarty Firth, Scotland, first operated in March, 1974. It measures 408 feet long, 50 feet high, with a 4-foot-thick base, and is made of reinforced concrete. With its sill, quoins and roundheads, it weighs a total of 17,882 tons.

Longest Jetty

The longest deep-water jetty in the world is the Quai Hermann du Pasquier at Le Havre, France, with a length of 5,000 feet. Part of an enclosed basin, it has a constant depth of water of 32 feet on both sides.

Longest Pier

The world's longest pier is the Dammam Pier in El Hasa, Saudi Arabia, on the Persian Gulf. A rock-filled causeway 4.84 miles long joins the steel trestle pier 1.80 miles long, which joins the Main Pier (744 feet long), giving an overall length of 6.79 miles. The work was begun in July, 1948, and completed on March 15, 1950.

Longest Breakwater

The world's longest breakwater is that which protects the port of Galveston, Texas. The granite south breakwater is 6.74 miles long.

Lighthouses

Brightest. The lighthouse with the most powerful light in the world is Créac'h d'Ouessant lighthouse, established in 1638 and last altered in 1939 on l'Île d'Ouessant, Finistère, Brittany, France. It is 163 feet tall and, in times of fog, has a luminous intensity of up to 500,000,000 candelas.

The lights with the greatest visible range are those 1,092 feet above the ground on the Empire State Building, New York City. Each of the four-arc mercury bulbs has a rated candlepower of 450,000,000, visible 80 miles away on the ground and 300 miles away from aircraft. They were switched on on March 31, 1956.

Tallest. The world's tallest lighthouse is the steel tower 348 feet tall near Yamashita Park in Yokohama, Japan. It has a power of 600,000 candles and a visibility range of 20 miles.

Windmills

Earliest. The earliest recorded windmills are those used for grinding corn in Iran (Persia) in the 7th century A.D. The oldest Dutch mill is the towermill at Zeddam, Gelderland, built *c.* 1450.

Largest. The biggest windmill in the world is the Tvind windmill, 173 feet 10½ inches tall, in Ulfborg, Denmark. Completed in February, 1978 at a cost of nearly $600,000, it has 3 blades which sweep a 177-foot-2-inch-diameter circle. The generating capacity is 2,000 kW. A windmill with 200-foot blades is reportedly planned at Boone, North Carolina.

The largest Dutch windmill is the Dijkpolder in Maasland, built

LONGEST WALL: It has been estimated that it took 300,000 laborers over a decade to build the Great Wall of China.

in 1718. The sails measure 95¾ feet from tip to tip. The tallest wind-mill in the Netherlands is De Walvisch in Schiedam built to a height of 108 feet in 1794.

Waterwheel

The largest waterwheel is the Mohammadieh Noria wheel at Hama, Syria, with a diameter of 131 feet. It dates from Roman times.

Longest Stairs

The world's longest stairs are reputedly at the Aura power station, Sienndal, western Norway. Built of wood in 1952, these are 4,101 feet in length, rising in 3,875 steps at an angle of 41° inside the pressure shaft. The T'ai Chan temple stairs of 6,600 steps in the Shantung Mountains, China, ascend 4,700 feet over a distance of 5 miles.

Longest Wall

The Great Wall of China, completed during the Ch'in dynasty, reign of Shih Huang-ti (246–210 B.C.), has a main-line length of 2,150 miles with a further 1,780 miles of branches and spurs, with a height of from 15 to 39 feet and up to 32 feet thick. It runs from Shanhaikuan, on the Gulf of Pohai, to Yümên-kuan and Yang-kuan and was kept in repair up to the 16th century.

Longest Fence

The longest fence in the world is the dingo-proof fence enclosing the main sheep areas of Queensland, Australia. The wire fence is 6 feet high, goes one foot underground, and stretches for 3,437 miles, more than the distance from Seattle to New York.

LARGEST SCIENTIFIC BUILDING: A 363-foot-high Saturn V space vehicle stands alongside the Vehicle Assembly Building at the Kennedy Space Center in Florida.

Largest Maze

The world's largest maze is at Longleat, near Warminster, Wiltshire, England, with 1.61 miles of paths flanked by 16,180 yew trees. It was opened on June 6, 1978.

Largest Windows

The largest sheet of glass ever manufactured was one of 538.2 square feet, or 65 feet 7 inches by 8 feet 2½ inches, exhibited by the Saint Gobain Company in France at the *Journées Internationales de Miroiterie* in March, 1958. The largest single windows in the world are those in the Palace of Industry and Technology at Rondpoint de la Défense, Paris, with an extreme width of 715.2 feet and a maximum height of 164 feet.

Largest Doors

The largest doors in the world are the four in the Vehicle Assembly Building near Cape Canaveral (Kennedy), Florida, with a height of 460 feet. (See *Largest Buildings—Scientific*, page 253.)

Cemetery

The world's largest cemetery is one in Leningrad, U.S.S.R., which contains over 500,000 of the 1,300,000 victims of the German army's siege of 1941–42.

The largest crematorium is at the Nikolo-Arkhangelskoye Cemetery, East Moscow, completed to a British design in March, 1972. It has seven twin furnaces and several Halls of Farewell for atheists.

Largest Garbage Dump

Reclamation Plant No. 1, Fresh Kills, Staten Island, which opened in March, 1974, is the world's largest sanitary landfill. In its first 4 months, 500,000 tons of refuse from New York City was dumped on the site by 700 barges.

Largest Revolving Globe

The world's largest revolving globe is the 24-ton sphere (27 feet 11 inches in diameter) in the Coleman Map Building, Wellesley, Massachusetts, completed in 1956 at a cost of $200,000.

Largest Tent

The largest field tent ever erected covered an area of 188,368 square feet (4.32 acres), put up by the firm of Deuter from Augsburg, Germany, for the 1958 "Welcome Expo" in Brussels, Belgium.

Tallest Scaffolding

The greatest scaffolding structure ever erected was one 486 feet high, using 152 miles of tubing, for the reconstruction of Guy's Hospital, London, in 1971.

Largest Vat

The world's largest vat is named "Strongbow," used by H. P. Bulmer Ltd., a cider company in Hereford, England. It measures 64½ feet in height, 75½ feet in diameter, and has a capacity of 1,956,000 gallons.

Naturist Resorts

The oldest naturist resort (the term "nudist camp" is deplored by naturists) is Der Freilichtpark, Klingberg, West Germany, established in 1903. The largest in the world is the Centre Helio-Marin, Montalivet, near Bordeaux, France. Extending over 1¼ miles of coast and covering 420 acres, it has 1,200 chalets and 50,000 visitors per year. However, 100,000 people visit the smaller Centre Helio-Marin at Cap d'Agde, southern France, which covers 222 acres.

Advertising Signs

Largest. The greatest advertising sign ever erected was the electric Citroën sign on the Eiffel Tower, Paris. It was switched on on July 4, 1925, and could be seen 24 miles away. It was in six colors with 250,000 lamps and 56 miles of electric cables. The letter "N" which terminated the name "Citroën" between the second and third levels measured 68 feet 5 inches in height. The whole apparatus was taken down after 11 years in 1936.

The world's largest neon advertising sign was owned by the Atlantic Coast Line Railroad Company at Port Tampa, Florida. It measured 387 feet 6 inches long and 76 feet high, weighed 196 tons and contained about 4,200 feet of red neon tubing. It was demolished on February 19, 1970.

Broadway's largest current billboard is 11,426 square feet in area—equivalent to 107 feet by 107 feet. The world's largest working sign was in Times Square between 44 & 45th Streets, New York City, in 1966. It showed two 42½-foot-tall "bottles" of Haig Scotch Whisky and an 80-foot-long "bottle" of Gordon's Gin being "poured" into a frosted glass.

Highest. The highest advertising signs in the world are the four Bank of Montreal logos atop the 72-story 935-foot-tall First Canadian Place building in Toronto. Each sign, built by Claude Neon Industries Ltd., measures 20 feet by 22 feet, and was lifted into place by helicopter.

Largest Bonfire

A bonfire 120 feet high was built at Whitehaven, Cumbria, England. in 1902. It used 672 tons of wood and 2,400 gallons of petroleum.

Tallest Fountain

The world's tallest fountain is at Fountain Hills, Arizona, built at a cost of $1,500,000 for McCulloch Properties, Inc. At full pressure of 375 pounds per square inch and at a rate of 7,000 gallons a minute, the 560-foot column of water weighs more than 9 tons. The nozzle speed achieved by the three 600 h.p. pumps is 46.7 m.p.h.

10. Borings and Mines

Deepest. Man's deepest penetration into the earth's crust is under Rig No. 32 gas well at No. 1 Bertha Rogers Field, Washita County, Oklahoma. After 503 days of drilling, the Loffland Brothers Drilling Co. reached 31,441 feet (5.95 miles) on April 3, 1974. The hole temperature at the bottom was 475° F. A conception of the depth of this hole can be gained by the realization that it was sufficient in depth to lower the CN Tower in Toronto (the world's tallest) down it 17 times.

In May, 1976, drilling was begun at Saatly, Azerbaijan, U.S.S.R. in an attempt to reach the Mohorovicic discontinuity, a target depth of 49,212 feet.

The deepest recorded drilling into the sea bed by the *Glomar Challenger* of the U.S. Deep Sea Drilling Project is one of 5,709 feet, and the deepest site is one 20,483 feet below sea level.

The deepest oil exploration is in 4,346 feet of water, 50 miles west of Point Noire, Congo, by *Discoverer Seven Seas*, spudded in on January 14, 1978.

Oil Fields

Largest. The largest oil field in the world is the Ghawar Field, Saudi Arabia, developed by ARAMCO, which measures 150 miles by 22 miles. The Groningen gas field in the Netherlands, exploited since 1965, has reserves of 100 trillion cubic feet. This may be matched by the Dome find of 1972 off Qatar.

Greatest Gusher. The most prolific wildcat recorded is the 1,160-foot-deep Lucas No. 1, at Spindletop, about 3 miles south of Beaumont, Texas, on January 10, 1901. The gusher was heard more than a mile away and yielded 800,000 barrels during the 9 days it was uncapped. The surrounding ground subsequently yielded 142,000,000 barrels.

GREATEST GUSHER (above): The greatest wildcat gusher in oil industry history going full blast in January, 1901. LARGEST FOUNTAIN (top right): This 560-foot-column in Arizona uses 7,000 gallons a minute. DEEPEST PENETRATION (bottom right): This Loffland rig dug a hole deeper than Mt. Everest is high.

Oil Spill

Greatest. The worst oil spill in history was of 246,400 tons of crude light oil from the Liberian tanker *Amoco Cadiz*, commanded by Capt. Pasquale Barardi, which drifted onto the French Brittany coast at Portsall on March 16, 1978. The oil slick stretched more than 100 miles from Pointe St. Mathieu to Perros-Guirec.

Greatest Flare. The greatest gas fire ever burnt at Gassi Touil in the Algerian Sahara from noon on November 13, 1961 to 9:30 a.m. on April 28, 1962. The pillar of flame rose 450 feet and the smoke 600 feet. It was eventually extinguished by Paul Neal ("Red") Adair, aged 47, of Austin, Texas, using 550 lbs. of dynamite. His fee was understood to be about $1,000,000.

Largest Gas Tank. The world's largest gas tank is that at Fontaine l'Eveque, Belgium, where disused mines have been adapted to store up to 500 million cubic meters (17,650 million cubic feet) of gas at ordinary pressure. Probably the largest conventional gas tank is that at Wien-Semmering, Vienna, Austria, completed in 1968, with a height of 274 feet 8 inches and a capacity of 10.59 million cubic feet.

Well

The world's deepest water well is the Stensvad Water Well 11-W1 7,320 feet deep drilled by the Great Northern Drilling Co. Inc. in Rosebud County, Montana, in October–November, 1961.

The Thermal Power Co. geothermal steam well begun in Sonoma County, California in 1955 is now down to 9,029 feet.

The highest recorded flow rate of any artesian well is 20,000 gallons per minute, certified in 1973 for a well 20 miles northwest of Orlando, Florida, by the Wekiva River.

Mines

Earliest. The earliest known mining operations were in the Ngwenya Hills of the Hhohho District of northwestern Swaziland where hematite (iron ore) was mined for body paint *c.* 41,000 B.C. The earliest known copper mines were reported in February, 1977, in the Timna Valley, north of Elath, Israel, tentatively dated *ante* 3000 B.C.

Deepest. The world's deepest mine is the Western Deep Levels Mine at Carletonville, South Africa. A depth of 12,600 feet (2.38 miles) was attained in May, 1975. At such extreme depths where the rock temperatures reach 131°F., refrigerated ventilation is necessary. The other great hazard is rock bursts due to the pressures.

Gold. The largest gold-mining area in the world is the Witwatersrand gold field extending 30 miles east and west of Johannesburg, South Africa. Gold was discovered there in 1886 by George Harrison and by 1944 more than 45 per cent of the world's gold was mined there by 320,000 Bantu and 44,000 Europeans. In 1975, 49.9 per cent of the world's supply came from this area. Production reached a peak in 1970 of 1,102 tons.

The largest gold mine in area is East Rand Proprietary Mines of South Africa, whose 8,785 claims cover 12,100 acres. The largest, by volume extracted, is Randfontein Estates Gold Mine Co., Ltd. with 170 million cubic yards—enough to cover Manhattan Island to a depth of 8 feet. The main tunnels if placed end to end would stretch a distance of 2,600 miles.

Richest. The richest gold mine historically has been Crown Mines with nearly 49.4 million ounces. The richest in yield per year in 1976 was West Driefontein with 0.71 oz. per ton milled, but Vaal Reefs produced the most with 2,240,000 oz. fine.

Iron. The world's largest iron mine is at Lebedinsky, U.S.S.R., in the Kursk Magnetic Anomaly which has altogether an estimated

22,400 million tons of rich (45–65 per cent) ore and 11,200,000 million tons of poorer ore in seams up to 2,000 feet thick. The world's greatest reserves are, however, those of Brazil, estimated to total 65,000 million tons, or 35 per cent of the world's total surface stock.

Copper. Historically the world's most productive copper mine has been the Bingham Canyon Mine, Utah, belonging to the Kennecott Copper Corporation with over 9,000,000 tons in the 65 years 1904–68. Currently the most productive is the Chuquicamata mine of the Anaconda Company 150 miles north of Antofagasta, Chile, with more than 330,000 tons.

The world's largest underground copper mine is the San Manuel Copper Mine in Arizona, owned by the Magma Copper Company, with 355.8 miles of underground workings, and an average annual extraction of over 193,000,000 tons of ore.

Silver, Lead and Zinc. The world's largest lead, zinc and silver mine is the Kidd Creek Mine of Texasgulf Canada Ltd., located at Timmins, Ontario, Canada.

Since 1970, the world's leading lead mine has been the Vibernum Trend in southeast Missouri with 489,397 tons in 1972, from which is extracted some 10 per cent of the world's output of lead.

The world's largest zinc smelter is the Cominco Ltd. plant at Trail, British Columbia, Canada, which has an annual capacity of 295,000 tons of zinc and 900 tons of cadmium.

Tungsten. The largest tungsten mine with published output figures is the Union Carbide mine in Mount Morgan, near Bishop, California. Opened in 1937, it has a capacity of 2,200 tons per day and a work force of 420.

Tin. The most productive dredging for tin ever recorded was 882.9 tons of concentrate (76.8 per cent pure tin) by Ayer Hitam No. 2 Dredge at Puchong, Malaysia in the 30 days of November, 1976, at 237 feet below surface level in a pond lowered 70 feet by pumping.

Platinum. The world's largest platinum refinery is the Impala plant at Springs Mine, South Africa. Largest producer is the Rustenburg Group, with more than 1,000,000 ounces per year.

Uranium. The world's largest uranium mine, located at Rossing in Namibia (South-West Africa) went into full production in 1978.

Excavation

The world's largest excavation is the Bingham Canyon Copper Mine, 30 miles south of Salt Lake City, Utah. From 1906 to mid-1976 the total excavation has been 3,700,000,000 tons over an area of 2.81 square miles to a depth of 2,540 feet. This is seven times the amount of material moved to build the Panama Canal. Three shifts of 900 men work around the clock with 39 electric shovels, 67 locomotives, 113 dump trucks and 17 drilling machines for the 31.3 tons of explosive used daily. The record daily extraction is 504,167 tons on October 13, 1974.

Manual Excavation. The world's deepest open pit of the pre-mechanical, pick-and-shovel era is the Kimberley Open Mine in South Africa, which took 43 years (1871 to 1914) to dig to a depth of nearly 1,200 feet, with a diameter of about 1,500 feet and a circumference of nearly a mile, covering an area of 36 acres. Over 3 tons (14,504,566 carats) of diamonds were extracted from the 28,000,000 tons of earth dug out. The inflow of water has now risen to a depth of 845 feet.

Strip Mine. The world's largest open cast mine is the Fortuna-Garsdorf lignite mine near Bergheim, West Germany. Since 1955 the cut has been extended to 2½ miles by 2 miles and 820 feet deep.

Largest Stone. The largest mined slab of quarried stone on record is one of 2,016 tons of slate at Spoutcrag Quarry, Langdale Valley, Cumbria, England, in May, 1969.

Spoil Dump. The world's largest artificial spoil dump is the New Cornelia Tailings at Ten Mile Wash, Arizona, with a volume of 274,026,000 cubic yards.

DEPTH 1000 FEET

GREATEST MANUAL EXCAVATION: Over a period of 43 years, the Kimberley Open Mine grew to nearly 1,200 feet in depth and nearly a mile in circumference.

Chapter Eight

THE MECHANICAL WORLD

1. Ships

Earliest. Evidence of seafaring between the Greek mainland and the island of Melos to trade obsidian *c.* 7250 B.C. was published in 1971. Oars found in bogs at Magle Mose, Sjaelland, Denmark, and Star Carr, North Yorkshire, England, have been dated to the 8th millennium B.C.

The oldest surviving boat is the 142-foot-long 40-ton Nile boat buried near the Great Pyramid of Khufu, Egypt, *c.* 2515 B.C., and now reassembled.

Earliest Power Vessels

Propulsion by steam engine was first achieved when the Marquis Jouffroy d'Abbans ascended a reach of the Saône River near Lyons, France, in 1783, in the 180-ton paddle steamer *Pyroscaphe.*

The tug *Charlotte Dundas* was the first successful power-driven vessel. She was a paddlewheel steamer built in Scotland in 1801–02 by William Symington (1763–1831), using a double-acting condensing engine constructed by James Watt (1736–1819).

The earliest regular steam run was by the *Clermont*, built by Robert Fulton (1765–1815), a U.S. engineer, which maintained a service from New York to Albany (150 miles in 32 hours) from August 17, 1807.

The oldest active steam ship is the *Skibladner*, which has plied Lake Mjøsa, Norway, since 1856. Originally built in Motala, Sweden, she has had two major refittings.

Earliest Turbine

The first turbine ship was the *Turbinia*, built in 1894, at Wallsend-on-Tyne, Tyne and Wear, England, to the design of the Hon. Sir Charles Algernon Parsons (1854–1931). The *Turbinia* was 100 feet long and of 44½ tons displacement with machinery consisting of three steam turbines totaling about 2,000 shaft horsepower. At her first public demonstration in 1897 she reached a speed of 34.5 knots (39.7 m.p.h.).

Atlantic Crossings

Earliest. The earliest crossing of the Atlantic by a power vessel, as opposed to an auxiliary-engined sailing ship, was a 22-day voyage, begun in April, 1827, from Rotterdam, Netherlands, to the West Indies by the *Curaçao*. She was a 127-foot wooden paddle boat of 438 tons, built in Dundee, Tayside, Scotland, in 1826, and purchased by the Dutch Government for the West Indian mail service. The earliest Atlantic crossing entirely under steam (with intervals for desalting the boilers) was by H.M.S. *Rhadamanthus* from Plymouth, England, to Barbados in 1832. The earliest crossing of the Atlantic under continuous steam power was by the condenser-fitted packet ship *Sirius* (703 tons) from Queenstown (now Cobh), Ireland, to Sandy Hook, New Jersey, in 18 days 10 hours on April 4–22, 1838.

Fastest. The fastest Atlantic crossing was made by the *United States* (then 51,988, later 38,216, gross tons), former flagship of the United States Lines. On her maiden voyage between July 3 and 7, 1952, from New York City, to Le Havre, France, and Southampton, England, she averaged 35.59 knots, or 40.98 m.p.h., for 3 days 10 hours 40 minutes (6:36 p.m. G.M.T. July 3, to 5:16 a.m. July 7) on a route of 2,949 nautical miles from the Ambrose Light Vessel to the Bishop Rock Light, Isles of Scilly, Cornwall, England. During this run, on July 6–7, 1952, she steamed the greatest distance ever covered by any ship in a day's run (24 hours)—868 nautical miles, hence averaging 36.17 knots (41.65 m.p.h.). The maximum speed attained from her 240,000 shaft horsepower engines was 38.32 knots (44.12 m.p.h.) in trials on June 9–10, 1952.

Submerged. The fastest disclosed submerged Atlantic crossing is 6 days 11 hours 55 minutes by the U.S. nuclear-powered submarine *Nautilus*, which traveled 3,150 miles from Portland, Dorset, England, to New York City, arriving on August 25, 1958.

Pacific Crossing

The fastest crossing of the Pacific Ocean (4,840 nautical miles) was 6 days 1 hour 27 minutes by the containership *Sea-Land Commerce* (50,315 tons) from Yokohama, Japan, to Long Beach, California, in 1973, at an average speed of 33.27 knots (38.31 m.p.h.).

Southernmost

The farthest south ever reached by a ship was achieved on February 15, 1912, when the *Fram* reached latitude 78° 41′ S., off the Antarctic coast.

Largest Passenger Liner

When in operation, R.M.S. *Queen Elizabeth* (82,998, formerly 83,673 gross tons), of the Cunard fleet, was the largest passenger vessel ever built and also had the largest displacement of any liner in the world. She had an overall length of 1,031 feet and was 118 feet 7 inches in breadth. She was powered by steam turbines which developed 168,000 h.p. The *Queen Elizabeth's* normal sea speed was 28½ knots (32.8 m.p.h.). Her last passenger voyage ended on November 15, 1968. In 1970, she was removed to Hong Kong to serve as a floating marine university and renamed *Seawise University*. On January 9, 1972, she caught fire in three places simultaneously. Most of the gutted hull had been cut up and removed by December, 1977.

The largest active liner is R.M.S. *Queen Elizabeth 2* of 66,851 gross tons and an overall length of 963 feet, completed for the Cunard Line Ltd. in 1969. She set a "turnaround" record of 8 hours 3 minutes at New York on May 17, 1972. In her 1979 World Cruise the Queen Mary and Queen Elizabeth suites were priced at $181,193.

Fastest Warship

The world's fastest warship is the 112-ton U.S. Navy test vehicle SES-100B, which attained a speed of 88.88 knots (102.35 m.p.h.) in 1976.

Largest Battleship

The Japanese battleships *Yamato* (sunk southwest of Kyushu by U.S. planes on April 7, 1945) and *Musashi* (sunk in the Philippine Sea by 11 bombs and 16 torpedoes on October 24, 1944) were the largest battleships ever commissioned, each with a full-load displacement of 72,809 tons. With an overall length of 863 feet, a beam of 127 feet and a full-load draught of 35½ feet, they mounted nine 18.1-inch guns in three triple turrets. Each gun weighed 181 tons and was 75 feet in length, firing a 3,200-lb. projectile.

The largest battleship now is the U.S.S. *New Jersey*, with a full-load displacement of 59,000 tons and an overall length of 888 feet. She was the last fire support ship on active service in the world and was decommissioned on December 17, 1969.

Largest Aircraft Carrier

The warships with the largest full-load displacement in the world are the U.S. Navy aircraft carriers U.S.S. *Nimitz* and *Dwight D. Eisenhower* at 91,400 tons. They are 1,092 feet in length overall and have a speed well in excess of 30 knots with their nuclear-powered 280,000 shaft horsepower reactors. They have to be refuelled after about 900,000 miles steaming. Their complement is 6,300. The total cost of the *Eisenhower*, commissioned on October 18, 1977, exceeded $2 billion excluding the more than 90 aircraft carried. U.S.S. *Enterprise* is, however, 1,102 feet long and thus still the longest warship ever built.

Most Powerful Cruiser

The Fleet Escort Ships (formerly cruisers) with the greatest fire power are the three Albany class ships, U.S.S. *Albany, Chicago* and *Columbus* of 13,700 tons and 673 feet overall. They carry 2 twin Talos and 2 twin Tartar surface-to-air missiles and an 8-tube Asroc launcher.

The largest cruiser was the U.S.S. *Newport News* of 21,500 tons full load, commissioned on January 29, 1949, and since then extensively modified as a flagship.

Fastest Destroyer

The highest speed attained by a destroyer was 45.02 knots (51.84 m.p.h.) by the 3,750-ton French destroyer *Le Terrible* in 1935. She was powered by four Yarrow small-tube boilers and two geared turbines giving 100,000 shaft horsepower. She was removed from the active list at the end of 1957.

Submarines

Largest. The $1,250,000,000 nuclear-powered submarine U.S.S. *Ohio* was commissioned at Groton, Connecticut, in April, 1979, with

24 Trident I missiles of 4,600-mile range and a submerged displacement of 18,700 tons. She is 560 feet in length. The U.S.S.R. Delta II class submarines, first reported in November, 1973, with 16 SSN 8 missiles may be even larger. Four or five were in service by January, 1977, when still larger submarines were reported under construction.

Fastest. The world's fastest submarines are the U.S. Navy's teardrop hulled nuclear vessels of the *Los Angeles* class. They have been listed officially as capable of a speed of "30 plus knots" but the true figure is believed to be dramatically higher. The first 4 were commissioned in 1975–76, with an additional 19 by 1979–80.

Deepest. The two U.S. Navy vessels able to descend 12,000 feet are the 3-man *Trieste II* (DSV 1) of 303 tons, recommissioned in November, 1973, and the DSV 2 (Deep submergence vessel) U.S.S. *Alvin*. The *Trieste II* was reconstructed from the record-breaking bathyscaphe *Trieste*, but without the Krupp-built sphere, which enabled it to descend to 35,820 feet.

Largest and Longest Tanker

The world's largest tanker and ship of any kind is the French *Pierre Guillaumat* of 555,031 tons deadweight (274,838 g.r.t.), completed for Compagnie Nationale de Navigation on November 9, 1977. She is 1,359 feet long with a beam of 206.6 feet, has a draught of 93.8 feet, and is powered by 4 turbines delivering 65,000 s.h.p. She can maintain a speed of 18.4 m.p.h. *Bellamya* (completed for Société Maritime Shell on December 31, 1976) is 275,276 g.r.t. but 553,662 dwt.

Globtik Tankers U.S., Inc. expects to receive the first of three 600,000 dwt. nuclear-powered tankers from Newport News Shipbuilding and Dry Dock Co. in 1985, at a cost of $318,000,000 each. These 1,303-foot-long tankers will have an annual carrying capacity of 25 million barrels or 5 million tons of crude oil at 22 knots.

Some idea of the length of these ships can be conveyed by the thought that it would take a golfer, standing on the stem, a full-powered drive and a chip shot to reach the stern.

Largest Cargo Vessel

The largest vessel in the world capable of carrying dry cargo is the Liberian ore/oil carrier *World Gala* of 286,981 deadweight tons with a length of 1,109 feet and beam of 179 feet. She is owned by Liberian Trident Transports Inc. and was completed in 1973.

Fastest-Built. During the Second World War "Liberty Ships" of prefabricated welded steel construction were built at seven shipyards on the Pacific coast, under the management of Henry J. Kaiser (1882–1967). The record time for assembly of one ship of 7,200 gross tons (10,500 tons deadweight) was 4 days 15½ hours. In January, 1968, some 900 Liberty Ships were still in service.

Most Powerful Tugs

The world's largest and most powerful tugs are the *S.A. Wolraad Waltemade* and her sister ship *John Ross* (2,822 g.r.t.) rated at 19,200

LARGEST FERRY: The GTS *Finnjet* can attain a speed of 30.5 knots as it crosses the Baltic Sea, carrying up to 350 cars and 1,532 passengers.

horsepower and with a bollard pull of 150 tons. They have an overall length of 278 feet 10 inches and a beam of 49 feet 10 inches. They were built to handle the largest oil tankers, and were completed respectively in April, 1976 (Leith, Scotland) and in October, 1976 (Durban, South Africa).

Largest Car Ferry

The world's largest car and passenger ferry is the 30.5 knot, 24,600 g.r.t. GTS *Finnjet* which entered service across the Baltic between Helsinki and Travemünde, West Germany, on May 13, 1977. She can carry 350 cars and 1,532 passengers.

Largest Hydrofoil

The world's largest naval hydrofoil is the 212-foot-long *Plainview* (310 tons full load), launched by Lockheed Shipbuilding and Construction Company at Seattle, Washington, on June 28, 1965. She has a service speed of 50 knots (57 m.p.h.).

Three 165-ton Supramar PTS 150 Mk. III hydrofoils, carrying 250 passengers at 40 knots, ply the Malmö-Copenhagen crossing, between Sweden and Denmark. They were built by Westermoen Hydrofoil Ltd. of Mandal, Norway.

A 500-ton wing ground effect vehicle capable of carrying 990 tons has been reported to be plying a U.S.S.R. river.

Most Powerful Dredger

The world's most powerful dredger is the 468.4-foot-long *Prins der Nederlanden* of 10,586 g.r.t. Using two suction tubes, she can dredge 22,400 tons of sand from a depth of 115 feet in less than one hour.

Most Powerful Icebreaker

The world's most powerful icebreaker is the U.S.S.R.'s 25,000-ton atomic-powered icebreaker *Arktika*, able to smash through ice up to nearly 13 feet thick. On August 9, 1977, she sailed from Murmansk and reached the North Pole at 2 a.m. G.M.T. on August 17.

The largest converted icebreaker is the 1,007-foot-long S.S. *Manhattan* (43,000 s.h.p.), which was converted by the Humble Oil Co. into a 150,000-ton icebreaker with an armored prow 69 feet 2 inches long. She made a double voyage through the Northwest Passage in arctic Canada to Alaska from August 24 to November 12, 1969. The Northwest Passage was first navigated in 1906.

Most Expensive Yacht

The ultimate in luxury yachts is the 20-knot, 212-foot *Al Riyadh*, built at van Lent's yard, Keeg, Netherlands, for King Khalid of Saudi Arabia at a cost above $10 million. It has a helicopter pad, satellite communications, a pool and an operating theatre.

Largest Whale Factory

The largest whale factory ship is the U.S.S.R.'s *Sovietskaya Ukraina* (32,034 gross tons), with a summer deadweight of 46,000 tons, completed in October, 1959. She is 713.6 feet in length and 94 feet 3 inches in the beam.

Wooden Ships

The heaviest wooden ship ever built was the *Richelieu*, 333 feet 8 inches long, of 8,534 tons, launched in Toulon, France, on December 3, 1873.

The longest modern wooden ship ever built was the New York-constructed *Rochambeau* (1867–72) formerly the *Dunderberg*, which measured 377 feet 4 inches overall.

The biblical length of Noah's Ark was 300 cubits or, at 18 inches to a cubit, 450 feet.

Longest Dug-out Canoe

The world's longest canoe is the 117-foot-long, 20-ton Kauri wood Maori war canoe *Nga Toki Matawhaorua*, built with adzes at Kerikeri Inlet, New Zealand, in 1940 to hold a crew of 70 or more.

Sailing Ships

Largest. The largest sailing vessel ever built was the *France II* (5,806 gross tons), launched at Bordeaux in 1911. The *France II* was a steel-hulled, five-masted barque (square-rigged on four masts and fore and aft rigged on the aftermost mast). Her hull measured 418 feet overall. Although principally designed as a sailing vessel with a stump topgallant rig, she was also fitted with two steam engines. She was wrecked in 1922.

The only 7-masted sailing vessel ever built was the 375.6-foot-long *Thomas W. Lawson* (5,218 gross tons), built at Quincy, Massachusetts, in 1902. She was lost in the English Channel on December 15, 1907.

LONGEST DUGOUT CANOE: This 20-ton Kauri wood Maori war canoe, built in New Zealand in 1940, is 117 feet long and seats more than 70 paddlers.

Largest Junks. The largest junk on record was the seagoing *Cheng Ho* of *c.* 1420, flagship of Admiral Cheng Ho's 62 treasure ships, with a displacement of 3,100 tons and a length variously estimated up to 538 feet. It was believed to have had 9 masts.

A river junk 361 feet long, with treadmill-operated paddlewheels, was recorded in 1161 A.D. In *c.* 280 A.D. a floating fortress 600 feet square, built by Wang Chün on the Yangtze, took part in the Chin-Wu river war. Modern junks do not, even in the case of the Chiang-su traders, exceed 170 feet in length.

Longest Day's Run Under Sail. The longest day's run claimed by any sailing ship was one of 465 nautical miles (535.45 statute miles) in 23 hours 17 mins. by the *Champion of the Seas* (2,722 registered tons)

FULL RIGGED SEVEN-MASTED SHIP was unique. Built in Massachusetts, she served only 5 years before being lost at sea.

on her maiden voyage on December 11–12, 1854. She was on passage in the south Indian Ocean under Capt. Alex. Newlands, running before a northwesterly gale. She averaged 19.97 knots.

Slowest Voyage. Perhaps the slowest passage on record was that of the *Red Rock* (1,600 tons), which was posted missing at Lloyd's of London after taking 112 days for a 950-mile passage across the Coral Sea from February 20 to June 12, 1899, at an average speed of less than 0.4 of a knot.

Largest Sails. The largest spars ever carried were those in the British Royal Navy battleship *Temeraire*, completed at Chatham, Kent, on August 31, 1877. The fore and main yards measured 115 feet in length. The mainsail contained 5,100 square feet of canvas, weighing 2 tons, and the total sail area was 25,000 square feet.

Deepest Anchorage

The deepest anchorage ever achieved is one of 24,600 feet in the mid-Atlantic Romanche Trench by Capt. Jacques-Yves Cousteau's research vessel *Calypso*, with a 5½-mile-long nylon cable, on July 29, 1956.

Largest Propeller

The largest ship's propeller ever cast has been one for the Kuwaiti oil tanker *Al Rawdatain* (328,000 dwt.), being built at Chantiers Naval de la Ciotat, France. It weighs 82.13 tons, has a diameter of 31 feet 8 inches and was constructed by Heliphoc of Marseilles, France, in 1976.

Wrecks

The largest ship ever wrecked has been the $50 million tanker *Olympic Bravery* of 275,000 dwt. which ran aground off Ushant Island, N.W. France, on January 24, 1976. She broke in two on March 12, 1976.

The oldest shipwreck ever found is one of a Cycladic trading vessel, located off the islet of Dhokos, near the Greek island of Hydra, reported in May, 1975, and dated to 2450 B.C. ± 250.

Largest Collision

The closest approach to an irresistible force striking an immovable object occurred on December 19, 1977, 22 miles off the coast of southern Africa, when the tanker *Venoil* (330,954 dwt.) struck her sister ship *Venpet* (330,869 dwt.).

Greatest Roll

The ultimate in rolling was recorded in heavy seas off Coos Bay, Oregon, on November 13, 1971, when the U.S. Coast Guard motor lifeboat *Intrepid* made a 360-degree roll.

Largest Oil Platforms

The deepest fixed-leg oil platform in the world sits in 1,025 feet of water 100 miles southeast of New Orleans, Louisiana. The overall height of the $275 million structure is 1,265 feet.

The world's most massive oil platform is the Central Ninian production and storage platform built at Loch Kishorn, Highland, Scotland. When towed out to the North Sea site on May 5, 1978, it was the heaviest object ever moved at 660,000 tons ballasted weight. She was towed by 8 tugs with a combined strength of 92,000 h.p. The height of the concrete structure is 509 feet and the overall height is 820 feet.

2. Road Vehicles

Coaches. Before the widespread use of tarred road surfaces from 1845 coach-riding was slow and hazardous. The zenith in speed was reached on July 13, 1888, when J. Selby, Esq., drove the "Old Times" coach 108 miles from London to Brighton and back with 8 teams and 14 changes in 7 hours 50 minutes to average 13.79 m.p.h. Four-horse carriages could maintain a speed of $21\frac{1}{4}$ m.p.h. for nearly an hour.

CARS

Most Cars. In 1978 it was estimated that in the United States 138 million drivers drove 147 million vehicles 1,480,000,000,000 miles, or 206.2 miles per week per driver.

Earliest Automobile. The earliest car of which there is record is a two-foot-long steam-powered model, constructed by Ferdinand Verbiest (died 1687), a Belgian Jesuit priest, described in his *Astronomia Europaea*. His 1668 model was possibly inspired either by Giovanni Branca's description of a steam turbine, published in 1629, or by writings on "fire carts" during the Chu dynasty (*c.* 800 B.C.) in the library of the Emperor K'ang-hi of China, to whom he was an astronomer during the period *c.* 1665–80.

The earliest mechanically-propelled passenger vehicle was the first of two military steam tractors completed in Paris in 1769 by Nicolas-Joseph Cugnot (1725–1804). This reached about $2\frac{1}{4}$ m.p.h. Cugnot's second, larger tractor, completed in 1771, today survives in the *Conservatoire national des arts et métiers* in Paris.

The first true internal-combustion-engined vehicle was built by a Londoner, Samuel Brown, whose 4-h.p. 2-cylinder-engined carriage climbed Shooters Hill, Blackheath, Kent, England, in May, 1826.

Earliest Gasoline-Driven Cars. The first successful gasoline-driven car, the Motorwagen, built by Karl-Friedrich Benz (1844–1929) of Karlsruhe, ran at Mannheim, Germany, in late 1885. It was a 560-lb. 3-wheeler reaching 8–10 m.p.h. Its single-cylinder chain-drive engine (bore 91.4 mm., stroke 160 mm.) delivered 0.85 h.p. at 200 r.p.m. It was patented on January 29, 1886. Its first 1-kilometer road test was reported in the local newspaper, the *Neue Badische Landeszeitung*, of June 4, 1886, under the heading "Miscellaneous." Two were built in 1885 of which one has been preserved in "running order" at the Deutsches Museum, Munich.

Most Durable Car

The highest recorded mileage for a car is 1,184,880 authenticated miles by August, 1978, for a 1957 Mercedes 180D owned by Robert O'Reilly of Olympia, Washington.

Earliest Registrations. The world's first plates were probably introduced by the Parisian police in France in 1893. The first American plates were in 1901 in New York State. Registration plates were introduced in Britain in 1903. The original A1 plate was secured by the 2nd Earl Russell (1865–1931) for his 12-h.p. Napier. This plate, willed to Mr. Trevor Laker of Leicester, was sold in August, 1959, for £2,500 ($7,000) in aid of charity. It was reported in April, 1973, that a "cherished" number plate changed hands in a private sale for £14,000 ($35,000).

Fastest Cars

Rocket-Engined. The highest speed attained by any wheeled land vehicle is 631.367 m.p.h. over the first measured kilometer by *The Blue Flame*, a liquid natural gas-powered 4-wheeled vehicle driven by Gary Gabelich (b. San Pedro, California, August 29, 1940) on the Bonneville Salt Flats, Utah, on October 23, 1970. Momentarily Gabelich exceeded 650 m.p.h. The tires were made by Goodyear. The car was powered by a liquid natural gas/hydrogen peroxide rocket engine delivering 22,000 lbs. s.t. maximum, and theoretically capable of 900 m.p.h.

Jet. The highest speed attained by any jet-engined car is 613.995 m.p.h. over a flying 666.386 yards by the 34-foot-7-inch-long, 9,000-lb. *Spirit of America—Sonic I*, driven by Norman Craig Breedlove (born March 23, 1938, Los Angeles) on Bonneville Salt Flats, Utah, on November 15, 1965. The car was powered by a General Electric J79 GE-3 jet engine, developing 15,000 lbs. static thrust at sea level.

Wheel-Driven. The highest speed attained is 429.311 m.p.h. over a flying 666.386 yards by Donald Malcolm Campbell (1921–

67), a British engineer, in the 30-foot-long *Bluebird*, weighing 9,600 lbs., on the salt flats at Lake Eyre, South Australia, on July 17, 1964. The car was powered by a Bristol-Siddeley Proteus 705 gas-turbine engine developing 4,500 s.h.p. Its peak speed was *c.* 445 m.p.h. It was rebuilt in 1962, after a crash at about 360 m.p.h. on September 16, 1960.

Piston-Engined. The highest speed attained is 418.504 m.p.h. over a flying 666.386 yards by Robert Sherman Summers (born April 4, 1937, Omaha, Nebraska) in *Goldenrod* at Bonneville Salt Flats, Utah, on November 12, 1965. The car, measuring 32 feet long and weighing 5,500 lbs., was powered by four fuel-injected Chrysler Hemi engines (total capacity 27,924 c.c.) developing 2,400 b.h.p.

Diesel-Engined. The prototype 230-h.p., 3-liter Mercedes C 111/3 attained 203.3 m.p.h. in tests on the Nardo Circuit, Southern Italy, October 5–15, 1978.

Fastest Racing Car. The world's fastest racing car yet produced was the Porsche 917/30 Can-Am car powered by a 5,374-c.c. flat 12 turbo-charged engine developing 1,100 b.h.p. On the Paul Ricard circuit near Toulon, France, in August, 1973, Mark Donohue (U.S.) reached a speed of 257 m.p.h. The two models built took 2.2 seconds to go from 0 to 60 m.p.h., 4.3 seconds from 0 to 100 m.p.h., and 12.6 seconds from 0 to 200 m.p.h. In 1973, the UOP Shadow Can-Am car's 8.1-liter turbo-charged Chevrolet V-8 engine developed 1,240 b.h.p.

FASTEST CARS: *The Blue Flame* (top), a rocket-engined car driven by Gary Gabelich, attained the highest speed of any wheeled land vehicle. Craig Breedlove's *Spirit of America—Sonic I* (bottom) holds the speed record for a jet-engined car.

Fastest Production Car. The fastest production road car (as claimed by a manufacturer) is 195.7 m.p.h. for the Lamborghini Countach P400. The Ferrari BB Berlinetta Boxer has the highest independently (*Autocar*) road-tested speed for a production car at 163 m.p.h. The Aston Martin Vantage has an *estimated* maximum speed of 170 m.p.h. The fastest road-tested acceleration reported is 0–60 in 5.3 seconds and 0–100 in 12.3 seconds for a Porsche 3,299-c.c. Turbo at Ehra-Lessien, West Germany.

Fastest Truck. The U.S. stock truck class A diesel record was set on the Bonneville Salt Flats, Utah, on September 9, 1975, when Harold Miller, 26, and Larry Lange, 38, drove their 17,500-lb. rig, powered by a 1,150 cu. in. Cummins turbo-charged diesel engine, to a speed of 132.154 m.p.h.

Longest in Production

The longest any car has been in production is 42 years (1910–52), including wartime interruptions, in the case of the Jowett "Flat Twin," produced in Britain.

The Volkswagen "Beetle" series, originally designed by Ferdinand Porsche, ceased production on January 19, 1978, with 19,200,000 cars produced since May, 1938.

Largest Cars

Of cars produced for private road use, the largest ever was the Bugatti "Royale" Type 41, known as the "Golden Bugatti," of which only six (not seven) were made at Molsheim, France, by the Italian, Ettore Bugatti, and some survive. First built in 1927, this machine has an 8-cylinder engine of 12.7-liter capacity, and measures over 22 feet in length. The hood is over 7 feet long.

CAPACIOUS CADILLAC; The 29-foot-6-inch-long 1976 Fleetwood Cadillac specially built for Joel Nelson is equipped with such necessities of life as a bar, videotape equipment and 4 telephones. (The exterior of the car is shown on page D.)

LARGEST CAR: This 1931 Type 41 "Royale" Bugatti, called the "Golden Bugatti," was over 22 feet long. Only six were made.

A special $100,000 "stretched" 1976 Fleetwood Cadillac built for Joel D. Nelson of Bakersfield, California, exhibited in April, 1979, measures 29 feet 6 inches long. It is fitted inside with 2 color TV sets, an 8-speaker stereo system, a sink, refrigerator, bar, videotape recorder and camera, 4 telephones and a safe.

The longest present-day limousine is the Stageway Coaches Inc. (U.K.) 10-door "Travelall" 18-seat model, measuring 25 feet 4¼ inches overall.

The heaviest standard production car is the U.S.S.R.'s Zil 114, which weighs 7,000 lbs.

(For cars not intended for private use, see *Largest Engines*.)

Most Expensive Used Cars

The greatest price paid for a used car is $421,040 for a 1936 Mercedes-Benz Roadster from the M. L. Cohn collection, by a telephone bidder in Monaco at Christie's sale on February 25, 1979, at the Los Angeles Convention Center.

The greatest collection of vintage cars is the William F. Harrah Collection of 1,700, estimated to be worth more than $4,000,000, in Reno, Nevada. Mr. Harrah was still looking for a Chalmers-Detroit 1909 Tourabout, an Owen car of 1910–12, and a Nevada Truck of 1915 when he died in 1978.

Most Expensive Special Cars

The most expensive car ever built is the Presidential 1969 Lincoln Continental Executive delivered to the U.S. Secret Service on October 14, 1968. It has an overall length of 21 feet 6.3 inches with a 13-foot-4-inch wheelbase and, with the addition of two tons of armor plate, weighs 12,000 lbs. The cost for research, development and manufacture was estimated at $500,000, but it is rented for a mere $5,000 per annum. Even if all four tires were to be shot out it can travel at 50 m.p.h. on inner rubber-edged steel discs.

Carriage House Motor Cars Ltd. of New York City in March, 1978, completed four years' work on converting a 1973 Rolls-Royce, including lengthening it by 30 inches. The price tag was $500,000.

Most Inexpensive. The cheapest car of all-time was the 1922 Red Bug Buckboard, built by Briggs and Stratton Co. of Milwaukee, Wisconsin, listed at $150–$125. It had a 62-inch wheel base and weighed 245 lbs. The cheapest model listed in *Autocar's* New Car Prices feature of May 5, 1979, was the Fiat 126 at £1,783 ($3,566) including tax. The early models of the King Midget cars were sold in kit form for self-assembly for as little as $100 as late as 1948.

Largest Engines

The highest engine capacity of a production car was $13\frac{1}{2}$ liters (824 cubic inches), in the case of the Pierce-Arrow 6–66 Raceabout of 1912–18, the Peerless 6–60 of 1912–14 and the Fageol of 1918. The largest currently available is the V-8 engine of 500.1 cubic inches (8,195 c.c.), developing 235 b.h.p. net, used in the 1972 Cadillac Fleetwood Eldorado.

The largest car ever used was the "White Triplex," sponsored by J. H. White of Philadelphia. Completed early in 1928, after two years' work, the car weighed about $4\frac{1}{2}$ tons and was powered by three Liberty V-12 aircraft engines with a total capacity of 81,188 c.c., developing 1,500 b.h.p. at 2,000 r.p.m. It was used to break the world speed record, but crashed at Daytona, Florida, on March 13, 1929.

Currently, the most powerful car on the road is the 6-wheeled Jameson-Concorde, powered by a 27,000-c.c. 1,760-h.p. Rolls-Royce V12 Merlin aero-engine, governed down to a maximum speed of 185 m.p.h. It has a range of 300 miles with tanks of 72-gallon capacity. The vehicle weighs 2.96 tons overall.

The world's most powerful piston-engine car is "Quad A1." It was designed and built in 1964 by Jim Lytle and was first shown in May, 1965, at the Los Angeles Sports Arena. The car features 4 Allison V-12 aircraft engines with a total of 6,840 cu. in. (112,087 c.c.) displacement and 12,000 horsepower. The car has 4-wheel drive, 8 wheels and tires, and dual 6-disc clutch assemblies. The wheelbase is 160 inches. It weighs 5,860 lbs. and has 96 spark plugs and 96 exhaust pipes.

Gasoline Consumption

The world record for fuel economy on a closed circuit course (one of 14.076 miles) was set by Ben Visser (U.S.) in a highly modified 90.8 cu. in. 1959 Opel CarAvan Station Wagon in the annual Shell Research Laboratory contest at Wood River, Illinois, driven by Ben and Carolyn Visser on October 2, 1973, with 451.90 ton-miles per gallon and 376.59 miles on one gallon of gasoline. The tire pressure was 200 lbs. per square inch and the maximum speed was 12 m.p.h.

On July 30, 1977, on the Hockenheim Ring, West Germany, a 200-c.c. diesel-engined 3-wheeler covered 417.9 miles on 1 liter of fuel, which is equivalent to over 1,580 miles to the gallon.

Gas Station Pumping

The highest gallonage sold through a single pump is claimed by the Mornington Motors Ltd., Dunedin, New Zealand, for dispensing 7,813.77 Imperial gallons (9,376.5 U.S. gallons) in 24 hours on June 25, 1977.

LONGEST BUS: Stepping to the rear would involve quite a journey in this 76-foot-long bus. Built by the Wayne Corporation, it can carry 187 passengers.

Most Massive Vehicle

The most massive vehicle ever constructed is the Marion 8-caterpillar crawler used for conveying *Saturn V* rockets to their launching pads at the John F. Kennedy Space Center, Cape Canaveral, Florida. It measures 131 feet 4 inches by 114 feet and two of them built at the same time cost $12,300,000. The loaded train weight is 9,000 tons. Its windshield wipers with 42-inch blades are the world's largest.

Buses

Earliest. The first municipal motor bus service in the world was inaugurated on April 12, 1903, between the Eastbourne railway station and Meads, East Sussex, in England. A steam-powered bus named *Royal Patent* ran between Gloucester and Cheltenham, England, for 4 months in 1831.

Longest Route. The longest regularly scheduled bus route is Greyhound's "Supercruiser" Miami-to-San Francisco route over 3,240 miles in 81 hours 50 minutes (average speed of travel 39.59 m.p.h.). The total Greyhound fleet numbers 5,500 buses.

Longest. The longest buses in the world are the 12-ton, 76-foot-long articulated buses, with 121 passenger seats and room for an additional 66 "strap-hangers," built by the Wayne Corporation of Richmond, Indiana for use in the Middle East.

Largest Dump Truck

The world's largest dump truck is the Terex Titan 33–19 manufactured by the Terex Division of the General Motors Corporation. It has a loaded weight of 604.7 tons and a capacity of 350 tons. When unloading, its height is 56 feet. The 16-cylinder engine delivers 3,300 h.p. The fuel tank holds 1,560 gallons. It went into service in November, 1974.

Most Powerful Fire Engine

The world's most powerful fire appliance is the 860-h.p. 8-wheel Oshkosh fire truck used for aircraft fires. It can discharge 49,920 gallons of foam through 2 turrets in just 150 seconds. It weighs 66 tons.

Largest Bulldozer

The world's most powerful bulldozer is the 152½-ton VCON V220 diesel electric bulldozer, completed by the Marion Power Shovel Co., Inc. of Dallas, Texas, in 1975. The blade is 26 feet wide and can push 90 cubic yards of earth. The machine is 52 feet long and 23½ feet high, with 500 h.p. on each of the four 10-foot-2-inch-diameter wheels.

Most Powerful Wrecker

The world's most powerful wrecker is the Vance Corporation 28-ton 30-foot-long Monster No. 2 stationed at Hammond, Indiana. It can lift in excess of 179 tons on its short boom.

Largest Earth Mover

The Balderson "Double Dude" plow harnessed to a Caterpillar SXS D9H 820 flywheel horsepower tractor can cast 14,185 cubic yards of earth in one hour.

Largest Tractor

The world's largest tractor is the $325,000, 65-ton Northern Manufacturing Co. 8-wheeled 16V-747. It is 14 feet tall and 20 feet 7 inches wide with an 848.6-gallon tank. It was launched in October, 1978.

Longest Motor Trip

The longest continuous trailer tour is one of 143,716 miles by Harry B. Coleman and Peggy Larson in a Volkswagen Camper from August 20, 1976, to April 20, 1978, through 113 countries. Saburo Ouchi (b. Feb. 7, 1942) of Tokyo, Japan, drove 167,770 miles in 91 countries from December 2, 1969, to February 10, 1978. He said Queensland, Australia, has the worst roads in the world for his Volkswagen "Kombi."

Largest Road Load

The world's record road load is one of 830 tons when a nuclear reactor vessel was moved from Seneca to Marseilles, Illinois, on a 384-wheel Schearele trailer by the Reliance Truck Co. on February 12, 1977.

LARGEST BULLDOZER: The VCON V220 is 52 feet long and carries a 26-foot-wide blade.

The greatest weight moved on wheels anywhere in the world was a 2,399-ton module for the Claymore field North Sea oil platform measuring 200 feet by 50 feet by 28 feet on a 640-wheeled Magnaload platform at Willington Quay, Wallsend, England in August, 1976.

Largest Tires

The world's largest tires are manufactured in Topeka, Kansas, by the Goodyear Co. for giant dump trucks. They are 11 feet 6 inches in diameter, weigh 12,500 pounds and cost more than $50,000. A tire 17 feet in diameter is believed to be the practical upper limit.

LARGEST TIRE: This monster weighs 12,500 pounds and costs more than $50,000.

Most Countries in 24 Hours

Ralph C. Johnson, Dean Rittenhouse and Herman Oldigs drove a rented Mercedes 280S 1,262.6 miles in 23 hours 33 minutes on May 11, 1977. They started in the Netherlands, crossed into Belgium, then Luxembourg, France, West Germany, Switzerland, Liechtenstein, Austria, Italy, Monaco and Spain, finishing in Andorra, for a total of 11 countries in their whirlwind tour.

Amphibious Vehicle

The only transatlantic crossing by an amphibious vehicle was achieved by Ben and Elinore Carlin (Australia and U.S. respectively) in an amphibious jeep called "Half-Safe." Mr. Carlin completed the leg across the English Channel on August 24, 1951, and the complete circumnavigation of the world on May 8, 1958, after having covered 39,000 miles by land and 9,600 miles by river and sea.

Longest Skid Marks

The longest recorded skid marks on a public road were 950 feet long, left by a Jaguar car involved in an accident on the M.1 near Luton, Bedfordshire, England, on June 30, 1960. Evidence given in the High Court case *Hurlock v. Inglis and others* indicated a speed "in excess of 100 m.p.h." before the application of the brakes.

The skid marks made by the jet-powered *Spirit of America*, driven by Craig Breedlove, after the car went out of control at Bonneville Salt Flats, Utah, on October 15, 1964, were nearly 6 miles long.

Fastest Round-the-World Driving

The fastest circumnavigation embracing more than an equator's length of driving (26,514.23 road miles) was one of 102 days 18 hours 26 minutes 54.7 seconds by Johnnie Parsons in the U.S. Bicentennial Global Record Run, July 4–October 15, 1976, in a Pontiac Grand Prix from National Car Rental. He averaged 47.22 m.p.h.

Paula Murphy (*nee* Mulhauser) drove the same race in a Pontiac Sunbird, finishing on October 17, 1976, with 26,412.20 miles in 105 days 2 hours 29 minutes 25.0 seconds. Gasoline purchased on the trip through 28 countries varied from 18¢ to $2.00 a gallon.

ONLY AMPHIBIOUS CIRCUMNAVIGATION OF THE WORLD: In this jeep, "Half-Safe," Ben Carlin (Australia) arrived in London after crossing the English Channel on one leg of his journey across the Atlantic.

MOST SUCCESSFUL RACING CAR MECHANIC: Leo Villa (left) visits with Donald Campbell.

Largest Taxi Fleet and Longest Cab Ride

The largest taxi fleet was that of New York City, which amounted to 29,000 cabs in October, 1929, compared with the present figure of 12,500, plus an equal number of "gypsy" cabs.

The longest cab ride on record is one of 6,753.3 miles by Fred Hamby, hired by Charles Dailie and Herbert Sedinger, through 16 U.S. states on September 9–25, 1978. They started in Lanette, Alabama.

Driving in Reverse

Charles Creighton (1908–70) and James Hargis of Maplewood, Missouri, drove their Ford Model A 1929 roadster in reverse from New York City to Los Angeles (3,340 miles), July 26–August 13, 1930, *without* stopping the engine once. They arrived back in New York on September 5, again in reverse, thus completing 7,180 miles in 42 days.

Gerald Hoagland drove a 1969 Chevrolet Impala 501 miles non-stop in 17 hours 38 minutes at Chemung Speed Drome, New York, July 9–10, 1976.

Most Successful Mechanic

Leopold Alfonso Villa (1899–1979) was a racing mechanic or chief engineer for Malcolm and Donald Campbell when they set 21 world speed records (10 land, 11 water) from 1924 to 1964.

Longest Tow

The longest tow on record was one of 4,759 miles from Halifax, Nova Scotia, to Canada's Pacific coast, when Frank J. Elliott and George A. Scott of Amherst, Nova Scotia, persuaded 168 passing motorists in 89 days to tow their Model T Ford (in fact, engineless) to win a $1,000 bet on October 15, 1927.

Lawn Mowers

Largest. The widest gang mower on record is the 5.6-ton 60-foot-wide Big Green Machine (made up of 27 units), used by the sod

WIDEST LAWN MOWER: The 27 units that make up the Big Green Machine can cut a swath 60 feet wide and mow an acre of grass in only one minute.

farmer Jay Edgar Frick of Monroe, Ohio. It mows an acre in 60 seconds.

Duration. From March 28 to April 1, 1959, a Ransome *Matador* motorized mower was driven for 99 hours non-stop over 375 miles from Edinburgh to London.

MOTORCYCLES

Earliest. The earliest internal-combustion-engined motorized bicycle was a wooden-framed machine built in 1885 by Gottlieb Daimler (1834–1900) of Germany at Bad Cannstett and first ridden by Wilhelm Maybach (1846–1929). It had a top speed of 12 m.p.h. and developed one-half of one horsepower from its single cylinder 264-c.c. four-stroke engine at 700 r.p.m. The earliest factory which made motorcycles in quantity was opened in 1894 by Heinrich and Wilhelm Hildebrand and Alois Wolfmüller at München (Munich), Germany. In its first two years this factory produced over 1,000 machines, each having a water-cooled 1,488-c.c. twin-cylinder four-stroke engine developing about 2.5 b.h.p. at 600 r.p.m.—the highest capacity motorcycle engine ever put into production.

Fastest Road Motorcycle. The highest speed returned in an independent road test for a catalogued road machine is 154.2 m.p.h. for a Dunstall Suzuki GS 1000 CS.

Fastest Track Motorcyle. There is no satisfactory answer to the identity of the fastest track machine, other than to say that the current Kawasaki, Suzuki and Yamaha machines have all been geared to attain speeds marginally in excess of 186.4 m.p.h. under race conditions.

Most on One Machine. Nineteen men from the Huntington Park (California) Elks stunt-and-drill team, captained by Carl Wickes, mounted and rode a 1,200-c.c. Harley Davidson on August 1, 1979 in Los Angeles, California.

Circumnavigation. Ernest O'Gaffney, 41, departed from New York City on his Kawasaki KZ 1000 "Spirit of America" on November 27, 1978, and arrived back 79 days later on February 15, 1979, having traversed 25 countries in a 35,000-mile circumnavigation.

BICYCLES AND UNICYCLES

Earliest. The first design for a machine propelled by cranks and pedals, with connecting rods, has been attributed to Leonardo da Vinci (1452–1519) or one of his pupils, dated *c.* 1493.

The first machine of such design actually built was in 1839–40 by Kirkpatrick Macmillan (1810–78) of Dumfries, Scotland. It is now in the Science Museum, London.

Longest Bicycle. The longest tandem bicycle ever built is the 1½-ton Vestergaard multipede built at Koege, Denmark, in April, 1976. It seats 35 and measures 72 feet in length and has an additional stabilizing wheel.

Largest Tricycle. The largest tricycle ever made was manufactured in 1897 for the Woven-Hose and Rubber Company of Boston, Massachusetts. Its side wheels were 11 feet in diameter and it weighed over 2,000 lbs. It could carry eight riders.

Largest Bicycle. A classic ordinary bicycle with a 64-inch-diameter front wheel and a 20-inch-diameter back wheel was built *c.* 1886 by the Pope Manufacturing Co. of Massachusetts. It is now owned by Paul Niquette of Connecticut.

Smallest Bicycle. The world's smallest wheeled rideable bicycle is one with 2⅛-inch wheels, weighing 2 lbs., built and ridden by Charlie Charles at Circus Circus Hotel, Las Vegas, Nevada.

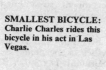

SMALLEST BICYCLE: Charlie Charles rides this bicycle in his act in Las Vegas.

TALLEST UNICYCLE EVER RIDDEN
(left): Carlho S. Abrahams atop his 45-foot-
10-inch unicycle in Paramaribo, Surinam.
LARGEST BICYCLE (above): Paul Niquette
of New Canaan, Connecticut, rides his classic
Ordinary bicycle with its 64-inch diameter front
wheel.

Fastest. The world speed records for human-powered vehicles
are 49.38 m.p.h. (single rider) by Ralph Therrio in 1977, and 54.43
m.p.h. (multiple riders) by Jan Russell and Butch Stanton aboard
"White Lightning," their supine-supine recumbent streamlined
tricycle, at the Ontario Speedway, California, on May 7, 1978. (See
photo, page D.)

Unicycle Records. The tallest unicycle ever mastered is one
45 feet 10 inches tall ridden (without a safety belt or mechanic) by
Carlho Sem Abrahams (born Paramaribo, Surinam, December 3,
1962) in Paramaribo for 23 feet on November 26, 1977.

Robert Neil "Bob" McGuinness (b. 1951) unicycled 3,976 miles
across Canada from Halifax to Vancouver in 79 days, June 6–August
24, 1978.

Frank R. Williams, 20, of the U.S. Air Force, set a speed record
for 100 miles from south of Austin to Waco, Texas, in 12 hours 50
minutes on September 5, 1977.

3. Railroads

Earliest. Railed trucks were used for mining as early as 1550 at Leberthal, Alsace, near the French-German border, and at the Broseley Colliery, Salop (Shropshire), England, in October, 1605, but the first self-propelled locomotive ever to run on rails was built by Richard Trevithick (1771–1833) for the 3-foot-gauge plateway at Coalbrookdale, Salop, in 1803.

The earliest established railway to have a steam-powered locomotive was the Middleton Colliery Railway, set up by an Act of June 9, 1758, running between Middleton Colliery and Leeds Bridge, Yorkshire, England. This line was converted to the use of steam locomotives (gauge 4 feet 1 inch), built by Matthew Murray (1765–1826), in 1812. The Stockton and Darlington Railway, Cleveland, England, which ran from Shildon through Darlington to Stockton, opened on September 27, 1825. The 7.8-ton *Locomotion* could pull 54 tons at a speed of 15 m.p.h. It was designed and driven by George Stephenson (1781–1848).

The first regular steam passenger run was inaugurated over a one-mile section on the 6¼-mile track from Canterbury to Whitstable, Kent, England, on May 3, 1830, hauled by the engine *Invicta*.

The first electric railway was Werner von Siemen's 600-yard-long Berlin electric track opened for the Berlin Trades Exhibition on May 31, 1879.

Fastest

The record for the fastest rail speed in the world was set by the U.S. Federal Railroad Administration LIMRV (Linear Induction Motor Research Vehicle), built by the Garrett Corporation, on the 6.2- mile-long Pueblo, Colorado, test track, when it attained a speed of 254.76 m.p.h. on August 14, 1974.

Steam. The highest speed ever ratified for a steam locomotive is 126 m.p.h. over 440 yards by the London & North Eastern Railway 4-6-2 No. 4468 *Mallard*, which hauled seven coaches weighing 268.8 tons gross down Stoke Bank, near Essendine, between Grantham, Lincolnshire, and Peterborough, Cambridgeshire, England, on July 3, 1938. Driver Duddington was at the controls with Fireman T. Bray. The engine suffered severe damage. On June 12, 1905, a speed of 127.06 m.p.h. was claimed for the "Pennsylvania Special" near Ada, Ohio, but this has never been accepted by leading experts.

Fastest Regular Run. The fastest point-to-point schedule in the world is that of the Kings Cross–Berwick section of British Rail's Eastern Region HST Service introduced on May 14, 1979, at 106.25 m.p.h. Speeds of 186.4 m.p.h. are planned for the SNCF Paris-Lyon line by 1982.

Most Powerful Locomotive. The world's most powerful steam locomotive, measured by tractive effort, was No. 700, a triple-articulated or triplex 2-8-8-8-4 six-cylinder engine which the Baldwin Locomotive Co. built in 1916 for the Virginian Railway. It had a tractive force of 166,300 lbs. working compound and 199,560 lbs. working simple.

Probably the heaviest train ever hauled by a single engine was one of 17,100 tons made up of 250 freight cars stretching 1.6 miles by the *Matt H. Shay* (No. 5014), a 2-8-8-8-2 engine which ran on the Erie Railroad from May, 1914, until 1929.

Railroad Handcar Pumping. "World" Championships pumped over a 220-yard shuttle course sponsored by the Jaycees of Jacksonville, Illinois, on September 12, 1976, produced best times of 62.177 seconds for men (Jerry Johnson and Tom Sheehan) and 81.123 seconds for women (Chris Ruyle and Jeanne McCulloch).

Steepest Grade

The world's steepest standard gauge gradient by adhesion is 1:11 between Chedde and Servoz on the meter gauge electric Chamonix line of the French National Railways.

Busiest Railroad

The world's most crowded rail system is the Japanese National Railways, which in 1976 carried 19,487,000 passengers daily. Professional pushers are employed in the Tokyo service to squeeze in passengers before the doors can be closed. Among articles reported lost in the crush in 1970 were 419,929 umbrellas, 250,630 eyeglasses and hats, 172,106 shoes, and also an assortment of false teeth and artificial eyeballs.

Widest and Narrowest Gauges

The widest gauge in standard use is 5 feet 6 inches. This width is used in India, Pakistan, Bangladesh, Sri Lanka, Argentina and Chile. In 1885, there was a lumber railway in Oregon with a gauge of 8 feet.

The narrowest gauge in use is 1 foot 3 inches on the Ravenglass & Eskdale Railway, Cumbria, England (7 miles), and the Romney, Hythe & Dymchurch line in Kent, England (14 miles).

Longest Straight Length. The longest straight in the world is on the Commonwealth Railways Trans-Australian line over the Nullarbor Plain from Mile 496 between Nurina and Loongana, Western Australia, to Mile 793 between Ooldea and Watson, South Australia, 297 miles dead straight although not level.

Highest Track

The highest standard gauge (4 feet 8½ inches) track in the world is on the Peruvian State Railways at La Cima, on the Morocoha Branch at 15,806 feet above sea level. The highest point on the main line is 15,688 feet in the Galera tunnel.

Longest Line

The world's longest run is one of 5,864½ miles on the Trans-Siberian Line between Moscow and Nakhodka in the Soviet Far East. There are 97 stops on the journey, which takes 8 days 4 hours 25 minutes. The new Baykal-Amur Magistral (BAM) northern line, begun with forced labor in 1938, is expected to be open in 1983, and will cut 310 miles off the route around the southern end of Lake Baykal. A total of 10,000,000,000 cubic feet of earth must be removed and 3,700 bridges built in this $14,400,000,000 project.

Freight Trains

Longest. The longest and heaviest freight train on record was one about 4 miles in length, consisting of 500 coal cars with three 3,600-h.p. diesels pulling, with three more pushing on the Iaeger, West Virginia, to Portsmouth, Ohio, stretch of 157 miles on the Norfolk and Western Railway on November 15, 1967. The total weight was more than 47,000 tons.

Greatest Load. The heaviest single pieces of freight ever conveyed by rail are limited by the capacity of the rolling stock. The only rail carrier with a capacity of 937 tons is a 36-axle "Schnabel," 283 feet 1½ inches long, built for a U.S. railway by Krupp, West Germany, in 1978.

In 1975, the 16th-century Church of the Virgin Mary at Most, Czechoslovakia, weighing nearly 12,000 tons, was moved because it was in the way of mining for coal deposits. It was moved on rails 800 yards at 0.0013 m.p.h. over a period of 4 weeks at a cost of $15,300,000.

Stations

Largest. The world's biggest railroad station is Grand Central Terminal, New York City, built 1903–13. It covers 48 acres on two levels with 41 tracks on the upper level and 26 on the lower. On average, more than 550 trains and 180,000 people per day use it, with a peak of 252,288 on July 3, 1947.

Highest. The highest station in the world on standard gauge railways is Condor, Bolivia, at 15,705 feet on the Rio Mulato-to-Potosí line.

Waiting Rooms. The world's largest waiting rooms are in Peking Station, Chang'an Boulevard, Peking, China, opened in September, 1959, with a capacity of 14,000.

Longest Platform. The longest railroad platform in the world is the Khargpur platform, West Bengal, India, which measures 2,733 feet in length. The State Street Center subway platform staging in "The Loop" in Chicago, measures 3,500 feet in length.

Subways

The oldest (first section opened January 10, 1863) underground railway system in the world, and one of the most extensive, is that of the London Transport Executive, with 255 miles of route, of which 77 miles is bored tunnel and 22 miles is "cut and cover." This whole system is operated by a staff of 11,700 serving 278 stations. The 484 trains comprising 4,323 cars carried 546,000,000 passengers in 1977. The record for a day is 2,073,134 on VE Day, May 8, 1945. The greatest depth is 221 feet near Hampstead. The record for touring 277 stations (all at that time) was 15 hours precisely, by Leslie R. V. Burwood on September 3, 1968.

The busiest subway in the world is operated by the New York City Transit Authority with a total of 229.76 miles of track and 1,018,833,642 passengers in 1978. The stations are close set and total 458. The record for traveling the whole system was 21 hours 8¼ minutes by Mayer Wiesen and Charles Emerson on October 8, 1973.

Monorail

Highest Speed. The highest speed ever attained on rails is 3,090 m.p.h. (Mach 4.1) by an unmanned rocket-powered sled on the 6.62-mile-long captive track at the U.S. Air Force Missile Development Center at Holloman, New Mexico, on February 19, 1959. The highest speed reached carrying a chimpanzee is 1,295 m.p.h.

The highest speed attained by a tracked hovercraft is 255.3 m.p.h. by the jet-powered *L'Aérotrain 02,* invented by Jean Bertin.

An experimental, magnetically levitated Japanese National Railway train on a test track near Miyazaki reached 215 m.p.h. on November 10, 1978, and is expected to touch 310 m.p.h. in 1979.

Model Train

The non-stop duration record for a model train (locomotive plus six coaches) is 864 hours 30 minutes from June 1 to July 7, 1978, covering 678 miles, organized by Roy Catton at "Pastimes" Toy Store, Mexborough, S. Yorkshire, England.

The longest train ever operated was one of 501 cars with 9 HO-scale engines by The Model Railroad Club of New Jersey at Union, New Jersey, July 22, 1978, when it traversed its own length.

RAPID TRANSIT: This experimental, magnetically levitated Japanese National Railway monorail train reached 215 m.p.h. in November, 1978.

NON-STOP ROUND TRIP: Roy Catton organized the record model train marathon, running an engine and six cars for 864 hours 30 minutes and covering 678 miles.

4. Aircraft

Note.—The use of the Mach scale for aircraft speeds was introduced by Prof. Ackeret of Zurich, Switzerland. The Mach number is the ratio of the velocity of a moving body to the local velocity of sound. This was first employed by Dr. Ernst Mach (1838–1916) of Austria in 1887. Thus Mach 1.0 equals 760.98 m.p.h. at sea level at 15° C. (59°F.) and is assumed, for convenience, to fall to a constant 659.78 m.p.h. in the stratosphere, *i.e.* above 11,000 meters (36,089 feet).

Earliest Flight. The first controlled and sustained power-driven flight occurred near Kill Devil Hill, Kitty Hawk, North Carolina, at 10:35 a.m. on December 17, 1903, when Orville Wright (1871–1948) flew the 12-h.p. chain-driven *Flyer I* at an airspeed of 30 m.p.h., a ground speed of 6.8 m.p.h. and an altitude of 8–12 feet for 12 seconds, watched by his brother Wilbur (1867–1912) and three members of the Coast Guard and two others. Both brothers, from Dayton, Ohio, were bachelors because, as Orville put it, they had not the means to "support a wife as well as an airplane." The plane is now in the Smithsonian Institution, Washington, D.C.

The first hop by a man-carrying airplane entirely under its own power was made when Clément Ader (1841–1925) of France flew in his *Eole* for about 164 feet at Armainvilliers, France, on October 9, 1890.

Richard William Pearce (1877–1953) flew for at least 50 yards along the Main Waitohi Road, South Canterbury, New Zealand, in a home-built petrol-engined monoplane, probably on March 31, 1903.

The earliest "rational design" for a flying machine (according to the British Royal Aeronautical Society) was published by Emanuel Swedenborg (1688–1772) in Sweden in 1717.

Cross-Channel Flight. The earliest flight across the English Channel by an airplane was made on July 25, 1909, when Louis Blériot (1872–1936), of France, flew his *Blériot XI* monoplane, powered by a 23-h.p. Anzani engine, from Les Baraques, France, to a meadow near Dover Castle, England, in 36½ minutes, after taking off at 4:41 a.m.

Transatlantic Flight. The first crossing of the North Atlantic by air was made by Lt.-Cdr. (later Rear Admiral) Albert C. Read (1887–1967) and his crew (Stone, Hinton, Rodd, Rhoads and Breese) in an 84-knot Curtiss flying boat NC-4 of the U.S. Navy, from Newfoundland, Canada, *via* the Azores, to Lisbon, Portugal, on May 16 to 27, 1919. The whole flight of 4,717 miles originating from Rockaway Air Station, Long Island, N.Y., on May 8, required 53 hours 58 minutes, terminating at Plymouth, England, on May 31. The Newfoundland-Azores leg (1,200 miles) took 15 hours 18 minutes at 81.7 knots.

The first non-stop transatlantic flight was achieved from 4:13 p.m. G.M.T. on June 14, 1919, from Lester's Field, St. John's, Newfoundland, 1,960 miles to Derrygimla bog near Clifden, County Galway, Ireland, at 8:40 a.m. G.M.T. June 15, when Capt. John William Alcock, D.S.C. (1892–1919), and Lt. Arthur Whitten Brown (1886–1948) flew across in a Vickers *Vimy*, powered by two 360-h.p. Rolls-Royce *Eagle VII* engines. Both men were given knighthoods on June 21, 1919, when Alcock was only 26 years 227 days old. They won a £10,000 (then $50,000) prize given by a London newspaper.

The first solo transatlantic flight was achieved by Capt. (later Colonel) Charles A. Lindbergh (1902–74), who took off in his 220-h.p. Ryan monoplane *Spirit of St. Louis* at 12:52 p.m. G.M.T. on May 20, 1927, from Roosevelt Field, Long Island, New York. He landed at 10:21 p.m. G.M.T. on May 21, 1927, at Le Bourget airfield, Paris, France. His flight of 3,610 miles lasted 33 hours 29½ minutes and he won a prize of $25,000. He was the 79th man to achieve a transatlantic flight, but the first to fly alone.

The record for the most transatlantic flights is held by Capt. John M. Winston, a senior British Airways pilot, who flew 1,277 transatlantic flights from May 10, 1947, to December 14, 1978—a total of 20,100 hours.

The transatlantic flight speed record is 1 hour 54 minutes 56.4 seconds by Major James V. Sullivan, 37, and Major Noel F. Widdifield, 33, flying a Lockheed SR-71A eastwards on September 1, 1974. The average speed, slowed by refueling by a KC-135 tanker aircraft, for the New York-London stage of 3,461.53 miles was 1,806.963 m.p.h. The solo record (Gander to Gatwick) is 8 hours 47 minutes 32 seconds by Captain John J. A. Smith in a Rockwell 685 on March 12, 1978.

Transpacific Flight. The first non-stop Pacific flight was by Major Clyde Pangborn and Hugh Herdon in the Bellanca cabin plane *Miss Veedol* from Sabishiro Beach, Japan, 4,558 miles to Wenatchee, Washington, in 41 hours 13 minutes on October 3–5, 1931. (For earliest crossing see 1924 flight below.)

Circumnavigational Flights. A strict circumnavigation of the earth requires passing through two antipodal points and is thus a

FIRST FLIGHTS AROUND THE WORLD: The *Chicago* and the *New Orleans* made aviation history with the first circumnavigational flights in 1924.

minimum distance of 24,859.75 miles. (The F.A.I. recognizes flights which exceed the length of the Tropic of Cancer or Capricorn (22,858.754 miles).)

The earliest such flight (26,345 miles) was made by two U.S. Army Douglas D.W.C. amphibians in 57 "hops." The *Chicago* was piloted by Lt. Lowell H. Smith and Lt. Leslie P. Arnold. The *New Orleans* was piloted by Lt. Erik H. Nelson and Lt. John Harding. The planes took off from Seattle, Washington, on April 6, 1924, and landed back there on September 28, 1924.

The earliest solo claim was by Wiley Hardemann Post (1898–1935) (U.S.) in the Lockheed Vega *Winnie Mae*, starting and finishing at Floyd Bennett Field, New York City, July 15–22, 1933, in 10 "hops." His distance of 15,596 miles in a flying time of 115 hours 36 minutes was, however, at too high a latitude to qualify as completely circumnavigational.

The fastest circumnavigation of the globe was a non-stop eastabout flight by three U.S.A.F. B-52 Stratofortresses, led by Maj.-Gen. Archie J. Old, Jr., from Castle Air Force Base, Merced, California, on January 16, arriving 45 hours 19 minutes later at March Air Force Base, Riverside, California, on January 18, 1957, after a flight of 24,325 miles. They averaged 525 m.p.h. with 4 in-flight refuelings by KC-97 aerial tankers.

The smallest aircraft to complete a circumnavigation is a 20-foot 11-inch single-engined 180-h.p. Thorp T-18, built in his garage by its pilot Donald P. Taylor of Sage, California. His 26,190-mile flight in 37 stages took 176 flying hours, ending in Oshkosh, Wisconsin, on September 30, 1976.

Circum-Polar Flight. The first circum-polar flight was flown solo by Captain Elgen M. Long, 44, in a Piper Navajo, November 5 to December 3, 1971. He covered 38,896 miles in 215 flying hours. The cabin temperature sank to −40°F. over Antarctica.

Jet-Engine Flight. Proposals for jet propulsion date back to Captain Marconnet (1909) of France and Henri Coanda (1886–1972) of Rumania, and to the turbojet proposals of Maxime Guillaume in

LIGHTEST AIRPLANE: The Tally Birdman TL-1, weighing only 288 lbs. at take-off, is the lightest powered airplane ever flown.

1921. The earliest testbed run was that of the British Power Jets Ltd.'s experimental W.U. (Whittle Unit) on April 12, 1937, invented by Flying Officer (now Air Commodore Sir) Frank Whittle (born June 1, 1907), who had applied for a patent on jet propulsion in 1930.

The first flight by an airplane powered by a turbojet engine was made by the Heinkel He 178, piloted by Flugkapitän Erich Warsitz, at Marienehe, Germany, on August 27, 1939. It was powered by a Heinkel He S3b engine (834-lb. s.t. as installed with long tailpipe) designed by Dr. Hans von Ohain and first tested in August, 1937.

Supersonic Flight. The first supersonic flight was achieved on October 14, 1947, by Capt. (later Brigadier-General) Charles ("Chuck") E. Yeager (born February 13, 1923), U.S.A.F. ret., over Edwards Air Force Base, Muroc, California, in a U.S. Bell XS-1 rocket plane (*Glamorous Glennis*), with Mach 1.015 (670 m.p.h.) at a height of 42,000 feet.

Planes

Largest. The aircraft with the largest wing span ever constructed was Howard R. Hughes' H.2 *Hercules* flying boat, which rose 70 feet into the air in a test run of 1,000 yards off Long Beach Harbor, California, on November 2, 1947. The 8-engined 213-ton aircraft had a wing span of 320 feet and a length of 219 feet. It never flew again. The craft cost $40,000,000, and was piloted by Howard Hughes himself on its one run. It was not scrapped until April, 1976.

Heaviest. The third Boeing E-4A, advanced airborne command post version of the Boeing 747-200B transport, flew for the first time on June 6, 1974, powered by four General Electric F103-GE-100 turbofan engines with a total thrust of 210,000 lbs. The all-up weight has been put at 425 tons and the cost at $117 million, making it the heaviest and most expensive aircraft of all time.

Lightest. The lightest mechanically-powered plane ever flown was the prototype Birdman TL-1, a single-seat monoplane designed and built by Emmet M. Tally III of Daytona Beach, Florida, and first flown on January 25, 1975. It had a wing span of 34 feet, an empty weight of 100 lbs. and a normal take-off weight of 288 lbs. It was powered by a 15-h.p. Tally M.C. 101DT single-cylinder two-stroke engine driving a pusher propeller, and had a maximum speed of 60 m.p.h. and a range of 200 miles on 4 gallons of fuel. The pilot sat on an open seat.

The lightest and smallest twin-engined airplane is the prototype MC10 Cricri single-seat monoplane designed and built by Michel Colomban of Rueil-Malmaison, France, and first flown on July 19, 1973, by 68-year-old Robert Buisson. It has a wing span of 16 feet 4¾ inches, an empty weight of 139 pounds and a take-off weight (including the pilot) of 375 pounds. Two 9-h.p. Rowena two-stroke engines give it a maximum speed of 130 m.p.h. and a range of 248 miles. The Cricri is aerobatic.

Smallest. The smallest airplane ever flown is the Stits *Skybaby* biplane, designed and built by Ray Stits at Riverside, California, and first flown by Robert H. Starr on May 26, 1952. It was 9 feet 10 inches long, with a wing span of 7 feet 2 inches, and weighed 452 lbs. empty. Powered by an 85-h.p. Continental C85 engine, it had a top speed of 185 m.p.h.

Bombers

Heaviest. The world's heaviest bomber is the 8-jet sweptwing Boeing B-52H Stratofortress, which has a maximum takeoff weight of 488,000 lbs. It has a wing span of 185 feet and is 157 feet 6¾ inches in length, with a speed of over 650 m.p.h. The B-52 can carry 12 SRAM thermonuclear short-range attack missiles or 24 750-lb. bombs under its wings and 8 more SRAMs or 84 500-lb. bombs in the fuselage.

The 10-engined Convair B-36J, weighing 205 tons, has a greater wing span, at 230 feet, but is no longer in service. It had a top speed of 435 m.p.h.

SMALLEST AIRPLANE: Ray Stits' "Skybaby" was only 9 feet 10 inches long. It could fly at speeds up to 185 m.p.h.

Fastest. The world's fastest operational bombers are the French Dassault Mirage IV, which can fly at Mach 2.2 (1,450 m.p.h.) at 36,000 feet; the American General Dynamics FB-111A, with a maximum speed of Mach 2.5; and a swing-wing Russian Tupolev Tu-26 bomber known to NATO as "Backfire," which has an estimated over-target speed of Mach 2.0 and a combat radius of up to 3,570 miles.

Airliners

Largest. The highest capacity jet airliner is the Boeing 747, "Jumbo Jet," first flown on February 9, 1969. It has a capacity of from 385 to 500 passengers with a maximum speed of 608 m.p.h. Its wing span is 195.7 feet and its length, 231.3 feet. It entered service on January 22, 1970.

FASTEST AIRLINER: The Soviet's Tu-144, of which 8 have been built, has a capacity of 140 passengers, is able to attain 1,585 m.p.h. and began passenger flights in 1977.

Fastest. The supersonic BAC/Aerospatiale Concorde, first flown on March 2, 1969, with a capacity of 128 passengers, cruises at up to Mach 2.2 (1,450 m.p.h.). It flew at Mach 1.05 on October 10, 1969, exceeded Mach 2 for the first time on November 4, 1970, and became the first supersonic airliner used for passenger service on January 21, 1976, when Air France and British Airways opened service simultaneously between, respectively, Paris—Rio de Janeiro and London—Bahrain. Service between London/New York (record 3 hours 6 minutes) and Paris/New York began on November 22, 1977.

The U.S.S.R.'s Tu-144, which first flew on December 31, 1968, began passenger operations between Moscow and Alma-Ata (2,190 miles) on November 1, 1977, offering an average speed of 1,245 m.p.h. (Mach 1.9).

Most Capacious. The capacity of the commercial adaptation of the U.S.A.F. Lockheed C-5A Galaxy known as the Lockheed 500-3 is 51,707 cubic feet. The wing span is 222.7 feet and the length is 245.9 feet.

LARGEST AIR-SUPPORTED ROOF: The roof of the octagonal Pontiac Silverdome Stadium in Michigan measures a total 10 acres in area. (Photo courtesy of Irvin Industries)

SMALLEST TV: The Sinclair Microvision weighs only 28 oz. It has a screen which measures 2 inches diagonally.

RICHEST MUSEUM (above): The J. Paul Getty Museum in California has an endowment of $1,400,000,000. The oil billionaire's personal fortune was estimated at over $1,750,000,000 at the time of his death, in 1976.

MOST EXPENSIVE SCULPTURE (right): Known as the "Getty Bronze" and enmeshed in controversy regarding its acquisition, this statue from the 4th century B.C. was sold for a record $3,900,000 in 1977.

LARGEST BLANKET
(above): Made from 20,160
squares knitted by readers
of a women's magazine in
England, this blanket
measured 6,800 square feet
and weighed 600 lbs. (Photo
courtesy of BBC-TV
"Record Breakers")

LARGEST VASE (right):
This 8-foot-high vase was
made by Sebastian Maglio
in Dundee, Illinois, in 1976.

BIGGEST BOOT: This leather leviathan, constructed in England in 1887, is 4 feet 3½ inches long and weighs 81 lbs.

DEAREST DOLLS: The Victoria and Albert Museum in London paid $36,800 for this pair of painted wooden dolls in April, 1974. (Photo courtesy of Victoria and Albert Museum)

H

FAST SHUTTLE: The Space Shuttle Orbiter, when flown into space, will take off like a rocket and orbit like a spacecraft at speeds up to 17,600 m.p.h.

Highest Speed

The official air speed record is 2,193.167 m.p.h. by Capt. Eldon W. Joersz and Maj. George T. Morgan, Jr., in a Lockheed SR-71A near Beale Air Force Base, California, on July 28, 1976 over a 15-25-km. (10-15-mile) course.

The fastest fixed-wing aircraft in the world was a North American Aviation X-15A-2, which flew for the first time (after modification) on June 28, 1964, powered by a liquid oxygen and ammonia rocket propulsion system. Ablative materials on the airframe enabled a temperature of 3,000°F. to be withstood. The landing speed was 210 knots (242 m.p.h.) momentarily. The highest speed attained was 4,534 m.p.h. (Mach 6.72) when piloted by Major William J. Knight, U.S.A.F. (b. 1930) on October 3, 1967. An earlier version piloted by Joseph A. Walker (1920–66) reached 354,200 feet (67.08 miles) also over Edwards Air Force Base, California, on August 22, 1963. The program was suspended after the final flight of October 24, 1968.

Potentially the fastest aircraft ever flown is the Space Shuttle Orbiter built for N.A.S.A. by Rockwell International, and first flown piggyback atop a converted Boeing 747 on February 18, 1977. When flown into space, from 1979, the Orbiter will take off like a rocket, operate in orbit like a spacecraft (at up to 17,600 m.p.h.) and land at speeds as high as 223 m.p.h.

Fastest Jet. The world's fastest jet aircraft is the Lockheed SR-71 reconnaissance aircraft which first flew on December 22, 1964, and attained a speed of 2,193.167 m.p.h. in July, 1976. It is reportedly capable of attaining an altitude ceiling of close to 100,000 feet. The SR-71 has a span of 55.6 feet and a length of 107.4 feet and weighs 170,000 lbs. at takeoff. Its reported range is 2,982 miles at Mach 3 at 78,750 feet. At least 30 are believed to have been built.

The fastest combat aircraft in service is the U.S.S.R. Mikoyan MIG-25 *alias* E-266 fighter (code name "Foxbat"). The reconnaissance "Foxbat-B" has been tracked by radar at a speed of about Mach 3.2 (2,110 m.p.h.). When armed with four large underwing air-to-air missiles known to NATO as "Acrid," the "Foxbat-A" is limited to Mach 2.8 (1,845 m.p.h.). The single-seat "Foxbat-A" spans 45 feet 9 inches, is 73 feet 2 inches long, and has a maximum takeoff weight of 79,800 lbs.

Fastest Biplane. The fastest recorded biplane was the Italian Fiat C.R.42B, with a 1,010-h.p. Daimler-Benz DB601A engine, which attained 323 m.p.h. in 1941. Only one was built.

Fastest Piston-Engined Aircraft. The fastest speed at which a piston-engined plane has ever been measured was for a cut-down privately owned Hawker *Sea Fury* which attained 520 m.p.h. in level flight over Texas in August, 1966, piloted by Mike Carroll (d. 1969) of Los Angeles. The official record is 482.463 m.p.h. over Edwards Air Force Base, California, by Darryl C. Greenamyer, 33, in a Grumman F8F-2 *Bearcat* on August 16, 1969.

Fastest Propeller-Driven Aircraft. The Soviet Tu-114 turbo-prop transport is the world's fastest propeller-driven airplane. It has achieved average speeds of more than 545 m.p.h. carrying heavy payloads over measured circuits. It is developed from the Tupolev Tu-95 bomber, known in the West as the "Bear," and has 14,795-horsepower engines. The Republic XF-84H prototype U.S. Navy fighter which flew on July 22, 1955, had a top design speed of 670 m.p.h., but was abandoned.

Largest Propeller

The largest aircraft propeller ever used was the 22-foot 7½-inch diameter Garuda propeller, fitted to the Linke-Hofmann R II built in Wroclaw, Poland, which flew in 1919. It was driven by four 260-h.p. Mercedes engines and turned at only 545 r.p.m.

Greatest Altitude

The official altitude record by an aircraft which took off from the ground under its own power is 123,524 feet (23.39 miles) by Aleksandr Fedotov (U.S.S.R.) in a Mikoyan E-266M (MIG-25) aircraft, powered by two 30,865-lb. thrust turbojet engines on August 31, 1977.

The greatest recorded height by any pilot without a pressure cabin or even a pressure suit has been 49,500 feet by British Squadron Leader G. W. H. Reynolds, D.F.C., in a Spitfire Mark VC over Libya in 1942.

Flight Duration

The flight duration record is 64 days, 22 hours, 19 minutes and 5 seconds, set by Robert Timm and John Cook in a Cessna 172 "Hacienda." They took off from McCarran Airfield, Las Vegas, Nevada, just before 3:53 p.m. local time on December 4, 1958, and landed at the same airfield just before 2:12 p.m. on February 7, 1959. They covered a distance equivalent to six times around the world with continued refueling without landing.

FLEDGLING FLIER: One of the youngest pilots ever, Clark Pelaez flew solo at age 10 years 11 months.

The record for duration without refueling is 84 hours 32 minutes, set by Walter E. Lees and Frederic A. Brossy in a Bellanca monoplane with a 225-h.p. Packard Diesel engine, at Jacksonville, Florida, May 25–28, 1931.

Longest Scheduled Flight. The longest scheduled non-stop flight is the weekly Pan-Am Sydney-San Francisco non-stop Flight 816 (13 hours 25 minutes) in a Boeing 747 SP, opened in December, 1976, over 7,475 statute miles. The longest delivery flight by a commercial jet is 8,936 nautical miles or 10,290 statute miles from Seattle, Washington, to Capetown, South Africa, by South African Airway's Boeing 747 SP *Matroosberg*. She made the 17-hour 22½ minute flight loaded with 196.5 tons of pre-cooled fuel on March 23–29, 1976.

Shortest Scheduled Flight. The shortest scheduled flight is made by Loganair between the Orkney Islands (Scotland) of Westray and Papa Westray, which has been flown since September, 1967. Though scheduled for 2 minutes, in favorable wind conditions it is accomplished in 58 seconds by Captain Andrew D. Alsop. It is flown with twin-engined 10-seat Britten-Norman Islander transports.

Youngest and Oldest Pilots

The youngest age at which anyone has ever qualified as a military pilot is 15 years 5 months in the case of Sgt. Thomas Dobney (born May 6, 1926) of the British Royal Air Force. He had lied about his age (14 years) on induction.

Miss Betty Bennett took off, flew and landed solo at the age of 10 on January 4, 1952, in Cuba. Clark O. Pelaez (b. May 4, 1957) flew a Piper Tri-Pacer solo at Cebu City, Philippines, on April 24, 1968, aged 10 years 11 months.

The world's oldest pilot is Ed McCarty (born September 18, 1885) of Kimberly, Idaho, who in 1977 was flying his rebuilt 30-year-old Ercoupe at the age of 92. Glenn E. Messer of Birmingham, Alabama, has been flying "steady" since May 13, 1911. Albert E. Savoy (born February 22, 1895) was issued his first private pilot's license on November 8, 1977, aged 82 years 8 months.

Most Flying Hours. Max Conrad (1903–1979) (U.S.) logged 52,929 hours 40 minutes of flight time, a total of more than 6 years airborne, between 1928 and mid-1974. He completed 150 transatlantic crossings in light aircraft.

Most Takeoffs and Landings. Douglas Blair, 34, and Dennis Oliver made 138 takeoffs and daylight landings in 14 hours 54 minutes on June 21, 1978, from Milwaukee, Wisconsin, to Urbana, Ohio, in a single-engine Beechcraft Bonanza.

Airports

Largest. The world's largest airport is the Dallas/Fort Worth Airport, Texas, which extends over 17,500 acres in the Grapevine area. Opened in January, 1974, at an initial cost of nearly $800,000,000, the present 4 runways and 5 terminal buildings are planned to be extended to 9 runways and 13 terminals with 260 gates with an ultimate capacity of 150,000,000 passengers per year.

The total airport reserve area of Mirabel, Montreal's airport, is 88,960 acres, of which 17,300 acres is operational.

The planned area of the Jeddah airport in Saudi Arabia, due to be completed at a cost of $6,460,000,000 by 1982, has been published at 26,250 acres.

Busiest. The world's busiest airport is the Chicago International Airport, O'Hare Field, with a total of 754,986 movements in fiscal 1978 and 49,151,449 passengers in calendar 1978. This represents a takeoff or landing every 41.8 seconds around the clock. Heathrow Airport outside London handles more *international* traffic than any other.

The busiest landing area ever has been Bien Hoa Air Base, South Vietnam, which handled more than 1,000,000 takeoffs and landings in 1970. The world's largest "helipad" was An Khe, South Vietnam, which serviced U.S. Army and Air Force helicopters.

Farthest and Nearest to City Centers. The airport farthest from the city center it allegedly serves is Mirabel, Quebec, Canada, which is 33 miles from Montreal. The Gibraltar airport is 800 yards from the center.

Highest and Lowest. The highest airport in the world is La Sa (Lhasa) Airport in Tibet at 14,315 feet. The highest landing ever made by a fixed-wing plane was at 19,947 feet on Dhaulagri in the Nepal Himalayas by a Pilatus Porter, named *Yeti*, supplying the 1960 Swiss Expedition. The lowest landing field is El Lisan on the east shore of the Dead Sea, 1,180 feet below sea level. The lowest international airport is Schiphol, Amsterdam, Netherlands, at 13 feet below sea level.

Longest Runway. The longest runway in the world is 7 miles in length (of which 15,000 feet is concreted) at Edwards Air Force Base on the bed of Rogers Dry Lake at Muroc, California. The whole test center airfield extends over 65 square miles. In an emergency, an auxiliary 12-mile strip is available along the bed of the Dry Lake.

The world's longest civil airport runway is one of 16,076 feet (3.04 miles) at Upington, South Africa.

Helicopters

Fastest. A Bell YUH-1B Model 533 compound research helicopter, boosted by two auxiliary turbojet engines, attained an unofficial speed record of 316.1 m.p.h. over Arlington, Texas, in April, 1969. The official world speed record for a pure helicopter is 228.9 m.p.h. set by Gourguen Karapetyan in a Mil A-10 on a 15–25 kilometer course near Moscow, U.S.S.R., on September 21, 1978.

Largest. The world's largest helicopter is the Soviet Mil Mi-12 ("Homer"), also known as the V-12, which set an international record by lifting a payload of 88,636 lbs. to a height of 7,398 feet on August 6, 1969. It is powered by four 6,500-h.p. turboshaft engines, and has a span of 219 feet 10 inches over its rotor tips with a fuselage length of 121 feet 4½ inches and weighs 115.7 tons.

Highest. The altitude record for helicopters is 40,820 feet by an Aerospatiale SA 315 B Lama over France on June 21, 1972.

The highest recorded landing has been at 23,000 feet, below the southeast face of Everest, in a rescue sortie in May, 1971.

The World Trade Center Helipad is 1,385 feet above street level in New York City, on the South Tower, making it the highest helicopter landing site in regular use.

Smallest. The Aerospace General Co. one-man rocket-assisted mini-copter weighs about 160 lbs. and can cruise 250 miles at 85 m.p.h.

SMALLEST HELICOPTER: Shown here ready for takeoff, this rocket-assisted mini-copter can be packed into an aerial delivery container and parachuted to rescue the stranded.

PEDAL POWER: Bryan Allen pedaled his way to the first human-powered flight across the English Channel in the *Gossamer Albatross*. The extraordinary vehicle was designed by Dr. Paul MacCready.

Autogyros

The autogyro or gyroplane, a rotorcraft with an unpowered rotor turned by the airflow in flight, preceded the practical helicopter with engine-driven rotor. Juan de la Cierva (Spain) made the first successful autogyro flight with his model C.4 (commercially named an *Autogiro*) at Getafe, Spain, on January 9, 1923. On December 6, 1955, Dr. Igor B. Bensen (U.S.) flew his very simple open-seat Gyro-Copter and then made his design available in kit form to amateur builders and pilots.

Wing Commander Kenneth H. Wallis (G.B.) holds the straight-line distance record of 543.27 miles, set in his WA-116F autogyro on September 28, 1975 (non-stop from Lydd, Kent, England, to Wick, Highland, Scotland).

Wallis flew his WA-116 to a record altitude of 15,220 feet on May 11, 1968, and to a record speed of 111.2 m.p.h. over a 3-km. (1.86 mile) straight course on May 12, 1969.

Flying Boat

The fastest flying boat ever built has been the Martin XP6M-1 Seamaster, the U.S. Navy 4-jet-engined minelayer, flown in 1955–59 with a top speed of 646 m.p.h. In September, 1946, the Martin JRM-2 Mars flying boat set a payload record of 68,327 lbs.

The official flying-boat speed record is 566.69 m.p.h., set by Nikolai Andrievsky and a crew of two in a Soviet Beriev M-10, powered by two AL-7 turbojets, over a 15–25-km. (10–15 mile) course on August 7, 1961. The M-10 holds all 12 records listed for jet-powered flying boats, including an altitude of 49,088 ft. set by Georgiy Buryanov and crew over the Sea of Azov on September 9, 1961.

LONGEST BALLOON FLIGHTS:
The helium-filled *Double Eagle II*
(right), photographed over the
French coast, completed the first
transatlantic balloon flight. The
Cameron balloon *Sungas* (above) set
the world's distance record for a
hot-air balloon with a flight of
350.7 miles.

Human-Powered Flight

The world distance record for human-powered flight was set on
June 12, 1979, by Dr. Paul MacCready's man-powered aircraft
Gossamer Albatross, piloted and pedaled by Bryan Allen. The
Albatross took off from Folkestone, England and landed at Cap Gris-
Nez, France, 2 hours 49 minutes later, a flight spanning 23 miles,
winning the £100,000 ($200,000) prize offered by Henry Kremer.

Balloons

The earliest recorded ascent was by a model hot-air balloon invented by Father Bartolomeu de Gusmão (*né* Lourenço) (b. Santos,
Brazil, 1685), which was flown indoors at the Casa da India, Terreiro
do Paço, Portugal, on August 8, 1709.

Distance Record. The American Yost HB-72 helium-filled balloon *Double Eagle II* completed the first transatlantic crossing with
a flight of 3,107.61 miles, landing at Coquerel Farm, Miserey,
France, at 5:48 p.m. G.M.T. on August 17, 1978. It also set a record
for the longest duration at 137 hours 5 minutes 50 seconds. The
takeoff was from Sprague Farm, Presque Isle, Maine, on August 11.
The crew were Ben Abruzzo, 48, Max Anderson, 44, and Larry
Newman, 31, all of Albuquerque, New Mexico.

For hot-air ballooning the world's distance record is 350.7 miles by Philip Charles Clark (G.B.), set on January 25, 1978, in the Cameron balloon *Sungas* from Bristol, England, to Châlons-sur-Marne, France. The altitude record is 45,837 feet by Julian Nott and co-pilot Felix Pole (both G.B.) over Bhopal, India, in *Daffodil II*, a 375,000-cu. ft. Cameron A-375 balloon, on January 25, 1974. The largest hot-air balloon ever built is the U.K. Cameron A-500 of 500,000 cu. ft. capacity *Gerard A. Heineken,* first flown on August 18, 1974. The endurance record is 18 hours 56 minutes from Dorset, England, to Angers, France, on November 21–22, 1975, by Donald Allan Cameron (G.B.) and Le Comte Jean Costa de Beauregard (France), in a Cameron A-500.

Highest Manned. The greatest altitude reached in a manned balloon is the unofficial 123,800 feet by Nicholas Piantanida (1933–66) of Bricktown, New Jersey, from Sioux Falls, South Dakota, on February 1, 1966. He landed in a cornfield in Iowa but did not survive.

The official record is 113,740 feet by Commander Malcolm D. Ross, U.S.N.R., and the late Lt.-Commander Victor E. Prather, U.S.N., in an ascent from the deck of U.S.S. *Antietam* on May 4, 1961, over the Gulf of Mexico.

The record altitude in an open basket is 38,789 feet by Kingswood Sprott Jr. over Lakeland, Florida, on September 27, 1975.

Highest Unmanned. The highest altitude attained by an unmanned balloon was 170,000 feet, by a Winzen Research balloon of 47,800,000 cubic feet, launched at Chico, California, in October, 1972.

Largest. The largest balloon built is one with an inflatable volume of 70,000,000 cubic feet, by Winzen Research Inc., Minnesota.

Airships

The earliest flight of an airship was by Henri Giffard from Paris in his coal-gas 88,300-cu. ft. 144-foot-long rigid airship on September 24, 1852.

The largest non-rigid airship ever constructed was the U.S. Navy ZPG 3-W. It had a capacity of 1,516,300 cubic feet, was 403.4 feet long and 85.1 feet in diameter, with a crew of 21. It first flew on July 21, 1958, but crashed into the sea in June, 1960.

The largest rigid airship was the 236-ton German *Graf Zeppelin II* (LZ130), with a length of 803.8 feet and a capacity of 7,062,100 cubic feet. She made her maiden flight on September 14, 1938 and in May and August, 1939, made radar spying missions in British air space. She was dismantled in April, 1940. Her sister ship, the *Hindenburg,* was 5.6 feet longer.

The most people ever carried in an airship was 207 in the U.S. Navy *Akron* in 1931. The transatlantic record is 117 by the German *Hindenburg* in 1937.

The distance record for airships is 3,967.1 miles, set by the German *Graf Zeppelin,* captained by Dr. Hugo Eckener between October 29 and November 1, 1928.

Hovercraft

The inventor of the ACV (air-cushion vehicle) is Christopher S. Cockerell (born June 4, 1910), a British engineer who had the idea in 1954, published his Ripplecraft Report 1/55 on October 25, 1955, and patented it on December 12, 1955. The earliest patent relating to an air-cushion craft was taken out in 1877 by John I. Thornycroft (1843–1928) of Chiswick, London. The first flight by a hovercraft was made by the 4½-ton Saunders Roe SR-N1 at Cowes, Isle of Wight, on May 30, 1959. With a 1,500-lb. thrust Viper turbojet engine, this craft reached 68 knots in June, 1961. The first hovercraft public service was opened across the Dee Estuary, Great Britain, by the 60-knot 24-passenger Vickers-Armstrong VA-3 in July, 1962.

The world's largest hovercraft is the 342-ton British-built SRN 4 MK III with a capacity of 416 passengers and 60 cars. It is 186 feet in length, powered by 4 Siddeley Marine Proteus engines which give a maximum speed in excess of the permitted operating speed of 65 knots.

The fastest is the 78-foot 112-ton U.S. Navy test vehicle SES-100B (the fastest warship). She attained 88.88 knots (102.35 m.p.h.) in speed trials in 1976. A contract for a 3,360-ton Large Surface Effect Ship (LSES) was placed by the U.S. Department of Defense with Bell Aerospace in September, 1977, for delivery in mid-1981.

The greatest altitude at which a hovercraft is operating is on Lake Titicaca, Peru, where, since 1975, an HM2 Hoverferry hovers 12,506 feet above sea level.

The longest hovercraft journey was one of 5,000 miles through 8 West African countries between October 15, 1969, and January 3, 1970, by the British Trans-African Hovercraft Expedition.

Model Aircraft

The world record for altitude is 26,929 feet by Maynard L. Hill (U.S.) on September 6, 1970, using a radio-controlled model. The speed record is 213.70 m.p.h. by V. Goukoune and V. Myakinin (both U.S.S.R.) with a radio-controlled model at Klementyeva, U.S.S.R., on September 21, 1971. The record duration flight is one of 28 hours 28 minutes by B. Laging at Ballarat, Victoria, Australia, on October 1, 1978.

The first model helicopter to fly across the English Channel was an 11-lb. model Bell 212 radio-controlled helicopter piloted by Dieter Ziegler for the 32 miles between Ashford, Kent, England, and Amble-teuse, France, on July 17, 1974.

Paper Airplane

The flight duration record for a paper aircraft over level ground is 15.0 seconds by William Harlan Pryor in the Municipal Auditorium, Nashville, Tennessee, on March 26, 1975. A paper plane was reported and witnessed to have flown 1¼ miles after a throw by "Chick" C. O. Reinhart from a 10th-story office window at 60 Beaver Street, New York City, across the East River to Brooklyn, New York, in August, 1933. It was helped by a thermal updraft from a coffee-roasting plant.

An indoor distance record of 113 feet 11 inches was recorded by Brad Mickelson in Eby Fieldhouse, Coe College, Cedar Rapids, Iowa, on April 2, 1979.

5. Power Producers

Largest Power Plant

The world's largest power station is the U.S.S.R.'s hydro-electric station at Krasnoyarsk on the Yenisey River, U.S.S.R., with a power of 6,096,000 kilowatts. Its third generator turned in March, 1968, and the twelfth became operative by December, 1970. The turbine hall completed in June, 1968, is 1,378 feet long. The reservoir backed up by the dam was reported in November, 1972, to be 240 miles long.

The largest power plant now planned is the Itaipu on the Paraná River on the Brazil-Paraguay border, with an ultimate power of 12,600,000 kW. from 18 turbines.

Nuclear Power

The world's first atomic pile was built in an abandoned squash court at the University of Chicago. It "went critical" at 3:25 p.m. on December 2, 1942.

The world's largest atomic power station is the Ontario Hydro's Pickering station which in 1973 attained full output of 2,160 MW.

Largest Reactor

The largest single nuclear reactor in the world is the 1,098 MW Brown's Ferry Unit 1 General Electric boiling-water-type reactor located on the Wheeler Reservoir near Decatur, Alabama, which became operative in 1973. The Grand Gulf Nuclear Station at Port Gibson, Mississippi, will have a capacity of 1,290 MW in 1979.

Largest Generator

Generators in the 2,000,000 kW (or 2,000 MW) range are now in the planning stages both in the U.K. and the U.S. The largest under construction is one of 1,300 MW by the Brown Boveri Co. of Switzerland for the Tennessee Valley Authority.

Biggest Blackout

The greatest power failure in history struck seven northeastern U.S. states and Ontario, Canada, on November 9–10, 1965. About 30,000,000 people in 80,000 square miles were plunged into darkness. Only two were killed. In New York City the power failed at 5:27 p.m. on November 9, and was not fully restored for 13½ hours. The total losses resulting from another New York City power failure, on July 13, 1977, which lasted as long as 25 hours in some areas, have been estimated at more than $1 billion, including losses due to looting.

Tidal Power Station

The world's first major tidal power station is the *Usine marèmotrice de la Rance*, officially opened on November 26, 1966, at the Rance estuary in the Golfe de St. Malo, Brittany, France. Built in five years, at a cost of $75,600,000, it has a net annual output of 544,000,000 kilowatt-hours. The 880-yard barrage contains 24 turbo-alternators. This harnessing of the tides has imperceptibly slowed the earth's rate of revolution.

LARGEST POWER STATION: The hydro-electric station at Krasnoyarsk can generate a total of 6,096,000 kW.

Biggest Boiler

The largest boilers ever designed are those ordered in the U.S. from the Babcock & Wilcox Company, with a capacity of 1,330 MW, so involving the evaporation of 9,330,000 lbs. of steam per hour.

Largest Turbines

The largest turbines are those rated at 820,000 h.p. with an overload capacity of 1,000,000 h.p., 32 feet in diameter, with a 449-ton runner and a 350-ton shaft, for the Grand Coulee "Third Powerplant."

Largest Pump Turbine

The world's largest integral reversible pump turbine was made by Allis-Chalmers for the $50,000,000 Taum Sauk installation of the Union Electric Co. in St. Louis, Missouri. It has a rating of 240,000 h.p. as a turbine and a capacity of 1,320,000 gallons per minute as a pump. The Tehachapi Pumping Plant in California, completed in 1972, pumps 21,960,000 gallons per minute over 1,700 feet up.

Oldest Steam Engine

The oldest steam engine in working order is the 1812 Boulton & Watt 26-h.p. 42-inch bore beam engine on the Kennet & Avon Canal at Great Bedwyn, Wiltshire, England. It was restored by the Crofton Society in 1971.

Solar Power Plant

The largest solar furnace in the world is the 5-megawatt Solar Thermal Test Facility at the Sandia Laboratories, Albuquerque, New Mexico, completed in December, 1977. Sunlight from 222 heliostats is concentrated on a target 114 feet up in the power tower.

LARGEST MOBILE LAND MACHINE: The 13,440-ton Bucyrus-Erie 4250W walking dragline is the world's largest mobile land machine. It has a bucket capacity of 220 cubic yards.

6. Engineering

The earliest machinery still in use is the *dâlu*—a water-raising instrument known to have been in use in the Sumerian civilization which originated *c*. 3500 B.C. in Lower Iraq—even earlier than the *Saqiyas* of the Nile.

Largest Press

The world's two most powerful production machines are forging presses in the U.S. The Loewy closed-die forging press, in a plant leased from the U.S. Air Force by the Wyman-Gordon Company at North Grafton, Massachusetts, weighs 10,600 tons and stands 114 feet 2 inches high, of which 66 feet is sunk below the operating floor. It has a rated capacity of 50,000 tons, and went into operation in October, 1955. The other similar press is at the plant of the Aluminum Company of America at Cleveland, Ohio. There has been a report of a press in the U.S.S.R. with a capacity of 82,500 tons, at Novo Kramatorsk.

The Bêché and Grohs counterblow forging hammers, manufactured in West Germany, are rated at 66,120 tons.

Lathe

The world's largest lathe is the 72-foot-long 431-ton giant lathe built by the Dortmunder Rheinstahl firm of Wagner, in Germany, in 1962. The face plate is 15 feet in diameter and can exert a torque of 289,000 ft.-lbs. when handling objects weighing up to 225 tons.

Excavator

Largest. The world's largest excavator is the 14,325-ton bucket wheel excavator being assembled at the open cast lignite mine of Hambach, West Germany, with a rating of 260,000 cubic yards per 20-hour working day. It is 690 feet in length and 269 feet tall. The wheel is 222 feet in circumference with 6.5-cubic-yard buckets.

Dragline Excavator

The Ural Engineering Works at Ordzhonikdze, U.S.S.R., completed in March, 1962, has a dragline known as the ES–25(100) with a boom of 100 meters (328 feet) and a bucket with a capacity of 31.5 cubic yards. The world's largest walking dragline is the Bucyrus-Erie 4250W with an all-up weight of 13,440 tons and a bucket capacity of 220 cubic yards on a 310-foot boom. This, the largest mobile land machine, is now operating on the Central Ohio Coal Company's Muskingum site in Ohio.

Blast Furnace

The world's largest blast furnace is one with an inner volume of 179,040 cubic feet and a 48-foot 6½-inch diameter hearth at the Oita Works, Kyushu, Japan, completed in October, 1976, with an annual capacity of 4,905,600 tons.

Largest Forging

The largest forging on record is a generator shaft 55 feet long, weighing 450,600 lbs., forged by Bethlehem Steel in October, 1973, for a General Electric Company nuclear power station in Japan.

FORGING AHEAD: This 55-foot-long, 450,600-lb. generator shaft is the largest forging on record, completed in 1973 by the Bethlehem Steel Corporation.

Longest Pipelines

Oil. The longest crude oil pipeline in the world is the Interprovincial Pipe Line Company's installation from Edmonton, Alberta, Canada, to Buffalo, New York, a distance of 1,775 miles. Along the length of the pipe 13 pumping stations maintain a flow of 8,280,000 gallons of oil per day.

The eventual length of the Trans-Siberian Pipeline will be 2,319

miles, running from Tuimazy through Omsk and Novosibirsk to Irkutsk. The first 30-mile section was opened in July, 1957.

The world's most expensive pipeline is the Alaska pipeline running 798 miles from Prudhoe Bay to Valdez. By completion of the first phase in 1977 it had cost at least $6 billion. The pipe is 48 inches in diameter and will eventually carry up to 2,000,000 barrels of crude oil per day.

The longest submarine pipeline is the Ekofisk-Emden line stretching 260 miles under the North Sea, completed in July, 1975.

Natural Gas. The longest natural gas pipeline in the world is the Trans-Canada Pipeline which by 1974 had 5,654 miles of pipe up to 42 inches in diameter.

Largest Oil Tank

The largest oil tank ever constructed is the Million Barrel Ekofisk Oil Tank completed in Norway in 1973 and implanted in the North Sea. It measures $92 \times 92 \times 102$ meters (301.8 ft. sq., 335 ft. high) and contains 8,800 tons of steel and 222,700 tons of concrete. Its capacity of 209,272 cu. yds. is equivalent to 1.42 times the amount of oil which escaped from the *Torrey Canyon*, in the largest oil spill from a ship.

Largest Cat Cracker

The world's largest catalytic cracker is the Exxon Company's Bayway Refinery plant at Linden, New Jersey, with a fresh feed rate of 5,040,000 gallons per day.

Largest Padlock

The largest standard padlock made is ERA No. 1212 Close Shackle Clever Lock produced by J. E. Reynolds of Willenhall, England. It weighs 100 lbs.

Largest Nut

The largest nuts ever made weigh 5,264 lbs. each and have an outside diameter of $50\frac{1}{2}$ inches and a $31\frac{1}{2}$-inch thread. Known as Moorthrust, they are manufactured by Doncaster Moorside Ltd. of Oldham, England, for securing propellers.

Largest Valve

The world's largest valve is the 14-foot diameter Pratt-Triton XL butterfly valve made in Aurora, Illinois, for water and power systems.

Smallest Monkeywrench

The smallest standard ratchet monkeywrench is the No. 0 model made by the precision engineers, Leytool Ltd. of London E.10, England, with a head outside diameter of $\frac{1}{2}$ inch and a width of $\frac{1}{4}$ inch.

Fastest Printer

The world's fastest printer is the Radiation Inc. electro-sensitive system at the Lawrence Radiation Laboratory, Livermore, California. Recording of up to 30,000 lines per minute each containing 120 alphanumeric characters is attained by controlling electronic pulses through chemically impregnated recording paper which is rapidly moving under closely spaced fixed styli. It can thus print the wordage of the whole Bible (773,692 words) in 65 seconds— 3,333 times as fast as the world's fastest typist.

Highest Ropeway

The highest and longest aerial ropeway in the world is the Teleférico Mérida (Mérida téléphérique) in Venezuela, from Mérida City (5,379 feet) to the summit of Pico Espejo (15,629 feet), a rise of 10,250 feet. The ropeway is in four sections, involving 3 car changes in the 8-mile ascent in one hour. The fourth span is 10,070 feet in length. The two cars work on the pendulum system—the carrier rope is locked and the cars are hauled by means of three pull ropes powered by a 230-h.p. motor. They have a maximum capacity of 45 persons and travel at 32 feet per second (21.8 m.p.h.).

The longest single-span ropeway is the 13,500-foot-long span from the Coachella Valley to Mt. San Jacinto (10,821 feet), California, opened on September 12, 1963.

Fastest Passenger Elevators

The fastest domestic passenger elevators in the world are the express elevators to the 60th floor of the 787.4-foot-tall "Sunshine 60" building, Ikebukuro, Tokyo, Japan, completed April 5, 1978. They were built by Mitsubishi Corp. and operate at a speed of 2,000 feet per minute, or 22.72 m.p.h.

Much higher speeds are achieved in the winding cages of mine shafts. A hoisting shaft 6,800 feet deep, owned by Western Deep Levels Ltd. in South Africa, winds at speeds of up to 40.9 m.p.h. (3,595 feet per minute). Otitis-media (popping of the ears) presents problems at speeds much above even 10 m.p.h.

First and Longest Escalators

The name "escalator" was registered in the U.S. on May 28, 1900, but the earliest "Inclined Elevator" was installed by Jesse W. Reno on the pier at Coney Island, New York, in 1896.

The longest escalators are on the Leningrad Underground, U.S.S.R., which have a vertical rise of 195 ft.

The world's longest "moving sidewalks" are those installed in 1970 in the Neue Messe Centre, Düsseldorf, West Germany, which measure 738 feet between comb plates.

Largest Transformer

The world's largest single-phase transformers are rated at 1,500,000 kV of which 8 are in service with the American Electric Power Service Corporation. Of these, 5 step down from 765 to 345 kV.

Transmission Lines

Longest. The longest span between pylons of any power line in the world is that across the Sogne Fjord, Norway, between Rabnaberg and Fatlaberg. Erected in 1955 by the Whitecross Co. Ltd. of Warrington, England, as part of the high-tension power cable from Refsdal power station at Vik, it has a span of 16,040 feet and a weight of 13 tons. In 1967, two further high-tensile steel/aluminum lines 16,006 feet long, and weighing 37 tons, manufactured by Whitecross and British Insulated Callender's Cables Ltd., were erected here.

Highest. The world's highest are those across the Straits of Messina, with towers of 675 feet (Sicily side) and 735 feet (Calabria) and 11,900 feet apart.

Highest Voltages. The highest voltages now carried are 1,330,000 volts on the D.C. Pacific Inter-tie in the U.S. for a distance of 1,224 miles. The Ekibastuz D.C. transmission lines in Kazakhstan, U.S.S.R., are planned to be 1,490 miles long with a 1,500,000-volt capacity.

Longest Conveyor Belt

The world's longest single-flight conveyor belt is one of 9 miles installed near Uniontown, Kentucky, by Cable Belt Ltd. of Camberley, Surrey, England. It has a weekly capacity of 140,000 tons of coal on a 42-inch-wide 800-feet-per-minute belt and forms part of a 12½-mile-long system.

The world's longest multi-flight conveyor is one of 62 miles between the phosphate mine near Bucraa and the Atlantic port of El Aaiun, Morocco, built by Krupp and completed in 1972. It has 11 flights of between 5.6 and 6.8 miles in length and is driven at 10.06 m.p.h.

Smallest Tubing

The smallest tubing in the world is made by Accles and Pollock, Ltd., of Warley, England. Made of pure nickel with an outside diameter of 0.0005 of an inch, and an inside diameter of 0.00013 of an inch, it was announced on September 9, 1963. The average human hair measures from 0.002 to 0.003 of an inch in diameter. The tubing, which is stainless, can be used for the artificial insemination of bees and "feeding" nerves, and weighs only 5 ounces per 100 miles.

Longest Wire Rope

The longest wire rope ever spun in one piece was one measuring 46,653 feet (8.83 miles) long and $3\frac{1}{8}$ inches in circumference, with a weight of $31\frac{1}{2}$ tons, manufactured by British Ropes Ltd., of Doncaster, England.

The thickest ever made are spliced crane strops $11\frac{1}{4}$ inches thick, made of 2,392 individual wires in March, 1979, by British Ropes at Willington Quay, Tyneside, England.

Largest Radar Installations

The largest of the three installations in the U.S. Ballistic Missile Early Warning System is that near Thule, Greenland, 931 miles from the North Pole, completed in 1960 at a cost of $500,000,000. Its sister stations are at Cape Clear, Alaska, completed in July, 1961, and a $115,000,000 installation at Fylingdales Moor, North Yorkshire, England, completed in June, 1963. The largest scientific radar installation is the 21-acre ground array at Jicamarca, Peru.

Most Powerful Cranes

The world's most powerful crane is the 60,000-ton 584-foot-long converted tanker *Odin*, owned by Heerema Engineering Service of The Hague, Netherlands. On May 26, 1976, she made a test lift of 3,360 tons at a radius maximum of 105 feet in the Calard Canal, Europoort, Holland.

The most powerful gantry crane is the 92.3-foot-wide Rahco (R. A. Hanson Disc. Ltd.) gantry crane at the Grand Coulee Dam Third Powerplant, which was tested to lift a load of 2,500 tons in 1975. It successfully lowered a 3,944,000-lb. generator rotor with an accuracy of $\frac{1}{32}$ of an inch.

Greatest Lift

The heaviest lifting operation in engineering history was of the 41,000-ton roof of the Velodrome in Montreal, Canada, in 1975. It was raised by jacks some 4 inches to strike its centering.

Tallest Mobile Crane

The tallest is the 890-ton Rosenkranz K10001 with a lifting capacity of 1,100 tons and a combined boom and jib height of 663 feet. It is carried on 10 trucks, each limited to 75 feet 8 inches and an axle weight of 130 tons. It can lift 33.6 tons to a height of 525 feet.

Clocks

Oldest. The earliest mechanical clock, that is, one with an escapement, was completed in China in 725 A.D. by I Hsing and Liang Ling-tsan.

The oldest surviving working clock is the faceless clock dating from 1386, or possibly earlier, at Salisbury Cathedral, Wiltshire, England, which was restored in 1956 having struck the hours for 498 years and ticked more than 500,000,000 times. Earlier dates, ranging back to *c.* 1335, have been attributed to the weight-driven clock in

Wells Cathedral, Somerset, England, but only the iron frame is original. A model of Giovanni de Dondi's heptagonal astronomical clock of 1348–64 was completed in 1962.

Largest. The world's most massive clock is the Astronomical Clock in the Cathedral of St. Pierre, Beauvais, France, constructed between 1865 and 1868. It contains 90,000 parts and measures 40 feet high, 20 feet wide and 9 feet deep. The Su Sung clock, built in China at K'aifeng in 1088–92, had a 22-ton bronze armillary sphere for $1\frac{3}{4}$ tons of water. It was removed to Peking in 1126 and was last known to be working in its 40-foot-high tower in 1136.

Public Clocks. The largest four-faced clock in the world is that on the building of the Allen-Bradley Company of Milwaukee, Wisconsin. Each face has a diameter of 40 feet $3\frac{1}{2}$ inches with a minute hand 20 feet in overall length.

The tallest four-faced clock in the world is that of the Williamsburgh Savings Bank, Brooklyn, New York City. It is 430 feet above street level.

Most Accurate. The most accurate and complicated clock in the world is the Olsen clock, installed in the Copenhagen Town Hall, Denmark. The clock, which has more than 14,000 units, took 10 years to make and the mechanism of the clock functions in 570,000 different ways. The celestial pole motion of the clock will take 25,753 years to complete a full circle, the slowest moving designed mechanism in the world. The clock is accurate to 0.5 seconds in 300 years—50 times more accurate than the previous record holder.

Watches

Oldest. The oldest watch (portable clockwork timekeeper) is one made of iron by Peter Henlein in Nürnberg (Nuremberg), Bavaria,

MOST EXPENSIVE POCKET WATCH (left): The Swiss "Grande Complication" retails for $76,000. SMALLEST WATCH (right): Just over a half inch long, the dial of this watch is not much larger than a match head.

THINNEST WRISTWATCH: Delirium I, the thinnest watch in the world, is only $\frac{1}{16}$ inch thick and retails for $4,400.

Germany, *c.* 1504, and now in the Memorial Hall, Philadelphia The earliest wristwatches were those of Jacquet-Droz and Leschot of Geneva, Switzerland, dating from 1790.

Smallest. The smallest watches in the world are produced by Jaeger Le Coultre of Switzerland. Equipped with a 15-jeweled movement, they measure just over half an inch in length and three-sixteenths of an inch in width. The movement, with its case, weighs under a quarter of an ounce.

Most Expensive. Excluding watches with jeweled cases, the most expensive standard men's pocket watch is the Swiss *Grande Complication* by Audemars-Piguet, which retailed for $76,000 in May, 1979.

On June 1, 1964, a record £27,500 ($77,000) was paid for the Duke of Wellington's watch made in Paris in 1807 by Abraham Louis Bréguet, at the salesrooms of Sotheby & Co., London, by the dealer Mr. Ronald Lee for a Portuguese client.

The Patek Philippe 18-carat-gold minute-repeater perpetual-calendar pocket watch, launched by Tiffany's of New York on September 28, 1976, is priced at $100,000.

Thinnest. The world's thinnest wristwatch is the Delirium I by Concord Watch Corporation, New York. The quartz timepiece measures $\frac{1}{16}$ inch thick and retails with its lizard strap for $4,400. It is manufactured in Bienne, Switzerland.

Most Accurate Time Measurer

The most accurate time-keeping devices are the twin atomic hydrogen masers installed in 1964 in the U.S. Naval Research Laboratory, Washington, D.C. They are based on the frequency of the hydrogen atom's transition period of 1,420,450,751,694 cycles per second. This enables an accuracy to within one second per 1,700,000 years.

Chapter Nine

THE BUSINESS WORLD

In this chapter, the pound sterling has been converted, unless otherwise noted, at the fixed mean rate of £1 = $2.00 for early 1979, and at the prevailing rates for earlier dates.

1. Commerce

Oldest Industry

Agriculture is often described as "the oldest industry in the world," whereas in fact there is no evidence that it was practiced before *c.* 11,000 B.C. The oldest known industry is flint knapping, involving the production of chopping tools and hand axes, dating from about 1,750,000 years ago. Salt panning is of comparable antiquity.

Oldest Company. The oldest company in the world is the Faversham Oyster Fishery Co. of England, referred to in the Faversham Oyster Fishing Act of 1930 as existing "from time immemorial," *i.e.* from before 1189.

Greatest Assets. The business with the greatest amount in physical assets is the Bell System, which comprises the American Telephone and Telegraph Company, with headquarters at 195 Broadway, New York City, and its subsidiaries. The Bell System's total assets on the consolidated balance sheet on February 28, 1979 were valued at $104,926,359,000. The plant involved included 134,300,000 telephones. The number of employees is 993,000. A total of 20,109 attended the annual meeting in April, 1961, thereby setting a world record.

The first company to have assets in excess of $1 billion was the United States Steel Corporation with $1,400,000,000 at the time of its creation by merger in 1900.

Greatest Sales and Capital. The first company to surpass the $1 billion mark in annual sales was the United States Steel Corporation in 1917. Now there are some 250 corporations with sales exceeding $2,000,000,000 (143 of which are in the U.S.). The list is headed by General Motors of Detroit with $63,221,100,000 in 1978.

Greatest Profit and Loss. The greatest net profit made by an industrial company in a year is $3,508,000,000 by General Motors in 1978.

The greatest loss ever recorded by any enterprise in a year was £443,000,000 ($841,700,000) by the British Steel Corporation in 1977–78.

The Bethlehem Steel Corporation lost $477,000,000 for the third quarter of 1978.

Biggest Work Force. The greatest payroll of any single civilian organization in the world is that of the U.S.S.R. National Railway system with a total work force of 2,031,200 in 1976.

Largest Take-Over. The largest take-over in world commercial history has been the bid of £438,000,000 ($1,051,200,000) by Grand Metropolitan Hotels Ltd., England, for the brewers Watney Mann on June 17, 1972. Watney Mann was then valued at £378,000,000 ($907,200,000).

Largest Write-Off. The largest reduction of assets in the history of private enterprise was the $800,000,000 write-off of Tristar aircraft development costs by Lockheed announced on November 23, 1974.

Advertising Agency

The largest international single-name advertising agency in the world as listed in *Advertising Age* is Dentsu Incorporated of Tokyo, which in 1978 had estimated total worldwide billings of $2,210,000,000.

Biggest Advertiser

The world's biggest advertiser is Sears, Roebuck and Co., with $528,771,000 spent in 1978, excluding its catalogue.

Aircraft Manufacturer

The world's largest aircraft manufacturer is the Boeing Company of Seattle, Washington. The corporation's annual sales totaled $5,463,000,000 in 1978, and it had 92,200 (down from a 120,500 top) employees and assets valued at $1,473,600,000 on April 1, 1979. Cessna Aircraft Company of Wichita, Kansas, produced a record 9,197 civil aircraft in 1978, with total sales of $759,000,000. The company has produced more than 150,000 aircraft since Clyde Cessna's first was built in 1911.

Airlines

Largest. The largest airline in the world is the U.S.S.R. State airline "Aeroflot," so named since 1932. This was instituted on February 9, 1923, with the title of Civil Air Fleet of the Council of Ministers of the U.S.S.R., abbreviated to "Dobrolet." It operates 1,300 aircraft over about 560,000 miles of routes, employs 400,000 people and carries 100,000,000 passengers to 67 countries.

The commercial airline carrying the greatest number of passengers in 1978 was United Airlines (formed 1926), with 41,676,260 passengers. The company had 53,831 employees and a fleet of 336 jet planes.

Oldest. The oldest existing national airline is Koninklijke-Luchtvaart-Maatschappij N.V. (KLM) of the Netherlands, which opened its first scheduled service (Amsterdam-London) on May 17, 1920, having been established on October 7, 1919. One of the original constituents of B.O.A.C., Handley-Page Transport Ltd., was founded in May, 1919, and merged into Imperial Airways in 1924. Delag (Deutsche Luftschiffahrt A.G.) was founded at Frankfurt am Main on November 16, 1909, and started a scheduled airship service in June, 1910. Chalk's International Airline has been flying amphibians between Miami, Florida, and the Bahamas since July, 1919. Albert "Pappy" Chalk flew from 1911 to 1975.

Aluminum Producer

The world's largest producer of primary aluminum is the Aluminum Company of America (Alcoa) of Pittsburgh, with its affiliated companies. In 1978, the company had an output of 1,937,784 tons, and set a new world record for highest sales in the industry, with $4,051,800,000.

The Aluminum Company of Canada, Ltd. owns the largest aluminum smelter in the western world, at Arvida, Quebec, with a capacity of 465,000 tons per annum.

Art Auctioneering

The largest and oldest firm of art auctioneers is the Sotheby Parke Bernet Group of London and New York, founded in 1744. Their turnover in 1977–78 was $322,194,000. The highest total for any house sale auction was Sotheby's on May 18–27, 1977, at the 6th Earl of Rosebery's home at Mentmore, Buckinghamshire, England, which reached £6,389,933 ($10,900,000).

The highest total of any sale of fine art is $34,100,000 for a collection ranging from medieval art to impressionist paintings from the estate of Baron Robert von Hirsch, in a 7-day auction conducted by Sotheby's in London from June 19-27, 1978.

Barbers

The largest barbering establishment is Norris of Houston at 3303 Audley, Houston, Texas, which employs 60 barbers.

Bicycle Factory

The 64-acre plant of TI Raleigh Industries Ltd. at Nottingham, England, is the largest factory in the world producing complete bicycles, components and wheeled toys. The factory employs 10,000 and has the capacity to make more than 2,000,000 bicycles and 850,000 wheeled toys per year.

Bookshop

The bookshop with the greatest selection of books is that of W. & G. Foyle, Ltd., of London, W.C.2. First established in 1904 in a small shop in Islington, the company is now at 119–125 Charing Cross Road, which has an area of 75,825 square feet. It has a record 30 miles of shelving.

The most capacious bookstore in the world measured by square footage is Barnes & Noble Bookstore on Fifth Avenue at 18th Street in New York City. It covers 154,250 square feet with 12.87 miles of shelving.

The world's largest second-hand bookseller is Richard Booth (Bookseller) Ltd., Hay-on-Wye, Powys, Wales, with 8.30 miles of shelving and a running stock of 900,000 to 1,100,000 in 30,091 square feet of selling space.

Brewery

The oldest brewery is the Weihenstephan Brewery in Freising, near Munich, West Germany, founded in 1040.

The largest single brewer is Anheuser-Busch, Inc. of St. Louis. In 1978, the company sold 41,600,000 barrels, the greatest annual volume ever produced by a brewing company. The company's St. Louis plant covers 100 acres and after completion of current modernization projects will have an annual capacity in excess of 12,000,000 barrels.

The largest brewery on a single site is Adolph Coors Co. of Golden, Colorado, which sold 12,800,000 barrels in 1978.

Arthur Guinness, Son & Co., Ltd., founded in 1759, is the largest exporter of beer, ale and stout in the world. Exports of Guinness from the Republic of Ireland in the 52 weeks ending March 17, 1979, were 937,068 bulk barrels (1 bulk barrel = 36 Imperial gallons) which is equivalent to 1,482,833 half-pint glasses per day. The brewery extends over 57.22 acres at St. James's Gate, Dublin, Ireland.

Brickworks

The largest brickworks in the world is the London Brick Company plant at Stewartby, Bedfordshire, England. The works, established in 1898, now cover 221 acres and produce 16,000,000 bricks and brick equivalent every week.

Car Manufacturer

The largest car manufacturing company in the world (and largest manufacturer of any kind) is General Motors Corporation of Detroit. During its peak year of 1978, worldwide sales totaled $63,221,100,000. Its assets on December 31, 1978, were valued at $30,598,300,000. Its total 1978 payroll was $17,195,500,000 to an average of 839,000 employees. Dividends paid in 1978 were $1,725,500,000.

Largest Plant. The largest single automobile plant in the world is the Volkswagenwerk, Wolfsburg, West Germany, with 55,000 employees and a capacity of over 4,500 vehicles daily. The surface area of the factory buildings is 368 acres and that of the whole plant, with 43.5 miles of rail sidings, is 4,880 acres.

Greatest Salesman. The all-time record for automobile salesmanship in individual units sold is 1,425 in 1973, by Joe Girard of Detroit, Michigan, author of "How to Sell Anything to Anybody" and winner of the Number One Car Salesman title every year from 1966 to 1977. His commissions in 1976 totaled $180,000. His lifetime total of one-at-a-time "belly to belly" selling was 13,001 units sold, all retail. He retired on January 1, 1978, to teach others his art.

Chocolate Factory

The world's largest chocolate factory is that built by Hershey Foods Corp. of Hershey, Pennsylvania, in 1903-05. It now has 2,000,000 square feet of floor space.

Computer Company

The world's largest computer firm is International Business Machines Corporation (IBM) which, in a 1975 court decision,

FIRST "FIVE AND TEN": This store in Lancaster, Pennsylvania, gave birth to a 5,788-store marketing empire.

was held to have a 36.7 per cent share in the value of "electronic computers and peripheral equipment, except parts" based on 1971 shipments. In 1978, assets were $20,771,374,000, with sales of $20,076,089,000.

Department Stores

F. W. Woolworth celebrated its centenary year by announcing a total of 5,788 stores worldwide. Frank W. Woolworth opened his first Five and Ten Cent Store in Lancaster, Pennsylvania, on June 21, 1879. The 1978–79 earnings were a record $130,300,000.

Largest Single Store. The world's largest store is R. H. Macy & Co. Inc. at Broadway and 34th Street, New York City. It has a floor space of 50.5 acres, and 12,000 employees who handle 400,000 items. The sales of the company and its subsidiaries totaled $1,834,100,000 in 1978. Mr. Rowland Hussey Macy's sales on his first day at his fancy goods store on 6th Avenue, on October 27, 1858, were recorded as $11.06.

Fastest-Moving Merchandise. The department store with the fastest-moving stock is the Marble Arch store of Marks & Spencer Ltd. at 458 Oxford Street, London, England. The figure of more than $1,275-worth of goods per square foot of selling space (total 97,400 square feet) per year is believed be an understatement. The company has 253 branches in the U.K. and nearly 6,000,000 square feet of selling space. It now has branches in Continental Europe and Canada.

Distillery

The world's largest distilling company is The Seagram Company Limited of Canada. Its sales in the year ending July 31, 1978, totaled $2,272,584,000, of which $1,886,727,000 were from sales by Joseph E. Seagram & Sons, Inc. in the United States. The group employs about 15,000 people, including about 10,800 in the United States.

The largest of all Scotch whisky distilleries is Carsebridge at Alloa, Central Region, Scotland, owned by Scottish Grain Distillers Limited. This distillery is capable of producing more than 20,000,000 proof gallons per annum. The largest establishment for blending and bottling Scotch whisky is owned by John Walker & Sons Limited at Kilmarnock, Strathclyde, where over 3,000,000 bottles are filled each week. "Johnnie Walker" is the world's largest-selling brand of Scotch whisky. The largest malt Scotch whisky distillery is the Tomatin Distillery, Highland, Scotland, established at 1,028 feet above sea level in 1897, with an annual capacity of 5 million proof gallons. The world's largest-selling brand of gin is Gordon's.

Drug Store Chain

The largest chain is that of Boots The Chemists, which has 1,157 retail branches. The firm was founded in England by Jesse Boot (1850–1931), the 1st Baron Trent.

Fisheries

The world's highest recorded catch of fish was 65,700,000 metric tons in 1973. Peru had the largest ever national haul with 12,160,000 metric tons in 1970, comprising mostly anchoveta.

The world's largest fishmongers are MacFisheries, a subsidiary of Unilever Ltd., England, with 173 retail outlets in April, 1979.

Largest Net. The largest net yet manufactured is one that can fish 8,800,000 cubic yards per hour, announced in West Germany in March, 1974.

Games Manufacturer

The largest manufacturer of games is probably Parker Bros. Inc. of Salem, Massachusetts. The company's top-selling item is the real estate game "Monopoly," acquired in 1935. Almost 80,000,000 sets were sold by July, 1974. The print of "money" by the company for all its games is $18,500,000,000,000 per year, more than the total of real paper money printed in the entire world. The streets are named after those in Atlantic City, New Jersey, where the game's then unemployed inventor, Charles Darrow (1889–1967), spent his vacations.

The longest game of Monopoly approved by the Monopoly Marathon Records Documentation Committee is 1,008 hours by relays of 34 people in Denver, Colorado, from June 18 to July 31, 1974. The longest game by four players is 288 hours by Valerie Schmoltze, Karen Schmidt, Bob Schmidt and Paul Boyer of Ashland, Pennsylvania, August 17–29, 1978.

The Milton Bradley Company of Springfield, Massachusetts, claims to be larger than Parker Bros. but its sales of games are not segregated from sales of toys and school supplies, and Parker Bros., since it became part of General Mills, does not issue a separate statement, so exact comparisons are impossible.

General Merchandise

The largest general merchandising firm in the world is Sears, Roebuck and Co. (founded by Richard W. Sears in the North Redwood railroad station in Minnesota in 1886) of Chicago. The net sales were $17,946,000,000 in the year ending January 31, 1979, when the corporation had 866 retail stores and 2,861 catalogue, retail and telephone sales offices and independent catalogue merchants in the U.S., and total assets valued at $15,262,112,000.

Grocery Stores

The largest grocery chain in the world is Safeway Stores Incorporated, Oakland, California, with sales in 1978 amounting to $12,550,569,000 and total current assets valued at $1,183,390,000 as of December 30, 1978. The company has 2,436 stores totaling 57,461,000 square feet. The total payroll covers 144,243 people.

Hotels

The top revenue-earning hotel business is Holiday Inns, Inc., with 1978 revenues of $2,800,000,000 from 1,731 inns (284,000 rooms) in 59 countries. The business was founded by Charles Kemmons Wilson with his first inn on Summer Avenue in Memphis, Tennessee, in 1952.

Insurance

The company with the highest volume of insurance in force in the world is the Prudential Insurance Company of America, Newark, New Jersey, with $330,864,000,000 as of December 31, 1978. The admitted assets are $50,054,000,000.

It was estimated in 1978 that the total premiums paid in the United States had surpassed $100 billion or $1,400 per household.

Largest Association. The largest single association in the world is the Blue Cross, the medical insurance organization, with a membership at December 31, 1978, in the U.S. and Canada of 83,256,601. Benefits paid out totaled $19,406,109,000.

Marine Insurance. The largest marine insurance loss ever was the 125,000 g.r.t. VLCC (Very Large Crude Carrier) *Olympic Bravery*, insured at Lloyd's of London and valued at £25,000,000 ($50,000,000), which ran aground off Ushant, France, on January 24, 1976. The 83,000 g.r.t. LNG (Liquid Natural Gas) Carrier *Aquarius*, built in 1977 by General Dynamics Co., is currently insured for $175,000,000. This vessel is owned by Wilmington Trust Company, Delaware, and chartered to the Burmah Oil Co. Ltd.

Highest Life Insurance Pay-out. Linda Mullendore, wife of a murdered Oklahoma rancher, received some $18,000,000 as of November 14, 1970, the largest pay-out on a single life. Her husband had paid $300,000 in premiums in 1969.

Mineral Water

The world's largest mineral water firm is Source Perrier near Nîmes, France, with an annual production of more than 2,100,000,000 bottles, of which 1,000,000,000 now come from

TOP-SELLING SOFT DRINK: The familiar Coca-Cola bottle has not always been the same.

Perrier and Contrexéville. The French drink 50 liters (106 pints) of mineral water per person per year.

Soft Drinks

The world's top-selling soft drink is Coca-Cola with over 235,000,000 sold per day by the end of 1978 in more than 135 countries. "Coke" was invented by Dr. John S. Pemberton of Atlanta, Georgia, in 1886, the company was formed in 1892, and its famous bottle was patented in 1915.

Oil Company and Refinery

The world's largest oil company is the Exxon Corporation (formerly Standard Oil Company (New Jersey)), with 130,000 employees and assets valued at $41,530,804,000 on January 1, 1979. The world's largest refinery is the Amerada Hess refinery at St. Croix, Virgin Islands, with a capacity of 33,800,000 tons.

Paper Mill

The world's largest paper mill is that established in 1936 by the Union Camp Corporation at Savannah, Georgia, with a record output of 1,002,967 tons in 1974.

Pharmaceutical Company

The world's leading pharmaceutical company is Hoechst of West Germany, with drug sales in 1977 of $9,860,000,000.

Popcorn Plant

The largest popcorn plant is The House of Clarks Ltd. of Dagenham, Barking, England (instituted in 1933), which in 1977-78 produced 65,000,000 packets of popcorn.

Public Relations

The world's largest public relations firm is Hill and Knowlton, Inc. of 633 Third Avenue, New York City, and ten other U.S. cities. The firm employs a full-time staff of over 700 and also maintains offices in 22 cities overseas.

The world's pioneer public relations publication is *Public Relations News*, founded by Mrs. Denny Griswold in 1944. It now has readers in 86 countries.

Publishing

The publishing company generating most net revenue is Time, Inc., of New York City with $1,697,600,000 in 1978. The largest book publishing concern in the world is the Book Division of McGraw-Hill, Inc., of New York City, with sales of $305,321,000 in 1978.

Restaurant Chain

The largest restaurant chain is McDonald's Corporation in Oakbrook, Illinois, started on April 15, 1955, in Des Plaines, a suburb of Chicago, by Ray A. Kroc, B.H. (Bachelor of Hamburgerology). By January 1, 1979, the number of restaurants licensed and owned in 25 countries reached 5,185 with an aggregate output of 22 billion 100 per cent beef hamburgers. Sales systemwide in 1978 were $4,577,000,000.

The world's largest fish and chip shop is Harry Ramsdens, White Cross, Guiseley, West Yorkshire, England, with a staff of 180 serving 1,510,000 customers each year, who consumed 348 tons of fish and 504 tons of potatoes.

Shipbuilding

In 1978, there were 18,194,120 tons gross of ships, excluding sailing ships, barges, and vessels of less than 100 tons, completed throughout the world, excluding the U.S.S.R. and the People's Republic of China. Japan completed 6,307,155 tons gross (34.67 per cent of the world's total).

The world's leading shipbuilding firm in 1977 was the Mitsubishi Heavy Industries Co. of Japan, which launched 81 merchant ships totaling 1,377,342 tons gross.

Shipping Line

The largest shipping owners and operators are the Royal Dutch/Shell Group of Companies, whose fleets of owned/managed and chartered ships comprised 232 oil tankers (totaling 30,000,000 d.w.t.), 11 gas carriers (totaling 732,000 cubic meters capacity) and 7 dry bulk carriers (600,000 d.w.t.) as of December 31, 1978.

Shopping Center

The world's largest shopping center is the Lakewood Center, California, with a gross building area of 2,451,438 square feet on a 168-acre site. There is parking for 12,500 cars.

The world's first shopping center was Roland Park Shopping Center in Baltimore, Maryland, built in 1896.

The world's largest wholesale merchandise market is the Dallas Market center, located on Stemmons Freeway, Dallas, Texas, with more than 7,000,000 square feet in 6 buildings. The complex covers 135 acres with some 3,000 permanent showrooms displaying merchandise of more than 22,000 manufacturers. The center attracts 500,000 buyers each year to its 27 annual markets and trade shows.

Sporting Goods Chain Stores

Herman's World of Sporting Goods, comprising 72 stores in 13 states and the District of Columbia, reported sales of $171,000,000 in 1971.

Steel Company

The world's largest producer of steel has been Nippon Steel of Tokyo, Japan, which produced 59,600,000 tons of steel and steel products in 1977-78. The Fukuyama Works of Nippon Kokan has a capacity of more than 16,000,000 metric tons per annum. Its January, 1978, work force was 76,034.

Tobacco Company

The world's largest tobacco company is the British-American Tobacco Company Ltd. (founded 1902) of London. The company's subsidiaries and affiliates operate 118 tobacco factories in 53 countries. Consolidated turnover in 1977-78 was $10,269,500,000 and total assets were $5,622,100,000 on September 30, 1978. The Group's sales in 1978 topped 550,000,000,000 cigarettes.

The world's largest cigarette plant is the $200,000,000 Philip Morris plant at Richmond, Virginia, which opened in October, 1974. It employs 4,500 people producing 485,000,000 cigarettes a day.

Toy Manufacturer

The world's largest single toy manufacturer is Mattel Inc. of Hawthorne, California, founded in 1945. Its total sales in the year ending February 3, 1979, were $496,563,000 for 6 divisions, of which Mattel Toys is the largest.

Toy Store

The world's biggest toy store is Hamley's of Regent Street Ltd., founded in 1760 in Holborn, England, and moved to Regent Street, London, in 1901. It has selling space of 30,000 square feet on 11 floors with over 300 employees during the Christmas season. It was taken over by Debenhams on May 12, 1976, and also has a Sport and Leisure Centre (occupying 50,000 square feet) in Wigmore Street, London, and Model Centres in London and Bristol.

Wine Company

The oldest champagne firm is Ruinart Père et Fils, founded in 1729. The oldest cognac firm is Augier Frères & Cie., established in 1643.

LAND

The world's largest land owner is the United States Government, with a holding of 762,192,000 acres (1,190,000 square miles), which is nearly the area of India. The world's largest private landowner is reputed to be International Paper Co., based in New York City, with 9,000,000 acres.

Land Values

Highest. Currently the most expensive land in the world is that in the City of London. The freehold price on small prime sites reached £1,950 ($4,875) per square foot in mid-1973.

China Square Inch Land Ltd., at a charity auction on December 2, 1977, sold 1 square centimeter (0.155 square inch) of land at Sha Tau Kok for $2,000 Hong Kong (the equivalent of $17,405,833,737 per acre). The purchasers were Stephen and Tony Nicholson.

The real estate value per square meter of the two topmost French vineyards, the Grande and Petite Cognac vineyards in Bordeaux, has not been recently estimated.

Greatest Auction

The greatest auction ever was that at Anchorage, Alaska, on September 11, 1969, for 179 tracts of 450,858 acres of the oil-bearing North Slope, Alaska. An all-time record bid of $72,277,133 for a 2,560-acre lease was made by the Amerada Hess Corporation-Getty Oil consortium. The bid indicated a price of $28,233 per acre.

Highest Rent. The highest recorded rentals in the world are for shop premises in Hong Kong at $20 per square foot *per month*. The freehold price for a grave site with excellent *Fung Shui* (a choice location) in Hong Kong may cost $200,000 Hong Kong (U.S. $40,000) for 4 by 10 feet.

Lowest Rent. The rent for a 3-room apartment in the Fuggerei in Augsburg, West Germany, since it was built by Jacob Fugger in 1519, has been 1 Rhine guilder (now 1.72 deutsche marks or 90¢) per month. Fugger was the extremely wealthy philanthropist who pioneered social welfare.

STOCK EXCHANGES

The oldest Stock Exchange in the world is that in Amsterdam, in the Netherlands, founded in 1602. There were 138 throughout the world as of June 27, 1977.

Highest Value

The highest price quoted was for a share of F. Hoffmann-La Roche of Basel, Switzerland, worth 101,000 Swiss francs ($38,486) on April 23, 1976.

New York Stock Exchange Records

The highest index figure on the Dow Jones average (instituted October 8, 1896) of selected industrial stocks at the close of a day's trading was 1,051.70 on January 11, 1973, when the average of the daily "highs" of the 30 component stocks was 1,067.20.

The old record trading volume in a day on the New York Stock Exchange of 16,410,030 shares on October 29, 1929, the "Black Tuesday" of the famous "crash," was not surpassed until the first 20-million-share day (20,410,000) was achieved on April 10, 1968, when the ticker tape fell 47 minutes behind. The current record for a day's trading is 66,370,000 shares on August 3, 1978.

The Dow Jones industrial average, which had reached 381.71 on September 3, 1929, plunged 30.57 points on October 29, 1929, on its way to the Depression's lowest point of 41.22 on July 8, 1932.

The largest decline in one day, 38.33 points, occurred on October 28, 1929. The total lost in security values from September 1, 1929, to June 30, 1932 was $74,000,000,000.

The greatest paper loss in a year was $209,957,000,000 in 1974.

The record-setting daily increase of 28.40 on October 30, 1929, was most recently bettered on November 1, 1978, when the Dow Jones index increased 35.34 points to 827.79.

The largest transaction on record "share-wise" was on March 14, 1972, for 5,245,000 shares of American Motors at $7.25 each.

The largest stock trade in the history of the New York Exchange was a 1,874,300-share block of Cutler-Hammer stock at $55 per share in a $103,086,500 transaction on June 12, 1978.

The highest price paid in a transaction for a seat on the New York Stock Exchange was $625,000 in 1929. The lowest 20th century price was $17,000 in 1942.

Largest New Issue

The largest security offering in history was one of $1,375,000,000 in American Telephone and Telegraph Company stock in a rights offer on 27,500,000 shares of convertible preferred stock on June 2, 1971.

Largest Equity

The greatest aggregate market value of any corporation is $33,500,000,000, given the closing price of 206⅝ on December 31, 1975, for IBM, multiplied by the 149,533,813 shares outstanding.

Largest Investment House

The largest investment company in the U.S., and once the world's largest partnership (124 partners before becoming a corporation in 1959), is Merrill Lynch, Pierce, Fenner & Smith, Inc. (founded January 6, 1914) of New York City. It has 23,535 employees, 450 offices, 1,770,000 separate accounts and assets of $8,600,000,000. The firm is referred to in stock exchange circles as "We" or "We, the people" or "The Thundering Herd."

Largest Bank

The International Bank for Reconstruction and Development (founded December 27, 1945), the United Nations "World Bank" at 1818 H Street N.W., Washington, D.C., has an authorized share capital of $34,000,000,000. There were 130 members with a subscribed capital of $25,903,100,000 on December 31, 1977. The International Monetary Fund in Washington, D.C., had 138 members with total quotas of SDR39,011,000,000 ($49,934,000,000) on April 30, 1979.

The private commercial bank with the greatest deposits is the Bank of America National Trust and Savings Association, of San Francisco, with $75,828,044,000 on December 31, 1978. Its total resources on that date were $94,902,460,000.

The bank with the most branches is The State Bank of India with 7,262 on January 1, 1979, with assets of $12,144,244,790.

Largest Bank Building

The world's tallest bank building is the Bank of Montreal's First Bank Tower, Toronto, Canada, which has 72 stories and stands 935 feet high. The largest bank vault in the world, measuring 350 × 100 × 8 feet and weighing 984 tons, is in the Chase Manhattan Building,

LARGEST ANTIQUE: London Bridge was sold for almost $2½ million and moved to Lake Havasu City, Arizona. When it was all in place, an official balloon was launched for the celebration.

New York City, completed in May, 1961. Its six doors weigh up to 44.7 tons apiece, but each can be closed by the pressure of a forefinger.

Most Directorships

The record for directorships was set in 1961 by Hugh T. Nicholson, formerly senior partner of Harmood Banner & Co., London, who, as a liquidating chartered accountant, became a director of all 451 companies of the Jasper Group in 1961 and had 7 other directorships.

MANUFACTURED ARTICLES

Largest Antique

The largest antique ever sold has been the London Bridge in March, 1968. The sale was made by Ivan F. Luckin of the Court of Common Council of the Corporation of London to the McCulloch Oil Corporation of Los Angeles, California, for $2,460,000. Over 10,000 tons of facade stonework were re-assembled at a cost of $6,900,000 at Lake Havasu City, Arizona, and "re-dedicated" on October 10, 1971.

Armor

The highest price paid for a suit of armor is £25,000 (equivalent to $125,000 at that time) paid in 1924 for the Pembroke suit of armor, made in the 16th century for the 2nd Earl of Pembroke.

Largest Beds

In Bruges, Belgium, Philip, Duke of Burgundy, had a bed 12½ feet wide and 19 feet long erected for the perfunctory *coucher officiel* ceremony with Princess Isabella of Portugal in 1430. The largest bed in existence is the Great Bed of Ware, dating from *c.* 1580, from the

Crown Inn, Ware, Hertfordshire, England, now preserved in the Victoria and Albert Museum, London. It is 10 feet 8½ inches wide, 11 feet 1 inch long and 8 feet 9 inches tall. The largest bed currently marketed is the Super Size Diplomat bed, 9 feet wide and 9 feet long, sold in England for £2,200 ($4,400), including tax.

The heaviest bed is a waterbed 9 feet 7 inches wide and 9 feet 10 inches long, owned by Milan Vacek of Canyon Country, California, since 1977. The thermostatically-heated water alone weighs 4,205 lbs.

Beer Cans and Coasters

Beer cans date from a test marketing by Krueger Beer of Richmond, Virginia, in 1935. The largest collection is claimed by John F. Ahrens of Mt. Laurel, New Jersey, with over 12,000 *different* cans.

The world's largest collection of beer coasters is owned by Leo Pisker of Vienna, who had collected 76,000 different coasters from 144 countries by April, 1979.

Stuffed Bird

The highest price ever paid for a stuffed bird is £9,000 ($23,400). This was given on March 4, 1971, in the salesrooms of Sotheby & Co., London, by the Iceland Natural History Museum for a specimen of the Great Auk (*Alca impennis*) in summer plumage, which was taken in Iceland *c.* 1821; this particular specimen stood 22½ inches high. The Great Auk was a flightless North Atlantic seabird, which was finally exterminated on Eldey, Iceland, in 1844, becoming extinct through hunting.

Blanket

The largest blanket ever made measured 68 feet long and 100 feet wide, weighing 600 lbs. It was knitted in 20,160 6-inch squares in 10 months (October, 1977–July, 1978) by the English *Woman's Weekly* readers for Action Research for The Crippled Child. It was shown on the BBC-TV *Record Breakers* show in October, 1978. (See photo, page G.)

Candle

A candle 80 feet high and 8½ feet in diameter was exhibited at the 1897 Stockholm Exhibition by the firm of Lindahls. The overall height was 127 feet.

Carpets and Rugs

Earliest. The earliest carpet known (and still in existence) is a woollen pile-knotted carpet, red on a white ground, excavated at Pazyryk, U.S.S.R. in 1947 and dated to the 5th century B.C., and now preserved in Leningrad. Of ancient carpets the largest on record was the gold-enriched silk carpet of Hashim (dated 743 A.D.) of the Abbasid caliphate in Baghdad, Iraq. It is reputed to have measured 180 feet by 300 feet.

Largest. The world's largest carpet now consists of 88,000 square feet (over two acres) of maroon carpeting in the Coliseum exhibition hall, Columbus Circle, New York City. This was first used for the International Automobile Show on April 28, 1956.

Most Expensive. The most magnificent carpet ever made was the Spring carpet of Khusraw made for the audience hall of the Sassanian palace at Ctesiphon, Iraq. It was about 7,000 square feet of silk and gold thread, encrusted with emeralds. It was cut up as booty by military looters in 635 A.D. and from the known realization value of the pieces must have had an original value of some $2,400,000,000.

In 1946 the Metropolitan Museum of Art in New York City privately paid $1,000,000 for the 26.5-foot by 13.6-foot Anholt Medallion Carpet made in Tabriz or Kashan, Persia *c.* 1590. The highest price ever paid at auction for a carpet is $229,900 for a Mamluk carpet 12 feet 5 inches by 7 feet 3 inches, presumed woven in Cairo *c.* 1500 and sold at Sotheby's Bond Street salesrooms in London on March 29, 1978.

Most Finely Woven. The most finely woven carpet known is one with more than 2,490 knots per square inch from a fragment of an Imperial Mughal prayer carpet of the 17th century, now in the Altman collections in the Metropolitan Museum of Art, New York City.

Ceramics

The auction record for any ceramic object is £420,000 ($1,008,000) for the 16½-inch Ming blue and white bottle dated 1403–24 acquired by Mrs. Helen Glatz, a London dealer, at Sotheby Parke Bernet on April 2, 1974.

Chair

The world's largest chair measures 29 feet 6½ inches tall, 13 feet 9¼ inches wide, and has stood outside the Edsbyverken furniture factory in Edsbyn, Sweden, since 1944.

The highest price ever paid for a single chair is $85,000 for the John Brown Chippendale mahogany corner chair attributed to John Goddard of Newport, Rhode Island, and made *c.* 1760. This piece was included in the collection of Mr. Lansdell K. Christie dispersed by Sotheby Parke Bernet, New York City, on October 21, 1972.

Chandelier

The largest chandelier was built in Murano, Italy, in 1953 for the Casino Knokke, Belgium. It measures 26 feet 3 inches in circumference and 23 feet in height and weighs 3.9 tons with 1,896 electric lights.

Cigars

Largest and Most Expensive. The largest smokable cigar in existence is 9 feet 1½ inches long, 12¾ inches in circumference and weighs 60 lbs. 3 oz. It was made by J. P. Schmidt Jr., Fredericia, Denmark, and exhibited in May, 1979.

The largest standard brand of cigar in the world is the 9¾-inch-long "Partagas Visible Immensas." The Partagas factory in Havana, Cuba, manufactures special gift cigars 19.7 inches long for gift purposes, which retail in Europe for more than $13 each.

Russo's Restaurant, Union Street, San Francisco has the largest known collection of cigar bands with some 5,000, dating from 1860.

The most expensive standard cigar in the world is the Montecristo "A," which retails in Great Britain at a suggested £5.48 ($11.00).

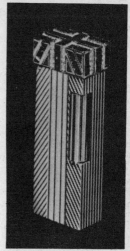

LUXURIOUS LIGHTER (left): The ornamentation of this $20,000 pocket lighter
includes 73 precious stones (see page 356). MILLION-DOLLAR BOTTLE (right):
This blue and white Ming bottle, decorated in underglaze red and blue, was sold at
auction for $1,008,000 in 1974.

Most Voracious Smoker. Paul Mears of the University of
Winnipeg, Manitoba, Canada, won a contest in 1975 by smoking
35 full-size cigars simultaneously.

Scott Case smoked 110 cigarettes simultaneously for 30 seconds at
the Oddball Olympics in Los Angeles in May, 1974.

In New York City on September 23, 1973, Simon Argevitch of
Oakland, California, retained his record for the more esoteric art of
smoking 14 cigars while simultaneously whistling.

Cigarettes

Consumption. The heaviest smokers in the world are the people
of the U.S. where about 665,000,000,000 cigarettes (an average of
3,900 per adult) were consumed at a cost of some $15,000,000,000
in 1978. The people of China, however, were estimated to consume
725,000,000,000 in 1977.

Largest Collection. The world's largest collection of cigarettes is
that of Robert E. Kaufman, M.D., of 950 Park Avenue, New York
City 10028. In May, 1979, he had 7,225 different brands of
cigarettes with 43 kinds of tips made in 167 countries. The oldest
brand represented is "Lone Jack," made in the U.S. in *c.* 1885. Both
the longest and shortest (see below) are represented.

Cigarette Packs. The world's largest collection of cigarette
packs is that of Niels Ventegodt of Copenhagen, Denmark. He had

52,021 different packets from 210 countries by March, 1974. The countries supplying the largest numbers were the United Kingdom (6,861) and the United States (3,981). The earliest is the Finnish "Petit Canon" packet for 25, made by Tollander & Klärich in 1860. The rarest is the Latvian 700-year-anniversary (1201–1901) Riga packet, believed to be unique.

Most Popular. The world's most popular cigarette is "Marlboro," a filter cigarette made by Philip Morris, which sold 186,598,000,000 units in 1978.

Longest and Shortest. The longest cigarettes ever marketed were "Head Plays," each 11 inches long and sold in packets of five in the U.S. in about 1930, to save tax. The shortest were "Lilliput" cigarettes, each $1\frac{1}{4}$ inches long and $\frac{1}{8}$ inch in diameter, made in Great Britain in 1956.

Cigarette Lighter. The most expensive pocket cigarette lighter is the 18 carat gold and platinum Dunhill lighter, featuring the Union Jack comprising 73 precious stones (diamonds, rubies and sapphires) and selling for $20,000 at Dunhill's in New York in 1979. The 18-carat lighthouse table lighter made by Alfred Dunhill, Ltd., of London, set on an island of amethyst retails for a record £32,500 ($65,000).

Cigarette Cards. The earliest known and most valuable tobacco card is "Vanity Fair," dated 1876, issued by Wm. S. Kimball & Co., Rochester, New York.

The largest known collection belongs to Mr. Edward Wharton-Tigar of London, with a collection of more than 1,000,000 cigarette and trade cards in about 45,000 sets. The highest price paid for a set is $4,600 on October 11, 1975, for Taddy's "Clowns," purchased by Ian Graham of Leeds, England, at auction in London.

Finest Cloth

The most expensive of all cloths is Shatoosh (or Shatusa), a brown-gray wool from the throat hair of Indian goats. It is sold by Neiman-Marcus of Dallas, at $1,000 per yard, and is both more expensive and finer than vicuña.

Credit Card Collection

The largest collection of valid credit cards, as of May 1, 1979, is one of 932, all different, by Walter Cavanagh (b. 1943) of Santa Clara, California. The cost of acquisition was nil, and he keeps them in the world's largest wallet, 250 feet long, weighing 28 lbs., and worth more than $1,000,000 in credit.

Largest Curtain

The largest curtain ever built was the bright orange-red $4\frac{1}{2}$-ton 185-foot-high curtain suspended 1,350 feet above and across the Rifle Gap, Grand Hogback, Colorado, by the Bulgarian-born sculptor Christo (né Javacheff), 36, on August 10, 1971. It blew apart in a 50-m.p.h. gust of wind 27 hours later. The total cost of displaying this work of art was $750,000.

Dolls

The highest price paid at auction for dolls is £16,000 ($36,800) for a pair of William and Mary painted wooden dolls in original clothes 22 inches high at Sotheby's, London, on April 19, 1974. After an export license was refused, they were purchased, after a public subscription, by the Victoria and Albert Museum, London. (See photo, page H.)

A rag doll 23 feet high was made at Monterey Adult Education Center, Bronx, New York, in April-June, 1977.

Most Expensive Dress

On January 23, 1977, a dress designed by Serge Lepage was exhibited in the Schiaparelli spring/summer collection in Paris. Called "The Birth of Venus" and studded with 512 diamonds, it carried a record price tag of $1,500,000.

Emperor Jean-Bédel Bokassa's coronation robe, with a 39-foot-long train, was encrusted with 785,000 pearls and 1,220,000 crystal beads by Guiselin of Paris for $144,500 for use at Bangui, Central African Empire in December, 1977.

Most Expensive Bikini

A platinum bikini valued at $9,500 was made by Mappin and Webb Jewelers, London. It was worn by Miss United Kingdom in the 1977 Miss World beauty pageant.

Fabric

The oldest surviving fabric discovered from Level VI A at Çatal Hüyük, Turkey, has been radio-carbon dated to 5900 B.C.

The most expensive fabric obtainable is an evening-wear fabric $37\frac{1}{2}$ inches wide, hand embroidered and sequinned on a pure silk ground in a classical flower pattern. It has 194,400 tiny sequins per yard, and is designed by Alan Hershman of London; it cost $550 per meter in May, 1978.

Largest Fireworks

The most powerful firework obtainable is the Bouquet of Chrysanthemums *hanabi*, marketed by the Marutamaya Ogatsu Fireworks Co. Ltd., of Tokyo, Japan. It is fired to a height of over 3,000 feet from a 36-inch caliber mortar. Their chrysanthemum and peony flower shells produce a spherical flower with "twice-thrice changing colors," 2,000 feet in diameter.

The world's lowest firework was George Plimpton's $40\frac{1}{2}$-inch 720-lb. Roman candle "Fat Man," which was supposed to break the record over Long Island, N.Y., in February, 1975. Instead, it sizzled, hissed and exploded, leaving a crater 10 feet deep.

Flags

Oldest. The crest in the center of the Austrian flag has its origins in the 11th century, while that of Malta dates from 1090. The origins of the Iranian flag, with its sword-carrying lion and sun, are obscure, but "go beyond the 12th century." The study of flags is known as vexillology.

Largest. The largest flag in the world was the Stars and Stripes designed by The Great American Flag Company of Warren,

LARGEST FLAG: This Stars and Stripes flown on the Verrazano Bridge covered an area equivalent to almost two football fields and weighed about 1½ tons.

Vermont, to be displayed on the Verrazano-Narrows Bridge, New York City, on July 3, 1976, as part of the celebration of the Bicentennial of the American Revolution. It measured 193 by 366½ feet (1.64 acres), weighed about 1½ tons, with 15-foot-wide stripes, and stars 11 feet in diameter. It was torn apart after a few hours during a test hanging on June 28, 1976.

Largest Float

The longest float used in any street carnival is the 200-foot-long dragon *Sun Loon* used in Bendigo, Victoria, Australia. It has 65,000 mirror scales. Six men are needed to carry its head alone.

The largest float is the 150-foot-long, 22-foot-wide "Agree" Float, bearing 51 All-American Homecoming Queens, used at the Orange Bowl parade, Miami, Florida, on December 29, 1977.

Furniture

The highest price ever paid for a single piece of furniture is 7,600,000 francs ($1,700,000) for a 10-foot-high marquetry and ormolu Louis XV corner cabinet made by Dubois, sold at Sotheby Parke Bernet, Monte Carlo, on June 25, 1979. On May 18, 1977, a bureau *en pente* of *c.* 1735 by Bernard van Risen Burgh was sold at Mentmore Towers, England, for £280,000 ($476,000).

FOREMOST FLOAT (left): This 150-foot-long float carried 51 beauty queens at the 1977 Orange Bowl Parade in Miami. TOP HAT (above): Worn by Napoleon, this hat sold for almost $30,000 in 1970 (see page 360).

The largest item of furniture is the Long Sofa—a wooden bench for old seafarers—measuring 236 feet in length, at Oskarshamn, Sweden. The largest marketed sofa is the King Talmage Sofa, 12 feet 2 inches in length, made by Talmageville Furniture manufacturers in California.

Glass

The most priceless example of the art of glass-making is usually regarded as the Portland Vase which dates from late in the first century B.C. or 1st century A.D. It was made in Italy and was in the possession of the Barberini family in Rome from at least 1642. It was eventually bought by the Duchess of Portland in 1792, but smashed while in the British Museum in 1847.

An auction record was set at Sotheby's in London, on June 4, 1979, when a 4th century Roman cage cup measuring 7 inches in diameter and 4 inches in height from the collection of Andrew Constable-Maxwell was sold for £520,000 ($1,040,000).

Gold Plate

The world's highest auction price for a single piece of gold plate is £40,000 ($112,000) for a 20.2-oz. George II teapot made by James Ker of Edinburgh, for the King's Plate horserace for 100 guineas at Leith, Scotland, in 1736. The sale was by Christie's of London on December 13, 1967, to a dealer from Boston, Massachusetts.

The gold coffin of the 14th century B.C. Pharaoh Tutankhamun, discovered by Howard Carter on February 16, 1923, in Luxor, western Thebes, Egypt, weighed 2,448 pounds.

Golf Club

The most valuable golf club, and the most valuable item of manual sports equipment in the world, is a putter presented to golfer Don Byrd by Claude A. Akkaoui of Egypt valued at $136,000; it has a white mink grip, solid gold head, and a shaft encrusted with 1,044 20-point diamonds.

Gun

The highest price ever paid for a single gun is £125,000 ($312,500) given by the London dealers, F. Partridge, for a French flintlock fowling piece made for Louis XIII, King of France, in *c.* 1615 and attributed to Pierre le Bourgeoys of Lisieux, France (d. 1627). This piece was included in the collection of the late William Goodwin Renwick (U.S.) sold by Sotheby's, London, on November 21, 1972.

Most Expensive Hat

The highest price ever paid for a hat is 165,570 francs (including tax) ($29,471) at an auction by Maîtres Liery, Rheims et Laurin, France, on April 23, 1970, for one last worn by Emperor Napoleon I (1769–1821) on January 1, 1815. It was bought by Moët et Chandon, a champagne house.

Most Expensive Jade

The highest price ever paid for an item in jade is 1,250,000 Swiss francs ($390,625) for a necklace set with 31 graduated beads of Imperial green jade. This was sold by Christie's at the Hotel Richmond, Geneva, Switzerland, on May 9, 1973. The highest price paid for jade objects is H.K.$1.4 million ($297,000 U.S.) for a pair of 19th-century green jadeite table screens $17\frac{1}{4}$ inches in height sold by Sotheby's in Hong Kong on November 2, 1976.

Largest Jig-Saw Puzzle

The largest jig-saw puzzle ever made is one 48 feet $\frac{1}{16}$ inch by 24 feet $\frac{1}{8}$ inch, built with 9,111 large pieces by the 75th Field Artillery Group, U.S. Army, at Fort Sill, Oklahoma, and exhibited on November 3, 1975. The *Festival of Britain* jig-saw by Efroc Ltd., now in Montserrat, though of much less area, contains an estimated 40,000 pieces.

Knife with Most Blades

The penknife with the greatest number of blades is the Year Knife made by the cutlers Joseph Rodgers & Sons Ltd., of Sheffield, England, whose trademark was granted in 1682. The knife was built in 1822 with 1,822 blades, and was designed to match the year of the Christian era until 2000 A.D., but had to halt at 1,973 because there was no more room.

Matchbox Labels

The oldest matchbox label is that of John Walker, Stockton-on-Tees, Cleveland, England, in 1827. Collectors of labels are phillumenists, of bookmatch covers philliberumenists, and of matchboxes cumyxaphists. Several labels, such as the Byron Match from Roche & Co., Marseilles, France, and the Canadian Allumettes Frontenac from the Eddy Match Co., are unique. Both of these are in the Frank J. Mrazik Collection in Quebec, Canada.

GOLFERS' DREAMS: The mink-lined golf shoes shown above, with ruby-tipped gold spikes, sell for $6,800 per pair. They are on display at the Guinness Museums and Exhibit Halls (see page 362). The precious putter at right is valued at $136,000.

Medal or Decoration

The highest price paid at auction for an order or decoration is £17,000 ($34,000) on March 21, 1979 at Sotheby's, London, for the group, including the V.C. and the M.M., won by Capt. George Burdon McKean of the 14th Canadian Infantry Bn., Quebec Regt., awarded for gallantry in the Gavrelle sector in France on April 27–28, 1918.

Sheerest Nylon

The lowest denier nylon yarn ever produced is the 6 denier used for stockings exhibited at the Nylon Fair in London in February, 1956. The sheerest stockings normally available are 9 denier. An indication of the thickness is that a hair from the average human head is about 50 denier.

Paperweight

The highest price ever paid for a glass paperweight is £48,000 ($96,000) at Christie's, London, on July 10, 1979, for a St. Louis 19th century paperweight. The earliest paperweights were made in Italy in the 15th century.

Pens

The most expensive writing pens are the 18-carat pair of pens (one fiber-tipped and one ballpoint) capped by diamonds of 3.88 carats sold by Alfred Dunhill Ltd., London, for £9,943 ($22,969) the pair (including taxes).

Most Expensive Pipe

A briar root pipe made by Julius Vesz of Toronto, Canada, with a silver mounting decorated with Canadian motifs and silver chains, with an ivory pushtype stem, is priced at $7,500.

Most Expensive Pistols

The highest price paid for a pair of pistols at auction is the £78,000 ($178,400) given by the London dealer Howard Ricketts at Sotheby Parke Bernet, London, on December 17, 1974, for a pair of English Royal flintlock holster pistols made *c.* 1690–1700 by Pierre Monlong. They were sent for sale by Anne, Duchess of Westminster.

Playing Cards

The rarest pack of playing cards is the 17th century "Lives of the Saints," published by the Bowles family and estimated to be worth $4,000. A 7 of diamonds signed by Edward Gibbon, who wrote *The Decline and Fall of the Roman Empire*, in 1786 as an IOU for £320 has been sold for $1,000.

Porcelain

The highest price ever paid for a single piece of English porcelain is £32,000 (about $77,000) for a Chelsea Boar's Head (of the red anchor period) sold at Sotheby's, London, on November 13, 1973.

The record for English pottery is £15,015 ($30,030) for a Staffordshire 18th-century salt-glaze pew group sold at Christie's, London, on December 15, 1975.

The highest price paid for a pot lid is £2,600 ($5,200) for a 19th century Staffordshire porcelain example purchased by Richard Cashmore at Phillips, London, on October 18, 1978.

Largest and Longest Ropes

The largest rope ever made was a coir fiber launching rope with a circumference of 47 inches, made in 1858 for the British liner *Great Eastern* by John and Edwin Wright. It consisted of four strands, each of 3,780 yards.

The longest fiber rope ever made without a splice was one of 10,000 fathoms (11.36 miles) of 6½-inch circumference manila by Frost Brothers (now British Ropes Ltd.) in London in 1874.

Most Expensive Shoes

The most expensive standard shoes obtainable are the mink-lined golf shoes with 18-carat gold embellishments and ruby-tipped gold spikes by Stylo Matchmakers International Ltd. of Northampton, England, which retail for £3,575 ($6,800) per pair.

The largest shoes ever sold, excluding those made for cases of elephantiasis, are a pair of size 42 built for the giant Harley Davidson, of Avon Park, Florida. The largest shoes normally available are size 14.

The 1887 Jubilee Boot made for the Newark trades procession, Nottinghamshire, England, is 4 feet 3½ inches long and weighs 81¾ lbs. It is a size 141, and is owned by Clarks Shoe, Somerset, England. (See photo, page H.)

Silver

The highest price ever paid for silver was £612,500 ($1,163,750) for the Duke of Kingston tureens made in 1735 by Meissonier and sold by Christie's, Geneva, on November 8, 1977.

HIGHEST-PRICED SNUFF BOX (above):
This gold and lapis lazuli box brought over
$200,000 at auction in 1974. **MOST EXPEN-
SIVE SWORD (right):** This gold sword of
honor, presented to General Lafayette by the
Continental Congress of the United States in
1779, was sold at auction for a record $145,000
nearly 200 years later.

Snuff Box

The highest price ever paid for a snuff box is $205,475 paid by
Kenneth Snowman of Wartski's in a sale at Christie's in London on
June 26, 1974. This was for a gold and lapis lazuli example uniquely
signed by Juste-Oreille Meissonier (d. 1750), the French master
goldsmith, and dated Paris, 1728. It was made for Marie-Anne de
Vaviere-Neubourg, the wife of Charles II of Spain, and measures
$3\frac{1}{4}$ by $2\frac{1}{4}$ inches.

Apostle Spoons

The highest price ever paid for a set of 12 apostle spoons is £70,000
($161,000) paid by Mrs. How in a sale at Christie's, London, on
June 26, 1974. They are Elizabethan silver-gilt spoons, made by
Christopher Wace in 1592, and are known as the "Tichborne
Celebrities."

Sword

The highest price recorded for a sword is $145,000 paid for the
gold sword of honor presented by the Continental Congress of 1779
to General Marie Jean Joseph Lafayette, sold at Sotheby Parke
Bernet, New York City, on November 20, 1976.

Tablecloth

The world's largest tablecloth is one 219 yards long by 2 yards wide
double damask, made by John S. Brown & Sons Ltd. of Belfast,
Northern Ireland, and shipped to a royal palace in the Middle East.
There was also an order for matching napkins for 450 places.

Tapestry

Earliest. The earliest known examples of tapestry-woven linen
are three pieces from the tomb of Thutmose IV, the Egyptian
pharaoh, which date from 1483 to 1411 B.C.

Most Expensive. The highest price paid for a set of tapestries is £200,000 ($560,000) for four Louis XV pieces at Sotheby & Co., London, on December 8, 1967.

Largest. The largest single piece of tapestry ever woven is "Christ in His Majesty," measuring 72 feet by 39 feet, designed by Graham Vivian Sutherland (b. August 24, 1903), for an altar hanging in Coventry Cathedral, West Midlands, England. It cost $29,400, weighs ⅞ of a ton, and was delivered from Pinton Frères of Felletin, France, on March 1, 1962.

Longest. The longest of all antique tapestries is Queen Matilda of England's famous Bayeux tapestry of embroidery, a hanging 19½ inches wide by 231 feet in length. It depicts events of the period 1064–66 in 72 scenes and was probably worked in Canterbury, Kent, in *c.* 1086. It was "lost" from 1476 until 1724.

An uncompleted embroidery depicting scenes from C. S. Lewis's Narnia children's stories has been worked by Mrs. Margaret Pollard of Truro, Cornwall, England, to the order of Mr. Michael Maine. It measures 8 inches wide by 1,065 feet long.

Earliest Tartan

The earliest evidence of tartan is the so-called Falkirk tartan, found stuffed in a jar of coins in Bells Meadow, Falkirk, Scotland. It is a dark and light brown pattern and dates from *c.* 245 A.D. The earliest reference to a specific named tartan has been to a Murray tartan in 1618 although Mackay tartan was probably worn earlier.

Time Capsule

The world's largest time capsule is the Tropico Time Tunnel measuring 10,000 cubic feet in a cave in Rosamond, Calfornia, sealed by the Kern Antelope Historical Society on November 20, 1966, and intended for opening in the year 2866.

Urn or Vase

The most expensive urn or vase is the Greek urn painted by Veuphromios and thrown by Euxitheos in *c.* 530 B.C., which was bought by the Metropolitan Museum of Art, New York City, for $1,300,000 in August, 1972, in a private transaction.

The largest vase on record is one 8 feet high, weighing 650 lbs., thrown by Sebastino Maglio at Haeger Potteries of Dundee, Illinois (founded 1872) during August, 1976. (See photo, page G.)

Wreaths

The most expensive wreath on record was that sent to the funeral of President Kennedy in Washington, D.C. on November 25, 1963, by the civic authority of Paris. It was handled by Interflora Inc. and cost $1,200. The only rival was a floral tribute sent to the Mayor of Moscow in 1970 by Umberto Formichello, general manager of Interflora, which is never slow to scent an opportunity.

Writing Paper

The most expensive writing paper in the world is that sold by Cartier, Inc., on Fifth Avenue, New York City, at $8,000 per 100 sheets with envelopes. It is of handmade paper from Finland with deckle edges and a "personalized" portrait watermark. Second thoughts and misspellings can be costly.

2. Agriculture

Origins. It has been estimated that only 21 per cent of the world's land surface is cultivatable and that only 7.6 per cent is actually under cultivation.

Evidence adduced in 1971 from Nok Nok Tha and Spirit Cave, Thailand, tends to confirm that plant cultivation and animal domestication was part of the Hoabinhian culture *c.* 11,000 B.C.

The earliest attested evidence for the cultivation of grain comes from Ali Kosh, Iran, and Jericho, *c.* 7000 B.C. Goats were domesticated at Asiab, Iran, by *c.* 8050 B.C. and dogs at Star Carr, North Yorkshire, by *c.* 7700 B.C. The earliest definite date for sheep is *c.* 7200 B.C. at Argissa-Magula, Thessaly, Greece, and for pigs and cattle *c.* 7000 B.C. at the same site. The earliest date for horses is *c.* 4350 B.C. from Dereivka, Ukraine, U.S.S.R.

Reindeer may have been domesticated as early as *c.* 18,000 B.C., but definite evidence is lacking.

Farms

The largest farms in the world are collective farms in the U.S.S.R. These have been reduced in number from 235,500 in 1940 to only 36,000 in 1969, and have been increased in size so that units of over 60,000 acres are not uncommon.

The pioneer farm of Laucidio Coelho near Campo Grande, Mato Grosso, Brazil, *c.* 1901 was 3,358 square miles (2,150,000 acres) with 250,000 head of cattle at the time of his death in 1975.

Largest Wheat Field. The world's largest single fenced field sown with wheat was one of 35,000 acres, sown in 1951 near Lethbridge, Alberta, Canada.

Largest Hop Field. The largest hop field in the world is one of 3,945 acres at Toppenish, Washington, owned by John I. Haas, Inc., the world's largest hop growers, with hop farms in British Columbia (Canada), California, Idaho, Oregon and Washington, with a total net area of 37,650 acres.

Largest Vineyard. The world's largest vineyard extends over the Mediterranean façade between the Rhone and the Pyrenees in the départements (provinces) of Aude, Hérault, Gard and Pyrénées-Orientales. It has an area of 2,075,685 acres of which 52.3 per cent is *monoculture viticole*.

Largest Cattle Station. The world's largest cattle station is Alexandria Station, Northern Territory, Australia, selected in 1873 by Robert Collins, who rode 1,600 miles to reach it. It now has 82 wells, a staff of 90 and originally extended over 7,207,608 acres. The present area is 6,500 square miles which is stocked with 60,000 shorthorn cattle. Until 1915 the Victoria River Downs Station, Northern Territory, was over three times larger, with an area of 22,400,000 acres (35,000 square miles).

Largest Sheep Station. The largest sheep station in the world is Commonwealth Hill, in the northwest of South Australia. It grazes between 70,000 and 90,000 sheep, about 700 cattle and 25,000 uninvited kangaroos, in an area of 4,080 square miles (2,611,200 acres). The largest sheep move on record occurred when 27 horsemen moved a mob of 43,000 sheep 40 miles from Barcaldine to Beaconsfield Station, Queensland, Australia, in 1886.

Largest Chicken Ranch. The world's largest chicken ranch is the 520-acre "Egg City," in Moorpark, California, established by Julius Goldman in 1961. Some 2,000,000 eggs are laid daily by by 3,160,000 hens.

Largest Turkey Farm. The turkey farm of Bernard Matthews Ltd., centered at Great Witchingham, Norfolk, England, has 1,076 workers tending 5,400,000 turkeys.

Largest Piggery. The world's largest piggery is at Sljeme, Yugoslavia, which is able to process 300,000 pigs in a year. Even bigger units may exist in Rumania, but details are lacking.

Mushroom Farm. The largest mushroom farm in the world is Butler County Mushroom Farm, Inc., founded in 1937 in a disused limestone mine near West Winfield, Pennsylvania. It has over 1,000 employees working underground, in a maze of galleries 110 miles long, producing about 45,000,000 lbs. of mushrooms per year.

Largest Community Garden. The largest recorded community garden project is that operated by the City Beautiful Council, and the Benjamin Wegerzyn Garden Center in Dayton, Ohio. It comprises 1,173 allotments, each of 812¼ square feet.

Crop Yields

Wheat. Crop yields for highly tended small areas are of little significance. The greatest recorded wheat yield is 89.8 cwt. per acre from 20.4 acres by A. S. Clark of Langley Mawn, Saffron Walden, Essex, England, in 1977, using Maris Hobbit winter wheat.

Barley. A yield of 82.61 cwt. per acre of Clermont Spring Barley was achieved in 1972 by John Graham of Kirkland Hall, Wigton, Cumbria, England, from a 13.52-acre field.

Corn. The record yield is 352.64 U.S. bushels (15½ per cent moisture) from an acre using De Kalb XL-54, by Roy Lynn, Jr. near Kalamazoo, Michigan, on September 30, 1977.

Sugar Beet. The highest recorded yield for sugar beet is 62.4 tons per acre by Andy Christensen and Jon Giannini in the Salinas Valley, California.

Plowing

The world championship (instituted 1953) has been staged in 17 countries and won by plowmen of 10 nationalities, of which the United Kingdom has been most successful with 6 championships. The only man to take the title 3 times has been Hugh Barr of Northern Ireland in 1954-55-56.

The fastest recorded time for plowing an acre (minimum 32 right-hand turns and a depth of 9 inches) is 13 minutes 34 seconds by Leslie Painter at West Farm, Appleton, Oxfordshire, England, using a Bamford 5-furrow 12-inch plow towed by a Massey Ferguson 1155 tractor on November 18, 1977.

The greatest recorded acreage plowed in 24 hours is 123.4 acres by David Griffiths and Pat Neylan using a Lamborghini R-1056 DT tractor with a 6-furrow plow to a depth of 7 inches in the Nakuru District, Kenya, on July 6-7, 1978.

John Frisby of Stoke Golding near Nuneaton, Warwickshire, England, plowed for 80 hours on November 3-6, 1978.

Potato Picking

The most U.S. barrels picked in a 9½-hour day is 235 by Walter Sirois (b. 1917) of Caribou, Maine, on September 30, 1950.

Largest Hay Rick

A rick of some 23,500 straw bales was completed by Birch and Pearman at Billesley, Warwickshire, England, in September, 1977.

Dimensions and Prolificacy

Cattle. Of heavyweight cattle the heaviest on record was a Holstein-Durham cross named "Mount Katahdin," exhibited by A. S. Rand of Maine in 1906–1910, and frequently weighed at an even 5,000 lbs. He was 6 feet 2 inches at the shoulder with a 13-foot girth, and died in a barn fire *c.* 1923.

The largest breed of heavyweight cattle is the Chianini, which were brought to India from the Middle East in pre-Roman times. Mature bulls average 5 feet 8 inches at the forequarters and 2,865 lbs. In 1955, a bull named "Donetto" tipped the scales at 3,834 lbs. at the Arezzo show—a world record for any bull of any breed.

The highest recorded birthweight for a calf is 225 lbs. from a British Friesian cow at Rockhouse Farm, Bishopston, Swansea, West Glamorgan, Wales, in 1961.

On April 25, 1964, it was reported that a cow named "Lyubik" had given birth to seven calves at Mogilev, U.S.S.R. A case of five live calves at one birth was reported in 1928 by T. G. Yarwood of Manchester, Lancashire, England. The lifetime prolificacy record is 30 in the case of a cross-bred cow owned by G. Page of Warren Farm, Wilmington, Sussex, England, which died in November, 1957, aged 32. A cross-Hereford calved in 1916 and owned by A. J. Thomas of West Hook Farm, Marloes, Dyfed, Wales, produced her 30th calf in May, 1955, and died in May, 1956, aged 40.

Pigs. The highest recorded number of piglets in one litter is 34, thrown on June 25–26, 1961, by a sow owned by Aksel Egedee of Denmark. This record was equalled by a litter of 34 in England in 1955, but 30 of the piglets were born dead.

The heaviest pig ever recorded was "Big Bill," a hog weighing 2,552 lbs. and measuring 9 feet long, raised in Henderson County, Tennessee, and killed in 1933. He was mounted and displayed by the Wells family in Jackson, Tennessee, until 1946.

The highest recorded weight for a piglet at weaning (8 weeks) is 81 lbs. for a boar, one of 9 piglets farrowed on July 6, 1962, at Kettle Lane Farm. Trowbridge, Wiltshire, England.

Sheep. The highest recorded birthweight for a lamb is 38 lbs., in the case of a lamb delivered in 1975 at Clearwater, Miner County, near Howard, Kansas, but neither this lamb nor the ewe survived.

A case of eight lambs at a birth was reported by D. T. Jones of Priory Farm, Monmouthshire, Wales, in June, 1956, but none lived.

A grey face ewe at Moss Side Farm, Longtown, Cumbria, England, gave birth to live sextuplets in March, 1977.

A case of a sheep living to 26 years was recorded in flock book records by H. Poole, Wexford, Ireland.

Egg-Laying

The highest authenticated rate of egg-laying by a hen is 361 eggs in 364 days by a Black Orpington in an official test at Taranaki, New Zealand, in 1930. The heaviest egg *reported* is one of 16 ounces, with double yolk and double shell, laid by a white Leghorn at Vineland, New Jersey, on February 25, 1956. The largest *recorded* was one of "nearly 12 ounces" for a 5-yolked egg, $12\frac{1}{4}$ inches around the long axis and 9 inches around the shorter axis, laid by a Black Minorca at Mr. Stafford's Damsteads Farm, Mellor, Lancashire, England, in 1896.

The highest claim for the number of yolks in a chicken's egg is 9, reported by Mrs. Diane Hainsworth of Hainsworth Poultry Farms, Mount Morris, New York, in July, 1971, and also from a hen in Kirghizia, U.S.S.R., in August, 1977.

The white goose "Speckle," owned by Donny Brandenberg of Goshen, Ohio, laid a 24-ounce egg measuring $13\frac{1}{2}$ inches by $9\frac{1}{2}$ inches in circumference on May 3, 1977.

The highest recorded annual average for a flock is 313 eggs in 52 weeks from a flock of 1,000 Warren-Stadler SSL layers (from 21 weeks of age) by Eric Savage, White Lane Farm, Surrey, England, in 1974-75.

Milk Yields

The world lifetime record yield of milk is 340,578 lbs. at 3.3 per cent butterfat by the Holstein cow "Or-Win Masterpiece Riva," owned by Willard and Gary Behm at Adrian, Michigan, up to April 10, 1975.

The greatest recorded yield for one lactation (365 days) is 55,661 lbs. by the Holstein "Beecher Arlinda Ellen," owned by Mr. and Mrs. Harold L. Beecher of Rochester, Indiana, in 1975.

The probable record milk yield in a day is $198\frac{1}{4}$ lbs. by R. A. Pierson's British Friesian "Garsdon Minnie" in 1948.

The highest recorded milk yield for any goat is 7,546 lbs. in 365 days by "Waiora Frill Q*," bred by Mr. and Mrs. E. L. Collins of Swanson, Auckland, New Zealand, in 1972.

Butterfat

The world record butterfat yield in a lifetime is 14,651 lbs. by the Jersey cow "Sunny King Berna" (calved March 5, 1950) in 5,726 days to January, 1979, on the J. W. Coppini estate, Ferndale, California.

The world's lactation (365-day) yield record is 2,230 lbs. by the Holstein "Breezewood Patsy Bar Pontiac" owned by the Gelbke brothers of Vienna, Ohio, announced on October 8, 1976.

Cheese

The most active cheese-eaters are the people of France, with an annual average in 1978 of 37.7 lbs. per person. The world's biggest producer is the United States with a factory production of 3,344,300,000 lbs. in 1977.

Oldest. The oldest and most primitive cheeses are the Arabian *kishk*, made of the dried curd of goat's milk. There are today 450 named cheeses of 18 major varieties, but many are merely named after different towns and differ only in shape or the method of packing. France has 240 varieties.

Most Expensive. The world's most expensive cheese is La Baratte from the Loire Valley, France, at 140 francs per kilogram ($17.20 per lb.).

Largest. The largest cheese ever made was a cheddar of 34,591 lbs., made in 43 hours, January 20–22, 1964, by the Wisconsin Cheese Foundation for exhibition at the New York World's Fair. It was transported in a specially designed 45-foot-long refrigerated tractor trailer "Cheese-Mobile."

Livestock Prices

Note: Some exceptionally high livestock auction prices are believed to result from collusion between buyer and seller to raise the ostensible price levels of the breed concerned. Others are marketing and publicity exercises with little relation to true market prices.

Bull. The highest price ever paid for a bull is $2,500,000 for the beefalo (⅜ buffalo, ⅜ Charolais, ¼ Hereford) "Joe's Pride," sold by D. C. Basolo of Burlingame, California, to the Beefalo Cattle Co. of Canada in Calgary, Alberta, on September 9, 1974.

On February 5, 1963, James R. Dick, co-manager of Black Watch Farms, Scotland, paid £63,000 (then $176,400) for the bull "Lindertis Evulse." The bull subsequently failed a fertility test in August, 1963, when it was 20 months old, and thus became the world's most expensive piece of beef.

Cow. The highest price ever paid for a cow is $235,000 Canadian for the Holstein-Friesian "Hanover Hill Barb" by a U.S.-Canadian syndicate at the Sale of Stars, Oakville, Ontario, Canada, on November 8, 1976.

Sheep. The highest price ever paid for a sheep is $46,000 Australian ($50,000) for a Merino ram from John Collins & Sons, Mount Bryan, South Australia, by Mr. Perce L. Puckridge of White River, Port Lincoln, South Australia, on September 2, 1976.

The highest price ever paid for wool is $A46 per kilogram ($29 per lb.) for a bale of superfine Merino fleece from the Launceton, Tasmania, Australia, sales in February, 1973. It was sold by Mr. C. Stephen of Mount Morriston estate to Fujii Keori Ltd., of Osaka, Japan.

Pig. The highest price ever paid for a pig is $42,500 for a Duroc boar, owned by Blaize Durocs of Stamford, Texas, by Wilbert and Myron Meinhart of Iowa on February 24, 1978.

Horse. The highest price ever paid for a farm horse is $47,500 paid for the 7-year-old Belgian stallion "Farceur," by E. G. Good at Cedar Falls, Iowa, on October 16, 1917.

Donkey. Perhaps the lowest price ever for livestock was at a sale at Kuruman, Cape Province, South Africa, in 1934, where donkeys were sold for less than 4d. (4 cents) each.

Chicken Plucking

The fastest recorded time for plucking chickens was set in the 1976 contest at Masaryktown, Florida, on October 9, when a team of four women (Doreena Cary, Diane Grieb, Kathy Roads and Dorothy McCarthy) plucked 12 birds naked in 32.9 seconds. Leaving a single feather produces the cry "Fowl!"

Ernest Hausen (1877-1955) of Fort Atkinson, Wisconsin, died undefeated after 33 years as a champion. On January 19, 1939, he was timed for one chicken at 4.4 seconds, and reportedly twice did 3.5 seconds a few years later.

Turkey Plucking

Vincent Pilkington of Cootehill, County Cavan, Ireland, killed and plucked 100 turkeys in 7 hours 32 minutes on December 15, 1978.

Hand Milking

Andy Faust at Collinsville, Oklahoma, in 1937, achieved 120 gallons in 12 hours.

Sheep Shearing

The highest recorded speed for sheep shearing in a working day was that of G. Phillips, who machine-sheared 694 lambs (average 77.1 per hour) in 9 hours at Tymawr Farms, Libanus, Powys, Wales, on June 25, 1975. The hand-shearing record for a 9-hour day is 353 by Peter Casserly of Christchurch, New Zealand, on February 13, 1976.

The sheep shearer with the largest lifetime total is believed to be LaVor Taylor (b. February 27, 1896) of Ephraim, Utah, who, with annual totals varying between 8,000 and 22,000 sheep, sheared 510,000 head in 60 years.

In a shearing marathon, 4 men machine-sheared 1,649 sheep in 24 hours at Brecon, Powys, Wales, on July 13-14, 1977.

Sheep Survival

On March 2, 1978, Peter Boa of Seiberscross, Strath Brora, Sutherland, Scotland, dug out 9 sheep buried in snow for 33 days. Two ewes were alive.

Chapter Ten

THE HUMAN WORLD

1. Political and Social

The land area of the earth is estimated at 57,270,000 square miles (including inland waters), or 29.08 per cent of the world's surface area.

Largest Political Division

The British Commonwealth of Nations, a free association of 39 independent sovereign states together with their dependencies, covers an area of 13,095,000 square miles with a population which in 1978 just surpassed 1,000,000,000.

COUNTRIES

The total number of separately administered territories in the world is 221, of which 164 were independent countries as of August 1, 1979. Of these, 39 sovereign and 42 non-sovereign are insular countries. Only 29 sovereign countries are entirely without a sea-board. Territorial waters vary between extremes of 3 miles (*e.g.* Australia, France, Ireland, and the United Kingdom) up to 200 miles (*e.g.* U.S., Argentina, Ecuador, El Salvador and Panama).

Largest. The country with the greatest area is the Union of Soviet Socialist Republics (the Soviet Union), comprising 15 Union (constituent) Republics with a total area of 8,649,500 square miles, or 15.0 per cent of the world's total land area, and a total coastline (including islands) of 66,090 miles. The country measures 5,580 miles from east to west and 2,790 miles from north to south.

Smallest. The smallest independent country in the world is the State of the Vatican City (Stato della Città del Vaticano), which was made an enclave within the city of Rome, Italy, on February 11, 1929. The enclave has an area of 108.7 acres (0.17 square miles).

The maritime country with the shortest coastline is Monaco with 3.49 miles excluding piers and breakwaters.

The smallest colony in the world is Gibraltar, with an area of 2½ square miles. Pitcairn Island, the only inhabited (70 people in 1977) island of a group of 4 (total area 18½ square miles), has an area of 1½ square miles, or 960 acres.

The world's smallest republic is Nauru, less than 1 degree south of the equator in the Western Pacific. It became independent on January 31, 1968, has an area of 5,263 acres (8.2 square miles) and a population of 8,000 (latest estimate, mid-1976). Tuvalu, a British dependency in Oceania, has an area of 6,080 acres (9.5 square miles), with a population of only 6,000.

The official residence, since 1834, of the Grand Master of the Order of the Knights of Malta totaling 3 acres and comprising the Villa del Priorato di Malta on the lowest of Rome's seven hills (the 151-foot Aventine) retains certain diplomatic privileges as does 68 Via Condotti. The order has accredited representatives to foreign governments. Hence, it is sometimes cited as the smallest state in the world.

Flattest and Most Elevated. The country with the lowest highest point is the Republic of the Maldives, which attains 13 feet above sea level. The country with the highest lowest point is Lesotho. The egress of the Senqu (Orange) riverbed is 4,530 feet above sea level.

Frontiers

Most. The country with the most land frontiers is China, with 13—Mongolia, U.S.S.R., North Korea, Hong Kong, Macau, Vietnam, Laos, Burma, India, Bhutan, Nepal, Pakistan, and Afghanistan.

France, if all her *Départements d'outre-mer* are included, may, if her territorial waters are extended, have 20 frontiers.

Longest. The longest *continuous* frontier in the world is that between Canada and the U.S., which (including the Great Lakes boundaries) extends for 3,987 miles (excluding 1,538 miles with Alaska).

Shortest. The "frontier" of the Holy See in Rome measures 2.53 miles. The land frontier between Gibraltar and Spain at La Linea, closed since 1969, measures 1,672 yards. Zambia, Rhodesia, Botswana and Namibia (South-West Africa) meet at a point.

Most Frequently Crossed. The frontier which is crossed most frequently is that between the U.S. and Mexico. It extends for 1,933 miles and has more than 120,000,000 crossings every year. The Sino-Soviet frontier, broken by the Sino-Mongolian border, extends for 4,500 miles with no reported figures of crossings.

Most Impenetrable Boundary. The 858-mile-long "Iron Curtain," dividing the Federal Republican (West) and the Democratic Republican (East) parts of Germany, utilizes 2,230,000 land mines and 50,000 miles of barbed wire, in addition to many watchtowers containing detection devices. The whole 270-yard-wide strip occupies 133 square miles of East German territory.

POPULATIONS

Estimates of the human population of the world largely hinge on the accuracy of the component figure for the population of the People's Republic of China, which in its mid-1979 census (the first published since 1953) claimed a population of 958,040,000. The U.N. estimate for 1978 accorded more closely than hitherto with the U.S. Bureau of the Census at 930,000,000.

The daily increase in the world's population has been estimated at 221,900 per day or 154 per minute. It was estimated that about

286 were born and about 114 died every minute in 1977–78. The world's population has doubled in the last 49 years and is now doubling at a rather faster rate.

WORLD POPULATION—PROGRESSIVE ESTIMATES

Date	Millions	Date	Millions
10000 B.C.	c. 5	1930	2,070
1 A.D.	c. 200	1940	2,295
1000	c. 275	1950	2,533*
1250	375	1960	3,049*
1500	420	1970	3,704*
1650	550–600	1975	4,090*
1700	615	1976	4,163*
1750	720	1977	4,314*
1800	900	1978	4,375**
1900	1,625	1980	4,470*
1920	1,862	2000	6,351***

* U.S. Bureau of Census Forecast made on medium variants.
** The mid-1978 provisional estimate by the U.N. is 4.205 billion.
*** Some demographers maintain that the figure will (or must) stabilize at 10 to 15 billion, but above 8 billion during the 21st century. The Tsui-Bogue estimate from the University of Chicago for 2000 A.D. is 5.8 billion.

It is estimated that 75,000,000,000 humans have been born and died in the last 600,000 years.

Largest. The country with the largest population in the world is China, which in *pinyin* is written Zhogguo. The mid-1977 U.N. estimate was 865,677,000. The rate of natural increase in the People's Republic of China is now estimated between 1.5 and 1.66 per cent and thus the 1,000,000,000 mark will be reached during 1980 by U.S. estimates, but will not be reached until 1986 by U.N. estimates. The Yugoslav news agency Tanjug reported that on May 1, 1978, the Chinese claimed a population of 900,000,000.

Smallest. The independent state with the smallest population is the Vatican City or the Holy See (see *Smallest Country*), with 723 inhabitants in mid-1977, and a zero birth rate.

Densest. The most densely populated territory in the world is the Portuguese province of Macau (or Macao), on the southern coast of China. It has an estimated population of 279,000 (mid-1977) in an area of 6.2 square miles, giving a density of 44,990 per square mile.

Of territories with an area of more than 400 square miles, Hong Kong (405 square miles) contains 4,525,000 people (estimated mid-1977), giving the territory a density of 11,362 per square mile. Hong Kong is now the most populous of all colonies. The name "Hong Kong" is only the transcription of the local pronunciation of the Peking dialect version of Xiang gang (a port for incense). Kowloon, on the mainland, had a density which reached 219,559 per square mile in 1961. On the Wah Fu estate, there are 55,000 people living on 24 acres, giving an unsurpassed spot density of more than 1,466,600 per square mile. In 1959, at the peak of the housing crisis, it was reported that in one house designed for 12 people the number of occupants was 459, including 104 in one room and 4 living on the roof.

The Principality of Monaco, on the south coast of France, has a population of 25,000 (estimated June 30, 1977) in an area of 369.9 acres, giving a density of 35,800 per square mile. This is being relieved by marine infilling which will increase her area to 447 acres.

Singapore has 2,334,000 (mid-1978 estimate) people in an inhabited area of 73 square miles.

Of countries over 1,000 square miles, the most densely populated is Bangladesh with a population of 84,655,000 (mid-1978 estimate) living in 55,126 square miles at a density of 1,535 per square mile.

The Indonesian island of Java (with an area of 48,763 square miles) had a population of 69,037,000 (estimate for 1971), giving a density of 1,415 per square mile.

Sparsest. Antarctica became permanently occupied by relays of scientists as of October, 1956. The population varies seasonally and reaches 1,500 at times.

The least populated territory, apart from Antarctica, is Greenland, with a population of 56,000 (estimate of mid-1977) in an area of 840,000 square miles, giving a density of one person to every 15.0 square miles. The ice-free area of the island is only 132,000 square miles, as some 84.3 per cent of the island comprises an ice-cap.

Cities

Most Populous. The most populous city in the world is Tokyo, Japan, with a population in 1977 of 11,649,000. At the census of 1977, the "Keihin Metropolitan Area" (Tokyo-Yokohama Metropolitan Area) of 1,081 square miles contained 27,717,000 people.

The world's largest city not built by the sea or on a river is Greater Mexico City (Ciudad de México), the capital of Mexico, with an estimated population of 11,943,100 in 1976.

Oldest. The oldest known walled town is Jericho, about 5 miles north of the Dead Sea. Radio-carbon dating on specimens from the lowest levels reached by archeologists indicate habitation there by perhaps 3,000 people as early as 7800 B.C. The village of Zawi Chemi Shanidar, discovered in 1957 in northern Iraq, has been dated to 8910 B.C. The oldest capital city in the world is Dimashq (Damascus), capital of Syria. It has been continuously inhabited since *c.* 2500 B.C.

Highest. The highest capital city in the world, before the domination of Tibet by China, was Lhasa, at an elevation of 12,087 feet above sea level.

La Paz, the administrative and *de facto* capital of Bolivia, stands at an altitude of 11,916 feet above sea level. The city was founded in 1548 by Capt. Alonso de Mendoza on the site of an Indian village named Chuquiapu. It was originally called Ciudad de Nuestra Señora de La Paz (City of Our Lady of Peace), but in 1825 was renamed La Paz de Ayacucho, its present official name. Sucre, the legal capital of Bolivia, stands at 9,301 feet above sea level.

The new town of Wenchuan, founded in 1955 on the Chinghai-Tibet road, north of the Tangla Range, is the highest in the world at

16,732 feet above sea level. The highest dwellings in the world are those at Basisi, India, near the Tibetan border, at *c.* 19,700 feet.

Lowest. The settlement of Ein Bokek, which has a synagogue, on the shores of the Dead Sea, is the lowest town in the world at 1,299 feet below sea level.

Towns

Largest in Area. The world's largest town, in area, is Mount Isa, Queensland, Australia. The area administered by the City Council is 15,822 square miles.

Northernmost. The world's northernmost town with a population of more than 10,000 is the Arctic port of Dikson, U.S.S.R., at 73° 32′ N.

The northernmost village is Ny Ålesund (78° 55′ N.), a coal mining settlement on King's Bay, Vest Spitsbergen, in the Norwegian territory of Svalbard, inhabited only during the winter season.

The northernmost capital is Reykjavik, Iceland, at 64° 08′ N. Its population was estimated to be 84,772 in 1974. The northernmost permanent human occupation is the base at Alert (82° 31′ N.), on Dumb Bell Bay, on the northeast coast of Ellesmere Island, northern Canada.

Southernmost. The world's southernmost village is Puerto Williams (population about 350), on the north coast of Isla Navarino, in Tierra del Fuego, Chile, about 680 miles north of Antarctica. Wellington, North Island, New Zealand, is the southernmost capital city at 41° 17′ S. The world's southernmost administrative center is Port Stanley (51° 43′ S.), in the Falkland Islands, off southern South America.

Most Remote from Sea. The largest town most remote from the sea is Wulumuch'i (Urumchi) formerly Tihwa, Sinkiang, capital of the Uighur Autonomous Region of China, at a distance of about 1,400 miles from the nearest coastline. Its population was estimated to be 320,000 in 1974.

Emigration

More people emigrate from Mexico than from any other country. An estimated 800,000 emigrated illegally into the U.S. in 1976 alone.

Immigration

The country which regularly receives the most legal immigrants is the United States with 462,315 in 1977. It has been estimated that in the period 1820–1977, the U.S. received 42,063,523 *official* immigrants. One person in every 24 in the U.S. is an *illegal* immigrant.

Birth Rate

Highest and Lowest. The highest 1970–75 figure is 52.2 per 1,000 for the Niger Republic. The rate for the whole world was 30.4 per 1,000 in 1975.

Excluding Vatican City, where the rate is negligible, the lowest recorded rate is 7.5 for Monaco (1977).

Death Rate

Highest and Lowest. The highest of the latest available recorded death rates is 28.1 deaths per each 1,000 of the population in Bangladesh in 1970–75. The rate for the whole world was 12.3 per 1,000 in 1975. The lowest of the latest available recorded rates is 1.7 deaths per 1,000 in Tonga in 1976.

Natural Increase

The highest of the latest available recorded rates of natural increase is 40.6 (45.4–4.8) per 1,000 in Syria. The rate for the whole world was 30.4 — 12.3 = 18.1 in 1975.

The lowest rate of natural increase in any major independent country is West Germany with a negative figure of —2.0 per 1,000 for 1977 (9.5 births and 11.5 deaths).

Marriage Ages

The country with the lowest average ages for marriage is India, with 20.0 years for males and 14.5 years for females. At the other extreme is Ireland, with 31.4 for males and 26.5 years for females. In the People's Republic of China, the recommended age for marriage for men has been 28 and for women 25.

Sex Ratio

There were estimated to be 1,003.5 men in the world for every 1,000 women in 1975. The country with the largest recorded female surplus is the U.S.S.R., with 1,143 females to every 1,000 males in the 1979 census. The country with the largest recorded woman shortage is Pakistan, with 885 to every 1,000 males in 1972. The figures are, however, probably under-enumerated due to *purdah*, a policy that keeps women from appearing in public.

Divorces

The country with the most divorces is the United States with a total of 1,090,000 in 1977—a rate of 50.09 per cent of the current annual total of marriages.

Infant Mortality

Based on deaths before one year of age, the lowest of the latest available recorded rates is 8.0 deaths per 1,000 live births in Sweden, in 1977. The world rate in 1975 was 98.

The highest recorded infant mortality rate reported has been 195 to 300 per 1,000 live births for Burma in 1952, and 259 for Zaire in 1950.

Many countries have apparently ceased to make returns. In Ethiopia the infant mortality rate was unofficially estimated to be nearly 550 per 1,000 live births in 1969.

Life Expectation

There is evidence that life expectation in Britain in the 5th century A.D. was 33 years for males and 27 years for females. In the decade

1890–1900 the expectation of life among the population of India was 23.7 years.

Based on the latest available data, the highest recorded expectation of life at age 12 months is 73.0 years for males and 79.2 years for females in Iceland (1975–76).

The lowest recorded expectation of life at birth is 27 years for both sexes in the Vallée du Niger area of Mali in 1957 (sample survey, 1957–58). The figure for males in Gabon was 25 years in 1960–61, but 45 for females.

STANDARDS OF LIVING

National Incomes

The country with the highest income per native citizen in 1977 was Abu Dhabi, with some $70,000 each. In 1977, the U.S. reached $9,430 per head.

Housing Units

For comparison, a dwelling unit is defined as a structurally separated room or rooms occupied by private households of one or more people and having separate access or a common passageway to the street. The country with the greatest recorded number of private dwelling units is India, with 100,251,000 occupied in 1972.

Hospitals

Largest. The largest medical center in the world is the District Medical Center in Chicago. It covers 478 acres and includes five hospitals, with a total of 5,600 beds, and eight professional schools with more than 3,000 students.

The largest mental hospital in the world is the Pilgrim State Hospital, West Brentwood, Long Island, New York, with 3,816 beds. It formerly contained 14,200 beds.

The busiest maternity hospital in the world is the Mama Yemo Hospital in Kinshasha, Zaire, with 41,930 deliveries in 1976. The record "birthquake" occurred on one day in May, 1976, with 175 babies born. It has 599 beds.

Longest Stay. Martha Nelson was admitted to the Columbus State Institute for the Feeble-Minded in Ohio in 1875. She died in January, 1975, aged 103 years 6 months, in the Orient State Institution, Ohio, after spending more than 99 years in institutions.

Physicians

The country with the most physicians is the U.S.S.R., with 831,300, or one to every 307 persons. The country with the lowest recorded proportion is Upper Volta, with 58 physicians (one for every 92,759 people) in 1970.

China has more than a million para-medical personnel known as "barefoot doctors."

DEDICATED DOCTOR: Dr. Frederick Dawson was the only practicing centenarian physician in the world.

Eight sons of John Robertson of Dumbarton, Scotland, graduated as medical doctors between 1892 and 1914. The family of David L. Bernie of Dayton, Ohio, contains 27 members who are qualified M.D.s, with 5 more in medical school.

The oldest doctor to continue practice was Frederick Walter Whitney Dawson (1876–1977), who was the first doctor to receive his license in the 20th century in London, England, on January 1, 1901, and who was still practicing in Whangerai, New Zealand, in his 101st year.

Dentists

The country with the most dentists is the U.S., where 131,000 were registered members of the American Dental Association in 1978.

Psychiatrists and Psychologists

The country with the most psychiatrists is the U.S. The registered membership of the American Psychiatric Association was 22,000 in 1978. The membership of the American Psychological Association was 45,000 in 1978.

ROYALTY

Oldest Ruling House. The Emperor of Japan, Hirohito (born April 29, 1901), is the 124th in line from the first Emperor, Jimmu Tenno or Zinmu, whose reign was traditionally from 660 to 581 B.C., but probably from *c.* 40 to *c.* 10 B.C.

Reigns

Longest. The longest recorded reign of any monarch is that of Pepi II, a Sixth Dynasty Pharaoh of ancient Egypt. His reign began in *c.* 2310 B.C., when he was aged 6, and lasted *c.* 94 years.

Currently the longest reigning monarch in the world is King Sobhuza II (born July 4, 1899), the *Ngwenyama* (Paramount Chief) of Swaziland, who began his reign at the age of 5 months. The country was placed under United Kingdom protection at that time, December, 1899, and became independent on September 6, 1968. At the last published count in 1972, he had 112 wives. Emperor Hirohito of Japan (see page 378) began his reign on December 25, 1926.

The longest reign of any major European monarch was that of King Louis XIV of France, who ascended the throne on May 14, 1643, aged 4 years 231 days, and reigned for 72 years 110 days until his death on September 1, 1715, four days before his 77th birthday. Grand Duke Karl Friedrich of Baden (1728–1811) ruled from May 12, 1738, for 73 years 29 days.

Musoma Kanijo, chief of the Nzega district of western Tanganyika (now part of Tanzania), reputedly reigned for more than 98 years from 1864, when aged 8, until his death on February 2, 1963.

The 6th Japanese Emperor Koo-an traditionally reigned for 102 years (from 392 to 290 B.C.), but probably his actual reign was from about 110 A.D. to about 140 A.D. The reign of the 11th Emperor Suinin was traditionally from 29 B.C. to 71 A.D. (99 years), but probably was from 259 to 291 A.D.

Shortest. King Vikramabahu II of the Kalinga Kshatriya dynasty of Ceylon (Sri Lanka) was assassinated a few hours after he was crowned at Polonnaruwa in 1196.

Youngest King or Queen. Of the world's 25 monarchies, the one with the youngest king is Bhutan (in the Himalayas) where King Jigme Singye Wangchuk (b. November 11, 1955) succeeded to the throne on July 24, 1972.

Heaviest Monarch. The world's heaviest monarch is the 6-foot 3-inch-tall King Taufa'ahau of Tonga, who in September, 1976, was weighed on the only adequate scale in the country (at the airport) at 462 lbs.

Longest-Lived Royalty. The longest life among the "blood royal" of Europe is the 98 years 206 days of H.R.H. Princess Alicia of Bourbon, who was born June 29, 1876, and died on January 20, 1975.

The longest-lived Queen on record has been the Queen Grandmother of Siam, Queen Sawang (born September 10, 1862), 27th daughter of King Mongkut (Rama IV), who died on December 17, 1955, aged 93 years 3 months.

H.R.H. Princess Alice Mary, Countess of Athlone (b. February 25, 1883), became the longest-lived British "royal" on July 15, 1977, and celebrated her 96th birthday on February 25, 1979.

Most Prolific. The most prolific monogamous "royals" have been Prince Hartmann of Liechtenstein (1613–1686) who had 24 children, of whom 21 were live born, by Countess Elisabeth zu Salm-Reifterscheidt (1623–1688). H.R.H. Duke Roberto I of Parma also had 24 children, but by two wives.

Highest Regnal Number. Count Heinrich LXXV Reuss (1800–1801) briefly enjoyed the highest post-nominal number (75). All male members of this German family are called Heinrich and are successively numbered from I upwards *each* century.

LEGISLATURES

Parliaments

Oldest. The earliest known legislative assembly was a bicameral one in Erech, Iraq, *c.* 2800 B.C. The oldest legislative body is the *Alpingi* (Althing) of Iceland, founded in 930 A.D. This body, which originally comprised 39 local chieftains, was abolished in 1800, but restored by Denmark to a consultative status in 1843 and a legislative status in 1874. The legislative assembly with the oldest continuous history is the Tynwald Court of the Isle of Man, in the Irish Channel, which is believed to have originated more than 1,000 years ago.

The earliest known use of the term "parliament" in an official English royal document, in the meaning of a summons to the King's council, dates from December 19, 1241.

Largest. The largest legislative assembly in the world is the National People's Congress of the People's Republic of China. The fourth Congress, which was convened in January, 1975, had 3,500 members.

Smallest Quorum. The British House of Lords has the smallest quorum, expressed as a percentage of eligible voters, of any legislative body in the world, namely less than one-third of one per cent. To transact business there must be three peers present, including the Lord Chancellor or his deputy.

Highest-Paid Legislators. The most highly paid of all the world's legislators are U.S. Congressmen, who receive a basic annual salary of $57,500. Of this, up to $3,000 is deductible from Federal income tax as an amount expended for additional living expenses. In addition, Senators are allowed from $508,221 to $1,021,167 per year, depending on the population of the state, for clerk-hire, with a salary limit of $49,941 for any one staff member per annum. Senators are authorized from $33,000 to $143,000 per year, depending on the state, for an Official Office Expense Account from which are paid official travel expenses, telegrams, long-distance telephone calls, air-mail postage, stationery, subscriptions to newspapers, and office expenses in the home state. When abroad they have access to "counterpart funds."

Filibusters. The longest continuous speech in the history of the U.S. Senate was that of Senator Wayne Morse of Oregon on April 24–25, 1953, when he spoke on the Tidelands Oil Bill for 22 hours 26 minutes without resuming his seat. Senator Strom Thurmond, Democrat (South Carolina), spoke against the Civil Rights Bill for 24 hours 19 minutes on August 28–29, 1957, interrupted only briefly by the swearing-in of a new senator.

OLDEST AND YOUNGEST PRESENT HEADS OF STATE: Jean-Claude Duvalier (left) succeeded his father as President of Haiti in 1971. Marshal Tito, at age 87, continues to govern Yugoslavia (see page 382).

The record for a filibuster in any legislature is 43 hours by Texas State Senator Bill Meier from Euless, who spoke against non-disclosure of industrial accidents in May, 1977.

Longest Membership. The longest span as a legislator was 83 years by József Madarász (1814–1915). He first attended the Hungarian Parliament in 1832–36 as *oblegatus absentium* (*i.e.* on behalf of an absent deputy). He was a full member in 1848–50 and from 1861 until his death on January 31, 1915.

Attendance Record. U.S. Congressman William H. Natcher, a Democrat from Bowling Green, Kentucky, on January 6, 1979, completed his 25th year (1954–1979) without missing a single vote (3,748 quorum calls and 7,000 roll-call votes to April 9, 1979).

State Representative Lucille H. McCollough was elected to the Michigan House of Representatives on January 1, 1955, and had a perfect attendance record as of June, 1979.

Longest Term. Members of Taiwan's National Assembly, elected in 1947, have been extended in office and include several hundred who celebrated their 32nd year in 1979.

Prime Ministers and Heads of State

Oldest. The longest-lived Prime Minister of any country is believed to have been Christopher Hornsrud, Prime Minister of Norway from January 28 to February 15, 1928. He was born on November 15, 1859 and died on December 13, 1960, aged 101 years 28 days.

El Hadji Mohammed el Mokri, Grand Vizier of Morocco, died on September 16, 1957, at a reputed age of 116 Muslim (*Hijri*) years, equivalent to 112.5 Gregorian years.

The oldest age of appointment has been 81 years in the case of Morarji Ranchhodji Desai (born February 29, 1896) in March, 1977.

Oldest and Youngest Living Heads of State. The oldest head of state is Marshal Tito of Yugoslavia (b. Josip Broz, May 25, 1892), now aged 87. The youngest non-royal head of state is Jean-Claude Duvalier (b. July 3, 1951), President of Haiti since April 21, 1971.

Longest Term of Office. Prof. Dr. António de Oliveira Salazar (1889–1970) was the President of the Council of Ministers (*i.e.* Prime Minister) of Portugal from July 5, 1932, for 36 years and 84 days until superseded on September 27, 1968, eleven days after going into a coma.

The longest-serving democratically elected premier was Tage Erlander of Sweden for 22 years 357 days, from October 10, 1946 to October 1, 1969.

Elections

Largest. The largest election ever held was that for the Indian *Lok Sabha* (House of the People) on March 16–20, 1977. There were 373,000 polling places for the 320,000,000 voters. The outgoing Prime Minister, Mrs. Indira Gandhi, was better known by her symbol (a cow) than by her name.

Closest. The ultimate in close general elections occurred in Zanzibar (now part of Tanzania) on January 18, 1961, when the Afro-Shirazi Party won by a single seat, after the seat of Chake-Chake on Pemba Island had been gained by a single vote.

Most One-Sided. North Korea recorded a 100 per cent turn-out of electors and a 100 per cent vote for the Workers' Party of Korea in the general election of October 8, 1962. The previous record had been set in the Albanian election of June 4, 1962, when all but seven of the electorate of 889,875 went to the polls—a 99.9992 per cent turn-out. Of the 889,868 voters, 889,828 voted for the candidates of the Albanian Party of Labor, *i.e.* 99.9955 per cent of the total poll.

The highest personal majority by any politician has been 424,545 votes from a total electorate of 625,179 achieved by Ram Bilas Paswan, the Janata candidate for Hajipur in Bihar, India, in March, 1977.

Most Rigged. In his book *Journey Without Maps*, Graham Greene recounts the case of the 1928 presidential election of Liberia, in which the president, Charles D. B. King, was returned to office with an officially announced majority over his opponent (Thomas J. Faulkner of the People's Party) of 600,000 votes. The total electorate at the time was less than 15,000.

Smallest Vote. Mr. Wideon Pyfrom (Free National Party), standing for the Rolleville constituency in the Bahamas, received no votes in the July, 1977 elections.

Communist Parties. The largest national Communist party outside the U.S.S.R. (which had 15,000,000 members in 1975) and Communist states has been the Partito Communista Italiano (Italian

Communist Party), with a membership of 2,300,000 in 1946. The total fell to 1,700,000 by 1976. The membership in mainland China was estimated to be 28,000,000 in 1974.

Voting Ages. The eligibility extremes for voting are 15 years in the Philippines and 25 years in Andorra.

Mayoralty. Harold E. Johnson has been elected mayor of Hatton, Washington, each year since 1931.

2. Military and Defense

WAR

Longest. The longest of history's countless wars was the "Hundred Years' War" between England and France, which lasted from 1338 to 1453 (115 years), although it may be said that the Holy War, comprising nine Crusades from the First (1096–1104) to the Ninth (1270–91), extended over 195 years.

Shortest. The shortest war on record was that between the United Kingdom and Zanzibar (now part of Tanzania) from 9:02 to 9:40 a.m. on August 27, 1896. The U.K. battle fleet under Rear-Admiral (later Admiral Sir) Harry Holdsworth Rawson (1843–1910) delivered an ultimatum to the self-appointed Sultan Sa'id Khalid to evacuate his palace and surrender. This was not forthcoming until after 38 minutes of bombardment. Admiral Rawson received the Brilliant Star of Zanzibar (first class) from the new Sultan Hamud ibn Muhammad. It was proposed at one time that elements of the local populace should be compelled to defray the cost of the ammunition used.

Bloodiest. By far the most costly war in terms of human life was World War II (1939–45), in which the total number of fatalities, including battle deaths and civilians of all countries, is estimated to have been 54,800,000, assuming 25,000,000 U.S.S.R. fatalities and 7,800,000 Chinese civilians killed. The country which suffered most was Poland with 6,028,000 or 22.2 per cent of her population of 27,007,000 killed. The total death toll from World War I was 9,700,000, only 17.7 per cent of that of World War II.

In the Paraguayan war of 1864–70 against Brazil, Argentina, and Uruguay, the Paraguayan population was reduced from 1,400,000 to 220,000, of whom only 30,000 were adult males.

Most Costly. The material cost of World War II far transcended that of the rest of history's wars put together and has been estimated at $1.5 trillion. In the case of the United Kingdom the cost was over five times as great as that of World War I. The total cost of World War II to the Soviet Union was estimated semi-officially in May, 1959, at 2,500,000,000,000 roubles ($280 billion) while a figure of $530 billion has been estimated for the United States.

Bloodiest Battle. The battle with the greatest recorded number of fatalities was the First Battle of the Somme from July 1 to November 19, 1916, with more than 1,030,000—614,105 British and French and *c.* 420,000 (*not* 650,000) German. The gunfire was heard as far away as Hampstead Heath, London. The greatest battle of World War II and the greatest conflict ever of armor was the Battle of Kursk and Oryol which raged for 50 days from July 5 to August 23, 1943, on the Eastern front, which involved 1,300,000 Red Army troops with 3,600 tanks, 20,000 guns and 3,130 aircraft in repelling a German Army Group which had 2,700 tanks. The final invasion of Berlin by the Red Army in 1945 is, however, said to have involved 3,500,000 men, 52,000 guns and mortars, 7,750 tanks and 11,000 aircraft on both sides.

Modern historians give no credence to the casualty figures attached to ancient battles, such as the 250,000 reputedly killed at Plataea (Greeks *vs.* Persians) in 479 B.C. or the 200,000 allegedly killed in a single day at Châlons-sur-Marne, France, in 451 A.D. This view is on the grounds that it must have been logistically quite impossible to maintain forces of such a size in the field at that time.

Bloodiest Civil War. The bloodiest civil war in history was the T'ai-p'ing ("Great Peace") rebellion, in which peasant sympathizers of the Southern Ming dynasty fought the Manchu Government troops in China from 1851 to 1864. The rebellion was led by the deranged Hung Hsiu-ch'üan (executed in June, 1864), who imagined himself to be a young brother of Jesus Christ. His force was named *T'ai-p'ing T'ien Kuo* (Heavenly Kingdom of Great Peace). According to the best estimates, the loss of life was between 20,000,000 and 30,000,000 including more than 100,000 killed by Government forces in the sack of Nanking on July 19–21, 1864.

Greatest Invasion

Seaborne. The greatest invasion in military history was the Allied land, air and sea operation against the Normandy coast of France on D-day, June 6, 1944. Thirty-eight convoys of 745 ships moved in on the first three days, supported by 4,066 landing craft, carrying 185,000 men and 20,000 vehicles, and 347 minesweepers. The air assault comprised 18,000 paratroopers from 1,087 aircraft. The 42 available divisions possessed an air support from 13,175 aircraft. Within a month 1,100,000 troops, 200,000 vehicles and 840,000 tons of stores were landed.

The Allied invasion of Sicily on July 10–12, 1943, involved the landing of 181,000 men in 3 days.

Airborne. The largest airborne invasion was the Anglo-American assault of three divisions (34,000 men), with 2,800 aircraft and 1,600 gliders, near Arnhem, in the Netherlands, on September 17, 1944.

Greatest Evacuation

The greatest evacuation in military history was that carried out by 1,200 Allied naval and civil craft from the beachhead at Dunkerque (Dunkirk), France, between May 27 and June 4, 1940. A total of 338,226 British and French troops were taken off.

Worst Sieges

The longest recorded siege was that of Azotus (now Ashdod), Israel, which, according to Herodotus, was besieged by Psamtik I of Egypt for 29 years in the period 664–610 B.C.

The worst siege in history was the 880-day siege of Leningrad, U.S.S.R., by the German Army from August 30, 1941, until January 27, 1944. The best estimate is that between 1.3 and 1.5 million defenders and citizens died.

Largest Armed Forces

Numerically, the country with the largest regular armed force is the People's Republic of China with 4,325,000. Her paramilitary forces of armed and unarmed militias have been estimated by the Institute of Strategic Studies at some 115,000,000. Their mid-1978 estimates for the world's two principal military powers are 3,638,000 for the U.S.S.R. and 2,068,800 for the U.S.

Defense

The estimated level of spending on armaments throughout the world in 1978 was $400 billion. This represents $96 per person per annum, or more than 6 per cent of the world's total production of goods and services. It was estimated in 1978 that there were 22,500,000 full-time armed force regulars or conscripts.

The budgeted expenditure on defense by the government of the United States in the year ending June 30, 1979, was $126,000,000,000 or 6.9 per cent of the country's gross national product.

The official Chinese estimate for 1977 was that the defense burden on the U.S.S.R.'s G.N.P. was in excess of 15 per cent of the gross national product, *i.e.* more than double that of the U.S.

At the other extreme is Andorra, whose defense budget, voted in 1972, was reduced to $5.

Treaty

The world's oldest treaty is the Anglo-Portuguese Treaty of Alliance, signed in London over 600 years ago on June 16, 1373. The text was confirmed "with my usual flourish" by John de Banketre, Clerk.

NAVIES

Largest. The largest navy in the world in terms of manpower is the U.S. Navy, with 532,000 sailors and 191,500 Marines in mid-1978. The active strength in 1978 included 13 aircraft carriers, 68 attack nuclear submarines and 10 diesel attack submarines, 41 strategic missile submarines, 71 guided missile warships (26 cruisers, 39 destroyers, and 6 frigates), and 62 amphibious warfare ships.

The U.S.S.R. Navy has a larger submarine fleet of 360 boats, of which 85 are nuclear-powered, 90 of them carrying strategic atomic missiles. It has 243 major surface combat ships.

Greatest Naval Battles

The greatest number of ships and aircraft ever involved in a sea-air action was 231 ships and 1,996 aircraft in the Battle of Leyte Gulf, in the Philippines. It raged from October 22 to 27, 1944, with 166 Allied and 65 Japanese warships engaged, of which 26 Japanese and 6 U.S. ships were sunk. In addition, 1,280 U.S. and 716 Japanese aircraft were engaged.

The greatest naval battle of modern times was the Battle of Jutland on May 31, 1916, in which 151 British Royal Navy warships were involved against 101 German warships. The Royal Navy lost 14 ships and 6,097 men and the German fleet 11 ships and 2,545 men.

The greatest of ancient naval battles was the Battle of Salamis, Greece, on September 23, 480 B.C. There were an estimated 800 vessels in the defeated Persian fleet and 310 in the victorious Greek fleet with a possible involvement of 190,000 men.

The death roll at the Battle of Lepanto on October 7, 1571, has been estimated at 33,000.

ARMIES

Largest. Numerically, the largest army is the People's Republic of China's, with a total strength of about 3,625,000 in mid-1978. The total size of the U.S.S.R.'s army in mid-1978 was estimated by the International Institute of Strategic Studies at 1,825,000 men, believed to be organized into about 170 divisions with a maximum strength of 12,700 each.

OLDEST OLD SOLDIER: John Salling, who served in the Confederate Army during the Civil War, lived to be 113 years old.

FASTEST TANK: The prototype of this American XM-1 tank reached 45 m.p.h.

Oldest. The oldest army in the world is the 83-strong Swiss Guard in the Vatican City, with a regular foundation dating back to January 21, 1506. Its origins, however, extend back before 1400.

Oldest Old Soldier. The oldest age to which a veteran soldier has lived is 113 years 1 day by John B. Salling of the Army of the Confederate States of America and the last accepted survivor of the U.S. Civil War (1861–65). He died in Kingsport, Tennessee, on March 16, 1959.

Youngest Soldiers. President Francisco Macias Nguema of Equatorial Guinea decreed in March, 1976, compulsory military service for all boys between 7 and 14. Any parent refusing to hand over his or her son "will be imprisoned or shot."

Tallest Soldier. The tallest soldier of all time was Väinö Myllyrinne (1909–63) who was inducted into the Finnish Army when he was 7 feet 3 inches and later grew to 8 feet 1¼ inches.

Tanks

Earliest. The first fighting tank was "Mother," alias "Big Willie," built by William Foster & Co. Ltd. of England, and completed on September 8, 1915. The tank was first taken into action by the Machine Gun Corps (Heavy Section), which later became the Royal Tank Corps, at the battle of Flers, in France, on September 15, 1916. Known as the Mark I Male, it was armed with a pair of 6-lb. guns and two machine-guns. It weighed 31.4 tons and, driven by a motor developing 105 horsepower, had a maximum road speed of 3 to 4 m.p.h.

Heaviest. The heaviest tank ever constructed was the German Panzer Kampfwagen Maus II, which weighed 212 tons. By 1945, it had reached only the experimental stage and was not proceeded with.

The heaviest operational tank used by any army was the 91.3-ton 13-man French Char de Rupture 2C bis of 1923. It carried a 155-mm. howitzer and had two 250-h.p. engines giving a maximum speed of 8 m.p.h.

The world's fastest tank is the $1,800,000 XM-1, due for U.S. Army service. The prototype reached 45 m.p.h. The 3,600,000 deutsche mark ($1,900,000) German Leopard 2 has the greatest firepower with a 120-mm. (4.72-inch) gun.

Guns

Earliest. Although it cannot be accepted as proved, the best opinion is that the earliest guns were constructed in North Africa, possibly by Arabs, in *c.* 1250. The earliest representation of an English gun is contained in an illustrated manuscript dated 1326 at Oxford. The earliest anti-aircraft gun was an artillery piece on a high-angle mounting used in the Franco-Prussian War of 1870 by the Prussians against French balloons.

Largest. The remains of the most massive gun ever constructed were found near Frankfurt am Main, Germany, in 1945. It was the "Schwerer Gustav" or "Dora," which had a barrel 94.7 feet long, with a caliber of 800 millimeters (31.5 inches), and a breech weighing 121 tons. The maximum charge was 4,409 lbs. of cordite to fire a shell weighing 5.28 tons a distance of 34 miles. The maximum projectile was one of 7.8 tons with a range of 22 miles. Each gun with its carriage weighed 1,481 tons and required a crew of 1,500 men.

Greatest Range. The greatest range ever attained by a gun is by the H.A.R.P. (High Altitude Research Project) gun consisting of two 16.5-inch caliber barrels in tandem, 119.4 feet long and weighing 165 tons, at Yuma, Arizona. On November 19, 1966, a 185-lb. projectile was fired to an altitude of 111.8 miles (590,550 feet). The static V.3 underground firing tubes built by the Germans in 50-degree shafts at Mimoyecques, near Calais, France, to bombard London were never operative, due to R.A.F. bombing.

The famous long-range gun which shelled Paris in World War I was the *Kaiser Wilhelm Geschütz*, with a caliber of 220 mm. (8.66 inches), a designed range of 79.5 miles and an achieved range of 76 miles. The "Big Berthas" were mortars of 420-mm. (16.53-inch) caliber with a range of less than 9 miles.

Largest Cannon

The highest caliber cannon ever constructed is the *Tsar Puchka* (King of Cannons), now housed in the Kremlin, Moscow, U.S.S.R. It was built in the 16th century with a bore of 36.2 inches (920 mm.) and a barrel 10 feet 5 inches long. It weighs 44 tons.

The Turks fired up to seven shots per day from a bombard 26 feet long, with an internal caliber of 42 inches, against the walls of Constantinople (now Istanbul) from April 12 to May 29, 1453. It was dragged by 60 oxen and 200 men and fired a stone cannonball weighing 1,200 lbs.

Mortars

The largest mortars ever constructed were Mallets mortar (Woolwich Arsenal, London, England, 1857), and the "Little David" of World War II, made in the U.S. Each had a caliber of 36¼ inches (920 mm.), but neither was ever used in action.

The heaviest mortar used was the tracked German 600-mm. (23.6-inch) siege piece known as "Karl" used in the siege of Stalingrad.

Military Engines

The largest military catapults, or onagers, were capable of throwing a missile weighing 60 lbs. a distance of 500 yards.

March

Longest. The longest march in military history was the famous Long March by the Chinese Communists in 1934–35. In 368 days, of which 268 days were of movement, from October to October, their force of 90,000 covered 6,000 miles northward from Kiangsi to Yenan in Shensi *via* Yünnan. They crossed 18 mountain ranges and six major rivers and lost all but 22,000 of their force in continual rearguard actions against Nationalist Kuo-min-tang (K.M.T.) forces.

Most Rapid. The most rapid recorded march by foot-soldiers was one of 42 miles covered in 11 hours 49 minutes in a night march by 9 soldiers in full battle dress carrying 40 lbs., from B Company, 4th Infantry Battalion of the Irish Army, on September 12–13, 1944.

Greatest Mutiny

In World War I, 56 French divisions, comprising some 650,000 men and their officers, refused orders in the Nivelles sector.

AIR FORCES

The earliest autonomous air force is the Royal Air Force of Great Britain, whose origins began with the Royal Flying Corps (created May 13, 1912); the Air Battalion of the Royal Engineers (April 1, 1911) and the Corps of Royal Engineers Balloon Section (1878) which was first operational in Bechuanaland (now Botswana) in 1884. The Prussian Army used a balloon near Strasbourg, France, as early as September 24, 1870.

Largest. The greatest air force of all time was the U.S. Army Air Force (now called the U.S. Air Force), which had 79,908 aircraft in July, 1944, and 2,411,294 personnel in March, 1944. The U.S. Air Force, including strategic air forces, had 571,000 personnel and 3,400 combat aircraft in mid-1978. The U.S.S.R. Air Force, including Air Defense Forces with about 1,005,000 men in mid-1978, had 7,370 combat aircraft. In addition, the U.S.S.R.'s Offensive Strategic Rocket Forces had about 375,000 operational personnel in mid-1977.

Bombs

The heaviest conventional bomb ever used operationally was the British Royal Air Force's "Grand Slam," weighing 22,000 lbs. and measuring 25 feet 5 inches long, dropped on Bielefeld railway viaduct, Germany, on March 14, 1945. In 1949, the U.S. Air Force tested a bomb weighing 42,000 lbs. at Muroc Dry Lake, California.

Atomic. The two atom bombs dropped on Japan by the U.S. in 1945 each had an explosive power equivalent to that of 20,000 tons (20 kilotons) of trinitrotoluene, called T.N.T. The one dropped on Hiroshima, known as "Little Boy," was 10 feet long and weighed 9,000 lbs.

The most powerful thermonuclear device so far tested is one with a power equivalent to 57,000,000 tons of T.N.T., or 57 megatons, detonated by the U.S.S.R. in the Novaya Zemlya area at 8:33 a.m. G.M.T. on October 30, 1961. The shock wave was detected to have circled the world three times, taking 36 hours 27 minutes for the first circuit. Some estimates put the power of this device at between 62 and 90 megatons. On August 9, 1961, Nikita Khrushchev, then the Chairman of the Council of Ministers of the U.S.S.R., declared that the Soviet Union was capable of constructing a 100-megaton bomb, and announced the possession of one in East Berlin, Germany, on January 16, 1963. It has been estimated that such a bomb would make a crater 19 miles in diameter and would cause serious fires at a range of from 36 to 40 miles.

Atom bomb theory began with Albert Einstein's publication of the $E = mc^2$ formula in *Annalen der Physik* in Leipzig on May 14, 1907. It became practical with the mesothorium experiments of Otto Hahn, Fritz Strassman, and Lise Meitner on December 17, 1938. Work started in the U.S.S.R. on atomic bombs in June, 1942, although the first chain reaction was not achieved until December, 1945, by Dr. Igor Vasilyevich Kurchatov.

The patent for the fusion or H-bomb was filed in the U.S. on May 26, 1946, by Dr. Janos (John) von Neumann (1903–57), a Hungarian-born mathematician, and Dr. Klaus Julius Emil Fuchs (born in Germany, 1911), the physicist who defected to Russia from England.

Largest Nuclear Arsenal

The most powerful ICBM's are the U.S.S.R.'s SS-18's, each with up to 10 one-megaton M.I.R.V.'s (multiple independently targetable re-entry vehicles); thus each has power 50 times as great as the Hiroshima bomb. The U.S. Minuteman III has 3 M.I.R.V.'s, each of 335 kiloton force.

No official estimate has been published of the potential power of the device known as Doomsday, but this far surpasses any tested weapon. If it were practicable to construct, it is speculated that a 50,000-megaton cobalt-salted device could wipe out the entire human race except people who were deep underground and did not emerge for more than five years.

Largest "Conventional" Explosion. The largest use of conventional explosive was for the demolition of the fortifications at Heligoland, Germany, on April 18, 1947. A charge of 4,476 tons was detonated by Commissioned Gunner E. C. Jellis of the Royal Navy aboard H.M.S. *Lasso* lying 9 miles out to sea.

3. Judicial

LEGISLATION AND LITIGATION

Statutes

Oldest. The earliest known judicial code was that of King Ur-Nammu during the Third Dynasty of Ur, Iraq, in *c.* 2145 B.C.

Most Inexplicable

Certain passages in several laws have always defied interpretation and the most inexplicable must be a matter of opinion. A judge of the Court of Session of Scotland has sent the editors of this book his candidate which reads, "In the Nuts (unground), (other than ground nuts) Order, the expression nuts shall have reference to such nuts, other than ground nuts, as would but for this amending Order not qualify as nuts (unground) (other than ground nuts) by reason of their being nuts (unground)."

Most Protracted Litigation

The longest contested lawsuit ever recorded ended in Poona, India, on April 28, 1966, when Balasaheb Patloji Thorat received a favorable judgment on a suit filed by his ancestor Maloji Thorat 761 years earlier in 1205. The suit involved rights of presiding over public functions and precedences at religious festivals.

Longest Impeachment

The British Parliament's impeachment of Warren Hastings (1732–1818), for maladministration of India, began in 1788 and dragged on for seven years, until his acquittal on April 23, 1795. The trial itself lasted only 149 days.

Best-Attended Trial

The greatest attendance at any trial was at that of Major Jesús Sosa Blanco, aged 51, for an alleged 108 murders. At one point in the $12\frac{1}{2}$-hour trial (5:30 p.m. to 6 a.m., January 22–23, 1959), 17,000 people were present in the Havana Sports Palace, Cuba.

Shortest Trial

On March 1, 1977, an ill-founded prosecution (under the 1974 British Air Navigation Order) brought against a pilot at Edinburgh airport was timed at No. 1 Sheriff Court, Edinburgh, Scotland, to have lasted 7 seconds. Sheriff Skae uttered two words—"Not Guilty."

Highest Bail

The highest amount ever demanded as bail was $46,500,000 against Antonio De Angelis in a civil damages suit by the Harbor Tank Storage Co. filed in the Superior Court, Jersey City, New Jersey, on January 16, 1964, in the Salad Oil Swindle. He was released on June 4, 1973.

Abul Hassen Ebtehaj, later Chairman of the Iranian Bank in Teheran, was granted bail in 1977 in excess of $50,000,000.

Greatest Damages

Loss of Life. The highest damages ever actually paid have been $14,387,674 following the crash of a private aircraft at South Lake Tahoe, California, on February 21, 1967, to the sole survivor Ray Rosendin, 45, by the Santa Clara Superior Court on March 8, 1972. Rosendin received $1,069,374 for the loss of both legs and disabling arm injuries; $1,213,129 for the loss of his wife and $10,500,000 punitive damages against Avco-Lycoming Corporation which allegedly violated Federal regulations when it rebuilt the aircraft engine owned by Rosendin Corporation.

Breach of Contract. The greatest damages ever awarded for a breach of contract were £610,392 ($1,709,000), awarded on July 16, 1930, to the Bank of Portugal against the printers Waterlow & Sons, Ltd., of London, arising from their unauthorized printing of 580,000 five-hundred escudo notes in 1925. This award was upheld in the House of Lords on April 28, 1932. One of the perpetrators, Arthur Virgilio Alves Reis, served 16 years (1930–46) in jail.

Personal Injury. The greatest damages for personal injury ever awarded went to Janelle Lynn Stearns, 12, against Park Avenue Hospital Inc. and Dr. Howard K. Gifford, an anesthetist, in settlement for alleged medical malpractice resulting in severe brain damage following a tonsillectomy at Pomona, California, in May, 1973. If she lives to the average expectation of 63.9 additional years, the payments will total $26,541,832.

The largest single cash payment settlement for a single person has been $6,800,000 to John Coates, 42, a lawyer from Austin, Texas, against Remington Arms Co. Inc. *et al.*, on October 23, 1978. The case concerned severe injury from a defectively made hunting rifle.

Divorce. The highest alimony awarded by a court has been $2,261,000 against George Storer, Sr., 74, in favor of his third wife Dorothy, 73, in Miami, Florida, on October 29, 1974. Mr. Storer, a broadcasting executive, was also ordered to pay his ex-wife's attorney $200,000 in fees.

Defamation. A sum of $16,800,000 was awarded to Dr. John J. Wild, 58, at the Hennepin District Court of Minnesota on November 30, 1972, against the Minnesota Foundation and others for defamation, bad-faith termination of a contract, and interference with professional business relationships, plus $10,800,000 in punitive damages. These amounts have not to date been appealed.

Greatest Compensation

On August 12, 1975, William De Palma (born 1938) of Whittier, California, agreed to a $750,000 settlement for 16 months' wrongful imprisonment in McNeil Island Federal Prison, Washington. He had been given a 15-year sentence for armed robbery in Buena Park, California, on forged fingerprint evidence in 1968.

Highest Settlement

Divorce. The greatest amount ever reported in a divorce settlement is half of the estimated $100,000,000 wealth of the publisher

James Kent Cooke (b. 1913) of Las Vegas, Nevada, decreed by a Los Angeles court in March, 1979, in favor of his wife, Mrs. Jeannie Cooke (b. 1917), after 42 years of marriage.

Patent Case. The greatest settlement ever made in a patent-infringement suit is $9,250,000, paid in April, 1952, by the Ford Motor Company to the Ferguson Tractor Co. for a claim filed in January, 1948.

Libel. The largest libel settlement made has been one of $600,000 by the Hearst Corporation, publishers of the *San Francisco Examiner*, in response to a $32,000,000 suit brought by the Synanon Foundation Inc. and its founder Charles E. Dederich on July 1, 1976, for adverse news articles.

Greatest Lien. The greatest lien ever imposed by a court is 40,000,000,000 lire ($64,800,000) on April 9, 1974, in Milan, upon Vittorio and Ida Riva for back taxes allegedly due on a chain of cotton mills around Turin, Italy, inherited by their brother Felice (who left for Beirut) in 1960.

Longest Lease. Part of the Cattle Market, Dublin, Ireland, was leased by John Jameson to the city's Corporation on a lease for 100,000 years, expiring on January 21, 101,863 A.D.

Most Literal Legal Interpretation

Eugene Schneider of Carteret, New Jersey, allegedly cut his $80,000 home in half with a chain saw in July, 1976, after his wife sued him for divorce, thus fulfilling in his eyes the equal division of property required by New Jersey law.

Most Successful Complainer

Ralph Charell, a New York City media executive, claims to have been successful in collecting for every misadventure that has damaged him. His total receipts in settlement for such complaints as poor telephone and car rental service, gas and electric overcharges, failure to deliver on time, imperfect goods, improper installation, landlord disputes, and the like, have come to $80,710.46 as of June 15, 1977—and he is still complaining! His latest complaint is against the *Guinness Book* for failing to list his 51 consecutive profitable transactions in "option trading," a category this book does not cover.

Largest Suit

The highest amount of damages ever sought is $675,000,000,000,000,000 (then equivalent to 10 times the U.S. national wealth) in a suit by Mr. I. Walton Bader brought in the U.S. District Court, New York City on April 14, 1971, against General Motors and others for polluting all 50 States.

Wills

Shortest. The shortest valid will in the world is "Vse zene," the Czech for "All to wife," written and dated January 19, 1967, by Herr Karl Tausch of Langen, Hesse, Germany. The shortest will contested but subsequently admitted to probate in English law was the case of *Thorn v. Dickens* in 1906. It consisted of the three words "All for Mother."

Longest. The longest will on record was that of Mrs. Frederica Cook (U.S.), in the early part of the century. It consisted of four bound volumes containing 95,940 words.

Most Durable Judge

The oldest recorded active judge was Judge Albert R. Alexander (born November 8, 1859), of Plattsburg, Missouri, magistrate and probate judge of Clinton County. He retired on July 9, 1965, at the age of 105 years 8 months, and died on March 30, 1966. James Russell McElroy (b. October 1, 1901) served 49 years 125 days (1927–1977) on the Circuit Court of Alabama.

Judge Vernon D. Hitchings of Norfolk, Virginia, disposed of his millionth traffic case from January, 1954 to January 19, 1977. Of these some 965,000 of his verdicts were unappealed or upheld on appeal.

Youngest Judge

No collated records on the ages of judicial appointments exist. However, Thomas J. Boynton (born Amherst, Ohio, on August 31, 1838) is known to have been appointed Federal Judge at Key West, Florida, on January 20, 1864, aged 25 years 142 days. Judge Susan I. Broyles (b. Alamosa, Colorado, on June 25, 1949) was appointed County Judge of Conejos County, Colorado, on January 9, 1973, aged 23 years 198 days.

Most Successful Criminal Lawyer

Sir Lionel Luckhoo, senior partner of Luckhoo and Luckhoo, of Georgetown, Guyana, succeeded in getting his 225th successive murder charge acquittal by May, 1979.

Deadliest Prosecutor

Joe Freeman Britt, District Attorney in the Sixteenth Judicial District in North Carolina, obtained 23 death verdicts in 28 months to mid-1976, when he had 13 defendants simultaneously on death row.

CRIME AND PUNISHMENT

Greatest Mass Killings

China. The greatest massacre in human history ever attributed to any nation is that of 26,300,000 Chinese during the regime of Mao Tse-tung between 1949 and May, 1965. This accusation was made by an agency of the U.S.S.R. government in a radio broadcast on April 7, 1969. The broadcast broke down the figure into four periods: 2.8 million (1949–52); 3.5 million (1953–57); 6.7 million (1958–60); and 13.3 million (1961–May, 1965). The highest reported death figures in single monthly announcements on Peking radio were 1,176,000 in the provinces of Anhwei, Chekiang, Kiangsu, and Shantung, and 1,150,000 in the Central South Provinces. Po I-po, Minister of Finance, is alleged to have stated in the organ *For a lasting peace, for a people's democracy* "in the past three years

COURT RECORDS: Judge Alexander of Plattsburg, Missouri (left), served on the bench well into his 105th year. A more fearsome example of American jurisprudence is Judge Hitchings of Norfolk, Virginia (right), whose verdicts stood in 96.5% of the traffic cases he tried.

(1950–52) we have liquidated more than 2 million bandits." General Jacques Guillermaz, a French diplomat, estimated the total executions between February, 1951, and May, 1952, at between 1 million and 3 million. In April, 1971, the Executive *Yuan* or cabinet of the implacably hostile government of The Republic of China in Taipei, Taiwan, announced its official estimate of the mainland death roll in the period 1949–69 as "at least 39,940,000." This figure, however, excluded "tens of thousands" killed in the Great Proletarian Cultural Revolution, which began in late 1966. The Walker Report published by the U.S. Senate Committee of the Judiciary in July, 1971, placed the total death roll within China since 1949 between 32.25 and 61.7 million. An estimate of 63,784,000 was published by Jean-Pierre Dujardin in *Figaro Magazine* of November 19–25, 1978.

U.S.S.R. The death roll in the Great Purge, or *Yezhovshchina*, in the U.S.S.R., in 1936–38, has never been published, though evidence of its magnitude may be found in population statistics which show a deficiency of males from before the outbreak of the 1941–45 war. The reign of terror was administered by the *Narodny Kommissariat Vnutrennykh Del* (N.K.V.D.), or People's Commissariat of Internal Affairs, the Soviet security service headed by Nikolay Ivanovich Yezhov (1895–1939), described by Nikita Khrushchev in 1956 as "a degenerate." S. V. Utechin, an expert on Soviet affairs, regarded estimates of 8,000,000 or 10,000,000 victims as "probably not exaggerations." On August 17, 1942, Stalin indicated to Churchill in Moscow that 10 million *kulaks* (farmers with excessive wealth according to Communist standards) had been liquidated.

Nazi Germany. At the S.S. (*Schutzstaffel*) extermination camp known as Auschwitz-Birkenau (Oswiecim-Brzezinka), near Oswiecim, in southern Poland, where a minimum of 920,000 people (Soviet estimate is 4,000,000) were exterminated from June 14, 1940 to January 18, 1945, the greatest number killed in a day was 6,000. The man who operated the release of the "Zyklon B" cyanide pellets into the gas chambers there during this time was Sergeant-Major Moll (or Mold). The Nazi Commandant during the period 1940–43 was Rudolf Franz Ferdinand Höss, who was tried in Warsaw from March .11 to April 2, 1947, and hanged, aged 47, at Oswiecim on April 15, 1947.

Obersturmbannführer (Lt.-Col.) Karl Adolf Eichmann (born 1906) of the S.S. was hanged in a small room inside Ramleh Prison, near Tel Aviv, Israel, at just before midnight (local time) on May 31, 1962, for his complicity in the deaths of an indeterminably massive number of Jews during World War II, under the instruction given in April, 1941, by Adolf Hitler (1889–1945) for the "Final Solution" (*Endlösung*).

Forced Labor

No official figures have been published of the death roll in Corrective Labor Camps in the U.S.S.R., first established in 1918. The total number of such camps was known to be more than 200 in 1946, but in 1956 many were converted to less severe Corrective Labor Colonies. An estimate published in the Netherlands puts the death roll between 1921 and 1960 at 19,000,000. The camps were administered by the *Cheka* until 1922, the O.G.P.U. (1922–34), the N.K.V.D. (1934–1946), the M.V.D. (1946–1953) and the K.G.B. since 1953. Solzhenitsyn's best estimate is an aggregate number of 66 million inmates. The study by S. Grossu, published 1975, stated there were then 2,000,000 political prisoners in 96 camps.

In China, there are no published official figures on the numbers undergoing *Lao Jiao* (Education through Labor) or *Lao Dong Gai Zao* (Reform through Manual Labor). An estimate published by Bao Ruo-wang, who was released in 1964 because his father was a Corsican, was 16,000,000, which was then almost 3 per cent of the population.

Largest Criminal Organization

The largest syndicate of organized crime is the Mafia (meaning "swank," from a Sicilian word) or La Cosa Nostra ("our thing") which is said to have infiltrated the executive, judiciary and legislative branches of the U.S. Government. It consists of some 3,000 to 5,000 individuals in 24 "families" federated under "The Commission," with an estimated annual turnover in vice, gambling, protection rackets, cigarettes, bootlegging, hijacking, narcotics, loan-sharking, prostitution and some legitimate businesses estimated in May, 1977, at $48 billion per annum, of which some $25,300,000,000 is profit. This is nearly 7½ times more than the profit shown by G.M. (see page 340).

The biggest Mafia killing was on September 11–13, 1931, when the topmost man, Salvatore Maranzano, *Il Capo di Tutti Capi*, and 40 allies were liquidated.

The Mafia is said to have got its start in the U.S. after the lynching of 11 Mafiosi in New Orleans in 1890, for which a naive U.S. government paid $30,000 compensation to the widows. This money was seized and used as the initial funding to prime the whole operation.

Murder

Highest Rate. The country with the highest recorded murder rate is Mexico with 46.3 registered homicides per 100,000 of the population in 1970. It has been estimated that the total number of murders in Colombia during *La Violencia* (1945–62) was about 300,000, giving a rate over a 17-year period of nearly 48 per day. A total of 592 deaths was attributed to one bandit leader, Teófilo ("Sparks") Rojas, aged 27, between 1948 and his death in an ambush near Armenia on January 22, 1963. Some sources attribute 3,500 slayings to him.

The highest homicide rates recorded in New York City have been 58 in a week in July, 1972, and 13 in a day in August, 1972. In 1973, the total for Detroit, Michigan (population then 1,500,000) was 751.

Lowest Rate. The country with the lowest officially recorded rate in the world is Spain, with 39 murders (a rate of 1.23 per million population) in 1967, or one murder every 9 days. In the Indian protectorate of Sikkim, in the Himalayas, murder is, however, practically unknown, while in the Hunza area of Kashmir, in the Karakoram, only one definite case by a Hunzarwal has been recorded since 1900.

Most Prolific Murderers. It was established at the trial of Buhram, the Indian Thug, that he had strangled at least 931 victims with his yellow and white cloth *ruhmal* in the Oudh district between 1790 and 1840. It has been estimated that at least 2,000,000 Indians were strangled by Thugs (*burtotes*) during the reign of the Thugee cult (pronounced "tugee") from 1550 until its final suppression by the British *raj* in 1853.

The greatest number of victims ascribed to a murderess has been 610 in the case of Countess Erszebet Bathory (1560–1614) of Hungary. At her trial which began on January 2, 1611, a witness testified to seeing a list of her victims in her own handwriting totaling this number. All were alleged to be young girls from the neighborhood of her castle at Csejthe, where she died on August 21, 1614. She was walled up in her room for 3½ years, after being found guilty.

This century's top candidate for most prolific one-at-a-time murderer is the German, Bruno Lüdke (born 1909), who confessed to 85 murders of women between 1928 and January 29, 1943. He was executed by injection without trial in a hospital in Vienna on April 8, 1944.

Frans Hooijmaijers, 40, a male nurse at the Luckerheide Geriatric Clinic, Kerkrade, Netherlands, admitted to murders of 14 patients in August, 1976. From November, 1969, his section of the clinic had seen 245 other deaths of a suspicious nature, as well as an inordinately high consumption of insulin and Valium. He was sentenced to 18 years in April, 1977.

John Wayne Gacy was charged with murdering 7 youths and, according to the police, admitted to assaulting and strangling 25 others. The first of 29 bodies was found on December 21, 1978, under his house in Park Ridge, Illinois.

Gang Murders. During the period of open gang warfare in Chicago, the peak year was 1926, when there were 76 unsolved killings. The 1,000th gang murder in Chicago since 1919 occurred on February 1, 1967. Only 13 cases have ended in convictions.

Suicide

The estimated daily rate of suicides throughout the world surpassed 1,000 in 1965. The country with the highest recorded suicide rate is Hungary, with 42.6 per 100,000 of the population in 1977. The country with the lowest recorded rate is Jordan, with a single case in 1970 and hence a rate of 0.04 per 100,000.

Capital Punishment

Capital punishment was first abolished *de facto* in Liechtenstein in 1798.

Between the 5-to-4 U.S. Supreme Court decision against capital punishment in June, 1972, and April, 1975, 32 of the 50 states voted to restore the death penalty. Gary Gilmore, a convicted murderer, became the first man to be executed in the U.S. since 1967, when he faced a firing squad in Utah on January 17, 1979. On May 25, 1979, John Spenkelink, 30, became the first man to be electrocuted since 1967, at Railford Jail, Florida.

"Smelling-Out." The greatest "smelling-out" (ritualistic execution) recorded in African history occurred before Shaka (chief of the Zulu tribes, 1787–1828) and 30,000 of his subjects near the Umhlatuzana River, Zululand (now Natal, South Africa) in March, 1824. After 9 hours, over 300 were "smelt-out" as guilty of smearing the Royal *Kraal* with blood. Their "discoverers" were 150 witchfinders led by the hideous female *isangoma* Nobela. The victims were declared innocent when Shaka admitted to having the smearing done himself to expose the falsity of the power of his diviners. Nobela poisoned herself with atropine ($C_{17} H_{23} NO_3$), but the other 149 witchfinders were thereupon skewered or clubbed to death.

Last Guillotinings

The last person to be publicly guillotined in France was the murderer Eugen Weidmann before a large crowd at Versailles, near Paris, at 4:50 a.m. on June 17, 1939.

Dr. Joseph Ignace Guillotin (1738–1814) died a natural death. He had advocated the use of the machine designed by Dr. Antoine Louis in 1789 in the French constituent assembly.

Largest Hanging

The most people hanged from one gallows was 38 Sioux Indians by William J. Duly outside Mankato, Minnesota, for the murder of unarmed citizens on December 26, 1862.

Most Hanging Attempts

In 1803 it was reported that Joseph Samuels was reprieved in Sydney, Australia, after three unsuccessful attempts to hang him in which the rope broke twice.

Longest on Death Row

The longest stay on "death row" in the U.S. has been one of more than 14 years by Edgar Labat, aged 44, and Clifton A. Paret, aged 38, in Angola Penitentiary, Louisiana. In March, 1953, they were sentenced to death, after being found guilty of rape in 1950. They were released on May 5, 1967, only to be immediately re-arrested on an indictment arising from the original charge.

Caryl Whittier Chessman, aged 38, convicted of 17 felonies, was executed on May 2, 1960, in the gas chamber at the California State Prison, San Quentin, California. In 11 years 10 months and one week on "death row," Chessman had won eight stays of execution.

Longest Prison Sentences

The longest recorded prison sentences were ones of 7,109 years awarded to two confidence tricksters by an Iranian court on June 15, 1969. The duration of sentences are proportional to the amount of the defalcations involved. A sentence of 384,912 years was demanded at the prosecution of Gabriel March Grandos, 22, at Palma de Mallorca, Spain, on March 11, 1972, for failing to deliver 42,768 letters.

Juan Corona, a Mexican-American, was sentenced on February 5, 1973, at Fairfield, California, to 25 consecutive life terms for murdering 25 migrant farm workers he had hired, killed and buried in 1970–71 near Feather River, Yuba City, California. His 20th century record for number of murder victims was surpassed with the discovery on August 13, 1973, of the body of the 27th victim of Dean Corll, 33, of Houston, Texas.

Longest Time Served

Paul Geidel, given a life sentence for murder on September 5, 1911 and imprisoned in New York State, overtook the 66-year-11-month total of time served by Johnson VanDyke Grigsby (1908-74 plus 7 months in 1976) in August, 1977. Geidel was still serving in April, 1979.

Most Parking Tickets

Henry Rabin, 40, of Skokie, Illinois, was arrested in July, 1975, for failing to pay 468 parking tickets in $2\frac{1}{2}$ years. This top "scofflaw" was fined $5,000.

Most Appearances in Court

There are no collected records on the greatest number of convictions on an individual, but the highest recently reported is 1,433 for the gentlemanly but alcoholic Edward Eugene Ebzery, who died in Brisbane Jail, Queensland, Australia, on September 23, 1967.

Lynchings

The worst year in the 20th century for lynchings in the U.S. was 1901, with 130 lynchings (105 Negroes, 25 whites), while the first year with no reported cases was 1952.

Longest Prison Escape

The longest recorded escape by a prisoner who was eventually recaptured was that of Leonard T. Fristoe, 77, who escaped from Nevada State Prison, on December 15, 1923, and was turned in by his son on November 15, 1969, at Compton, California. He had 46 years of freedom under the name Claude R. Willis. He had killed two sheriff's deputies in 1920.

Greatest Jail Break

In February, 1979, retired U.S. Army Colonel Arthur "Bull" Simons led a band of 14 to break into Gasre prison, Teheran, Iran, to rescue two fellow Americans. Some 11,000 other prisoners took advantage of this (and the Islamic revolution) in history's largest jail break.

In July, 1971, Raoul Sendic and 105 other Tupamaro guerrillas escaped from a Uruguayan prison through a tunnel 298 feet long.

Robbery

The greatest robbery on record was that of the Berlin Reichsbank's reserves during April and May, 1945. The Westphalia bearer bonds repayable in gold totaled $400 million. Gold coins and bullion then valued at $3,434,626 and jewels, foreign exchange and securities valued at 23 million gold marks were stolen from the Reichsbank.

Art. The greatest recorded robbery by market valuation was the removal of 19 paintings, valued at $19,200,000, taken from Russborough House, Blessington, Ireland, the home of Sir Alfred and Lady Beit, by 4 men and a woman, on April 26, 1974. They included the $6.9 million Vermeer *Lady Writing a Letter with her Maid*. The paintings were recovered on May 4, 1974, near Glandore, Ireland. Dr. Rose Bridgit Dugdale (born 1941) was subsequently convicted.

It is arguable that the value of the "Mona Lisa" at the time of its theft from the Louvre on August 21, 1911, was greater than this figure. It was recovered in Italy in 1913 when Vincenzo Perruggia was charged with its theft.

On September 1, 1964, antiquities reputedly worth $23,000,000 were recovered from 3 warehouses near the Pyramids in Egypt.

Bank. During the extreme civil disorder prior to January 22, 1976, in Beirut, Lebanon, a guerrilla force blasted the vaults of the British

LARGEST ART ROBBERY (left): Dr. Rose Dugdale and her accomplices made off with 19 paintings, valued at almost $20 million. YOUNGEST KIDNAP VICTIM (right): Carolyn Wharton of Beaumont, Texas, was kidnapped when she was only 29 minutes old.

Bank of the Middle East in Bab Idriss and cleared out safe deposit boxes with contents valued by former Finance Minister Lucien Dahadah at $50,000,000, and by another source at an "absolute minimum" of $20,000,000.

Industrial Espionage. It has been alleged that a division of the American Cyanamid Company about 1966 lost some papers and vials of micro-organisms through industrial espionage, allegedly organized from Italy, which data had cost them $24,000,000 in research and development.

Jewel. The greatest recorded theft of jewels was from safe deposit boxes in the Palm Towers, Palm Beach, Florida, on April 14, 1976, estimated by police at about $6,000,000 plus an additional $1,000,000 in other items.

Jewels are believed to have constituted a major part of the Hotel Pierre, New York City, "heist" on December 31, 1971. An unofficial estimate ran as high as $5,000,000.

Train. The greatest recorded train robbery occurred between 3:03 a.m. and 3:27 a.m. on August 8, 1963, when a General Post Office mail train from Glasgow, Scotland, was ambushed at Sears Crossing and robbed at Bridego Bridge near Mentmore, Buckinghamshire, England. The gang escaped with about 120 mailbags containing £2,631,784 ($6,053,103) worth of bank notes being taken to London for pulping. Only £343,448 ($961,654) was recovered.

Greatest Kidnapping Ransom

Historically, the greatest ransom paid was that for their chief, Atahualpa, by the Incas to the Spanish conquistador Francisco

Pizarro, in 1532–33 at Cajamarca, Peru, which constituted a hall full of gold and silver worth in modern money some $170 million.

The greatest ransom ever extorted is $60,000,000 for the release of two businessmen, the brothers Jorge Born, 40, and Juan Born, 39, of Argentina, paid to the left-wing urban guerrilla group Montoneros in Buenos Aires on June 20, 1975.

The youngest person ever kidnapped has been Carolyn Wharton, who was born at 12:46 p.m. on March 19, 1955, in the Baptist Hospital, Beaumont, Texas, and kidnapped by a woman disguised as a nurse at 1:15 p.m., aged 29 minutes.

Greatest Hijack Ransom

The highest amount ever paid to hijackers has been $4,800,000 in small denomination notes by the West German government to Popular Front for the Liberation of Palestine representatives 30 miles outside Beirut, Lebanon, on February 23, 1972. In return, a Lufthansa Boeing 747, which had been bound for Athens when it was hijacked an hour out of New Delhi and forced down at Aden, was released, along with its 14 crew members.

The longest air piracy has been one of 8,800 miles by three Filipino Moslem separatists from the southern Philippines in a BAC 111, changing to a DC8 at Bangkok, Thailand, and arriving at Benghazi, Libya, a week later on April 14, 1976.

Largest Narcotics Haul

The heaviest recorded haul of narcotics was made in the Bahamas on August 16, 1975, when 1,049 sacks (43.14 tons) of high-grade Colombian marijuana were discovered, worth an estimated $24,000,000. The most valuable haul was of 937 lbs. of pure heroin worth $106¼ million retail seized aboard the 60-ton shrimp boat *Caprice des Temps* at Marseilles, France, on February 28, 1972. The captain, Louis Boucan, 57, tried to commit suicide, but was sentenced to 15 years on January 5, 1973.

Thailand's Prime Minister Gen. Kriangsak Chammanand personally ignited a 13 × 33-foot pit containing heroin (3,585 lbs.), marijuana (4,409 lbs.), amphetamines (2,679 lbs.) and 7,253 lbs. of other drugs in Bangkok on January 31, 1979. The street worth of the seizures, made in 1975–78, was put at "billions of dollars."

In raids on the Gunjira peninsula, Colombia, on April 27–29, 1978, authorities seized 574 tons of marijuana, with an estimated wholesale value of $200,000,000.

It was revealed on January 31, 1973, that 398 lbs. of heroin and cocaine with a street value of $73,000,000 had been stolen from safekeeping by the New York City Police Department—a record for any law enforcement agency.

The British Home Office disclosed on December 23, 1977, that 13 million LSD tablets with a street value approaching $170 million had been destroyed at the conclusion of "Operation Julie."

Largest Bribe

An alleged bribe of $84,000,000 offered to Shaikh Zaid ibn Sultan of Abu Dhabi, United Arab Emirates, by a Saudi Arabian official in

August, 1955, is the highest on record. The affair concerned oil concessions in the disputed territory of Buraimi on the Persian Gulf.

Greatest Banknote Forgery

The greatest recorded forgery was the German Third Reich government's forging operation, code name "Bernhard," engineered by *S.S. Sturmbannführer* Alfred Naujocks in 1940–41. It involved £150,000,000 (now about $300,000,000) worth of Bank of England £5 notes.

Welfare Swindle

The greatest welfare swindle yet worked was that of the gypsy Anthony Moreno, on the French Social Security in Marseille. By forging birth certificates and school registration forms, he invented 197 fictitious families and 3,000 children on which he claimed benefits from 1960 to mid-1968. Moreno, nicknamed "El Chorro" (the fountain), was last reported free of extradition worries and living in luxury in his native Spain having absquatulated with an estimated $6,440,000.

Biggest Bank Fraud

The largest amount of money named in a defalcation case has been a gross £33,000,000 ($75,900,000) at the Lugano, Switzerland, branch of Lloyd's Bank International Ltd., on September 2, 1974. Mark Colombo was arrested pending charges including falsification of foreign currency accounts and suppression of evidence.

Computer Fraud

Between 1964 and 1973, some 64,000 fake insurance policies were created on the computer of the Equity Funding Corporation involving $2,000,000,000.

Passing Bad Checks

Mrs. Ann Lorraine Ohlschlager, *alias* Ann Kosak, of Los Angeles, was charged in January, 1974, with writing $37,000,000 in bad checks between January and October, 1973, netting a total of $463,000 from the United California Bank.

Fines

It was reported in January, 1979, that Carlo Ponti, husband of Sophia Loren, was to be fined the equivalent of $26,400,000 by the Italian courts in connection with claims for taxes alleged to be unpaid.

Largest Court

The largest judicial building in the world is the Johannesburg Central Magistrates' Court, opened in 1941, at the junction of Fox and West Streets, Johannesburg, South Africa. There are 42 courtrooms (8 civil and 34 criminal), with a further seven criminal courtrooms under construction. The court has a panel of 70 magistrates and deals with an average of 2,500 criminal cases every week, excluding those petty cases in which guilt has been admitted in writing.

MOST EXPENSIVE PRISON: Spandau Prison in Berlin contains only one inmate, Nazi war criminal Rudolf Hess.

Penal Camps

The largest penal camp systems in the world were those near Karaganda and Kolyma, in the U.S.S.R., each with a population estimated in 1958 at between 1,200,000 and 1,500,000. The largest labor camp in the U.S.S.R. is now said to be the Dubrovlag Complex of 15 camps centered on Pot'ma, Mordovian Republic, U.S.S.R. The official NATO estimate for all Soviet camps was "more than one million" in March, 1960, compared with a peak of probably 12 million during the Stalinist era.

Devil's Island. The largest French penal settlement was that of St. Laurent du Maroni, which included the notorious Île du Diable, Royale and St. Joseph (for incorrigibles) off the coast of French Guiana, South America. It remained in operation for 99 years from 1854 until the last group of repatriated prisoners, including Théodore Rouselle, who had served 50 years, was returned to Bordeaux on August 22, 1953. It has been estimated that barely 2,000 of the 70,000 deportees ever returned. These included the executioner Ladurelle (imprisoned 1921–37), who was murdered in Paris in 1938.

Prisons

Largest. The largest prison in the world is Kharkov Prison, in the U.S.S.R., which has at times accommodated 40,000 prisoners.

Most Secure. After it became a maximum security Federal prison in 1934, no convict was known to have lived to tell of a successful escape from the prison on Alcatraz ("Pelican") Island in San Francisco Bay. A total of 23 men attempted it, but 12 were recaptured, 5 shot dead, one drowned and 5 presumed drowned. On December 16, 1962, three months before the prison was closed, one man reached the mainland alive, only to be recaptured on the spot. John Chase was imprisoned for a record 26 years on Alcatraz.

Most Expensive. Spandau Prison, Berlin, built 100 years ago for 600 prisoners, is now used solely for the Nazi war criminal Rudolf Hess (born April 26, 1894). The cost of maintenance of the staff of 105 has been estimated at $415,000 per annum.

4. Economic

MONETARY AND FINANCE

Largest Budget

The greatest annual expenditure budgeted by any country has been $500,200,000,000 by the U.S. Government (federal expenditure) in the fiscal year ending September 30, 1979. The highest budgeted revenue in the U.S. was $439,600,000,000 in 1978–79.

In the U.S., the greatest surplus was $8,419,469,844 in 1947–48, and the greatest deficit was $61,800,000,000 in 1978–79.

Foreign Aid

The total net foreign aid given by the U.S. Government between July 1, 1945, and January 1, 1978, was $177,681,000,000.

The country which received most U.S. aid in 1977 was Israel with $1,476,000,000. U.S. foreign aid began with $50,000 to Venezuela for earthquake relief in 1812.

Taxation

Highest Tax Rates. The country with the most confiscatory taxation is Norway, where in January, 1974, the Labor Party and Socialist Alliance abolished the 80 per cent limit so that some 2,000 citizens were listed in the *Lignings Boka* as paying more than 100 per cent of their taxable income. The shipping magnate Hilmer Reksten was assessed at 491 per cent.

Least Taxed. The lowest income tax in the world is paid by the citizens of Bahrain, Kuwait, and Qatar, where the rate, regardless of income, is zero.

There is no income tax paid by residents on Lundy Island off North Devon, England. This 1,062.4-acre island issued its own unofficial currency of Puffins and Half Puffins between the Wars, for which offense the owner was prosecuted.

National Debt

The largest national debt of any country in the world is that of the U.S., where the gross federal public debt surpassed the half-trillion dollar mark in 1975 and reached $721,800,000,000 by January 1, 1978. This amount in dollar bills would make a pile 39,166 miles high, weighing 614,543 tons.

Biggest Savers

The world's top savers are the Swiss, with deposits averaging $11,225 per head.

National Wealth

The richest nation, measured by average income per capita (5,000 people), is Abu Dhabi, a state of Trucial Oman on the Arabian peninsula, with $70,000 in 1976. The U.S., which took the lead in 1910, was third behind Sweden and Switzerland in the 1977 figures.

It has been estimated that the value of all physical assets in the U.S. in 1976 was $6.2 trillion, or $28,800 per person.

Poorest Country

The lowest *published* annual income per capita of any country is Rwanda, with $70 per person.

Gross National Product

The estimated free world aggregate of Gross National Products in 1975 was about $10,200,000,000,000. The country with the largest Gross National Product is the U.S., running at $1,965,100,000,000 as of January 1, 1978.

Gold Reserves

The country with the greatest monetary gold reserve is West Germany, whose Treasury had $39,700,000,000 on hand in January, 1978. The United States Bullion Depository at Fort Knox, 30 miles southwest of Louisville, Kentucky, is the principal depository of U.S. gold. Gold is stored in standard mint bars of 400 troy ounces (439 oz. avoirdupois), measuring 7 inches by $3\frac{5}{8}$ inches by $1\frac{5}{8}$ inches, and each worth $16,888.

The greatest accumulation of the world's central banks' $50,000,000,000 of gold bullion is now in the Federal Reserve Bank at 33 Liberty Street, New York City. Some $17 billion or 15,680 tons is stored 80 feet below street level, in a vault 50 feet by 100 feet behind a steel door weighing nearly 100 tons.

Worst Inflation

The world's worst inflation occurred in Hungary in June, 1946, when the 1931 gold pengö was valued at 130 quintillion (1.3×10^{20}) paper pengös. Notes were issued for szazmillio billion (1 followed by 20 zeros or 10^{20}) pengös on June 3 and withdrawn on July 11, 1946. Notes for 1 sextillion or 10^{21} pengös were printed but not circulated.

In Germany, on November 6, 1923, the circulation of Reichsbank marks reached 400,338,326,350,700,000,000, a level of inflation 755,700 million times the 1913 figures.

Currency

Paper money is an invention of the Chinese, first tried in 910 A.D. and prevalent by 970 A.D. The world's earliest bank notes (*banco-sedlar*) were issued in Stockholm, Sweden, in July, 1661. The oldest surviving bank note is one for 5 dalers dated December 6, 1662.

Largest and Smallest. The largest paper money ever issued was the one kwan note of the Chinese Ming dynasty issue of 1368–99, which measured 9 inches by 13 inches. The smallest bank note ever

HIGHEST EXISTING DENOMINATION CURRENCY is this $10,000 bill with the portrait of Salmon P. Chase. Only 400 are circulating today.

issued was the 10 bani note of the Ministry of Finance of Rumania, issued in 1917. It measured (printed area) 1.09 inches by 1.49 inches.

Highest Denominations. The highest denomination notes in circulation are U.S. Federal Reserve Bank notes for $10,000. They bear the head of Salmon Portland Chase (1808–73). None have been printed since July, 1944, and the U.S. Treasury announced in 1969 that no further notes higher than $100 would be issued. Only some 400 $10,000 bills remain in circulation.

Lowest Denomination. The 1-cent Hong Kong note is worth one-fifth of a U.S. cent.

Largest Check

The greatest amount paid by a single check in the history of banking was one equivalent to $2,046,700,000, handed over by Daniel P. Moynihan, the U.S. Ambassador to India, in New Delhi on February 18, 1974.

An internal U.S. Treasury check for $4,176,969,623.57 was drawn on June 30, 1954.

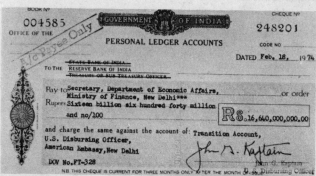

LARGEST CHECK: This check for 16,640,000,000 Indian rupees, drawn on February 18, 1974, is equivalent to more than $2 billion U.S.

Highest Denomination Bond

There exists a U.S. Treasury note for $500,000,000 bearing interest at 6¼ per cent for 14 years. Each annual interest payment is $31,250,000. An example is held by the Bureau of Engraving and Printing in Washington, D.C.

COINS

Oldest. The earliest certainly dated coins are the electrum (alloy of gold and silver) staters of Lydia, in Asia Minor (now Turkey), which were coined in the reign of King Gyges (c. 685–652 B.C.). Primitive uninscribed "spade" money of the Chou dynasty of China is now *believed* to date from c. 770 B.C. A discovery at Tappeh Nush-i-jan, Iran, of silver ingot currency in 1972 has been dated to as early as 760 B.C. The earliest dated coin is the Danish coin of the Bishop of Roskilde, dated MCCXXXIIII (1234), of which 6 are known.

Smallest. The smallest coins in the world have been the Nepalese ¼ dam or Jawa, struck c. 1740 in silver in the reign of Jeya Prakash Malla. The Jawa, which weighed between 0.008 and 0.014 of a gram and measured about 2 × 2 mm., was sometimes cut into ½ and even ¼ Jawa, thus weighing 0.002 of a gram, or 14,000 to the ounce.

Heaviest. The Swedish copper 10 daler coin of 1644 attained a weight of 43 lbs. 7¼ oz. Of primitive exchange tokens, the most massive are the holed stone discs, or *Fé*, from the Yap Islands, in the western Pacific Ocean, with diameters of up to 12 feet, weighing up to 185 pounds. A medium-sized one was worth one Yapese wife or an 18-foot canoe.

Coinless Country. Laos is the only country presently without coins (paper money only).

Denominations

Highest. The 1654 Indian gold 200 mohur ($1,400) coin of the Mughul Emperor Khurram Shihab-ud-din Muhammad, Shah Jahan (reigned 1628–57), had the greatest intrinsic worth ever struck. It weighed 2,177 grams (70 troy oz.) and hence has an intrinsic worth of $5,320. It had a diameter of 5⅜ inches. The only known example disappeared in Patna, Bihar, India, in c. 1820, but a plaster cast of this coin exists in the British Museum, London.

Currently the highest denomination is the Bahamian $2,500 1977 gold coin, 72 millimeters (2.8 inches) in diameter, struck by the Royal Canadian Mint, Ottawa. Each of the 250 examples struck contains 1 lb. troy of 22 carat gold.

Lowest. Lowest in face value today is the 5 aurar piece of Iceland issued in 1971. At today's currency rates, it would take 3,955 5-aurars to equal one U.S. dollar.

Quarter farthings (sixteen to the British penny) were struck in copper at the Royal Mint, London, in the Imperial coinage for use in Ceylon, in 1839 and 1851–53.

**HIGHEST
DENOMINATION COIN:**
This $2,500 Bahamian gold
coin contains a pound of
22 carat gold.

Most Expensive Coin

The highest price paid at auction for a single coin is $272,000
or $314,000 inclusive of commission for an Athenian silver
decadrachm in Zurich, Switzerland, on May 28, 1974, by Constantinople Fine Arts Inc.

The unique U.S. 1907 $20 gold double eagle Indian head pattern
from the Dr. Wilkison Collection was sold by private treaty by coin
dealer Steven C. Markoff of Beverly Hills, California, for $500,000
in May, 1979.

Rarest

A number of coins are unique. An example of a unique coin of
threefold rarity (in alloy, denomination and reign) is one of the rare
admixture of bronze with inlaid gold of Kaleb I of Axum (*c.* 500 A.D.).
Only 700 Axumite coins of any sort are known.

Greatest Collection

The highest price paid for a coin collection is $7,300,000 by Steve
Markoff of A-Mark Coin Co., Inc. of Beverly Hills, California,
for a hoard of 407,000 U.S. silver dollars from the La Vere
Redfield estate in a courtroom auction in Reno, Nevada, on
January 27, 1976.

Largest Treasure Trove

The largest hoard ever found was one of about 80,000 aurei in
Brescello near Modena, Italy, in 1814, believed to have been
deposited *c.* 37 B.C.

The numerically largest hoard ever found was the Brussels hoard
of 1908 containing *c.* 150,000 coins.

It is believed that the greatest undersea recovery of treasure will
be made from the wreck of the 140-foot-long Spanish ship *Nuestra
Señora de Concepción* which capsized off the north coast of the
Dominican Republic in 1641. The first part of possibly $40,000,000
of treasure was found by Seaquest International on November 30,
1978.

NINETY-YEAR CAREER: Edward King Gaylord began working as a strawberry picker when he was 11 years old, and worked his way up until, at age 101, he was the millionaire president of a publishing firm.

Largest Mint

The largest mint in the world is the U.S. Mint built in 1965–69 on Independence Mall, Philadelphia, covering 500,000 square feet (11½ acres) with an annual capacity on a 3-shift 7-day-a-week production of 8 billion coins. A single stamping machine can produce coins at a rate of 10,000 per hour.

TRADE UNIONS

The world's largest union is the Industrie-Gewerkschaft Metall (Metal Workers' Union) of West Germany, with a membership of 2,695,312 on January 1, 1979. The union with the longest name is probably the International Association of Marble, Slate and Stone Polishers, Rubbers and Sawyers, Tile and Marble Setters' Helpers and Marble Mosaic and Terrazzo Workers' Helpers (Washington, D.C.).

Longest Working Week. The longest working week (maximum possible 168 hours) is up to 139 hours at times by some housemen and registrars in some hospitals in England. This allowed only 4 hours 8½ minutes sleep per night, according to evidence given in November, 1971.

Shortest Working Week. Some contracts for university lecturers in England call for a 3-hour week, that is, a 72-hour year spread over 24 weeks.

Labor Disputes

Earliest. The earliest recorded strike was one by an orchestra leader from Greece named Aristos in Rome *c.* 309 B.C. The cause was meal breaks. A labor dispute concerning monotony of diet and working conditions was recorded in 1153 B.C. in Thebes, Egypt.

Longest. The world's longest recorded strike ended on January 4, 1961, after 33 years. It concerned the employment of barbers' assistants in Copenhagen, Denmark. The longest recorded major strike was one at the plumbing fixtures factory of the Kohler Co. in Sheboygan, Wisconsin, between April, 1954, and October, 1962. The strike is alleged to have cost the United Automobile Workers union about $12,000,000 to sustain.

Employment

Lowest Unemployment. In Switzerland in December, 1973 (population 6,600,000), the total number of unemployed was reported to be 81.

Working and Jobs. The longest recorded working career in one job was that of Miss Polly Gadsby who started at the age of 9 and worked 86 years wrapping elastic for the same company until she died in 1932 at the age of 95.

Edward King Gaylord (b. March 5, 1873 in Muscotah, Kansas) worked for 90 years, starting as a strawberry picker at age 11 until, at the age of 101, he was serving as the millionaire president of the Oklahoma Publishing Co. He died on May 30, 1974.

FOOD CONSUMPTION

The figures relating to net food consumption per person are based on gross available food supplies at retail level, less waste, animal feed and that used for industrial purposes, divided by the total population. The figures given are the latest available.

Calories. Of all countries in the world, based on the latest available data, Belgium and Luxembourg have the largest available total of calories per person. The net supply averaged 3,645 per day in 1974. The lowest *reported* figure is 1,728 calories per day in Upper Volta in 1974. The highest calorific value of any foodstuff is that of pure animal fat, with 930 calories per 100 grams (3.5 oz.). Pure alcohol provides 710 calories per 100 grams.

Protein. Australia and New Zealand have the highest recorded consumption of protein per person, an average of 106 grams (3.79 oz.) per day in 1969.

Cereals. The greatest consumers of cereal products—flour, milled rice, etc.—are the people of Egypt, with an average of about 500 lbs. per person annually (600 grams per day) in 1966–67. Figures for 1977 from China suggest a possible consumption (including rice) of 890 grams (31.3 oz.).

Starch. The greatest eaters of starchy food are the people of the U.S., who consumed 4.02 lbs. per person per day in 1972.

Sugar. The greatest consumers of sugars are the people of Bulgaria, with an average of 6.26 oz. per person per day in 1977.

Meat. The greatest meat eaters in the world—figures include organs and poultry—are the people of the U.S., with an average consumption of 10.89 oz. per person per day in 1977.

Soft Drinks. The people of the U.S. undoubtedly consume more carbonated soft drinks than any other people—30.3 gallons per person in 1972, up from 16.8 gallons in 1962. Coffee consumption in the U.S. in the same period dropped from 39.2 gallons to 35.6 gallons per person in 1972, but tea increased from 6.1 to 7.2 gallons. Cold juices (not included in the soft drink totals) reached 5 gallons per person in 1972.

Alcoholic Beverages

Beer. Of reporting countries, the nation with the highest beer consumption per person is West Germany, with 39.2 U.S. gallons per person in 1977. In the Northern Territory of Australia, however, the annual intake has been estimated to be as high as 62.4 U.S. gallons per person. A society for the prevention of alcoholism in Darwin had to disband in June, 1966, for lack of support.

Wine. The greatest wine drinkers are the French, who consumed 26.6 gallons per person for the year 1977.

Spirits. The greatest consumers of spirits are the people of Poland, who, in 1977, consumed an average of 1½ gallons per person per year.

Prohibition. The longest-lasting imposition of prohibition against consumption of alcoholic beverages has been 26 years in Iceland (1908–34). Other prohibitions have been in Russia, later the U.S.S.R. (1914–24), and the United States (1920–33). The Faroe Islands have had a public (as opposed to private licensed) prohibition since 1918.

Biggest Round. The largest round of drinks ever recorded was one for 1,222 people stood by the *Sunday Sun* and shouted by Jack Amos in Newcastle upon Tyne, England, in October, 1974, at the conclusion of the Jack o' Clubs road show.

Largest Dish

The largest single dish in the world is roasted camel, prepared occasionally for Bedouin wedding feasts. Cooked eggs are stuffed in fish, the fish stuffed in cooked chickens, the chickens stuffed into a roasted sheep carcass and the sheep stuffed into a whole camel.

Largest Banquet

The greatest outdoor banquet ever staged was that by President Loubet, President of France, in the gardens of the Tuileries, Paris, on September 22, 1900. He invited the mayors of France and their deputies, ending up with 22,295 guests. With the Gallic penchant for round numbers, the event has always been referred to as "le banquet des 100,000 maires." It was estimated that some 30,000 attended a military feast at Radewitz, Poland, on June 25, 1730, thrown by King August II (1709–1733).

LARGEST DOUGHNUT (above): It took 8 people to lift this 74-lb. doughnut out of a 3-foot-deep cooking vat. Baked by the Holly Drive Baptist Church of Richardson, Texas, on July 9, 1978, the glazed doughnut had a 5-foot-9-inch diameter. LONGEST BREAKFAST TABLE (right): Breakfast for 17,000 was served at this table, stretching 2,000 feet through the streets of Battle Creek, Michigan, on June 9, 1979.

The greatest number of people served indoors at a single sitting was 18,000 municipal leaders at the Palais de l'Industrie, Paris, on August 18, 1889.

The menu for the main 5½-hour banquet at the Imperial Iranian 2,500th anniversary gathering at Persepolis in October, 1971 (see *Party Giving* in Chapter 11), was probably the most expensive ever compiled. It comprised quail eggs stuffed with Iranian caviar, a mousse of crayfish tails in Nantua sauce, stuffed rack of roast lamb, with a main course of roast peacock stuffed with *foie gras*, fig rings, and raspberry sweet champagne sherbet. Wines included *Château Lafite Rothschild* 1945 at $100 per bottle from the cellars of Maxim's, Paris.

Most Expensive Food

The most expensive non-seasonal food is white truffle of Alba, Italy, which sells according to its rarity for as high as $200 per lb. on the U.S. market. Truffles from oak roots in the Périgord district of France require drought between mid-July and mid-August. Only 7 of Europe's 70 species of this hypogeous mycorrhizal fungus are considered edible.

Most Expensive Fruit

One pound of strawberries (30 berries) was sold at auction on April 5, 1977, by John Synnott of Ashford, Ireland, to restaurateur Mr. Leslie Cooke in the Dublin Fruit Market for £530 ($900) or $30 per berry.

Largest Pies

The largest apple pie ever baked was that in a 16-foot-8-inch-diameter dish at the Orleans County Fair, New York State, on August 2–3, 1977. Baking time of the 300 bushels of apples and 5,950 lbs. of sugar was 4 hours 40 minutes. The total weight was 21,210 lbs.

The largest cherry pie weighed 7 tons and contained 4,950 lbs. of cherries. It measured 14 feet 4 inches in diameter, 24 inches in depth and was baked on the grounds of the Medusa Cement Corporation, Charlevoix, Michigan, on May 15, 1976, as part of the town's Bicentennial celebration.

The largest mince pie was one of 2,260 lbs., measuring 20 feet by 5 feet, baked at Ashby-de-la-Zouch, Leicestershire, England, on October 15, 1932.

The largest meat pie ever baked weighed 6.4 tons, measuring 18 feet by 6 feet and 18 inches deep, in Denby Dale, West Yorkshire, England, and was baked on September 5, 1964. This was the eighth in a series begun in 1788, baked to commemorate important events in the history of the English monarchy. The fourth, for Queen Victoria's Jubilee in 1887, went a bit "off" and had to be buried in quicklime.

Biggest Barbecue

The most monumental barbecue was one for over 4,000 people at Brisbane, California, on September 16, 1973, with a rotisserie with a 12-foot spit length impaling 7 buffaloes with a dressed weight of 3,755 lbs. John De Marco supervised the 26-hour roast.

The 1979 annual Lancaster Sertoma in Pennsylvania served 20,500 barbecued chickens.

Longest Bread

The longest one-piece loaf ever baked was one of 684 feet 6 inches baked by Buttercup Bakeries, Unanderra, New South Wales, Australia, on July 22, 1978, and sold to the public by the Apex Club of Corrimal.

Largest Cakes

The largest cake ever assembled was the Baltimore City, Maryland, Bicentennial Cake of July 4, 1976, with ingredients weighing 69,860 lbs. It contained an estimated 10,000 dozen eggs, 21,600 lbs. of sugar, and a 415-lb. pinch of salt.

The tallest recorded free-standing wedding cake was one of 39 tiers, 23 feet 7 inches tall, baked and constructed by Mrs. Rhoda Murray and Roy Butterworth on October 20, 1978, in the Halifax Shopping Center, Halifax, Nova Scotia, Canada.

Largest Chocolate Easter Egg

The largest Easter egg ever made was one of 4,484 lbs. made on March 2–16, 1978, by Red Tulip Chocolates Pty. Ltd. of Prahran, Victoria, Australia. It was 10 feet 2½ inches high and 24 feet 9 inches in circumference.

LARGEST HAMBURGER: The 2,859-lb. beefburger is paraded through the streets of Perth, Western Australia in 1975.

Largest Pancake

The largest pancake ever flipped intact on any griddle was one of 12 feet in diameter by the Liberal Jaycees at Liberal, Kansas, on February 9, 1975. Due to difficulties in establishing appropriate guidelines for judging, this category is now discontinued and no further entries will be considered.

Largest Hamburger

The largest burger (made of beef) on record is one of 2,859 lbs., 27½ feet in circumference, exhibited by Tip Top Butchers and Noonan's Bakery Pty. Ltd. at the Perth Royal Show, Western Australia, on September 24, 1975.

Largest Omelette

The largest omelette ever made was one produced with 12,440 eggs in a pan measuring 30 feet by 10 feet, cooked by students at Conestoga College, Kitchener, Ontario, Canada, on June 29, 1979.

Largest Pizza

The largest pizza ever baked was one measuring 80 feet 1 inch in diameter, 5,027 square feet in area, and 18,664 lbs. in weight at the Oma Pizza Restaurant, Glens Falls, New York, owned by Lorenzo Amato, on October 8, 1978. It was cut into 60,318 slices. (See photo, page K.)

Largest Popsicle®

The world's largest iced lollipop on a stick was one of 5,750 lbs. constructed for the Westside Assembly of God Church, Davenport, Iowa, on September 7, 1975.

Biggest Salami

The largest salami on record is one 18 feet 10 inches long with a circumference of 28 inches, weighing 457 lbs., made by La Ron Meat Co., Cosby, Missouri on January 29, 1978.

Longest Sausage

The longest sausage ever recorded was one of 2 miles made by Dewhurst's at Thamesmead, England, on May 28, 1979, and cooked by Scouts at The Great Children's Party in Hyde Park, May 30–31, 1979. It was made with pork and seasoning and weighed 2,740 lbs.

Largest Sundae

The most monstrous ice cream sundae ever concocted is one of 8,100 lbs. of ice cream plus 90 lbs. of walnuts, 160 lbs. of chocolate syrup and 12 gallons of whipped topping, constructed by the Class of '82 at Smith College, Northampton, Massachusetts, on April 29, 1979.

Longest Banana Split

The longest banana split ever made was 1 mile 99 yards in length, embracing 11,333 bananas, 34,000 scoops of ice cream, 260 Imperial gallons of topping, 160 lbs. of chopped nuts and 100 gallons of whipped cream, made at the annual fete of the Cleveland State High School, Queensland, Australia, on November 20, 1976.

Spices

Most Expensive. The most expensive of common spices is Mediterranean saffron (*Crocus sativus*). It takes 96,000 stigmas and therefore 32,000 flowers to make a pound. Packets of 0.045 oz. are retailed in England for about $6—equivalent to $2,133 per pound.

Prices for unprocessed ginseng (root of *Panax quinquefolius*), thought to have aphrodisiacal quality, were reported in September, 1977, to be as high as $2,000 per ounce.

"Hottest." The hottest of all spices is claimed to be Siling labuyo from the Philippines.

Rarest Condiment. The world's most prized condiment is Ca Cuong, a secretion recovered in minute amounts from beetles in North Vietnam. Owing to war conditions, the price rose to $100 per ounce before supplies virtually ceased in 1975.

Candy

The biggest candy eaters in the world are the people of Britain, with 7.8 oz. of confectionery per person per week in 1971. The figure for Scotland alone is more than 9 oz. in 1968.

The world's top-selling candies are Life Savers, with 25,000 million rolls between 1913 and November 14, 1973. The aggregate depth of the "hole in the middle" exceeds 1,000,000 miles. Paul Shirley, 21, of Sydney, Australia, made one last for 4 hours 40 minutes on February 15, 1979.

The world's greatest coffee drinkers are the people of Sweden, who consumed 17.34 lbs. of coffee per person per year in 1978.

The most expensive coffee is Jamaican High Mountain Supreme, which is retailed in the U.S. at prices varying from $5 per lb. upwards, when most coffees are selling at $2.50 per lb.

Tea

The world's greatest tea drinkers are the people of Ireland, who consumed 8.21 lbs. of tea per person per year in 1977.

The most expensive tea marketed is "Oolong Leaf Bud," specially imported by Fortnum and Mason of Piccadilly, London, where in May, 1978, it retailed for $28.90 per lb. It is blended from very young Formosan leaves.

Fresh Water

The world's greatest consumers of fresh water are the people and industrial users of the U.S., whose average consumption was 1,855 gallons per person per day in 1974.

ENERGY

To express the various forms of available energy (coal, liquid fuels and water power, etc., but omitting vegetable fuels and peat), it is the practice to convert them all into terms of coal. On this basis the world average consumption was the equivalent of 4,528 lbs. of coal, or its energy equivalents, per person in 1974. The lowest recorded average for 1974 was 28.6 lbs. per person in Rwanda. In the same year, the U.S. had the highest average consumption at 25,320 lbs. per person.

COMMUNICATION AND TRANSPORTATION

Merchant Shipping

The world total of merchant shipping (excluding vessels of less than 100 tons gross, sailing vessels and barges) was 69,020 vessels of 406,001,979 tons gross on July 1, 1978. The largest merchant fleet in the world as of mid-1978 was under the flag of Liberia with 2,523 ships of 80,191,329 tons gross.

Largest and Busiest Ports

Physically, the largest port in the world is New York Harbor. The port has a navigable waterfront of 755 miles (460 miles in New York State and 295 miles in New Jersey) stretching over 92 square miles. A total of 261 general cargo berths and 130 other piers give a total berthing capacity of 391 ships at one time. The total warehousing floor space is 18,400,000 square feet (422.4 acres).

The world's busiest port and largest artificial harbor is the Rotterdam-Europoort in the Netherlands, which covers 38 square miles. It handled 31,042 sea-going vessels carrying a total of 280,000,000 metric tons of sea-going cargo, and about 200,000 barges, in 1978. It is able to handle 310 sea-going vessels simultaneously, of up to 318,000 metric tons and 68 feet draught.

Airlines

The country with the busiest airlines system is the U.S., where 193,218,837,000 revenue passenger miles were flown on scheduled domestic and local services in 1977. This was equivalent to an annual trip of 891.1 miles for every inhabitant of the U.S.

Railroads

The country with the greatest length of railroad is the U.S., with 200,000 miles of track on January 1, 1979.

Roads

The oldest trackway yet discovered in the world is the Sweet track, Shapwick, Somerset, England, which has been dated to 4000 B.C.

The country with the greatest length of road is the U.S. (50 states), with 3,814,970 miles of graded roads in 1977.

Busiest. The highest traffic volume of any point in the world is at East Los Angeles interchange (Santa Ana, Pomona, Golden State, and Santa Monica Freeways), California, with a 24-hour average on weekdays of 443,000 vehicles in 1976. The most heavily traveled stretch of road is between 43rd and 47th Street on the Dan Ryan Expressway in Chicago, with an average daily volume of 254,700 vehicles.

The territory with the highest traffic density in the world is Hong Kong. By January 1, 1977, there were 191,146 motor vehicles on 678 miles of serviceable roads giving a density of 6.24 yards per vehicle.

Traffic Jam. Probably the longest traffic jam in the world was one in Britain of 35 miles between Torquay and Yarcombe, Devon, on July 25, 1964, which was equaled by another in Britain on the A30 between Egham (Surrey) and Micheldever (Hampshire) on May 23, 1970.

Widest. The widest street in the world is the Monumental Axis, running for $1\frac{1}{2}$ miles from the Municipal Plaza to the Plaza of the Three Powers in Brasilia, the capital of Brazil. The six-lane boulevard was opened in April, 1960, and is 273.4 yards wide.

The Bay Bridge Toll Plaza has 23 lanes (17 westbound) serving San Francisco and Oakland.

Narrowest. The narrowest street in the world is in Port Isaac, Cornwall, England, where Temple Bar, at its junction with Dolphin Street, is $19\frac{5}{16}$ inches wide at its narrowest point. It is popularly known as "Squeeze-Belly Alley."

Shortest. The shortest true street in Britain and probably in the world is Tolbooth Street in Falkirk, Scotland, which is 58 feet long.

The shortest length of restricted road is probably Kelbrook Road, Salterforth, Lancashire with $336\frac{1}{2}$ feet between 30 m.p.h. signs.

LARGEST SQUARE: The Chairman Mao Memorial Hall stands in the middle of Tien An Men Square in Peking (see page 420).

Longest. The longest motorable road in the world is the Pan-American Highway, which will stretch 17,018 miles from northwest Alaska to southernmost Chile. There remains a gap of 250 miles, known as the Tapon del Darién in Panama, and as the Atrato Swamp where it is in Colombia. The first complete traverse was made by the 1972 British Trans-Americas Expedition led by Lt. Col. John Blashford-Snell, which emerged from the Atrato Swamp after 99 days. The Range Rover VXC 868 K which left Alaska on December 3, 1971, arrived in Tierra del Fuego on June 9, 1972.

The longest uninterrupted stretch of highway is the $3,500,000,000 Interstate 75, which opened on December 21, 1977, and now runs 1,564 miles from Sault Ste. Marie, Michigan, to Tampa, Florida, without a traffic light.

The longest designated street in the world is Yonge Street, which runs north and west from Toronto, Canada. The first stretch, completed on February 16, 1796, ran 34½ miles. Its official length, now extended to Rainy River at the Manitoba-Minnesota border, is 1,178.3 miles.

Steepest. The steepest streets in the world are Filbert Street, Russian Hill and 22nd Street, Dolores Heights, San Francisco, with gradients of 31.5 per cent or a rise of 1 foot for every 3.17 feet.

Crookedest. Lombard Street in San Francisco between Hyde and Leavenworth has 5 consecutive hairpin turns as it descends steeply one way.

Highest. The highest trail in the world is an 8-mile stretch of the Kang-ti-suu between Khaleb and Hsin-chi-fu, Tibet, which in two places exceeds 20,000 feet. The highest motor road in the world is one 733.2 miles long between Tibet and southwestern Sinkiang, completed in October, 1957, which includes passes of an altitude up to 18,480 feet above sea level.

DRIVE TO LEARN TO DRIVE: Mrs. Miriam Hargrave of Yorkshire, England continued taking and failing driving tests until she succeeded on her 40th attempt.

Lowest. The lowest road is that along the Israeli shores of the Dead Sea, 1,290 feet below sea level. The world's lowest pass is the Rock Reef Pass in Everglades National Park, Florida, which is 3 feet above sea level.

Biggest Square

The Tien An Men (Gate of Heavenly Peace) Square in Peking, described as the navel of China, extends over 98 acres.

Drivers' Licenses

Regular drivers' licenses are issuable as young as 15 without a driver education course only in Hawaii and Mississippi. Thirteen U.S. states issue restricted juvenile licenses at 14.

Oldest Driver

Roy M. Rawlins (born July 10, 1870) of Stockton, California, was warned for driving at 95 m.p.h. in a 55-m.p.h. zone in June, 1974. On August 25, 1974, he was awarded a California State license valid until 1978, but he died in 1975, aged 105. Maude Tull of Inglewood, California, who began driving after her husband's death, when she was aged 91, was issued a renewal of her license on February 5, 1976, then aged 104.

Most Failures on Learner's Test

The record for persistence in taking and failing a test for a driver's license is held by Mrs. Miriam Hargrave, 62, of Wakefield, Yorkshire, England, who finally passed her 40th driving test on August 3, 1970. She spent $720 on driving lessons and could no longer afford to buy a car. In 1978, she was reported to dislike right-hand turns.

Mrs. Fannie Turner (b. 1903) of Little Rock, Arkansas, passed her *written* test for a driver's license on her 104th attempt in October, 1978.

The world's easiest test for a driver's license is given in Egypt, where the ability to drive 6 meters (19.7 feet) forward and 6 meters in reverse has been deemed sufficient.

Worst Driver

It was reported that a 75-year-old *male* driver received 10 traffic tickets, drove on the wrong side of the road four times, committed four hit-and-run offenses and caused six accidents, all within 20 minutes, in McKinney, Texas, on October 15, 1966.

Earliest Traffic Lights

Semaphore-type traffic *signals* were set up in Parliament Square, London in 1868, with red and green gas lamps for night use. The first traffic light was installed in 1919 in Detroit.

Earliest Parking Meters

The earliest parking meters ever installed were those put in the business district of Oklahoma City, Oklahoma, on July 19, 1935. They were the invention of Carl C. Magee (U.S.).

Inland Waterways

The country with the greatest length of inland waterways is Finland. The total length of navigable lakes and rivers is about 31,000 miles.

Longest Navigable River. The longest navigable natural waterway in the world is the Amazon River, which sea-going vessels can ascend as far as Iquitos, in Peru, 2,236 miles from the Atlantic seaboard.

On a National Geographic Society expedition ending on March 10, 1969, Helen and Frank Schreider navigated downstream from San Francisco, Peru, 3,845 miles up the Amazon to Bélem.

Telephones

There were approximately 423,082,000 telephones in the world on January 1, 1978, it was estimated by the American Telephone and Telegraph Co. The country with the greatest number was the U.S., with 162,076,000 instruments, equivalent to 744 for every 1,000 people. The territory with fewest is Pitcairn Island with 32.

The country with the most telephones per head of population is Midway Islands, with 1,296 per 1,000 of the population on January 1, 1978. The countries with the least phones are Chad, Rwanda, Upper Volta and Nepal, each with less than 1 telephone per 1,000 people.

The greatest total of calls made in any country is in the U.S., with 221,482,530,600 in 1977.

The city with most telephones is New York City, with 5,936,829 (808 per 1,000 people) as of January 1, 1978. In 1978, Washington, D.C., reached the level of 1,495 telephones per 1,000 people, though in some small areas there are still higher densities, such as Beverly Hills, part of Los Angeles, with about 1,600 per 1,000.

Longest Cable. The world's longest submarine telephone cable is the Commonwealth Pacific Cable (COMPAC), which runs for more than 9,000 miles from Australia *via* Auckland, New Zealand,

and the Hawaiian Islands to Port Alberni, Canada. It cost about $98,000,000 and was inaugurated on December 2, 1963.

Busiest Phone. The pay phone with the heaviest usage in the world is one in the Greyhound bus terminal in Chicago, which averages 270 calls a day, and is thus used each 5 minutes 20 seconds around the clock all year.

Largest Incorrect Bill. On August 18, 1975, the landlord of the Blue Bell Inn, Lichfield, Staffordshire, England, received a telephone bill for $4,386,800,000. It was later found that this bill contained "an arithmetical error."

Postal Services

The country with the largest mail in the world is the U.S., whose people posted over 92 billion letters and packages in 1977. The U.S. Postal Service then employed 655,097 people.

The U.S. also takes first place in the average number of letters which each person mails during one year. The figure was 427 in 1977. Of all countries, the greatest discrepancy between incoming and outgoing mails is for the U.S. where, in 1970, only 887 million items were mailed abroad in comparison with 1,477,000,000 items received from foreign sources.

Postage Stamps

Earliest. The earliest adhesive postage stamps ever issued were the "Penny Blacks" of the United Kingdom, bearing the head of Queen Victoria, placed on sale on May 1 for use on May 6, 1840. A total of 68,158,080 were printed. The British National Postal Museum possesses a unique full proof sheet of 240 stamps printed in April, 1840, before the corner letters, plate numbers or marginal inscriptions were added.

Largest. The largest stamps ever issued were the special purpose 1913 Express Delivery stamps of China, which measured $9\frac{3}{4}$ inches by $2\frac{3}{4}$ inches.

The largest standard postage stamp was the 250 mils issue of Cyprus on July 2, 1974, which measured $4\frac{3}{8}$ by $3\frac{1}{2}$ inches.

Smallest. The smallest stamps ever issued were the 10 cents and 1 peso of the Colombian State of Bolívar in 1863–66. They measured 0.31 of an inch (8 mm.) by 0.37 of an inch (9.5 mm.).

The imperforate 4/4 schilling red of Mecklenburg-Schwerin issued on July 1, 1856, printed in Berlin, was divisible into four quarters. Thus a 1/4 section measured fractionally over 0.394 of an inch (10 mm.) square.

Highest and Lowest Denominations. The highest denomination stamp ever issued was a red and black stamp for £100 ($280) issued in Kenya in 1925–27. Although valid for postage, it was essentially for collection of revenue.

Owing to demonetization and inflation it is difficult to determine the lowest denomination stamp but it was probably the 1946 3000 pengö Hungarian stamp, worth at the time 1.6×10^{-14} parts of a cent.

EARLIEST STAMP: The first adhesive stamp was the "Penny Black," issued in May, 1840.

Largest Collection. The greatest private stamp collection ever auctioned was that of Maurice Burrus (died 1959) of Alsace, France, which realized between $3,250,000 and $4,000,000. He himself valued the collection at $10,000,000.

The largest national collection in the world is that at the British Museum, London, which has had the General Post Office collection on permanent loan since March, 1963. The British Royal collection, housed in 400 volumes, is also believed to be worth well in excess of £1,000,000 ($2,500,000). The collection of the Universal Postal Union (founded October 9, 1874) in Berne, Switzerland, started in 1878, has received 155,000 issued stamps and 2,400 miniature sheets, all of them different, from its member nations. The largest international collection open to the public is in the Swiss Postal Museum in Berne.

Highest Price. The highest price ever paid for a single philatelic item is 1,000,000 deutsche marks (about $520,000) for a Swedish

HIGHEST DENOMINATION STAMP: This red and black stamp can be used for postage, but was issued mostly for revenue collection.

3 skilling banco yellow color error of 1855. The item was bought by an anonymous buyer at an auction in Hamburg, West Germany, on October 17, 1978.

One of the world's rarest stamps, the unique 1-cent black on magenta British Guiana of 1856, was sold by F. T. Small to Irwin Weinberg by Robson Lawe in New York City on March 24, 1970. The stamp was priced in a 1979 catalogue at $700,000. This same stamp was bought from a British schoolboy, L. Vernon Vaughan, for 84 cents in 1873.

Postal Addresses

Earliest Numbering. The practice of numbering houses began in 1463 on the Pont Notre Dame, Paris, France.

Post Boxes. Pillar boxes were introduced at the suggestion of the English novelist Anthony Trollope (1815–82). The oldest original site still in service is one dating from February 8, 1853, at Union Street, St. Peter Port, Guernsey, Channel Islands. The present box is not the original.

Telegrams

The country where most telegrams are sent is the U.S.S.R., whose population sent about 478,535,000 telegrams in 1977.

5. Education

Illiteracy

Literacy is variously defined as "ability to read simple subjects" and "ability to read and write a simple letter." The looseness of definition and the scarcity of data for many countries preclude

LARGEST UNIVERSITY BUILDING: Located on the Lenin Hills south of Moscow, this 32-story structure contains 40,000 rooms.

OLDEST UNIVERSITY:
Shown is the principal
entry to the University of
Karueein, founded in
859.

anything more than approximations, but the extent of illiteracy
among adults (15 years old and over) is estimated to have been 34.7
per cent in 1969.

The continent with the greatest proportion of illiterates is Africa,
where 81.5 per cent of adults were illiterate. The last published
figure for Mali in 1960 showed 97.8 per cent of people over 15 were
unable to read.

Universities

Oldest. Probably the oldest educational institution in the world
is the University of Karueein, founded in 859 A.D. in Fez, Morocco.

Greatest Enrollment. The university with the greatest enrollment in the world is the State University of New York, with 344,000
students enrolled in 1978. Its oldest college, at Albany, New York,
was founded in 1844.

Largest. Bids for the $3,400,000,000 University of Riyadh, Saudi
Arabia, closed in June, 1978. The University will house 15,000
families and have its own mass transportation system.

The largest existing university building in the world is the
M. V. Lomonosov State University on the Lenin Hills, south of
Moscow, U.S.S.R. It stands 787.4 feet tall, has 32 stories and con-
tains 40,000 rooms. It was constructed in 1949–53.

Professors

Youngest. The youngest at which anybody has been elected to a
chair (full professorship) in a major university is 19, in the case of
Colin MacLaurin (1698–1746), who was admitted to Marischal
College, Aberdeen, Scotland, as Professor of Mathematics on
September 30, 1717. In 1725 he was made Professor of Mathematics
at Edinburgh University on the recommendation of Sir Isaac Newton.

In July, 1967, Dr. Harvey Friedman, Ph.D., was appointed Assistant Professor of Mathematics at Stanford University, California, when aged just 19 years.

Most Durable. The longest period for which any professorship has been held is 63 years, in the case of Thomas Martyn (1735–1825), Professor of Botany at Cambridge University from 1762 until his death. His father, John Martyn (1699–1768), had occupied the chair from 1732 to 1762.

Dr. Joel Hildebrand (b. November, 1881), Professor Emeritus of Physical Chemistry at the University of California, Berkeley, first became an Assistant Professor in 1913, and was still researching in 1978.

Most Durable Teachers

David Rhys Davies (1835–1928) taught as a pupil teacher, teacher and, from 1879 to his death, as headmaster of Dame Anna Child's School, Whitton, Powys, England, for a total of 76 years 2 months.

Colonel Ernest Achay Loftus (born January 11, 1884) served as a teacher over a span of 73 years, from September, 1901, in York, England, until February 18, 1975, in Zambia, when he retired, aged 91 years 38 days. This also qualified him as the world's oldest civil servant.

Most Eternal Students

After 23 years as a student, George A. Goulty of Guildford, Surrey, England, submitted his thesis for a Ph.D., after having acquired eight degrees previously.

Mrs. Sarah Ann Raw joined Hendon College, Greater London, on September 29, 1976, for further education in lip-reading, aged 102 years 9 months.

Miss Mabel Fitzgerald received an honorary M.A. degree from Oxford University on December 14, 1972, aged 100 years 113 days, in recognition of work done in the 19th century before the School of Physiology was open to women.

Youngest Undergraduate

The most extreme recorded case of academic juvenility was that of William Thomson (1824–1907), later Lord Kelvin, who entered Glasgow University aged 10 years 4 months in October, 1834, and matriculated on November 14, 1834.

Dr. Merrill Kenneth Wolf (born August 28, 1931) of Cleveland, Ohio, took his B.A. in music from Yale University in September, 1945, aged 14 years.

Schools

Largest. The largest school enrollment in the world was at De Witt Clinton High School in the Bronx, New York City, where it attained a peak of 12,000 in 1934. It was founded in 1897 and now has an enrollment of 4,500.

Most Expensive. L'Institut "Le Rosey" at Rolle, Switzerland, charges annual fees of at least 25,000 Swiss francs ($14,350).

Most Schools Attended

The documented record for the greatest number of schools attended by a pupil is 265 by Wilma Williams, now Mrs. R. J. Horton, from 1933 to 1943 when her parents were in show business in the U.S.

Lecture Agency

The world's largest lecture agency is the American Program Bureau of Boston with 400 personalities on 40 major subject areas and a turnover of some $5,000,000. The top rate is $4,000 per hour commanded by Ralph Nader, equivalent to $66.66 per minute.

6. Religions

Oldest

The oldest major formal religion is Hinduism. Its Vedic precursor was brought to India by Aryans *c.* 1500 B.C. The Rig Veda Hindu hymnal was codified *c.* 900 B.C. or earlier.

Largest. Religious statistics are necessarily only approximate. The test of adherence to a religion varies widely in rigor, while many individuals, particularly in the East, belong to two or more religions.

Christianity is the world's prevailing religion, with some 1,070,000,000 adherents in 1978. The Vatican statistics office reported that in 1978 there were 724,434,000 Roman Catholics including priests and nuns. The largest non-Christian religion is Islam (Muslim) with about 550,000,000 followers.

Largest Clergy. The world's largest religious organization is the Roman Catholic Church, with 1,494,090 clergy (1978 estimate), 401,168 priests and 956,734 nuns. The total number of cardinals, archbishops and bishops is 2,947. There are about 420,000 churches.

Jews. The total of world Jewry was estimated to be 14,300,000 in 1978. The highest concentration was in the U.S., with 5,800,000 of whom 2,000,000 are in the New York area. The total in Israel is 3,060,000, in Britain 410,000 (of whom 280,000 are in Greater London). The total in Tokyo, Japan, is less than 1,000.

Earliest Shrine

The earliest known shrine dates from the proto-neolithic Natufian culture in Jericho, where a site on virgin soil has been dated to the 9th millennium B.C. A simple rectilinear red-plastered room with a niche housing a stone pillar, believed to be the shrine of a pre-pottery fertility cult dating from *c.* 6500 B.C., was also uncovered in Jericho (also called Eriha) in the Israeli-occupied West Bank of Jordan. The oldest surviving Christian church in the world is Qal'at es Salihiye in eastern Syria, dating from 232 A.D.

Largest Temple. The largest religious building ever constructed is Angkor Wat (City Temple), covering 402 acres, in Cambodia. It was built to the God Vishnu by the Khmer King Suryavarman II in the period 1113–1150. Its curtain wall measures 1,400 yards by 1,400 yards and its population, before it was abandoned in 1432, was at times 80,000.

LARGEST BUDDHIST TEMPLE: The highly adorned and ornamented Borobudur in Indonesia covers the entire upper section of a large hill.

The largest Buddhist temple is Borobudur, near Jogjakarta, Indonesia, built in the 8th century.

The largest Mormon temple is in Kensington, Maryland, dedicated in November, 1974, with a floor area of 159,000 square feet.

Largest Mosque. The largest mosque ever built was the now ruined al-Malawiya mosque of al-Mutawakil in Samarra, Iraq, built in 842–852 A.D. and measuring 401,408 square feet (9.21 acres) with dimensions of 784 feet by 512 feet.

The world's largest mosque in use is the Umayyad Mosque in Damascus, Syria, built on a 2,000-year-old religious site measuring 515 feet by 318 feet, thus covering an area of 3.76 acres.

The largest mosque will be the Merdeka Mosque in Djakarta, Indonesia, which was begun in 1962. The cupola will be 147.6 feet in diameter and the capacity in excess of 50,000 people.

Largest Synagogue. The largest synagogue in the world is the Temple Emanu-El on Fifth Avenue at 65th Street, New York City. The temple, completed in September, 1929, has a frontage of 150 feet on Fifth Avenue and 253 feet on 65th Street. The sanctuary proper can accommodate 2,500 people, and the adjoining Beth-El Chapel seats 350. When all the facilities are in use, more than 6,000 people can be accommodated.

Cathedrals

Largest. The world's largest cathedral is the cathedral church of the Episcopalian Diocese of New York, St. John the Divine, with a floor area of 121,000 square feet and a volume of 16,822,000 cubic feet. The cornerstone was laid on December 27, 1892, and the Gothic building was still uncompleted in 1979. In New York it is referred to as "Saint John the Unfinished." The nave is the longest in the world, 601 feet in length, with a vaulting 124 feet in height.

The cathedral covering the largest area is that of Santa María de la Sede in Seville, Spain. It was built in Spanish Gothic style be-

LARGEST CATHEDRAL (above): New York's St. John the Divine cathedral was begun in 1892 and is still unfinished. **LARGEST SYNAGOGUE:** Temple Emanu-El can accommodate more than 6,000 worshippers.

tween 1402 and 1519 and is 414 feet long, 271 feet wide and 100 feet high to the vault of the nave.

See also *Largest Church.*

Smallest. The smallest cathedral in the world is the Cathedral Chapel of St. Francis of the American Catholic Church, built in 1933 at Laguna Beach, California, with an area of 1,008 square feet and seating for 42 people.

Churches

Largest. The largest church in the world is the basilica of St. Peter, built between 1492 and 1612 in the Vatican City, Rome. Its length, measured from the apse, is 611 feet 4 inches. Its area is 18,110 square yards. The inner diameter of the famous dome is 137 feet 9 inches and its center is 390 feet 5 inches high. The external height is 457 feet 9 inches.

The elliptical Basilique de St. Pie X at Lourdes, France, completed in 1957 at a cost of $5,600,000, has a capacity of 20,000 under its giant span arches and a length of 656 feet.

The crypt of the underground Civil War Memorial Church in the Guadarrama Mountains, 28 miles from Madrid, Spain, is 853 feet in length. It took 21 years (1937–58) to build, at a reported cost of $392,000,000 and is surmounted by a cross 492 feet tall.

Smallest. The world's smallest church is the Union Church at Wiscasset, Maine, with a floor area of 31½ square feet (7 feet by 4½ feet). Les Vauxbelets Church in Guernsey, Channel Islands, has an area of 16 feet by 12 feet, room for one priest and a congregation of two.

Tallest Spires. The tallest cathedral spire in the world is that of the Protestant Cathedral of Ulm in Germany. The building is early Gothic and was begun in 1377. The tower, in the center of the west façade, was not finally completed until 1890 and is 528 feet high.

The world's tallest church spire is that of the Chicago Temple of the First Methodist Church on Clark Street, Chicago. The building consists of a 22-story skyscraper (erected in 1924) surmounted by a parsonage at 330 feet, a "Sky Chapel" at 400 feet and a steeple cross at 568 feet above street level.

Tallest Minaret. The world's tallest minaret is the Qutb Minar, south of New Delhi, India, built in 1194 to a height of 238 feet.

Tallest Pagoda. The world's tallest pagoda is the 326-foot-tall Shwe Dagon Pagoda in Rangoon, Burma, which was increased to its present height by Hsinbyushin, King of Ava (1763–1776).

Oldest Pagoda. The oldest pagoda in China is Sung-Yo Ssu in Honan, built with 15 12-sided stories in 523 A.D.

Saints

There are 1,848 "registered" saints (including 60 St. Johns), of whom 628 are Italians, 576 French and 271 from the British Isles. The total includes 15 Popes. The first U.S.-born saint is Mother Elizabeth Ann Bayley Seton (1774–1821) who was canonized on September 14, 1975.

Most and Least Rapidly Canonized. The shortest interval that has elapsed between the death of a saint and his canonization was in the case of St. Anthony of Padua, Italy, who died on June 13, 1231, and was canonized 352 days later on May 30, 1232.

The other extreme is represented by St. Bernard of Tiron, for 20 years Prior of St. Sabinus, who died in 1117 and was made a saint in 1861—744 years later.

Popes

Longest Reign. The longest reign of any of the 264 Popes has been that of Pius IX (Giovanni Maria Mastai-Ferretti), who reigned for 31 years 236 days from June 16, 1846, until his death, aged 85, on February 7, 1878.

Shortest Reign. Pope Stephen II was elected on March 24, 752, and died two days later.

Oldest. It is recorded that Pope St. Agatho (reigned 678–681) was elected at the age of 103 and lived to 106, but recent scholars have expressed doubts. The oldest of recent Pontiffs has been Pope Leo XIII (Gioacchino Pecci), who was born on March 2, 1810, elected Pope at the third ballot on February 20, 1878, and died on July 20, 1903, aged 93 years 140 days.

Youngest. The youngest of all Popes was Pope Benedict IX (Theophylact), who had three terms as Pope: in 1032–44; April to May, 1045; and November 8, 1047 to July 17, 1048. It would appear that he was aged only 11 or 12 in 1032, though the Catalogue of the Popes admits only to his "extreme youth." He died in 1056.

Last Married. The last married Pope was Adrian II (867–872). Rodrigo Borgia was the father of at least six children before being elected Pope Alexander VI in 1492. The first 37 Popes had no

FIRST U.S. SAINT (above): Mother Elizabeth Ann Bayley Seton was canonized in September, 1975. OLDEST STAINED GLASS WINDOW: In Augsburg Cathedral, Germany, this window depicting the Prophets dates from c. 1050 (see page 432).

specific obligation to celibacy. Pope Hormisdas (514–523) was the father of Pope Silverius (536–537).

Last Non-Italian Pope. The current Pope John Paul II, elected on October 16, 1978 (born Karol Wojtyla, May 18, 1920, at Wadowice, near Krakow, Poland) is the first non-Italian Pope since Cardinal Adrian Florenz Boeyens (Pope Adrian VI) of the Netherlands, crowned on August 31, 1522.

Last Non-Cardinalate Pope. The last Pope elected from outside the College of Cardinals was Bartolomeo Prignano (1318–89), Archbishop of Bari, who was elected Pope Urban VI on April 8, 1378.

Slowest and Quickest Election. After 31 months without declaring "We have a Pope," the cardinals were subjected to a bread and water diet and the removal of the roof of their conclave by the Mayor of Viterbo before electing Teobaldo Visconti (c. 1210–76), the Archbishop of Liège, as Pope Gregory X at Viterbo, near Rome, on September 1, 1271. The papacy was, however, vacant for at least 3 years 214 days in 304–308.

The shortest conclave was that of October 21, 1503, for the election of Pope Julius II on the first ballot.

Cardinals

Oldest. On February 2, 1973, the College of Cardinals contained a record 145 declared members—compared with 135 on May 25, 1979. The oldest was James Francis L. McIntyre, former Archbishop of Los Angeles (1886–1979). The record length of service of any Cardinal has been 60 years 10 days by the Cardinal York, a grandson of James VII of Scotland and II of England, from July 3, 1747, to July 13, 1807. The oldest Cardinal of all time was probably Giorgio da Costa (born Portugal, 1406) who died in Rome on September 18, 1508, aged 102.

Youngest. The youngest Cardinal of all time was Luis Antonio de Bourbon (born July 25, 1727), created on December 19, 1735, aged 8 years 147 days. His son Luis was also made a Cardinal, but at age 23.

The youngest Cardinal is Jaime L. Sin, Archbishop of Manila (born August 31, 1928).

Bishops

Oldest. The oldest Roman Catholic bishop in recent years has been Bishop Angelo Teutonico, formerly Bishop of Aversa (born August 28, 1874), who died on May 30, 1978, aged 103 years 275 days. He had celebrated Mass about 24,800 times.

Bishop Herbert Welch of the United Methodist Church, who was elected a bishop for Japan and Korea in 1916, died on April 4, 1969, aged 106.

Youngest. The youngest bishop of all time was H.R.H. The Duke of York and Albany, the second son of King George III of England, who was elected Bishop of Osnabrück through his father's influence as Elector of Hanover, at the age of 196 days (less than 7 months old) on February 27, 1764. He resigned after 39 years' enjoyment.

Church Attendance

The most extreme recorded case of perfect Sunday School Church attendance is that of Roland E. Daab, currently the Vice President of the Consistory of St. Paul United Church of Christ, Columbia, Illinois, who on February 4, 1979, attended service on his 3,141st consecutive Sunday, an unbroken period of more than 60 years.

Choir Service

Alfred Ernest Pick served in the choir of St. Helen's Church, Wakefield, West Yorkshire, England from August, 1886 to April, 1973, a stretch of 86¾ years. He died on December 23, 1973, at age 95.

Stained Glass

Oldest. The oldest stained glass in the world represents the Prophets in a window of the cathedral of Augsburg, Bavaria, Germany, dating from *c.* 1050.

Largest. The largest stained glass window is the complete mural of The Resurrection Mausoleum, Justice, Illinois, measuring 22,381 square feet in 2,448 panels completed in 1971.

Monumental Brasses

The world's oldest monumental brass is that commemorating Bishop Ysowilpe in St. Andrew's Church, Verden, near Hanover, West Germany, dating from 1231.

Largest Crowd

The greatest recorded number of human beings assembled with a common purpose was an estimated 12,700,000 at the Hindu feast of Kumbh-Mela, which was held at the confluence of the Yamuna (formerly called the Jumna), the Ganges and the invisible "Sarasvati" at Allahabad, Uttar Pradesh, India, on January 19, 1977. The holiest time during this holiest day since 1833 was during the planetary alignment between 9:28 and 9:40 A.M., during which only 200,000 achieved immersion to wash away the sins of a lifetime.

Largest Funeral

The greatest attendance at any funeral is the estimated 4 million who thronged Cairo, Egypt, for the funeral of President Gamal Abdel Nasser (b. January 15, 1918) on October 1, 1970.

Biggest Demonstrations

A figure of 2,700,000 was published from China for the demonstration against the U.S.S.R. in Shanghai on April 3–4, 1969, following border clashes, and one of 10 million for the May Day celebrations of 1963 in Peking.

WORST ACCIDENTS AND DISASTERS IN THE WORLD

	Deaths		
Pandemic	75,000,000	The Black Death (bubonic, pneumonic and septicaemic plague)	1347–51
	21,640,000	Influenza	April–Nov. 1918
Famine	9,500,000[1]	Northern China Feb. 1877–Sept. 1878	
Flood	3,700,000	Yellow (Hwang-ho) River, China	Aug. 1931
Circular Storm	>1,000,000*	Ganges Delta islands, Bangladesh	Nov. 12–13, 1970
Earthquake	830,000	Shensi Province, China (duration 2 hours)	Jan. 23, 1556

---

* The figure published in 1972 of 1,000,000 was from Dr. Afzal, Principal Scientific Officer of the Atomic Energy Authority Centre, Dacca. One report asserted that less than half of the population of the 4 islands of Bhola, Charjabbar, Hatia and Ramagati (1961 Census 1.4 million) survived.

The most damaging hurricane recorded was the billion dollar Betsy (name now retired) in 1965 with an estimated insurance pay-out of $750 million.

Landslide	180,000	Kansu Province, China	Dec. 16, 1920
Atomic Bomb	141,000	Hiroshima, Japan	Aug. 6, 1945
Conventional Bombing[2]	c. 25,000	Dresden, Germany	Feb. 13–15, 1945
Alluvial Flood (Snow avalanche)	c. 25,000[6]	Yungay, Huascaran, Peru	May 31, 1970
Marine (single ship)	c. 7,700	Wilhelm Gustloff (25,484 tons) torpedoed off Danzig by U.S.S.R. submarine S-13	Jan. 30, 1945
Panic[11]	c. 4,000	Chungking, China (air raid shelter)	c. June 8, 1941
Dam Burst	2,209	Johnstown, Pennsylvania (South Fork dam)	May 31, 1889
Explosion	1,963[4]	Halifax, Nova Scotia, Canada	Dec. 6, 1917
Fire[3] (single building)	1,670	The Theatre, Canton, China	May, 1845
Mining[5]	1,572	Honkeiko Colliery, Manchuria, China (coal dust explosion)	April 26, 1942
Riot	c. 1,200	New York City (anti-conscription riots)	July 13–16, 1863
Crocodiles (disputed)	c. 900	Japanese soldiers, Ramree Island, Burma	Feb. 19–20, 1945
Fireworks	>800	Dauphine's wedding, Seine, Paris	May 16, 1770
Tornado	689	South Central States, U.S. (3 hours)	Mar. 18, 1925
Aircraft (Civil)	582	KLM-Pan Am Boeing 747 Ground Crash, Tenerife, Canary Islands	March 27, 1977
Railroad	543[7]	Modane, France	Dec. 12, 1917
Man-Eating Animal	436[8]	Champawat district, India, tigress shot by Col. Jim Corbett	1907
Hail	246	Moradabad, Uttar Pradesh, India	April 20, 1888
Submarine	129	U.S.S. Thresher off Cape Cod, Mass.	April 10, 1963
	129	Le Surcout rammed in Caribbean	Feb. 18, 1942
Road[9] (Single Vehicle)	127	A bus plunged into a canal at Sayyoum, Egypt	August 9, 1973

Helicopter	54	Israeli military "Sea Stallion," West Bank	May 10, 1977
Ski Lift (Cablecar)	42	Cavalese resort, Northern Italy	March 9, 1976
Mountaineering[10]	40	U.S.S.R. Expedition on Mount Everest	Dec., 1952
Lightning (Single Bolt)	21	Hut in Chinamasa Kraal near Umtali, Rhodesia	Dec. 23, 1975
Space	3	Apollo oxygen fire, Cape Kennedy, Fla.	Jan. 27, 1967
	3	Soyuz II re-entry over U.S.S.R.	June 29, 1971

Notes. 1.—In 1770 the great Indian famine carried away a proportion of the population estimated as high as one third, hence a figure of tens of millions. The figure for Bengal alone was probably about 10 million.
It has been estimated that more than 5,000,000 died in the post-World War I famine, in the U.S.S.R. The U.S.S.R. government in July, 1923, informed Mr. (later President) Herbert Hoover that the A.R.A. (American Relief Administration) had, since August, 1921, saved 20,000,000 lives from famine and famine diseases.

2.—The number of civilians killed by the bombing of Germany has been put variously as 593,000 and "over 635,000." A figure of c. 140,000 deaths in U.S.A.F. fire raids on Tokyo of May 10, 1945, has been attributed. Total Japanese fatalities were 600,000 (conventional) and 220,000 (nuclear).

3.—The worst-ever hotel fire killed 162 at the Hotel Taeyokake, Seoul, South Korea, December 25, 1971.

4.—Some sources maintain that the final death toll was over 3,000.

5.—The worst gold mining disaster in South Africa was 152 killed due to flooding in the Witwatersrand Gold Mining Co. gold mine in 1909.

6.—A total of 10,000 Austrian and Italian troops is reputed to have been lost in the Dolomite valley of Northern Italy on Dec. 13, 1916, in more than 100 avalanches. The total is probably exaggerated though bodies were still being found in 1952.

7.—Between 500 and 800 died in the Torro Tunnel, Léon, Spain, train disaster on January 3, 1944.

8.—In the period 1941–42 c. 1,500 Kenyans were killed by a pride of 22 man-eating lions. Eighteen of these were shot by a hunter named Rushby.

9.—The worst year ever for road deaths in the U.S. has been 1969 (about 56,000). The world's highest death rate is said to be in Queensland, Australia, but global statistics are not available. The U.S.'s 2 millionth victim since 1899 died in January, 1973. The global total dead by September, 1975, was put at 25,000,000.

10.—According to Polish sources, not confirmed by the U.S.S.R. On Mt. Fuji, Japan, 23 died in blizzard and avalanche on March 20, 1972.

11.—It was estimated that some 5,000 people were trampled to death in the stampede for free beer at the coronation celebration of Czar Nicholas II in Moscow in May, 1896.

PROGRESSIVE ABSOLUTE HUMAN ALTITUDE RECORDS

Feet	Pilot	Place	Date
80	Jean François Pilâtre de Rozier (France)	Hot Air Balloon (tethered) Fauxbourg, Paris	Oct. 15 & 17, 1783
200	J. F. Pilâtre de Rozier (France)	Hot Air Balloon (tethered) Fauxbourg, Paris	Oct. 19, 1783
250	J. F. Pilâtre de Rozier (France)	Hot Air Balloon (tethered) Fauxbourg, Paris	Oct. 19, 1783
c. 330	de Rozier and the Marquis François Laurent d'Arlandes	Hot Air Balloon (free flight) La Muette, Paris	Nov. 21, 1783
c. 3,000	Jacques Alexander César Charles and Aîné Robert (France)	Hydrogen Balloon Tuileries, Paris	Dec. 1, 1783
c. 9,000	J. A. C. Charles (France)	Hydrogen Balloon Nesle, France	Dec. 1, 1783
c. 20,000	E. G. R. Robertson (U.K.) and Loest (Germany)	Hydrogen Balloon Hamburg, Germany	July 18, 1803
27,950	H. T. Sivel, J. E. Crocé-Spinelli, Gaston Tissandier	Coal gas Balloon *Zenith* La Villette, Paris	Apr. 15, 1875
31,500	Prof. A. Berson (Germany)	Hydrogen Balloon *Phoenix* Strasbourg, France	Dec. 4, 1894
36,565	Sadi Lecointe (France)	Nieuport aircraft Issy, France	Oct. 30, 1923
43,166	Lt. Apollo Soucek (U.S. Army)	U.S.N. Wright *Apache* Washington, D.C.	June 4, 1930
51,961	Prof. Auguste Piccard (Switzerland) and Paul Kipfer	*F.N.R.S. I* Balloon Augsburg, Germany	May 27, 1931
53,139	Piccard and Dr. Max Cosyns (Belgium)	*F.N.R.S. I* Balloon Dübendorf nr. Zurich	Aug. 18, 1932
72,078[1]	Raul F. Fedoseyenko, A. B. Vasenko and E. D. Ususkin	*Osaviakhim* Balloon Moscow	Jan. 30, 1934
72,395	Capts. Orvill Anderson and Albert Stevens (U.S. Army)	U.S. *Explorer II* Helium Balloon Rapid City, S.D.	Nov. 11, 1935
79,600	William Barton Bridgeman (U.S.)	U.S. Douglas D558-II *Skyrocket* California	Aug. 15, 1951
83,235	Lt.-Col. Marion Carl, U.S.M.C.	U.S. Douglas D558 *Skyrocket* California	Aug. 21, 1953
c.93,000	Major Arthur Murray (U.S.A.F.)	U.S. *Bell X-1A* Rocket Plane California	Aug. 21, 1954
126,200	Capt. Iven C. Kincheloe (U.S.A.F.)	U.S. *Bell X-2* Rocket Plane California	Sept. 7, 1956
136,500	Major Robert M. White (U.S.A.F.)	U.S. *X-15* Rocket Plane California	Aug. 12, 1960
169,600	Joseph A. Walker (U.S.)	U.S. *X-15* Rocket Plane California	Mar. 30, 1961
Miles 203.2	Fl. Major Yuriy A. Gagarin (U.S.S.R.)	*Vostok I* capsule Orbital flight	Apr. 12, 1961
253.5	Col. Vladimir M. Komarov, Lt. Boris B. Yegorov and Konstantin P. Feoktistov (U.S.S.R.)	*Voskhod I* capsule Orbital flight	Oct. 12, 1964
309.2	Col. Pavel I. Belyayev and Lt.-Col. Aleksey A. Leonov (U.S.S.R.)	*Voskhod II* capsule Orbital flight	Mar. 18, 1965
474.4	Cdr. John W. Young (U.S.N.) and Major Michael Collins (U.S. Army)	U.S. *Gemini X* capsule Orbital flight	July 19, 1966
850.7	Cdr. Charles Conrad, Jr., and Lt.-Cdr. Richard F. Gordon, Jr. (U.S. Army)	U.S. *Gemini XI* capsule Orbital flight	Sept. 14, 1966
234,672	Col. Frank Borman, Capt. James A. Lovell, Jr., William A. Anders (U.S. Army)	U.S. *Apollo VIII* Command Module Circum-lunar flight	Dec. 25, 1968
248,433*	Cdr. Eugene A. Cernan (U.S.N.) and Lt.-Col. Thomas P. Stafford (U.S.A.F.)	U.S. *Apollo X* Lunar Module Circum-lunar flight	May 22, 1969
248,665	Capt. James Arthur Lovell (U.S.N.), John L. Swigert, Jr. (U.S.N.), and Frederick W. Haise	U.S. *Apollo XIII* Circum-lunar flight	April 15, 1970

[1]All died on descent. *Note: The moon was 6,150 miles *less* distant at the time of the lunar landing of July 20–21, 1969.

Chapter Eleven

HUMAN ACHIEVEMENTS

1. Endurance and Endeavor

Lunar Conquest

Neil Alden Armstrong (born Wapakoneta, Ohio, of Scotch-Irish-German ancestry, on August 5, 1930), command pilot of the Apollo XI mission, became the first man to set foot on the moon on the Sea of Tranquillity at 02:56 and 15 secs. a.m. G.M.T. on July 21, 1969. He was followed out of the Lunar Module *Eagle* by Col. Edwin Eugene Aldrin, Jr. (born Glen Ridge, New Jersey, of Swedish, Dutch and British ancestry, on January 20, 1930), while the Command Module *Columbia* piloted by Lt.-Col. Michael Collins (born Rome, Italy, of Irish and pre-Revolutionary American ancestry, on October 31, 1930) orbited above.

Eagle landed at 20:17 hrs. 42 secs. G.M.T. on July 20 and blasted off at 17:54 G.M.T. on July 21, after a stay of 21 hours 36 minutes. The *Apollo XI* had blasted off from Cape Kennedy, Florida at 13:32 G.M.T. on July 16 and was a culmination of the U.S. space program, which, at its peak, employed 376,600 people and attained in the year 1966–67 a peak budget of $5,900,000,000.

Altitude

Manned Flight. The greatest altitude attained by man was when the crew of the ill-fated *Apollo XIII* was at apocynthion (*i.e.* their furthest point behind the moon) 158 miles above its surface and 248,665 miles above the earth's surface at 6:21 a.m. E.S.T. on April 15, 1970. The crew consisted of Capt. James Arthur Lovell, Jr.,

THE EARTH AS SEEN FROM THE MOON (left): The view seen by Apollo XI astronauts, the first to land on the moon. FIRST FOOTPRINT (right): Neil Armstrong's first step on the lunar surface.

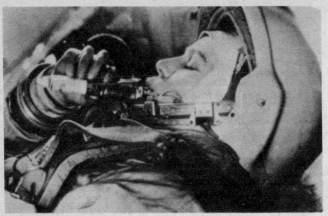

HIGHEST AND FASTEST FEMALE: On her historic journey in *Vostok VI* in 1963, Valentina Tereshkova-Nikolayev set all-time women's records for speed and altitude.

U.S.N. (b. Cleveland, Ohio, March 25, 1928); John L. Swigert, Jr., (b. Denver, Colorado, August 30, 1931); and Fred Wallace Haise, Jr. (b. Biloxi, Mississippi, November 14, 1933).

Woman. The greatest altitude attained by a woman is 143.5 miles by Jr. Lt. (now Lt. Col.) Valentina Vladimirovna Tereshkova-Nikolayev (born March 6, 1937), of the U.S.S.R., during her 48-orbit flight in *Vostok VI* on June 16–19, 1963. The record for a woman in an aircraft is 79,842 feet by Natalia Prokhanova (U.S.S.R.) (b. 1940) in an E-33 jet, on May 22, 1965.

Speed in Space

Man. The fastest speed at which any human has traveled is 24,791 m.p.h. when the Command Service Module (C.S.M.) of *Apollo X* carrying Col. (now Brig.-Gen.) Thomas Patten Stafford, U.S.A.F. (b. Weatherford, Okla., September 17, 1930), Commander Eugene Andrew Cernan (b. Chicago, March 14, 1934) and Commander (now Capt.) John Watts Young, U.S.N. (b. San Francisco, September 24, 1930) reached their maximum speed on their trans-earth return flight at an altitude of 400,000 feet on May 26, 1969.

Woman. The highest speed ever attained by a woman is 17,470 m.p.h. by Jr. Lt. (now Lt. Col.) Valentina Vladimirovna Tereshkova-Nikolayev (born March 6, 1937), of the U.S.S.R., during her 48-orbit flight in *Vostok VI* on June 16–19, 1963.

The highest speed ever achieved by a woman aircraft pilot is 1,669.89 m.p.h. by Svetlana Savitskaya (U.S.S.R.), reported on June 2, 1975.

Speed on Land

Man. The highest speed ever achieved on land is 650 m.p.h. momentarily during the faster of the two runs of *The Blue Flame* driven by Gary Gabelich (b. San Pedro, California, August 29, 1940) on Bonneville Salt Flats, Utah, on October 23, 1970 when setting the world land speed record of 622.287 m.p.h. (see *Mechanical World*). The car, built by Reaction Dynamics Inc. of Milwaukee, Wisconsin, is designed to withstand stresses up to 1,000 m.p.h. while the tires have been tested to speeds of 850 m.p.h.

Woman. The highest land speed recorded by a woman is 524.016 m.p.h. by Mrs. Kitty Hambleton, *née* O'Neil (U.S.), in the 48,000-h.p. rocket-powered 3-wheeled S.M.1 *Motivator* over the Alvard Desert, Oregon, on December 6, 1976. Her official 2-way record was 512.710 m.p.h. and she probably touched 600 m.p.h. momentarily.

Speed on Water

Man. The highest speed ever achieved on water is an estimated 300 knots (345 m.p.h.) by Kenneth Peter Warby (born May 9, 1939) on the Blowering Dam Lake, N.S.W., Australia on November 20, 1977, in his unlimited hydroplane *Spirit of Australia*. The official world water speed record is 319.627 m.p.h., set on October 8, 1978, by Kenneth Warby on the Blowering Dam Lake.

The world record for propeller-driven craft is 202.42 m.p.h. by Larry Hill in the supercharged hydroplane *Mr. Ed* at Long Beach, California, in August, 1971. On a one-way run, the *Climax* reached a speed of 205.19 m.p.h.

Woman. Sue Williams, 28, drove the unlimited hydroplane U-96 *KYYX* through a measured mile on Lake Washington, Seattle, at 163.043 m.p.h. on July 26, 1978, for a world record.

Most Traveled

The man who visited more countries than anyone else was Jesse Hart Rosdail (1914-77) of Elmhurst, Illinois. Of the 161

MOST TRAVELED MAN: Jesse Hart Rosdail of Illinois visited 221 different countries and territories—all but two in the whole world—a total of 1,626,605 miles.

sovereign countries and 60 non-sovereign territories (221 in all) *then* listed by the *U.N. Population Report,* he visited all but two, namely North Korea and French Antarctic Territories. He estimated his total mileage as 1,626,605 miles.

Though he has not visited so many currently existing countries, Mehmet S. Ersöz (born 1904, Turkey) has traveled much more widely within some 210 countries. His wife's total was 163 by mid-1978.

The most countries visited by a disabled person is 115 sovereign and 59 non-sovereign countries by Professor Daniel J. Crowley of Davis, California, who has been confined to a wheelchair since March, 1946.

The Methodist preacher Francis Asbury of Birmingham, England, traveled 264,000 miles by horseback in North America from 1771 to 1815, preaching 16,000 sermons.

The most traveled men in space are the third crew of *Skylab 4,* the space station, with 34,469,696 miles.

Most Isolated

Man. The farthest any human has been removed from his nearest living fellow man is 2,233.2 miles in the case of the Command Service Module pilot Alfred M. Worden on the U.S. Apollo XV lunar mission of July 30-August 1, 1971.

Fastest Round-the-World Trip

The fastest time for a round-the-world journey on scheduled flights for a circumnavigation is 53 hours 34 minutes by Alec E. Prior and Terry Sloane eastward from Sydney *via* Los Angeles, London, Bombay, Perth and Melbourne, March 10–12, 1978, over 24,161 miles.

The F.A.I. accepts any flight, taking off and landing at the same point, which is as long as the Tropic of Cancer (22,858.754 miles) as a circumnavigational flight.

Passports

The world's most expensive passports are those from the U.S.S.R., which in 1974 were priced at $540, payable in advance. If applications involved travel to the West or a whole family, however, the necessary accompanying visa was refused in 996 out of 1,000 applications.

Polar Conquests

South Pole. The first ships to cross the Antarctic circle (latitude 66° 30′ S.) were the 193-crew *Resolution* (462 tons) under Capt. James Cook (1728–79), the English navigator, and *Adventure* (336 tons) under Lt. T. Furneaux, at 39° E., on January 17, 1773.

The first person to sight the Antarctic *mainland*—on the best available evidence and against claims made for British and Russian explorers—was Nathaniel Brown Palmer (U.S.) (1799–1877). On November 17, 1820, he sighted the Orleans Channel coast of the Palmer Peninsula from his 45-ton sloop *Hero.*

The South Pole was first reached at 11 a.m. on December 16, 1911, by a Norwegian party, led by Roald Amundsen (1872–1928), after a

CONQUEST OF NORTH POLE: Commander Robert E. Peary (right) took the picture (left) of his companions after they reached the North Pole on April 6, 1909. Left to right are the Eskimos Ooqueah and Ootah; Matthew Henson, Peary's assistant; and the other two Eskimos, Eginwah and Seegloo.

53-day march with dog sleds from the Bay of Whales, to which he had penetrated in the *Fram*. Subsequent calculations showed that Olav Bjaaland (the last survivor, dying in June, 1961, aged 88) and Helmer Hanssen probably passed within 400–600 meters of the exact pole. The other two members of the party were Sverre H. Hassell and Oskar Wisting.

The first woman to set foot on Antarctica was Mrs. Klarius Mikkelsen on February 20, 1935. No woman stood on the South Pole until November 11, 1969, when Lois Jones, Kay Lindsay, Eileen McSavenay, Jean Pearson, Tarry Lee Tickhall and Pam Young, all of the U.S., arrived by air.

Antarctic Crossing. The first crossing of the Antarctic continent was completed at 1:47 p.m. on March 2, 1958, after a 2,158-mile trek lasting 99 days from November 24, 1957, from Shackleton Base to Scott Base *via* the Pole. The crossing party of 12 was led by Dr. (now Sir) Vivian Ernest Fuchs (born February 11, 1908).

North Pole. The claims of neither of the two U.S. Arctic explorers Dr. Frederick Albert Cook (1865–1940) and Rear Admiral Robert Edwin Peary, U.S.N. (1856–1920), in reaching the North Pole are subject to positive proof. Cook, accompanied by the Eskimos Ah-pellah and Etukishook, two sledges and 26 dogs, struck north from a point 60 miles north of Svarteoeg, on Axel Heiberg Is., Canada, 460 miles from the Pole on March 21, 1908, allegedly reaching Lat. 89° 31′ N. on April 19, and the Pole on April 21. Peary, accompanied by his Negro assistant, Matthew Alexander Henson (1866–1955), and the four Eskimos, Ooqueah, Eginwah, Seegloo, and Ootah (1875–1955), struck north from his Camp Bartlett (Lat. 87° 44′ N.) at 5 a.m. on April 2, 1909. After traveling another 134 miles, he allegedly established his final camp, Camp

FIRST ARCTIC SEA ICE CROSSING: The British Trans-Arctic Expedition went by sled from Point Barrow, Alaska, to near Spitzbergen, Norway, in 464 days.

Jessup, in the proximity of the Pole at 10 a.m. on April 6, and marched a further 42 miles quartering the sea ice before turning south at 4 p.m. on April 7. On excellent pack ice, Herbert's 1968–69 Expedition (see below) attained a best day's route mileage of 23 miles in 15 hours. Cook claimed 26 miles twice, while Peary claimed a surely unsustainable average of 38 miles for 8 consecutive days.

The earliest indisputable attainment of the North Pole over the sea ice was at 3 p.m. (Central Standard Time) on April 19, 1968, by Ralph Plaisted (U.S.) and three companions after a 42-day trek in four snowmobiles. Their arrival was independently verified 18 hours later by a U.S. Air Force weather aircraft. The sea bed is 13,410 feet below the North Pole.

Naomi Uemara (born 1941), the Japanese explorer and mountaineer, became the first person to reach the North Pole in a solo trek across the Arctic ice cap at 04:45 G.M.T. on May 1, 1978. He had traveled 450 miles, setting out on March 7 from Cape Edward, Ellesmere Island, in northern Canada. He averaged over 8 miles per day with his sled "Aurora" drawn by 17 huskies (he had hoped to average 10.5 miles per day).

The first woman to set foot on the North Pole was Mrs. Fran Phipps, wife of the Canadian bush pilot Weldy Phipps, on April 5, 1971. Galina Aleksandrovna Lastovskaya (b. 1941) and Lilia Vladislavovna Minina (b. 1959) were crew members of the U.S.S.R. atomic icebreaker *Arktika* which reached the pole on August 17, 1977.

Arctic Crossing. The first crossing of the Arctic sea ice was achieved by the British Trans-Arctic Expedition which left Point Barrow, Alaska, on February 21, 1968, and arrived at the Seven Island Archipelago northeast of Spitzbergen 464 days later on May 29, 1969, after a haul of 2,920 statute miles and a drift of 700 miles, compared with a straight-line distance of 1,662 miles. The team was Wally Herbert (leader), 34, Major Ken Hedges, 34, R.A.M.C.,

Allan Gill, 38, Dr. Roy Koerner, 36 (glaciologist), and 40 huskies. This was the longest sustained (sled) journey ever made on polar pack ice and the first undisputed conquest of the North Pole by sled. Temperatures sank to −47° F. during the trek.

Longest Sled Journey. The longest totally self-supporting polar sled journey ever made was one of 1,080 miles from west to east across Greenland, June 18–September 5, 1934, by Capt. M. Lindsay, Lt. Arthur Godfrey, Andrew Croft and 49 dogs.

The same crossing was first made with man-hauled sledges by the Inter Services 1974 Trans-Greenland Expedition, led by Flight Lt. D. R. Gleed, in 36 days.

Mountaineering

The conquest of the highest point on earth, Mount Everest (29,028 feet), was first achieved at 11:30 a.m. on May 29, 1953, by Edmund Percival Hillary (New Zealand) and the Sherpa Tenzing Norkhay (see *Mountaineering*, Chapter 12).

The female record was set by Mrs. Junko Tabei, 34, of Japan, on reaching Everest's summit on May 16, 1975.

Deep Diving Records

The record depth for the extremely dangerous activity of breath-held diving is 282 feet by Jacques Mayol (France) off Elba, Italy, on November 9, 1973. The pressure on Mayol's thorax was 136.5 lbs. of force per square inch, and his pulse fell to 36.

Enzo Maiorca (Italy) surfaced unconscious from his dive of 285 feet off Sorrento, Italy, on September 27, 1974.

The women's record is 147½ feet by Giuliana Treleani (Italy) off Cuba in September, 1967.

The record dive with scuba (self-contained underwater breathing apparatus) is 437 feet by John J. Gruener and R. Neal Watson (U.S.) off Freeport, Grand Bahama, on October 14, 1968.

The record dive utilizing gas mixtures is a simulated dive of 2,001 feet in a dry chamber by Patrice Chemin and Robert Gauret (France) at the Comex Chamber, Marseilles, France, reported in June, 1972.

Some divers have survived free swimming for short intervals at 1,400 feet.

Underwater Rescue

The deepest underwater rescue achieved was of the *Pisces III* in which Roger R. Chapman, 28, and Roger Mallinson, 35, were trapped for 76 hours when it sank to 1,575 feet, 150 miles southeast of Cork, Ireland, on August 29, 1973. She was hauled to the surface by the cable ship *John Cabot* after preliminary work by *Pisces V*, *Pisces II* and the remote control recovery vessel U.S. C.U.R.V., on September 1, 1973.

The greatest depth of an actual escape without any equipment has been from 225 feet by Richard A. Slater from the rammed submersible *Nekton Beta* off Catalina Island, California, on September 28, 1970.

MARINE CIRCUMNAVIGATION RECORDS (Compiled by Sq. Ldr. D. H. Clarke)

A true circumnavigation entails passing through two antipodal points (which are at least 12,429 statute miles apart).

CATEGORY*	VESSEL	NAME	START PLACE, DATE	FINISH DATE, DURATION
Earliest*	Vittoria Expedition of Fernao de Magalhaes (Magellan) (c. 1480–1521) 100 tons	Juan Sebastian de Elcano or Del Cano (k. 1526) and 17 crew	Seville, Spain Sept. 20, 1519	San Lucar, Spain Sept. 6, 1521, 30,700 miles
Earliest British	Golden Hind (ex Pelican) Etoile	Francis Drake (c. 1540–1596) (knighted April 4, 1581)	Plymouth, England, Dec. 13, 1577	Sept. 26, 1580
Earliest Woman		Crypto-female valet of M. de Commerson, named Baré	St. Malo, 1766	1769
Earliest Fore-and-Aft Rigged Vessel	Union, 98 tons (Sloop)	John Bolt Junior (U.S.)	Newport, R.I., 1794 (via Cape Horn westabout)	Newport, R.I., 1796
Earliest Yacht	Sunbeam, 170-foot-5.8-inch 3-mast topsail schooner	Lord and Lady Brassey (G.B.), passengers and crew	Cowes, Isle of Wight, 1876	Cowes, Isle of Wight, 1877
Earliest Solo	Spray, 36½-foot gaff yawl	Capt. Joshua Slocum, 51 (U.S.) (a non-swimmer)	Newport, R.I. via Magellan Straits, Apr. 24, 1895	July 3, 1898, 46,000 miles
Earliest Motorboat	Speejacks, 98 feet	Albert Y. Gowen (U.S.), wife and crew	New York City, 1921	New York City, 1922
Earliest Woman Solo	Mazurek, 31-foot Bermuda Sloop	Krystyna Chojnowska-Liskiewicz (Poland)	Las Palmas, Mar. 28, 1976 Westward via Panama	Tied knot Mar. 21, 1978
Earliest Woman Solo via Cape Horn	Express Crusader, 53-foot Bermuda sloop	Naomi James (N.Z./G.B.)	Dartmouth, England, Sept. 9, 1977 (Cape Horn, March 19, 1978)	Dartmouth, June 8, 1978 (266 days 19 hours)
Smallest Boat	Ahdori II, 20-foot-8-inch Bermuda yawl	Hiroshi Aoki (Japan)	Osaka, Japan, June 13, 1972 (Cape Horn, Jan. 12, 1973)	Osaka, July 29, 1974
Earliest Submarine	U.S.S. Triton	Capt. Edward L. Beach, U.S.N., plus 182 crew	New London, Connecticut, Feb. 16, 1960	May 10, 1960, 30,708 miles
Fastest Solo (Multihull)	Manureva, 70-foot trimaran (ex Pen Duick IV)	Alain Colas (France)	St. Malo via Sydney	March 29, 1974 (167 days)
Fastest Solo (Monohull)	Egregious, 37-foot Bermuda sloop	Webb Chiles (U.S.)	San Diego, Oct.18, 1974 (Cape Horn, Dec. 12, 1975)	San Diego, Oct. 1, 1976 (202 days)
Fastest	Great Britain II, 72-foot ketch	1st Mike Gill (13 crew) 2nd R. Mullender (15 crew)	Thames, Aug. 31, 1975 via Sydney (change crews)	67 days 5 hrs. 19 min. 66 days 22 hrs. 31 min. 26,380 miles

*Eduard Roditi, author of Magellan of the Pacific, advances the view that Magellan's slave Enrique was the first circumnavigator. He had been purchased in Malacca, but knew the Filipino dialect, Vizayan, when he reached the Philippines from the east in 1521.

MARINE CIRCUMNAVIGATION RECORDS (continued)

Fastest Solo Westabout via Cape Horn	Mermaid III, 28-foot sloop	Kenichi Horie (Japan)	Osaka, Japan, Aug. 1, 1973		May 5, 1974 (275 days 13 hrs.)
Fastest Ever via Cape Horn	Awahnee II, 53 feet	Bob Griffith (U.S.) and 5 crew		Bluff, N.Z., 1970 (eastward)	Bluff, N.Z., 1971 (84 days)
Earliest Non-stop Solo (Port-to-Port)	Suhaili, 32.4-foot Bermuda ketch	Robin Knox-Johnston (G.B.) (b. 1939)	Falmouth, England, June 14, 1968		Apr. 22, 1969 (312 days) Longest alone at sea

TRANSATLANTIC MARINE RECORDS (Compiled by Sq. Ldr. D. H. Clarke)

CATEGORY	CAPTAIN	VESSEL & SIZE	START	FINISH	DURATION	DATE
Earliest Canoe	"Finn-Man" (Eskimo)	Kayak, 11 ft. 10 in.	Greenland	Humber, England	Time not known	1613
Earliest Crossing (2 men)	C. R. Webb + 1 crew (U.S.)	Charter Oak, 43 ft.	New York	Liverpool	35 days	1857
Earliest Trimaran	John Mikes + 2 crew (U.S.)	Non Pareil, 25 ft.	New York (June 4)	Southampton, England	51 days	1868
Earliest Solo Sailing	Alfred Johnson (U.S.)	Centennial, 20 ft.	Gloucester, Mass.	Wales	46 days	1876
Earliest Woman Sailing (with U.S. husband)	Mrs. Joanna Crapo (Scot.)	New Bedford, 20 ft.	Chatham, Mass.	Newlyn, England	51 days	1877
Earliest Single-handed Race	J. W. Lawlor (U.S.)	Sea Serpent, 15 ft.	Boston (June 21)	Coverack, England	45 days	1891
Earliest Rowing (partial)	Six British deserters	Ship's boat, c. 20 ft.	St. Helena (June 10)	Belmonte, Brazil	28 days (83 m.p.d.)	1799
Earliest Rowing by 2 Men (Northern)	George Harbo and Frank Samuelson (U.S.)	Richard K. Fox, 18½ ft.	New York (June 6)	Isles of Scilly (Aug. 1)	55 days (56 m.p.d.)	1896
Fastest Solo Sailing West-East	J. V. T. McDonald (G.B.)	Inverarity, 38 ft.	Nova Scotia	Ireland	16 days	1922
Earliest Canoe (with sail)	F. Romer (Germany)	Deutscher Sport, 21½ ft.	Las Palmas (June 2)	St. Thomas, V.I.	58 days (47 m.p.d.)	1928
Earliest Woman Solo-Sailing West-East	Gladys Gradely (U.S.)	Lugger, 18 ft.	Nova Scotia	Hope Cove, Devon, England	60 days	1903
Earliest Woman Solo-Sailing East-West	Mrs. Ann Davison (G.B.)	Felicity Ann, 23 ft.	Las Palmas (November 20, 1952)	Portsmouth, Dominica	65 days	1952–53
Fastest Woman Solo	Clare Francis (G.B.)	Robertson's Golly, 37⅜ ft.	Plymouth, Eng.	Newport, R.I.	29 days 1 hr. 52 mins.	1976

TRANSATLANTIC MARINE RECORDS (continued)

Longest Non-Stop Woman Solo	Anna Woolf (S. Afr.)	Zama Zulu, 43 ft.	Capetown–Ascension Is.	Ascension Is.–Bowling, Scot.	1,800 miles/29 days, 7,120 miles/80 days	1976
Fastest Crossing Sailing (multihull)	Eric Tabarly (France) +2 crew	Pen Duick IV, 67 ft.	Tenerife, Canary Is.	Martinique	251.4 miles/day (10 days 12 hrs.)	1968
Fastest Crossing Sailing (monohull) East-West	Wilhelm Hirte and crew (Ger.)	Kriter II, 80 ft.	Canary Is.	Barbados	13 days, 8 hours	1977
Fastest Crossing Sailing (monohull) West-East	Wilson Marshall (U.S.) and crew	Atlantic, 185 ft.	Sandy Hook, N.J.	Lizard, Cornwall, Eng. (3,054 miles)	12 days 4 hrs. (fastest noon to noon 341 miles)	1905
Fastest Solo East-West (Northern) (monohull)	Jean-Yves Terlain (France)	Vendredi 13, 128 ft.	Plymouth, Eng. (June 13)	Newport, R.I. (July 8)	21 days 5¼ hrs.	1972
Fastest Solo East-West (Northern) (multihull)	Prof. Alain Colas (France)	Pen Duick IV, 70-ft. trimaran	Plymouth, Eng. (June 17)	Newport, R.I. (July 7)	20 days 13¼ hrs.	1972
Fastest Solo East-West (Southern) (monohull)	Sir Francis Chichester (G.B.)	Gipsy Moth V, 57 ft.	Portuguese Guinea	Nicaragua	179.1 miles/day (22.4 days)	1970
Fastest Solo Rowing East-West	Sidney Genders, 51 (G.B.)	Khaggavisana, 19½ ft.	Penzance, Eng.	Miami, Florida via Antigua	37.3 miles/day 162 days 18 hrs.	1970
Earliest Solo Rowing East-West	John Fairfax (G.B.)	Britannia, 22 ft.	Las Palmas, Canary Is. (Jan. 20)	Ft. Lauderdale, Florida (July 19)	180 days	1969
Earliest Solo Rowing West-East	Tom McClean (Ireland)	Super Silver, 20 ft.	St. John's, Newfoundland (May 17)	Black Sod Bay, Ireland (July 27)	70.7 days	1969
Smallest East-West (Southern)	Hugo S. Vihlen (U.S.)	The April Fool, 5 ft. 11⅞ in.	Casablanca (Mar. 29)	Ft. Lauderdale, Florida (June 21)	85 days	1968
Smallest West-East	Gerry Spiess, 39 (U.S.)	Yankee Girl, 10 ft.	Norfolk, Virginia (June 1)	Falmouth, England (July 24)	54 days (3,800 miles)	1979
Smallest (across 2 oceans)	John Riding (G.B.)	Sio As, 12 ft.	Plymouth via Panama	New Zealand, 1973	Lost in Tasman Sea	1964/1974
Youngest Solo Sailing	David Sandeman, 17½ years	Sea Raider, 35 ft.	Jersey, C.I.	Newport, R.I.	43 days	1976
Oldest Solo Sailing	Jean Gau, 72 years	Atom, 30 ft.	New York	France (wrecked N. Africa)	50 days	1975

TRANSPACIFIC MARINE RECORDS

Fastest	Bill Lee (U.S.)	*Merlin* 67-ft. sloop	Los Angeles	Honolulu	8 days 11 hrs. 1 min.	1977
Fastest Solo	Andrew Urbanczyk	*Nord III*, 27-ft. sloop	Yokosuka, Japan, April 23	San Francisco, June 11	49 days	1979
Earliest Solo (Woman)	Sharon Sites Adams (U.S.)	*Sea Sharp II*, 31 ft.	Yokohama	San Diego	75 days (5,911 miles)	1969
Earliest Rowing	John Fairfax (G.B.) Sylvia Cook (G.B.)	*Britannia II* 35 ft.	San Francisco Apr. 26, 1971	Hayman Is., Australia, Apr. 22, 1972	362 days	1971 /1972
Earliest Rowing Solo	Anders Svedlund (Sweden)	*Roslagena*, 20 ft.	Chile	Samoa	118 days	1974

N.B.—The earliest single-handed Pacific crossings were achieved East-West by Bernard Gilboy (U.S.) in 1882 in the 18-ft. double-ender *Pacific* and West-East by Fred Rebel (Latvia) in the 18-ft. *Elaine*, and Edward Miles (U.S.) in the 36½-ft. *Sturdy II*, both in 1932.

FIRST ATLANTIC ROW WEST-TO-EAST was made in this 20-foot dory, "Super Silver," by Tom McClean, who rowed for 70 days 17 hours from Newfoundland to Ireland.

Greatest Ocean Descent

The record ocean descent was achieved in the Challenger Deep of the Marianas Trench, 250 miles southwest of Guam, when the Swiss-built U.S. Navy bathyscaphe *Trieste*, manned by Dr. Jacques Piccard (b. 1914) and Lt. Donald Walsh, U.S.N., reached the ocean bed 35,820 feet (6.78 miles) down, at 1:10 p.m. on January 23, 1960. The pressure of the water was 16,883 lbs. per square inch (1,215.6 tons per square foot), and the temperature 37.4° F. The descent required 4 hours 48 minutes and the ascent 3 hours 17 minutes.

Salvaging

Deepest. The greatest depth at which salvage has been achieved is 16,500 feet by the bathyscaphe *Trieste II* (Lt. Commander Mel Bartels, U.S.N.) to attach cables to an "electronics package" on the sea bed 400 miles north of Hawaii on May 20, 1972.

Project Jennifer by U.S.S. *Glomar Explorer* in June–July, 1974, to recover a Golfclass U.S.S.R. submarine 750 miles northwest of Hawaii cost $550,000,000 but was not successful.

By Divers. The deepest salvage by flexible dress divers was on the wreck of the S.S. *Niagara*, sunk by a mine in 1940, 438 feet down off Bream Head, Whangarei, North Island, New Zealand. All but 6 per cent of the $6,300,000 of gold in her holds was recovered in 7 weeks. The record recovery was from the White Star Liner *Laurentic*, which struck a mine in 132 feet of water off Malin Head, Donegal, Ireland, in 1917, with $14,000,000 of gold ingots in her Second Class baggage room. By 1924, 3,186 of the 3,211 gold bricks had been recovered with immense difficulty.

Mining Depths

Man's deepest penetration into the ground is in the Western Deep Levels Mine at Carletonville, Transvaal, South Africa. By May, 1975, a record depth of 12,600 feet had been attained. The rock temperature at this depth is 131° F.

Shaft-Sinking Record. The one-month (31-day) world record is 1,251 feet for a standard shaft 26 feet in diameter at Buffelsfontein Mine, Transvaal, South Africa, in March, 1962.

Marriage and Divorce

Longest Engagement. The longest engagement on record is one of 67 years between Octavio Guillen, 82, and Adriana Martinez, 82. They finally took the plunge in June, 1969, in Mexico City.

Engagement "Faux Pas." If measured by financial consequence, the greatest *faux pas* on record was that of the young multi-millionaire James Gordon Bennett, committed on January 1, 1877, at the family mansion of his demure fiancée, one Caroline May, on Fifth Avenue, New York City. Bennett arrived late in a two-horse cutter and obviously in wine. By dint of intricate footwork, he gained the portals to enter the living room, where he was the cynosure of all eyes. He mistook the fireplace for a plumbing fixture more usually reserved for another purpose. The May family broke

DEEP SINKER: The U.S. Navy bathyscaphe "Trieste" reached the ocean floor 6.78 miles below the surface in a 1960 descent.

the engagement and Bennett was obliged to spend the rest of his footloose and fancy-free life based in Paris with the resultant non-collection of millions of tax dollars by the U.S. Treasury.

Most Divorces and Marriages. Mrs. Beverly Nina Avery, then aged 48, a barmaid from Los Angeles, set a monogamous world record in October, 1957, by obtaining her 16th divorce, this one from Gabriel Avery, her 14th husband. She alleged outside the court that five of the 14 had broken her nose.

The most often-marrying millionaire, Thomas F. Manville (1894–1967), contracted his 13th marriage to his 11th wife, Christine Erdlen Popa (1940–71), in New York City on January 11, 1960, when aged 65. His shortest marriage (to his seventh wife) effectively lasted only 7½ hours. His fortune of $20,000,000 came from asbestos, which he unfortunately could not take with him.

The greatest number of marriages in the monogamous world is 20 by the former minister of religion Mr. Glynn de Moss Wolfe (U.S.) (b. 1908) who, at age 71, filed his 23rd marriage license application since 1931, on June 22, 1979. His intended is Guadalupe Reyes Chavez, age 20. He believes he has 39 children. He has long kept two wedding dresses (different sizes) in his closet for ready use. He has suffered 16 mothers-in-law.

Oldest Bride and Bridegroom. Dyura Avramovich, reportedly aged 101, married Yula Zhivich, admitting to 95, in Belgrade, Yugoslavia, in November, 1963.

Longest Marriage. The longest recorded marriage is one of 86 years between Sir Temulji Bhicaji Nariman and Lady Nariman from 1853 to 1940 resulting from a cousin marriage when both were five. Sir Temulji (born September 3, 1848) died, aged 91 years 11 months, in August, 1940 in Bombay.

The only reliable instance of an 83rd anniversary celebrated by a couple marrying at normal ages is that between the late Edd (105) and Margaret (99) Hollen (U.S.) who celebrated their 83rd anniversary on May 7, 1972. They were married in Kentucky on May 7, 1889.

The most recent example of a marriage with both partners over the age of 100 was that of John and Harriet Orton, aged 102 and 100 respectively, of Great Gidding, Cambridgeshire, England, who celebrated their 78th anniversary on July 9, 1978.

Most Married. Jack V. and Edna Moran of Seattle, Washington, have married each other 40 times since the original and only really necessary occasion on July 27, 1937 in Seaside, Oregon. Subsequent ceremonies have included those at Banff, Canada (1952), Cairo, Egypt (1966) and Westminster Abbey, London (1975).

Mass Ceremony. The largest mass wedding ceremony was one of 1,800 couples officiated over by Sun Myung Moon of the Holy Spirit Association for the Unification of World Christianity in Seoul, South Korea, on February 14, 1975. The response to the question "Will you swear to love your spouse forever?" is "Ye."

STUNTS AND MISCELLANEOUS ENDEAVORS

Accordion Playing. Stas Szezesniak played an accordion for 64 hours 13 minutes in West Chester, Pennsylvania, on April 20–22, 1979.

Apple Peeling. The longest single unbroken apple peel on record is 172 feet 4 inches peeled by Kathy Wafler, 17, of Wolcott, New York, in 11 hours 30 minutes at the Long Ridge Mall, Rochester, N.Y., on October 16, 1976. The apple weighed 20 oz.

Apple Picking. The greatest recorded performance is 341 U.S. bushels picked in 8 hours by Geoffrey Cash at Batlow, N.S.W., Australia, on April 3, 1977.

Baby Carriage Pushing. The greatest distance covered in 24 hours in pushing a perambulator is 345.25 miles by Runner's Factory of Los Gatos, California, with an all-star team of 57 California runners on June 23–24, 1979. A team of 10 with an adult "baby" from "Flore Moderns" covered 226.1 miles at Flore, Northamptonshire, England, in 24 hours on June 28–29, 1975.

Bagpipes. The longest bagpipe performance was 100 hours by Neville Workman, Clive Higgins, Patrick Forth, and Paul Harris of Churchill School Pipe Band, Salisbury, Rhodesia, on July 9–13, 1976.

ONE-MAN BANDS: James Blain (left) is a university-certified octomusicologist. As Werner Hirzel (right) struts around, he plays 49 instruments, including the accordion, flute, saxophone, gong, duck, fox and goose callers, siren, oogal and cow horns, tambourines, cymbals, washboard, musical hose, toilet brush, bass drum and balloon pump.

Balancing on One Foot. The longest recorded duration for continuous balancing on one foot without any rests is 31 hours 45 minutes by Anton Christy of Jaffna, Sri Lanka, May 27–28, 1979. The disengaged foot may not be rested on the standing foot nor may any sticks be used for support or balance.

Balloon Flights. The longest reported toy balloon flight is one of 9,000 miles from Atherton, California (released by Jane Dorst) on May 21, 1972 and found on June 10 at Pietermaritzburg, South Africa.

Balloon Release. The largest balloon release on record was one of 130,000 helium balloons at Baltimore Memorial Stadium on October 10, 1976.

Ball Punching. Ron Renaulf (Australia) equaled his own world duration ball-punching record of 125 hours 20 minutes at 10:20 p.m. on December 31, 1955, at the Esplanade, Southport, Queensland, Australia.

Band, One-Man. The greatest number of musical instruments played simultaneously is 49 by Werner Hirzel (b. 1919), known as Schnickelgruber), who performed on ABC-TV with the David Frost Show on April 5, 1974.

The greatest number of instruments played in a single tune is 75 in 2 minutes 11.2 seconds by Rory Blackwell at the E.M.I. Bingo and Social Club, Derry's Cross, Plymouth, Devon, England, on September 6, 1977.

Rob Stewart of Kissimmee, Florida, played his one-man band (at least 3 instruments played simultaneously) for 38 hours 1 minute May 5–6, 1979.

Don Davis of Hollywood, California, was the first one-man band able to play 4 melody and 2 percussion instruments simultaneously without electronics, in 1974. For a rendition of the 4th movement of Beethoven's Fifth Symphony, he utilizes an 8-prong pendular perpendicular piano pounder and a semi-circular chromatic radially operated centrifugally sliding left-handed glockenspiel. A professor of music at the University of Connecticut certified on August 11, 1978, that James Blain played 8 instruments (4 melodic and 4 percussion) simultaneously.

Band Marathons. The longest recorded "blow-in" is 100 hours 2 minutes by the DuVal Senior High School band, Lanham, Maryland, on May 13–17, 1977.

Band, Pop. The playing duration record for a 4-man pop group is 144 hours by "Rocking Ricky and the Velvet Collars" at The Talardy Hotel, St. Asaph, Wales on November 12–18, 1976. The group at no time sank below a trio.

Barrel Jumping. The greatest reported distance achieved by a barrel-jumper on ice skates is 32 feet (over 13 barrels) by T. Karl Milne (born 1900) at Albany, New York, on January 13, 1930.

Barrel Rolling. The record for rolling a 43.2-gallon metal beer barrel over a measured mile is 9 minutes 52 seconds by a team of six from Haunchwood Collieries Institute and Social Club, Nuneaton, Warwickshire, England, on October 30, 1977.

Bathtub Racing. The record for the annual 36-mile Nanaimo to Vancouver, British Columbia, bathtub race is 1 hour 29 minutes 40 seconds by Gary Deathbridge, 25 (Australia), on July 30, 1978. Tubs are limited to 75 inches and 6-h.p. motors. The greatest distance for paddling a hand-propelled bathtub in 24 hours is 36 miles 1,072 yards by 25 Venture Scouts at Priory Park, Malvern, Hereford, and Worcester, England, on May 10–11, 1975.

Baton Twirling. Shelia Cline, Donnetta Cline and Rebeckah Peery of Tazewell High School, Tazewell, Virginia, twirled for 50 hours 30 minutes, December 2–4, 1978.

Beard of Bees. The heaviest recorded beard of bees was one of about 17,500 which swarmed around a queen bee on the chin of Don Cooke of Ohio, on the Guinness Spectacular TV show, filmed in Los Angeles on April 6, 1979. (See photo, page I.)

Bedmaking. The record time set under the rigorous rules of the Australian Bedmaking Championships is 28.2 seconds by Wendy Wall, 34, of Sydney, N.S.W., Australia, on November 30, 1978.

Bed of Nails. The duration record for non-stop lying on a bed of nails (sharp 6-inch nails 2 inches apart) is 65 hours 43 minutes 21 seconds by Tim Robinson (Strombo the Maniac) at Oval House Theatre Club, London, on June 16–19, 1977. Much longer durations are claimed by uninvigilated *fakirs*—the most extreme case being *Silki* who claimed 111 days in São Paulo, Brazil, ending on August 24, 1969.

The female endurance record is 30 hours non-stop set by Geraldine Williams (Miranda, Queen of the Fakirs) of Welwyn Garden City, Hertfordshire, England, on March 18–19, 1977.

Bed Pushing. The longest recorded push of a normally stationary object is 3,233 miles 1,150 yards in the case of a wheeled hospital bed by a team of 9 from Bruntsfield Bedding Centre, Edinburgh, Scotland, June 21–July 26, 1979.

Bed Racing. The record time for the annual Knaresborough Bed Race (established 1966) in Yorkshire, England is 14 minutes 7.0 seconds for the 1.96-mile course crossing the River Nidd, by the I. C. I. Fibres Flying Fiasco team on June 10, 1978.

Bell Ringing. The longest recorded handbell ringing recital has been one of 43 hours 2 minutes by the Bluebells of Paradise, United Church of Christ, Louisville, Ohio, June 8–10, 1978.

Best Best Man. The world's champion "best man" is Wally Gant, a bachelor fishmonger from Wakefield, Yorkshire, England, who officiated for the 50th time since 1931 in December, 1964.

Billiard Table Jumping. Joe Darby (1861–1937) cleared a 12-foot billiard table lengthwise, taking off from a 4-inch-high solid wooden block, at Wolverhampton, England, on February 5, 1892.

Bomb Defusing. The highest reported number of unexploded bombs defused by any individual is 8,000 by Werner Stephan in West Berlin, Germany, in the 12 years from 1945 to 1957. He was killed by a small grenade on the Grünewald blasting site on August 17, 1957.

Bond Signing. The greatest feat of bond signing was performed by L. E. Chittenden (died 1902), the Registrar of the United States Treasury. In 48 hours (March 20–22, 1863), he signed 12,500 bonds worth $10,000,000, which had to catch a steam packet to England. He suffered years of pain thereafter and the bonds were never used.

Boomerang Throwing. The earliest mention of a word similar to "boomerang" is "wo-mur-rang" in Collins *Account N.S. Wales Vocabulary*, published in 1798. The earliest certain Australian account of a returning boomerang (term established in 1827) was in 1831 by Major (later Sir) Thomas Mitchell.

Curved throwing sticks for hunting wild fowl were found in the tomb of Tutankhamen, dating from the mid-14th century B.C. World championships and codified rules were not established until 1970. Jeff Lewry won the world title in 1970–71–72–73, and the Australian title in 1974. The Boomerang Association of Australia's official record for distance reached before the boomerang returns is

289 feet 4 inches (orbital path 885 feet) by Leo Meier (Switzerland) at Darlington Point, N.S.W., Australia, on November 6, 1976. Herb A. Smith won a contest at Crawley, Sussex, England, on August 6, 1978, with a throw of 346.1 feet.

Brick Carrying. The record for carrying a brick (8 lbs. 15 oz.) in a nominated ungloved hand with the arm extended in an un-cradled downward pincer grip is 45 miles in 13 hours 7 minutes by David and Kym Barger of Lamar, Missouri on May 21, 1977.

The feminine record of 19.2 miles was set by Cynthia Ann Smolko of Denville, New Jersey, on May 14, 1977, using a 9 lb.-12 oz. brick.

Brick Throwing. The greatest reported distance for throwing a standard 5-lb. building brick is 146 feet 1 inch by Geoffrey Capes at Braybrook School, Cambridgeshire, England, on July 19, 1978.

Bubble Gum Blowing. In contests conducted across the U.S. in 1978–79 by the Bubble Yum gum company, the largest bubble blown measured 19¼ inches in diameter, created by Susan Montgomery of Fresno, California, in a contest held in Jacksonville, Florida. Each bubble in the competition was blown using 3 pieces of gum only, and all measurements were taken on a horizontal rather than a vertical basis, to eliminate any elongation due to gravity.

Camping Out. Graeme Hurry of Coventry, England completed 4 years of sleeping out on June 19, 1978. He had earlier shared first place in a *Scouting* magazine British national contest on June 19, 1975, but just carried on.

Card Throwing. Kevin St. Onge threw a standard playing card 185 feet at Henry Ford Community College, Dearborn, Michigan, on June 12, 1979.

Car Wrecking. The greatest number of cars wrecked in a stunting career is 1,470 to June 1, 1979, by Dick Sheppard of Gloucester, England.

Catapulting. The greatest recorded distance for a catapult shot is 1,362 feet by James F. Pfotenhauer, using a patented 16½-foot "Monarch IV Supershot" and a 53-caliber lead shot on Ski Hill, Escanaba, Michigan, on September 10, 1977.

Champagne Fountain. The tallest successfully filled column of champagne glasses is one 19 high, filled from the top by Martin Moore, Annabel Lee, Christine Price and Susan Brooklyn of Butlin's, Brighton, Sussex, England, on April 17, 1979.

Circus Cycling. The most on one cycle is 13, riding simultaneously, by the cyclist troupe from the Chinese Acrobatic Theatre of Shanghai which performs this trick regularly. (For other circus stunt records see page 456.)

Clapping. The duration record for continuous clapping (sustaining an average 140 claps per minute audible at 100 yards) is 39 hours 15 minutes by James Dutton, Steven Passmore, Melody Goodrich and Tammy Robertson of Richmond, Virginia, on August 19-20, 1977.

UNBEATABLE BALANCING: The Chinese Acrobatic Theatre in Shanghai features 12 on a bike at every performance, and sometimes 13. It took Alex Chervinsky 26 years of practice before he could achieve the ultimate balancing feat—130 coins perched on the edge of a silver dollar—as shown (right).

Club Swinging. Bill Franks set a world record of 17,280 revolutions (4.8 per second) in 60 minutes at Webb's Gymnasium, Newcastle, N.S.W., Australia, on August 2, 1934. M. Dobrilla swung continuously for 144 hours at Cobar, N.S.W., Australia, finishing on September 15, 1913.

Coal Bag Carrying. The greatest non-stop bag-carrying feat, carrying 1 cwt. (112 lbs.) of household coal in an open bag, is 22.2 miles by Brian Newton, 29, from Leicester to Rearsby, England, and back in 6 hours 7 minutes on November 12, 1976.

Coal Shoveling. The record for filling a 1,120-lb. hopper with stove-size pieces of coal is 42 secs. by Robert Taylor of Dobson, New Zealand, on February 3, 1979.

Coin Balancing. The greatest recorded feat of coin balancing is the stacking of 130 coins on top of a silver U.S. dollar on edge by Alex Chervinsky of Lock Haven, Pennsylvania in 1974, after 26 years' practice.

Coin Snatching. The greatest number of 25-cent pieces (quarters) caught by the same hand after being flipped from a pile or piles balanced on the back of the forearm is 120 by Gene Basta of Liverpool, New York, on May 12, 1978.

Contest Winnings. The largest recorded individual prize won was $307,500 by Herbert J. Idle, 55, of Chicago in an encyclopedia contest run by Unicorn Press, Inc., on August 20, 1953.

CIRCUS RECORDS

The following represent the greatest feats performed, either for the first time or, if marked with an asterisk, uniquely. A "mechanic" is a safety harness.

Category	Feat	Performer	Location	Year
Flying Trapeze	Earliest Act	Jules Leotard (France)	Circus Napoleon, Paris	1859
	Double back somersault	Eddie Silbon	Paris Hippodrome	1879
	Triple back somersault (female)	Lena Jordan (Latvia) to Lew Jordan (U.S.)	Sydney, Australia	1897
	Triple back somersault (male)	Ernest Clarke to Charles Clarke	Publiones Circus, Cuba	1909
	Triple and a half back somersault	Tony Steel to Lee Strath Marliees	Durango, Mexico	1962
	Quadruple back somersault (in practice)	*Ernest Clarke to Charles Clarke	Orrin Bros. Circus, Mexico City	1915
	Double Pass with back somersault	Buster and Anne Melzora with Paul Garee (catcher)	Latrobe, Pennsylvania	1935
	Triple back somersault with 1½ twists	Terry Cavarette Lemus (b. March 6, 1953).	Circus Circus Hotel, Las Vegas	1969
	Head to head stand on swinging bar (no holding)	*Ed. and Ira Millette (né Wolf)	Europe and U.S.	1910-20
Horseback	Downward circles or "muscle grinding"	306 by Denise La Grassa (U.S.)	Circus World Museum, Wisc	1976
	Highest Trapeze Act	Ryan Kelly (U.S.)	Calf-hang from helicopter	1978
	Running leaps on and off	*26 by "Poodles" Hanneford	New York City	1915
	Three-high column without "mechanic" with a pad	*Willy, Beby and Rene Fredianis.	Nouveau Cirque, Paris	1908
	Double back somersault mounted	(John or Charles) Frederick Clarke	Various	c. 1905
	Double back somersault from a 2-high to a trailing horse with "mechanic"	Aleksandr Sergey	Moscow Circus	1956
Fixed Bars	Pass from 1st to 3rd bar with a double back somersault	Phil Shevette, Andres Atayde	Woods Gymnasium, New York	1925-27
Giant Springboard	Triple flyaway to ground (male)	Phil Shevette	City-European tours	1896
	Triple flyaway to ground (female)	Loretto Twins, Ora and Pauline	Folies Bergere, Paris	1914
Risley (Human Juggling)	Running forward triple back somersault	John Cornish Worland (1855-1933) of the U.S.	Los Angeles	1874
	Back somersault feet to feet	Richard Risley Carlisle (1814-74) and son (U.S.)	Theatre Royal, Edinburgh	1844
Teeter Board	Quadruple back somersault to a chair	Sylvester Mezzetti(voltigeur) to ButchMezzetti (catcher) and Emilia Ivanova (Bulgaria)	Kehlavi Troupe at New York Hippodrome	1915-17
	Five-high column	The Yacopis (Argentina)	Ringling Bros., Barnum & Bailey	1941
	Six men-high perch pyramid	Emilia Ivanova (Bulgaria)	Inglewood, Calif	1976
Aerialist	One-arm swings or planges 305 (no net)	Janet May Klemke (U.S.)	Medina Shrine Circus, Chicago	1938
Wire-Juggling	16 hoops (hands and feet)	Ala Naito (Japan) (female)	Madison Square Garden, N.Y.C.	1937
Low Wire (7 feet)	Feet to feet forward somersault	Con Colleano	Empire Theatre, Johannesburg	1923
High Wire (30-40 feet)	Four-high column (with mechanic)	*The Solokhin Brothers (U.S.S.R.)	Moscow Circus	1962
	Three-layer, 7-man pyramid	Great Wallendas (Germany).	U.S.	1961
Ground Acrobatics	Stationary double back somersault	François Gouleau (France)	St. Petersburg, Florida	1905
Trampoline	Septuple twisting back somersault	Marco Canestrelli (U.S.)	Madison Square Garden, N.Y.C.	1979
	5 twisting back to shoulders	Marco to Belmonte Canestrelli	Madison Square Garden, N.Y.C.	1979
Flexible Pole	Double full-twisting somersault onto a 2-inch-diameter pole	The Robertos, Roberto Tabak (age 11)	Sarasota, Florida	1977

PERILOUS POLE FLIP: The Robertos mastered the double full-twisting somersault onto a 2-inch-diameter pole in 1977.

Cow Chip Tossing. The record distance for throwing a dried cow chip depends on whether the projectile may or may not be "molded into a spherical shape." Purists do not permit "sphericalization." The greatest distance achieved under the "non-alteration" rule (established in 1970) is 199 feet 1 inch by Robert D. Fleming, 25, of Taylorville, Illinois, on August 27, 1977. These increasing distances are anxiously studied by those who are also in support of a rule which precludes the common practice of mixing cement kiln dust into the cow feed prior to contests.

Crawling. The longest continuous voluntary crawl (progression with one or the other knee in unbroken contact with the ground) on record is 12.6 miles by Peter Holroyd of Bath University, Avon, England, on November 1, 1978. Wayne Forsyth equaled this mileage in Christchurch, New Zealand, on May 12, 1979.

The Baptist lay preacher Hans Mullikin, 39, arrived at the White House in Washington, D.C. on November 23, 1978, having crawled all but 8 of the 1,600 miles from Marshall, Texas.

Cucumber Slicing. Norman Johnson of the Blackpool College of Art and Technology, England, sliced 12 inches of a 1½-inch-diameter cucumber at 20 slices to the inch in 24.2 seconds, on the BBC-TV *Record Breakers* program, on September 28, 1973.

Custard Pie Throwing. The most-times champion in the annual World Custard Pie Championship at Coxheath, Kent, England (instituted 1967) has been "The Birds" and the "Coxheath Men," each with 3 wins. The target (face) must be 8 feet 3⅞ inches from the thrower, who must throw a pie no more than 10¾ inches in diameter. Six points are scored for a square hit full in the face.

Dancing. Marathon dancing must be distinguished from dancing mania, which is a pathological condition. The worst outbreak of dancing mania was at Aachen, Germany, in July, 1374, when hordes of men and women broke into a frenzied dance in the streets which lasted for hours till injury or complete exhaustion ensued.

The most severe marathon dance (staged as a public spectacle in the U.S.) was one lasting 4,152½ hours (24 weeks 5 days). This was completed by Tony Alteriri and Vera Mikus (now Mrs. Oglesby of Springfield, Pennsylvania) at Motor Square Garden, Pittsburgh, from June 6 to November 30, 1932. The rest allowance was progressively cut from 15 minutes per hour to only 3 minutes until this Marathon Dance "Classic" was finally stopped by the authorities. The prize of $1,000 was equivalent to 24 cents per hour.

Largest Dance. The largest dance ever held was that put on by the Houston Livestock Show at the Astro Hall, Houston, Texas, on February 8, 1969. The attendance was 16,500, with 4,000 turned away.

Dancing, Ballet. In the *entrechat* (a vertical spring from the fifth position with the legs extended criss-crossing at the lower calf), the starting and finishing position each count as one, such that in the *entrechat douze* there are *five* crossings and uncrossings. This was performed by Wayne Sleep for the BBC-TV *Record Breakers* program on January 7, 1973. He was in the air for 0.71 of a second.

The greatest number of spins called for in classical ballet choreography is the 32 *fouettés rond de jambe en tournant* in "Swan Lake" by Pyotr Ilyich Chaykovskiy (Tchaikovsky) (1840–93). Rowena Jackson (b. 1925) of New Zealand achieved 121 such turns at her class in Melbourne, Victoria, Australia, in 1940.

The greatest recorded number of curtain calls ever received by ballet dancers is 89 by Dame Margaret Evelyn Arias, *née* Hookham (born in Reigate, Surrey, England, May 18, 1919), *alias* Margot Fonteyn, and Rudolf Hametovich Nureyev (born in a train near Irkutsk, U.S.S.R., March 17, 1938), after a performance of "Swan Lake" at the Vienna Staatsoper, Austria, in October, 1964.

Dancing, Ballroom. The individual continuous world record is 106 hours 5 minutes 10 seconds by Carlos Sandrini in Buenos Aires, Argentina, in September, 1955. Three girls worked shifts as his partner.

The world's most successful professional ballroom dancing champions have been Bill Irvine and Bobbie Irvine, of London, who won 13 world titles, 1960–72.

The oldest competitive ballroom dancer is Albert J. Sylvester (born November 24, 1889) of Corsham, Wiltshire, England, who on April 26, 1977, won the topmost amateur Alex Moor award for a 10-dance test with his partner, Paula Smith, in Bath, England.

Dancing, Charleston. The Charleston duration record is 110 hours 58 minutes by Sabra Starr of Lansdowne, Pennsylvania, January 15–20, 1979.

Dancing, Conga. The longest recorded conga line was a "snake" of 8,128 people in Sidmouth, Devon, England, on August 25, 1978.

Dancing, Disco. The longest recorded disco dancing marathon is one of 329 hours 30 minutes by Keith Leriche of Port Aux Basques, Newfoundland, Canada, April 16–30, 1979.

JUST FOR KICKS:
Veronica Evans high-
kicked over 8,000 times
in a row at a British
movie studio in 1939.

Dancing, Flamenco. The fastest flamenco dancer ever measured is Solero de Jerez, aged 17, who, in Brisbane, Australia, in September, 1967, in an electrifying routine attained 16 heel taps per second or a rate of 1,000 a minute.

Dancing, Go-Go. The duration record for go-go dancing (Booga-loo or Reggae) is 200 hours 7 minutes by Nitro (Sabra Starr) and Rhiannon (Beverly Rainey) at Kelly's Bar, Wrightstown, New Jersey, July 1–8, 1978.

In future editions this category will be deleted and Disco Dancing will encompass this style of dance.

Dancing, High Kicking. The world record for high kicks is 8,005 in 4 hours 40 minutes by Veronica Evans (*née* Steen) (b. Liverpool, February 20, 1910) at the Pathétone Studios, Wardour Street, London, in the summer of 1939.

Dancing, Jive. The duration record for non-stop jiving is 96 hours 49 minutes by Richard Rimmer of Caterham, Surrey, England, November 20–24, 1978.

Dancing, Limbo. The lowest height for a flaming bar under which a limbo dancer has passed is $6\frac{1}{8}$ inches off the floor at Port of Spain Pavilion, Toronto, on June 24, 1973, by Marlene Raymond, 15.

Strictly no part of the body other than the sole or side of the foot should touch the ground, though brushing the shoulder blade does not, in fact, usually result in disqualification.

Dancing, Tap. The fastest *rate* ever measured for any tap dancer has been 1,440 taps per minute (24 per second) by Roy Castle on the BBC-TV *Record Breakers* program on January 14, 1973. The greatest assemblage of tap dancers ever is 528 from Brenda Kalatzes' Tap Studio, Los Angeles, performing on April 7, 1979, for the Guinness Spectacular ABC-TV program. The dancers ranged in age from 4 to 84 years.

SHALLOW HIGH DIVE SPECIALIST: Henri La Mothe, 70, shows how he dives from 40 feet up the Flatiron Building in New York City into a 12½-inch deep plastic wading pool of water.

Dancing the Twist. The duration record for the twist is 145 hours 30 minutes by Anetta Roussou of Simonstown, Cape Province, South Africa, December 12–18, 1977.

In future editions this category will be deleted and Disco Dancing will encompass this style of dance.

Dance Band. The most protracted session is one of 321 hours (13 days 9 hours) by the Black Brothers of Bonn, West Germany, ending on February 2, 1968. Never less than a quartet were in action during the marathon.

Demolition. Fifteen members of the International Budo Association led by Phil Milner (3rd dan karate) demolished a 6-room early Victorian house at Idle, Bradford, Yorkshire, England, by head, foot and empty hand in 6 hours on June 4, 1972. On completion they bowed to the rubble.

HIGHEST DIVE PERFORMED REGULARLY: At Acapulco, Mexico, professional divers fling themselves from La Quebrada ("the break in the rocks") 118 feet above the water to thrill the crowds. The water is only 12 feet deep. Since the base rocks extend 21 feet out from the take-off point, the divers have to jump 27 feet forward.

Disc Jockey. The longest continuous period of acting as a disc jockey is 2,016 hours by Dave Belmondo of Brocton, New York, from September 15–December 7, 1978. L.P.'s are limited to 50 per cent of total playing time.

This category will henceforth be retired. No further entries will be accepted or considered.

Diving, Highest Shallow. Henri La Mothe (b. 1904) set a record by diving 40 feet from the Flatiron Building, New York City, into 12½ inches of water in a child's wading pool on April 2, 1974.

Diving, High. The highest regularly performed dive is that of professional divers from La Quebrada ("the break in the rocks") at Acapulco, Mexico, a height of 118 feet. The leader of the 27 divers in the exclusive Club de Clavadistas is Raul Garcia (born 1928) with more than 35,000 dives. The base rocks are 21 feet out from the take-off, necessitating a leap 27 feet out. The water is only 12 feet deep.

On the *Wide World of Sports* television program, a record of 130 feet 6 inches was set jointly by Donnie Vick, Pat Sucher and John Tobler in March, 1974.

On May 18, 1885, Sarah Ann Henley, aged 24, jumped from the Clifton Suspension Bridge across the Avon, England. Her 250-foot fall was slightly cushioned by her voluminous dress and petticoat acting as a parachute. She landed, bruised and bedraggled, in the mud on the Gloucestershire bank and was carried to hospital by four policemen.

On February 11, 1968, Jeffrey Kramer, 24, leaped off the George Washington Bridge 250 feet above the Hudson River, New York City, and survived. Of the 511 people who made 240-foot suicide dives from the Golden Gate Bridge, San Francisco, California, from 1937 to April 25, 1974, only 7 survived.

On July 10, 1921, a stuntman named William H. Bailey leapt from a seaplane into the Ohio River at Louisville. The alleged altitude was 310 feet.

The celebrated dive, allegedly of 203 feet, made in 1919 by Alex Wickham from a rock into the Yarra River in Melbourne, Victoria, Australia, was in fact from a height of 96 feet 5 inches. Samuel Scott (U.S.) is reputed to have made a dive of 497 feet at Pattison Falls (now Manitou Falls) in Wisconsin in 1840, but this would have entailed an entry speed of 86 m.p.h. The actual height was probably 165 feet. Col. Harry A. Froboess (Switzerland) jumped 360 feet into the Bodensee from the airship *Graf Hindenburg* on June 22, 1936.

The greatest height reported for a dive into a flaming tank is 100 feet into $7\frac{1}{2}$ feet of water by Bill McGuire, 48, at the Holiday Inn in Chicago City Center, Michigan, on August 14, 1975.

Kitty O'Neil dived 127 feet from the 12th floor of the Valley Hilton Hotel, Sherman Oaks, California, onto an airbag, in March, 1979.

Domino Tumbling. The greatest number of dominoes toppled in a row is 169,713 by Michael Cairney, 23, of London, England, at the Mid-Hudson Civic Center, Poughkeepsie, New York, on June 9, 1979, under the auspices of the National Hemophilia Foundation. The dominoes, stretching 4.3 miles, fell at $2\frac{1}{4}$ m.p.h., after taking Cairney 13 days to set up.

Drumming. The world's duration drumming record is 720 hours by Clifford Marshall Van Buren of Ridgefield, Connecticut, December 26, 1977-January 25, 1978.

Ducks and Drakes. The best accepted ducks and drakes (stone-skipping) record is 24 skips (10 plinkers and 14 pitty-pats) by Warren Klope, 20, of Troy, Michigan, with 14 thin, flat, 4-inch limestones, at the annual Mackinac Island, Michigan, stone-skipping tournament on July 5, 1975. This was equaled by John S. Kolar of Birmingham, Michigan, and Glenn Loy Jr. of Flint, Michigan, on July 4, 1977.

Egg Drop. The greatest height from which fresh eggs landed without breaking was from 600 feet from a helicopter by David S. Donoghue and John Cartwright, on February 8, 1974.

DOMINO TUMBLING: Michael Cairney, a 23-year-old civil engineer from London, set off a 169,713-domino topple in which he had the tiles walk up a 7-foot ramp, dial a phone and touch off a microswitch which took a Polaroid picture.

Egg and Spoon Racing. Gerry O'Kane, 21, from Strathclyde, Scotland, completed a 27-mile fresh egg and dessert spoon marathon in 5 hours 27 minutes on April 7, 1977.

Egg Shelling. Two kitchen hands, Harold Witcomb and Gerald Harding, shelled 1,050 dozen eggs in a $7\frac{1}{4}$-hour shift at Bowyers, Trowbridge, Wiltshire, England on April 23, 1971. Both are blind.

Egg Throwing. The longest recorded distance for throwing a fresh hen's egg without breaking it is 323 feet $2\frac{1}{2}$ inches on the 12th exchange between Johnny Dell Foley and Keith Thomas at Leon High School, Jewett, Texas, on November 12, 1978.

Escapology. The most renowned of all escape artists has been Ehrich Weiss, *alias* Harry Houdini (1874–1926), who pioneered underwater escapes from locked, roped and weighted containers while handcuffed and shackled with irons.

One of the major manufacturers of straitjackets acknowledges that an escapologist "skilled in the art of bone and muscle manipulation" could escape from a standard jacket in seconds. The fastest acknowledged claim is 1.68 seconds by Bill Shirk at the Marion County Sheriff's Department Training Center in Indianapolis, Indiana, in 1979.

Bill Shirk was imprisoned in a cell in Hamilton County Jail, Indiana, on October 31, 1977. He was locked with 3 handcuffs behind his back, tied with a 5-millimeter chain, then fastened in footcuffs and a further 44 lbs. of 5-millimeter and 10-millimeter chain (tensile strength 6.65 tons). He broke out in 3 hours 49 minutes 42 seconds. Shirk also set the record for the highest escape suspended in a straitjacket below a helicopter at 1,610 feet over Indianapolis, on August 7, 1977. He freed himself in 22.5 seconds.

Mario Manzini, a 31-year-old escape artist from New York City, was suspended upside-down 20 feet above the ground securely tied in a Humane Restraint straitjacket and escaped within $8\frac{1}{2}$ seconds on August 8, 1979, on the "Guinness Game" TV show.

Family Tree. The largest family tree on record is the Borton tree of 6,820 names compiled by Nellaray "Borton" Holt of Union Gap, Washington, over 16 years. It measures 18 feet by 15 feet and extends back to 1562. She also constructed a 340-foot-long pedigree chart covering 16 generations, commissioned by Maxine Bremermans.

Fashion Show. The longest fashion show ever recorded was one which lasted for 48 hours on The Roseland Catwalk, Sydney, Australia, on June 16–18, 1977. Lyn Snowdon, Kay Hammond and Virginia Conner were compèred by Patrick Bollen. All walked 41.4 miles.

Adalene Ross of San Francisco, California, has produced and served as the commentator in over 4,610 fashion shows to mid-1979.

Feminine Beauty. Female pulchritude, being qualitative rather than quantitative, does not lend itself to records. It has been suggested that if the face of Helen of Troy (*c.* 1200 B.C.) was capable of launching 1,000 ships, then a unit of beauty sufficient to launch one ship should be called a millihelen.

The pioneer beauty contest was staged at Atlantic City, New Jersey, in 1921, and was won by a blue-eyed blonde with a 30-inch bust, Margaret Gorman. The Miss World contest, begun in 1951, had a winner in 1954, Miss Egypt (Antigone Costanda), who had the Junoesque measurements of 40–26–38. The United Kingdom is the only country to have produced four winners.

The world's largest beauty pageant is the annual Miss Universe contest, inaugurated in Long Beach, California, in 1952. The number of countries represented has reached 78, with Miss Venezuela reigning in 1979. The U.S. has been most successful, winning in 1954, 1956, 1960 and 1967.

Ferris Wheel Riding. The endurance record for big wheel riding is 37 days by Rena Clark and Jeff Block at Frontier Village Amusement Park, San Jose, California, July 1–August 7, 1978.

Fire Pumping. The greatest gallonage stirrup-pumped by a team of 8 in an 80-hour period is 8,995 U.S. gallons by the Witney Brigade, Oxfordshire, England, on August 26–30, 1977.

Fire Pump Pulling. The longest unaided tow of a fire appliance in excess of 1,120 lbs. in 24 hours is 217.5 miles by a team of 32 men from the Hamburg Fire Brigade in 23 hours 55 minutes on June 22–23, 1979.

Flute Marathon. The longest recorded time is 48 hours by flautist Joe Silmon on H.M.S. *Grampus* in Gosport, Hampshire, England, on February 19–20, 1977.

Frisbee Throwing. Competitive Frisbee throwing began in 1957. The International Frisbee Association *indoor* records are:

Men: 296.3 feet by Joseph Youngman on August 22, 1978, in Los Angeles.

FURRY FRISBEE CHAMPION: John Pickerill and "Martha Faye" display the form which gave Martha and Dave Johnson the world record for canine distance throw and catch, a remarkable 334.6 feet on June 11, 1978 in Wilmette, Illinois. Photo by Bob Madden.

Women: 222.5 feet by Monika Lou in Los Angeles on August 24, 1977.

John Kirkland holds the men's *outdoor* record with a throw of 444 feet on April 30, 1978 in Dallas, Texas. The women's outdoor record is 283.5 feet by Susane Lempert on July 24, 1976 in Boston.

The throw, run and catch record is 254.9 feet by Bob Reeve on March 24, 1979, in Santa Barbara, California.

The group marathon record is 1001 hours by the Alhambra Frisbee Disc Club on May 7-June 18, 1978, at Alhambra, California.

Gladiatorial Combat. Emperor Trajan of Rome (98-117 A.D.) staged a display involving 4,941 pairs of gladiators over 117 days. Publius Ostorius, a freedman, survived 51 combats in Pompeii.

Gold Panning. The fastest times recorded for "panning" 8 planted gold nuggets with a 10-inch-diameter pan is 14.45 seconds for men, by Lance Murray, and 15.27 seconds for women, by Mrs. Carolyn Box, both from Ahwahnee, California, in the 1978 18th World Gold Panning Championships held at Tropico Gold Mine, Rosamond, California, on March 4-5, 1978.

Golf Ball Balancing. Lang Martin, 16, of Charlotte, North Carolina, succeeded on July 10, 1977, in balancing 6 new golf balls vertically without using any adhesive.

Grape Catching. The longest recorded distance for catching a thrown grape in the mouth is 259 feet by Arden Chapman at Northeast Louisiana University, Louisiana, on November 7, 1977. The grape thrower was Benny David Jones.

Grave Digging. It is recorded that Johann Heinrich Karl Thieme, sexton of Aldenburg, Germany, dug 23,311 graves during a 50-year career. In 1826, his understudy dug *his* grave.

Guitar Playing. The longest recorded solo guitar-playing marathon is one of 200 hours 2 minutes by David Hathaway in Marion, Indiana, on July 20–28, 1978.

Hairdressing. Gerry Stupple of Dover, Kent, England, cut, set and styled hair continuously for 341 hours 58 minutes, March 5–19, 1979.

Hair Splitting. The greatest reported achievement in hair splitting has been that of the former champion cyclist and craftsman Alfred West (born London, April 14, 1901) who succeeded in splitting a human hair 15 times into 16 parts in 1977. This example of his work is on permanent display in the Guinness World Records Museum in Niagara Falls, Ontario.

Handshaking. The world record for handshaking was set by President Theodore Roosevelt (1858–1919), who shook hands with 8,513 people at a New Year's Day White House presentation in Washington, D.C., on January 1, 1907. Mayor Joseph Lazarow shook hands with 11,030 people on the Boardwalk, Atlantic City, New Jersey, in 11 hours 5 minutes on July 3, 1977. Outside public life this record has become meaningless because aspirants either shake hands with anyone passing by or else shake the same hands repetitively.

Hand-to-Hand Balancing. The longest horizontal dive achieved in any hand-to-hand balancing act is 22 feet by Harry Berry (top mounter) and the late Nelson Soule (understander) of the Bell-Thazer Brothers from Kentucky, who played at state fairs and in vaudeville from 1908 to 1917. Berry used a 10-foot tower and trampoline for impetus. For other circus stunt records, see page 456.

THUMBED FROM FLORIDA TO ALASKA: A young man named Ilmar Island of Pompano Beach, Florida, hitchhiked from Key West, Florida, to Fairbanks, Alaska, a distance of about 5,200 miles, setting out on June 2, 1979, and arriving at his destination on June 7, just 5 days 20 hours and 52 minutes later.

BALANCING STUNT: From 1908 to 1917, Harry Berry and Nelson Soule performed this exciting dive to a hand-to-hand stand.

Handwriting. The longest recorded handwritten letter writing marathon was one of 505 hours and more than 3,998 letters and their envelopes by Raymond L. Cantwell of Oxford, England (trying to raise money for the Radcliffe Infirmary), August 25-September 16, 1978.

Hiking. The longest recorded hike is one of 18,500 miles through 14 countries from Singapore to London by David Kwan, aged 22, which occupied 81 weeks from May 4, 1957, or an average of 32 miles a day.

Hitchhiking. The title of world champion hitchhiker is claimed by Devon Smith who from 1947 to 1971 thumbed lifts totaling 291,000 miles.

Raymond L. Anderson of Cuba, Missouri, hitchhiked across all 48 continental United States in 14 days, 4 hours 42 minutes and 5 seconds in 1976 to beat Devon Smith's record of 33 days.

Hoop Rolling. In 1968 it was reported that Zolilio Diaz (Spain) had rolled a hoop 600 miles from Mieres to Madrid and back in 18 days.

Hopscotch. The longest recorded hopscotch marathon is one of 54 hours 15 minutes by Sharon Wright and Sandra Burchett of Streamwood High School, Streamwood, Illinois, July 23–26, 1978.

Hot Water Bottle Bursting. The highest lung power measurement in bursting hot water bottles is $28\frac{1}{2}$ lbs. per square inch by

HE REALLY BLEW IT!: Champion bodybuilder Franco Columbu huffed and puffed and blew up a hot water bottle until it burst, in just 55 seconds, on the "Guinness Spectacular" television show in April, 1979, and then in August set a new record of 23 seconds on the "Guinness Game" TV show.

Mel Robson of Newcastle upon Tyne, England, in February, 1977. He and Stuart Hughes have both extended a Suba Seal Safety Bottle to 5 feet 6 inches before rupture. Franco Columbu burst this type of bottle in 23 seconds in Los Angeles in August, 1979, for the "Guinness Game" show.

House of Cards. The greatest number of stories achieved in building free-standing houses of cards is 61 in the case of a tower using 3,650 cards by James Warnock at Cantley, Quebec, Canada, on September 8, 1978. The height was 11 feet 7 inches.

Hula Hooping. The highest claim for sustaining gyrating hoops is 62 set by Jo Ann Barnes, 15, of Inglewood, California, co-champion of the 1976 U.S. National Contest at Six Flags Over Georgia, near Atlanta, on October 3, 1976. The longest recorded marathon is 54 hours by Kym Coberly of Denton, Texas, October 7–9, 1978.

Human Cannonball. The record distance for firing a human from a cannon is 175 feet in the case of Emanuel Zacchini in the Ringling Bros. and Barnum & Bailey Circus, in 1940. His muzzle velocity was estimated at 54 m.p.h. On his retirement the management was fortunate in finding that his daughter, Florinda, was of the same caliber.

An experiment on Yorkshire TV in England on August 17, 1978, showed that when Sue Evans, 17, was fired from a cannon, she was ⅜ inch shorter in height on landing.

In the Halifax explosion of December 6, 1917 (see *Worst Accidents*), A. B. William Becker (d. 1969) was blown some 1,600 yards and found, still alive, in a tree.

Human Fly. The greatest climb achieved on the face of a building occurred on May 26, 1977, when George Willig, 27, scaled the outside of the World Trade Center, New York City. He climbed

1,350 feet up in $3\frac{1}{2}$ hours at the rate of 6.4 feet per minute. He evaded police attempting to stop him as he climbed, but on descending by elevator from the 110th floor, he was led to a waiting police car, charged with criminal trespass and reckless endangerment. He was fined $1.10, one cent for each story he climbed.

The name of the masked "human fly" who rode at 240 m.p.h. atop a DC-8 jetliner in April, 1977 has not been disclosed. It is, however, believed unlikely that he is a member of the jet set.

Joke Telling. G. David Howard cracked jokes unremittingly for 16 hours in Clearwater Beach, Florida, July 14–15, 1979.

The duo duration record is 52 hours by Wayne Malton and Mike Hamilton at the Howard Johnson Motor Hotel, Toronto Airport, Canada, November 13–16, 1975.

Juggling. The only juggler in history able to juggle—as opposed to "shower"—10 balls or 8 plates was the Italian Enrico Rastelli, who was born in Samara, Russia, on December 19, 1896, and died in Bergamo, Italy, on December 13, 1931.

HUMAN CANNONBALL: Emanuel Zacchini and his daughter, Florinda, were regularly shot 175 feet from a cannon.

Karate Chop
Note: Claims for breaking bricks and wooden blocks are unsatisfactory because of the lack of any agreed standards of friability and the spacing of fulcrums upon which comparisons can be made. Karatekas have been measured to exert a force of 3,000 newtons (675 lbs. of force) and can develop a speed of 14.4 meters per second (32.2 m.p.h.).

Kissing. The most prolonged osculatory marathon in cinematic history is one of 185 seconds by Regis Toomey and Jane Wyman in *You're In the Army Now*, released in 1940.

In a smoochathon held in Pittsburgh, Pennsylvania, Bobbi Sherlock and Ray Blazina kissed for 130 hours 2 minutes (in aid, they say, of Cystic Fibrosis) on May 1–6, 1978. James Whale, 27, of Metro Radio, Newcastle upon Tyne, England, kissed 4,049 girls in 8 hours in Tyneside, England, on September 22, 1978—a rate of one per 7.11 seconds.

Kiss of Life. Five members of the St. John Ambulance, York, England, maintained a "kiss of life" (mouth-to-mouth resuscitation) for 132 hours with 140,742 inflations, December 26–31, 1978. The "patient" was a dummy. A 168-hour "kiss of life" marathon was completed by 108 members of the Hawthorne Ambulance Service, Farmington, Maine, September 17–24, 1978.

Kite Flying. The single kite record is 22,500 feet (minimum) to 28,000 feet (maximum) by Prof. Phillip R. Kunz of the University of Wyoming and Jay P. Kunz at Laramie, Wyoming, on November 21, 1967. A claim for a chain of 8 kites reaching 31,955 feet was made from Lindenburg (now East Germany) on August 1, 1919.

The longest recorded flight is one of 169 hours by The Sunrise Inn team, Fort Lauderdale, Florida, managed by Will Yolen, on April 30–May 7, 1977.

The most kites flown on a single line is 4,128 by Kazuhiko Asaba, 55, at Kamakura, Japan, on September 21, 1978.

The largest kite on record was built in Naruto City, Japan in 1936, of 3,100 panes of paper weighing 9½ tons. The largest hand-launched kite was one 91 feet long and 2,640 square feet in area, by Mr. and Mrs. Don Shearing at San Pedro, California, on October 17, 1975.

Knitting. The most prolific hand-knitter is Mrs. Gwen Matthewman (b. 1927) of Featherstone, Yorkshire, England, who in 1975 knitted 885 garments involving 10,530 oz. of wool (equivalent to the fleece of 85 sheep). She has been timed to average 108 stitches per minute in a 30-minute test. Her technique has been filmed by the world's only Professor of Knitting, from Japan.

Knot Tying. The fastest recorded time for tying the six Boy Scout Handbook knots (square knot, sheet bend, sheep shank, clove hitch, round turn and two half hitches and bowline) on individual ropes is 8.1 seconds by Clinton R. Bailey, Sr., 52, of Pacific City, Oregon, on April 13, 1977.

Leap Frogging. Fourteen students of Hanover High School, Hanover, New Hampshire, covered 555.25 miles in 148 hours, June 4–10, 1978.

LIGHTNING-STRUCK 7 TIMES: Roy Sullivan of Virginia doesn't know why he is so attractive to lightning, which has gone right through his hat.

Lecture. The longest recorded lecture was one of 56½ hours on "The Old Testament: Mirror of Theocracy" by Wayne P. Morrow at Grants Pass High School, Oregon, on June 3-5, 1978.

Life Saving. In November, 1974, the City of Galveston, Texas, and the Noon Optimist Club unveiled a plaque to the deaf-mute lifeguard Leroy Colombo (1905–74), who saved 907 people from drowning in the waters around Galveston Island from 1917 to his death.

Lightning-Struck. The only living man in the world to be struck by lightning 7 times is former Shenandoah Park Ranger Roy C. Sullivan (U.S.), the human lightning-conductor of Virginia. His attraction for lightning began in 1942 (lost big toe nail) and was resumed in July, 1969 (lost eyebrows), in July, 1970 (left shoulder seared), on April 16, 1972 (hair set on fire) and, *finally*, he hoped, on August 7, 1973: as he was driving along a bolt came out of a small, low-lying cloud, hit him on the head through his hat, set his hair on fire again, knocked him 10 feet out of his car, went through both legs, and knocked his left shoe off. He had to pour a pail of water over his head to cool off. Then, on June 5, 1976, he was struck again for the sixth time, his ankle injured. When he was struck for the *seventh* time on June 25, 1977, while fishing, he was sent to Waynesboro Hospital with chest and stomach burns. He can offer no explanation for his magnetism, but he has donated his lightning-burnt Ranger hats to the Guinness World Records Exhibit Halls in New York City and Myrtle Beach, South Carolina.

Lion Taming. The greatest number of lions mastered and fed in a cage simultaneously by an unaided lion-tamer was 40, by "Captain" Alfred Schneider in 1925.

Clyde (Raymond) Beatty (1903–65) likewise handled more than 40 "cats" (mixed lions and tigers) simultaneously. Beatty, top of the bill for 40 years, insisted on being called a lion-trainer. More than twenty lion-tamers have died of injuries since 1900.

Log Rolling. The record number of International Championships is 10 by Jubiel Wickheim (of Shawnigan Lake, British Columbia, Canada) between 1956 and 1969. At Albany, Oregon, on July 4, 1956, Wickheim rolled on a 140-inch log against Chuck Harris of Kelso, Washington for 2 hours 40 minutes before losing.

Merry-Go-Round. The longest marathon ride on record is one of 312 hours 43 minutes by Gary Mandau, Chris Lyons and Dana Dover in Portland, Oregon, on August 20–September 2, 1976.

Message in a Bottle. The longest recorded interval between drop and pick-up is 64 years, between August 7, 1910 ("please write to Miss Gladys Potter") in Grand Lake, and August, 1974, from Lake Huron. Miss Potter was traced and found to be Mrs. Oliver Scheid, 76, of Columbus, Ohio.

A bottle apparently bearing a message written on November 19, 1899, by Captain Charles Weieerishen of the S.S. *Crown Princess Cecilia* off Varberg, Sweden, was reportedly picked up on the coast of Victoria, B.C., Canada, on December 9, 1936.

Milk Bottle Balancing. The greatest distance walked by a person continuously balancing a full pint milk bottle on the head is 18 miles 880 yards by Willie Hollingsworth of Freeport, New York, on March 24, 1979.

Modeling. Miss Margaux Hemingway (born 1955) of Ketchum, Idaho, signed the largest contract in the history of modeling, for $1,000,000 for 5 years with Fabergé, on May 20, 1975. She is described as "corn-fed pretty" and describes her own height as "five foot twelve."

Lauren Hutton is reported to be at a higher *rate* at $500,000 for 2 years from Revlon. The modeling rate of Cheryl Tiegs (Mrs. Stan Dragoti), proponent of the California Look, was last reported to be $2,000 per day in early 1978.

Morse Code. The highest recorded speed at which anyone has received Morse code is 75.2 words per minute—over 17 symbols per second. This was achieved by Ted R. McElroy (U.S.) in a tournament at Asheville, North Carolina, on July 2, 1939.

Motorcycle and Car Stunting. The so-called T-bone dives or Dive Bomber crashes by cars off ramps over and onto parked cars are measured by the number of cars but, owing to their variable size, and because their purpose in landing on cars is purely to cushion the shock, distance is more significant. The longest recorded distance is 176 feet by Dusty Russell in a 1963 Ford Falcon in Athens, Georgia, in April, 1973.

The longest distance ever achieved for motorcycle long jumping is 212 feet by Alain Jean Prieur (born July 4, 1939) of France at Montlhéry near Paris, over 16 buses on February 6, 1977.

Evel Knievel (Robert Craig Knievel) (b. October 17, 1938, in Butte, Montana) suffered 433 bone fractures by his 1975 season. His abortive attempt to cross the Snake River Canyon, Idaho, on

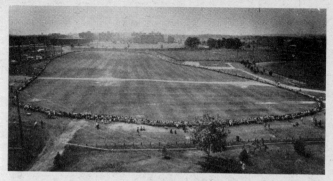

MUSIC GOES 'ROUND AND 'ROUND: This game of musical chairs in North Yorkshire, England, began with 3,728 people scrambling for a seat in the first round.

September 8, 1974, in a rocket, reputedly increased his lifetime earnings by $6,000,000.

The longest recorded jump in a car is one of 203 feet into water by stuntman Roland van de Putte (Belgium) in a Volkswagen on August 11, 1968.

The greatest endurance feat on a "wall of death" was 3 hours 4 minutes by the motorcyclist Louis W. "Speedy" Babbs (1908-1976) on a 32-foot diameter silo, refuelling in motion, at the Venice Amusement Pier, California, on October 11, 1929. In 1934, Babbs performed 1,003 consecutive loop-the-loops, sitting side-saddle in an 18-foot-diameter globe at Ocean Park Pier, California. In a life of stunting, Babbs, who proclaimed "Stuntmen are not fools," had broken 56 bones.

Musical Chairs. The largest game on record was one starting with 3,728 participants and ending with Paul Morgan on the last chair at Butlin's Holiday Centre, Filey, North Yorkshire, England, on July 20, 1978.

Needle Threading. The record number of strands of cotton threaded through a number 13 needle (eye $\frac{1}{2}$ inch by $\frac{1}{16}$ inch) in 2 hours is 3,795 by Brenda Robinson of the College of Further Education, Chippenham, Wiltshire, England, on March 20, 1971.

PARACHUTING RECORDS

Record	Person	Detail	Location	Date
First from Tower	Louis-Sébastien Lenormand (1757–1839)	quasi-parachute	Montpellier, France	1783
First from Balloon	André-Jacques Garnerin (1769–1823)	2,230 ft.	Monceau Park, Paris	Oct. 22, 1797
First from Aircraft (man)	Capt. Albert Berry		St. Louis	Mar. 1, 1912
(woman)	Mrs. Georgina "Tiny" Broadwick (b. 1893)		Griffith Park, Los Angeles	June 21, 1913
First Free Fall	Mrs. Georgina "Tiny" Broadwick	pilot, Glenn L. Martin	North Island, San Diego, California	Sept. 13, 1914
Lowest Escape	Squad. Leader T. Spencer, R.A.F.	30–40 ft.	Wismar Bay, Baltic Sea	Apr. 19, 1945
Longest Duration Fall	Lt. Col. Wm. H. Rankin, U.S.M.C.	40 mins., due to thermals	North Carolina	July 26, 1956
Highest Escape	Flt. Lt. J. de Salis and Fg. Off. P. Lowe, R.A.F.	56,000 ft.	Monyash, Derby, Eng.	Apr. 9, 1958
Longest Delayed Drop (man)	Capt. Joseph W. Kittinger*	84,700 ft. (16.04 miles) from balloon at 102,800 ft.	Tularosa, New Mexico	Aug. 16, 1960
(woman)	O. Kommissarova (U.S.S.R.)	46,250 ft.	over U.S.S.R.	Sept. 21, 1965
(civilian)	R. W. K. Beckett (G.B.)	30,000 ft. from 32,000	D. F. Malan Airport, Capetown, So. Afr.	Nov. 23, 1969
Most Southerly	Harry Ferguson (G.B.)	Operation Deep Freeze —39° F.	South Pole	Nov. 25, 1956
Most Northerly (man)	Tech. Sgt. Richard J. Patton, Ray Munro (Canada)		89° 39′ N.	Mar. 31, 1969
Career Total (man)	Anatolyi Osipov (U.S.S.R.)	8,000	over U.S.S.R.	April, 1978
(woman)	Patty Wilson	More than 1,000	Elsinore paracenter, California	to Nov., 1973
Highest Landing	Ten U.S.S.R. parachutists†	23,405 ft.	Lenina Peak	May, 1969
Heaviest Load	U.S.A.F. C-130 Hercules	25.22 tons steel plates 6 parachutes	El Centro, California	Jan. 28, 1970
Highest from Bridge	Donald R. Boyles	1,053 ft.	Royal Gorge, Colorado	Sept. 7, 1970
Highest Tower Jump	Herb Schmidtz (U.S.)	KTUL-TV Mast 1,984 ft.	Tulsa, Okla.	Oct. 4, 1970
Connected Free Fall	32-member Enquirer team	5 seconds connected (F.A.I. rules)	Tahlequah, Okla.	July 14, 1975
Highest Column	8-Member Enquirer team	170 ft.	over California	Oct., 1978
Most Traveled	Kevin Seaman from a Cessna Skylane (pilot, Charles Merritt)	12,186 miles	Jumps in all 50 U.S. States	July 26–Oct. 15, 1972
Oldest Man	Bob Broadbere (G.B.) (1892–1977)	85 years	Honiton, Devon, England	July 10, 1977
Oldest Woman	Mrs. Ardeth Shuler Evitt	first jump at 74 years 5 months	Mooresville, Indiana	Aug. 6, 1978
24-Hour Total‡	David Parchment (G.B.)	233 in 18 hrs. 7 mins.	Shobdon Air Centre, England	June 19, 1979

*Maximum speed in rarified air was 825.2 m.p.h. at 90,000 feet—marginally supersonic. †Four were killed.
‡First estimates of the sponsored income due for charity were £20,000 ($40,000).

PANCAKE TOSSING CHAMPIONS:
Brenda "Angel" Lavisso (above) of Fort
Worth, Texas, flipped a 9½-inch pancake
8,960 times in 65½ minutes on December
20, 1975. Marty Kraft (right) set a marathon record by flipping pancakes for 52
hours in Hyannis, Massachusetts, August
11-13, 1978.

Noodle Making. Stephen Yim (b. Shanghai, China, 1949) made
256 noodle strips (exceeding 5 feet) in 63 seconds on the BBC-TV
Record Breakers program on October 21, 1973.

Omelette Making. Howard Helmer of New York City cooked
217 two-egg omelettes in 30 minutes at Disneyland, Anaheim, California, on July 14, 1978.

Onion Peeling. The record for onion peeling is 50 lbs. in 25
minutes 7 seconds by Alan Benn at the E.M.I. Bingo and Social Club,
Newcastle upon Tyne, England, on March 29, 1979.

Organ Marathons. The longest church organ recital ever
sustained was one of 90 hours by Frank Hughes at Wesley College
Chapel, Dublin, Ireland on October 31-November 4, 1975.

The longest recorded electric organ marathon is 411 hours by
Vince Bull of Scunthorpe, England, at the Comet Hotel, Scunthorpe,
June 2-19, 1977.

Parachute, Longest Fall Without Parachute. The greatest
altitude from which anyone has bailed out without a parachute and
survived is 21,980 feet. This occurred in January, 1942, when Lt.
(now Lt.-Col.) I. M. Chisov (U.S.S.R.) fell from an Ilyushin 4 which
had been severely damaged. He struck the ground a glancing blow
on the edge of a snow-covered ravine and slid to the bottom. He
suffered a fractured pelvis and severe spinal damage. It is estimated
that the human body reaches 99 per cent of its low-level terminal
velocity after falling 1,880 feet, which takes 13-14 seconds. This is

117-125 m.p.h. at normal atmospheric pressure in a random posture, but up to 185 m.p.h. in a head-down position.

Vesna Vulovic, 23, a Jugoslavenski Aerotransport hostess, survived when her DC-9 blew up at 33,330 feet over the Czechoslovak village of Ceska Kamenice on January 26, 1972. She fell inside a section of tail unit. She was hospitalized for 16 months after emerging from a 27-day coma, having broken many bones.

Party Giving. The most expensive private party ever thrown was that of Mr. and Mrs. Bradley Martin of Troy, N.Y. It was staged at the Waldorf-Astoria Hotel, New York City, in February, 1897. The cost to the host and hostess was estimated to be $369,200 in the days when dollars were made of gold.

Estimates as high as $600,000,000 were made for the 49-nation Organization of African Unity summit conference staged in Libreville, Gabon, in July, 1977.

The "International Year of the Child" children's party in Hyde Park, London, England, was attended by 160,000 children, May 30–31, 1979.

Piano Playing. The longest piano-playing marathon has been one of 1,172 hours 27 minutes (48 days 20 hours 27 minutes) playing 22 hours every day (with 5-minute intervals each playing hour) from January 6 to February 24, 1978, by Roger Lavern at the Osborne Tavern, London.

The women's world record is 133 hours non-stop (5 days 13 hours) by Mrs. Marie Ashton, aged 40, in a theatre at Blyth, Northumberland, England, on August 18–23, 1958. This category has since been discontinued.

Piano Smashing. The record time for demolishing an upright piano and passing the entire wreckage through a circle 9 inches in diameter is 1 minute 37 seconds by six members of the Tinwald Rugby Football Club, Ashburton, New Zealand, led by David Young, on November 6, 1977.

Anthony Fukes, Mike Newman, Terry Cullington and Malcolm Large smashed a piano *with bare hands*, passing all wreckage through a 9-inch circle, in 7 minutes in Nottingham, England, on June 6, 1977, a record equaled by the foursome of C. Crain, R. Crain, O. Richards and M. Cording on December 16, 1978, also in Nottingham.

Piano Tuning. The record time for pitch raising (one semi-tone or 100 cents) and then returning a piano to a musically acceptable quality is 9 minutes 57 seconds by Sebastian Verdolino at the A. & C. Piano Craft Company in New York City, on February 9, 1979.

Pinball Marathon. The most protracted pinball marathon was one of 216 hours played by Jon Wood and David Irvine (each playing separately) of Luton, Bedfordshire, England, March 1–9, 1979.

Pipe Smoking. The duration record for keeping a pipe (3.3 grams of tobacco) continuously alight with only an initial match is 253 minutes 28 seconds by Yrjö Pentikäinen of Kuopio, Finland, on March 15–16, 1968.

HOP TO IT!: Michael Barban of Florissant, Missouri, displays the style which won him a pogo stick record with 105,338 bounces in 18 hours.

Plate Spinning. The greatest number of plates spun simultaneously is 53 by Shukuni Sasaki of Takamatsu, Japan, on January 3, 1979. (See color photo, page J.)

Pogo Stick Jumping. The greatest number of jumps achieved is 105,338 by Michael Barban in 18 hours on September 12, 1978, in Florissant, Missouri.

Scott Spencer, 13, of Wilmington, Delaware, covered 6 miles in 6½ hours in September, 1974.

Pole Sitting. There being no international rules, the "standards of living" atop poles vary widely. The record squat is 399 days by Frank Perkins from June 1, 1975, to July 4, 1976, in an 8- by 8-foot box atop a 50-foot telegraph pole in San Jose, California.

Modern records do not, however, compare with that of St. Simeon the Younger (c. 521–597 A.D.), called Stylites (Greek, *stylos* = pillar), a monk who spent his last 45 years on a stone pillar on the Hill of Wonders, Syria. This is probably the earliest example of record setting.

Potato Peeling. The peeling of 170 lbs. of potatoes to an institutional cookery standard by 5 teenagers (ages 14–16) with standard kitchen knives in 45 minutes was set in Sydney, Australia, on June 11, 1977. The peelers were Julie Morris, Chris Hughes, Kerry White, Angus McKinnon and Julian Morgan.

Psychiatrist, Fastest. The world's fastest "psychiatrist" was Dr. Albert L. Weiner of Erlton, New Jersey, who dealt with up to 50 patients a day in four treatment rooms. He relied heavily on narcoanalysis, muscle relaxants and electro-shock treatments. In December, 1961, he was found guilty on 12 counts of manslaughter from using unsterilized needles. He had been trained in osteopathy, which includes all varieties of medicine, but had no specialization in psychiatry.

Quoit Throwing. The world's record for rope quoit throwing is an unbroken sequence of 4,002 pegs by Bill Irby, Sr. of Australia in 1968.

Longest on a Raft. The longest recorded survival alone on a raft is 133 days (4½ months) by Second Steward Poon Lim (born Hong Kong) of the U.K. Merchant Navy, whose ship, the S.S. *Ben Lomond*, was torpedoed in the Atlantic 565 miles west of St. Paul's Rocks at Lat. 00° 30′ N. and Long. 38° 45′ W. at 11:45 a.m. on November 23, 1942. He was picked up by a Brazilian fishing boat off Salinópolis, Brazil, on April 5, 1943, and was able to walk ashore. In July, 1943, he was awarded the British Empire Medal, and now lives in New York City.

Maurice and Maralyn Bailey survived 118¼ days in an inflatable dinghy 4½ feet in diameter in the northeast Pacific from March 4 to June 30, 1973.

Riding in Armor. The longest recorded ride in full armor is one of 147.6 miles around East Grinstead, West Sussex, England, in 3 days 40 minutes (riding time 24 hours 25 minutes) by John Asmus and John Waller on August 26–30, 1976.

Riveting. The world's record for riveting is 11,209 in 9 hours by J. Moir at the Workman Clark Ltd. shipyard, Belfast, Northern Ireland, in June, 1918. His peak hour was his seventh with 1,409, an average of nearly 23½ per minute.

Rocking Chair. The longest recorded duration of a "Rockathon" is 432 hours by Mrs. Maureen Weston of Petreburgh Athletics Club, Peterborough, Cambridge, England, on April 14–May 2, 1977.

Roller Coasting. The endurance record for riding on a roller coaster is 168 hours by Jim King at Panama City, Florida, August 28-September 4, 1978. He covered a distance of 1,946.5 miles.

Rolling Pin. The record distance for a woman to throw a 2-lb. rolling pin is 157 feet 6 inches by Janet Thompson at West London Stadium, Wormwood Scrubs, London, England, on July 6, 1975.

Rope Tricks. The only man ever able to spin 14 ropes simultaneously is Frank Dean of Palmdale, California, on August 8, 1979, on the "Guinness Game" show. He used extenders attached to his knees and hips, as well as hand-held extenders.

Rummage Sale. The largest known rummage sale is that staged by the Winnetka Congregational Church in Illinois, which raised $73,200.79 in a one-day sale on May 10, 1979.

See-Saw. The most protracted session for see-sawing indoors is one of 1,101 hours 40 minutes on a suspension see-saw by George Partridge and Tamara Marquez of Auburn High School, Auburn, Washington, on March 28–May 13, 1977.

ROLLER COASTER MARATHON: Disc jockey Jim King of Panama City, Florida, raised money for Muscular Dystrophy as he rode a roller coaster for over a week, August 28–September 4, 1978. At top, a doctor makes sure Jim is still ready to roll after several days of riding.

Georgia Chaffin and Tammy Adams of Goodhope Junior High School, Cullman, Alabama, completed 730½ hours outdoors from June 25–July 25, 1975.

Sermon. The longest sermon on record was delivered by the Reverend Donald Thomas of Brooklyn, New York, for 93 hours, September 18–22, 1978.

From May 31 to June 10, 1969, the 14th Dalai Lama (born July 6, 1934, as Tenzin Gyalto), the exiled ruler of Tibet, preached a sermon on Tantric Buddhism for five to seven hours per day to total 60 hours, in India.

Shaving. The fastest demon barber on record is Gerry Harley, who shaved 130 men in 60 minutes with a cut-throat razor at The Plough, Gillingham, Kent, England, on April 1, 1971. In setting a marathon record he ran out of volunteer subjects.

Sheaf Tossing. The world's best performance for tossing an 8-lb. sheaf for height is 64.86 feet by Trond Ulleberg of Skolleborg, Norway, on November 11, 1978. Such pitchfork contests date from 1914.

Shoe Shining. In this category, limited to teams of 4 teenagers, an 8-hour time limit, and all shoes "on the hoof," the record is 6,334 pairs by the Bedford North (Newnham) Scout Group in England, on July 16, 1977.

Shorthand, Fastest. The highest recorded speeds ever attained under championship conditions are: 300 words per minute (99.64 per cent accuracy) for five minutes and 350 w.p.m. (99.72 per cent accuracy, that is, two insignificant errors) for two minutes by Nathan Behrin (U.S.), in New York City in December, 1922. Behrin (born 1887) used the Pitman system invented in 1837. Morris I. Kligman, official court reporter at the U.S. Court House, New York City, has taken 50,000 words in five hours (a sustained rate of 166.6 w.p.m.). Rates are dependent upon the nature, complexity, and syllabic density of the material.

G. W. Bunbury of Dublin, Ireland, held the unique distinction of writing at 250 w.p.m. for 10 minutes on January 23, 1894.

Showering. The most prolonged continuous shower bath on record is one of 336 hours by Arron Marshall of Rockingham Park, Western Australia, July 29–August 12, 1978.

The feminine record is 120 hours 1 minute by Penny Cresswell of Waikiki, Western Australia, September 7–12, 1977.

Desquamation can be a positive danger.

Singing. The longest recorded solo singing marathon is one of 134 hours 54 minutes by S. A. E. W. Perera of the Sri Lanka Army, May 8–13, 1979.

The marathon record for a choir is 61 hours by the Clinton High School Choir, Saline, Michigan, on January 20–22, 1979. Acharya Prem Bhikuji started chanting the Akhand Ram Dhum in 1964 and devotees took this up in rotation, completing their devotions 13 years later on July 31, 1977, at Jamnagar, India.

Skateboarding. "World" skateboard championships have been staged intermittently since 1966. The highest speed recorded on a skateboard is 66.5 m.p.h. over 50 yards under South African Skateboard Association surveillance on a course at Naturina near Johannesburg, flat on his back, by Peter Clark, 14, on December 19, 1977. The stand-up record is 53.45 m.p.h. by John Hutson, 23, at Signal Hill, Long Beach, California, on June 11, 1978. The high jump record is 5 feet by Bryan Beardsly (U.S.) at Signal Hill, September 24–25, 1977.

At the U.S. Skateboard Association championships, Tony Alva, 19, of Santa Monica, California, took off from a moving skateboard, jumped over 17 barrels (12-inch diameters) and landed on another skateboard.

Mike Kinney won a marathon contest at Reseda, California, on May 26, 1979, with 217.3 miles in 30 hours 35 minutes.

Slinging. The greatest distance recorded for a slingshot is 1,147 feet 4 inches using a 34-inch-long sling and a 7½-oz. stone by Melvyn Gaylor on the Newport Golf Course, Shide, Isle of Wight, England, on September 25, 1970.

Smoke-Ring Blowing. The highest recorded number of smoke rings formed from a single pull of a cigarette is 441 rings by Atsuhiro Nakamura of Nara, Japan, on December 21, 1978.

BEARD OF BEES: Don Cooke of Ohio "grew" a beard of approximately 17,500 Italian honey bees for the "Guinness Spectacular" TV show on April 6, 1979. The beard extended 17 inches from his sideburns to his waist as the bees clung to each other, attempting to reach the queen bee which was fastened to his chin. (Photo by Franklin Berger)

PLATE SPINNING: Shukuni Sasaki of Japan kept 53 plates spinning simultaneously on Japanese television, January 3, 1979.

A BIT OF A BATTLE: Pulling only with his teeth on the bit in his mouth, "Hercules" John Massis of Belgium prevented a helicopter from rising, despite the measured 375 pounds of upward pressure it exerted, in a man-versus-machine tug of war, for the "Guinness Spectacular" TV show on April 7, 1979. (Photo by Franklin Berger)

J

STEEPEST ASCENT: Farrell Hettig and Steve McPeak raced up a wire at a hazardous 39° angle for the "Guinness Spectacular" TV show. Hettig made it to the top first, but McPeak seconds later reached the lofty height as well. (Photo by Franklin Berger)

NICE PIZZA REAL ESTATE: The world's largest pizza is this mozzarella monster created in October, 1978, by Lorenzo Amato in Glens Falls, New York. It measured over 80 feet across and weighed more than 9 tons.

K

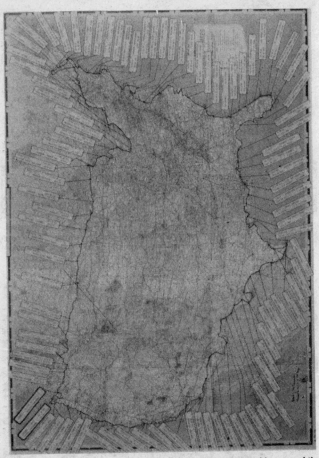

ITINERANT PEDALLER'S ITINERARY: The dark blue line stretching around the entire perimeter of the United States on this map traces the route of Richard J. DeBernardis, who bicycled around the country in a continuous journey of 12,092 miles. He began his 180-day trip on September 10, 1978 at 12:35 p.m. in Seattle, Washington, reached Portland, Maine, on November 3; Chiefland, Florida, by Christmas; Presidio, Texas, on January 26, 1979; and returned to Seattle on March 8.

HOLY SMOKE!: Atsuhiro Nakamura blew 441 smoke rings from a single pull on a cigarette on Japanese television.

Snowshoe Travel. The fastest officially recorded time for covering a mile is 6 minutes 23.8 seconds by Richard Lemay (Frontenac Club of Quebec, Canada) at Manchester, New Hampshire, in 1973.

Speech-Listening. The Guild of Professional Toastmasters (founded 1962) has only 12 members. Its founder, Ivor Spencer, listened to a speech in excess of 2 hours by the maudlin guest of honor of a retirement luncheon. The Guild also elects the most boring speaker of the year, but for professional reasons will not publicize the winners' names until a decent interval has elapsed.

Spinning. The duration record for spinning a clock balance wheel by hand is 5 minutes 26.8 seconds by Philip Ashley, aged 16, of Leigh, Lancashire, England, on May 20, 1968.

Spitting. The greatest distance achieved at the annual (July) tobacco-spitting classic (instituted 1955) at Raleigh, Mississippi, is 31 feet 1 inch by Don Snyder, 28, on July 26, 1975. In the 3rd International Spittin', Belchin' and Cussin' Triathlon, Harold Fielden reached 34 feet ¼ inch at Central City, Colorado, on July 13, 1973. Distance is dependent on the quality of salivation, absence of cross wind, two-finger pucker and the coordination of the back arch and neck snap. Sprays or wads smaller than a dime are not measured.

The record for projecting a melon seed under WCWSSCA rules is 59 feet 1½ inches by Brian Dunne at Savemore Centre, Yeppoon, Queensland, Australia, on December 11, 1976. The highest reported distance for a cherrystone spat from a sitting position is 49 feet 2 inches by William A. Mobley at Eau Claire, Michigan, on July 8, 1978. Spitters who care about their image wear 12-inch block-ended boots so practice spits can be measured without a tape.

MOVING UP IN THE WORLD: "Steady Eddy" Long (left) mastered 30-foot-3-inch stilts in Loyal, Wisconsin, in 1978. Richard Black (right) set a record for the vertical mile in July, 1978, by racing up and down the stairs at Lake Point Tower, Chicago.

Stair Climbing. The 100-story record for stair climbing was set by Dennis W. Martz in the Detroit Plaza Hotel, Detroit, Michigan, on June 26, 1978, at 11 minutes 23.8 seconds.

The record for running a vertical mile in continuous action is 1 hour 25 minutes 6 seconds in ascent and 44 minutes 39 seconds in descent, set by Richard Black in 9 round trips up and down the stairs of Lake Point Tower, Chicago, on July 13, 1978. *These records can only be attempted in buildings with a minimum of 70 stories.*

Jerry Rafferty, 26, raced up the 1,575 steps of the Empire State Building, New York City, in 12 minutes 19.8 seconds on February 15, 1979.

Standing Up. Swami Maujgiri Maharij stood up continuously for more than 17 years, from 1955 to November, 1973, while performing the "Tapasya" or penance in Shahjahanpur, India. He leaned against a plank to sleep.

Stilt Walking. Even with a safety wire, very high stilts are extremely dangerous—25 steps are deemed to constitute "mastery." Eddy Wolf, known as "Steady Eddy," of Loyal, Wisconsin, has mastered aluminum stilts 30 feet 3 inches tall.

Hop pickers use stilts up to 15 feet. In 1892, M. Garisoain of Bayonne, France, stilt-walked 4.97 miles into Biarritz in 42 minutes to average 7.1 m.p.h. In 1891, Sylvain Dornon stilt-walked from Paris to Moscow *via* Vilno in 50 days for the 1,830 miles. Another source gives his time as 58 days.

Stowaway. The most rugged stowaway was Socarras Ramirez, who escaped from Cuba on June 4, 1969, by stowing away in an unpressurized wheel well in the starboard wing of a Boeing 707 in a 5,600-mile Iberian Airlines flight from Havana to Madrid. He survived 8 hours at 30,000 feet where temperatures were −8°F. (−22.2°C.).

Stretcher Bearing. The longest recorded carry of a stretcher case with a 140-lb. "body" is 120 miles in 40 hours 12 minutes by two 4-man teams from the 1st Field Ambulance, Canadian Forces Base, Calgary, Alberta, Canada, May 5–7, 1979.

String Ball, Largest. The largest balls of string on record are 11 feet in diameter weighing 5½ tons, one of which was amassed by Francis A. Johnson of Darwin, Minnesota, since 1950, and another by Frank Stoeber of Cawker City, Kansas, since at least 1962.

Submergence. The longest submergence under water (excluding the use of diving bells) is 141 hours 24 minutes established by L/Cpl. Steven Cook, 22, of Romsey, near Birmingham, England, in a 5,950-gallon tank in Confederation Square, Ottawa, Canada, in 83°–84°F. water, August 12–18, 1978.

Suggestion Box. The most prolific suggestion box stuffer on record is John Drayton (born September 13, 1907) of Newport, Gwent,

ONE OF TWO LARGEST BALLS OF STRING: Francis Johnson of Darwin, Minnesota, began this string ball in 1950. It now measures 11 feet in diameter and weighs 5½ tons.

Wales, who plied British Rail and the companies from which it was formed with a total of 28,186 suggestions from 1924 to May, 1979. One out of every seven was accepted.

The U.S. Postal Service champion, John Kingston, has an acceptance rate of one in 5.3 (284 out of 1,500) to January, 1976.

Swinging. The record duration for continuous swinging is 185 hours by Mollie Jackson of Tarrytown, New York, March 25–April 1, 1979.

Tailoring. The highest speed in making a 2-piece wool suit, starting with shearing the sheep and ending with a finished article, is 1 hour 52 minutes 18.5 seconds by Bud Macken of Mascot, N.S.W., Australia, on December 23, 1931. The shearing took 35 seconds, the carding and teasing 19 minutes and the weaving 20 minutes.

Talking. The world record for non-stop talking is 150 hours by Raymond Cantwell at Trust Houses Forte Travel Lodge, Oxford, England, December 4–10, 1977.

The longest continuous political speech on record was one of 33 hours 5 minutes by Marvin Eakman of Minneapolis, Minnesota, November 6–7, 1978.

The women's non-stop talking record was set by Mrs. Mary E. Davis, who, on September 2–7, 1958, started talking at a radio station in Buffalo, New York, and did not stop until 110 hours 30 minutes 5 seconds later in Tulsa, Oklahoma.

Historically the longest after-dinner speech with unsuspecting victims was 3 hours, delivered by the Rev. Henry Whitehead (d. March, 1896) at the Rainbow Tavern in London, England, on January 16, 1874. Both Nicholas Parsons and Gyles Brandreth spoke from 8 p.m. to 7 a.m. February 13–14, 1978, at the Hyde Park Hotel, London, in aid of Action Research, to tie a longest after-dinner speech contest with 11-hour performances.

Pulling with Teeth. The "strongest teeth in the world" belong to "Hercules" John Massis (b. Wilfried Oscar Morbée, June 4, 1940) of Oostakker, Belgium, who on November 8, 1978, demonstrated the ability to pull 3 railroad cars weighing 140 tons on a level track outside Stockholm, Sweden, with a bit in his teeth. At Evry, France, on March 19, 1977, he raised a weight of $513\frac{5}{8}$ lbs. to a height of 6 inches from the ground with a bit in his teeth. Massis prevented a helicopter from taking off using only a mouth harness in Los Angeles on April 7, 1979, for the "Guinness Spectacular" ABC-TV show. (See photo, page J.)

Tightrope Walking. The greatest 19th century tightrope walker was Jean François Gravelet, *alias* Charles Blondin (1824–1897), of France, who made the earliest crossing of Niagara Falls on a 3-inch rope 1,100 feet long, 160 feet above the Falls on June 30, 1859. He also made a crossing with Harry Colcord pickaback on September 15, 1860, though other artists find it difficult to believe. Colcord was his agent.

The world tightrope endurance record is 185 days by Henri Rochetain (born 1926) of France on a wire 394 feet long, 82 feet above a supermarket in St. Etienne, France, from March 28 to

TIGHTROPE JUMPER: Javier Gomez (known as Valentino) from Cali, Colombia, jumped rope 54 times consecutively without a miss on a high wire stretched 33 feet above the ground on July 30, 1979, for the "Guinness Game" television show.

September 29, 1973. His ability to sleep on the wire has left doctors puzzled. During this time, he walked some 310 miles on the wire to keep fit.

The longest tightrope walk by any funambulist was achieved by Rochetain on a wire 3,790 yards long slung across a gorge at Clermont-Ferrand, France, on July 13, 1969. He required 3 hours 20 minutes to negotiate the crossing.

The highest high-wire act was performed by Steve McPeak (born September 1945), who made a 300-foot crossing on a wire 2,624 feet above the Yosemite Valley floor in California on July 5, 1976. McPeak also holds the record for the greatest tightrope ascent, with his 2,400-foot-long walk up a 1.7-inch cable to the top of Sugarloaf Mountain in Rio de Janeiro harbor, Brazil. The climb was 675 feet, accomplished in 65 minutes.

Farrell Hettig of Sarasota, Florida, beat Steve McPeak by five seconds in setting the record for the steepest high-wire ascent when they raced up a wire ascending to 57 feet at an angle of 39° in Los Angeles, on the "Guinness Spectacular" ABC-TV show in April, 1979. (See color photo, page K.)

McPeak has also successfully ridden a 41-foot-tall unicycle across a high wire which was itself suspended 40 feet above the ground.

The greatest height above street level in a high-wire performance was when Philippe Petit, 24, of Nemours, France, crossed on a wire 1,350 feet above the street in New York City between the newly constructed twin towers of the World Trade Center on August 7, 1974. He shot the 140-foot-long wire across by bow and arrow. He was charged with criminal trespass after a 75-minute display of at least 7 crossings. The police psychiatrist's verdict was, "Anyone who does this 110 stories up can't be entirely right."

Tire Stacking. The greatest number of car tires lifted at one time is 60 by Gary Windibank at Braishfield Country Fair, Romsey, England, on June 3, 1979. The total weight was 840 lbs. The tires were Michelin 155–13 XZX.

Treasure Finding. The most successful treasure hunter has been C. Fred Ahrendt of Dayton, Ohio, who, by August, 1976, had found with his metal detector 175 class rings (earliest, 1890) and 179 wedding rings of 14 or more carats. Employees of crematoria are officially excluded from the competition.

Tree Climbing. The fastest climb up a 100-foot fir spar pole and return to the ground is one of 31.1 seconds by Marvin Trudeau of Honeymoon Bay, B.C., Canada, at Haywood, Wisconsin, in July, 1977.

The fastest time up a 40-foot coconut tree barefoot is 8.4 seconds by Kini Marawai in Suva, Fiji, on September 2, 1977.

Tree Sitting. The duration record for sitting in a tree is 182 days 2 minutes by Glen T. Woodrich, 23, at Golf N' Stuff Amusement Park, Norwalk, California, January 1–July 2, 1978.

Typing, Fastest. The highest recorded speeds attained with a ten-word penalty per error on a manual machine are:

One Minute: 170 words, Margaret Owen (U.S.) (Underwood Standard), New York City, October 21, 1918.

One Hour: 147 words (net rate per minute), Albert Tangora (U.S.) (Underwood Standard), October 22, 1923.

The official hour record on an electric machine is 9,316 words (40 errors) on an I.B.M. machine, giving a net rate of 149 words per minute, by Margaret Hamma, now Mrs. Dilmore (U.S.), in Brooklyn, New York City, on June 20, 1941. Mrs. Barbara Blackburn of Everett, Washington, can maintain 150 words per minute for 50 minutes (37,500 key strokes) and attains a speed of 170 w.p.m. using the Dvorak Simplified Keyboard (D.S.K.) system.

In an official test in 1946, Stella Pajunas, now Mrs. Garnard, attained a speed of 216 words in a minute on an I.B.M. machine.

Typing, Slowest. Chinese typewriters are so complex that even the most skilled operator cannot select characters from the 1,500 offered at a rate of more than 11 words a minute. The Hoang typewriter produced in 1962 now has 5,850 Chinese characters. The keyboard is 2 feet wide and 17 inches high.

Typing, Longest. The world duration record for typing on an electric machine is 162 hours 1 minute by Robin Heil of Sherman E. Burroughs High School, Ridgecrest, California, April 6–13, 1976.

Mrs. Marva Drew, 51, of Waterloo, Iowa, between 1968 and November 30, 1974, typed the numbers 1 to 1,000,000 (in words) on a manual typewriter. She used 2,473 pages. When asked why, she replied, "But I love to type."

The longest duration typing marathon on a manual machine is 120 hours 15 minutes by Mike Howell, a 23-year-old blind office worker from Greenfield, Oldham, Greater Manchester, England, November 25–30, 1969, on an Olympia manual typewriter in Liverpool. In aggregating 561,006 strokes he performed a weight movement of 2,780 tons plus a further 174 tons in moving the carriage on line spacing.

Unsupported Circle. The highest recorded number of people who have demonstrated the physical paradox of all being seated without a chair in an unsupported circle is 3,394 for 60 seconds at Balment Park, Cranbrook, B.C., Canada, on May 14, 1978.

Walking-on-Hands. The duration record for walking-on-hands is 871 miles by Johann Hurlinger, who, in 55 daily 10-hour stints, averaged 1.58 m.p.h. from Vienna to Paris in 1900.

Cadet Thomas P. Hunt of the U.S.A.F. Academy, Colorado Springs, completed a 50-yard inverted sprint in 18.7 seconds on May 20, 1978. (See photo, page P.)

Wheelbarrow Pushing. The heaviest loaded wheelbarrow pushed for a minimum 20 feet is one loaded with 289 bricks weighing 2,347 lbs. pushed by Bill Richardson of Pontefract, Yorkshire, England, on June 30, 1979.

Whip Cracking. The longest stock whip ever "cracked" (*i.e.* the end made to travel above the speed of sound—760 m.p.h.) is one of 97 feet wielded by Noel Harris on the steps of Parliament House, Melbourne, Australia, on August 7, 1978. The dry weight of the red hide-plaited whip was 26.4 lbs.

Window Cleaning. The fastest time in the annual Top Shiner contest in England has been 46.5 seconds plus three ½-second smear penalties to equal 48 seconds by Richard Baterip for 3 standard 1040 × 1153-mm. (40.94 × 45.39-inch) office windows with a 300-mm.-long (11.8-inch) squeegee and 9 liters (15.83 pints) of water.

Wood Cutting. The earliest competitions date from Tasmania in 1874. The records set at the Lumberjack World Championships at Hayward, Wisconsin (founded 1960), are:

Power Saw	11.55 sec.	Ron Johnson (U.S.)	1976
One-Man Bucking	23.06 sec.	Ron Hartill (N.Z.)	1976
Standing Block Chop	26.9 sec.	Ron Wilson (Aust.)	1973
Underhand Block Chop	20.3 sec.	Jim Alexander (Aust.)	1973
Two-Man Bucking	10.40 sec.	Dave Green and	
		Rudy Dettmer (U.S.)	1976

White pine logs 14 inches in diameter are used for chopping and 20 inches for sawing.

Writing Small. In 1926, an account was published of Alfred McEwen's pantograph record in which the 56-word version of the Lord's Prayer was written by diamond point on glass in the space of 0.0016 by 0.0008 of an inch.

Frank C. Watts of Felmingham, Norfolk, England, demonstrated for photographers on January 24, 1968, the ability, without mechanical or optical aids, to write the Lord's Prayer 34 times (9,452 letters) within the size of a definitive postage stamp (0.84 × 0.71 of an inch).

Writing under Handicap. The ultimate feat in "funny writing" would appear to be the ability to write extemporaneously and decipherably backwards, upside down, laterally inverted (mirror-style) while blindfolded, with both hands simultaneously. One claim to this ability with both hands and feet simultaneously is under investigation.

Yodeling. The most protracted yodel on record was that of Donn Reynolds for 7 hours 29 minutes in Brampton, Ontario, Canada, on November 27, 1976.

Yo-Yo. The yo-yo originates from a Filipino jungle fighting weapon recorded in the 16th century weighing 4 lbs. with a 20-foot thong. The word means "come-come." The modern toy was first marketed by Donald F. Duncan of Chicago in 1926. The most difficult modern yo-yo trick is the "Whirlwind," incorporating both inside and outside horizontal loop-the-loops.

The individual continuous endurance record is 120 hours by John Winslow of Gloucester, Virginia, on November 23-28, 1977.

Dr. Allen Bussey in Waco, Texas, on April 23, 1977, completed 20,302 loops in 3 hours (including 6,886 in a single 60-minute period). He used a Duncan Imperial with a $34\frac{1}{2}$-inch nylon string.

EATING RECORDS

While no healthy person has been reported to have succumbed in any contest for eating or drinking non-alcoholic or non-toxic drinks, such attempts, from a medical point of view, must be regarded as *extremely* inadvisable, particularly among young people. Gastronomic record attempts should aim at improving the *rate* of consumption, rather than the volume. *Guinness* will not list any records involving the consumption of more than 2 liters (approximately 2 quarts) of beer or any at all involving liquor. Nor will this book list records for potentially dangerous categories such as consuming live ants, goldfish, quantities of chewing gum or marshmallows, or raw eggs in shells. The ultimate in stupidity—the eating of a bicycle—has, however, been recorded since it is unlikely to attract competition.

Records for eating and drinking by trenchermen do not match those suffering from the rare disease of bulimia (morbid desire to eat) and polydipsia (pathological thirst). Some bulimia patients have to spend 15 hours a day eating, with an extreme consumption of 384 lbs. 2 oz. of food in six days by Matthew Daking, aged 12, in 1743 (known as Mortimer's case). Fannie Meyer of Johannesburg, after a skull fracture, was stated in 1974 to be unsatisfied by less than 192 pints of water a day. By October, 1978, he was down to 62 pints. Miss Helge Andersson (b. 1908) of Lindesberg, Sweden, was reported in January, 1971, to have been drinking 48 pints of water a day since 1922—a total of 105,120 gallons.

The world's greatest trencherman is Edward Abraham ("Bozo") Miller (born 1909) of Oakland, California. He consumes up to 25,000 calories per day, or more than 11 times that recommended. He stands 5 feet 7½ inches tall but weighs from 280 to 300 lbs., with a 57-inch waist. He has been undefeated in eating contests since 1931 (see below).

The bargees (barge sailors) on the Rhine are reputed to be the world's heaviest eaters, with 5,200 calories per day. However, the New Zealand Sports Federation of Medicine reported in December, 1972, that a long-distance road runner consumed 14,321 calories in 24 hours.

Specific records have been claimed as follows:

Baked Beans. 2,353 cold beans one by one, with a cocktail stick, in 30 minutes by John Lawrence in Petersfield, Hampshire, England, on March 4, 1978.

Bananas. 17 (edible weight minimum 4½ ounces each) in 2 minutes by Dr. Ronald L. Alkana at the University of California, Irvine, on December 7, 1973.

Beer. Steven Petrosino drank one liter of beer in 1.3 seconds on June 22, 1977, at "The Gingerbread Man," in Carlisle, Pennsylvania.
Peter G. Dowdeswell (born in London, July 29, 1940) of Earls Barton, Northamptonshire, England, drank 2 liters in 6 seconds on February 7, 1975. He also holds the speed record for consuming 2 Imperial pints, in 2.3 seconds, on June 11, 1975.

Bicycle. 15 days by Monsieur "Mangetout" (M. Lotito), in the form of tires and metal filings, at Evry, France, March 17–April 2, 1977. No further entries in this category will be accepted.

Champagne. 1,000 bottles per annum by Bobby Acland of the "Black Raven," Bishopsgate, London, England.

Cheese. 16 oz. of hard English cheddar in 1 minute 13 seconds by Peter Dowdeswell (see Beer) in Earls Barton, Northamptonshire, England, on July 14, 1978.

Chicken. 27 (2-lb. pullets) by "Bozo" Miller (see above) at a sitting at Trader Vic's, San Francisco, California, in 1963.

Clams. 424 Little Necks in 8 minutes by Dave Barnes at Port Townsend Bay, Washington, on May 3, 1975.

Doughnuts. 29 (total of 2 lbs. 12½ oz.) in 7 minutes 16 seconds by Hany Rizk of Melbourne, Australia, on April 10, 1976.

Eels. 1 lb. of elvers (1,300) in 13.7 seconds by Peter Dowdeswell at Reeves Club, Bristol, England, on October 20, 1978.

Eggs. (Hard-boiled) 14 in 58 seconds by Peter Dowdeswell (see above) in Corby, England, on February 18, 1977. (Soft-boiled) 32 in 78 seconds by Peter Dowdeswell in Northamptonshire, England, on April 8, 1978. (Raw, without shells) 13 in 2.2 seconds by Peter Dowdeswell in Norwich, England, on January 26, 1978.

Frankfurters. 23 (2-ounce) in 3 minutes 10 seconds by Linda Kuerth, 21, at Veterans Stadium, Philadelphia, on July 12, 1977.

Gherkins. 1 lb. in 43.6 seconds by Rex Barker of Elkhorn, Nebraska, on October 30, 1975.

Grapes. 3 lbs. 1 oz. in 34.6 seconds by Jim Ellis of Montrose, Michigan, on May 30, 1976.

Hamburgers. 20¾ hamburgers (each weighing 3½ oz., totaling 4½ lbs. of meat) and buns in 30 minutes by Alan Peterson at Longview, Washington, on February 8, 1979.

Ice Cream. 3 lbs. 6 oz. in 90 seconds by Bennett D'Angelo at Dean Dairy, Waltham, Massachusetts, on August 7, 1977.

Lemons. 12 quarters (3 lemons) whole (including skin and seeds) in 22.9 seconds by Peter Dowdeswell at Reeves Club, Bristol, England, on October 20, 1978.

Meat. One whole roast ox in 42 days by Johann Ketzler of Munich, Germany, in 1880.

FASTEST WITH FAST FOOD: Burger-eating recordholder Alan Peterson devoured 20¾ in 30 minutes in February, 1979.

Milk. One Imperial quart (1.2 U.S. quarts) in 3.2 seconds by Peter Dowdeswell (see above) at Dudley Top Rank Club, West Midlands, England, on May 31, 1975.

Oysters. 218 in 5 minutes by Mickey Rigdon at Fat City, Metairie, Louisiana, on July 6, 1977.

The record for opening oysters is 100 in 3 minutes 1 second by Douglas Brown, 31, at Christchurch, New Zealand, on April 29, 1975.

Pancakes. 62 (each 6 inches in diameter, buttered and with syrup) in 6 minutes 58.5 seconds by Peter Dowdeswell (see above) in Northamptonshire, England, on February 9, 1977.

Peanuts. 100 (unshelled) singly in 47.32 seconds by Dan Blackwell in South Lake Tahoe, California, on February 10, 1979.

Pickled Onions. 91 (total weight 30 oz.) in 1 minute 8 seconds by Pat Donahue in Victoria, British Columbia, Canada, on March 9, 1978.

Potatoes. 3 lbs. in 1 minute 22 seconds by Peter Dowdeswell in Earls Barton, Northamptonshire, England, on August 25, 1978.

Potato Chips. 30 2-oz. bags in 24 minutes 33.6 seconds, without a drink, by Paul G. Tully of Brisbane University, Australia, in May, 1969.

Prunes. 144 in 65 seconds by Douglas Mein at Dundee University, Tayside, Scotland, on October 19, 1978.

Ravioli. 324 (first 250 in 70 minutes) by "Bozo" Miller (see above) at Rendezvous Room, Oakland, California, in 1963.

Sandwiches. 40 (jam and butter, $6 \times 3\frac{3}{4} \times \frac{1}{2}$ inch) in 17 minutes 53.9 seconds by Peter Dowdeswell (see above) on October 17, 1977, at the Donut Shop, Reedley, California.

Sausages. 96 1-oz. sausages in 6 minutes by Steve Meltzer of Brooklyn, New York, on October 14, 1974.

Shellfish. 81 (unshelled) whelks in 15 minutes by William Corfield at Helyar Arms, East Coker, Somerset, England, on September 6, 1969.

Shrimps. 3 lbs. in 4 minutes 8 seconds by Peter Dowdeswell (see above) of Earls Barton, Northamptonshire, England, on May 25, 1978.

Snails. 124 (Moroccan snails) in 15 minutes by Mrs. Nicky Bove at the 6th Great Escargot Eating Contest, Houston, Texas, April 1, 1974. The style prize was won by Rex Miller.

Spaghetti. 100 yards in 28.73 seconds by Steve Weldon of Austin, Texas, on May 1, 1977.

Tortillas. 74 (each $1\frac{1}{2}$ oz.) in 30 minutes by Tom Nall in the 2nd World Championship at Mariano's Mexican Restaurant, Dallas, Texas, on October 16, 1973.

WEALTH AND POVERTY

The comparison and estimation of extreme personal wealth are beset with intractable difficulties. Quite apart from reticence and the element of approximation in estimating the valuation of assets, as Jean Paul Getty (1892–1976) once said: "If you can count your millions, you are not a billionaire." The term "millionaire" was invented *c.* 1740 and "billionaire" in 1861.

The earliest dollar billionaires were John Davison Rockefeller (1839-1937); Henry Ford (1863-1947); and Andrew William Mellon (1855-1937).

Living Billionaires. There is currently only one surviving U.S. dollar billionaire of the seven U.S. citizens so described in the 20th century, namely Daniel K. Ludwig (b. South Haven, Michigan, June, 1897) whose fortune was estimated at $3 billion in 1977. Mr. Ludwig reportedly began in business at age 9 by buying a sunken boat for $25, and now has the world's third largest tanker fleet and much real estate.

H. (Henry) Ross Perot (b. Texarkana, Texas, 1930) was, in December, 1969, worth in excess of a billion dollars on paper.

The richest man in Great Britain today is reputed to be John Moores (b. Eccles, Lancashire, 1896), a football pool operator who pioneered in the field in 1923. In 1973, he was estimated to be worth £400 million (hence £850 million in 1979). His first job after leaving school at 14 was as a telephone operator.

Highest Income. The greatest income is derived from the collection of royalties per barrel by rulers of oil-rich sheikdoms who have not abrogated personal entitlement. Before his death in 1965, H.H. Sheikh Sir Abdullah as-Salim as-Sabah (b. 1895), the 11th Amir of Kuwait, was accumulating royalties payable at the rate of £2.6 million ($6.5 million) per week or £135 million ($337.5 million) a year.

Highest Gross. The highest gross income ever achieved in a single year by a private citizen is an estimated $105,000,000 in 1927

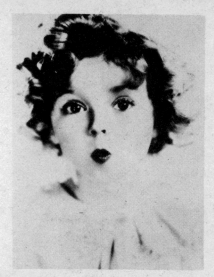

by the gangster Alphonse ("Scarface Al") Capone (b. Naples, Italy, 1899, d. Chicago, 1947). This was derived from illegal liquor trading and alky-cookers (illicit stills), gambling establishments, dog tracks, dance halls, "protection" rackets and vice. On his business card, Capone described himself as a "Second Hand Furniture Dealer."

Youngest Millionaire. The youngest person ever to accumulate a million dollars was the child film actor Jackie Coogan (born Los Angeles, October 26, 1914), co-star with Sir Charles Chaplin (1889–1977) in "The Kid," made in 1920.

Millionairesses. The world's wealthiest woman was probably Princess Wilhelmina Helena Pauline Maria of Orange-Nassau (1880–1962), formerly Queen of the Netherlands (from 1890 to her abdication, September 4, 1948), with a fortune which was estimated at over $550,000,000.

Mrs. Anna Dodge (later Mrs. Hugh Dillman), born in Dundee, Scotland, died in the U.S. on June 3, 1970, aged 103, and left an estate of about $96,000,000.

Shirley Temple (born April 23, 1928, Santa Monica, California), formerly Mrs. John Agar, Jr., now Mrs. Charles Black, accumulated wealth in excess of $1,000,000 before she was 10 years old. Her child actress career spanned the years 1934–39.

The earliest recorded self-made millionairess was Madame Charles Joseph Walker (*née* Sarah Breedlove on December 23, 1867), a black woman, whose fortune was founded on a hair straightener. She had been a scrubwoman and a laundress.

It was estimated in 1978 that 50.4 per cent of the United States' 250,000 millionaires are in fact millionairesses.

GREATEST MISER:
Hetty Green had more
than $31 million in one
bank alone in the early
1900's, but lived off
cold oatmeal because
she was too stingy to
heat it.

Greatest Miser. An estate of $95,000,000 was left by the notorious miser Henrietta (Hetty) Howland Green (*née* Robinson) (1835–1916). She had a balance of over $31,400,000 in one bank alone. She was so mean that her son had to have his leg amputated because of the delays in finding a *free* medical clinic. She herself lived off cold oatmeal because she was too mean to heat it, and died of apoplexy in an argument over the virtues of skimmed milk.

Richest Families. It has been tentatively estimated that the combined value of the assets nominally controlled by the Du Pont family of some 1,600 members may be on the order of $150 billion. The family arrived penniless in the U.S. from France on January 1, 1800.

Biggest Dowry. The largest recorded dowry was that of Elena Patiño, daughter of Don Simón Iturbi Patiño (1861–1947), the Bolivian tin millionaire, who in 1929 bestowed $22,400,000 from a fortune at one time estimated to be worth $350,000,000.

Longest Pension. Miss Millicent Barclay, daughter of Col. William Barclay of Great Britain, was born posthumously on July 10, 1872, and became eligible for a Madras Military Fund pension to continue until her marriage. She died unmarried on October 26, 1969, having drawn the pension for every day of her life of 97 years 3 months.

Highest Earnings. According to a *Business Week* survey the highest salary paid in the United States in 1978 was to David Mahoney, chairman of Norton Simon Inc., with $2,037,000.

Most Millionaires. The United States was estimated to have 250,000 millionaires in August, 1978.

Lowest Incomes. The poorest people in the world are the Tasaday tribe of cave-dwellers of central Mindanao, the Philippines, who were "discovered" in 1971 and live without any domesticated animals, agriculture, pottery, wheels or clothes.

Biggest Loss. The biggest recorded personal paper losses on stock values have been taken by Ray A. Kroc, chairman of McDonald's Corporation, with $64,901,718 on July 8, 1974, and Edwin H. Land, president of the Polaroid Corporation, with $59,397,355 on May 28–29, 1974, when Polaroid stock closed down $12.12 at 43¼.

Return of Cash. The largest amount of cash ever found and returned to its rightful owners was $500,000 found by Lowell Elliott, 61, on his farm at Peru, Indiana. It had been dropped in June, 1972, by a parachuting skyjacker.

Greatest Bequests. The greatest bequests in a lifetime of a millionaire were those of the late John Davison Rockefeller (1839–1937), who gave away sums totaling $750,000,000.

The Scottish-born U.S. citizen Andrew Carnegie (1835–1919) is estimated to have made benefactions totaling $350,000,000 in the last 18 years of his life. These included 7,689 church organs and 2,811 libraries. He had started in a bobbin factory at $1.20 per week.

The largest bequest made in the history of philanthropy was the $500,000,000 gift, announced on December 12, 1955, to 4,157 educational and other institutions by the Ford Foundation (established 1936) of New York City. The assets of the Foundation had a book value of $3,140,000,000 in 1974.

2. Honors, Decorations and Awards

Eponymous Record. The largest object to which a human name is attached is the universe itself—in the case of the "standard" cosmological model devised in 1922 by the Russian mathematician Aleksandr Aleksandrovich Friedman (1888–1925) and known as Friedman's Universe. The claim that Lord Rutherford named the proton (of which there are some 10^{85} in the observable universe) with the scientist William Prout in mind is not now supported.

Orders and Decorations

Oldest. The earliest of the orders of chivalry is the Venetian Order of St. Marc, reputedly founded in 831 A.D. The Castilian Order of Calatrava has an established date of foundation in 1158. The prototype of the princely Orders of Chivalry is the Most Noble Order of the Garter founded by King Edward III of England in *c.* 1348. A date of 809 A.D. has been attributed to the Most Ancient Order of the Thistle, but is of doubtful provenance.

Most Titles. The most titled person in the world is the 18th Duchess of Alba (Alba de Tormes), Doña María del Rosario Cayetana Fitz-James Stuart y Silva. She is 8 times a duchess, 15 times a marchioness, 21 times a countess and 19 times a Spanish grandee.

U.S. The highest U.S. decoration is the Congressional Medal of Honor. Five marines received both the Army and Navy Medals of Honor for the same acts in 1918 and 14 officers and men from 1863 to 1915 have received the medal on two occasions.

Top Jet Ace. The greatest number of kills in jet-to-jet battles is 16 by Capt. Joseph Christopher McConnell (U.S.A.F.) in the Korean War (1950–53). He was killed on August 25, 1954. It is possible that an Israeli ace may have surpassed this total in the period 1967–70, but the identity of pilots is subject to strict security.

Top Woman Ace. The record score for any woman fighter pilot is 12 by Jr. Lt. Lydia Litvak (U.S.S.R.) in the Eastern Front campaign of 1941–43. She was killed in action on August 1, 1943.

Top Scoring Air Aces

Country	World War I 1914–1918	World War II 1939–1945
World	80 Rittm. Manfred Freiherr (Baron) von Richthofen (Germany)	352[1] Major Erich Hartmann (Germany)
U.S.	26 Capt. Edward Vernon Rickenbacker, M.H., D.S.C. (7 o.l.c.), L. d'H., C. de G.	40 Major Richard I. Bong, M.H., D.S.C., S.S., D.F.C. (6 o.l.c.), A.M. (11 o.l.c.).
Canada	72 Lt.-Col. William Avery Bishop, V.C., C.B., D.S.O. and bar, M.C., D.F.C., L. d'H., C. de G.	31½ Sq.-Ldr. George F. Beurling, D.S.O., D.F.C., D.F.M. and bar.

[1]All but one of the aircraft in this unrivaled total were Soviet combat aircraft on the Eastern Front in 1942–1945.

MOST DECORATED SOLDIER IN WORLD WAR II: Audie Murphy, who died in 1971, was also a movie actor.

MOST DECORATED:
Ethiopian ruler Haile
Selassie wore over 50
medals in up to 14 rows.

MOST CLUSTERS AND GOLD STARS

Navy Cross	4 gold stars	Brig. Gen. Lewis B. Puller, U.S.M.C. Cdr. Ray M. Davenport, U.S.N.
Distinguished Service Cross	7 clusters	Capt. Edward Rickenbacker (died 1973)
Silver Star	8 clusters 2 gold stars	Col. David H. Hackworth, U.S.A. Lt. Col. Raymond L. Murray, U.S.M.C.
Distinguished Flying Cross	11 clusters 8 gold stars	Col. Francis S. Gabreski, U.S.A.F. Capt. Howard J. Finn, U.S.M.C.
Distinguished Service Medal (Army)	4 clusters	Gen. of the Army Douglas MacArthur (also one Naval award) Gen. of the Army Dwight D. Eisenhower
Distinguished Service Medal (Navy)	3 gold stars	Fleet Admiral William F. Halsey
Legion of Merit	5 clusters 4 gold stars	Maj. Gen. Richard Steinbach Lt. Gen. Claire E. Hutchin
Purple Heart	9 clusters	Sgt. Raymond E. Tirva

Most Decorated. Audie Murphy (1924–71) was the most
decorated soldier in World War II, receiving the Medal of Honor,
the Silver Star with 2 oak leaf clusters, the Bronze Star with an oak
leaf cluster, the Distinguished Service Cross, the French Croix de
Guerre, the Legion of Merit, the Purple Heart with 2 oak leaf
clusters, and the French Légion d'Honneur.

Most Bemedalled. The most bemedalled chest was that of
H.I.M. Haile Selassie (born as Ras Tafari Makonnen) (1892–1975),
ex-Emperor of Ethiopia, who had over 50 medal ribbons worn in
up to 14 rows.

NOBEL PRIZE: Alfred Nobel, the inventor of dynamite, established the prizes which bear his name under the terms of his will.

Most Statues. The world record for raising statues to oneself was set by Generalissimo Dr. Rafael Leónidas Trujillo y Molina (1891–1961), former President of the Dominican Republic. In March, 1960, a count showed that there were "over 2,000." The country's highest mountain was named Pico Trujillo (now Pico Duarte). One province was called Trujillo and another Trujillo Valdez. The capital was named Ciudad Trujillo (Trujillo City) in 1936, but reverted to its old name of Santo Domingo on November 23, 1961. Trujillo was assassinated in a car ambush on May 30, 1961, and May 30 is now celebrated annually as a public holiday.

The man to whom most statues have been raised is undoubtedly Vladimir Ilyich Ulyanov, *alias* Lenin (1870–1924), busts of whom have been mass-produced. Busts of Mao Tse-tung (b. December 26, 1893, d. 1976) and Ho Chi Minh (1890–1969) have also been mass-produced.

Greatest Reception. The greatest ticker-tape reception ever given in New York City was that for Lt.-Col. (now Col.) John Herschel Glenn, Jr. (born July 18, 1921), on March 1, 1962, after his return from his tri-orbital space flight. The New York City Street Cleaning Department estimated that 3,474 tons of paper descended. This total compared with 3,249 tons for General of the Army Douglas MacArthur (1880–1964) in 1951, and 1,800 tons for Col. Charles Augustus Lindbergh (1902–1974) in June, 1927.

Most Honorary Degrees. The greatest number of honorary degrees awarded to any individual is 89, given to Herbert Clark Hoover (1874–1964), former President of the United States (1929–33).

Nobel Prizes

The Nobel Foundation of $8,960,000 was set up under the will of Alfred Bernhard Nobel (1833–96), the unmarried Swedish chemist and chemical engineer who invented dynamite in 1866. The Nobel Prizes are presented annually on December 10, the anniversary of Nobel's death and the festival day of the Foundation. Since the first Prizes were awarded in 1901, the highest cash value of the award, in each of the six fields of Physics, Chemistry, Medicine and Physiology, Literature, Peace and Economics was $161,000 in 1978.

Most Awards by Countries. U.S. citizens have won outright or shared in the greatest number of awards (including those made in 1978) with a total of 144, made up of 39 for Physics, 21 for Chemistry, 52 for Medicine-Physiology, 9 for Literature, 17 for Peace and 6 for Economics.

By classes, the U.S. holds the records for Medicine-Physiology with 52, for Physics with 39, for Peace with 17 and Economics with 6; Germany and the U.S. for Chemistry with 21 each; and France for Literature with 12.

Individuals. Individually the only person to have won two Prizes outright is Dr. Linus Carl Pauling (born February 28, 1901), Professor of Chemistry since 1931 at the California Institute of Technology, Pasadena, California. He was awarded the Chemistry Prize for 1954 and the Peace Prize for 1962. Only two others have won two Prizes. One was Madame Marie Curie (1867–1934), who was born in Poland as Marja Sklodowska. She shared the 1903 Physics Prize with her husband, Pierre Curie (1859–1906), and Antoine Henri Becquerel (1852–1908), and won the 1911 Chemistry Prize outright. The other was Professor John Bardeen (b. May 23, 1908), who shared the Physics Prize in 1956 and 1972. The Peace Prize has been awarded three times to the International Committee of the Red Cross (founded October 29, 1863), of Geneva, Switzerland, namely in 1917, 1944 and in 1963, when it was shared with the International League of Red Cross Societies.

Oldest. The oldest prizeman was Professor Francis Peyton Rous (born in Baltimore, Maryland) (1879–1970), who worked at the Rockefeller Institute, New York City. He shared the Medicine Prize in 1966, at the age of 87.

Youngest. The youngest laureate has been Professor Sir William Lawrence Bragg (born in Adelaide, South Australia, 1890, died 1971), of the U.K., who, at the age of 25, shared the 1915 Physics Prize with his father, Sir William Henry Bragg (1862–1942), for work on X-rays and crystal structures. Bragg and also Theodore William Richards (1868–1928) of the U.S., who won the 1914 Chemistry Prize, carried out their prize work when aged 23. The youngest Literature prizeman was Rudyard Kipling (U.K.) (1865–1936) at the age of 41, in 1907. The youngest Peace prize winner was the Rev. Dr. Martin Luther King, Jr. (born January 15, 1929, assassinated April 4, 1968), of the U.S., in 1964 at the age of 35.

Who's Who

The longest entry of the 66,000 entries in *Who's Who in America* is that of Dr. Glen T. Seaborg (b. April 12, 1912), whose all-time record listing of 97 lines compares with the 16-line sketch on President Carter.

EVOLUTION OF SPORTS RECORDS IN THE 20TH CENTURY

	Start of the Century—January 1, 1901	*Middle of the Century—January* 1, 1951	*Present-Day Record—December*, 1978
Greatest Weight Lift	4,133 lbs.—Louis Cyr (Canada), 1896	4,133 lbs.—Louis Cyr (Canada), 1896	6,270 lbs.—Paul Anderson (U.S.), 1957
Fastest 100 meters	10.8 secs.—Luther Cary (U.S.) and 4 others, 1891–1900	10.3 secs.—Percy Williams (Canada) and 6 others, 1930–1935	9.95 secs. -James Ray Hines (U.S.), 1968
Fastest One Mile	4m 12.8s—W. G. George (U.K.), 1886	4m 01.3s—Gunder Hägg (Sweden), 1945	3m 49.0s—Sebastian Coe (G.B.), 1979
One Hour Running	11 miles 932 yds.—W. G. George (U.K.), 1884	12 miles 29 yds.—Viljo Heino (Finland), 1945	13 miles $24\frac{2}{3}$ yards—Jos Hermens (Netherlands), 1976
Highest High Jump	6′ $5\frac{5}{8}$″—M. Sweeney (U.S.), 1895	6′ 11″—Lester Steers (U.S.), 1941	7′ 8″—Vladimir Yashchenko (U.S.S.R.), 1978
Highest Pole Vault	11′ $10\frac{1}{2}$″—R. Clapp (U.S.), 1898	15′ $7\frac{3}{4}$″—Cornelius Warmerdam (U.S.), 1942	18′ $8\frac{1}{4}$″—David Roberts (U.S.), 1976
Long Jump	24′ $7\frac{3}{4}$″—P. O'Connor (U.K.), 1900	26′ $8\frac{1}{4}$″—Jesse Owens (U.S.), 1935	29′ $2\frac{1}{2}$″—Robert Beamon (U.S.), 1968
Longest Shot Put	48′ 2″—D. Horgan (U.K.), 1897	58′ $10\frac{3}{4}$″—Jim Fuchs (U.S.), 1950	72′ 8″—Udo Beyer (E. Germany), 1978
Longest Discus Throw	122′ $3\frac{1}{2}$″—R. Sheldon (U.S.), 1899	186′ 11″—Fortune Gordien (U.S.), 1949	233′ 5″—Wolfgang Schmidt (E. Germany), 1978
Longest Hammer Throw	169′ 4″—J. J. Flanagan (U.S.), 1900	196′ 5″—Imre Németh (Hungary), 1950	263′ 6″—Karl-Heinz Riehm (W. Germany), 1978
Longest Javelin Throw	161′ $9\frac{3}{4}$″—E. Lemming (Sweden), 1899	258′ 2″—Yrjo Nikkanen (Finland), 1938	310′ 4″—Miklos Németh (Hungary), 1976
One Hour Walking	8 miles 270 yds.—W. J. Sturgess (U.K.) (Amateur), 1895	8 miles 1,025 yds.—John Mikaelsson (Sweden), 1945	8 miles 1,700 yds.—Daniel Bautista (Mexico), 1978
Longest Ski Jump	$116\frac{1}{2}$′—O. Tanberg (Norway), 1900	$442\frac{3}{4}$′—Dan Netzell (Sweden), 1950	593′ 10″—Bogdan Norcic (Yugoslavia), 1977
Fastest 500 meters Ice Skating	45.2 sec.—P. Ostlund (Norway), 1900	41.8 sec.—Hans Engnestangen (Norway), 1938	37.00 sec.—Evgeni Kulikov (U.S.S.R.), 1975
Fastest 100 meters Swim (long course)	1m. 14.0s. (no turn)—J. Nutall (U.K.), 1893	55.8 sec.—Alexandre Jany (France), 1947	49.44 sec.—Jonty Skinner (S. Africa), 1976
Cycling Paced (m.p.h.)	62.27—C. M. Murphy (U.S.), 1899	>80—L. Vanderstuyft (Belgium), 1928	140.5—Allan V. Abbott (U.S.), 1973
Fastest 1 mile Racehorse (excluding straightaways)	1m. 35.5s.—*Salvator* in U.S., 1890	1m. 33.4s.—*Citation* in U.S., 1950	1m. 32.2s.—*Dr. Fager* in U.S., 1968
Highest Mountain Climbed (feet)	22,834—Aconcagua, Argentina, 1897	26,492—Annapurna I, Nepal, 1950	29,028—Everest, Nepal-Tibet, 1953

Chapter Twelve

SPORTS, GAMES AND PASTIMES

Earliest. The origins of sport stem from the time when self-preservation ceased to be the all-consuming human preoccupation. Archery was a hunting skill in Mesolithic times (by *c.* 8000 B.C.), but did not become an organized sport until about 300 A.D., among the Genoese. The earliest dated evidence for sport is *c.* 2450 B.C. for fowling with throwing sticks and hunting. Ball games by girls, depicted on Middle Kingdom murals at Beni Hasan, Egypt, have been dated to *c.* 2050 B.C.

Fastest. The highest speed reached in a non-mechanical sport is in sky-diving, in which a speed of 185 m.p.h. is attained in a head-down free-falling position, even in the lower atmosphere. In delayed drops, a speed of 614 m.p.h. has been recorded at high rarefied altitudes. The highest projectile speed in any moving ball game is *c.* 180 m.p.h. in pelota (jai-alai). This compares with 170 m.p.h. (electronically-timed) for a golf ball driven off a tee.

Slowest. In amateur wrestling, before the rules were modified toward "brighter wrestling," contestants could be locked in holds for so long that a single bout once lasted for 11 hours 40 min. In the extreme case of the 2-hour 41-minute pull in the regimental tug o'war in Jubbulpore, India, on August 12, 1889, the winning team moved a net distance of 12 feet at an average speed of 0.00084 m.p.h.

MOST PARTICIPANTS: 37,683 people on 8,304 rafts entered the "Ramblin' Raft Race" on the Chattahoochee River (see page 502).

Longest. The most protracted sporting test was an automobile duration test of 222,618 miles by Appaurchaux and others in a Ford Taunus. This was contested over 142 days in 1963. The distance was equivalent to 8.93 times around the equator.

The most protracted non-mechanical sporting event is the *Tour de France* cycling race. In 1926, this was over 3,569 miles, lasting 29 days. The total damage to the French national economy due to the interest in this annual event, now reduced to 23 days, is immense, and is currently estimated to be in excess of $2,000,000,000.

Largest Field. The largest field for any ball game is that for polo with 12.4 acres, or a maximum length of 300 yards and a width, without side-boards, of 200 yards.

Most Participants. The *Stramilano* 22-kilometer run around Milan, Italy, attracted over 50,000 runners on April 16, 1978.

In May, 1971, the "Ramblin' Raft Race" on the Chattahoochee River at Atlanta, Georgia, attracted 37,683 competitors on 8,304 rafts.

According to a report issued in 1978, 55 million people are actively involved in sports in the U.S.S.R., using 3,282 stadiums, 1,435 swimming pools and over 66,000 indoor gymnasiums. It is estimated that some 29 per cent of the East German population participates in sport regularly.

Worst Disasters. The worst disaster in recent history was when an estimated 604 were killed after some stands at the Hong Kong Jockey Club race course collapsed and caught fire on February 26, 1918. During the reign of Antoninus Pius (138–161 A.D.) the upper wooden tiers in the Circus Maximus, Rome, collapsed during a gladiatorial combat, killing 1,112 spectators.

Youngest and Oldest Sports Record Breakers. The youngest age at which any person has broken a world record is 12 years 298 days in the case of Gertrude Caroline Ederle (born October 23, 1906) of the United States, who broke the women's 880-yard freestyle swimming world record with 13 minutes 19.0 seconds at Indianapolis, Indiana on August 17, 1919.

The oldest person to break a world record is Irish-born John J. Flanagan (1868–1938), triple Olympic hammer throw champion for the U.S., 1900–1908, who set his last world record of 184 feet 4 inches at New Haven, Connecticut, on July 24, 1909, aged 41 years 196 days.

Youngest and Oldest Internationals. The youngest age at which any person has won international honors is 8 years in the case of Joy Foster, the Jamaican singles and mixed doubles table tennis champion in 1958. It would appear that the greatest age at which anyone has actively competed for his country is 72 years 280 days in the case of Oscar G. Swahn (Sweden) (1847–1927), who won a silver medal for shooting in the Olympic Games at Antwerp on July 26, 1920. He qualified for the 1924 Games, but was unable to participate because of illness.

Most Versatile Athletes. Charlotte (Lottie) Dod (1871–1960) won the Wimbledon singles title (1887 to 1893) five times, the

RECORD
RECORDBREAKER:
The mighty Vasili
Alexeev has broken
80 world weight-
lifting records.

British Ladies Golf Championship in 1904, an Olympic silver medal for archery in 1908, and represented England at hockey in 1899. She also excelled at skating and tobogganning.

Mildred (Babe) Didrikson Zaharias (U.S.) was an All-American basketball player, took the silver medal in the high jump, and gold medals in the javelin throw and hurdles in the 1932 Olympics. Turning professional, she first trained as a boxer, and then, switching to golf, eventually won 19 championships, including the U.S. Women's Open and All-American Open. She holds the women's world record also for longest throw of a baseball—296 feet.

Most Prolific Recordbreaker. Between January 24, 1970, and November 1, 1977, Vasili Alexeev (U.S.S.R.) (b. January 7, 1942) broke a total of 80 official world records in weightlifting.

Youngest and Oldest Champions. The youngest person to have successfully participated in a world title event was a French boy, whose name is not recorded, who coxed the winning Netherlands pair at Paris on Aug. 26, 1900. He was not more than 10 and may have been as young as 7. The youngest individual Olympic winner was Marjorie Gestring (U.S.), who took the springboard diving title at the age of 13 years 9 months at the Olympic Games in Berlin in 1936. Oscar G. Swahn (see above) was aged 65 years 258 days when he won the gold medal in the 1912 Olympic Running Deer team shooting competition.

Longest Reign. The longest reign as a world champion is 33 years (1829–62) by Jacques Edmond Barre (France, 1802–73) at real (royal) tennis.

400,000,000 FANS: The 1978 World Cup soccer final drew the largest television audience in sports history, excluding Olympic events.

Greatest Earnings. The greatest fortune amassed by an individual in sport is an estimated $60,000,000 by the boxer Muhammad Ali Haj to August, 1979. The most for a single event is a purse of $6,500,000 won by Ali in his title fight against Ken Norton, fought in New York City on September 28, 1976.

The highest-paid woman athlete in the world is ice skater Janet Lynn (*née* Nowicki) (U.S.) (born April 6, 1953) who in 1974 signed a $1,500,000 three-year contract. In 1974 she earned more than $750,000.

Largest Trophy. The world's largest trophy for a particular sport is the Bangalore Limited Handicap Polo Tournament Trophy. This massive cup is 6 feet tall and was presented in 1936 by the Raja of Kolanka.

Heaviest Sportsmen. The heaviest sportsman of all time was the wrestler William J. Cobb of Macon, Georgia, who in 1962 was billed as the 802-lb. "Happy Humphrey." The heaviest player of a ball game was Bob Pointer, the 487-lb. tackle, formerly on the 1967 Santa Barbara High School team.

Most Expensive. The most expensive of all sports is the racing of large yachts—"J" type boats and International 12-meter boats. The owning and racing of these is beyond the means of individual millionaires and is confined to multi-millionaires or syndicates.

Largest Crowd. The greatest number of live spectators for any sporting spectacle is the estimated 2,000,000 who lined the route of the New York Marathon in October, 1978. The race was won by Bill Rogers (U.S.) for the third consecutive time. However, spread over 23 days, it is estimated that more than 10,000,000 see the annual *Tour de France* along the route.

The largest crowd traveling to any sporting event is "more than 400,000" for the annual *Grand Prix d'Endurance* motor race on the Sarthe circuit near Le Mans, France. The record stadium crowd was one of 199,854 for the Brazil *vs.* Uruguay match in the Maracaña Municipal Stadium, Rio de Janeiro, Brazil, on July 16, 1950.

The largest television audience for a single sporting event (excluding Olympic events) was the 400,000,000 who watched the final of the 1978 World Cup soccer competition.

Aerobatics

Earliest. The first aerobatic maneuver is generally considered the sustained inverted flight in a Blériot of Célestin-Adolphe Pégoud, at Buc, France on September 21, 1913, but Lieut. Peter Nikolayevich Nesterov, of the Imperial Russian Air Service, performed a loop in a Nieuport Type IV monoplane at Kiev, U.S.S.R. on August 27, 1913.

World Championships. Held biennially since 1960 (excepting 1974), scoring is based on the system devised by Col. José Aresti of Spain. The competitions consist of two compulsory and two free programs.

Most Titles. The world championships team competition has been won on four occasions by the U.S.S.R. No individual has won more than one title, the most successful competitor being Igor Egorov (U.S.S.R.) who won in 1970, was second in 1976, fifth in 1972 and eleventh in 1968. The most successful in the women's competition has been Lidia Leonova (U.S.S.R.) with first place in 1976, second in 1978, third in 1972 and fifth in 1970.

Inverted Flight. The duration record for inverted flight is 2 hours 15 minutes 4 seconds by John Leggatt in a Champion Decathlon on May 28, 1974, over the Arizona Desert.

Loops. John "Hal" McClain performed $1,501\frac{1}{2}$ inside loops in a Pitts S-2A over Long Beach, California, on December 16, 1973. He also achieved 180 outside loops in a Bellanca Super Decathlon on September 2, 1978, over Houston, Texas.

Archery

Earliest References. The discovery of stone arrowheads at Border Cave, Northern Natal, South Africa, in deposits exceeding the Carbon 14 dating limit, indicates that the bow was invented *ante* 46,000 B.C. Archery developed as an organized sport at least as early as the 3rd century A.D. The world governing body is the *Fédération Internationale de Tir à l'Arc* (FITA), founded in 1931.

Flight Shooting. The longest flight shooting records are achieved in the footbow class. In the unlimited footbow division, the professional Harry Drake of Lakeside, California, holds the record at 1 mile 268 yards, shot at Ivanpah Dry Lake, California, on October 24, 1971. The crossbow record is 1,359 yds. 29 inches, held by Drake and set at the same venue on October 14–15, 1967. The unlimited handbow class (*i.e.* standing stance with bow of any weight) record is 1,164 yards 2 feet 9 inches by Don Brown (b. 1946) at Wendover, Utah, on September 18, 1977.

Sultan Selim III shot an arrow 1,400 Turkish *pikes* or *gez* near Istanbul, Turkey, in 1798. The equivalent English distance is somewhere between 953 and 972 yards.

Highest Scores. The world records for a single FITA round are: men, 1,318 points (of a possible 1,440) by Giancarlo Ferrari (Italy) at Viareggio, Italy, October 15–16, 1977; and women, 1,304 points (possible 1,440) by Zebiniso Rustamova (U.S.S.R.) at Milan, Italy, on October 3, 1977.

There are no world records for Double FITA rounds, but the highest scores achieved in either a world or Olympic championship are: men, 2,571 points (possible 2,880) by Darrell Pace (U.S.) posted at the 1976 Olympics at Montreal, Canada, July 27–30, 1976; women, 2,515 by Luann Ryon (U.S.) at Canberra, Australia, February 11–12, 1977.

Most Titles. The greatest number of world titles (instituted 1931) ever won by a man is four by Hans Deutgen (Sweden) in 1947–48–49–50. The greatest number won by a woman is seven by Mrs.

HOLDER OF THREE FLIGHT-SHOOTING RECORDS: Harry Drake is the master with the footbow (1 mile 268 yards), handbow and crossbow. Here he is trying to break his own unlimited footbow record.

RECORD ROUND: Zebiniso Rustamova shot a 1,304-point FITA round in Milan in 1977.

Janina Spychajowa-Kurkowska (Poland) in 1931–32–33–34, 1936, 1939 and 1947.

Oscar Kessels (Belgium) has participated in 21 world championships since 1931.

Olympic Medals. Hubert van Innis (Belgium) (1866–1961) won 6 gold and 3 silver medals in archery events at the 1900 and 1920 Olympic Games.

Greatest Pull. Gary Sentman of Roseburg, Oregon, drew a longbow weighing a record 176 lbs. to the maximum draw on the arrow (28¼ inches) at Forksville, Pennsylvania, on September 20, 1975.

Highest 24-Hour Score. The record over 24 hours by a pair of archers is 51,633 during 48 Portsmouth Rounds (60 arrows at 20 yards with a 2-inch diameter 10 ring) shot by Jimmy Watt and Gordon Danby at the Epsom Showgrounds, Auckland, New Zealand, on November 18–19, 1977.

Auto Racing

Earliest Races. There are various conflicting claims, but the first automobile race was the 201-mile Green Bay-to-Madison, Wisconsin, run in 1878, won by an Oshkosh steamer.

In 1887, Count Jules Felix Philippe Albert de Dion de Malfiance (1856–1946) won the *La Velocipede* 19.3-mile race in Paris in a De Dion steam quadricycle in which he is reputed to have exceeded 37 m.p.h.

The first "real" race was from Paris to Bordeaux and back (732 miles) June 11–13, 1895. The winner was Emile Levassor (1844–97)

(France) driving a Panhard-Levassor two-seater with a 1.2-liter Daimler engine developing $3\frac{1}{2}$ h.p. His time was 48 hours 47 min. (average speed 15.01 m.p.h.). The first closed circuit race was held over 5 laps of a mile dirt track at Narragansett Park, Cranston, Rhode Island, on September 7, 1896. It was won by A. H. Whiting, who drove a Riker electric.

The oldest auto race in the world still being regularly run is the R.A.C. Tourist Trophy (40th race held in 1976), first staged on the Isle of Man on September 14, 1905. The oldest continental race is the French Grand Prix (55th in 1977) first held on June 26–27, 1906. The Coppo Florio, in Sicily, has been irregularly held since 1900.

Fastest Circuits. The highest average lap speed attained on any closed circuit is 221.160 m.p.h. by Mark Donohue, Jr. (1937–75) (U.S.) who lapped the 2.66-mile 33-degree banked tri-oval at Alabama International Motor Speedway, Talladega, Alabama, in 43.299 seconds, driving a 5,374-c.c. turbocharged Porsche 917/30 Can-Am car on August 9, 1975.

The highest average race lap speed for a closed circuit is 214.158 m.p.h. by Mario Gabriele Andretti (U.S.) (b. Trieste, Italy, February 28, 1940) driving a 2.6-liter turbocharged Viceroy Parnelli-Offenhauser on the 2-mile 22-degree banked oval at Texas World Speedway, College Station, Texas, on October 6, 1973.

The fastest road circuit was the Francorchamps circuit near Spa, Belgium, then 14.10 kilometers (8 miles 1,340 yards) in length. It was lapped in 3 minutes 13.4 seconds (average speed of 163.086 m.p.h.) on lap seven of the Francorchamps 1,000-kilometer sports car race on May 6, 1973, by Henri Pescarolo (b. Paris, France, September 25, 1942) driving a 2,933-c.c. V12 Matra-Simca MS 670 Group 5 sports car. The race lap average speed record at Berlin's AVUS track was 171.75 m.p.h. by Bernd Rosemeyer (Germany) (1909–38) in a 6-liter V16 Auto Union in 1937.

The fastest world championship Grand Prix circuit in current use is the 2.932-mile course at Silverstone, Northamptonshire, England (opened 1948). The race lap record is 1 minute 14.40 seconds (average speed 141.87 m.p.h.) by Gianclaudio (Clay) Regazzoni (Switzerland) (b. September 5, 1939) driving a Saudia-Williams FW07 on July 14, 1979. The practice lap record is 1 minute 11.88 seconds (146.84 m.p.h.) by Alan Jones (Australia) (b. November 2, 1946) in a Saudia-Williams on July 12, 1979.

Fastest Races. The fastest race in the world is the NASCAR Grand National 125-mile event (a qualifying race for the Daytona 500) on the $2\frac{1}{2}$-mile 31-degree banked tri-oval at Daytona International Speedway, Daytona Beach, Florida. The record time is 40 minutes 55 seconds (average speed 183.295 m.p.h.) by William Caleb "Cale" Yarborough (born March 27, 1939) of Timmonsville, South Carolina, driving a 1969 Mercury V8, on February 19, 1970.

The fastest road race was the 1,000-kilometer (621-mile) sports car race held on the Francorchamps circuit (8 miles 1,340 yards) near Spa, Belgium. The record time for this 71-lap (622.055-mile) race was 4 hours 1 minute 9.7 seconds (average speed 154.765 m.p.h.) by Pedro Rodriguez (1940–71) of Mexico and Keith Jack "Jackie" Oliver

(b. Chadwell Heath, Essex, England, Aug. 14, 1942), driving a 4,998-c.c. flat-12 Porsche 917K Group 5 sports car on May 9, 1971.

Toughest Circuits. The Targa Florio (first run May 9, 1906) was widely acknowledged to be the most arduous race in the world. Held on the Piccolo Madonie Circuit in Sicily, it covered eleven laps (492.126 miles) and involved the negotiation of 9,350 corners over severe mountain gradients and narrow rough roads.

The record time was 6 hours 27 minutes 48.0 seconds (average speed 76.141 m.p.h.) by Arturo Francesco Merzario (b. Civenna, Italy, March 11, 1943) and Sandro Munari (Italy) driving a 2,998.5-c.c. flat-12 Ferrari 312 P Group 5 sports car in the 56th race on May 21, 1972. The lap record was 33 minutes 36.0 seconds (average speed 79.890 m.p.h.) by Leo Juhani Kinnunen (born Tampere, Finland, Aug. 5, 1943) on lap 11 of the 54th race in a 2,997-c.c. flat-8 Porsche 908/3 Spyder Group 6 prototype sports car on May 3, 1970.

The most gruelling and slowest Grand Prix circuit is that for the Monaco Grand Prix (first run on April 14, 1929), run through the streets and around the harbor of Monte Carlo. It is 3.312 km. (2.058 miles) in length and has 11 pronounced corners and several sharp changes of gradient. The race is run over 76 laps (156.4 miles) and involves on average about 1,600 gear changes.

The record for the race is 1 hour 55 minutes 22.48 seconds (average speed 81.338 m.p.h.) by Jody Scheckter (b. South Africa, January 29, 1950) driving a Ferrari 312T4 on May 27, 1979. The race lap record is 1 minute 28.65 seconds (average speed 83.67 m.p.h.) by Andreas-Nikolaus "Niki" Lauda (b. Austria, February 22, 1949) driving a Brabham-Alfa Romeo BT46 on May 7, 1978. The practice lap record is 1 minute 26.45 seconds (average speed 85.69 m.p.h.) by Jody Scheckter in a Ferrari 312T4 on May 26, 1979.

Le Mans

The greatest distance ever covered in the 24-hour *Grand Prix d'Endurance* (first held on May 26–27, 1923) on the old Sarthe circuit (8 miles 650 yards) at Le Mans, France, is 3,315.208 miles by Dr. Helmut Marko (b. Graz, Austria, April 27, 1943) and Jonkheer Gijs van Lennep (b. Bloemendaal, Netherlands, March 16, 1942) driving a 4,907-c.c. flat-12 Porsche 917K Group 5 sports car on June 12–13, 1971. The record for the current circuit is 3,134.52 miles by Didier Pironi (b. March 26, 1952) and Jean-Pierre Jaussaud (b. June 3, 1937) (average speed 130.60 m.p.h.) in an Alpine Renault, June 10–11, 1978. The race lap record (8.475 mile lap) is 3 minutes 34.2 seconds (average speed 142.44 m.p.h.) by Jean Pierre Jabouille (b. France, October 1, 1942) driving an Alpine Renault on June 11, 1978. (See photo, page M) The practice lap record is 3 minutes 27.6 seconds (average speed 146.97 m.p.h.) by Jacques-Bernard "Jacky" Ickx (b. Belgium, January 1, 1945) in a turbocharged 2.1-liter Porsche 936/78 on June 7, 1978.

Most Wins. The race has been won by Ferrari cars nine times, in 1949, 1954, 1958 and 1960–61–62–63–64–65. The most wins by one man is four by Oliver Gendebien (Belgium), who won in 1958,

1960–61–62, and by Jacky Ickx (Belgium), who won in 1969, 1975–76–77.

Indianapolis 500

The Indianapolis 500-mile race (200 laps) was inaugurated on May 30, 1911. The most successful driver has been Anthony Joseph "A.J." Foyt, Jr., who won in 1961, 1964, 1967 and 1977.

The record time is 3 hours 4 minutes 5.54 seconds (average speed 162.962 m.p.h.) by Mark Donohue (b. New Jersey, March 18, 1937, d. 1975) driving a 2,595-c.c. 900-b.h.p. turbocharged Sunoco McLaren M16B-Offenhauser on May 27, 1972. The record prize fund was $1,116,807 for the 61st race on May 29, 1977. The individual prize record is $271,697.72 by Al Unser (b. Albuquerque, New Mexico, May 29, 1939) on May 30, 1970.

The race lap record is 46.71 seconds (average speed 192.678 m.p.h.) by Danny Ongais of Costa Mesa, California, driving a 2.6-liter turbocharged Parnelli-Cosworth DFX on lap 42 of the race held on May 29, 1977. The 4-lap qualifying record is 2 minutes 58.08 seconds (average speed 202.156 m.p.h.) by Tom Sneva (b. U.S., June 1, 1948) driving a Penske-Cosworth DFX turbocharged PC6 on May 20, 1978.

QUICKEST QUALIFIER: Tom Sneva roared through the 4-lap qualifying round at Indy at 202.156 m.p.h. in 1978.

DRIVING CHAMPION: Juan-Manuel Fangio has won the World Drivers' Championships five times.

Fastest Pit Stop. Bobby Unser (U.S.) took 4 seconds to take on fuel on lap 10 of the Indianapolis 500 on May 30, 1976.

Duration Record

The greatest distance ever covered in one year is 400,000 kilometers (248,548.5 miles) by François Lecot (1879–1949), an innkeeper from Rochetaillée, France, in a 1,900-c.c. 66-b.h.p. Citroën 11 sedan mainly between Paris and Monte Carlo, from July 22, 1935 to July 26, 1936. He drove on 363 of the 370 days allowed.

The world's duration record is 185,353 miles 1,741 yards in 133 days 17 hours 37 minutes 38.64 seconds (average speed 58.07 m.p.h.) by Marchand, Presalé and six others in a Citroën on the Montlhéry track near Paris, during March–July, 1933.

Most Successful Drivers

Based on the World Drivers' Championships, inaugurated in 1950, the most successful driver is Juan-Manuel Fangio y Cia (born Balcarce, Argentina, June 24, 1911), who won five times in 1951–54–55–56–57. He retired in 1958, after having won 24 Grand Prix races (2 shared).

The most successful driver in terms of race wins is Richard Lee Petty (born Randleman, North Carolina, July 2, 1937) with 186 NASCAR Grand National wins from 1960 to April, 1979. His best year was 1967 with 27 victories.

The most Grand Prix victories is 27 by Jackie Stewart of Scotland between September 12, 1965 and August 5, 1973. Jim Clark, O.B.E. (1936–1968) of Scotland holds the record of Grand Prix victories in one year with 7 in 1963. He won 61 Formula One and Formula Libre races between 1959 and 1968. The most Grand Prix starts is 176 (out of a possible 184) between May 18, 1958, and Jan. 26, 1975, by Norman Graham Hill, O.B.E. (1929–1975). He took part in 90 *consecutive* Grands Prix between November 20, 1960 and October 5, 1969.

Oldest and Youngest World Champions. The oldest was Juan-Manuel Fangio, who won his last World Championship on August 18, 1957, aged 46 years 55 days. The youngest was Emerson Fittipaldi (Brazil) who won his first World Championship on September 10, 1972, aged 25 years 273 days.

Oldest and Youngest Grand Prix Winners and Drivers. The youngest Grand Prix winner was Bruce Leslie McLaren (1937–70) of New Zealand, who won the U.S. Grand Prix at Sebring, Florida, on December 12, 1959, aged 22 years 104 days. The oldest Grand Prix winner was Tazio Giorgio Nuvolari (1892–1953) of Italy, who won the Albi Grand Prix at Albi, France, on July 14, 1946, aged 53 years 240 days. The oldest Grand Prix driver was Louis Alexandre Ghiron (Monaco, 1899–1979), who finished 6th in the Monaco Grand Prix on May 22, 1955, aged 55 years 292 days.

The youngest Grand Prix driver was Christopher Arthur Amon (b. Bulls, New Zealand, July 20, 1943) who took part in the Belgian Grand Prix on June 9, 1963, aged 19 years 324 days.

Land Speed Records

The highest speed ever recorded by a wheeled vehicle was achieved by Gary Gabelich (b. San Pedro, California, August 29, 1950), at Bonneville Salt Flats, Utah, on October 23, 1970. He drove the Reaction Dynamics *The Blue Flame*, weighing 4,950 lbs. and measuring 37 feet long, powered by a liquid natural gas-hydrogen peroxide rocket engine developing a maximum static thrust of 22,000 lbs. On his first run, at 11:23 a.m. (local time), he covered the measured kilometer in 3.543 seconds (average speed 631.367 m.p.h.) and the mile in 5.829 seconds (617.602 m.p.h.). On the return run, at 12:11 p.m., his times were 3.554 seconds for the kilometer (629.413 m.p.h.) and 5.739 seconds for the mile (627.287 m.p.h.). The average times for the two runs were 3.5485 seconds for the kilometer (630.388 m.p.h.) and 5.784 seconds for the mile (622.407 m.p.h.). During the attempt only 13,000 lbs. s.t. was used and a peak speed of 650 m.p.h. was momentarily attained.

The most successful land speed record breaker was Major Sir Malcolm Campbell (1885–1948) (U.K.). He broke the official record nine times between September 25, 1924, with 146.157 m.p.h. in a Sunbeam, and September 3, 1935, when he achieved 301.129 m.p.h. in the Rolls-Royce-engined *Bluebird*.

The world speed record for compression-ignition-engined cars is 190.344 m.p.h. (average of two runs over measured mile) by Robert Havemann of Eureka, California, driving his *Corsair* streamliner, powered by a turbocharged 6,981-c.c. 6-cylinder GMC 6-71 diesel engine developing 746 b.h.p., at Bonneville Salt Flats, Utah, in August, 1971. The faster run was made at 210 m.p.h.

Dragging

Piston-Engined. The lowest elapsed time recorded by a piston-engined dragster is 5.637 seconds by Donald Glenn "Big Daddy" Garlits (born 1932) of Seffner, Florida, driving his rear-engined AA-F dragster, powered by a 7,948-c.c. supercharged Dodge V8

THREE-TIME HEAVYWEIGHT CHAMP: Muhammad Ali is the only man in boxing history to win the world heavyweight crown on three separate occasions, defeating Sonny Liston in February, 1964, George Foreman in October, 1974, and Leon Spinks in September, 1978. He is shown here landing a punishing right to the jaw of Ken Norton. (Photo courtesy of Jim Jacobs)

LE MANS SPEEDSTER: Jean Pierre Jabouille drove his Alpine Renault to a race lap record at an average speed of 142.44 m.p.h. with his 3-minute 34.2-second lap in the 1978 French Grand Prix. (Photo by Sporting Pictures)

BLAZING BLADES:
Winner of two Olympic
gold medals, Tatiana
Averina of the U.S.S.R.
holds the women's speed
skating record at 1,000
meters with a time of 1
minute 23.46 seconds.
(Photo by Tony Duffy,
All-Sport Photographic)

NO RINKY-DINK RINK: The Fujikyo Highland Promenade Rink in Japan provides the largest artifical outdoor ice skating facility in the world, with an area of over 6½ acres. (Photo courtesy of Fujikyo Amusement Park)

SOARING SARA: Italian Sara Simeoni set the women's high jump record with a 6-foot-7-inch leap on August 4, 1978, at Brescia, Italy.

LONG-RUNNING RECORD: Michael Eufemia pocketed 625 balls in a row in an exhibition in Brooklyn, New York, in 1960.

PROFITABLE RACKET: Guillermo Vilas had the most financially successful year in tennis history in 1977, when he won $800,642. (Photo courtesy of Syndication International)

FAST HANDS: Cadet Thomas P. Hunt of the U.S. Air Force Academy sprinted 50 yards on his hands in just 18.7 seconds in May, 1978, to set a new mark for manual locomotion.

SNOW TREK: Fritz Sprandel made an extraordinary journey across the continental United States, beginning in Washington State on December 4, 1977, and arriving in Maine on February 6, 1978.

P

HIGHEST TERMINAL VELOCITY: Shirley Muldowney broke her own record with a 255.58-m.p.h. run in January, 1979.

engine, during the National Hot Rod Association's Supernationals at Ontario Motor Speedway, California, on October 11, 1975.

The highest terminal velocity recorded is 255.58 m.p.h. by Shirley Muldowney (U.S.) at Pomona, California, in January, 1979.

The world record for two runs in opposite directions over 440 yards from a standing start is 6.70 seconds by Dennis Victor Priddle (b. 1945) of Yeovil, Somerset, England, driving his 6,424-c.c. supercharged Chrysler dragster, developing 1,700 b.h.p. using nitromethane and methanol, at Elvington Airfield, England, on October 7, 1972. The faster run took 6.65 seconds.

Rocket or Jet-Engined. The highest terminal velocity recorded by any dragster is 377.754 m.p.h. (elapsed time 4.65 seconds) by Norman Craig Breedlove (b. March 23, 1938) of Los Angeles, California, driving his *English Leather Special* rocket dragster at Bonneville Salt Flats, Utah, in Sept. 1973. The lowest elapsed time recorded by any dragster is 3.94 seconds by Sam Miller (b. April 15, 1945) of Wayne, New Jersey, in Miami, Florida, in February, 1979.

Terminal velocity is the speed attained at the end of a 440-yard run made from a standing start and elapsed time is the time taken for the run.

Stock Car Racing

Richard Petty of Randleman, North Carolina, was the first stock car driver to attain $1,000,000 lifetime earnings on August 1, 1971. His earnings through the 1976 season were over $2,500,000. Petty also holds the NASCAR records for most races won (180) and most victories in a single season (27 in 1967).

Rallies

Earliest. The earliest long rally was promoted by the Parisian daily *Le Matin* in 1907 from Peking, China to Paris, over a route of about 7,500 miles. Five cars left Peking on June 10. The winner, Prince Scipione Borghese, arrived in Paris on August 10, 1907 in his 40 h.p. Itala accompanied by his chauffeur, Ettore, and Luigi Barzini.

Longest. The world's longest ever rally event was the *Singapore Airlines* London–Sydney Rally run over 19,329 miles starting from Covent Garden, Greater London, on August 14, 1977, ending at the Sydney Opera House, passing through 17 countries. It was won on September 28, 1977, by Andrew Cowan, Colin Malkin and Michael Broad in a Mercedes 280E.

The longest rally held annually is the East African Safari (first run 1953 through Kenya, Tanzania and Uganda), which is up to 3,874 miles long, as in the 17th Safari held on April 8–12, 1971. It has been won a record three times by Joginder Singh (Kenya) in 1965, 1974 and 1976.

Monte Carlo. The Monte Carlo Rally (first run 1911) has been won a record four times by Sandro Munari (Italy) in 1972, 1975–77. The smallest car to win was an 851-c.c. Saab driven by Erik Carlsson (b. Sweden, March 5, 1929) and Gunnar Häggbom of Sweden, on January 25, 1962, and by Carlsson and Gunnar Palm on January 24, 1963.

Pikes Peak Race

The Pikes Peak Auto Hill Climb, Colorado (instituted 1916) has been won by Bobby Unser 13 times between 1956 and 1974 (10 championship, 2 stock and 1 sports car title). On June 30, 1968, in the 46th race, he set an absolute record of 11 minutes 54.9 seconds in his 5,506-c.c. Chevrolet championship car over the 12.42-mile course, rising from 9,402 to 14,110 feet through 157 curves.

Badminton

Origins. A game similar to badminton was played in China in the 2nd millennium B.C. The modern game was devised *c.* 1863 at Badminton Hall in Avon, England, the seat of the Dukes of Beaufort. The oldest club is the Newcastle Badminton Club, England, formed as the Armstrong College Club, on January 24, 1900.

International Championships. The International Championship or Thomas Cup (instituted 1948) has been won seven times by Indonesia, in 1957–58, 1960–61, 1963–64, 1969–70, 1972–73, 1975–76 and 1978–79.

The Ladies International Championship or Uber Cup (instituted 1956) has been won four times by Japan (1966, 1969, 1972 and 1978).

Most Titles Won. The record number of All-England Championship (instituted 1899) titles won is 21 by Sir George Thomas (1881–1972) between 1903 and 1928. The record for men's singles is 8 by Rudy Hartono of Indonesia (1968–74, 76). The most, including doubles, by women is 17, a record shared by Mary Lucas (1899–1910) and Mrs. G. C. K. Hashman (*née* Judy Devlin) (U.S.), whose wins came from 1954 to 1967, including a record 10 singles titles.

Shortest Game. In the 1969 Uber Cup in Djakarta, Indonesia, Miss N. Takagi (Japan) beat Miss P. Tumengkol in 9 minutes.

Marathons. The longest singles match is 65 hours by Phil Duffy and Aiden Taffe at the Star & Crescent Recreation Centre, Drogheda, Co. Lough, Ireland, on April 6–9, 1979.

Longest Hit. Frank Rugani drove a shuttlecock 79 feet 8½ inches in indoor tests at San Jose, California, on February 29, 1964.

HOME RUN CHAMP:
Japanese baseball star
Sadaharu Oh beat
Hank Aaron's record with
number 756 on
September 3, 1977.

Baseball

Origins. The Reverend Thomas Wilson, of Maidstone, Kent, England, wrote disapprovingly, in 1700, of baseball being played on Sundays. It is also referred to in *Northanger Abbey* by Jane Austen, *c.* 1798.

Earliest Games. The earliest game on record under the Cartwright rules was on June 19, 1846, in Hoboken, N.J., where the "New York Nine" defeated the Knickerbockers 23 to 1 in 4 innings. The earliest all-professional team was the Cincinnati Red Stockings in 1869.

Home Runs

Henry L. (Hank) Aaron broke the major league record set by George H. (Babe) Ruth of 714 home runs in a lifetime when he hit No. 715 on April 8, 1974. Between 1954 and 1974 he hit 733 home runs in the National League. In 1975, he switched over to the American League and in that year and 1976, when he finally retired, he hit 22 more, bringing his lifetime total to 755, the major league record.

The Japanese slugger Sadaharu Oh (b. May 20, 1940), of the Yomiuri Giants, hit his 820th home run on July 7, 1979, to break a tie in the 8th inning in a game against the Hanshin Tigers in Tokyo.

An all-league record of 800 in a lifetime has been claimed for Josh Gibson (1911–47) of the Homestead Grays of the Negro League, who

FASTEST PITCHER:
L. Nolan Ryan (California AL),
who can throw a pitch 100.9
m.p.h., set a new modern record
with 383 strikeouts in the 1973
season. He has also tied Sandy
Koufax with 4 no-hit games.

was elected in 1972 to the Baseball Hall of Fame in Cooperstown, New York. Gibson hit 84 round-trippers in one season.

The longest home run ever measured was one of 618 feet by Roy Edward "Dizzy" Carlyle (1900–56) in a minor league game at Emeryville Ball Park, California, on July 4, 1929. Babe Ruth hit a 587-foot homer in a Boston Red Sox vs. New York Giants game at Tampa, Florida, in 1919.

Fastest Pitcher

The fastest pitcher in the world is L. Nolan Ryan of the California Angels who, on August 20, 1974, in Anaheim Stadium, was electronically clocked at a speed of 100.9 m.p.h.

Longest Throw

The longest throw of a 5–5¼-oz. baseball is 445 feet 10 inches by Glen Gorbous (b. Canada) on August 1, 1957. Mildred "Babe" Didrikson (later Mrs. George Zaharias) (1914–56) threw a ball 296 feet at Jersey City, New Jersey, on July 25, 1931.

Do-Nothing Record

Toby Harrah of the Texas Rangers (AL) played an entire double-header at shortstop on June 26, 1976, without having a chance to make any fielding plays, assists or putouts.

Hit by Pitch

Ron Hunt, an infielder who played with various National League teams from 1963 to 1974, led the league in getting hit by pitched balls for a record seven consecutive years. His career total is 243, also a major league record.

Fastest Base Runner

Ernest Evar Swanson (1902–73) took only 13.3 seconds to circle the bases at Columbus, Ohio, in 1932, averaging 18.45 m.p.h.

Youngest Player

The youngest major league player of all time was the Cincinnati pitcher Joe Nuxhall, who started his career in June, 1944, aged 15 years 10 months 11 days.

Largest Stadium

The Cleveland Municipal Stadium in Cleveland, Ohio, has a seating capacity of 76,977.

MAJOR LEAGUE
ALL-TIME RECORDS
(including 1978 season)

Individual Batting

Highest percentage, lifetime (5,000 at-bats)
.367 Tyrus R. Cobb, Det. AL, 1905–26; Phil. AL, 1927–28

Highest percentage, season (500 at-bats)
(Leader in each league)
.438 Hugh Duffy, Bos. NL, 1894
.422 Napoleon Lajoie, Phil. AL, 1901

Most games played
3,298 Henry L. Aaron, Mil. NL, 1954–65, Atl. NL, 1966–74; Mil. AL, 1975–76

Most consecutive games played
2,130 Henry Louis Gehrig, N.Y. AL, June 1, 1925 through Apr. 30, 1939

Most runs, lifetime
2,244 Tyrus R. Cobb, Det. AL, 1905–1926; Phil. AL, 1927–28; 24 years

Most runs batted in, season
190 Lewis R. (Hack) Wilson, Chi. NL., 155 games, 1930

Most runs batted in, game
12 James L. Bottomley, St. L. NL, Sept. 16, 1924

Most runs batted in, inning
7 Edward Cartwright, St. L. AA, Sept. 23, 1890

Most base hits
4,191 Tyrus R. Cobb, Det. AL, 1905–26; Phil. AL, 1927–28; 24 years

Most runs, season
196 William R. Hamilton, Phil. NL, 131 games, 1894

HIGHEST BATTING AVERAGE for a season in the American League was .422 by Nap Lajoie of Philadelphia in 1901.

Most runs batted in, lifetime
2.297 Henry L. Aaron, Mil. NL, 1954–65, Atl. NL, 1966–74; Mil. AL, 1975–76

Most base hits, season
257 George H. Sisler, St. L. AL, 154 games, 1920

HOME RUN KING: Henry
L. (Hank) Aaron played in the
National League for 21
seasons before switching to
the American League for his
last two seasons (1975–76). He
hit a record 755 home runs in
his career and also holds
records for lifetime runs batted
in (2,297) and most total
bases (6,856).

Individual Batting Records (continued)

Most hits in succession
12 M. Frank (Pinky) Higgins, Bos.
AL, June 19–21 (4 games), 1938;
Walter Dropo, Det. AL, July 14,
July 15, 2 games, 1952

Most base hits, consecutive, game
7 Wilbert Robinson, Balt. NL,
June 10, 1892, 1st game (7-ab),
6-1b, 1-2b

Renaldo Stennett, Pitt. NL,
Sept. 16, 1975 (7-ab), 4-1b,
2-2b, 1-3b

Cesar Gutierrez, Det. AL, June
21, 1970, 2nd game (7-ab) 6-1b,
1-2b (extra-inning game)

Most consecutive games batted safely,
season
56 Joseph P. DiMaggio, N.Y. AL
(91 hits—16-2b, 4-3b, 15 hr),
May 15 to July 16, 1941

Most long hits, season
119 George H. (Babe) Ruth, N.Y.
AL (44-2b, 16-3b, 59 hr), 152
games, 1921

Most total bases, lifetime
6,856 Henry L. Aaron, Mil. NL,
1954–65, Atl. NL, 1966–74; Mil.
AL, 1975–76

Most total bases, season
457 George H. (Babe) Ruth, N.Y. AL,
152 g. (85 on 1b, 88 on 2b, 48 on
3b, 236 on hr), 1921

Most total bases, game
18 Joseph W. Adcock, Mil. NL
(1-2b, 4-hr), July 31, 1954

Sluggers' percentage
(The percentage is obtained by dividing
the "times at bat" into total bases.)
Highest slugging percentage, lifetime
.690 George H. (Babe) Ruth, Bos.-
N.Y. AL, 1914–34; Bos. NL,
1935

Triple-Crown winners
(Most times leading league in batting,
runs batted in and home runs.)
2 Rogers Hornsby, St. L. NL, 1922,
1925
Theodore S. Williams, Bos. AL,
1942, 1947

Most one-base hits (singles), season
202 William H. Keeler, Balt. NL,128
games, 1898

Most two-base hits, season
67 Earl W. Webb, Bos. AL, 151
games, 1931

Most three-base hits, season
36 J. Owen Wilson, Pitts. NL, 152
games, 1912

Most home runs, season (154-game
schedule)
60 George H. (Babe) Ruth, N.Y. AL
(28 home, 32 away), 151 gs, 1927

Most home runs, season (162-game
schedule)
61 Roger E. Maris, N.Y. AL (30
home, 31 away), 161 gs. 1961

Most home runs, lifetime
 755 Henry L. Aaron, Mil. NL, 1954
   (13), 1955 (27), 1956 (26), 1957
   (44), 1958 (30), 1959 (39), 1960
   (40), 1961 (34), 1962 (45), 1963
   (44), 1964 (24), 1965 (32); Atl.
   NL, 1966 (44), 1967 (39), 1968
   (29), 1969 (44), 1970 (38), 1971
   (47), 1972 (34), 1973 (40), 1974
   (20); Mil. AL, 1975 (12), 1976
   (10)

Most home runs, bases filled, lifetime
 23 Henry Louis Gehrig, N.Y. AL,
   1927–1938

Most home runs with bases filled, season
 5 Ernest Banks, Chi. NL, May 11,
   19, July 17 (1st game), Aug. 2,
   Sept. 19, 1955
   James E. Gentile, Balt. AL, May
   9 (2), July 2, 7, Sept. 22, 1961

Most home runs, with bases filled, same
game
 2 Anthony M. Lazzeri, N.Y. AL,
   May 24, 1936
   James R. Tabor, Bos. AL (2nd
   game), July 4, 1939
   Rudolph York, Bos. AL, July 27,
   1946
   James E. Gentile, Balt. AL, May
   9, 1961 (consecutive at-bats)
   Tony L. Cloninger, Atl. NL,
   July 3, 1966
   James T. Northrup, Det. AL, June
   24, 1968 (consecutive at-bats)
   Frank Robinson, Balt. AL, June
   26, 1970 (consecutive at-bats)

Most bases on balls, game
 6 James E. Foxx, Bos. AL, June 16,
   1938

Most bases on balls, season
 170 George H. (Babe) Ruth, N.Y.
   AL, 152 games, 1923

Most home runs, one month
 18 Rudolph York, Det. AL, Aug.
   1937

Most consecutive games hitting home
runs
 8 R. Dale Long, Pitt. NL, May 19–
   28, 1956

Most home runs, one doubleheader
 5 Stanley F. Musial, St. L. NL, 1st
   game (3), 2nd game (2), May 2,
   1954
   Nathan Colbert, S.D. NL, 1st
   game (2), 2nd game (3), Aug. 1,
   1972

Most consecutive pinch hits, lifetime
 9 David E. Philley, Phil. NL, Sept.
   9, 11, 12, 13, 19, 20, 27, 28, 1958;
   Apr. 16, 1959

RECORD SLUGGER: Babe Ruth
(New York AL) still holds the record
for 60 home runs in a 154-game season,
most long hits (119), most total bases
(457), and most bases on balls (170)
in a season and had a lifetime slugging
percentage of .690.

Most Valuable Player, as voted by
Baseball Writers Association

3 times James E. Foxx, Phil. AL, 1932,
   33, 38
   Joseph P. DiMaggio, N.Y. AL,
   1939, 41, 47
   Stanley F. Musial, St. L. NL,
   1943, 46, 48
   Lawrence P. (Yogi) Berra, N.Y.
   AL, 1951, 54, 55
   Roy Campanella, Bklyn. NL,
   1951, 53, 55
   Mickey C. Mantle, N.Y. AL,
   1956, 57, 62

MVP THREE TIMES: Mickey
Mantle (New York AL) also holds
World Series records for most runs (42),
most runs batted in (40), and most home
runs (18) in total series games.

Base Running

Most stolen bases, lifetime
937 William R. Hamilton, K.C. AA,
1888–89; Phil. NL 1890–95;
Bos. NL 1896–1901

Most stolen bases, lifetime since 1900
917 Louis C. Brock, Chi.-St. L. NL,
1961–78

Most stolen bases, season since 1900
118 Louis C. Brock, St. L. NL, 153
games, 1974

Most stolen bases, game
7 George F. (Piano Legs) Gore,
Chi. NL, June 25, 1881
William R. (Sliding Billy)
Hamilton, Phil. NL, 2nd game,
8 inn., Aug. 31, 1894

Most times stealing home, game
2 by 9 players

Most times stealing home, lifetime
35 Tyrus R. Cobb, Det.-Phil. AL,
1905–28

Fewest times caught stealing, season
(50+ attempts)
2 Max Carey, Pitt. NL, 1922 (53
atts.)

Pitching

Most games, lifetime
1,070 J. Hoyt Wilhelm, N.Y.-St. L.-
Atl.-Chi.-L.A. (448) NL,
1952–57, 69–72; Clev.-Balt.-
Chi.-Cal. (622) AL, 1957–69

Most complete games, lifetime
751 Denton T. (Cy) Young, Clev.-
St. L.-Bos. NL (428); Bos.-Clev.
AL (323), 1890–1911

Most complete games, season
74 William H. White, Cin. NL, 1879

Most innings pitched, game
26 Leon J. Cadore, Bklyn. NL, May
1, 1920
Joseph Oeschger, Bos. NL, May
1, 1920

Lowest earned run average, season
0.90 Ferdinand M. Schupp, N.Y. NL,
1916 (140 inn)
1.01 Hubert B. (Dutch) Leonard, Bos.
AL, 1914 (222 inn)
1.12 Robert Gibson, St. L. NL, 1968
(305 inn)

LONGEST-LASTING PITCHER:
Hoyt Wilhelm, knuckleball pitcher for 9
teams in both leagues, played in 1,070
major league games between 1952 and
1972, and had a lifetime ERA of 2.52.

Most games won, lifetime
511 Denton T. (Cy) Young, Clev. NL
(239) 1890–98; St. L. NL 1899–
1900; Bos. AL (193) 1901–08;
Clev. AL (29) 1909–11; Bos. NL
(4) 1911

Most games won, season
60 Charles Radbourne, Providence
NL, 1884

Most consecutive games won, lifetime
24 Carl O. Hubbell, N.Y. NL, 1936
(16); 1937 (8)

Most consecutive games won, season
19 Timothy J. Keefe, N.Y. NL, 1888
Richard W. Marquard, N.Y. NL,
1912

Most shutout games, season
16 George W. Bradley, St. L. NL,
1876
Grover C. Alexander, Phil. NL,
1916

Most shutout games, lifetime
113 Walter P. Johnson, Wash. AL, 21
years, 1907–27

Most consecutive shutout games, season
6 Donald S. Drysdale, L.A. NL,
May 14, 18, 22, 26, 31, June 4,
1968

Most consecutive shutout innings
58 Donald S. Drysdale, L.A. NL,
May 14–June 8, 1968

Most strikeouts, lifetime
3,508 Walter P. Johnson, Wash. AL, 1907–27

Most strikeouts, season
505 Matthew Kilroy, Balt. AA, 1886 (Distance 50 ft)
383 L. Nolan Ryan, Cal. AL, 1973 (Distance 60 ft 6 in.)

Most strikeouts, game (9 inn) since 1900:
19 Steven N. Carlton, St. L. NL vs N.Y., Sept. 15, 1969 (lost)
G. Thomas Seaver, N.Y. NL vs S.D., Apr. 22, 1970
L. Nolan Ryan, Cal. AL, vs Bos., Aug. 12, 1974

Most strikeouts, extra-inning game
21 Thomas E. Cheney, Wash. AL vs Balt. (16 inns), Sept. 12, 1962 (night)

Most no-hit games, lifetime
4 Sanford Koufax, L.A. NL, 1962–63–64–65
L. Nolan Ryan, Cal. AL, 1973(2)-74-75

Most consecutive no-hit games
2 John S. Vandermeer, Cin. NL, June 11–15, 1938

Perfect game—9 innings

1880 John Lee Richmond, Worcester vs Clev. NL, June 12 1–0
John M. Ward, Prov. vs Buff. NL, June 17 AM...... 5–0
1904 Denton T. (Cy) Young, Bos. vs Phil. AL, May 5 ... 3–0
1908 Adrian C. Joss, Clev. vs Chi. AL, Oct. 2...................... 1–0
†1917 Ernest G. Shore, Bos. vs Wash. AL, June 23 (1st g.) 4–0
1922 C. C. Robertson, Chi. vs Det. AL, April 30............ 2–0
**1956 Donald J. Larsen, N.Y. AL vs Bklyn. NL, Oct. 8...... 2–0
1964 James P. Bunning, Phil. NL vs N.Y., June 21 (1st g.) 6–0
1965 Sanford Koufax, L.A. NL vs Chi., Sept. 9................ 1–0
1968 James A. Hunter, Oak. AL vs Minn., May 8............ 4–0

Special mention
1959 Harvey Haddix, Jr., Pitt. vs Mil. NL, May 26, pitched 12 "perfect" innings, allowed hit in 13th and lost.

†Starting pitcher, "Babe" Ruth, was banished from game by Umpire Owens after giving first batter, Morgan, a base on balls. Shore relieved and while he pitched to second batter, Morgan was caught stealing. Shore then retired next 26 batters to complete "perfect" game.
**World Series game.

Club Batting

Highest percentage, season
.343 Phil. NL, 132 games, 1894

Highest percentage, season since 1900
.319 N.Y. NL, 154 games, 1930

Most runs, one club, game
36 Chi. NL (36) vs Louisville (7), June 29, 1897

Most runs, one club, inning
18 Chi. NL, 7th inning, Sept. 6, 1883

Most runs, both clubs, inning
19 Wash. AA (14), Balt. (5), 1st inn., June 17, 1891
Clev. AL (13), Bos. (6), 8th inn., April 10, 1977

Most hits, one club, 9 inning game
36 Phil. NL, Aug. 17, 1894

Most hits, one club, inning
18 Chi. NL, 7th inning, Sept. 6, 1883

Fewest hits, both clubs, game
1 Chi. NL (0) vs L.A. (1), Sept. 9, 1965

Most home runs, one club, season (154-game schedule)
221 N.Y. NL, 155 games, 1947
Cin. NL, 155 games, 1956

Most home runs, one club, season (162-game schedule)
240 N.Y. AL, 163 games, 1961

Fewest home runs (135 or more games), one club, season
3 Chi. AL, 156 games, 1908

Most stolen bases (1900 to date), one club, season
347 N.Y. NL, 154 games, 1911

Most stolen bases, one club, inning
8 Wash. AL, 1st inning, July 19, 1915
Phil. NL, 9th inning, 1st g., July 7, 1919

Club Fielding

Highest percentage, one club, season
.985 Balt. AL, 1964

Fewest errors, season
95 Balt. AL, 163 games, 1964
Cin. NL, 162 games, 1977

Most double plays, club, season
217 Phil. AL, 154 games, 1949

Most double plays, club, game
7 N.Y. AL, Aug. 14, 1942
Houst. NL, May 4, 1969

General Club Records

Shortest and longest game by time
51 minutes N.Y. NL (6), Phil. (1), 1st
g., Sept. 28, 1919
7:23 S.F. NL (8) at N.Y. (6) 23 inn.,
2nd g., May 31, 1964

Longest 9-inning game
4:18 S.F. NL (7) at L.A. (8), Oct. 2,
1962

Fewest times shutout, season
0 Bos. NL, 1894 (132 g.)
Phil. NL, 1894 (127 g.)
N.Y. AL, 1932 (155 g.)

Most consecutive innings shutting out opponents
56 Pitt. NL, June 1–9, 1903

Highest percentage games won, season
.798 Chi. NL (won 67, lost 17), 1880
.763 Chi. NL (won 116, lost 36), 1906
.721 Clev. AL (won 111, lost 43), 1954

Most games won, season (154-game schedule)
116 Chi. NL, 1906

Most consecutive games won, season
26 N.Y. NL, Sept. 7 (1st g.) to Sept.
30 (1 tie), 1916

Most pitchers used in a game, 9 innings, one club
9 St. L. AL vs Chi., Oct. 2, 1949

Managers' consecutive championship records
5 years Charles D. (Casey) Stengel,
N.Y. AL, 1949–50–51–52–53

World Series Records

Most series played
14 Lawrence P. (Yogi) Berra, N.Y.,
AL, 1947, 49–53, 55–58, 60–63

Highest batting percentage (20 g. min.), total series
.391 Louis C. Brock, St. L. NL, 1964,
67–68 (g-21, ab-87, h-34)

Highest batting percentage, 4 or more games, one series
.625 4-game series, George H. (Babe)
Ruth, N.Y. AL, 1928

Most runs, total series
42 Mickey C. Mantle, N.Y. AL,
1951–53, 55–58, 60–64

Most runs, one series
10 Reginald M. Jackson, N.Y. AL,
1977

Most runs batted in, total series
40 Mickey C. Mantle, N.Y., AL,
1951–53, 55–58, 60–64

Most runs batted in, game
6 Robert C. Richardson, N.Y. AL,
(4) 1st inn., (2) 4th inn., Oct. 8,
1960

Most runs batted in, consecutive times at bat
7 James L. (Dusty) Rhodes, N.Y.
NL, first 4 times at bat, 1954

Most base hits, total series
71 Lawrence P. (Yogi) Berra, N.Y.
AL, 1947, 49–53, 55–58, 60–61

Most home runs, total series
18 Mickey C. Mantle, N.Y. AL,
1952 (2), 53 (2), 55, 56 (3), 57,
58 (2), 60 (3), 63, 64 (3)

Most home runs, one series
5 Reginald M. Jackson, N.Y. AL,
1977

Most home runs, game
3 George H. (Babe) Ruth, N.Y.
AL, Oct. 6, 1926; Oct. 9, 1928
Reginald M. Jackson, N.Y. AL,
1977

Pitchers' Records

Pitching in most series
11 Edward C. (Whitey) Ford, N.Y.
AL, 1950, 53, 55–58, 60–64

Most victories, total series
10 Edward C. (Whitey) Ford, N.Y.
AL, 1950 (1), 55 (2), 56 (1),
57 (1), 60 (2), 61 (2), 62 (1)

All victories, no defeats
6 Vernon L. (Lefty) Gomez, N.Y.
AL, 1932 (1), 36 (2), 37 (2), 38 (1)

Most games won, one series
3 games in 5-game series
Christy Mathewson, N.Y. NL,
1905
J. W. Coombs, Phil. AL, 1910
Many others won 3 games in series of
more games.

Most shutout games, total series
4 Christy Mathewson, N.Y. NL.
1905 (3), 1913

Most shutout games, one series
3 Christy Mathewson, N.Y. NL.
1905

Most strikeouts, one pitcher, total series
94 Edward C. (Whitey) Ford, N.Y.
AL, 1950, 53, 55–58, 60–64

Most strikeouts, one series
23 in 4 games Sanford Koufax, L.A.
NL, 1963

WORLD SERIES RUNS: Reggie Jackson belted 3 homers in a game and 5 in the 6-game series in 1977.

18 in 5 games Christy Mathewson,
    N.Y. NL, 1905

20 in 6 games C. A. (Chief) Bender,
    Phil. AL, 1911

35 in 7 games Robert Gibson, St. L.
    NL, 1968

28 in 8 games W. H. Dinneen, Bos.
    AL, 1903

Most strikeouts, one pitcher, game
  17 Robert Gibson, St. L. NL, Oct. 2,
     1968

Highest attendance
420,784 L.A. NL, World Champions
    vs Chi. AL, 4–2, 1959

Most Series Won
  22 New York AL, 1923, 1927, 1928,
     1932, 1936, 1937, 1938, 1939,
     1941, 1943, 1947, 1949, 1950,
     1951, 1952, 1953, 1956, 1958,
     1961, 1962, 1977, 1978

*Baseball records by Seymour Siwoff,
Elias Sports Bureau.*

World Series Attendance

The World Series record attendance is 420,784 (6 games with total receipts of $2,626,973.44) when the Los Angeles Dodgers beat the Chicago White Sox 4 games to 2, October 1–8, 1959.

The single game record is 92,706 for the fifth game (receipts $552,774.77) at the Memorial Coliseum, Los Angeles, on October 6, 1959.

Basketball

Origins. *Ollamalitzli* was a 16th-century Aztec precursor of basketball played in Mexico. If the solid rubber ball was put through a fixed stone ring placed high on one side of the stadium, the player was entitled to the clothing of all the spectators. The captain of the losing team often lost his head (by execution). Another game played much earlier, in the 10th century B.C. by the Olmecs in Mexico, called *Pok-ta-Pok*, also resembled basketball in its concept of a ring through which a round object was passed.

Modern basketball (which may have been based on the German game of *Korbball*) was devised by the Canadian-born Dr. James A. Naismith (1861–1939) at the Training School of the International Y.M.C.A. College at Springfield, Massachusetts, in December, 1891. The first game played under modified rules was on January 20, 1892. The first public contest was on March 11, 1892.

The International Amateur Basketball Federation (F.I.B.A.) was founded in 1932.

Most Accurate Shooting. The greatest goal-shooting demonstration was made by a professional, Ted St. Martin, now of Jacksonville, Florida, who, on June 25, 1977, scored 2,036 consecutive free throws.

In a 24-hour period, May 31–June 1, 1975, Fred L. Newman of San Jose, California, scored 12,874 baskets out of 13,116 attempts (98.15 per cent). Newman has also made 88 consecutive free throws while blindfolded at the Central Y.M.C.A., San Jose, California, on February 5, 1978.

Longest Field Goal. The longest recorded field goal in a game was made from a measured distance of 89 feet by Rudy Williams (b. December 16, 1957) at Providence College, Rhode Island, on February 17, 1979.

Tallest Players

The tallest player of all time is reputed to be Suleiman Ali Nashnush (b. 1943) who played for the Libyan team in 1962 when he measured 8 feet tall. The tallest woman player is Iuliana Semenova (U.S.S.R.) who is reputed to stand 7 feet 2 inches tall and weigh 281 lbs. The tallest N.B.A. player is Tom Burleson, who is 7 feet 4 inches tall.

Greatest Attendances. The Harlem Globetrotters played an exhibition to 75,000 in the Olympic Stadium, West Berlin, Germany, in 1951. The largest indoor basketball crowd was at the Astrodome, Houston, Texas, where 52,693 watched a game on January 20, 1968, between the University of Houston and U.C.L.A.

The Harlem Globetrotters have traveled over 6,000,000 miles, visited 94 countries on six continents, and have been watched by an estimated 80,000,000 spectators. They have won over 12,000 games,

MILLIONS OF FANS:
Meadowlark Lemon was a star player for the Harlem Globetrotters, who have performed before an estimated 80 million people.

losing less than 350, but many were not truly competitive. The team was founded by Abraham M. Saperstein (1903–66) of Chicago, and their first game was played at Hinckley, Illinois, on January 7, 1927.

Olympic Champions

The U.S. won all seven Olympic titles from the time the sport was introduced to the Games in 1936 until 1968, without losing a single match. In 1972, in Munich, their run of 64 consecutive victories was broken when they lost 51–50 to the U.S.S.R. in a much-disputed final match. They regained the Olympic title in Montreal in 1976, again without losing a game.

World Champions

Brazil, the U.S.S.R. and Yugoslavia are the only countries to win the World Men's Championship (instituted 1950) on more than one occasion. Brazil won in 1959 and 1963; the U.S.S.R. in 1967 and 1974; Yugoslavia in 1970 and 1978.

In 1975, the U.S.S.R. won the women's championship (instituted 1953) for the fifth consecutive time since 1959.

Marathon

The longest game is 89 hours by two teams of five at Kwinana High School, Western Australia, on May 18–21, 1979.

NATIONAL BASKETBALL ASSOCIATION
Regular Season Records
Including 1978–79 *Season*

The National Basketball Association's Championship series was established in 1947. Prior to 1949, when it joined with the National Basketball League, the professional circuit was known as the Basketball Association of America.

SERVICE

Most Games, Lifetime
1,270 John Havlicek, Bos. 1963–78

Most Games, Consecutive, Lifetime
844 John Kerr, Syr.-Phil.-Balt., Oct. 31, 1954–Nov. 4, 1965

Most Complete Games, Season
79 Wilt Chamberlain, Phil. 1962

Most Complete Games, Consecutive, Season
47 Wilt Chamberlain, Phil. 1962

Most Minutes, Lifetime
47,859 Wilt Chamberlain, Phil.-S.F.-L.A. 1960–73

Most Minutes, Season
3 882 Wilt Chamberlain, Phil. 1962

SCORING

Most Seasons Leading League
7 Wilt Chamberlain, Phil. 1960–62; S.F. 1963–64; S.F.-Phil. 1965; Phil. 1966

Most Points, Lifetime
31,419 Wilt Chamberlain, Phil.-S.F.-L.A. 1960–73

Most Points, Season
4,029 Wilt Chamberlain, Phil. 1962

Most Seasons 1000+ Points
16 John Havlicek, Bos. 1963–78

Most Points, Game
100 Wilt Chamberlain, Phil. vs. N.Y., Mar. 2, 1962

Most Points, Half
59 Wilt Chamberlain, Phil. vs. N.Y., Mar. 2, 1962

Most Points, Quarter
33 George Gervin, S.A. vs. N.O. Apr. 9, 1978

Most Points, Overtime Period
13 Earl Monroe, Balt. vs. Det., Feb. 6, 1970
Joe Caldwell, Atl. vs. Cin., Feb. 18, 1970

Highest Scoring Average, Lifetime (400 + games)
30.1 Wilt Chamberlain, Phil.-S.F.-L.A. 1960–73

Highest Scoring Average, Season
50.4 Wilt Chamberlain, Phil. 1962

Field Goals Made

Most Field Goals, Lifetime
12,681 Wilt Chamberlain, Phil.-S.F.-L.A. 1960–73

Most Field Goals, Season
1,597 Wilt Chamberlain, Phil. 1962

Most Field Goals, Consecutive, Season
35 Wilt Chamberlain, Phil. Feb. 17–28, 1967

Most Field Goals, Game
36 Wilt Chamberlain, Phil. vs. N.Y., Mar. 2, 1962

Most Field Goals, Half
22 Wilt Chamberlain, Phil. vs. N.Y., Mar. 2, 1962

Most Field Goals, Quarter
13 David Thompson, Den. vs. Det., Apr. 9, 1978

Field Goals Attempted

Most Field Goal Attempts, Lifetime
23,930 John Havlicek, Bos. 1963–1978

Most Field Goal Attempts, Season
3,159 Wilt Chamberlain, Phil. 1962

Most Field Goal Attempts, Game
63 Wilt Chamberlain, Phil. vs. N.Y., Mar. 2, 1962

Most Field Goal Attempts, Half
37 Wilt Chamberlain, Phil. vs. N.Y., Mar. 2, 1962

Most Field Goal Attempts, Quarter
21 Wilt Chamberlain, Phil. vs. N.Y., Mar. 2, 1962

Field Goal Percentage

Most Seasons Leading League
9 Wilt Chamberlain, Phil. 1961; S.F. 1963; S.F.-Phil. 1965; Phil. 1966–68; L.A. 1969, 72–73

Highest Percentage, Lifetime
.551 Kareem Abdul-Jabbar, Mil.-L.A. 1970–79

Highest Percentage, Season
.727 Wilt Chamberlain, L.A. 1973

LONGEST SERVICE: John Havlicek played in a record 1,270 games for the Boston Celtics.

Free Throws Made

Most Free Throws Made, Lifetime
7,694 Oscar Robertson, Cin.-Mil. 1961–74

Most Free Throws Made, Season
840 Jerry West, L.A. 1966

Most Free Throws Made, Consecutive, Season
60 Rick Barry, G.S. Oct. 22–Nov. 16, 1976

Most Free Throws Made, Game
28 Wilt Chamberlain, Phil. vs. N.Y., Mar. 2, 1962

Most Free Throws Made (No Misses), Game
19 Bob Pettit, St.L. vs. Bos., Nov. 22, 1961

Most Free Throws Made, Half
19 Oscar Robertson, Cin. vs. Balt., Dec. 27, 1964

Most Free Throws Made, Quarter
14 Rick Barry, S.F. vs. N.Y., Dec. 6, 1966

FREE THROW LEADER: Jerry West sank 840 free throws in his 1966 season for L.A.

Basketball (N.B.A.) continued

Free Throws Attempted

Most Free Throw Attempts, Lifetime
11,862 Wilt Chamberlain, Phil.-S.F.-L.A. 1960–73

Most Free Throw Attempts, Season
1,363 Wilt Chamberlain, Phil. 1962

Most Free Throw Attempts, Game
   34 Wilt Chamberlain, S.F. vs. N.Y., Nov. 27, 1963

Most Free Throw Attempts, Half
   22 Oscar Robertson, Cin. vs. Balt., Dec. 27, 1964

Most Free Throw Attempts, Quarter
   16 Oscar Robertson, Cin. vs. Balt., Dec. 27, 1964
      Stan McKenzie, Phoe. vs. Phil., Feb. 15, 1970
      Pete Maravich, Atl. vs. Chi., Jan. 2, 1973

Free Throw Percentage

Most Seasons Leading League
   7 Bill Sharman, Bos. 1953–57, 59, 61

Highest Percentage, Lifetime
  .899 Rick Barry, S.F.-G.S.-Hou. 1966–67, 73–79

Highest Percentage, Season
  .947 Rick Barry, Hou. 1979

REBOUNDS

Most Seasons Leading League
   11 Wilt Chamberlain, Phil. 1960–62; S.F. 1963; Phil. 1966–68; L.A. 1969, 71–73

Most Rebounds, Lifetime
23,924 Wilt Chamberlain, Phil.-S.F.-L.A. 1960–73

Most Rebounds, Season
2,149 Wilt Chamberlain, Phil. 1961

Most Rebounds, Game
   55 Wilt Chamberlain, Phil. vs. Bos., Nov. 24, 1960

Most Rebounds, Half
   32 Bill Russell, Bos. vs. Phil., Nov. 16, 1957

Most Rebounds, Quarter
   18 Nate Thurmond, S.F. vs. Balt., Feb. 28, 1965

Highest Average (per game), Lifetime
  22.9 Wilt Chamberlain, Phil.-S.F.-L.A. 1960–73

Highest Average (per game), Season
  27.2 Wilt Chamberlain, Phil. 1961

ASSISTS

Most Seasons Leading League
   8 Bob Cousy, Bos. 1953–60

Most Assists, Lifetime
9,887 Oscar Robertson, Cin.-Mil. 1961–74

Most Assists, Season
1,099 Kevin Porter, Det. 1979

Most Assists, Game
   29 Kevin Porter, N.J. vs. Hou. Feb. 24, 1978

Most Assists, Half
   19 Bob Cousy, Bos. vs. Minn., Feb. 27, 1959

ASSIST SPECIALIST: Oscar Robertson holds the record for setting up plays with 9,887 assists in his lifetime, and also has the highest average (9.5) per game lifetime.

Most Assists, Quarter
12 Bob Cousy, Bos. vs. Minn., Feb. 27, 1959
    John Lucas, Hou. vs. Mil., Oct. 27, 1977
Highest Average (per game), Lifetime
9.5 Oscar Robertson, Cin.-Mil. 1961–74
Highest Average (per game), Season
13.4 Kevin Porter, Det. 1979

PERSONAL FOULS

Most Personal Fouls, Lifetime
3,855 Hal Greer, Syr.-Phil. 1959–73
Most Personal Fouls, Season
367 Bill Robinzine, K.C. 1979
Most Personal Fouls, Game
8 Don Otten, T.C. vs. Sheb., Nov. 24, 1949
Most Personal Fouls, Half
6 By many. Last:
   Cedric Maxwell, Bos. vs. San Diego, March 2, 1979
Most Personal Fouls, Quarter
6 Connie Dierking, Syr. vs. Cin., Nov. 17, 1959
   Henry Akin, Seattle vs. Phil., Dec. 20, 1967
   Bud Ogden, Phil. vs Phoe., Feb. 15, 1970
   Don Smith, Hou. vs. Clev., Feb. 8, 1974
   Roger Brown, Det. vs. G.S., Mar. 25, 1977

DISQUALIFICATIONS
(Fouling Out of Game)

Most Disqualifications, Lifetime
127 Vern Mikkelsen, Minn., 1950–59
Most Disqualifications, Season
26 Don Meineke, Ft. W. 1953
Most Games, No Disqualifications, Lifetime
1,045 Wilt Chamberlain, Phil.-S.F.-L.A. 1960–73 (Entire Career)

TEAM RECORDS
(ot = overtime)

Most Seasons, League Champion
13 Boston 1957, 59–66, 68–69, 74, 76
Most Seasons, Consecutive, League Champion
8 Boston 1959–66
Most Seasons, Division Champion
14 Boston 1957–65, 72–76
Most Seasons, Consecutive, Division Champion
9 Boston 1957–65
Most Games Won, Season
69 Los Angeles, 1972
Most Games Won, Consecutive, Season
33 Los Angeles Nov. 5, 1971–Jan. 7, 1972
Most Games Won, Consecutive, Start of Season
15 Washington Nov. 3–Dec. 4, 1948

REBOUND RECORD-HOLDER:
Wilton Norman (the Stilt) Chamberlain is probably the greatest basketball player of all time. He made 55 rebounds in one game, 2,149 in a season. He also set records of 100 points in a game, 4,029 points in a season, most free throws made (28) in a game, and other records.

Most Games Won, Consecutive, End of Season
14 Milwaukee Feb. 28–Mar. 27, 1973
Most Games Lost, Season
73 Philadelphia 1973
Most Games Lost, Consecutive, Season
20 Philadelphia Jan. 9–Feb. 11, 1973
Most Games Lost, Consecutive, Start of Season
15 Denver Oct. 29–Dec. 25, 1949
   Cleveland Oct. 14–Nov. 10, 1970
   Philadelphia Oct. 10–Nov. 10, 1973
Highest Percentage, Games Won, Season
.841 Los Angeles 1972
Lowest Percentage, Games Won, Season
.110 Philadelphia 1973

Team Scoring

Most Points, Season
10,143 Philadelphia 1967
Most Games, 100+ Points, Season
81 Los Angeles 1972
Most Games, Consecutive, 100+ Points, Season
77 New York 1967
Most Points, Game
173 Boston vs Minn. Feb. 27, 1959
Most Points, Both Teams, Game
316 Phil. (169) vs N.Y. (147) Mar. 2, 1962
   Cin.(165) vs San Diego (151) Mar. 12, 1970
Most Points, Half
97 Atlanta vs San Diego Feb. 11, 1970

Basketball (N.B.A.) continued

Most Points, Quarter
58 Buffalo vs Bos. Oct. 20, 1972
Widest Victory Margin, Game
63 Los Angeles (162) vs Golden State (99) Mar. 19, 1972

Field Goals Made

Most Field Goals, Season
3,972 Milwaukee 1971
Most Field Goals, Game
72 Boston vs Minn. Feb. 27, 1959
Most Field Goals, Both Teams, Game
134 Cin. (67) vs San Diego (67) Mar. 12, 1970
Most Field Goals, Half
40 Boston vs Minn. Feb. 27, 1959
Syracuse vs Det. Jan. 13, 1963
Most Field Goals, Quarter
23 Boston vs Minn. Feb. 27, 1959
Buffalo vs Bos. Oct. 20, 1972

Field Goals Attempted

Most Field Goal Attempts, Season
9,295 Boston 1961
Most Field Goal Attempts, Game
153 Philadelphia vs. L.A. Dec. 8, 1961 (3 ot)
150 Boston vs Phil. Feb. 3, 1960
Most Field Goal Attempts, Both Teams, Game
291 Phil. (153) vs L.A. (138) Dec. 8, 1961 (3 ot)
274 Bos. (149) vs Det. (125) Jan. 27 1961
Most Field Goal Attempts, Half
83 Philadelphia vs Syr. Nov. 4, 1959
Boston vs Phil. Dec. 27, 1960
Most Field Goal Attempts, Quarter
47 Boston vs Minn. Feb. 27, 1959
Highest Field Goal Percentage, Season
.517 Los Angeles 1979

Free Throws Made

Most Free Throws Made, Season
2,434 Phoenix 1970
Most Free Throws Made, Game
59 Anderson vs Syr. Nov. 24, 1949 (5 ot)
Most Free Throws Made, Both Teams, Game
116 And. (59) vs Syr. (57) Nov. 24, 1949 (5 ot)
Most Free Throws Made, Half
36 Chicago vs Phoe. Jan. 8, 1970
Most Free Throws Made, Quarter
24 St. Louis vs Syr. Dec. 21, 1957

Free Throws Attempted

Most Free Throw Attempts, Season
3,411 Philadelphia 1967
Most Free Throw Attempts, Game
86 Syracuse vs And. Nov. 24, 1949 (5 ot)
71 Chicago vs Phoe. Jan. 8, 1970

Most Free Throw Attempts, Both Teams, Game
160 Syr. (86) vs And. (74) Nov. 24, 1949 (5 ot)
127 Ft. W. (67) vs Minn. (60) Dec. 31, 1954
Most Free Throw Attempts, Half
48 Chicago vs. Phoe. Jan. 8, 1970
Most Free Throw Attempts, Quarter
30 Boston vs Chi. Jan. 9, 1963
Highest Free Throw Percentage, Season
.821 K.C.-Omaha 1975

Rebounds

Most Rebounds, Season
6,131 Boston 1961
Most Rebounds, Game
112 Philadelphia vs Cin. Nov. 8, 1959
Boston vs Det. Dec. 24, 1960
Most Rebounds, Both Teams, Game
215 Phil. (110) vs L.A. (105) Dec. 8, 1961 (3 ot)
196 Bos. (106) vs Det. (90) Jan. 27, 1961
Most Rebounds, Half
62 Boston vs Phil. Nov. 16, 1957
New York vs Phil. Nov. 19, 1960
Philadelphia vs Syr. Nov. 9, 1961
Most Rebounds, Quarter
40 Philadelphia vs Syr. Nov. 9, 1961

Assists

Most Assists, Season
2,562 Milwaukee 1979
Most Assists, Game
60 Syracuse vs Balt. Nov. 15, 1952 (1 ot)
53 Milwaukee vs. Det. Dec. 26, 1978
Most Assists, Both Teams, Game
89 Det. (48) vs Clev. (41) Mar. 28, 1973 (1 ot)
88 Phoe. (47) vs San Diego (41) Mar. 15, 1969
Most Assists, Half
30 Milwaukee vs. Det. Dec. 26, 1978
Most Assists, Quarter
19 Milwaukee vs. Det. Dec. 26, 1978

Personal Fouls

Most Personal Fouls, Season
2,470 Atlanta 1978
Most Personal Fouls, Game
66 Anderson vs Syr. Nov. 24, 1949 (5 ot)
Most Personal Fouls, Both Teams, Game
122 And. (66) vs Syr. (56) Nov. 24, 1949 (5 ot)
97 Syr. (50) vs N.Y. (47) Feb. 15, 1953
Most Personal Fouls, Half
30 Rochester vs Syr. Jan. 15, 1953
Most Personal Fouls, Quarter
18 Portland vs. Atl., Jan. 16, 1977

RIGHT ON CUE:
Willie Hoppe
was undisputed
master of
3-cushion
billiards from
1906 through 1952.

Billiards

Earliest Mention. The earliest recorded mention of billiards was in France in 1429, while Louis XI, King of France, 1461–83, is reported to have had a billiards table. The first recorded public room for billiards in England was the Piazza, Covent Garden, London, in the early part of the 19th century.

Rubber cushions were introduced in 1835 and slate beds in 1836.

Highest Breaks. Tom Reece (England) made an unfinished break of 499,135, including 249,152 cradle cannons (2 points each), in 85 hours 49 minutes against Joe Chapman at Burroughes' Hall, Soho Square, London, between June 3 and July 6, 1907. This was not recognized because press and public were not continuously present. The highest certified break made by the anchor cannon is 42,746 by W. Cook (England) from May 29 to June 7, 1907. The official world record under the then baulk-line rule is 1,784 by Joe Davis in the United Kingdom Championship on May 29, 1936. Walter Lindrum (Australia) made an official break of 4,137 in 2 hours 55 minutes against Joe Davis at Thurston's, London, on January 19–20, 1932, before the baulk-line rule was in force. The amateur record is 1,149 by Michael Ferreira (India) at Calcutta, India, on December 15, 1978.

Fastest Century. Walter Lindrum (1898–1960) of Australia made an unofficial 100 break in 27.5 seconds in Australia on October 10, 1952. His official record is 100 in 46.0 seconds, set in Sydney in 1941.

Most World Titles. The greatest number of world championship titles (instituted 1870) won by one player is eight by John Roberts, Jr. (1847–1919) (England) in 1870 (twice), 1871, 1875 (twice), 1877 and 1885 (twice). Willie Hoppe (U.S.) won 51 "world" titles in the U.S. variant of the game between 1906 and 1952.

Most Amateur Titles. The record for world amateur titles is four by Robert Marshall (Australia) in 1936–38–51–62. The record number of women's titles is eight by Vera Selby, 1970–78.

Pool

Pool or championship pocket billiards with numbered balls began to become standardized *c.* 1890. The greatest exponents were Ralph Greenleaf (U.S.) (1899–1950), who won the "world" professional title 19 times (1919–1937), and William Mosconi (U.S.), who dominated the game from 1941 to 1957.

Michael Eufemia holds the record for the greatest continuous run, pocketing 625 balls without a miss on February 2, 1960 before a large crowd at Logan's Billiard Academy, Brooklyn, New York. (See photo, page O.)

Patrick Young pocketed 10,752 balls in 24 hours, a rate of one per 8.03 seconds, at the Camden Arms in London on May 2–3, 1978.

The longest game is 151 hours by Roy Sadd and Richard Smith at The Sandringham, Brislington, Bristol, Avon, England, on April 12–19, 1979.

3-Cushion Billiards

This pocketless variation dates back to 1878. The world governing body, *Union Mondiale de Billiard*, was formed in 1928. The most successful exponent, 1906–52, was William F. Hoppe (b. October 11, 1887, Cornwall-on-Hudson, New York; d. February 1, 1959) who won 51 billiards championships in all forms. The most U.M.B. titles have been won by Raymond Ceulemans (Belgium) (b. 1937) with 14 (1963–66, 1968–73, 1975–78), with a peak average of 1.479 in 1973.

Bobsledding and Tobogganing

Origins. The oldest known sled is dated *c.* 6500 B.C. and came from Heinola, Finland. The first known bobsled race took place at Davos, Switzerland, in 1889. The International Federation of Bobsleigh and Tobogganing was formed in 1923, followed by the International Bobsleigh Federation in 1957.

Olympic and World Titles. The Olympic four-man bob title (instituted 1924) has been won four times by Switzerland (1924, 36, 56, 72). The U.S. (1932, 1936), Italy (1956, 1968) and West Germany (1952 and 1972) have won the Olympic boblet event (instituted 1932) twice. The most medals won by an individual is six (two gold, two silver, two bronze) by Eugenio Monti (Italy) from 1956 to 1968.

TOBOGGAN CHAMPION: Nino Bibbia of Italy has won 8 Grand National titles, 8 Curzon Cup titles, and the gold medal in the 1948 Olympic Games.

The world four-man bob has been won 12 times by Switzerland (1924–36–39–47–54–55–56–57–71–72–73–75). Italy won the two-man title 14 times (1954–56–57–58–59–60–61–62–63–66–68–69–71–75). Eugenio Monti (Italy) (b. January 23, 1928) has been a member of 11 world championship crews, eight two-man and three four-man.

Tobogganing

The word toboggan comes from the Micmac American Indian word *tobaakan*. The oldest tobogganing club in the world, founded in 1887, is at St. Moritz, Switzerland, home of the Cresta Run and site of the introduction of the skeleton one-man racing toboggan.

The skeleton one-man toboggan dates, in its present form, from 1892. On the Cresta Run at St. Moritz, dating from 1884, the record from the Junction (2,913 feet) is 42.96 seconds (average 63.08 m.p.h.) by Poldi Berchtold of Switzerland on February 22, 1975. The record from the top (3,977 feet long with a drop of 514 feet) is 53.24 seconds (average speed 50.92 m.p.h.), also by Berchtold on February 9, 1975. Speeds of 90 m.p.h. are occasionally attained.

The greatest number of wins in the Grand National (instituted 1885) is eight by the 1948 Olympic champion Nino Bibbia (Italy) (b. September 9, 1924) in 1960–61–62–63–64–66–68–73. The greatest number of wins in the Curzon Cup (instituted in 1910) is eight by Bibbia in 1950–57–58–60–62–63–64–69 who hence won the double in 1960–62–63–64. The most descents made in a season is 7,832 during 65 days in 1976.

Lugeing

In lugeing the rider adopts a sitting, as opposed to a prone position. Official international competition began at Klosters, Switzerland, in 1881. The first European championships were at Reichenberg (now East) Germany, in 1914 and the first world championships at Oslo, Norway, in 1953. The International Luge Federation was formed in 1957. Lugeing became an Olympic sport in 1964.

Most World Titles. The most successful rider in the world championships is Thomas Köhler (East Germany) (b. June 25, 1940), who won the single-seater title in 1962, 1964 (Olympic), 1966, and 1967, and shared in the two-seater title in 1967 and 1968 (Olympic). Margit Schumann (East Germany) (b. September 14, 1952) has won the women's championship 5 times—in 1973, 1974, 1975, 1976 (Olympic) and 1977.

Highest Speed. The fastest luge run is at Krynica, Poland, where speeds of more than 80 m.p.h. have been recorded.

Bowling

Origins. Bowling can be traced to articles found in the tomb of an Egyptian child of 5200 B.C. where there were nine pieces of stone to be set up as pins at which a stone "ball" was rolled. The ball first had to roll through an archway made of three pieces of marble. There is also resemblance to a Polynesian game called *ula maika* which utilized pins and balls of stone. The stones were rolled a distance of 60 feet. In the Italian Alps about 2,000 years ago, the underhand tossing of stones at an object is believed the beginnings of *bocci*, a game still widely played in Italy and similar to bowling. The ancient Germans played a game of nine-pins called *Heidenwerfen* —knock down pagans. Martin Luther is credited with the statement that nine was the ideal number of pins. In the British Isles, lawn bowls was preferred to bowling at pins. In the 16th century, bowling at pins was the national sport in Scotland. How bowling at pins came to the United States is a matter of controversy. Early British settlers probably brought lawn bowls and set up what is known as Bowling Green at the tip of Manhattan Island in New York but perhaps the Dutch under Henry Hudson were the ones to be credited. Some historians say that in Connecticut the tenth pin was added to evade a legal ban against the nine-pin game in 1845 but others say that ten pins was played in New York City before this and point to Washington Irving's "Rip Van Winkle," written about 1818, as evidence.

Lanes. In the U.S. there were 8,698 bowling establishments with 151,725 lanes in 1977 and about 65,000,000 bowlers.

The world's largest bowling center (now closed) was the Tokyo World Lanes Center, Japan, with 252 lanes.

Organizations. The American Bowling Congress (ABC) comprises 4,700,000 men who bowl in leagues and tournaments. The Women's International Bowling Congress (WIBC) has a membership of 4,100,000. The Professional Bowlers Association (PBA), formed in 1958, numbers nearly 1,900 of the world's best bowlers.

World Championships

The Fédération Internationale des Quilleurs world championships were instituted in 1954. The highest pinfall in the individual men's event is 5,963 for 28 games by Ed Luther (U.S.) at Milwaukee, Wisconsin, on August 28, 1971.

In the women's event (instituted 1963) the record is 4,615 pins in 24 games by Annedore Haefker (West Germany) at Tolworth, Surrey, England, on October 11, 1975.

League Scores

Highest Men's. The highest individual score for three games is 886 by Allie Brandt of Lockport, New York, in 1939. Maximum possible is 900 (three perfect games). Highest team score is 3,858 by Budweisers of St. Louis in 1958.

The highest season average attained in sanctioned competition is 239 by Jim Lewis of Schenectady, New York, in 88 games in a 3-man league in 1975–76.

Highest Women's. The highest individual score for three games is 818 by Bev Ortner (now of Tucson, Arizona) in Galva, Iowa in 1968. Highest team score is 3,379 by Freeway Washer of Cleveland in 1960. (Highest in WIBC tournament play is 737 by D. D. Jacobson in 1972.)

Consecutive Strikes. The record for consecutive strikes in sanctioned match play is 33 by John Pezzin (born 1930) at Toledo, Ohio, on March 4, 1976.

Most Perfect Scores. The highest number of sanctioned 300 games is 27 (through 1978) by Elvin Mesger of Sullivan, Missouri. The maximum 900 for a three-game series has been recorded three times in unsanctioned games—by Leo Bentley at Lorain, Ohio, on March 26, 1931; by Joe Sargent at Rochester, New York, in 1934; and by Jim Murgie in Philadelphia, on February 4, 1937.

ABC Tournament Scores

Highest Individual. Highest three-game series in singles is 801 by Mickey Higham of Kansas City, Missouri, in 1978. Best three-game total in any ABC event is 804 by Lou Veit of Milwaukee, Wisconsin, in team in 1977. Jim Godman of Vero Beach, Florida, holds the record for a nine-game All-Events total with 2,184 (731–749–704) set in Indianapolis, Indiana, in 1974. ABC Hall of Famers Fred Bujack of Detroit, Michigan, and Bill Lillard of Houston, Texas, have won the most championships with 8 each. Bujack shared in 3 team and 4 team All-Events titles between 1949 and 1955, and also won the individual All-Events title in 1955. Lillard bowled on Regular and team All-Events champions in 1955 and 1956, the Classic team champions in 1962 and 1971, and won regular doubles and All-Events titles in 1956.

Highest Doubles. The ABC record of 558 was set in 1976 by Les Zikes of Chicago and Tommy Hudson of Akron, Ohio. The record score in a doubles series is 1,453, set in 1952 by John Klares (755) and Steve Nagy (698) of Cleveland.

Perfect Scores. Les Schissler of Denver scored 300 in the Classic team event in 1967, and Ray Williams of Detroit scored 300 in

Regular team play in 1974. In all, there have been only thirty-four 300 games in the ABC tournament. There have been 19 perfect games in singles, 12 in doubles, and three in team play.

Best Finishes in One Tournament. Les Schissler of Denver won the singles, All-Events, and was on the winning team in 1966 to tie Ed Lubanski of Detroit and Bill Lillard of Houston as the only men to win three ABC crowns in one year. The best four finishes in one ABC tournament were third in singles, second in doubles, third in team and first in All-Events by Bob Strampe, Detroit, in 1967, and first in singles, third in team and doubles and second in All-Events by Paul Kulbaga, Cleveland, in 1960.

Attendance. Largest attendance on one day for an ABC tournament was 5,257 in Milwaukee in 1952. The total attendance record was set at Reno, Nevada, in 1977 with 174,953 in 89 days.

Youngest and Oldest Winners. The youngest champion was Harold Allen of Detroit who was a 1915 doubles winner at the age of 18. The oldest champion was Eddie Nicholas of Austin, Texas, who, at the age of 70, was a winner in the 1978 Booster team event. The oldest doubles team in ABC competition totaled 165 years in 1955: Jerry Ameling (83) and Joseph Lehnbeutter (82), both from St. Louis.

Professional Bowlers Association Records

Most Titles. Earl Anthony of Kent, Washington, has won a lifetime total of 31 PBA titles. The record number of titles won in one PBA season is 8, by Mark Roth of North Arlington, New Jersey, in 1978.

Consecutive Titles. Only three bowlers have ever won three consecutive professional tournaments—Dick Weber in 1961, Johnny Petraglia in 1971, and Mark Roth in 1977.

Highest Earnings. The greatest lifetime earnings on the Professional Bowlers Association circuit have been won by Earl Anthony of Kent, Washington, who has taken home $704,691 through August 1, 1979. Mark Roth of North Arlington, New Jersey, won a record $134,500 in the 1978 season.

Perfect Games. A total of 100 perfect (300-point) games were bowled in PBA tournaments through August 1, 1979. Dick Weber rolled 3 perfect games in one tournament (Houston, Texas) in 1965, as did Billy Hardwick of Louisville, Kentucky (in the Japan Gold Cup competition) in 1968, Roy Buckley of Columbus, Ohio (at Chagrin Falls, Ohio) in 1971, and John Wilcox (at Detroit) in 1979.

Don Johnson of Las Vegas, Nevada, bowled at least one perfect game in 11 consecutive seasons (1965–1975).

Strikes and Spares in a Row

In the greatest finish to win an ABC title, Ed Shay set a record of 12 strikes in a row in 1958, when he scored a perfect game for a total of 733 in the series.

The most spares in a row is 23, a record set by Lt. Hazen Sweet of Battle Creek, Michigan, in 1950.

Longest Career. William H. Bailey (born January 4, 1891) has been bowling in the Hamilton City Ten Pin League, Ontario, Canada, for 72 consecutive years.

Marathons

Tom Destowet bowled for 150 hours 15 minutes in Dublin, California, April 2–8, 1978. He bowled 709 games with a 16-lb. ball.

EARLY CODIFIER: Jack Broughton (left) wrote the earliest prize ring rules in the 18th century.

Boxing

Earliest References. Boxing with gloves was depicted on a fresco from the Isle of Thera, Greece, which has been dated 1520 B.C. The earliest prize-ring code of rules was formulated in England on August 16, 1743, by the champion pugilist Jack Broughton (1704–89), who reigned from 1729 to 1750. Boxing, which had in 1867 come under the Queensberry Rules, formulated for John Sholto Douglas, 9th Marquess of Queensberry, was not established as a legal sport in Britain until after a ruling of Mr. Justice Grantham following the death of Billy Smith (Murray Livingstone) as the result of a fight on April 24, 1901, at Covent Garden, London.

Longest Fight. The longest recorded fight with gloves was between Andy Bowen of New Orleans and Jack Burke in New Orleans, on April 6–7, 1893. The fight lasted 110 rounds and 7 hours 19 minutes from 9:15 p.m. to 4:34 a.m., but was declared a no contest (later changed to a draw) when both men were unable to continue. The longest recorded bare knuckle fight was one of 6 hours 15 minutes between James Kelly and Jack Smith at Fiery Creek, Dalesford, Victoria, Australia, on December 3, 1855. The greatest recorded number of rounds is 276 in 4 hours 30 minutes, when Jack Jones beat Patsy Tunney in Cheshire, England, in 1825.

Shortest Fight. There is a distinction between the quickest knockout and the shortest fight. A knockout in 10½ seconds (including a 10-second count) occurred on September 26, 1946, when Al Couture struck Ralph Walton while the latter was adjusting a gum shield in his corner at Lewiston, Maine. If the time was accurately taken it is clear that Couture must have been more than half-way across the ring from his own corner at the opening bell.

The shortest fight on record appears to be one in a Golden Gloves tournament in Minneapolis, Minnesota, on November 4, 1947, when Mike Collins floored Pat Brownson with his first punch and the contest was stopped, without a count, 4 seconds after the bell.

The shortest world heavyweight title fight occurred when Tommy Burns (1881–1955) (né Noah Brusso) of Canada knocked out Jem Roche in 1 minute,28 seconds in Dublin, Ireland, on March 17, 1908. The duration of the Clay *vs.* Liston fight at Lewiston, Maine, on May 25, 1965, was 1 minute 52 seconds (including the count) as timed from the video tape recordings despite a ringside announcement giving a time of 1 minute. The shortest world title fight was when Al McCoy knocked out George Chip in 45 seconds for the middleweight crown in New York on April 7, 1914.

Tallest. The tallest boxer to fight professionally was Gogea Mitu (born 1914) of Rumania in 1935. He was 7 feet 4 inches and weighed 327 lbs. John Rankin, who won a fight in New Orleans, in November, 1967, was reputedly also 7 feet 4 inches.

World Heavyweight Champions

Longest and Shortest Reigns. The longest reign of any world heavyweight champion is 11 years 8 months and 7 days by Joe Louis (born Joseph Louis Barrow, in Lafayette, Alabama, May 13, 1914), from June 22, 1937, when he knocked out James J. Braddock in the 8th round at Chicago until announcing his retirement on March 1, 1949. During his reign Louis made a record 25 defenses of his title. The shortest reign was by Leon Spinks (U.S.) (born July 11, 1953) for 212 days from February 15–September 15, 1978.

Heaviest and Lightest. The heaviest world champion was Primo Carnera (Italy) (1906–67), the "Ambling Alp," who won the title from Jack Sharkey in 6 rounds in New York City, on June 29, 1933. He scaled 267 lbs. for this fight but his peak weight was 270 lbs. He had the longest reach at 85½ inches (fingertip to fingertip) and also the largest fists with a 14¾-inch circumference. He had an expanded chest measurement of 53 inches. The lightest champion was Robert James Fitzsimmons (1863–1917), who was born at Helston, Cornwall, England, and, at a weight of 167 lbs., won the title by knocking out James J. Corbett in 14 rounds at Carson City, Nevada, on March 17, 1897.

The greatest differential in a world title fight was 86 lbs. between Carnera (270 lbs.) and Tommy Loughran (184 lbs.) of the U.S., when the former won on points at Miami, Florida, on March 1, 1934.

Tallest and Shortest. The tallest world champion was Primo Carnera, who was measured at 6 feet 5.4 inches by the Physical Education Director at the Hemingway Gymnasium of Harvard, although

LONGEST AS CHAMPION: Joe Louis (left) was the heavyweight champion of the world for 11 years 8 months 7 days.

he was widely reported and believed in 1933 to be 6 feet 8½ inches tall. Jess Willard (1881–1968), who won the title in 1915, often stated as 6 feet 6¼ inches tall, was in fact 6 feet 5¼ inches. The shortest was Tommy Burns (1881–1955) of Canada, world champion from February 23, 1906, to December 26, 1908, who stood 5 feet 7 inches, and weighed 179 lbs.

Oldest and Youngest. The oldest man to win the heavyweight crown was Jersey Joe Walcott (born Arnold Raymond Cream, January 31, 1914, at Merchantville, New Jersey), who knocked out Ezzard Charles on July 18, 1951, in Pittsburgh, when aged 37 years

HEAVIEST CHAMPION: Primo Carnera, scaling about 270 lbs., held the heavyweight title for just 350 days.

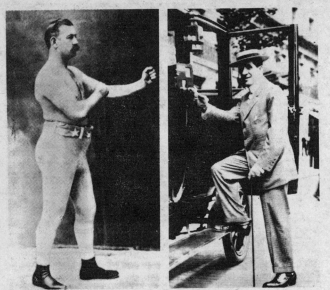

THE EARLIEST TITLE FIGHT pitted John L. Sullivan (left) against "Gentleman Jim" Corbett (right). It took 21 rounds for Corbett to win the fight.

5 months 18 days. Walcott was the oldest title holder at 38 years 7 months 23 days when he lost to Rocky Marciano on September 23, 1952. The youngest age at which the world title has been won is 21 years 331 days by Floyd Patterson (born Waco, North Carolina, January 4, 1935). After the retirement of Rocky Marciano, Patterson won the vacant title by beating Archie Moore in 5 rounds in Chicago, on November 30, 1956.

Most Recaptures. Muhammad Ali Haj is the only man to regain the heavyweight title twice. Ali first won the title on February 25, 1964, defeating Sonny Liston. He defeated George Foreman on October 30, 1974, having been stripped of his title by the world boxing authorities on April 28, 1967. He lost his title to Leon Spinks on February 15, 1978, but regained it on September 15, 1978 by defeating Spinks in New Orleans. (See photo, page M.)

Undefeated. Rocky Marciano (b. Rocco Francis Marchegiano) (1923–69) is the only heavyweight champion to have been undefeated in his entire professional career (1947–56).

Longest-Lived. Jess Willard was born December 29, 1881, at St. Clere, Kansas, and died in Pacoima, California, on December 15, 1968, aged 86 years 351 days.

Earliest Title Fight. The first world heavyweight title fight, with gloves and 3-minute rounds, was between John L. Sullivan (1858–1918) and "Gentleman" James J. Corbett (1866–1933) in New Orleans, on September 7, 1892. Corbett won in 21 rounds.

World Champions (any weight)

Longest and Shortest Reign. Joe Louis's heavyweight duration record stands for all divisions. The shortest reign has been 54 days by the French featherweight Eugène Criqui from June 2 to July 26, 1923. The disputed flyweight champion Emile Pladner (France) reigned only 47 days from March 2 to April 18, 1929, as did the disputed featherweight champion Dave Sullivan from September 26 to November 11, 1898.

Youngest and Oldest. The youngest at which any world championship has been claimed is 17 years 180 days by Wilfredo Benitez (born September 8, 1958) of Puerto Rico, who won the W.B.A. light-welterweight title in San Juan on March 6, 1976.

The oldest world champion was Archie Moore (b. Archibald Lee Wright, Collinsville, Illinois, December 13, 1913 or 1916), who was recognized as a light-heavyweight champion up to February 10, 1962, when his title was removed. He was then between 45 and 48. Bob Fitzsimmons (1863–1917) had the longest career of any official world titleholder with over 32 years from 1882 to 1914. He won his last world title aged 40 years 183 days in San Francisco on November 25, 1903. He was an amateur from 1880 to 1882.

Greatest "Tonnage." The greatest "tonnage" recorded in any fight is 700 lbs., when Claude "Humphrey" McBride of Oklahoma at 340 lbs. knocked out Jimmy Black of Houston at 360 lbs. in the 3rd round at Oklahoma City on June 1, 1971.

The greatest "tonnage" in a world title fight was 488¾ lbs. when Carnera (259¼ lbs.) fought Paolino Uzcudun (229½ lbs.) of Spain in Rome, Italy, on October 22, 1933.

Smallest Champions. The smallest man to win any world title has been Pascual Perez (1926–1977) who won the flyweight title in Tokyo on November 26, 1954, at 107 lbs. and 4 feet 11½ inches tall. Jimmy Wilde (b. Merthyr Tydfil, 1892, d. 1969, U.K.) who held the flyweight title from 1916 to 1923 was reputed never to have fought above 108 lbs.

Longest Fight. The longest world title fight (under Queensberry Rules) was between the lightweights Joe Gans (1874–1910), of the U.S., and Oscar "Battling" Nelson (1882–1954), the "Durable Dane," at Goldfield, Nevada, on September 3, 1906. It was terminated in the 42nd round when Gans was declared the winner on a foul.

Most Recaptures. The only boxer to win a world title five times at one weight is Sugar Ray Robinson (b. Walker Smith, Jr., in Detroit, May 3, 1920) who beat Carmen Basilio (U.S.) in the Chicago Stadium on March 25, 1958, to regain the world middleweight title for the fourth time. The other title wins were over Jake LaMotta

(U.S.) in Chicago on February 14, 1951, Randy Turpin (U.K.) in New York on September 12, 1951, Carl "Bobo" Olson (U.S.) in Chicago on December 9, 1955, and Gene Fullmer (U.S.) in Chicago on May 1, 1957. The record number of title bouts in a career is 33 or 34 (at bantam and featherweight) by George Dixon (1870–1909), *alias* "Little Chocolate," of Canada, between 1890 and 1901.

Most Titles Simultaneously. The only man to hold world titles at three weights simultaneously was Henry ("Homicide Hank") Armstrong (born December 12, 1912), now the Rev. Henry Jackson, of the U.S., at featherweight, lightweight and welterweight from August to December, 1938.

Most Knockdowns in Title Fights. Vic Toweel (South Africa) knocked down Danny O'Sullivan of London 14 times in 10 rounds in their world bantamweight fight at Johannesburg, on December 2, 1950, before the latter retired.

All Fights

Largest Purse. Muhammad Ali Haj (born Cassius Marcellus Clay, in Louisville, Kentucky, January 17, 1942) won a reported $6,500,000 in his successful defense of the heavyweight title against Ken Norton (U.S.), held in Yankee Stadium, New York City, on September 28, 1976.

The largest stake ever fought for in the bare-knuckle era was $22,500 in a 27-round fight between Jack Cooper and Wolf Bendoff at Port Elizabeth, South Africa, on July 29, 1889.

Highest Attendances. The greatest paid attendance at any boxing fight has been 120,757 (with a ringside price of $27.50) for the Tunney vs. Dempsey world heavyweight title fight at the Sesquicentennial Stadium, Philadelphia, on September 23, 1926. The indoor record is 63,360 for the Spinks vs. Ali world heavyweight title fight at the Louisiana Superdome in New Orleans, on September 15, 1978. The gate receipts exceeded $6,000,000, a record total. The highest non-paying attendance is 135,132 at the Tony Zale vs. Billy Pryor fight at Juneau Park, Milwaukee, Wisconsin, on August 18, 1941.

Lowest. The smallest attendance at a world heavyweight title fight was 2,434 at the Clay vs. Liston fight at Lewiston, Maine, on May 25, 1965.

Highest Earnings in Career. The largest known fortune ever made in a fighting career (or any sports career) is an estimated $60,000,000 (including exhibitions) amassed by Muhammad Ali from October, 1960 to August, 1979, in 59 fights comprising 529 rounds.

Most Knockouts. The greatest number of knockouts in a career is 141 by Archie Moore (1936 to 1963). The record for consecutive K.O.'s is 44, set by Lamar Clark of Utah at Las Vegas, Nevada, on January 11, 1960. He knocked out 6 in one night (5 in the first round) in Bingham, Utah, on December 1, 1958.

Most Fights. The greatest recorded number of fights in a career is 1,024 by Bobby Dobbs (U.S.), (1858–1930), who is reported to have fought from 1875 to 1914, a period of 39 years. Abraham Hollandersky, *alias* Abe the Newsboy (U.S.), is reputed to have had 1,309 fights in the fourteen years from 1905 to 1918, but many of them were exhibition bouts.

Most Fights Without Loss. Hal Bagwell, a lightweight, of Gloucester, England, was reputedly undefeated in 180 consecutive fights, of which only 5 were draws, between August 15, 1938, and November 29, 1948. His record of fights in the wartime period (1939–46) is very sketchy, however. Of boxers with complete records, Packey McFarland (1888–1936) went undefeated in 97 fights from 1905 to 1915.

Longest Career. The heavyweight Jem Mace, known as "the gypsy" (born at Norwich, England, April 8, 1831), had a career lasting 35 years from 1855 to 1890, but there were several years in which he had only one fight. He died, aged 79, in Jarrow on November 30, 1910. Walter Edgerton, the "Kentucky Rosebud," knocked out John Henry Johnson, aged 45, in 4 rounds at the Broadway A.C., New York City, on February 4, 1916, when aged 63. (See also *Most Fights,* above.)

Most Olympic Gold Medals. The only amateur boxer ever to win three Olympic gold medals is the southpaw László Papp (born 1926 in Hungary), who took the middleweight (1948) and the light-middleweight titles (1952 and 1956). The only man to win two titles in one meeting was Oliver L. Kirk (U.S.), who took both the bantam and featherweight titles at St. Louis, Missouri, in 1904, when the U.S. won all the titles. Harry W. Mallin (Great Britain) was in 1924 the first boxer ever to defend an Olympic title successfully when he retained the middleweight crown.

The oldest man to win an Olympic gold medal in boxing was Richard K. Gunn (born 1870) of Great Britain who won the featherweight title on October 27, 1908, in London, aged 38.

Bullfighting

In the latter half of the second millennium B.C., bull leaping was practiced in Crete. Bullfighting in Spain was first reported by the Romans in Baetica (Andalusia) in the third century B.C.

The first renowned professional *espada* (bullfighter) was Francisco Romero of Ronda, in Andalusia, Spain, who introduced the *estoque* and the red *muleta c.* 1700. Spain now has some 190 active matadors. Since 1700, 42 major matadors have died in the ring.

Largest Stadiums. The world's largest bullfighting ring, the Plaza, Mexico City, with a capacity of 48,000, was closed in March, 1976. The largest of Spain's 312 bullrings is Las Ventas, Madrid, with a capacity of 24,000.

Most Successful Matadors. The most successful matador measured by bulls killed was Lagartijo (1841–1900), born Rafael Molina, whose lifetime total was 4,867.

The longest career of any full matador was that of Bienvenida (1922–75) (*né* Antonio Mejías) from 1942 to 1974. (Recent Spanish law requires compulsory retirement at age 55.)

Most Kills in a Day. In 1884, Romano set a record by killing 18 bulls in a day in Seville, and in 1949 El Litri (Miguel Báes) set a Spanish record with 114 *novilladas* in a season.

Highest Paid Matadors. The highest paid bullfighter in history is El Cordobés (born Manuel Benitez Pérez, probably on May 4, 1936, in Palma del Rio, Spain), who became a multimillionaire in 1965, during which year he fought 111 *corridas* up to October 4, receiving over $15,000 for each half hour in the ring. In 1970, he received an estimated $1,800,000 for 121 fights.

Paco Camino (b. December 19, 1941) has received $27,200 (2,000,000 *pesetas*) for a *corrida*. He retired in 1977.

Canoeing

Origins. The acknowledged pioneer of canoeing as a modern sport was John Macgregor, a British barrister, in 1865. The Canoe Club was formed on July 26, 1866.

Most Olympic Gold Medals. Gert Fredriksson (b. November 21, 1919) of Sweden has won the most Olympic gold medals with six in 1948–52–56–60. In addition to his six Olympic titles he has won three other world titles in non-Olympic years for a record total of nine. This has been equaled by Yuri Lobanov (U.S.S.R.) (b. September 29, 1952) from 1972 to 1977, and Ludmila Pinayeva, who added six other world titles to her three Olympic golds, from 1966 to 1973.

LONGEST JOURNEY: Randy Bauer (left) and Jerry Mimbach (right) traveled 7,516 miles by paddle and portage in less than 2 years.

ESKIMO ROLLS: Bruce Parry turned in a record 1,000 rolls in 65 minutes 39.3 seconds in 1977.

The most by a woman is 3 by Ludmila Pinayeva (*née* Khvedosyuk, born January 14, 1936) (U.S.S.R.) in the 500-meter K.1 in 1964 and 1968, and the 500-meter K.2 in 1972.

The Olympic 1,000-meter best performance of 3 minutes 06.46 seconds by the 1976 Spanish K.4 represents an average speed of 11.99 m.p.h., and a rate of about 125 strokes per minute.

Longest Journey

The longest canoe journey in history was one of 7,516 miles around the eastern U.S. by paddle and portage, from Lake Itasca, Minnesota, *via* New Orleans, Miami, New York and Lake Ontario, by Randy Bauer (born August 15, 1949) and Jerry Mimbach (born May 22, 1952) of Coon Rapids, Minnesota, from September 8, 1974, to August 30, 1976.

The longest journey without portage or aid of any kind is one of 6,102 miles by Richard H. Grant and Ernest Lassey circumnavigating the eastern U.S. from Chicago to New Orleans to Miami to New York, returning back to Chicago *via* the Great Lakes, from September 22, 1930, to August 15, 1931.

Eskimo Rolls. The record for Eskimo rolls is 1,000 in 65 minutes 39.3 seconds by Bruce Parry (b. September 25, 1960) on Lake Lismore, New South Wales, Australia, on December 17, 1977. A "hand-rolling" record of 100 rolls in 3 minutes 58.7 seconds was set in the Bootham School Pool, York, England, on June 14, 1975, by David A. Clapham, 15.

English Channel Crossing. Andrew William Dougall Samuel (Scotland) paddled from Dover, England, to Wissant, France, in 3 hours 33 minutes 47 seconds on September 5, 1976.

The doubles record is 3 hours 20 minutes 30 seconds by Capt. William Stanley Crook and the late Ronald Ernest Rhodes, in their fiberglass K.2 *Accord*, from Dover, England, to Cap Blanc Nez, France, on September 20, 1961.

The record for a double crossing is 12 hours 47 minutes in K.1 canoes by nine members of the Canoe Camping Club of Great Britain on May 7, 1976.

Longest Open Sea Voyage. Beatrice and John Dowd, Ken Beard and Steve Benson (Richard Gillett replaced him mid-journey) paddled 1,559 miles out of a total journey of 2,010 miles from Venezuela to Miami, Florida, via the West Indies from August 11, 1977, to April 29, 1978, in two Klepper Aerius 20 kayaks.

Highest Altitude. In September, 1976, Dr. Michael Jones (1951–78) and Michael Hopkinson of the British Everest Canoe Expedition canoed down the Dudh Kosi River in Nepal from an altitude of 17,500 feet.

Longest Race. The longest regularly held canoe race in the U.S. is the Texas Water Safari (instituted 1963) which covers the 419 miles from San Marcos to Seadrift, Texas, on the San Marcos and Guadalupe rivers. Robert Chatham and Butch Hodges set the record of 37 hours 18 minutes on June 5–6, 1976.

Downstream Canoeing

River	Miles	Canoer	Location	Duration
Mississippi	2,500	Royal Air Force team of three two-man canoes (G.B.)	Lake Itasca, Minnesota, to Gulf of Mexico, Aug. 23–Oct. 4, 1978	42 days 5 hours
Mississippi-Missouri	3,810	Nicholas Francis (G.B.)	Three Forks, Montana, to New Orleans, July 13–Nov. 25, 1977	135 days
Congo	2,600	John and Julie Batchelor (G.B.)	Moasampanga to Banana, May 8–Sept. 12, 1974	128 days
Amazon	3,400	Stephan Z. Bezuk (U.S.) (kayak)	Atalaya to Ponta do Céu, June 21–Nov. 4, 1970	136 days
Nile	4,000	John Goddard (U.S.), Jean Laporte and André Davy (France)	Kagera to the Delta, Nov., 1953–July, 1954	9 months

Cave Exploration *(Spelunking)*

Duration. The endurance record for staying in a cave is 463 days by Milutin Veljkovic (b. 1935) (Yugoslavia) in the Samar Cavern, Svrljig Mountains, northern Yugoslavia from June 24, 1969, to September 30, 1970.

PROGRESSIVE CAVING DEPTH RECORDS

Feet	Cave	Cavers	Date
453	Macocha, Moravia, Czech.	J. Nagel *et al*	1748
741	Grotta di Padriciano, Trieste, Italy	Antonio Lindner *et al.*	1839
1,076	Grotta di Trebiciano, Trieste	Antonio Lindner *et al.*	April 6, 1841
1,509	Geldloch, Austria	—	1923
1,574	Antro di Corchia, Tuscany, Italy	E. Fiorentino Club	1934
1,978	Trou du Glaz, Isère, France	P. Chevalier *et al.*	1947
2,418	Reseau de la Pierre St. Martin, Básses-Pyrénées, France	Georges Lépineux *et al.*	July, 1953
2,962	Gouffre Berger, Isère, France	*F. Petzl and 6 men	Sept. 25, 1954
3,123	Gouffre Berger, Isère, France	L. Potié, G. Garby *et al.*	Aug., 1955
3,681	Gouffre Berger, Isère, France	F. Petzl and others	July, 1956
3,715	Gouffre Berger, Isère, France	K. Pearce	Aug., 1963
3,842	Reseau de la Pierre Saint Martin	Ass. de Rech. Spéléo Internationale	Aug., 1966
4,370	Reseau de la Pierre Saint Martin	A.R.S.I.P.	Aug., 1975

N.B.—The Reseau de la Pierre St. Martin was explored via a number of entrances, and was never entirely descended at any one time until 1978. Consequently, after Aug., 1963, the "sporting" records for greatest descent into a cave should read:

3,743	Gouffre Berger, Isère, France	Spéléo Club de Seine	July, 1968
4,370	Reseau de la Pierre St. Martin	P. Courbon *et al.*	Sept. 1978

Cricket

Origins. The earliest evidence of the game of cricket is from a drawing depicting two men playing with a bat and ball dated *c.* 1250. The game was played in Guildford, Surrey, at least as early as 1550. The earliest major match of which the score survives was one in which a team representing England (40 and 70) was beaten by Kent (53 and 58 for 9) by one wicket at the Artillery Ground in Finsbury, London, on June 18, 1744. Cricket was played in Australia as early as 1803.

CRICKET (First Class Matches Only)

Batting—Team Scores

Highest Innings
1,107 Victoria vs. N.S.W., Australia, Dec. 27–28, 1926

Highest Innings, Test
903 for 7 dec. England vs. Australia (5th Test), Aug. 20–23, 1938

Batting—Individual Scores

Highest Innings
499 Hanif Mohammad (Pakistan), Jan. 8–11, 1959

Highest Innings, Test
365 no Garfield Sobers (West Indies), Feb. 27–Mar. 1, 1958

Most Runs, Over (6 ball)
36 Garfield Sobers (Nottinghamshire), Aug. 31, 1968

Most Runs, Season
3,816 Denis Compton (Middlesex and England), 1947

Most Runs, Career
61,237 John (Jack) Hobbs (Surrey and England), 1905–34

Most Runs, Tests
8,032 Garfield Sobers (West Indies), 1953–1974

Test Match Average
99.94 (80 inn.) Donald Bradman (Australia), 1928–1948

Career Average
95.14 (338 inn.) Donald Bradman (Australia), 1927–1949

Bowling

Most Wickets, Innings
10 Numerous occasions

CHAMPION BATSMAN: Sir Garfield Sobers holds records for highest innings (365 not out) and most runs (8,032) in test matches.

Bowling (continued)

Most Wickets, Match
19   Jim Laker (Surrey), July 26–31, 1956

Most Wickets, Season
304   Alfred "Tich" Freeman (Kent), 1928

Most Wickets, Career
4,187   Wilfred Rhodes, 1898–1930

Most Wickets, Tests
309   Lance Gibbs (West Indies), 1958–1976

Wicket Keeping

Most Dismissals, Season
127   Leslie Ames (Kent), 1929

Most Dismissals, Career
1,527   John Murray (Middlesex), 1952–1975

Most Dismissals, Tests
252   Alan Knott (England), 1967–1977

Miscellaneous

Fastest Century
35 min.   Percy Fender (Surrey), Aug. 26, 1920

Fastest Bowler
99.7 m.p.h.   Jeff Thompson (Australia), Dec. 1975

Most Test Appearances
114   Colin Cowdrey (England), 1954–1975

Longest Cricket Ball Throw (5½ oz. ball)
422 ft.   Robert Percival, Apr. 18, 1881

Cross-Country Running

International Championships. The earliest international cross-country race was run between England and France on a course 9 miles 18 yards long from Ville d'Avray, outside Paris, on March 20, 1898. The inaugural International Cross-Country Championships took place at the Hamilton Park Racecourse, Glasgow, Scotland, on March 28, 1903. Since 1973 the race has been run under the auspices of the International Amateur Athletic Federation.

The greatest margin of victory in the International Cross-Country Championships has been 56 seconds, or 390 yards, by Jack T. Holden (England) at Ayr Racecourse, Scotland, on March 24, 1934. The narrowest win was that of Jean-Claude Fayolle (France) at Ostend, Belgium, on March 20, 1965, when the timekeepers were unable to separate his time from that of Melvyn Richard Batty (England), who was placed second.

Most Appearances. The runner with the largest number of international championship appearances is Marcel Van de Wattyne of Belgium, who participated in 20 competitions in the years 1946–65.

Most Wins. The greatest number of victories in the International Cross-Country Race is four by Jack Holden (England) in 1933, 1934, 1935 and 1939, by Alain Mimoun-o-Kacha (France) in 1949, 1952, 1954 and 1956, and Gaston Roelants (Belgium) in 1962, 1967, 1969 and 1972. England has won 43 times to 1977. Doris Brown-Heritage (U.S.) (b. September 17, 1942) has won the women's race five times, 1967–71.

Largest Field. The largest recorded field was one of 7,036 starters in the 18.6-mile Lidingöloppet, near Stockholm, Sweden, on October 10, 1978. There were 6,299 finishers.

Curling

Origins. Although a 15th century bronze figure in the Florence Museum appears to be holding a curling stone, the earliest illustration of the sport was in one of the winter scenes by the Flemish painter Pieter Brueghel, *c.* 1560. The club with the earliest records, dating back to 1716, is that at Kilsyth, Scotland. The game was introduced into Canada in 1759. Organized administration began in 1838 with the formation of the Grand (later Royal) Caledonian Curling Club, the international legislative body until the foundation of the International Curling Federation in 1966. The first indoor ice rink to introduce curling was at Southport, England, in 1879.

The U.S. won the first Gordon International Medal series of matches, between Canada and the U.S., at Montreal in 1884. The first Strathcona Cup match between Canada and Scotland was won by Canada in 1903. Although demonstrated at the Winter Olympics of 1924, 1932 and 1964, curling has never been included in the official Olympic program.

Largest Rink. The world's largest curling rink is the Big Four Curling Rink, Calgary, Alberta, Canada, opened in 1959 at a cost of Can. $2,250,000. Each of the two floors has 24 sheets of ice, the total accommodating 96 teams and 384 players.

Most Titles. The record for the Air Canada Silver Broom (instituted 1959) is 12 wins by Canada, in 1959–60–61–62–63–64–66–68–69–70–71–72. The most Strathcona Cup wins is seven by Canada (1903–09–12–23–38–57–65) against Scotland.

Perfect Games. A unique achievement is claimed by Mrs. Bernice Fekete of Edmonton, Alberta, Canada, who skipped her rink to two consecutive eight-enders on the same sheet of ice at the Derrick Club, Edmonton, on January 10 and February 6, 1973.

Marathon. The longest recorded curling match is one of 64 hours 28 minutes by eight members of the Pine Point Curling Club, N.W.T., Canada, on January 13–15, 1979. The duration record for 2 curlers is 24 hours 5 minutes by Eric Olesen and Warren Knuth at Racine Curling Club, Racine, Wisconsin on March 30–31, 1978. The weight handled was 27.72 tons each.

Longest Bonspiel. The longest bonspiel in the world is the Manitoba Bonspiel held in Winnipeg, Canada. There were 728 teams of 4 players in the February, 1977 tournament.

GREATEST ONE-HOUR RIDE: Leon Vanderstuyft of Belgium rode more than 76 miles in 60 minutes in 1928.

Cycling

Earliest Race. The earliest recorded bicycle race was a velocipede race over two kilometers (1.24 miles) at the Parc de St. Cloud, Paris, on May 31, 1868, won by James Moore (G.B.).

Slow Cycling. David Steed of Tucson, Arizona, stayed stationary without support for 9 hours 15 minutes on November 25, 1977.

Highest Speed. The highest speed ever achieved on a bicycle is 140.5 m.p.h. by Dr. Allan V. Abbott, 29, of San Bernardino, California, behind a windshield mounted on a 1955 Chevrolet over ¾ of a mile at Bonneville Salt Flats, Utah, on August 25, 1973. His speed over a mile was 138.674 m.p.h. Considerable help is provided by the slipstreaming effect of the lead vehicle. Charles Minthorne Murphy (born 1872) achieved the first mile-a-minute behind a pacing locomotive on the Long Island Railroad on June 30, 1899. He took only 57.8 seconds, so averaging 62.28 m.p.h.

Allan Abbott recorded an official unpaced 9.22 sec. for 200 meters (48.52 m.p.h.) at Ontario, California, on April 30, 1977.

The greatest distance ever covered in one hour is 76 miles 604 yards by Leon Vanderstuyft (Belgium) on the Montlhéry Motor Circuit, France, on September 30, 1928. This was achieved from a standing start paced by a motorcycle. The 24-hour record behind pace is 860 miles 367 yards by Hubert Opperman in Australia in 1932.

The greatest distance covered in 60 minutes unpaced is 30 miles 1,258 yards by Eddy Merckx at Mexico City, Mexico, on October 25, 1972. The 24-hour record on the road is 515.8 miles by Teuvo Louhivuori of Finland on September 10, 1974.

Most Olympic Titles. Cycling has been on the Olympic program since the revival of the Games in 1896. The greatest number of gold medals ever won is three by Paul Masson (France) in 1896, Francisco Verri (Italy) in 1906 and Robert Charpentier (France) in 1936. Marcus Hurley (U.S.) won four events in the "unofficial" cycling competition in the 1904 Games.

Tour de France

The greatest number of wins in the Tour de France (inaugurated 1903) is five by Jacques Anquetil (born January 8, 1934) of France, who won in 1957, 1961, 1962, 1963, and 1964, and Eddy Merckx (b. Belgium, June 17, 1945) who won five titles (1969–70–71–72–74).

The closest race ever was that of 1968 when after 2,898.7 miles over 25 days (June 27–July 21) Jan Jannssen (Netherlands) (born May 19, 1940) beat Herman van Springel (Belgium) in Paris by 38 seconds. The longest course was 3,569 miles on June 20–July 18, 1926. The length of the course is usually about 3,000 miles, but varies from year to year.

TOUR DE FRANCE CHAMPIONS: Jacques Anquetil of France (left) and Eddy Merckx of Belgium (right) have each achieved 5 Tour de France victories.

BICYCLING AROUND THE U.S.: Richard DeBernardis, a former college teacher who bicycled around the perimeter of the United States in 180 days, here takes a brief rest stop on Highway 8 west of Yuma, Arizona. For a map of his route, see page L.

The fastest average speed was 23.2 m.p.h. by Anquetil in 1962.

The longest race was 3,569 miles in 1926, and the greatest number of participants was in 1928, when 162 started and only 41 finished.

World Titles

The only four male cyclists to have won 7 world titles in any single world championship event are Leon Meredith (G.B.) who won the Amateur 100-kilometer paced event in 1904–05–07–08–09–11–13; Jeff Scherens (Belgium) who won the Professional sprint title in 1932–33–34–35–36–37 and 1947; Antonio Maspes (Italy) who won the Professional sprint title in 1955–56–59–60–61–62–64; and Daniel Morelon (France) who won the Amateur sprint title in 1966–67–69–70–71–73–75.

Yvonne Reynders (Belgium) won a total of 7 titles in women's events, the pursuits in 1961–64–65 and the road title in 1959–61–63–66. Beryl Burton (G.B.) equaled this total by winning the pursuits title in 1959–60–62–63–66 and the road title in 1960–67.

Endurance

Tommy Godwin (G.B.) in the 365 days of 1939 covered 75,065 miles or an average of 205.65 miles per day. He then completed 100,000 miles in 500 days to May 14, 1940.

The longest cycle tour on record is the more than 402,000 miles amassed by Walter Stolle (b. Sudetenland, 1926), an itinerant lecturer. From January 24, 1959 to December 12, 1976, he covered 159 countries, had 5 bicycles stolen and suffered 231 other robberies, along with over 1,000 flat tires. From 1922 to December 25, 1973, Tommy Chambers (b. 1903) of Glasgow, Scotland, had ridden a verified total of 799,405 miles. On Christmas Day he was badly injured and has not ridden since.

Ray Reece, 41, of Alverstoke, England, circumnavigated the world by bicycle (13,325 road miles) between June 14 and November 5 (143 days) in 1971.

John Hathaway of Vancouver, Canada, covered 50,600 miles, visiting every continent from November 10, 1974 to October 6, 1976.

Vivekananda Selva Kumar Anandan of Sri Lanka cycled for 187 hours 28 minutes non-stop around Vihara Maha Devi Park, Colombo, Sri Lanka, May 2–10, 1979.

U.S. Touring Records

The transcontinental record is 13 days 1 hour 20 minutes, from Santa Monica, California, to New York City by John Marino (b. 1948), August 13–26, 1978. He covered 2,956 miles.

Stan N. Kuhl (born December 31, 1955) and Steve Jeschien (born August 6, 1956) of Sunnyvale, California, traveled 8,026.7 miles on a tandem bicycle around the U.S. from June 29 to October 3, 1976.

Richard J. DeBernardis of Los Angeles bicycled around the perimeter of the continental United States in 180 days, beginning in Seattle, Washington, on September 10, 1978, and returning on March 8, 1979. His 12,092-mile continuous journey was accomplished without resorting to other means of transportation at any point. (See photo of route, page L.)

Equestrian Sports

Origin. Evidence of horse riding dates from a Persian engraving dated *c.* 3000 B.C. Pignatelli's academy of horsemanship at Naples dates from the sixteenth century. The earliest jumping competition was at the Agricultural Hall, London, in 1869. Equestrian events have been included in the Olympic Games since 1912.

MOST OLYMPIC GOLD: Hans Winkler of West Germany won 5 gold medals, 1956–72.

LONGEST JUMP: "Heatherbloom," the first horse to jump 8 feet high, has also been credited with a distance leap of 37 feet. Here she clears an 8-foot-2-inch barrier in a demonstration.

Most Olympic Medals. The greatest number of Olympic gold medals is 5 by Hans-Günter Winkler (West Germany), who won 4 team gold medals as captain in 1956, 1960, 1964 and 1972, and won the individual Grand Prix in 1956. The most team wins in the Prix des Nations is 5 by Germany in 1936, 1956, 1960, 1964, and 1972.

The lowest score obtained by a winner was no faults, by Frantisek Ventura (Czechoslovakia) on *Eliot* in 1928, and by Alwin Schocke-möhle (West Germany) on *Warwick Rex* in 1976. Pierre Jonqueres d'Oriola (France) is the only two-time winner of the individual gold medal, in 1952 and 1964.

World Titles. The men's world championship (instituted 1953) has been won twice by Hans-Günter Winkler of West Germany in 1954 and 1955, and Raimondo d'Inzeo of Italy in 1956 and 1960. The women's title (instituted 1965) has been won twice by Jane "Janou" Tissot (*née* Lefebvre) of France on *Rocket* in 1970 and 1974.

Jumping Records. The official *Fédération Equestre Internationale* high jump record is 8 feet 1¼ inches by *Huasó*, ridden by Capt. A. Larraguibel Morales (Chile) at Santiago, Chile, on February 5, 1949, and 27 feet 2¾ inches for long jump over water by *Amado Mio* ridden by Lt.-Col. Lopez del Hierro (Spain), at Barcelona, Spain, on November 12, 1951. *Heatherbloom*, ridden by Dick Donnelly, was reputed to have covered 37 feet in clearing an 8-foot-3-inch *puissance* jump at Richmond, Virginia, in 1903. H. Plant on *Solid Gold* cleared 36 feet 3 inches over water at the Wagga Show, N.S.W., Australia, on August 28, 1936. *Jerry M* allegedly cleared 40 feet over water at Aintree, Liverpool, England, in 1912.

At Cairns, Queensland, *Golden Meade* ridden by Jack Martin cleared an unofficially measured 8 feet 6 inches on July 25, 1946.

Ben Bolt was credited with clearing 9 feet 6 inches at the 1938 Royal Horse Show, Sydney, Australia. The Australian record however is 8 feet 4 inches by C. Russell on *Flyaway* in 1939 and A. L. Payne on *Golden Meade* in 1946. The world's unofficial best for a woman is 7 feet 8 inches by Katrina Towns (now Musgrove) (Australia) on *Big John* at Cairns, Queensland, Australia, in 1978.

The greatest recorded height reached bareback is 6 feet 7 inches by *Silver Wood* at Heidelberg, Victoria, Australia, on December 10, 1938.

Longest Ride. Aimé Felix Tschiffely rode 10,000 miles from Buenos Aires, Argentina, to Washington, D.C., in 504 days, starting on April 23, 1925, with two horses, *Mancha* and *Gato*.

The Bicentennial "Great American Horse Race," begun on May 31, 1976, from Saratoga Springs, New York, to Sacramento, California (3,500 miles) was won by Virl Norton on *Lord Fauntleroy*—a mule—in 98 days. His actual riding time was 315.47 hours.

Marathon. Michael Grealy (Australia) rode at all paces (including jumping) for 55 hours 26 minutes at Blackwater, Queensland, Australia, on May 5–7, 1978.

MOST OLYMPIC MEDALS: In a competitive career spanning 24 years, Edoardo Mangiarotti won 13 Olympic medals.

Fencing

Origins. Fencing (fighting with single sticks) was practiced as a sport in Egypt as early as *c.* 1360 B.C. The first governing body for fencing in Britain was the Corporation of Masters of Defence founded by Henry VIII before 1540 and fencing was practiced as sport, notably in prize fights, since that time. The foil was the practice weapon for the short court sword from the 17th century. The épée was established in the mid-19th century and the light sabre was introduced by the Italians in the late 19th century.

Most Olympic Titles. The greatest number of individual Olympic gold medals won is three by Ramón Fonst (Cuba) (b. 1883) in 1900 and 1904 (2) and Nedo Nadi (Italy) (1894–1952) in 1912 and 1920 (2). Nadi also won three team gold medals in 1920 making a then unprecedented total of five gold medals at one Olympic meet.

Edoardo Mangiarotti (Italy) (born April 7, 1919) holds the record of 13 Olympic medals (6 gold, 5 silver, 2 bronze), won in the foil and épée competitions from 1936 to 1960.

The most gold medals by a woman is four (three individual, one team) by Elena Novikova-Belova (U.S.S.R.) (b. July 28, 1947) from 1968 to 1976, and the record for all medals is 7 (2 gold, 3 silver, 2 bronze) by Ildikó Sagine-Retjoo (formerly Ujlaki-Retjö) (Hungary) (b. May 11, 1937) from 1960 to 1976.

Most World Titles. The greatest number of individual world titles won is four by d'Oriola (see table below), but note that d'Oriola also won 2 individual Olympic titles. Likewise, of the three women foilists with 3 world titles (Helene Mayer, Ellen Müller-Preiss and Ilona Schacherer-Elek) only Elek also won 2 individual Olympic titles.

Ellen Müller-Preiss (Austria) won the women's foil in 1947 and 1949 and shared it in 1950. She also won the Olympic title in 1932.

Most Olympic and Most World Titles

Event	Olympic Gold Medals	World Championships (not held in Olympic years)
Men's Foil, Individual	2 Christian d'Oriola (France) b. Oct. 3, 1928 (1952, 56)	4 Christian d'Oriola (France) (1947, 49, 53, 54)
	2 Nedo Nadi (Italy) 1894–1952 (1912, 20)	
Men's Foil, Team	5 France (1924, 32, 48, 52, 68)	12 Italy (1929–31, 33–35, 37, 38, 49, 50, 54, 55)
Men's Epée, Individual	2 Ramón Fonst (Cuba) b. 1883 d. 1959 (1900, 04)	3 Georges Buchard (France) b. Dec. 21, 1893 (1927, 31, 33)
		3 Aleksey Nikanchikov (U.S.S.R.) b. July 30, 1940 (1966, 67, 70)
Men's Epée, Team	6 Italy (1920, 28, 36, 52, 56, 60)	10 Italy (1931, 33, 37, 49, 50, 53 55, 57, 58)
Men's Sabre, Individual	2 Jean Georgiadis (Greece) b. 1874 (1896, 1906)	3 Aladar Gerevich (Hungary) (1935, 51, 55)
	2 Dr. Jenö Fuchs (Hungary) b. Oct. 29, 1882 (1908, 12)	3 Jerzy Pawlowski (Poland) b. Oct. 25, 1932 (1957, 65, 66)
	2 Rudolf Kárpáti (Hungary) b. July 17, 1920 (1956, 60)	3 Yacov Rylsky (U.S.S.R.) (1958, 61, 63)
Men's Sabre, Team	9 Hungary (1908, 12, 28, 32, 36, 48, 52, 56, 60)	15 Hungary (1930, 31, 33–35, 37, 51, 53–55, 57, 58, 66, 73, 78)
Women's Foil, Individual	2 Ilona Schacherer-Elek (Hungary) b. 1907 (1936, 48)	3 Helene Mayer (Germany) 1910–53 (1929, 31, 37)
		3 Ilona Schacherer-Elek (Hungary) b. 1907 (1934, 35, 51)
		3 Ellen Müller-Preiss (Austria) b. May 6, 1912 (1947, 49, 50 (shared))
Women's Foil, Team	4 U.S.S.R. (1960, 68, 72, 76)	12 Hungary (1933–35, 37, 52–55, 59, 62, 67, 73)
		U.S.S.R. (1956, 58, 61, 65–66, 70–71, 74–75, 77–78)

Field Hockey

Origin. A representation of two players with curved snagging sticks apparently in an orthodox "bully" position was found in Tomb No. 17 at Beni Hasan, Egypt, and has been dated to *c.* 2050 B.C. There is a reference to the game in Lincolnshire, England, in 1277. The first country to form a national association was England (The Hockey Association) on April 16, 1875.

Earliest International. The first international match was the Wales *vs.* Ireland match on January 26, 1895. Ireland won 3–0.

Highest International Score. The highest score in international field hockey was when India defeated the U.S. 24–1 at Los Angeles, in the 1932 Olympic Games. The Indians were Olympic Champions from the re-inception of Olympic hockey in 1928 until 1960, when Pakistan beat them 1–0 at Rome. They had their seventh win in 1964. Of the 6 Indians who have won 3 Olympic gold medals, two have also won a silver medal—Leslie Claudius in 1948, 1952, 1956 and 1960 (silver), and Udham Singh in 1952, 1956, 1964 and 1960 (silver).

The highest score in a women's international match occurred when England defeated France 23–0 at Merton, Surrey, on February 3, 1923.

The World Cup has been won twice by Pakistan, in 1971 and 1978.

Longest Game. The longest international game on record was one of 145 minutes (into the sixth period of extra time), when Netherlands beat Spain 1–0 in the Olympic tournament at Mexico City on October 25, 1968.

Marathon. Two teams of eleven from Newmarket Hockey Club played for 27 hours 10 minutes on May 19–20, 1979, at Coldhams Common, Cambridge, England.

Fishing

Largest Catches. The largest fish ever caught on a rod is an officially ratified man-eating great white shark (*Carcharodon carcharias*) weighing 2,664 lbs., and measuring 16 feet 10 inches long, caught by Alf Dean at Denial Bay, near Ceduna, South Australia, on April 21, 1959. Capt. Frank Mundus (U.S.) harpooned and landed a 17-foot-long 4,500-lb. great white shark, after a 5-hour battle, off Montauk Point, Long Island, New York, on June 6, 1964. He was assisted by Peter Brandenberg, Gerald Mallow, Frank Bloom and Harvey Ferston.

A white pointer shark weighing 3,388 lbs. was caught on a rod by Clive Green off Albany, Western Australia, on April 26, 1976, but this will remain unratified as whale meat was used as bait.

The largest marine animal ever killed by *hand* harpoon was a blue whale 97 feet in length, killed by Archer Davidson in Twofold Bay, New South Wales, Australia, in 1910. Its tail flukes measured 20 feet across and its jaw bone 23 feet 4 inches.

Fishing

(Sea and Freshwater fish records taken by tackle as ratified by the International Game Fish Association to January, 1979.)

Species	Weight in lbs. oz.		Name of Angler	Location	Date
Amberjack	149	0	Peter Simons	Bermuda	June 21, 1964
Barracuda†	83	0	K. J. W. Hackett§§	Lagos, Nigeria	Jan. 13, 1952
Bass (Giant Sea)	563	8	James D. McAdam, Jr.	Anacapa Island, California	Aug. 20, 1968
Black Runner (Cobia)	110	5	Eric Tinworth	Off Mombasa, Kenya	Sep. 8, 1964
Carp†	55	5	Frank J. Ledwein	Clearwater Lake, Minnesota	July 10, 1952
Cod	98	12	Alphonse J. Bielevich	Isle of Shoals, New Hampshire	June 8, 1969
Marlin (Black)	1,560	0	Alfred C. Glassell, Jr.	Cabo Blanco, Peru	Aug. 4, 1953
Marlin (Atlantic Blue)	1,282	0	Larry Martin	St. Thomas, U.S. Virgin Islands	Aug. 6, 1977
Marlin (Pacific Blue)	1,153	0	Greg D Perez	Ritidian Point, Guam	Aug. 21, 1969
Marlin (Striped)	417	8	Phillip Bryers	Cavalli Isles, New Zealand	Jan. 14, 1977
Marlin (White)	174	3	Otavia Cunha Reboucas	Vitoria, Brazil	Nov. 1, 1976
Pike (Northern)	46	2	Peter Dubuc	Sacandaga Reservoir, New York	Sept. 15, 1940
Sailfish (Atlantic)	128	1	Harm Steyn	Luanda, Angola	Mar. 27, 1974
Sailfish (Pacific)	221	0	C. W. Stewart	Santa Cruz I., Galapagos Is.	Feb. 12, 1947
Salmon (Chinook)§	93	0	Howard C. Rider	Kelp Bay, Alaska	June 24, 1977
Shark (Blue)	437	0	Peter Hyde	Catherine Bay, N.S.W., Australia	Oct. 2, 1976
Shark (Mako)**	1,061	0	James B. Penwarden	Mayor Island, New Zealand	Feb. 17, 1970
Shark (White or Man-Eating)	2,664	0	Alfred Dean	Ceduna, South Australia	Apr. 21, 1959
Shark (Porbeagle)	465	0	Jorge Potier	Cornwall, England	July 23, 1976
Shark (Thresher)‡	739	0	Brian Galvin	Tutukaka, New Zealand	Feb. 17, 1975
Shark (Tiger)	1,780	0	Walter Maxwell	Cherry Grove, South Carolina	June 14, 1964
Sturgeon (White)†‡	360	0	Willard Cravens	Snake River, Idaho	Apr. 24, 1956
Swordfish	1,182	0	L. E. Marron	Iquique, Chile	May 7, 1953
Tarpon	283	0	M. Salazar	Lago de Maracaibo, Venezuela	Mar. 19, 1965
Trout (Lake)‖	65	0	Larry Daunis	Great Bear Lake, Northwest Terr., Canada	Aug. 8, 1970
Tuna (Allison or Yellowfin)	388	12	Curt Wiesenhutter	San Benedicto Islands, Mexico	Apr. 1, 1977
Tuna (Atlantic Big-eyed)	375	8	Cecil Browne	Ocean City, Maryland	Aug. 26, 1977
Tuna (Pacific Big-eyed)	435	0	Dr. Russel V. A. Lee	Cabo Blanco, Peru	Apr. 17, 1957
Tuna (Bluefin)	1,235	0	Michael MacDonald	North Lake, P.E.I., Canada	Oct. 17, 1978
Wahoo	149	0	John Pirovano	Cat Cay, Bahamas	June 15, 1962

† A carp weighing 83 lbs. 8 oz. was taken (not by rod) near Pretoria, South Africa. A 60 lb. specimen was taken by bow and arrow by Ben A. Topham in Wythe Co., Virginia, on July 5, 1970. § A salmon weighing 126 lbs. 8 oz. was taken (not by rod) near Petersburg, Alaska.‖ A 102-lb. trout was taken from Lake Athabasea, northern Saskatchewan, Canada, on August 8, 1961. ** A 1,295-lb. specimen was taken by two anglers off Natal, South Africa, on March 17, 1939, and a 1,500-lb. specimen harpooned inside Durban Harbour, South Africa, in 1933. ‡ W. W. Dowding caught a 922-lb. thresher shark in 1937 on an untested line. †† A barracuda weighing 103 lbs. 4 oz. was caught on an untested line by Chester Benet at West End, Bahamas, on August 11, 1932. Another weighing 48 lbs. 6 oz. was barehanded by Thomas B. Pace at Panama City Beach, Florida, on April 19, 1974. §§ Hackett was only 11 years 137 days old at the time. ‡‡ Glenn Howard caught a sturgeon weighing 394 lbs. on the Snake River, Idaho, in 1954.

Smallest Catch. The smallest fish ever to win a competition was a smelt weighing $\frac{1}{16}$ of an ounce, caught by Peter Christian at Buckenham Ferry, Norfolk, England, on January 9, 1977. This beat 107 other competitors.

Spear-fishing. The largest fish ever taken underwater was an 804-lb. giant black grouper by Don Pinder of the Miami Triton Club, Florida, in 1955.

Freshwater Casting. The longest freshwater cast ratified under I.C.F. (International Casting Federation) rules is 574 feet 2 inches by Walter Kummerow (West Germany), for the Bait Distance Double-Handed 30-gram event held at Lenzerheide, Switzerland, in the 1968 Championships.

The longest Fly Distance Double-Handed cast is 257 feet 2 inches by S. Sheen of Norway, also set at Lenzerheide in 1968.

Longest Fight. The longest recorded fight with a fish by an individual is 32 hours 5 minutes by Donal Heatley (b. 1938) (New Zealand) with a black marlin (estimated length 20 feet and weight 1,500 lbs.) off Mayor Island off Tauranga, New Zealand, January 21–22, 1968. It towed the 12-ton launch 50 miles before breaking the line.

Marathon. John Reader fished for 504 hours at Hutton Pond, Weston-super-Mare, England, on August 20–September 10, 1978.

Football

Origins. The origin of modern football stems from the "Boston Game" as played at Harvard. Harvard declined to participate in the inaugural meeting of the Intercollegiate Football Association in New York City in October, 1873, on the grounds that the proposed rules were based on the non-handling "Association" code of English football. Instead, Harvard accepted a proposal from McGill University of Montreal, Canada, who played the more closely akin English Rugby Football. The first football match under the Harvard Rules was thus played against McGill at Cambridge, Mass., in May, 1874. In November, 1876, a New Intercollegiate Football Association, based on modern football, was inaugurated at Springfield, Mass., with a pioneer membership of five colleges.

Professional football dates from the Latrobe, Pa. *vs.* Jeannette, Pa. match at Latrobe, in August, 1895. The National Football League was founded in Canton, Ohio, in 1920, although it did not adopt its present name until 1922. The year 1969 was the final year in which professional football was divided into separate National and American Leagues, for record purposes.

Longest Service Coach

The longest service head coach was Amos Alonzo Stagg, who served Springfield in 1890–91, Chicago from 1892 to 1932 and College of Pacific from 1933 to 1946, making a total of 57 years.

MODERN MAJOR-COLLEGE INDIVIDUAL RECORDS
(Through 1978 Season)

Points
Most in a Game........................43...Jim Brown (Syracuse)........................1956

Most in a Season....................174...Lydell Mitchell (Penn State)...............1971

Most in a Career....................356...Tony Dorsett (Pittsburgh)...............1973–76

Touchdowns
Most in a Game..........................7...Arnold Boykin (Mississippi)...............1951

Most in a Season......................29...Lydell Mitchell (Penn State)...............1971

Most in a Career......................59...Glenn Davis (Army)....................1943–46

                            59...Tony Dorsett (Pittsburgh) 1973–76

Field Goals
Most in a Game..........................6...Frank Nester (West Virginia)...............1972

                           6...Charlie Gogolak (Princeton)...........1965

                           6...Vince Fusco (Duke)...................1976

Most in a Season......................22...Matt Bahr (Penn State)......................1978

Most in a Career......................56...Tony Franklin (Texas A & M).........1975–78

SEASON RECORDS

Total Offense ....3,343 yds....Bill Anderson (Tulsa)...............1965

Most Rushing and Passing Plays...........580...Bill Anderson (Tulsa)...............1965

Most Times Carried.........................358...Steve Owens (Oklahoma) 1969

Yards Gained Rushing.................1,948 yds....Tony Dorsett (Pittsburgh).........1976

Highest Average Gain per Rush...9.35 yds....Greg Pruitt (Oklahoma)............1971

Most Passes Completed ....296...Bill Anderson (Tulsa) 1965

Most Touchdown Passes ....39...Dennis Shaw (San Diego St.)......1969

Highest Completion Percentage.........69.3%...Chris Kupec (North Carolina)....1974

Most Yards Gained Passing........3,464 yds....Bill Anderson (Tulsa)...............1965

Most Passes Caught ....134...Howard Twilley (Tulsa)............1965

Most Yards Gained on Catches...1,779 yds....Howard Twilley (Tulsa)............1965

Most Touchdown Passes Caught...........18...Tom Reynolds (San Diego St.)....1969

Most Passes Intercepted by.................14...Al Worley (Washington).........1968

College Series Records

The oldest collegiate series is that between Princeton and Rutgers dating from 1869, or 7 years before the passing of the Springfield rules. The most regularly contested series is between Lafayette and Lehigh, who have met 114 times between 1884 and the end of 1978.

Longest Streaks

The longest winning streak is 47 straight by Oklahoma. The longest unbeaten streak is 63 games (59 won, 4 tied) by Washington from 1907 to 1917.

Highest Score

The most points ever scored in a college football game was 222 by Georgia Tech, Atlanta, Georgia, against Cumberland University of Lebanon, Tennessee, on October 7, 1916. Tech also set records for the most points scored in one quarter (63), most touchdowns (32) and points after touchdown (30) in a game, and the largest victory margin (Cumberland did not score). There were no first downs.

All-America Selections

The earliest All-America selections were made in 1889 by Caspar Whitney of *The Week's Sport* and later of *Harper's Weekly*.

KICKING MARATHON:
Vince Rovetti, a florist from
San Francisco, kicked 1,035
field goals out of 1,135 tries
from 20 yards out—barefoot!
It took him 2 hours 30 minutes
4 seconds on December 9, 1978,
at Candlestick Park in
San Francisco.

All-Star Games

The reigning N.F.L. Champions first met an All-Star College
selection in the annual August series in Chicago in 1934. The highest
scoring match was that of 1940 in which Green Bay beat the All-
Stars 45–28. The biggest professional win was in 1949 when Philadelphia won 38–0, and the biggest All-Stars win was in 1943 when
Washington was defeated 27–7.

ALL-TIME PROFESSIONAL INDIVIDUAL RECORDS
(Through 1978 Season)

Service

Most Seasons, Active Player
26 George Blanda, Chi. Bears 1949–
58; Balt. 1950; AFL: Hou.
1960–66; Oak. 1967–75

Most Games Played, Lifetime
340 George Blanda, Chi. Bears 1949–
58; Balt. 1950; AFL: Hou.
1960–66; Oak. 1967–75

**Most Consecutive Games Played, Life-
time**
266 Jim Marshall, Clev. 1960; Minn.
1961–78

Most Seasons, Head Coach
40 George Halas, Chi. Bears 1920–
29, 33–42, 46–55, 58–67

Scoring

Most Seasons Leading League
5 Don Hutson, Green Bay 1940–44
.Gino Cappelletti, Bos. 1961, 63–
66 (AFL)

Most Points, Lifetime
2,002 George Blanda, Chi. Bears 1949–
58; Balt. 1950; AFL: Hou.
1960–66; Oak. 1967–75 (9-td,
943-pat, 335-fg)

Most Points, Season
176 Paul Hornung, Green Bay 1960
(15-td, 41-pat, 15-fg)

Most Points, Rookie, Season
132 Gale Sayers, Chi. 1965 (22-td)

GREAT RUNNER:
O. J. Simpson scored the
most touchdowns in one
season (23) and rushed for
most yards gained in one
season (2,003 yards in
1973).

N.F.L. Records (continued)

Most Points, Game
40 Ernie Nevers, Chi. Cards vs Chi.
Bears, Nov. 28, 1929 (6-td, 4-pat)

Most Points, One Quarter
29 Don Hutson, Green Bay vs Det.,
Oct. 7, 1945 (4-td, 5-pat) 2nd
Quarter

Touchdowns

Most Seasons Leading League
8 Don Hutson, Green Bay, 1935–
38, 41–44

Most Touchdowns, Lifetime
126 Jim Brown, Cleve. 1957–65
(106-r, 20-p)

Most Touchdowns, Season
23 O. J. Simpson, Buff. 1975 (16-r,
7-p)

Most Touchdowns, Rookie Season
22 Gale Sayers, Chi. 1965 (14-r, 6-p,
1-prb, 1-krb)

Most Touchdowns, Game
6 Ernie Nevers, Chi. Cards vs Chi.
Bears, Nov. 28, 1929 (6-r)
William (Dub) Jones, Cleve. vs
Chi. Bears, Nov. 25, 1951 (4-r,
2-p)
Gale Sayers, Chi. vs S. F., Dec.
12, 1965 (4-r, 1-p, 1-prb)

Most Consecutive Games Scoring
Touchdowns
18 Lenny Moore, Balt. 1963–65

Points after Touchdown

Most Seasons Leading League
8 George Blanda, Chi. Bears 1956;
AFL: Hou. 1961–62; Oak. 1967–
69, 72, 74

Most Points After Touchdown, Lifetime
943 George Blanda, Chi. Bears 1949–
58; Balt. 1950; AFL: Hou.
1960–66; Oak. 1967–75

Most Points After Touchdown, Season
64 George Blanda, Hou. 1961 (AFL)

Most Points After Touchdown, Game
9 Marlin (Pat) Harder, Chi. Cards
vs N. Y., Oct. 17, 1948
Bob Waterfield, L. A. vs Balt.,
Oct. 22, 1950
Charlie Gogolak, Wash. vs N. Y.,
Nov. 27, 1966

Most Consecutive Points After Touchdown
234 Tommy Davis, S. F. 1959–65

Most Points After Touchdown (no
misses), Season
56 Danny Villanueva, Dall. 1966

Most Points After Touchdown (no
misses), Game
9 Marlin (Pat) Harder, Chi. Cards
vs N. Y., Oct. 17, 1948
Bob Waterfield, L. A. vs Balt.,
Oct. 22, 1950

Field Goals

Most Seasons Leading League
5 Lou Groza, Cleve., 1950, 52–54, 57

Most Field Goals, Lifetime
335 George Blanda, Chi. Bears 1949–58; Balt. 1950; AFL: Hou. 1960–66; Oak. 1967–75

Most Field Goals, Season
34 Jim Turner N.Y. 1968 (AFL)

Most Field Goals, Game
7 Jim Bakken, St. L. vs Pitt., Sept. 24, 1967

Most Consecutive Games, Field Goals
31 Fred Cox, Minn. 1968–70

Most Consecutive Field Goals
16 Jan Stenerud, K.C. 1969 (AFL)
Don Cockroft, Clev. 1974–75
Garo Yepremian, Mia. 1978

Longest Field Goal
63 yds. Tom Dempsey, New Orl. vs Det. Nov. 8, 1970

Rushing

Most Seasons Leading League
8 Jim Brown, Cleve. 1957–61, 63–65

Most Yards Gained, Lifetime
12,312 Jim Brown, Cleve., 1957–65

Most Yards Gained, Season
2,003 O. J. Simpson, Buff., 1973

Most Yards Gained, Game
275 Walter Payton, Chi. vs. Minn., Nov. 20, 1977

Longest Run from Scrimmage
97 yards Andy Uram, Green Bay vs Chi. Cards, Oct. 8, 1939 (td)
Bob Gage, Pitt. vs Chi. Bears, Dec. 4, 1949 (td)

Highest Average Gain, Lifetime (700 att.)
5.2 Jim Brown, Cleve. 1957–65 (2,359–12,312)

Highest Average Gain, Season (100 att.)
9.9 Beattie Feathers, Chi. Bears, 1934 (101–1004)

Highest Average Gain, Game (10 att.)
17.1 Marion Motley, Cleve. vs Pitt., Oct. 29, 1950 (11–188)

Most Touchdowns Rushing, Lifetime
106 Jim Brown, Cleve., 1957–65

Most Touchdowns Rushing, Season
19 Jim Taylor, Green Bay, 1962

Most Touchdowns Rushing, Game
6 Ernie Nevers, Chi. Cards vs Chi. Bears, Nov. 28, 1929

Passing

Most Seasons Leading League
6 Sammy Baugh, Wash., 1937, 40, 43, 45, 47, 49

Most Passes Attempted, Lifetime
6,467 Fran Tarkenton, Minn. 1961–66, 72–78; N.Y. Giants 1967–71 (3,686 completions)

Most Passes Attempted, Season
572 Fran Tarkenton, Minn. 1978 (345 completions)

Most Passes Attempted, Game
68 George Blanda, Hou. vs Buff., Nov. 1, 1964 (AFL) (37 completions)

Most Passes Completed, Lifetime
3,686 Fran Tarkenton, Minn. 1961–66, 72–78; N.Y. Giants 1967–71 (6,467 attempts)

Most Passes Completed, Season
345 Fran Tarkenton, Minn. 1978 (572 attempts)

Most Passes Completed, Game
37 George Blanda, Hou. vs Buff., Nov. 1, 1964 (AFL) (68 attempts)

Most Consecutive Passes Completed
17 Bert Jones, Balt. vs. N.Y. Jets, Dec. 15, 1974

Passing Efficiency, Lifetime (1,500 att.)
59.6 Ken Stabler, Oak. 1970–78 (1,983–1,182)

Passing Efficiency, Season (100 att.)
70.3 Sammy Baugh, Wash., 1945 (182–129)

Passing Efficiency, Game (20 att.)
90.9 Ken Anderson, Cin. vs. Pitt., Nov. 10, 1974 (22–20)

Shortest Pass Completion for Touchdown
2″ Eddie LeBaron (to Bielski), Dall. vs Wash., Oct. 9, 1960

Longest Pass Completion (all TDs)
99 Frank Filchock (to Farkas), Wash. vs Pitt., Oct. 15, 1939
George Izo (to Mitchell), Wash. vs Cleve., Sept. 15, 1963
Karl Sweetan (to Studstill), Det. vs Balt., Oct. 16, 1966
C. A. Jurgensen (to Allen), Wash. vs Chi., Sept. 15, 1968

Most Yards Gained Passing, Lifetime
47,003 Fran Tarkenton, Minn. 1961–66, 72–78; N.Y. Giants 1967–71

Most Yards Gained Passing, Season
4,007 Joe Namath, N. Y. 1967 (AFL)

Most Yards Gained Passing, Game
554 Norm Van Brocklin, L. A. vs N. Y. Yanks, Sept. 28, 1951 (41–27)

LONGEST FIELD GOAL in NFL competition (63 yards) was kicked by a man with only half a foot—Tom Dempsey of the New Orleans Saints, who wears a special shoe over his foot, and has only part of his right arm. His record kick beat the Detroit Lions, 19-17, on the last play of the game on November 8, 1970.

N.F.L. Records (continued)

Most Touchdown Passes, Lifetime
342 Fran Tarkenton, Minn. 1961–66, 72–78; N.Y. Giants 1967–71

Most Touchdown Passes, Season
36 George Blanda, Hou. 1961 (AFL) Y. A. Tittle, N. Y. 1963

Most Touchdown Passes, Game
7 Sid Luckman, Chi. Bears vs N. Y Nov. 14, 1943
Adrian Burk, Phil. vs Wash., Oct. 17, 1954
George Blanda, Hou. vs N. Y., Nov. 19, 1961 (AFL)
Y. A. Tittle, N. Y. vs Wash., Oct. 28, 1962
Joe Kapp, Minn. vs Balt., Sept. 28, 1969

Most Consecutive Games, Touchdown Passes
47 John Unitas, Balt., 1956–60

Passes Had Intercepted

Fewest Passes Intercepted, Season (Qualifiers)
1 Joe Ferguson, Buff. 1976 (151 attempts)

Most Consecutive Passes Attempted, None Intercepted
294 Bryan (Bart) Starr, Green Bay, 1964–65

Most Passes Intercepted, Game
8 Jim Hardy, Chi. Cards vs Phil., Sept. 24, 1950 (39 attempts)

Lowest Percentage Passes Intercepted, Lifetime (1,500 att.)
3.31 Roman Gabriel, L.A. 1962–72; Phil. 1973–77 (4,498–149)

Lowest Percentage Passes Intercepted, Season (Qualifiers)
0.66 Joe Ferguson, Buff. 1976 (151–1)

Pass Receptions

Most Seasons Leading League
8 Don Hutson, Green Bay, 1936–37, 39, 41–45

Most Pass Receptions, Lifetime
649 Charley Taylor, Wash. 1964–75, 77

Most Pass Receptions, Season
101 Charley Hennigan, Hou. 1964 (AFL)

TOUCHDOWN PASS RECORD RECEIVER: Elroy (Crazy Legs) Hirsch caught 17 in a season, and had an 11-game streak.

Most Pass Receptions, Game
  18 Tom Fears, L. A. vs Green Bay, Dec. 3, 1950 (189 yds.)

Longest Pass Reception (all TDs)
  99 Andy Farkas (Filchock), Wash. vs Pitt., Oct. 15, 1939
      Bobby Mitchell (Izo), Wash. vs Cleve., Sept. 15, 1963
      Pat Studstill (Sweetan), Det. vs Balt., Oct. 16, 1966
      Gerry Allen (Jurgensen), Wash. vs Chi., Sept. 15, 1968

Most Consecutive Games, Pass Receptions
  105 Dan Abramowicz, N.O. 1967–73; S.F. 1973–74

Touchdowns Receiving

Most Touchdown Passes, Lifetime
  99 Don Hutson, Green Bay, 1935–45

Most Touchdown Passes, Season
  17 Don Hutson, Green Bay, 1942
      Elroy (Crazy Legs) Hirsch, L. A., 1951
      Bill Groman, Hou. 1961 (AFL)

Most Touchdown Passes, Game
  5 Bob Shaw, Chi. Cards vs Balt., Oct. 2, 1950

Most Consecutive Games, Touchdown Passes
  11 Elroy (Crazy Legs) Hirsch, L.A., 1950–51
      Gilbert (Buddy) Dial, Pitt., 1959–60

Pass Interceptions

Most Interceptions by, Lifetime
  79 Emlen Tunnell, N. Y. (74), 1948–58; Green Bay (5), 1959–61

Most Interceptions by, Season
  14 Richard (Night Train) Lane, L. A., 1952

Most Interceptions by, Game
  4 By many players

Interception Yardage

Most Yards Gained, Lifetime
1,282 Emlen Tunnell, N. Y., 1948–58; Green Bay, 1959–61

Most Yards Gained, Season
  349 Charley McNeil, San Diego, 1961 (AFL)

Most Yards Gained, Game
  177 Charley McNeil, San Diego vs Hou., Sept. 24, 1961 (AFL)

Longest Gain (all TDs)
  102 Bob Smith, Det. vs Chi. Bears, Nov. 24, 1949
       Erich Barnes, N. Y. vs Dall., Oct. 22, 1961
       Gary Barbaro, K.C. vs. Sea., Dec. 11, 1977

Touchdowns on Interceptions

Most Touchdowns, Lifetime
  9 Ken Houston, Hou. 1967–72; Wash. 1973–78

Most Touchdowns, Season
  4 Ken Houston, Hou. 1971
     Jim Kearney, K.C. 1972

Punting

Most Seasons Leading League
  4 Sammy Baugh, Wash., 1940–43
     Jerrel Wilson, AFL: K.C., 1965, 68; NFL: K.C. 1972–73

LONGEST PUNTER: Steve O'Neal (N.Y. Jets) kicked 98 yards in the AFL in 1969.

MOST TOUCHDOWN PASSES: Y. A. Tittle threw a record 36 touchdown passes in 1963 and 7 in one game in 1962. Both marks have been equaled by other quarterbacks.

N.F.L. Records (continued)

Most Punts, Lifetime
1,072 Jerrel Wilson, AFL: K.C. 1963–69; NFL: K.C. 1970–77; N.E. 1978

Most Punts, Season
109 John James, Atl. 1978

Most Punts, Game
14 Dick Nesbitt, Chi. Cards. vs Chi. Bears, Nov. 30, 1933
Keith Molesworth, Chi. Bears vs G.B., Dec. 10, 1933
Sammy Baugh, Wash. vs Phil., Nov. 5, 1939
John Kinscherf, N. Y. vs Det., Nov. 7, 1943
George Taliaferro, N. Y. Yanks vs L. A., Sept. 28, 1951

Longest Punt
98 yards Steve O'Neal, N. Y. Jets vs. Den., Sept. 21, 1969 (AFL)

Average Yardage Punting

Highest Punting Average, Lifetime (300 punts)
45.1 yards Sammy Baugh, Wash., 1937–52 (338)

Highest Punting Average, Season (20 punts)
51.4 yards Sammy Baugh, Wash., 1940 (35)

Highest Punting Average, Game (4 punts)
61.8 yards Bob Cifers, Det. vs. Chi. Bears, Nov. 24, 1946

Punt Returns
·   Yardage Returning Punts

Most Yards Gained, Lifetime
2,209 Emlen Tunnell, N.Y. Giants 1948–58; G.B. 1959–61

Most Yards Gained, Season
655 Neal Colzie, Oak. 1975

Most Yards Gained, Game
205 George Atkinson, Oak. vs. Buff., Sept. 15, 1968

Longest Punt Return (all TDs)
98 Gil LeFebvre, Cin. vs. Brk., Dec. 3, 1933
Charlie West, Minn. vs. Wash., Nov. 3, 1968
Dennis Morgan, Dall. vs. St. L., Oct. 13, 1974

Average Yardage Returning Punts

Highest Average, Lifetime (75 returns)
13.4 Billy (White Shoes) Johnson, Hou. 1974–78

Highest Average, Season (Qualifiers)
23.0 Herb Rich, Balt. 1950

Highest Average, Game (3 returns)
47.7 Chuck Latourette, St. L. vs. N.O., Sept. 29, 1968

Touchdowns Returning Punts

Most Touchdowns, Lifetime
8 Jack Christiansen, Det. 1951–58

Most Touchdowns, Season
4 Jack Christiansen, Det. 1951
Rick Upchurch, Den. 1976

Most Touchdowns, Game
2 Jack Christiansen, Det. vs. L.A., Oct. 14, 1951; vs. G.B., Nov. 22, 1951
Dick Christy, N.Y. Titans vs. Den., Sept. 24, 1961
Rick Upchurch, Den. vs Clev., Sept. 26, 1976

Kickoff Returns
Yardage Returning Kickoffs

Most Yards Gained, Lifetime
6,922 Ron Smith, Chi. 1965, 70–72;
Atl. 1966–67; L.A. 1968–69;
S.D. 1973; Oak. 1974

Most Yards Gained, Season
1,317 Bobby Jancik, Hou. 1963 (AFL)

Most Yards Gained, Game
294 Wally Triplett, Det. vs L. A.,
Oct. 29, 1950 (4)

Longest Kickoff Return for Touchdown
106 Al Carmichael, Green Bay vs.
Chi. Bears, Oct. 7, 1956
Noland Smith, K.C. vs Den.,
Dec. 17, 1967 (AFL)

Average Yardage Returning Kickoffs

Highest Average, Lifetime (75 returns)
30.6 Gale Sayers, Chi. 1965–71

Highest Average, Season (15 returns)
41.1 Travis Williams, Green Bay, 1967
(18)

Highest Average, Game (3 returns)
73.5 Wally Triplett, Det. vs L. A.,
Oct. 29, 1950 (4-294)

Touchdowns Returning Kickoffs

Most Touchdowns, Lifetime
6 Ollie Matson, Chi. Cards, 1952
(2), 54, 56, 58 (2)
Gale Sayers, Chi., 1965, 66 (2),
67 (3)
Travis Williams, G.B., 1967 (4),
69, 71

Most Touchdowns, Season
4 Travis Williams, Green Bay, 1967
Cecil Turner, Chi. 1970

Most Touchdowns, Game
2 Thomas (Tim) Brown, Phil. vs
Dall., Nov. 6, 1966
Travis Williams, Green Bay vs
Cleve., Nov. 12, 1967

Fumbles

Most Fumbles, Lifetime
105 Roman Gabriel, L.A. 1962–72;
Phil. 1973–77

Most Fumbles, Season
17 Dan Pastorini, Hou., 1973

Most Fumbles, Game
7 Len Dawson, K.C. vs San Diego,
Nov. 15, 1964 (AFL)

Most Own Fumbles Recovered, Lifetime
43 Fran Tarkenton, Minn. 1961–66,
72–78; N.Y. Giants 1967–71

Most Own Fumbles Recovered, Season
8 Paul Christman, Chi. Cards,1945;
Bill Butler, Minn., 1963

Most Own Fumbles Recovered, Game
4 Otto Graham, Cleve. vs N. Y.,
Oct. 25, 1953
Sam Etcheverry, St. L. vs N. Y.,
Sept. 17, 1961
Roman Gabriel, L. A. vs S. F.,
Oct. 12, 1969
Joe Ferguson, Buff. vs. Miami,
Sept. 18, 1977

Most Opponents' Fumbles Recovered,
Lifetime
28 Jim Marshall, Clev. 1960; Minn.
1961–78

Most Opponents' Fumbles Recovered,
Season
9 Don Hultz, Minn., 1963

Most Opponents' Fumbles Recovered,
Game
3 Corwin Clatt, Chi. Cards vs Det.,
Nov. 6, 1949
Vic Sears, Phil. vs Green Bay,
Nov. 2, 1952
Ed Beatty, S. F. vs L. A., Oct. 7,
1956
Ron Carroll, Hou. vs Cin., Oct.
27, 1974
Maurice Spencer, N.O. vs. Atl.,
Oct. 10, 1976
Steve Nelson, N.E. vs. Phil.,
Oct. 8, 1978

Longest Fumble Run
104 Jack Tatum, Oak. vs G.B., Sept.
24, 1972

Miscellaneous

Most Drop Kick Field Goals, Game
4 John (Paddy) Driscoll, Chi. Cards
vs Columbus, Oct. 11, 1925 (23,
18, 50, 35 yards)
Elbert Bloodgood, Kansas City
vs Duluth, Dec. 12, 1926 (35, 32,
20, 25 yards)

Longest Drop Kick Field Goal
50 Wilbur (Pete) Henry, Canton vs
Toledo, Nov. 13, 1922
John (Paddy) Driscoll, Chi. Cards
vs Milwaukee, Sept. 28, 1924;
vs Columbus, Oct. 11, 1925

Most Yards Returned Missed Field
Goal
101 Al Nelson, Phil. vs Dall., Sept. 26,
1971 (TD)

SEASON RECORDS—OFFENSE

(Playoff games not included)

Most Seasons League Champion
11 Green Bay, 1929–31, 36, 39, 44,
61–62, 65–67

Most Consecutive Games Without
Defeat (Regular Season)
24 Canton, 1922–23 (Won–21, Tied–
3)
Chicago Bears, 1941–43 (Won–
23, Tied–1)

Most Consecutive Victories (All Games)
18 Chicago Bears (1933–34; 1941–42)
Miami (1972–73)

Most Consecutive Victories (Regular Season)
17 Chicago Bears, 1933–34

Most Consecutive Victories, One Season (All Games)
17 Miami, 1972

Most Consecutive Shutout Games Won
7 Detroit, 1934

Scoring

Most Seasons Leading League
9 Chicago Bears, 1934–35, 39, 41–43, 46–47, 56

Most Points, Season
513 Houston, 1961 (AFL)

Most Points, Game
72 Washington vs N. Y., Nov. 27, 1966

Most Touchdowns, Season
66 Houston, 1961 (AFL)

Most Touchdowns, Game
10 Philadelphia vs Cin., Nov. 6, 1934
Los Angeles vs Balt., Oct. 22, 1950
Washington vs N. Y., Nov. 27, 1966

Most Touchdowns, Both Teams, Game
16 Washington (10) vs N. Y. (6), Nov. 27, 1966

Most Points After Touchdown, Season
65 Houston, 1961 (AFL)

Most Points After Touchdown, Game
10 Los Angeles vs Balt., Oct. 22, 1950

Most Points After Touchdown, Both Teams, Game
14 Chicago Cards (9) vs N. Y. (5), Oct. 17, 1948
Houston (7) vs Oakland (7), Dec. 22, 1963 (AFL)
Washington (9) vs N. Y. (5), Nov. 27, 1966

Most Field Goals Attempted, Season
49 Los Angeles, 1966
Washington, 1971

Most Field Goals Attempted, Game
9 St. Louis vs Pitt., Sept. 24, 1967

Most Field Goals Attempted, Both Teams, Game
11 St. Louis (6) vs Pitt. (5), Nov. 13, 1966
Washington (6) vs Chi. (5), Nov. 14, 1971
Green Bay (6) vs Det. (5), Sept. 29, 1974
Washington (6) vs. N.Y. Giants (5), Nov. 14, 1976

Most Field Goals, Season
34 New York, 1968 (AFL)

Most Field Goals, Game
7 St. Louis vs Pitt., Sept. 24, 1967

Most Field Goals, Both Teams, Game
8 Cleveland (4) vs St. L. (4), Sept. 20, 1964
Chicago (5) vs Phil. (3), Oct. 20, 1968
Washington (5) vs Chi. (3), Nov. 14, 1971
Kansas City (5) vs. Buff. (3), Dec. 19, 1971
Detroit (4) vs G.B. (4), Sept. 29, 1974
Cleveland (5) vs Den. (3), Oct. 19, 1975
New England (4) vs S.D. (4), Nov. 9, 1975

Most Consecutive Games Scoring Field Goals
31 Minnesota, 1968–70

First Downs

Most Seasons Leading League
9 Chicago Bears, 1935, 39, 41, 43, 45, 47–49, 55

Most First Downs, Season
345 Seattle, 1978

Most First Downs, Game
38 Los Angeles vs N. Y., Nov. 13, 1966

Most First Downs, Both Teams, Game
58 Los Angeles (30) vs Chi. Bears (28), Oct. 24, 1954
Denver (34) vs K.C. (24), Nov. 18, 1974

Most First Downs, Rushing, Season
181 New England, 1978

Most First Downs, Rushing, Game
25 Philadelphia vs Wash., Dec. 2, 1951

Most First Downs, Passing, Season
186 Houston, 1964 (AFL)
Oakland, 1964 (AFL)

Most First Downs, Passing, Game
25 Denver vs K.C., Nov. 18, 1974

Net Yards Gained (Rushes and Passes)

Most Seasons Leading League
12 Chicago Bears, 1932, 34–35, 39, 41–44, 47, 49, 55–56

Most Yards Gained, Season
6,288 Houston, 1961 (AFL)

Most Yards Gained, Game
735 Los Angeles vs N. Y. Yanks, Sept. 28, 1951 (181-r, 554-p)

Most Yards Gained, Both Teams, Game
1,133 Los Angeles (636) vs N. Y. Yanks (497), Nov. 19, 1950

Rushing

Most Seasons Leading League
12 Chicago Bears, 1932, 34–35, 39–42, 51, 55–56, 68, 77

Most Rushing Attempts, Season
681 Oakland, 1977

Most Rushing Attempts, Game
72 Chicago Bears vs Brk., Oct. 20, 1935

Most Rushing Attempts, Both Teams, Game
108 Chicago Cards (70) vs Green Bay (38), Dec. 5, 1948

Most Yards Gained Rushing, Season
3,165 New England, 1978

Most Yards Gained Rushing, Game
426 Detroit vs Pitt., Nov. 4, 1934

Most Yards Gained Rushing, Both Teams, Game
595 L. A. (371) vs N. Y. Yanks (224), Nov. 18, 1951

Highest Average Gain Rushing, Season
5.7 Cleveland, 1963

Most Touchdowns Rushing, Season
36 Green Bay, 1962

Most Touchdowns Rushing, Game
7 Los Angeles vs. Atlanta, Dec. 4, 1976

Most Touchdowns Rushing, Both Teams, Game
8 Los Angeles (6) vs N. Y. Yanks (2), Nov. 18, 1951
   Cleveland (6) vs L. A. (2), Nov. 24, 1957

Passing

Most Seasons Leading League
10 Washington, 1937, 39–40, 42–45, 47, 67, 74

Most Passes Attempted, Season
592 Houston, 1964 (AFL)
     Minnesota, 1978

Most Passes Attempted, Game
68 Houston vs Buffalo, Nov. 1, 1964 (AFL) (37 comp.)

Most Passes Attempted, Both Teams, Game
98 Minn. (56) vs Balt. (42), Sept. 28, 1969

Most Passes Completed, Season
352 Minnesota, 1978

Most Passes Completed, Game
37 Houston vs Buffalo, Nov. 1, 1964 (AFL) (68 att.)

Most Passes Completed, Both Teams, Game
56 Minn. (36) vs Balt. (20), Sept. 28, 1969

Most Yards Gained Passing, Season
4,392 Houston, 1961 (AFL)

Most Yards Gained Passing, Game
554 Los Angeles vs N. Y. Yanks, Sept. 28, 1951

Most Yards Gained Passing, Both Teams, Game
834 Philadelphia (419) vs St. L. (415), Dec. 16, 1962

Most Seasons Leading League (Completion Pct.)
11 Washington, 1937, 39–40, 42–45, 47–48, 69-70

Most Touchdowns Passing, Season
48 Houston, 1961 (AFL)

Most Touchdowns Passing, Game
7 Chicago Bears vs N. Y., Nov. 14, 1943
   Philadelphia vs. Wash., Oct. 17, 1954
   Houston vs N. Y., Nov. 19, 1961 and Oct. 14, 1962 (AFL)
   New York vs Wash., Oct. 28, 1962
   Minnesota vs Balt., Sept. 28, 1969

Most Touchdowns Passing, Both Teams, Game
12 New Orleans (6) vs St. Louis (6), Nov. 2, 1969

Most Passes Had Intercepted, Season
48 Houston, 1962 (AFL)

Fewest Passes Had Intercepted, Season
5 Cleveland, 1960 (264-att.)
   Green Bay, 1966 (318-att.)

Most Passes Had Intercepted, Game
9 Detroit vs Green Bay, Oct. 24, 1943
   Pittsburgh vs Phil., Dec. 12, 1965

Punting

Most Seasons Leading League (Avg. Distance)
6 Washington, 1940–43, 45, 58

Highest Punting Average, Season
47.6 Detroit, 1961

Punt Returns

Most Seasons Leading League
8 Detroit, 1943–45, 51–52, 62, 66, 69

Most Yards Gained Punt Returns, Season
781 Chicago Bears, 1948

Most Yards Gained Punt Returns, Game
231 Detroit vs S. F., Oct. 6, 1963

Highest Average Punt Returns, Season
20.2 Chicago Bears, 1941

Most Touchdowns Punt Returns, Season
5 Chicago Cards, 1959

Most Touchdowns Punt Returns, Game
2 Detroit vs L. A., Oct. 14; vs Green Bay, Nov. 22, 1951
   Chicago Cards vs Pitt., Nov. 1; vs N. Y., Nov. 22, 1959
   New York Titans vs Den., Sept. 24, 1961 (AFL)
   Denver vs. Clev., Sept. 26, 1976

Kickoff Returns

Most Seasons Leading League
6 Washington, 1942, 47, 62–63, 73–74

Most Yards Gained Kickoff Returns, Season
1,824 Houston, 1963 (AFL)

Most Yards Gained Kickoff Returns, Game
362 Detroit vs L. A., Oct. 29, 1950

Most Yards Gained Kickoff Returns, Both Teams, Game
560 Detroit (362) vs L. A. (198) Oct. 29, 1950

Highest Average Kickoff Returns. Season
29.4 Chicago, 1972

Most Touchdowns Kickoff Returns, Season
4 Green Bay, 1967
   Chicago, 1970

Most Touchdowns Kickoff Returns, Game
2 Chicago Bears vs Green Bay, Sept. 22, 1940–Nov. 9, 1952
   Philadelphia vs Dall., Nov. 6, 1966
   Green Bay vs Cleve., Nov. 12, 1967

Fumbles

Most Fumbles, Season
56 Chicago Bears, 1938
    San Francisco, 1978

Fewest Fumbles, Season
8 Cleveland, 1959

Most Fumbles, Game
10 Phil/Pitts vs N. Y., Oct. 9, 1943
    Detroit vs Minn., Nov. 12, 1967
    Kansas City vs Hou., Oct. 12, 1969 (AFL)
    San Francisco vs. Det., Dec. 17, 1978

Most Fumbles, Both Teams, Game
14 Chicago Bears (7) vs Cleve. (7), Nov. 24, 1940
    St. Louis (8) vs N. Y. (6), Sept. 17, 1961
    Kansas City (10) vs Hou. (4), Oct. 12, 1969 (AFL)

Most Opponents' Fumbles Recovered, Season
31 Minnesota, 1963 (50 fumbles)

Most Opponents' Fumbles Recovered, Game
8 Washington vs St. L., Oct. 25 1976

Most Own Fumbles Recovered, Season
37 Chicago Bears, 1938 (56 fumbles)

Most Fumbles (Opponents' and Own) Recovered, Season
58 Minnesota, 1963 (95 fumbles)

Most Fumbles (Opponents' and Own), Recovered, Game
10 Denver vs Buff., Dec. 13, 1964 (AFL)
    Pittsburgh vs Hou., Dec. 9, 1973
    Washington vs St. L., Oct. 25, 1976

Penalties

Most Seasons Leading League, Fewest Penalties
9 Pittsburgh, 1946–47, 50–52, 54, 63, 65, 68

Most Penalties, Season
133 Los Angeles, 1978

Fewest Penalties, Season
19 Detroit, 1937 (139 yards)

Most Penalties, Game
22 Brooklyn vs Green Bay, Sept. 17, 1944 (170 yards)
    Chicago Bears vs Phil., Nov. 26, 1944 (170 yards)

Fewest Penalties, Game
0 By many teams

Fewest Penalties, Both Teams, Game
0 Brooklyn vs Pitt., Oct. 28, 1934; vs Bos., Sept. 28, 1936
   Cleveland Rams vs Chi. Bears, Oct. 9, 1938
   Pittsburgh vs Phil., Nov. 10, 1940

Most Yards Penalized, Season
1,274 Oakland, 1969 (AFL)

Fewest Yards Penalized, Season
139 Detroit, 1937 (19 pen.)

Most Yards Penalized, Game
209 Cleveland vs Chi. Bears, Nov. 25, 1951 (21 pen.)

DEFENSE

Fewest Points Allowed, Season (since 1932)
44 Chicago Bears, 1932

Fewest Touchdowns Allowed, Season (since 1932)
6 Chicago Bears 1932
   Brooklyn, 1933

Fewest First Downs Allowed, Season
77 Detroit, 1935

Fewest First Downs Allowed, Rushing, Season
35 Chicago Bears, 1942

Fewest First Downs Allowed, Passing, Season
33 Chicago Bears, 1943

Fewest Yards Allowed, Season
1,539 Chicago Cards, 1934

Fewest Yards Allowed Rushing, Season
519 Chicago Bears, 1942

Fewest Touchdowns Allowed, Rushing, Season
2 Detroit, 1934
Dallas, 1968
Minnesota, 1971

Fewest Yards Allowed Punt Returns, Season
22 Green Bay, 1967

Fewest Yards Allowed Kickoff Returns, Season
225 Brooklyn, 1943

Fewest Yards Allowed Passing, Season
545 Philadelphia, 1934

Most Opponents Tackled Attempting Passes, Season
67 Oakland, 1967 (AFL)

Fewest Touchdowns Allowed, Passing, Season
1 Portsmouth, 1932
Philadelphia, 1934

Most Seasons Leading League, Interceptions Made
9 New York Giants, 1933, 1937-39, 44, 48, 51, 54, 61

Most Pass Interceptions Made, Season
49 San Diego, 1961 (AFL)

Most Yards Gained, Interceptions, Season
929 San Diego, 1961 (AFL)

Most Yards Gained, Interceptions, Game
314 Los Angeles vs S. F., Oct. 18, 1964

Most Touchdowns, Interception Returns, Season
9 San Diego, 1961 (AFL)

Most Touchdowns, Interception Returns, Game
3 Baltimore vs Green Bay, Nov. 5, 1950
Cleveland vs Chi., Dec. 11, 1960
Philadelphia vs Pitt., Dec. 12, 1965
Baltimore vs Pitt., Sept. 29, 1968
Buffalo vs N. Y., Sept. 29, 1968 (AFL)
Houston vs S.D., Dec. 19, 1971
Cincinnati vs Hou., Dec. 17, 1972
Tampa Bay vs. N.O., Dec. 11, 1977

Gambling

World's Biggest Win. The world's biggest gambling win is $2,451,549 for a bet of two cruzeiros ($.58) in the Brazilian football pools Loteria Esportiva by Miron Vieira de Sousa, 30, of Ivolandia, Brazil, on the results of 13 games in October, 1975. The first thing he bought was a set of false teeth.

By winning a state lottery in January, 1976, Eric C. Leek, of North Arlington, New Jersey, won $1,776 a week for life. Aged 26, he will receive a total of $4.6 million should he live a further 50 years.

World's Biggest Loss. An unnamed Italian industrialist was reported to have lost $1,920,000 in five hours at roulette in Monte Carlo, Monaco, on March 6, 1974. A Saudi Arabian prince was reported to have lost more than $1 million in a single session at the Metro Club, Las Vegas, Nevada, in December, 1974.

Largest Casino. The largest casino in the world is the Casino, Mar del Plata, Argentina, with average daily attendances of 14,500 rising to 25,000 during carnivals. The Casino has more than 150 roulette tables running simultaneously.

BIGGEST "BANDIT" OF ALL: When playing Super Bertha, the world's largest slot machine, eight 7's add up to much more than 56.

Bingo

Origins. Bingo is a lottery game which, as keno, was developed in the 1880's from lotto, whose origin is thought to be the 17th century Italian game *tumbule*. It has long been known in the British Army (called Housey-Housey) and the Royal Navy (called Tombola). The winner was the first to complete a random selection of numbers from 1–90. The U.S. version of Bingo differs in that the selection is from 1–75. There are six million players in the United Kingdom alone.

Largest House. The largest "house" in Bingo sessions was at the Empire Pool, Wembley, Brent, Greater London, on April 25, 1965, when 10,000 attended.

Most Cards. The highest recorded number of cards played simultaneously (with a call rate of 31.7 seconds per call) has been 346 by Robert A. Berg at Pacific Beach, California, on November 16, 1973.

Bingo-Calling Marathon. A session of 240 hours 30 minutes was held at the Top Rank Social Club, Kingston-upon-Thames, Surrey, England, on May 1–4, 1979, with Philip Carter and Timothy Mann calling.

Slot Machines

Largest. The world's biggest slot machine (or one-armed bandit) is Super Bertha (555 cubic feet) installed by Si Redd at the Four

Queens Casino, Las Vegas, Nevada, in September, 1973. Once in every 25,000,000,000 plays it may yield $1 million for a $10 investment.

Biggest Win. The biggest beating handed to a "one-armed bandit" was $285,000 by Brian Flattery (U.S.) at the Flamingo Hilton Hotel, Las Vegas, Nevada, on June 23, 1979.

The total gambling "take" in 1978 in Nevada casinos was estimated at $1,800,000,000.

Horse Racing

Topmost Tipster. The only recorded instance of a racing correspondent forecasting ten out of ten winners on a race card was at Delaware Park, Wilmington, Delaware, on July 28, 1974, by Charles Lamb of the *Baltimore News American*.

Most Complicated Bet. The most complicated bet is the Harlequin, a British compound wager on four horses with 2,028 possible ways of winning. It was invented by Monty H. Preston of London who has been reputed to be the fastest settler of bets in the world. He once completed 3,000 bets in a $4\frac{1}{2}$-hour test.

Largest Bookmaker. The world's largest bookmaker is Ladbrokes of London, with a turnover from gambling in 1978 of $780,000,000.

See also *Harness Racing* and *Horse Racing*.

Blackjack

Marathon. Earl Arnall, a dealer at the King 8 Casino in Las Vegas, Nevada, spent 190 hours at the blackjack table, June 22–30, 1977. Ardeth Hardy set the women's mark of 169 hours 47 minutes of continuous dealing during the same period. Both took 5-minute rest breaks within each hour.

Roulette

Longest Run. The longest run on an ungaffed (*i.e.* true) wheel reliably recorded is six successive coups (in No. 10) at El San Juan Hotel, Puerto Rico, on July 9, 1959. The odds with a double zero were 1 in 38^6 or 3,010,936,383 to 1.

Longest Marathon. The longest "marathon" on record is one of 31 days from April 10 to May 11, 1970, at The Casino de Macao, to test the validity or invalidity of certain contentions in 20,000 spins.

Games and Pastimes
Bridge (Contract)

Earliest References. Bridge (corruption of Biritch) is thought to be of Levantine origin, similar games having been played there in the early 1870's. The game was known in London in 1886 under the title of "Biritch or Russian Whist." Whist, first referred to in 1529, was the world's premier card game until 1930. Its rules had been standardized in 1742.

Auction bridge (highest bidder names trump) was invented *c.* 1902. The contract principle, present in several games (notably the French game *Plafond, c.* 1917), was introduced to bridge by Harold S. Vanderbilt (U.S.) on November 1, 1925, during a Caribbean voyage aboard the S.S. *Finland.* The new version became a world-wide craze after the U.S. vs. Great Britain challenge match between Rumanian-born Ely Culbertson (1891–1955) and Lt.-Col. Walter Thomas More Buller (1887–1938) at Almack's Club, London, September, 1930. The U.S. won the 200-hand match by 4,845 points.

Perfect Deals. The mathematical odds against dealing 13 cards of one suit are 158,753,389,899 to 1, while the odds against receiving a "perfect hand" consisting of all 13 spades are 635,013,559,596 to 1. The odds against each of the 4 players receiving a complete suit (a "perfect deal") are 2,235,197,406,895,366,368,301,559,999 to 1.

Highest Possible Scores (excluding penalties for rules infractions)

Opponents bid 7 of any suit or no trump, doubled and redoubled and vulnerable. Opponents make no trick.		Bid 1 no trump, doubled and redoubled, vulnerable.	
Above Line 1st undertrick	400	*Below Line* 1st trick (40×4)	160
12 subsequent undertricks at 600 each	7,200	*Above Line* 6 overtricks (400×6)	2,400
All Honors	150	2nd game of 2-Game Rubber	*350
		All Honors (4 aces)	150
		Bonus for making redoubled contract	50
	7,750	(Highest Possible Positive Score)	3,110

* In practice, the full bonus of 700 points is awarded after the completion of the second game, rather than 350 after each game.

World Titles. The World Championship (Bermuda Bowl) has been won most often by Italy's "Blue Team" (Squadra Azzurra) (1957–58–59, 1961–62–63, 1965–66–67, 1969, 1973–74–75), which also won the Olympiad in 1964, 1968 and 1972. Giorgio Belladonna was on all 16 winning teams.

Most Master Points. In 1971, a new World Ranking List based on Master Points was instituted. The leading male player is Giorgio Belladonna (see above) with 1,712 points as of March, 1978, followed by 5 more Italians. The world's leading woman player is Mrs. Rixi Markus (G.B.) with 269 points to March, 1978.

Bridge Marathon. The longest recorded bridge session is one of 180 hours by four students at Edinburgh University, Scotland, April 21–28, 1972.

Checkers

Origins. Checkers, known as draughts in some countries, has origins earlier than chess. It was played in Egypt in the second millennium B.C. The earliest book on the game was by Antonio Torquemada of Valencia, Spain in 1547.

There have been three U.S. *vs.* Great Britain international matches. The earliest, in 1905, was won by the Scottish Masters, 73–

34, with 284 draws. The U.S. won in 1927 in New York, 96–20 with 364 draws, and won again in the most recent match, in 1973.

The only man to win 5 British Championships has been Jim Marshall (Fife, Scotland) in 1948–50–52–54–66. The longest tenure of invincibility was that of Melvin Pomeroy (U.S.), who was internationally undefeated from 1914 until his death in 1933.

Longest and Shortest Games. In competition, the prescribed rate of play is not less than 30 moves per hour with the average game lasting about 90 minutes. In 1958 a match between Dr. Marian Tinsley (U.S.) and Derek Oldbury (G.B.) lasted 7½ hours.

The shortest possible game is one of 20 moves composed by Alan M. Beckerson (G.B.) on November 2, 1977.

Most Opponents. Newell W. Banks (b. Detroit, October 10, 1887) played 140 games simultaneously, winning 133 and drawing 7 in Chicago in 1933. His playing time was 145 minutes so averaging about one second per move.

Chess

Origins. The name chess is derived from the Persian word *shah*. It is a descendant of the game *Chaturanga*. The earliest reference is from the Middle Persian Karnamak (*c.* 590–628), though there are grounds for believing its origins are from the 2nd century, owing to the discovery, announced in December, 1972, of two ivory chessmen in the Uzbek Soviet Republic, datable to that century. The game reached Britain in *c.* 1255. The *Fédération Internationale des Echecs* was established in 1924. There were an estimated 7,000,000 registered players in the U.S.S.R. in 1973.

World Champions. François André Danican, *alias* Philidor (1726–95), of France claimed the title of "world champion" from 1747 until his death. World champions have been generally recognized since 1886. The longest undisputed tenure was 27 years by Dr. Emanuel Lasker (1868–1941) of Germany, from 1894 to 1921. Robert J. (Bobby) Fischer (b. Chicago, March 9, 1943) is

GRANDEST GRANDMASTER: Anatoli Karpov (left), shown defending his title against Victor Korchnoi, had lost less than 5 per cent of his games to the end of 1977.

WOMEN'S CHESS CHAMPION: Nona Gaprindashvili of the U.S.S.R. is the current champion, a title she has held since 1962.

reckoned on the officially adopted Elo system to be the greatest Grandmaster of all time. He has an I.Q. of 187 and became at 15 the youngest ever International Grandmaster.

The women's world championship has been most often won by Vera Menchik-Stevenson (1906–44) (G.B.) from 1927 till her death, and was successfully defended a record 7 times. Nona Gaprindashvili (U.S.S.R.) has held the title since 1962, and defended 4 times.

Winning Streak. Bobby Fischer (see above) won 20 games in succession in Grandmaster chess from December 2, 1970 (*vs.* Jorge Rubinetti of Argentina) to September 30, 1971 (*vs.* Tigran Petrosian of the U.S.S.R.). Anatoli Karpov (U.S.S.R.) lost only 4.3 per cent of his 597 games to December, 1977.

Longest Games. The most protracted master game on record was one drawn on the 191st move between H. Pilnik (Argentina) and Moshe Czerniak (Israel) at Mar del Plata, Argentina, in April, 1950. The total playing time was 20 hours. A game of 21½ hours, but drawn on the 171st move (average over 7½ minutes per move), was played between Makagonov and Chekhover at Baku, U.S.S.R., in 1945.

The slowest recorded move (before modern rules) was one of 11 hours between Paul Charles Morphy (1837–84), the U.S. champion 1852–1862, and the German chess master Louis Paulsen (1833–91).

Marathon. The longest recorded session is one of 158 hours 24 minutes by Lori Daulton, Marian Selby, Charlotte Rugar and Gayle Fields (two separate pairs) from Dinwiddie County Junior High School, Dinwiddie, Virginia, on December 17–23, 1977.

Most Opponents. The record for most opponents tackled (with replacements as they are defeated) is held by Branimir Brebrich

(Canada) who played 575 games (winning 533, drawing 27 and losing 15) in Edmonton, Alberta, Canada, January 27–28, 1978 in 28 hours of play.

Vlastimil Hort (b. January 12, 1944) (Czechoslovakia) in Seltjarnarnes, Iceland, on April 23–24, 1977, simultaneously tackled 201 opponents and did not lose a game.

Georges Koltanowski (Belgium, later of U.S.) tackled 56 opponents "blindfold" and won 50, drew 6, lost 0 in 9¾ hours at the Fairmont Hotel, San Francisco, on December 13, 1960.

Cribbage

Origins. The invention of this game (once called "Cribbidge") is credited to the English dramatist John Suckling (1609–42). It is played by an estimated 10 million people in the U.S. alone.

Rare Hands. F. Art Skinner of Alberta, Canada, is reported to have had five maximum 29-point hands. Paul Nault of Athol, Massachusetts, had two such hands within eight games in a tournament on March 19, 1977. At Blackpool, England, Derek Hearne dealt two hands of six clubs with the remaining club being the turn-up on February 8, 1976. Bill Rogers of Burnaby, B.C., Canada, scored 29 in the crib in 1975.

Marathon. Four members of the Barley Mow Forever Legless Society of England played for 60 hours on February 6–8, 1979.

Darts

Origins. Darts date from the use by archers of heavily weighted 10-inch throwing arrows for self-defense in close fighting. "Dartes" were used in Ireland in the 16th century, and darts was played on the *Mayflower* by the Pilgrims in 1620. Today, more people in Great Britain (6,000,000) play darts than any other single sport.

Lowest Possible Scores. Under English rules, the lowest number of darts needed to achieve standard scores is: 201, four darts; 301, six darts; 401, seven darts; 501, nine darts; 1,001, seventeen darts. The four- and six-dart "possibles" have been achieved many times, the nine-dart 501 occasionally, but the seventeen-dart 1,001 has never been accomplished. The lowest number of darts thrown for a score of 1,001 is 19 by Cliff Inglis at the Bromfield Men's Club, Devon, England, on November 11, 1975.

Fastest Match. The fastest time taken for a match of 3 games of 301 is 1 minute 58 seconds by Ricky Fusco at the Perivale Residents Association Club, Middlesex, England, on December 30, 1976.

Million-and-One. Eight players from The Golden Fleece, Edmonton, England, scored 1,000,001 with 41,214 darts in one session, May 26–28, 1979.

Marathon. Stephen Ablett and Chris Dare played for 101 hours at Nienburg Weser, West Germany, on March 29–April 2, 1975.

Dominoes

Origins. The National Museum in Baghdad, Iraq, contains artifacts from Ur called "dominoes" dated *c.* 2450 B.C. The game remains unstandardized. Eskimos play with 148 pieces, while the European game uses only 28.

Marathon. The longest session by 2 players is 123 hours 4 minutes by Alan Mannering and David Harrison of Stoke on Trent, England, on February 8–13, 1978.

Tiddlywinks

Origins. This game was first espoused by adults in 1955, when Cambridge University (England) issued a challenge to Oxford.

Speed Records. The record for potting 24 winks from a distance of 18 inches is 21.8 seconds by Stephen Williams in May, 1966. Allen R. Astles of the University of Wales potted 10,000 winks in 3 hours 51 minutes 46 seconds in February, 1966.

Marathons. The most protracted game on record is one of 240 hours by six players from St. Anselm's College, Birkenhead, Merseyside, England, August 2–12, 1977.

Gliding

Emanuel Swedenborg (1688–1772) of Sweden made sketches of gliders *c.* 1714.

The earliest man-carrying glider was designed by Sir George Cayley (1773–1857) and carried his coachman (possibly John Appleby) about 500 yards across a valley near Brompton Hall, Yorkshire, England, in the summer of 1853. Gliders now attain speeds of 168 m.p.h. and the Jastrzab aerobatic sailplane is designed to withstand vertical dives at up to 280 m.p.h.

Most World Titles

World individual championships (instituted 1948) have been won 5 times by West Germans.

Hang-Gliding

In the 11th century, the monk Elmer is reported to have flown from the 60-foot-tall tower of Malmesbury Abbey, Wiltshire, England. The earliest modern pioneer was Otto Lilienthal (1848–96) of Germany who made numerous flights between 1893 and 1896. Professor Francis Rogallo of the U.S. National Space Agency developed a "wing" in the 1950's from his research into space capsule re-entries.

The official F.A.I. record for the farthest distance covered is 95 miles by George Worthington (U.S.) in an ASG-21 (Rogallo) over California, on July 21, 1977.

The official F.A.I. height gain record is 11,700 feet, recorded by George Worthington (U.S.) over Bishop, California, on July 22, 1978.

The greatest altitude from which a hang-glider has descended is 31,600 feet by Bob McCaffrey, 18, who was released from a balloon over the Mojave Desert, California, on November 21, 1976.

Championships. The First World Team Championships, held at Chattanooga, Tennessee, in October, 1978, were won by Great Britain.

Parasailing

The longest recorded flight being towed is 15 hours 45 minutes 10 seconds by Gary Edelen and Charlie Skeen on the Columbia River Course, Washington State, on June 23, 1979.

GLIDING WORLD RECORDS
(Single-Seaters)

DISTANCE	907.7 miles	Hans-Werner Grosse (W. Germany) in an ASW-12 on April 25, 1972.
DECLARED GOAL FLIGHT	799.4 miles	Bruce Drake, David Speight, S. H. "Dick" Georgeson (all N.Z.) all in Nimbus 2s, from Te Anau to Te Araroa, January 14, 1978.
ABSOLUTE ALTITUDE	46,266 feet	Paul F. Bikle, Jr. (U.S.) in a Schweizer SGS 1-23E over Mojave, Calif. (released at 3,963 feet) on Feb. 25, 1961 (also record altitude gain—42,303 feet).
GOAL AND RETURN	1,015.7 miles	Karl H. Striedieck (U.S.) in an ASW-17 from Lock Haven, Penn. to Tennessee on May 9, 1977.
SPEED OVER TRIANGULAR COURSE		
100 km.	102.74 m.p.h.	Ross Briegleb (U.S.) in a Kestrel 17 over the U.S. on July 18, 1974.
300 km.	95.95 m.p.h.	Walter Neubert (W. Germany) in a Kestrel 604 over Kenya on March 3, 1972.
500 km.	88.82 m.p.h.	Edward Pearson (G.B.) in a Nimbus 2 over Namibia on November 27, 1976.
750 km.	87.69 m.p.h.	G. Eckle (W. Germany) in a Nimbus 2 over South Africa on January 7, 1978.
1,000 km.	90.28 m.p.h.*	Hans-Werner Grosse (W. Germany) in an ASW-17 over Australia, on January 3, 1979.

*Awaiting official confirmation

Golf

Origins. Although a stained glass window in Gloucester Cathedral, Scotland, dating from 1350 portrays a golfer-like figure, the earliest mention of golf occurs in a prohibiting law passed by the Scottish Parliament in March, 1457, under which "golff be utterly cryit doune and not usit." The Romans had a cognate game called *paganica*, which may have been carried to Britain before 400 A.D. The Chinese National Golf Association claims the game is of Chinese origin ("*Ch'ui Wan*—the ball-hitting game") from the 3rd or 2nd century B.C. Gutta-percha balls succeeded feather balls in 1848, and were in turn succeeded in 1902 by rubber-cored balls, invented in 1899 by Haskell (U.S.). Steel shafts were authorized in 1929.

Clubs

Oldest. The oldest club of which there is written evidence is the Gentleman Golfers (now the Honourable Company of Edinburgh Golfers) formed in March, 1744—10 years prior to the institution of the Royal and Ancient Club of St. Andrews, Fife, Scotland. The oldest existing club in North America is the Royal Montreal Club (1873) and the oldest in the U.S. is St. Andrews, Westchester County, New York (1888). An older claim is by the Foxbury Country Club, Clarion County, Pennsylvania (1887).

Courses

Highest. The highest golf course in the world is the Tuctu Golf Club in Morococha, Peru, which is 14,335 feet above sea level at its lowest point. Golf has, however, been played in Tibet at an altitude of over 16,000 feet.

Lowest. The lowest golf course in the world was that of the now defunct Sodom and Gomorrah Golfing Society at Kallia (Qulya), on the northern shores of the Dead Sea, 1,250 feet below sea level.

Longest Hole. The longest hole in the world is the 17th hole (par 6) of 745 yards at the Black Mountain Golf Club, North Carolina. It was opened in 1964. In August, 1927, the 6th hole at Prescott Country Club in Arkansas measured 838 yards.

Largest Green. Probably the largest green in the world is the 5th green at International G.C., Bolton, ·Massachusetts, with an area greater than 28,000 square feet.

Biggest Bunker. The world's biggest trap is Hell's Half Acre on the 7th hole of the Pine Valley course, New Jersey, built in 1912 and generally regarded as the world's most trying course.

Longest Course. The world's longest course is the 8,101-yard Dub's Dread Golf Club course (par 78) in Piper, Kansas.

Longest "Course." Floyd Satterlee Rood used the whole United States as a course when he played from the Pacific surf to the Atlantic surf from September 14, 1963 to October 3, 1964, in 114,737 strokes. He lost 3,511 balls on the 3,397.7-mile trip.

Lowest Scores

9 holes and 18 holes—Men. The lowest recorded score on any 18-hole course with a par of 70 or more is 55 first achieved by Alfred Edward Smith (b. 1903), the English professional, at Woolacombe on January 1, 1936. The course measured 4,248 yards. The detail was 4, 2, 3, 4, 2, 4, 3, 4, 3=29 out, and 2, 3, 3, 3, 3, 2, 5, 4, 1=26 in.

At least three players are recorded to have played a long course (over 6,000 yards) in a score of 58.

Nine holes in 25 (4, 3, 3, 2, 3, 3, 1, 4, 2) was recorded by A. J. "Bill" Burke in a round of 57 (32+25) on the 6,389-yard par 71 Normandie course in St. Louis on May 20, 1970. The tournament record is 27 by Jose Maria Canizares (Spain) (b. February 18, 1947)

LOWEST SCORES: Gary Player (left) has scored a record 59 in the non-P.G.A. Brazilian Open (1974), and a 64 in the U.S. Masters (1978). Mickey Wright (right) shot a 62 on an 18-hole course in Texas in November, 1964.

for the first nine of the third round in the 1978 Swiss Open on the 6,811-yard Crans-Sur-Sierre course.

The United States P.G.A. tournament record for 18 holes is 59 (30 + 29) by Al Geiberger (b. September 1, 1937) in the second round of the Danny Thomas Classic, on the 72-par, 7,249-yard course at Memphis, Tennessee, on June 10, 1977.

In non-P.G.A. tournaments, Sam Snead had 59 in the Greenbrier Open (now called the Sam Snead Festival), at White Sulphur Springs, West Virginia, on May 16, 1959; Gary Player (South Africa) (born November 1, 1935) carded 59 in the second round of the Brazilian Open in Rio de Janeiro on November 29, 1974; and David Jagger (G.B.) also had 59 in a Pro-Am tournament prior to the 1973 Nigerian Open.

36 holes. The record for 36 holes is 122 (59 + 63) by Sam Snead in the 1959 Greenbrier Open (now called the Sam Snead Festival) (non-P.G.A.) (see above) May 16–17, 1959. Horton Smith (see below) scored 121 (63+58) on a short course on December 21, 1928.

72 holes. The lowest recorded score on a first-class course is 257 (27 under par) by Mike Souchak (born May 10, 1927) in the Texas Open at Brackenridge Park, San Antonio in February, 1955, made up of 60 (33 out and 27 in), 68, 64, 65 (average 64.25 per round), exhibiting, as one critic said, his "up and down form." Horton Smith (1908–63), twice U.S. Masters Champion, scored 245 (63, 58, 61 and 63) for 72 holes on the 4,700-yard course (par 64) at Catalina Country Club, California, to win the Catalina Open on December 21–23, 1928.

The lowest 72 holes in a national championship is 262 by Percy Alliss (1897–1975) of Britain, with 67, 66, 66 and 63 in the Italian Open Championship at San Remo in 1932, and by Liang Huan Lu (b. 1936) (Taiwan) in the 1971 French Open at Biarritz. Kelvin D. G. Nagle (b. December 21, 1920) of Australia shot 261 in the Hong Kong Open in 1961.

Women. The lowest recorded score on an 18-hole course (over 6,000 yards) for a woman is 62 (30+32) by Mary (Mickey) Kathryn

Wright (born February 14, 1935), of Dallas, on the Hogan Park Course (6,282 yards) at Midland, Texas, in November, 1964.

Wanda Morgan (b. March 22, 1910) recorded a score of 60 (31 + 29) on the Westgate-on-Sea and Birchington Golf Club course (England) over 18 holes (5,002 yards) on July 11, 1929.

Highest Round Score. It is recorded that Chevalier von Cittern went round 18 holes at Biarritz, France, in 1888 in 316 strokes—an average of 17.55 shots per hole.

Steven Ward took 222 strokes for the 6,212-yard Pecos Course, Reeves County, Texas, on June 18, 1976—but he was only aged 3 years 286 days.

Highest Single-Hole Scores. The highest score recorded for a single hole in the British Open is 21 by a player in the inaugural meeting at Prestwick in 1860. Double figures have been recorded on the card of the winner only once, when Willie Fernie (1851–1924) scored a 10 at Musselburgh, Lothian, Scotland, in 1883. Ray Ainsley of Ojai, California, took 19 strokes for the par-4 16th hole during the second round of the U.S. Open at Cherry Hills Country Club, Denver, Colorado, on June 10, 1938. Most of the strokes were used in trying to extricate the ball from a brook. Hans Merrell of Mogadore, Ohio, took 19 strokes on the par-3 16th (222 yards) during the third round of the Bing Crosby National Tournament at the Cypress Point course, Del Monte, California, on January 17, 1959.

Most Shots—Women. A woman player in the qualifying round of the Shawnee Invitational for Ladies at Shawnee-on-Delaware, Pennsylvania, in c. 1912, took 166 strokes for the 130-yard 16th hole. Her tee shot went into the Binniekill River and the ball floated. She put out in a boat with her exemplary, but statistically minded, husband at the oars. She eventually beached the ball 1½ miles downstream, but was not yet out of the woods. She had to play through a forest on the home stretch. In a competition at Peacehaven, Sussex, England, in 1890, A. J. Lewis had 156 putts on one green without holing out.

Most Rounds in a Day

The greatest number of rounds played on foot in 24 hours is 22 rounds plus 5 holes (401 holes) by Ian Colston, 35, at Bendigo G.C., Victoria, Australia (6,061 yards) on November 27–28, 1971. He covered more than 100 miles.

The most holes played on foot in a week (168 hours) is 1,102 by David Shepardson (U.S.), 17, at Maple Grove Golf Club, Wisconsin, in August, 1976.

Fastest and Slowest Rounds

With such variations in the lengths of courses, speed records, even for rounds under par, are of little comparative value.

Bob Williams at Eugene, Oregon, completed 18 holes (6,010 yds.) in 27 minutes 48.2 seconds in 1971, but this test permitted him to stroke the ball while it was still moving. The record for a still ball is

LONGEST DRIVE (left): Tommie Campbell hit a 392-yard drive in July, 1964.
MOST WINS (right): Byron Nelson won 19 out of 31 tournaments in the 1945 season.

30 minutes 10 seconds by Dick Kimbrough (U.S.) (b. 1931) at North Platte C.C., Nebraska (6,068 yards), on August 8, 1972, using only a 3-iron.

On June 11, 1976, forty-three players representing Borger High School, Huber, Texas, completed the 18-hole 6,109-yard Huber Golf Course in 10 minutes 11.4 seconds.

The slowest stroke-play tournament round was one of 6 hours 45 minutes by South Africa in the first round of the 1972 World Cup at the Royal Melbourne Golf Club, Australia. This was a 4-ball medal round, everything holed out.

Longest Drive

In long-driving contests 330 yards is rarely surpassed at sea level.

The world record is 392 yards by a member of the Irish P.G.A., Tommie Campbell, made at Dun Laoghaire, Co. Dublin, in July, 1964.

The United States P.G.A. record is 341 yards by Jack William Nicklaus (born Columbus, Ohio, January 21, 1940), then weighing 206 lbs., in July, 1963.

Valetin Barrios (Spain) drove a ball 568½ yards on an airport runway at Palma, Majorca, on March 7, 1977.

The longest on an ordinary course is 515 yards by Michael Hoke Austin (born February 17, 1910) of Los Angeles, in the U.S. National Seniors Open Championship at Las Vegas, Nevada, on September 25, 1974. Aided by an estimated 35-m.p.h. tailwind, the 6-foot-2-inch 210-lb. golfer drove the ball on the fly to within a yard of the green on the par-4, 450-yard 5th hole of the Winterwood Course. The ball rolled 65 yards past the hole.

FIVE MAJOR TITLES:
Jack Nicklaus has won
17 major tournaments,
including the Masters
Championship 5 times.

Arthur Lynskey claimed a drive of 200 yards out and 2 miles down off Pikes Peak, Colorado, on June 28, 1968.

A drive of 2,640 yards (1½ miles) across ice was achieved by an Australian meteorologist named Nils Lied at Mawson Base, Antarctica, in 1962. On the moon, the energy expended on a mundane 300-yard drive would achieve, craters permitting, a distance of a mile.

Longest Hitter. The golfer regarded as the longest consistent hitter the game has ever known is the 6-foot-5-inch-tall, 230-lb. George Bayer (U.S.), the 1957 Canadian Open Champion. His longest measured drive was one of 420 yards at the fourth in the Las Vegas Invitational in 1953. It was measured as a precaution against litigation since the ball struck a spectator. Bayer also drove a ball pin high on a 426-yard hole in Tucson, Arizona. Radar measurements show that an 87-m.p.h. impact velocity for a golf ball falls to 46 m.p.h. in 3.0 seconds.

Longest Putt

The longest recorded holed putt in a major tournament was one of 86 feet on the vast 13th green at the Augusta National, Georgia, by Cary Middlecoff (b. January, 1921) in the 1955 Masters Tournament.

Bobby Jones was reputed to have holed a putt in excess of 100 feet on the 5th green in the first round of the 1927 British Open at St. Andrews, Scotland.

Most Tournament Wins

The record for winning tournaments in a single season is 19, including a record 11 consecutively, by Byron Nelson (born February 4, 1912) (U.S.) in 1945.

Sam Snead has won 84 official U.S.P.G.A. tour events to December, 1978, and has been credited with a total 134 tournament victories since 1934.

Mickey Wright (U.S.) won 82 professional tournaments up to December, 1978.

Jack Nicklaus (U.S.) is the only golfer who has won five major titles, including the U.S. Amateur, twice, and a record total 17 major tournaments (1962–78). His remarkable record in the British Open is three firsts, five seconds and two thirds.

Most Titles

U.S. Open	Willie Anderson (1880–1910)	4	1901–03–04–05
	Robert Tyre Jones, Jr. (1902–71)	4	1923–26–29–30
	Ben W. Hogan (b. Aug. 13, 1912)	4	1948–50–51–53
U.S. Amateur	R. T. Jones, Jr.	5	1924–25–27–28–30
British Open	Harry Vardon (1870–1937)	6	1896–98–99, 1903, 1911, 1914
British Amateur	John Ball (1861–1940)	8	1888–90–92–94–99, 1907–10, 1912
P.G.A. Championship (U.S.)	Walter C. Hagen (1892–1969)	5	1921–24–25–26–27
Masters Championship (U.S.)	Jack W. Nicklaus (b. Jan. 21, 1940)	5	1963–65–66–72–75
U.S. Women's Open	Miss Elizabeth (Betsy) Earle-Rawls (b. May 4, 1928)	4	1951–53–57–60
	Miss "Mickey" Wright (b. Feb. 14, 1935)	4	1958–59–61–64
U.S. Women's Amateur	Mrs. Glenna Vare (née Collett) (b. June 20, 1903)	6	1922–25–28–29–30–35

U.S. Open

This championship was inaugurated in 1894. The lowest 72-hole aggregate is 275 (71, 67, 72 and 65) by Jack Nicklaus on the Lower Course (7,015 yards) at Baltusrol Golf Club, Springfield, New Jersey, on June 15–18, 1967, and by Lee Trevino (b. Horizon City, Texas, December 1, 1939) at Oak Hill Country Club, Rochester, New York, on June 13–16, 1968. The lowest score for 18 holes is 63 by Johnny Miller (b. April 29, 1947) of California on the 6,921-yard, par-71 Oakmont (Pennsylvania) course on June 17, 1973.

U.S. Masters

The lowest score in the U.S. Masters (instituted at the 6,980-yard Augusta National Golf Course, Georgia, in 1934) was 271 by Jack Nicklaus in 1965 and Raymond Floyd (born 1942) in 1976. The lowest rounds have been 64 by Lloyd Mangrum (1914–74) (1st round, 1940), Jack Nicklaus (3rd round, 1965), Maurice Bembridge (G.B.) (b. February 21, 1945) (4th round, 1974), Hale Irwin (b. June 3, 1945) (4th round, 1975), Gary Player (S. Africa) (4th round, 1978), and Miller Barber (b. March 31, 1931) (2nd round, 1979).

U.S. Amateur

This championship was inaugurated in 1893. The lowest score for 9 holes is 30 by Francis D. Ouimet (1893–1967) in 1932.

The Open (British)

The Open Championship was inaugurated in 1860 at Prestwick, Strathclyde, Scotland. The lowest score for 9 holes is 29 by Tom Haliburton (Wentworth) and Peter W. Thomson (Australia), in the first round at the Open on the Royal Lytham and St. Anne's course at Lytham St. Anne's, Lancashire, England, on July 10, 1963. Tony Jacklin (G.B., b. July, 1944) also shot a 29 in the first round of the 1970 Open at St. Andrews, Scotland.

The lowest scoring round in the Open itself is 63 by Mark Hayes (U.S., b. July 12, 1949) at Turnberry, Strathclyde, Scotland, in the second round on July 7, 1977. Henry Cotton (G.B.) at Royal St. George's, Sandwich, Kent, England, completed the first 36 holes in 132 (67+65) on June 27, 1934.

The lowest 72-hole aggregate is 268 (68, 70, 65, and 65) by Tom Watson (U.S.) (b. September 4, 1949) at Turnberry, Scotland, on July 9, 1977.

British Amateur

The lowest score for nine holes in the British Championship (inaugurated in 1885) is 29 by Richard Davol Chapman (born March 23, 1911) of the U.S. at Sandwich in 1948. Michael Francis Bonallack (b. 1934) shot a 61 (32+29) on the 6,905-yard par-71 course at Ganton, Yorkshire, on July 27, 1968, on the 1st 18 of the 36 holes in the final round.

World Cup (formerly Canada Cup)

The World Cup (instituted 1953) has been won most often by the U.S. with 14 victories between 1955 and 1978. The only men on six winning teams have been Arnold Palmer (b. Sept. 10, 1929) (1960, 62–63–64, 66–67) and Jack Nicklaus (1963–4, 66–67, 71, 73). The only man to take the individual title three times is Jack Nicklaus (U.S.) in 1963–64–71. The lowest aggregate score for 144 holes is 545 by Australia (Bruce Devlin and David Graham) at San Isidro, Buenos Aires, Argentina, on November 12–15, 1970, and the lowest score by an individual winner was 269 by Roberto de Vicenzo, 47, on the same occasion.

Walker Cup

The U.S. versus Great Britain–Ireland series instituted in 1921 (for the Walker Cup since 1922), now biennial, has been won by the U.S. 25½–2½ to date (July, 1978). Joe Carr (G.B.–I.) played in 10 contests (1947–67).

Ryder Trophy

The biennial Ryder Cup (instituted 1927) professional match between the U.S. and G.B. had been won by the U.S. 18½–3½ to July, 1978. Billy Casper has the record of winning most matches, with 20 won (1961–75).

Biggest Victory Margin

Randall Colin Vines (b. June 22, 1945) of Australia won the Tasmanian Open in 1968 with a score of 274, with a margin of 17 strokes over the second-place finisher.

TOP MONEY WINNER:
In 1978, only her second year on the L.P.G.A. tour, Nancy Lopez won a record $189,814.

Longest Tie

The longest delayed result in any National Open Championship occurred in the 1931 U.S. Open at Toledo, Ohio. George von Elm and Billy Burke tied at 292, then tied the first playoff at 149. Burke won the second playoff by a single stroke after 72 extra holes.

Highest Earnings

The greatest amount ever won in official U.S. P.G.A. golf prizes is $3,349,393 by Jack Nicklaus to the end of 1978.

The record for a year is $362,429 by Tom Watson (U.S.) in 1978.

The highest career earnings by a woman is $822,214 by Kathy Whitworth (b. September 27, 1939) through the end of 1978.

Nancy Lopez (now Mrs. T. Melton) (b. January 6, 1957) won a record $189,814 in the 1978 season.

Youngest and Oldest Champions. The youngest winner of the British Open was Tom Morris, Jr. (b. 1851, d. December 25, 1875) at Prestwick, Ayrshire, Scotland, in 1868, aged 17 years 5 months. The youngest winners of the British Amateur title were John Charles Beharrel (b. May 2, 1938) at Troon, Strathclyde, Scotland, on June 2, 1956, and Robert (Bobby) Cole (S. Africa) (b. May 11, 1948) at Carnoustie, Tayside, Scotland, on June 11, 1966, both aged 18 years 1 month. The oldest winner of the British Amateur was the Hon. Michael Scott at Hoylake, Cheshire, England, in 1933, when 54. The oldest Open Champion was "Old Tom" Morris (1821–1908) who was aged 46 years 99 days when he won in 1867. In modern times, the 1967 champion Roberto de Vicenzo (b. Buenos Aires, Argentina, April 14, 1923) was aged 44 years 93 days. The oldest U.S. Amateur Champion was Jack Westland (born 1905) at Seattle, Washington, in 1952, aged 47.

SHOT HIS AGE: Sam Snead is the first player to shoot a round lower than his age on the P.G.A. tour. Two months after turning 67 he shot a 67 in tournament play, and two days later scored a 66.

Shooting Your Age

Sam Snead holds the record for shooting the lowest score in professional competition less than the player's age in years with a 64 on the Onion Creek Golf Club, Austin, Texas (par 70) of 6,585 yards in April, 1978, when he was one month short of his 66th birthday. He was also the first player on record to score his age on the P.G.A. tour, by hitting a 67 in the second round of the Ed McMahon Quad Cities Open at Oakwood Country Club, Coal Valley, Illinois, on June 20, 1979. He bettered this mark two days later, with a 66 in the final round. Snead turned 67 on May 27, 1979.

The oldest player to score his age is C. Arthur Thompson (1869–1975) of Victoria, British Columbia, Canada, who scored 103 on the Uplands course of 6,215 yards when aged 103 in 1973.

The youngest player to score his age is Robert Leroy Klingaman (born October 22, 1914) who shot a 58 when aged 58 on the 5,654-yard course at the Caledonia Golf Club, Fayetteville, Pennsylvania, on August 31, 1973. Bob Hamilton, age 59, shot 59 on the 6,233-yard blue course, Hamilton Golf Club, Evansville, Indiana, on June 3, 1975.

Throwing the Golf Ball

The lowest recorded score for throwing a golf ball around 18 holes (over 6,000 yards) is 82 by Joe Flynn, 21, at the 6,228-yard Port Royal Course, Bermuda, on March 27, 1975.

Most Peripatetic Golfer

George S. Salter of Carmel, California, has played in 116 different "countries" around the world from 1964 to 1977.

Richest Prize

The greatest first place prize money was $100,000 (total purse $500,000) in the 144-hole "World Open" played at Pinehurst, North Carolina, on November 8–17, 1973, won by Miller Barber, 42, of Texas. The World Series of Golf also carries a prize of $100,000.

Largest Tournament

The annual Ford Amateur Golf Tournament in Great Britain had a record 100,030 competitors in 1978.

Holes-in-One

In 1975, *Golf Digest* was notified of 26,267 holes-in-one, so averaging over 71 per day.

Longest. The longest straight hole shot in one is the 10th hole (444 yards) at Miracle Hills Golf Club, Omaha, Nebraska. Robert Mitera achieved a hole-in-one there on October 7, 1965. Mitera, aged 21 and 5 feet 6 inches tall, weighed 165 lbs. A two-handicap player, he normally drove 245 yards. A 50-m.p.h. gust carried his shot over a 290-yard drop-off. The group in front testified to the remaining 154 yards.

The longest dogleg achieved in one is the 480-yard 5th hole at Hope Country Club, Arkansas, by L. Bruce on November 15, 1962.

The women's record is 393 yards by Marie Robie of Wollaston, Massachusetts, on the first hole of the Furnace Brook Golf Club, September 4, 1949.

Most. The greatest number of holes-in-one in a career is 41 by Art Wall, Jr. (born November 23, 1923).

Douglas Porteous, 28, aced 4 holes over 36 consecutive holes—the 3rd and 6th on September 26 and the 5th on September 28 at Ruchill Golf Club, Glasgow, Scotland, and the 6th at the Clydebank and District Golf Club Course on September 30, 1974. Robert Taylor holed the 188-yard 16th hole at Hunstanton, Norfolk, England, on three successive days—May 31, June 1 and 2, 1974. Joe Lucius, 59, aced the 138-yard 15th at the Mohawk Golf Club, Tiffin, Ohio, for the eighth time on November 16, 1974.

Consecutive. There is no recorded instance of a golfer performing three consecutive holes-in-one, but there are at least 15 cases of "aces" being achieved in two consecutive holes of which the greatest was Norman L. Manley's unique "double albatross" on two par-4 holes (330-yard 7th and 290-yard 8th) on the Del Valle Country Club course, Saugus, California, on September 2, 1964.

The only woman ever to card consecutive aces is Sue Prell, on the 13th and 14th holes at Chatswood Golf Club, Sydney, Australia, on May 29, 1977.

The closest recorded instances of a golfer getting 3 consecutive holes-in-one were by the Rev. Harold Snider (b. July 4, 1900) who aced the 8th, 13th and 14th holes of the par-3 Ironwood course in Phoenix, Arizona, on June 9, 1976, and Dr. Joseph Boydstone on the 3rd, 4th and 9th at Bakersfield G.C., California on October 10, 1962.

Youngest and Oldest. The youngest golfer recorded to have shot a hole-in-one was Coby Orr (aged 5) of Littleton, Colorado, on the 103-yard fifth hole at the Riverside Golf Course, San Antonio, Texas, in 1975. The oldest golfers to have performed the feat are George Miller, 93, at the 11th (116 yards) at Anaheim Golf Club, California, on December 4, 1970, and Charles Youngman, 93, at the Tam O'Shanter Club, Toronto, in 1971.

Greyhound Racing

Earliest Meeting. In September, 1876, a greyhound meeting was staged at Hendon, North London, England, with a railed hare operated by a windlass. Modern greyhound racing originated with the perfecting of the mechanical hare by Owen P. Smith at Emeryville, California, in 1919.

Fastest Dog. The highest speed at which any greyhound has been timed is 41.72 m.p.h. (410 yards in 20.1 secs.) by *The Shoe* for a track record at Richmond, New South Wales, Australia, on April 25, 1968. It is estimated that he covered the last 100 yards in 4.5 seconds or at 45.45 m.p.h. The fastest *photo*-timing is 28.99 seconds over 500 meters or 38.58 m.p.h. by *Linacre* on July 30, 1977, at Brighton and Hove Stadium, Sussex, England. The fastest phototiming over hurdles is 29.71 seconds (37.64 mp.h.) by *Watchit Buster* on August 22, 1978, also at Brighton.

Winning Streak. An American greyhound, *Real Huntsman*, won a world record 28 consecutive victories in 1950–51.

Gymnastics

Earliest References. A primitive form of gymnastics was widely practiced in ancient Greece and Rome during the period of the ancient Olympic Games (776 B.C. to 393 A.D.), but Johann Friedrich Simon was the first teacher of modern gymnastics, at Basedow's School, Dessau, Germany, in 1776.

World Championships. The greatest number of individual titles won by a man in the World Championships is 10 by Boris Shakhlin (U.S.S.R.) between 1954 and 1964. He was also on three winning teams. The women's record is 10 individual wins and 5 team titles by Larissa Semyonovna Latynina (born December 27, 1934, retired 1966) of the U.S.S.R., between 1956 and 1964.

Japan has won the men's team title a record five times (1962–66–70–74–78) and the U.S.S.R. has won the women's title on six occasions (1954–58–62–70–74–78).

Olympic Games. Japan has won the most men's titles with 5 victories (1960, 1964, 1968, 1972, 1976). The U.S.S.R. has won 7 women's team titles (1952–1976).

The only man to win six individual gold medals is Boris Shakhlin (U.S.S.R.), with one in 1956, four (two shared) in 1960 and one in 1964. He was also a member of the winning Combined Exercises team in 1956.

GYMNASTIC PERFECTION: Nelli Kim (left) and Nadia Comaneci (right) were each awarded unprecedented perfect scores at the 1976 Olympic Games.

The most successful woman has been Vera Caslavska-Odlozil (Czechoslovakia), with seven individual gold medals, three in 1964 and four (one shared) in 1968. Larissa Latynina of the U.S.S.R. won six individual and three team gold medals, five silver, and four bronze for an all-time record total of 18 Olympic medals.

Nadia Comaneci (b. 1961, Rumania) became the first gymnast to be awarded a perfect score of 10.00 in the Olympic Games, in the 1976 Montreal Olympics. She ended the competition with a total of seven such marks (four on the uneven parallel bars, three on the balance beam). Nelli Kim (U.S.S.R., b. July 29, 1957) was also awarded two perfect scores during the same competition.

Youngest International Competitor. Anita Jokiel (Poland) was aged 11 years 2 days when she competed at Brighton, East Sussex, England, on December 6, 1977.

World Cup. In the first World Cup Competition in London in 1975, Ludmilla Tourisheva (now Mrs. Valery Borzov) (born October 7, 1952) of the U.S.S.R. won all five available gold medals.

Chinning the Bar. The record for 2-arm chins from a dead hang position is 120 by Lee Chin-yong (b. August 15, 1925) at the YMCA Gym Hall, Seoul, Korea, on March 1, 1979. William Aaron Vaught (b. 1959) did 20 one-arm chin-ups at Finch's Gymnasium, Houston, Texas, on January 3, 1976. It is believed that only one person in 100,000 can chin a bar one-handed.

Francis Lewis (born 1896) of Beatrice, Nebraska, in May, 1914, achieved 7 consecutive chins using only the middle finger of his left hand. His bodyweight was 158 lbs.

Rope Climbing. The U.S. Amateur Athletic Union records are tantamount to world records: 20 feet (hands alone) 2.8 secs., Don

Perry, at Champaign, Illinois, on April 3, 1954; 25 feet (hands alone), 4.7 secs., Garvin S. Smith at Los Angeles, on April 19, 1947.

Parallel Bar Dips. Peter Herbert performed a record 239 consecutive parallel bar dips on June 27, 1979, at the Tasker Milward School gymnasium, Dyfed, Wales. Jack La Lanne is reported to have done 1,000 in Oakland, California, in 1945.

Push-Ups. Henry C. Marshall (b. 1946) did 7,650 consecutive push-ups in 3 hours 55 minutes, on his way to 9,075 in 5 hours, in San Antonio, Texas, on September 5, 1977.

Troy Lapic (b. March 30, 1966), of Corsicana, Texas, did 1,834 push-ups, the most in 30 minutes, on August 19, 1978. Noel Barry Mason of Burton-on-Trent, England, did 267 fingertip push-ups in 1 minute 50 seconds on June 10, 1979. Robert Goldman of Arverne, New York, did 80 consecutive handstand push-ups in 43 seconds on August 31, 1978, at the Brickman Hotel in New York.

James L. Palmer (aged 19) performed 240 one-armed push-ups at Brock University, St. Catharines, Ontario, Canada, on September 22, 1978.

Sit-Ups. The greatest recorded number of consecutive sit-ups on a hard surface without feet pinned or knees bent is 26,000 in 11 hours 44 minutes by Angel Bustamonte (b. February 28, 1959) in Sacramento, California, on December 17, 1977. On November 20, 1975, Dr. David G. Jones recorded 123 sit-ups at Bolling A.F.B., Maryland, in 2 minutes under the same conditions.

Jumping Jacks. The greatest number of side-straddle hops is 20,088, performed in 4 hours 30 minutes (more than 1 per sec.) by Chris B. Luther (b. 1947) at Beechwood School, Fort Lewis, Washington on November 12, 1977.

Vertical Jump. The greatest height reached in a vertical jump (the difference between standing and jumping fingertip reach) is 42 inches by David Thompson (6 feet 4 inches) of North Carolina in 1972. Higher jumps reported by athletes Franklin Jacobs (U.S.) and Greg Joy (Canada) were probably made with an initial run. Olympic Pentathlon champion Mary E. Peters (G.B.) reportedly jumped 30 inches in California in 1972.

Greatest Tumbler. James Chelich (b. Fairview, Alberta, Canada, March 12, 1957) performed 8,450 forward rolls in 8.3 miles on September 21, 1974.

Ian Michael Miles (born July 6, 1960) of Corsham, Wiltshire, England, made a successful diving front somersault with a tuck over 33 men at Harrogate, North Yorkshire on July 27, 1977.

Rope Jumping. The longest recorded non-stop rope-jumping marathon was one of 6 hours 12 minutes (58,869 turns) by Katsumi Suzuki of Saitama, Japan, on January 1, 1979.

SKIPPING SCHOOL: These 62 youngsters from Air Academy High School in Colorado skipped a single long rope in January, 1979.

Other rope-jumping records made without a break:

Most turns in one jump	5	Katsumi Suzuki	Saitama, Japan May 29, 1975
Most turns in 1 minute	290	Brian D. Christensen	East Ridge, Tenn. May 30, 1978
Most turns in 10 seconds	108	A. Rayner	Wakefield, Eng. June 28, 1978
Most doubles (with cross)	386	K. A. Brooks	Queensland, Australia Dec. 23, 1978
Double turns	6,851	Katsumi Suzuki (Japan)	Tokyo July 4, 1976
Treble turns	381	Katsumi Suzuki (Japan)	Saitama May 29, 1975
Quadruple turns	51	Katsumi Suzuki (Japan)	Saitama May 29, 1975
Duration	1,264 miles	Tom Morris (Aust.)	Brisbane-Cairns 1963
Most children single rope (11 turns)	62	from Air Academy High School	Colorado Springs, Colorado Jan. 31, 1979

Largest Gymnasium. The world's largest gymnasium is Yale University's Payne Whitney Gymnasium at New Haven, Connecticut, completed in 1932 and valued at $18,000,000. The building, known as the "Cathedral of Muscle," has nine stories with wings of five stories each. It is equipped with 4 basketball courts, 3 rowing tanks, 28 squash courts, 12 handball courts, a roof jogging track and a 25-yard by 14-yard swimming pool on the first floor and a 55-yard-long pool on the third floor.

Largest Crowd. The largest recorded crowd was some 18,000 people who packed the Forum, Montreal, Canada for the finals of the women's individual apparatus competitions at the XXI Olympic Games on July 22, 1976.

Comparable audiences are reported at the Shanghai Stadium, People's Republic of China.

HANDBALL MASTER:
Jim Jacobs of New York
City has won a total of
12 U.S. National titles.

Handball (Court)

Origin. Handball is a game of ancient Celtic origin. In the early 19th century only a front wall was used, but later side and back walls were added. The court is now standardized 60 feet by 30 feet in Ireland, Ghana and Australia, and 40 feet by 20 feet in Canada, Mexico and the U.S. The game is played with both a hard and soft ball in Ireland, and a soft ball only elsewhere.

The earliest international contest was in New York City in 1887, between the champions of the U.S. and Ireland.

Championship. World championships were inaugurated in New York in October, 1964, with competitors from Australia, Canada, Ireland, Mexico and the U.S. The U.S. is the only nation to have won twice, with victories in 1964 and 1967 (shared).

Most Titles. The most successful player in the U.S.H.A. National Four-Wall Championships has been James Jacobs (U.S.), who won a record 6 singles titles (1955–56–57–60–64–65) and shared in 6 doubles titles (1960–62–63–65–67–68). Martin Decatur has also shared in 6 doubles titles (1962–63–65–67–68–75), 5 of these with Jacobs as his partner.

Handball (Field)

Origins. Field handball was first played *c.* 1895. The earliest international match was when Sweden beat Denmark on March 8, 1935. It was introduced into the Olympic Games at Berlin in 1936 as an 11-a-side outdoor game, but when reintroduced in 1972 it was an indoor game with 7-a-side, which has been the standard team size since 1952. Field handball is played somewhat like soccer but with hands instead of feet.

By 1977 there were some 70 countries affiliated with the International Handball Federation, a World Cup competition, and an estimated 10,000,000 participants.

Olympic Games. The U.S.S.R. won both men's and women's titles at the competition in Montreal in 1976.

World Titles. The most victories in the world championship (instituted 1938) competition are by Rumania with four men's and three women's titles from 1956 to 1974.

Harness Racing

Origins. Trotting races were held in Valkenburg, Netherlands, in 1554. In England the trotting gait (the simultaneous use of the diagonally opposite legs) was known in the 16th century. The sulky first appeared in harness racing in 1829. Pacers thrust out their fore and hind legs simultaneously on one side.

Highest Price. The highest price paid for a trotter is $3,200,000 for *Green Speed* by the Pine Hollow Stud of New York from Beverly Lloyds of Florida, in 1977. The highest for a pacer is $3,600,000 for *Nero* in March, 1976, and *Falcon Almahurst* in 1978.

Greatest Winnings. The greatest amount won by a trotting horse is $1,960,945 by *Bellino II* (France) to retirement in 1977. The record for a pacing horse is $1,360,887 by *Rambling Willie* (U.S.) to the end of the 1978 season.

Most Successful Driver

The most successful sulky driver in North America has been Herve Filion (Canada) (b. Quebec, February 1, 1940) who reached a record of 6,705 wins by the end of the 1978 season, after a record 637 victories and winnings of $3,474,315 in the 1974 season. Filion won the North American championship for the tenth time in 1978.

William Haughton had won a record $27,100,000 in his career to the end of 1978.

RECORDS AGAINST TIME
TROTTING

World (mile track)	1:54.8	Nevele Pride (U.S.), Indianapolis	Aug. 31, 1969

PACING

World (mile track)	1:52.0	Steady Star (Canada), Lexington, Ky.	Oct. 1, 1971

RECORDS SET IN RACES

Trotting	1:55.0	Speedy Somolli (U.S.) at Du Quoin, Ill.	Sept. 2, 1978
	1:55.0	Florida Pro (U.S.) at Du Quoin, Ill.	Sept. 2, 1978
Pacing	1:53.2	Warm Breeze (U.S.) at Sacramento, California	June 26, 1977

Hockey

Origins. There is pictorial evidence of a hockey-like game being played on ice in the Netherlands in the early 16th century. The game probably was first played in 1855 at Kingston, Ontario, Canada, but Halifax also lays claim to priority.

The International Ice Hockey Federation was founded in 1908. The National Hockey League was inaugurated in 1917. The World Hockey Association was formed in 1971.

Olympic Games. Canada has won the Olympic title six times (1920–24–28–32–48–52) and the world title 19 times, the last being at Geneva in 1961. The longest Olympic career is that of Richard Torriani (Switzerland) from 1928 to 1948. The most gold medals won by any player is three; this was achieved by four U.S.S.R. players in the 1964–68–72 Games—Vitaliy Davidov, Aleksandr Ragulin, Anatoliy Firssov and Viktor Kuzkin.

Stanley Cup. This cup, presented by the Governor-General Lord Stanley (original cost $48.67), became emblematic of world professional team supremacy 33 years after the first contest at Montreal in 1893. It has been won most often by the Montreal Canadiens, with 22 wins in 1916, 1924, 1930, 1931, 1944, 1946, 1953, 1956, 1957, 1958, 1959, 1960, 1965, 1966, 1968, 1969, 1971, 1973, 1976, 1977, 1978 and 1979. Henri Richard played in his eleventh finals in 1973.

Longest Match. The longest match was 2 hours 56 minutes 30 seconds when the Detroit Red Wings eventually beat the Montreal Maroons 1–0 in the 17th minute of the sixth period of overtime at the Forum, Montreal, at 2:25 a.m. on March 25, 1936.

Longest Career. Gordie Howe skated a record 25 years for the Detroit Red Wings from 1946–47 through the 1970–71 season, playing in a record total of 1,687 N.H.L. games. During that time he also set records for most career goals, assists, and scoring points, and collected 500 stitches in his face. After leaving the Red Wings, he has played for 5 more seasons with the Houston Aeros and the New England Whalers of the World Hockey Association.

Most Consecutive Games. Garry Unger, playing for Toronto, Detroit and St. Louis, has skated in 883 consecutive games without a miss—11 complete seasons from 1968–69 through the end of 1978–79. The most consecutive complete games by a goaltender is 502, set by Glenn Hall (Detroit, Chicago), beginning in 1955 and ending when he suffered a back injury in a game against Boston on November 7, 1962.

Longest Season. The only man ever to play 82 games in a 78-game season is Ross Lonsberry. He began the 1971–72 season with the Los Angeles Kings where he played 50 games. Then, in January, he was traded to the Philadelphia Flyers (who had played only 46 games at the time) where he finished out the season (32 more games).

Dennis Owchar (with Pittsburgh and Colorado) and Jerry Butler (with St. Louis and Toronto) played 82 games in an 80-game season in 1977–78.

MOST GOALS: Reggie Leach of the Philadelphia Flyers scored 80 goals in the 1975-76 season (including playoffs).

Most Wins and Losses

The Montreal Canadiens had the winningest season in N.H.L. history in 1976–77. They ended the regular 80-game season with a record 132 point' earned, with an all-time record of 60 victories and 12 ties against only 8 losses.

The Washington Capitols set the record for seasonal losses with 67 in their maiden season in the league (1974–75). They won only 8 games.

Longest Winning Streak. In the 1929–30 season, the Boston Bruins won 14 straight games. The longest a team has ever gone without a defeat is 28 games, set by Montreal from December 18, 1977, to February 20, 1978 (23 wins, 5 ties).

Longest Losing Streak. The Washington Capitols went from February 18 to March 26, 1975, without gaining a point—a total of 17 straight defeats. The longest time a team has gone without a win was when the Kansas City Scouts played 27 games before scoring a victory. Starting February 12, 1976, they lost 21 games and tied 6 games before ending the drought on April 4, 1976.

Team Scoring

Most Goals. The greatest number of goals recorded in a World Championship match has been 47–0 when Canada beat Denmark on February 12, 1949.

The Boston Bruins set all-time records for goal production in the 1970–71 season with a total of 399. Added to a record 697 assists they tallied a record total of 1,096 points. One line alone (Esposito, Hodge, Cashman) accounted for 336 points—a record itself.

Guy Lafleur, Steve Shutt, and Jacques Lemaire of the Montreal Canadiens produced a total of 150 goals in the 1976–77 season—a record for a single line.

The N.H.L. record for both teams is 21 goals, scored when the Montreal Canadiens beat the Toronto St. Patricks at Montreal 14–7 on January 10, 1920. The most goals ever scored by one team in a single game was set by the Canadiens, when they defeated the Quebec Bulldogs on March 3, 1920 by a score of 16–3.

The Detroit Red Wings scored 15 consecutive goals without an answering tally when they defeated the New York Rangers 15–0 on January 23, 1944.

Fastest Scoring. Toronto scored 8 goals against the New York Americans in 4 minutes 52 seconds on March 19, 1938.

The fastest goals that have ever been scored from the opening whistle both came at 6 seconds of the first period: by Henry Boucha of the Detroit Red Wings on January 28, 1973, against Montreal; and by Jean Pronovost of the Pittsburgh Penguins on March 25, 1976, against St. Louis. Claude Provost of the Canadiens scored a goal against Boston after 4 seconds of the opening of the second period on November 9, 1957.

Kim D. Miles scored a goal after only 3 seconds of play for the University of Guelph, playing the University of Western Ontario on February 11, 1975.

The fastest scoring record is held by Bill Mosienko (Chicago) who scored 3 goals in 21 seconds against the New York Rangers on March 23, 1952.

Gus Bodnar (Toronto Maple Leafs) scored a goal against the New York Rangers at 15 seconds of the first period of *his first N.H.L. game* on October 30, 1943. Later in his career, while with Chicago, Bodnar again entered the record book when he assisted on all 3 of Bill Mosienko's quick goals.

Individual Scoring

Most Goals and Points. The career record in the N.H.L. for goals is 786 by Gordie Howe of the Detroit Red Wings. Howe scored 1,809 points in his N.H.L. career, with 1,023 assists.

Reggie Leach (Philadelphia Flyers) scored a total of 80 goals in the 1975–76 season including the playoffs.

Phil Esposito (Boston Bruins) scored 76 goals on a record 550 shots in the 1970–71 regular season. Esposito also holds the record for most points in a season at 152 (76 goals, 76 assists), set in the same season.

Phil Esposito has also scored 100 or more points in 6 different seasons, and 50 or more goals in 5 consecutive years. Bobby Orr had 6 *consecutive* 100-or-more-point seasons from 1969–70 to 1974–75. Bobby Hull (Chicago) had five 50-or-more-goal years when he left the N.H.L.

Anders Hedberg (born in Sweden, February 25, 1951) set a W.H.A. mark, scoring 83 goals for the Winnipeg Jets in 1976–77.

Marc Tardif (b. June 12, 1949) set a W.H.A. record for most points in a season with 169 (71 goals and 98 assists) for the Quebec Nordiques in 1977–78.

The most goals ever scored in one game is 7 by Joe Malone of the Quebec Bulldogs against the Toronto St. Patricks on January 31, 1920. Four different men have scored 4 goals in one period—Harvey Jackson (Toronto), Max Bentley (Chicago), Clint Smith (Chicago), and Red Berenson (St. Louis).

The most points scored in one N.H.L. game is 10, a record set by Darryl Sittler of the Toronto Maple Leafs, on February 7, 1976, against the Boston Bruins. He had 6 goals and 4 assists.

Jim Harrison, playing for Alberta, set a W.H.A. record for points with 10 (3 goals, 7 assists) against Toronto on January 30, 1973.

In 1921–22, Harry (Punch) Broadbent of the Ottawa Senators scored 25 goals in 16 consecutive games to set an all-time "consecutive game goal-scoring streak" record.

Most Assists. Bobby Orr of Boston assisted on 102 goals in the 1970–71 season for a record. His average of 1.31 assists per game is also a league record.

The most assists recorded in one game is 7 by Billy Taylor of Detroit on March 16, 1947 against Chicago. Detroit won 10–6.

Most 3-Goal Games. In his 15-year N.H.L. career, Bobby Hull of Chicago scored 3 or more goals in 28 games. Four of these were 4-goal efforts. The term "hat-trick" properly applies when 3 goals are scored consecutively by one player in a game without interruption by either an answering score by the other team or a goal by any other player on his own team. In general usage, a "hat-trick" is any 3-goal effort by a player in one game.

Goaltending

The longest any goalie has gone without a defeat is 33 games, a record set by Gerry Cheevers of Boston in 1971–72. The longest a goalie has ever kept successive opponents scoreless is 461 minutes 29 seconds by Alex Connell of the Ottawa Senators in 1927–28. He registered 6 consecutive shutouts in this time.

The most shutouts ever recorded in one season is 22 by George Hainsworth of Montreal in 1928–29 (this is also a team record). This feat is even more remarkable considering that the season was only 44 games long at that time, compared to the 80-game season currently used.

FAST-MOVING SCORER: In addition to his career record 28 "hat-tricks," Bobby Hull has also been hailed as the fastest man on ice at 29.7 m.p.h. His slap shot has been clocked at 118.3 m.p.h.

Terry Sawchuk registered a record 103 career shutouts in his 20 seasons in the N.H.L. He played for Detroit, Boston, Toronto, Los Angeles, and the New York Rangers during that time. He also appeared in a record 971 games.

Most Penalties

The most any team has been penalized in one season is the 1,980 minutes assessed against the Philadelphia Flyers in 1975–76.

The Los Angeles Kings and the Philadelphia Flyers set N.H.L. records for penalties (54) and penalty minutes (380) in a game on March 11, 1979. The Flyers were assessed 194 minutes in penalty time, a record for one team in a single game. Ten players, five from each team, were ejected from the game, including Randy Holt of the Kings, who accumulated 57 minutes in penalties, also a league record.

Bryan Watson (Montreal, Detroit, California, Pittsburgh, St. Louis and Washington) amassed a record total of 2,212 penalty minutes in 858 games over 16 seasons.

Dave Schultz of Philadelphia was called for a record 472 minutes in the 1974–75 season. Schultz averaged a record 346 minutes per year in penalties from 1972–73 through 1975–76 (1,386 minutes total).

Jim Dorey of the Toronto Maple Leafs set an all-time record in Toronto on October 16, 1968, in a game against the Pittsburgh Penguins. He was whistled down for a total of 9 penalties in the game, 7 of which came in the second period (also a record). The 4 minor penalties, 2 major penalties, 2 10-minute misconducts, and 1 game misconduct added up to a total of 48 minutes for one game.

Penalty Shots. Armand Mondou of the Montreal Canadiens was the first player in the N.H.L. to attempt a penalty shot on November 10, 1934. He did not score. Since then, about 40 per cent of those awarded have resulted in goals. The most penalty shots called in a single season was 29 in 1934–35.

Fastest Player. The highest speed measured for any player is 29.7 m.p.h. for Bobby Hull (Chicago Black Hawks) (b. January 3, 1939). The highest puck speed is also attributed to Hull, whose left-handed slap shot has been measured at 118.3 m.p.h.

Horse Racing

Origins. Horsemanship was an important part of the Hittite culture of Anatolia, Turkey, dating from about 1400 B.C. The 33rd ancient Olympic Games of 648 B.C. featured horse racing. The earliest horse race recorded in England was one held in *c.* 210 A.D. at Netherby, Yorkshire, among Arabians brought to Britain by Lucius Septimius Severus (146–211 A.D.), Emperor of Rome. The oldest race still being run annually is the Lanark Silver Bell, instituted in Scotland by William the Lion (1143–1214). Organized horse racing began in New York State at least as early as March, 1668.

The original Charleston Jockey Club, Virginia, was the first in the world, organized in 1734. Racing colors (silks) became compulsory in 1889.

Racecourses. The world's largest racecourse is the Newmarket course in England (founded 1636), on which the Beacon Course, the longest of the 19 courses, is 4 miles 397 yards long and the Rowley Mile is 167 feet wide. The border between Suffolk and Cambridgeshire runs through the Newmarket course. The world's largest racecourse grandstand was opened in 1968 at Belmont Park, Long Island, N.Y., at a cost of $30,700,000. It is 110 feet tall, 440 yards long and contains 908 mutuel windows. The greatest seating capacity at any racetrack is 40,000 at the Atlantic City Audit, New Jersey. The world's smallest is the Lebong racecourse, Darjeeling, West Bengal, India (altitude 7,000 feet), where the complete lap is 481 yards. It was laid out *c.* 1885 and used as a parade ground.

Longest Race

The longest recorded horse race was one of 1,200 miles in Portugal, won by *Emir*, a horse bred from Egyptian-bred Blunt Arab stock. The holder of the world's record for long distance racing and speed is *Champion Crabbet*, who covered 300 miles in 52 hours 33 minutes, carrying 245 lbs., in 1920.

In 1831, Squire George Osbaldeston (1787–1866), M.P. of East Retford, England, covered 200 miles in 8 hours 42 minutes at Newmarket, using 50 mounts, so averaging 22.99 m.p.h.

Most Entrants. The most horses entered in a single race was 66, in the Grand National Steeplechase of March 22, 1929, held at Aintree, England. The record for flat racing is 58 in the Lincolnshire Handicap in England, on March 13, 1948.

Victories. The horse with the best recorded win-loss record was *Kincsem*, a Hungarian mare foaled in 1874, who was unbeaten in 54 races (1876–79), including the English Goodwood Cup of 1878.

Camarero, owned by Don José Coll Vidal of Puerto Rico, foaled in 1951, had a winning streak of 56 races, 1953–55, and 73 wins in 77 starts altogether.

Greatest Winnings. The greatest amount ever won by a horse is $2,044,218 by *Affirmed* from 1977 to June, 1979.

The most won by a mare is $1,535,443 by *Dahlia*, from 1972 to 1976.

The most won in a year is $901,541 by *Affirmed* in 1978.

Triple Crown. Eleven horses have won all three races in one season which constitute the American Triple Crown (Kentucky Derby, Preakness Stakes and the Belmont Stakes). This feat was first achieved by *Sir Barton* in 1919, and most recently by *Seattle Slew* in 1977 and *Affirmed* in 1978.

The only Triple Crown winner to sire another winner was *Gallant Fox*, the 1930 winner, who sired *Omaha*, who won in 1935.

Tallest. The tallest horse ever to race is *Fort d'Or*, owned by Lady Elizabeth (Eliza) Nugent (*née* Guinness) of Berkshire, England, which stands 18.2 hands. He was foaled in April, 1963.

Most Valuable Horse

The most expensive horse ever is the 1978 Triple Crown winner *Affirmed* (foaled 1975). It was announced in November, 1978, that he would be syndicated for $14,400,000, in 36 shares of $400,000 each.

The highest price for a yearling is $1,500,000 for a colt by *Secretariat* out of *Charming Alibi*, subsequently named *Canadian Bound*, bought at Keeneland, Kentucky, on July 20, 1976.

Horses

Speed Records

Distance	Time m.p.h.		Name	Course	Date
¼ mile	20.8s.	43.26	*Big Racket* (Mex.)	Mexico City, Mex.	Feb. 5, 1945
½ mile	44.4s.	40.54	*Sonido* (Ven.)	‡Caracas, Ven.	June 28, 1970
⅝ mile	53.6s.	41.98†	*Indigenous* (G.B.)	‡*Epsom, England	June 2, 1960
	53.89s.	41.75††	*Raffingora* (G.B.)	‡*Epsom, England	June 5, 1970
	55.4s.	40.61	*Zip Pocket* (U.S.)	Phoenix, Arizona	Apr. 22, 1967
¾ mile	1m. 06.2s.	40.78	*Broken Tendril* (G.B.)	*Brighton, England	Aug. 6, 1929
	1m. 07.2s.	40.18	*Grey Papa* (U.S.)	Longacres, Wash.	Sept. 4, 1972
Mile	1m. 31.8s.	39.21	*Soueida* (G.B.)	*Brighton, England	Sept. 19, 1963
	1m. 31.8s.	39.21	*Loose Cover* (G.B.)	*Brighton, England	June 9, 1966
	1m. 32.2s.	39.04	*Dr. Fager* (U.S.)	Arlington, Ill.	Aug. 24, 1968
1¼ miles	1m. 57.4s.	38.33	*Double Discount*	Arcadia, Calif.	Oct. 9, 1977
1½ miles	2m. 23.0s.	37.76	*Fiddle Isle* (U.S.)	Arcadia, Calif.	Mar. 21, 1970
2 miles**	3m. 15.0s.	36.93	*Polazel* (G.B.)	Salisbury, England	July 8, 1924
2½ miles	4m. 14.6s.	35.35	*Miss Grillo* (U.S.)	Pimlico, Md.	Nov. 12, 1948
3 miles	5m. 15.0s.	34.29	*Farragut* (Mex.)	Aguascalientes, Mex.	Mar. 9, 1941

* Course downhill for ¼ of a mile.

** A more reliable modern record is 3m. 16.75 secs. by *Il Tempo* (N.Z.) at Trentham, Wellington, New Zealand, on January 17, 1970.

†Hand-timed.　††Electrically-timed.　‡Straight courses.

Dead Heats

There is no recorded case in turf history of a quintuple dead heat. The nearest approach was in the Astley Stakes, at Lewes, England,

TALLEST RACEHORSE: "Fort d'Or" stands 18.2 hands. He is owned by Lady Elizabeth Nugent of England (who was born in Ireland).

on August 6, 1880, when *Mazurka, Wandering Nun* and *Scobell* triple dead-heated for first place, just ahead of *Cumberland* and *Thora*, who dead-heated for fourth place. Each of the five jockeys thought he had won. The only three known examples of a quadruple dead heat were between *Honest Harry, Miss Decoy,* a filly by *Beningbrough* (later named *Young Daffodil*) and *Peteria* at Bogside, England, on June 7, 1808; between *Defaulter, The Squire of Malton, Reindeer* and *Pulcherrima* in the Omnibus Stakes at The Hoo, England, on April 26, 1851; and between *Overreach, Lady Go-Lightly, Gamester* and *The Unexpected* at the Houghton Meeting at Newmarket, England, on October 22, 1855.

Since the introduction of the photo-finish, the highest number of horses in a dead heat has been three, on several occasions.

Funeral Wreath. The largest floral piece honoring a horse was the tribute to the racehorse *Ruffian*, an 8½-foot-high, 8-foot-wide horseshoe made of 1,362 white carnations. It was made by Jay W. Becker Florist Inc. of Floral Park, New York, and decorated the grave of the horse in the infield at Belmont Race Track where she was buried in July, 1975.

Jockeys

The most successful jockey of all time is Willie Shoemaker (b. weighing 2½ lbs. on August 19, 1931) now weighing 98 lbs. and standing 4 feet 11½ inches, who beat Johnny Longden's lifetime record of 6,032 winners on September 7, 1970. From March, 1949, to the end of 1978 he rode 7,589 winners from some 32,184 mounts. His winnings have aggregated some $70,020,545.

Chris McCarron (U.S.), 19, won a total of 546 races in 1974.

The greatest amount ever won by any jockey in a year is $6,188,353 by Darrel McHargue (b. 1954) in the U.S. in 1978.

The oldest jockey was Levi Barlingame (U.S.), who rode his last race at Stafford, Kansas, in 1932, aged 80. The youngest jockey was Frank Wootton (English Champion jockey 1909–12), who rode his first winner in South Africa aged 9 years 10 months. The lightest recorded jockey was Kitchener (died 1872), who won the Chester Cup in England on *Red Deer* in 1844 at 49 lbs. He was said to have weighed only 40 lbs. in 1840.

Victor Morley Lawson won his first race at Warwick, England, on *Ocean King*, October 16, 1973, aged 67.

The most winners ridden on one card is 8 by Hubert S. Jones, 17, out of 13 mounts at Caliente, California, on June 11, 1944 (of which 5 were photo-finishes), and by Oscar Barattuci at Rosario City, Argentina, on December 15, 1957.

The longest winning streak is 12 races by Sir Gordon Richards (G.B.) who won the last race at Nottingham, England, on October 3, 1933, six out of six at Chepstow on October 4, and the first five races the next day at Chepstow.

Trainers. The greatest number of wins by a trainer in one year is 494 by Jack Van Berg in 1976. The greatest amount won in a year is $3,314,564 by Lazaro S. Barrera in 1978.

Owners. The most winners by an owner in one year is 494 by Dan R. Lasater (U.S.) in 1974, when he also won a record $3,022,960 in prize money.

Shortest Odds

The shortest odds ever quoted for any racehorse are 1 to 10,000 for *Dragon Blood*, ridden by Lester Piggott (G.B.) in the Premio Naviglio in Milan, Italy, on June 1, 1967. He won. Odds of 1 to 100 were quoted for the American horse *Man o' War* (foaled March 29, 1917, died November 1, 1947) on three separate occasions in 1920. In 21 starts in 1919–20 he had 20 wins and one second (on August 13, 1919, in the Sanford Memorial Stakes).

Pari-Mutuel Record

The U.S. pari-mutuel record pay-off is $941.75 to $1 on *Wishing Ring* at Latonia track, Kentucky, in 1912.

Largest Prizes. The richest race ever held is the All-American Futurity, a race for quarter-horses over 440 yards at Ruidoso Downs, New Mexico. The prizes in 1978 totaled $1,280,000.

The richest first prize was $437,500, won by *Moon Lark*, the winner of the 1978 All-American Futurity.

Horseshoe Pitching

Origin. This sport was derived by military farriers and is of great antiquity. The first formal World Championships were staged at Bronson, Kansas, in 1909.

Most Titles. The record for men's titles is 10 by Ted Allen (Boulder, Colorado) in 1933–34–35–40–46–53–55–56–57–59. The women's record is 9 titles by Vicki Chapelle Winston (LaMonte, Missouri) in 1956–58–59–61–63–66–67–69–75.

Highest Percentage. The record for percentage of ringers in one game is 95 by Ruth Hangen (Getzville, N.Y.) in 1973. The record for consecutive ringers is 72 by Ted Allen in 1951 for men, and 42 by Ruth Hangen in 1974 for women.

Most Ringers. The most ringers in a single game is 175 by Glen Henton of Maquoketa, Iowa, in 1965.

Marathon. The longest continuous session is 130 hours by a team of 6 playing in shifts in Tucson, Arizona, March 12–17, 1979. For a 4-man contest, two teams pitching continuously and without substitutions, the record is 76½ hours by Gary Alexander, Ralph Lewis, Steven Padgett and Stephen Moss, in Lakewood, Colorado, on July 1–4, 1979.

Ice Skating

Origins. The earliest reference to ice skating is in Scandinavian literature of the 2nd century, although its origins are believed, on archeological evidence, to be 10 centuries earlier still. The earliest English account of 1180 refers to skates made of bone. The earliest known illustration is a Dutch woodcut of 1498. The earliest skating club was the Edinburgh Skating Club, Scotland, formed in 1742. The earliest artificial ice rink in the world was opened at the Baker Street Bazaar, Portman Square, London, on December 7, 1842. The International Skating Union was founded in 1892.

Longest Race. The longest race regularly held is the "Elfstedentocht" ("Tour of the Eleven Towns") in the Netherlands. It covers 200 kilometers (124 miles 483 yards) and the fastest time is 7 hours 35 minutes by Jeen van den Berg (born January 8, 1928) on February 3, 1954.

Largest Rink. The world's largest indoor artificial ice rink is in the Moscow Olympic indoor arena which has an ice area of 86,800 square feet. The largest artificial outdoor rink is the quintuple complex of the Fujikyu Highland Promenade Rink, Japan (opened 1967), with an area of 285,244 square feet.

Figure Skating

World. The greatest number of individual world men's figure skating titles (instituted 1896) is ten by Ulrich Salchow (1877–1949), of Sweden, in 1901–05 and 1907–11. The women's record (instituted 1906) is also ten individual titles, by Sonja Henie (April 8, 1912–October 12, 1969), of Norway, between 1927 and 1936. Irina Rodnina (born September 12, 1949), of the U.S.S.R., has won ten pairs titles (instituted 1908)—four with Aleksiy Ulanov (1969–72) and six with her husband Aleksandr Zaitsev (1973–77). The most ice dance titles (instituted 1950) won is six by Aleksandr Gorshkov (born December 8, 1946) and Ludmilla Pakhomova (born December 31, 1946), both of the U.S.S.R., in 1970–71–72–73–74 and 1976.

Olympic. The most Olympic gold medals won by a figure skater is three by Gillis Grafstrom (1893–1938), of Sweden, in 1920, 1924, and 1928 (also silver medal in 1932); and by Sonja Henie (see above) in 1928, 1932 and 1936.

Most Difficult Jump. The first ever triple Axel performed in competition was by Vern Taylor (b. 1958) (Canada) in the World Championships at Ottawa on March 10, 1978.

A quadruple twist lift has been performed by only one pair, Sergei Shakrai (b. 1957) and Marina Tcherkasova (b. 1962) of the U.S.S.R., in an international championship at Helsinki, Finland, on January 26, 1977. They were also the first skaters to accomplish simultaneous triple jumps at that level, at Strasbourg, France, on February 1, 1978.

Highest Marks. The highest number of maximum six marks awarded for one performance in an international championship was 11 to Aleksandr Zaitsev and Irina Rodnina (U.S.S.R.) in the European pairs competition in Zagreb, Yugoslavia, in 1974.

Donald Jackson (Canada) was awarded 7 "sixes" (the most by a soloist) in the world men's championship at Prague, Czechoslovakia, in 1962.

Most Titles Speed Skating

World. The greatest number of world overall titles (instituted 1893) won by any skater is five by Oscar Mathisen (Norway) in 1908–09 and 1912–14, and Clas Thunberg (born April 5, 1893) of Finland, in 1923, 1925, 1928–29 and 1931. The most titles won by a woman is four by Mrs. Inga Voronina, *née* Artomonova (1936–66) of Moscow, U.S.S.R., in 1957, 1958, 1962 and 1965, and Mrs. Atje Keulen-Deelstra of the Netherlands (b. 1938) in 1970 and 1972–73–74.

DANCING FEAT:
Ludmilla Pakhomova and
Aleksandr Gorshkov have
won six ice dance
titles since 1970.

MOST DIFFICULT JUMPS: Sergei Shakrai and Marina Tcherkasova (left) are the only pair ever to perform the quadruple twist lift. Vern Taylor (right) performed the first triple Axel in competition in March 1978.

Olympic. The most Olympic gold medals won in speed skating is six by Lidia Skoblikova (born March 8, 1939), of Chelyabinsk, U.S.S.R., in 1960 (2) and 1964 (4). The male record is held by Clas Thunberg (see above) with 5 gold (including 1 tied gold) and also 1 silver and 1 tied bronze in 1924–28.

WORLD SPEED SKATING RECORDS
(Ratified by the I.S.U. as of June 1, 1979.)

Distance	min. sec.	Name and Nationality	Place	Date
Men				
500 meters	37.00*	Evgeni Kulikov (U.S.S.R.)	Medeo, U.S.S.R.	Mar. 29, 1975
1,000 meters	1:14.99	Eric Heiden (U.S.)	Salavan, Norway	Mar. 12, 1978
1,500 meters	1:55.18	Jan Egil Storholt (Norway)	Medeo, U.S.S.R.	Mar. 20, 1977
3,000 meters	4:04.06	Dmitri Ogloblin (U.S.S.R.)	Medeo, U.S.S.R.	Mar. 29, 1979
5,000 meters	6:56.90	Kay Stenshjemmel (Norway)	Medeo, U.S.S.R.	Mar. 19, 1977
10,000 meters	14:34.33	Viktor Leskine (U.S.S.R.)	Medeo, U.S.S.R.	Apr. 3, 1977
Women				
500 meters	40.68	Sheila Young (U.S.)	Inzell, W. Ger.	Mar. 13, 1976
1,000 meters	1:23.46	Tatiana Averina (U.S.S.R.)	Medeo, U.S.S.R.	Mar. 29, 1975
1,500 meters	2:07.18	Khalida Vorobyeva (U.S.S.R.)	Medeo, U.S.S.R.	Apr. 10, 1978
3,000 meters	4:31.00	Galina Stepanskaya (U.S.S.R.)	Medeo, U.S.S.R.	Mar. 23, 1976

*This represents an average speed of 30.22 m.p.h.

Longest Marathon. The longest recorded skating marathon is one of 109 hours 5 minutes by Austin McKinley of Christchurch, New Zealand, June 21–25, 1977.

Ice and Sand Yachting

Origin. The sport originated in the Low Countries (earliest patent is dated 1600) and along the Baltic coast. The earliest authentic record is Dutch, dating from 1768. The largest ice yacht built was *Icicle*, built for Commodore John E. Roosevelt for racing on the Hudson River, New York, *c.* 1870. It was 68 feet 11 inches long and carried 1,070 square feet of canvas.

Highest Speed. The highest speed officially recorded is 143 m.p.h. by John D. Buckstaff in a Class A stern-steerer on Lake Winnebago, Wisconsin, in 1938. Such a speed is possible in a wind of 72 m.p.h.

Sand Yachting. Land or sand yachts of Dutch construction were first reported on beaches (now in Belgium) in 1595. The earliest international championship was staged in 1914.

The fastest recorded speed for a sand yacht is 57.69 m.p.h. (measured mile in 62.4 secs.) by *Coronation Year Mk. II*, owned by R. Millett Denning and crewed by J. Halliday, Bob Harding, J. Glassbrook and Cliff Martindale at Lytham St. Anne's, England, in 1956.

A speed of 77.47 m.p.h. was attained by Jan Paul Lowe (born April 15, 1936) (U.S.) in *Sunkist*, at Ivanpaugh Dry Lake, California, on March 25, 1975.

FASTEST BALL GAME: The fastest-moving ball in any game is the pelota, which has been clocked at 180 m.p.h.

Jai-Alai *(Pelota)*

The game, which originated in Italy as *longue paume* and was introduced into France in the 13th century, is said to be the fastest of all ball games. Gloves were introduced *c.* 1840 and the *chistera* (basket-like glove) was invented *c.* 1860 by Jean "Gantchiki" Dithurbide of Ste. Pée. The long *grand chistera* was invented by Melchior Curuchague of Buenos Aires, Argentina, in 1888.

Various games are played in a *fronton* (enclosed stadium) the most popular being *main nue, remonte, rebot, pala, grand chistera* and *cesta punta*. The sport is governed by the Federacion Internacional de Pelota Vasca in Madrid, Spain.

The world's largest *fronton* is the World Jai-Alai in Miami, Florida, which had a record attendance of 15,052 on December 27, 1975.

The fastest throw of a (*pelota*) ball was made by José Ramon Areitio at an electronically measured speed of 180 m.p.h., recorded at the Palm Beach Jai-Alai, Florida, on February 2, 1978.

Longest Domination. The longest domination as the world's No. 1 player was enjoyed by Chiquito de Cambo (*né* Joseph Apesteguy) (France) (b. May 10, 1881–d. 1955), from the beginning of the century until succeeded in 1938 by Jean Urruty (France) (b. October 19, 1913).

Judo

Origin. Judo is a modern combat sport which developed out of an amalgam of several old (pre-Christian era) Japanese fighting arts, the most popular of which was *ju-jitsu* (*jiu-jitsu*), which is thought to be of pre-Christian Chinese origin. Judo has developed greatly since 1882, when it was first devised by Dr. Jigoro Kano (1860–1938). World Championships were inaugurated in Tokyo on May 5, 1956.

Highest Grades. The efficiency grades in Judo are divided into pupil (*kyu*) and master (*dan*) grades. The highest awarded is the extremely rare red belt *Judan* (10th *dan*), given only to seven men. The Judo protocol provides for a *Juichidan* (11th *dan*), who also would wear a red belt, and even a *Junidan* (12th *dan*), who would wear a white belt twice as wide as an ordinary belt, and even a *Shihan* (the highest of all), but these have never been bestowed.

Marathon. The longest recorded Judo marathon with continuous play by two of six Judoka in 5-minute stints is 200 hours by the Dufftown and District Judo Club, Banffshire, Scotland on July 9–17, 1977.

Champion. The only man to have won 4 world titles is Wilhelm Ruska of the Netherlands, who won the 1967 and the 1971 heavyweight and the 1972 Olympic heavyweight and Open titles.

Karate

Origins. Originally *karate* (empty hand) is known to have been developed by the unarmed populace as a method of attack on, and defense against, armed Japanese aggressors in Okinawa, Ryukyu Islands, based on techniques devised from the 6th century Chinese art of Shaolin boxing (Kempo). Transmitted to Japan in the 1920's by Funakoshi Gichin, this method of combat was refined and organized into a sport with competitive rules.

The five major schools of *karate* in Japan are *Shotokan, Wado-ryu, Goju-ryu, Shito-ryu,* and *Kyokushinkai,* each of which places different emphasis on speed, power, etc. Other styles include *Sankukai, Shotokai* and *Shukokai*. The military form of *Tae-kwan-do* with 9 *dans* is a Korean equivalent of *karate*. *Kung fu* is believed to have originated in Nepal or Tibet but was adopted within Chinese temples *via* India, and has in recent years been widely popularized through various martial arts films.

Wu shu is a comprehensive term embracing all Chinese martial arts.

Most Titles. The only winner of 3 All-Japanese titles has been Takeshi Oishi, who won in 1969–70–71.

The leading exponents among karatekas are a number of 10th *dans* in Japan.

Lacrosse

Origin. The game is of American Indian origin, derived from the inter-tribal game *baggataway*, and was played by Iroquois Indians in lower Ontario, Canada, and upper New York State, before 1492. The French named it after their game of *Chouler à la crosse*, known in 1381. The game was included in the Olympic Games of 1908, and featured as an exhibition sport in the 1928 and 1948 Games.

World Championship. The United States won the first two World Championships, in 1967 and 1974. Canada won the third in 1978, beating the U.S. 17–16 in overtime—this was the first drawn international match.

Highest Score. The highest score in any international match was U.S. over Canada, 28–4, at Stockport, England, on July 3, 1978.

Modern Pentathlon

The Modern Pentathlon (Riding, Fencing, Shooting, Swimming and Running) was inaugurated into the Olympic Games at Stockholm in 1912.

Point scores in riding, fencing, cross country and hence overall scores have no comparative value between one competition and another. In shooting and swimming (300 meters), where measurements are absolute, the point scores are of record significance. The records in these areas are listed below:

Points				
Shooting	1,132 Danieli Massala (Italy)	Jönkoping, Sweden	Aug. 21, 1978
Swimming	1,324 Robert Nieman (U.S.)	Montreal, Canada	July 21, 1976

Most World Titles. The record number of world titles won is 6 by András Balczó (Hungary) in 1963, 1965, 1966, 1967 and 1969, and the Olympic title in 1972, which also rates as a world title.

Olympic Titles. The greatest number of Olympic gold medals won is three by Balczó, a member of Hungary's winning team in 1960 and 1968, and the 1972 individual champion. Lars Hall (Sweden) uniquely has won two individual championships (1952 and 1956). Balczó has won a record number of five medals (3 gold and 2 silver).

Motorcycling

Earliest Races. The first motocycle race was held on an oval track at Sheen House, Richmond, Surrey, England, on November 29, 1897, won by Charles Jarrott (1877–1944) on a Fournier. The oldest motorcycle races in the world are the Auto-Cycle Union Tourist Trophy (T.T.) series, first held on the 15.81-mile "Peel" ("St. John's") course on the Isle of Man on May 28, 1907, and still run on the island, on the "Mountain" circuit (37.73 miles).

Longest Circuits. The 37.73-mile "Mountain" circuit, over which the two main T.T. races have been run since 1911, has 264 curves and corners and is the longest used for any motorcycle race.

Fastest Circuit. The highest average lap speed attained on any closed circuit is 160.288 m.p.h. by Yvon du Hamel (Canada) on a modified 903-c.c. four-cylinder Kawasaki Z1 on the 31-degree banked 2.5-mile Daytona International Speedway, Florida, in March, 1973. His lap time was 56.149 seconds.

The fastest road circuit is the Francorchamps circuit near Spa, Belgium. It is 14.12 kilometers (8 miles 1,340 yards) in length and was lapped in 3 minutes 50.3 seconds (average speed of 137.150 m.p.h.) by Barry S. F. Sheene (born Holborn, London, England, September 11, 1950) on a 495-c.c. four-cylinder Suzuki during the Belgian Grand Prix on July 3, 1977.

Fastest Race. The fastest race in the world was held at Grenzlandring, West Germany, in 1939. It was won by Georg Meier (b. Germany, 1910) at an average speed of 134 m.p.h. on a supercharged 495-c.c. flat-twin B.M.W.

The fastest road race is the 500-c.c. Belgian Grand Prix on the Francorchamps circuit (see above). The record time for this 10-lap 87.74-mile race is 38 minutes 58.5 seconds (average speed of 135.068 m.p.h.) by Barry Sheene (U.K.) on a 495-c.c. four-cylinder Suzuki on July 3, 1977.

Longest Race. The longest race is the Liège 24 Hours. The greatest distance ever covered is 2,761.9 miles (average speed 115.08 m.p.h.) by Jean-Claude Chemarin and Christian Leon of France on a 941-c.c. four-cylinder Honda on the Francorchamps circuit (8 miles 1,340 yards) near Spa, Belgium, August 14–15, 1976.

World Championships. Most world championship titles (instituted by the *Fédération Internationale Motorcycliste* in 1949) won are 15 by Giacomo Agostini (Italy) in the 350-c.c. class 1968, 69, 70, 71, 72, 73, 74 and in the 500-c.c. class 1966, 67, 68, 69, 70, 71, 72, 75. Agostini (b. 1942) is the only man to win two world championships in five consecutive years (350- and 500-c.c. titles in 1968–69–70–71–72). Agostini won 122 races in the world championship series between April 24, 1965, and August 29, 1976, including a record 19 in 1970, also achieved by Stanley Michael Bailey "Mike" Hailwood, (b. Oxford, England, April 2, 1940) in 1966.

Klaus Enders (Germany) (b. 1937) won six world side-car titles, 1967, 69–70, 72–74.

Joël Robert (b. Chatelet, Belgium, November 11, 1943) has won six 250-c.c. moto-cross (also known as "scrambles") world championships (1964, 68–72). Between April 25, 1964, and June 18, 1972, he won a record fifty 250-c.c. Grands Prix. He became the youngest moto-cross world champion on July 12, 1964, when he won the 250-c.c. championship aged 20 years 8 months.

Alberto "Johnny" Cecotto (born Caracas, Venezuela, January, 1956) was the youngest person to win a world championship. He was aged 19 years 211 days when he won the 350-c.c. title on August 24, 1975.

The oldest was Hermann-Peter Müller (1909–76) of West Germany, who won the 250-c.c. title in 1955, aged 46.

Most Successful Machines. Italian M.V.-Agusta motorcycles won 37 world championships between 1952 and 1973 and 276 world championship races between 1952 and 1976. Japanese Honda machines won 29 world championship races and five world championships in 1966. In the seven years Honda contested the championship (1961–67) its annual average was 20 race wins.

Speed Records

Official world speed records must be set with two runs over a measured distance within a time limit (one hour for F.I.M. records, two hours for A.M.A. records).

Donald Vesco (born 1939) of El Cajon, California, recorded an average speed of 303.810 m.p.h. over the measured mile at Bonneville Salt Flats, Utah, on September 28, 1975, to establish an A.M.A. record. Riding a 21-foot-long *Silver Bird* Streamliner powered by two 750-c.c. Yamaha TZ750 4-cylinder engines developing 180 b.h.p., he covered the first mile in 11.817 seconds (304.646 m.p.h.). On the second run his time was 11.882 seconds (302.979 m.p.h.). The average time for the two runs was 11.8495 (303.810 m.p.h.) for the A.M.A. record. On the same day, he set an F.I.M. record at an average speed of 302.928 m.p.h. Also on the same day, he covered a flying quarter mile in 2.925 seconds (307.692 m.p.h.), the highest speed ever achieved on a motorcycle.

The world record average speed for two runs over one kilometer (1,093.6 yards) from a standing start is 16.68 seconds by Henk Vink (Netherlands) on his supercharged 984-c.c. 4-cylinder Kawasaki, at Elvington Airfield, Yorkshire, England, on July 24, 1977. The faster run was made in 16.09 seconds.

The world record for two runs over 440 yards from a standing start is 8.805 seconds by Henk Vink on his supercharged 1,132-c.c. 4-cylinder Kawasaki, at Elvington Airfield, Yorkshire, England, on July 23, 1977. The faster run was made in 8.55 seconds.

The fastest time for a single run over 440 yards from a standing start is 7.62 seconds by Russ Collins of Gardena, California, riding his nitro-burning 2000-c.c. 8-cylinder Honda, *Sorcerer,* at the National Hot Rod Association's World Finals at Ontario Motor Speedway on

QUICK AS A VINK: Henk Vink of the Netherlands averaged 16.68 seconds in two one-kilometer runs in July, 1977.

October 7, 1978. The highest terminal velocity recorded at the end of a 440-yard run from a standing start is 199.55 m.p.h. by Russ Collins in the same run.

Marathon. The longest time a solo motorcycle has been kept in continuous motion is 500 hours by Owen Fitzgerald, Richard Kennett, and Don Mitchell in Western Australia, on July 10–31, 1977. They covered 8,432 miles.

Mountaineering

Origins. Although bronze-age artifacts have been found on the summit (9,605 feet) of the Riffelhorn, Switzerland, mountaineering, as a sport, has a continuous history dating back only to 1854. Isolated instances of climbing for its own sake exist back to the 13th century. The Atacamenans built sacrificial platforms near the summit of Llullaillaco in South America (22,058 feet) in late pre-Columbian times, *c.* 1490.

Greatest Wall. The highest final stage in any wall climb is that on the south face of Annapurna I (26,545 feet). It was climbed by the British expedition led by Christian Bonington April 2–May 27, 1970, when Donald Whillans, 36, and Dougal Haston, 27, scaled to the summit. They used 18,000 feet of rope.

The longest wall climb is on the Rupal-Flank from the base camp at 11,680 feet to the South Point (26,384 feet) of Nanga Parbat—a vertical ascent of 14,704 feet. This was scaled by the Austro-Germano-Italian Expedition led by Dr. Herrligkoffer in April, 1970.

The world's most demanding free climbs are in the Yosemite Valley, California, with a severity rating of 5.12.

Mount Everest. Mount Everest (29,028 feet) was first climbed at 11:30 a.m. on May 29, 1953, when the summit was reached by Edmund Percival Hillary (born July 20, 1919), of New Zealand, and the Sherpa, Tenzing Norgay (born, as Namgyal Wangdi, in Nepal in 1914, formerly called Tenzing Khumjung Bhutia). The successful expedition was led by Col. (later Hon. Brigadier) Henry Cecil John Hunt (born June 22, 1910).

Since the first ascent, another 85 climbers have succeeded to the end of June, 1979. Franz Oppurg (Austria) made the first solo climb on May 14, 1978. Three women have reached the summit, the first being Junko Tabei (b. 1939) (Japan) on May 16, 1975.

Olympic Games

Note: These records now include the un-numbered Games held at Athens in 1906, which some authorities ignore. Although inserted between the regular IIIrd Games in 1904 and the IVth Games in 1908, the 1906 Games were both official and were of a higher standard than all three of those that preceded them.

Origins.

Origins. The earliest celebration of the ancient Olympic Games of which there is a certain record is that of July, 776 B.C. (when Coroibos, a cook from Elis, won a foot race), though their origin probably dates from *c.* 1370 B.C. The ancient Games were terminated by an order issued in Milan in 393 A.D. by Theodosius I, "the Great" (*c.* 346–395), Emperor of Rome. At the instigation of Pierre de Fredi, Baron de Coubertin (1863–1937), the Olympic Games of the modern era were inaugurated in Athens on April 6, 1896.

Most Medals

In the ancient Olympic Games, victors were given a chaplet (head garland) of olive leaves. Leonidas of Rhodos won 12 running titles from 164–152 B.C.

Individual. The most individual gold medals won by a male competitor in the modern Games is 10 by Raymond Clarence Ewry (U.S.) (b. October 14, 1874, at Lafayette, Indiana; d. September 27, 1937), a jumper (see *Track and Field*). The female record is seven by Vera Caslavska-Odlozil (b. May 3, 1942) of Czechoslovakia (also see *Gymnastics*).

The only Olympian to win 4 consecutive individual titles in the same event has been Alfred A. Oerter (b. September 19, 1936, New York City) who won the discus title in 1956–60–64–68.

Most Olympic Gold Medals at One Games. Mark Spitz (U.S.), the swimmer who won 2 relay golds in Mexico in 1968, won 7 more (4 individual and 3 relay) at Munich in 1972. The latter figure is an absolute Olympic record for one celebration at any sport.

Youngest and Oldest Gold Medalists. The youngest woman to win a gold medal is Marjorie Gestring (U.S.) (b. November 18, 1922) aged 13 years 9 months, in the 1936 women's springboard event. The youngest winner ever was a French boy (whose name is not recorded) who coxed the Netherlands coxed pair in 1900. He was not more than 10 and may have been as young as 7. He substituted for Dr. Hermanus Brockmann, who coxed in the heats but proved too heavy.

Oscar G. Swahn was a member of the winning Running Deer shooting team in 1912, aged 65 years 258 days.

National. The total figures for most medals and most gold medals for all Olympic events (including those now discontinued) for the Summer (1896–1976) and Winter Games (1924–1976) are:

	Gold	Silver	Bronze	Total
1. U.S.A.	658*	511½	438½	1,608
2. U.S.S.R. (formerly Russia)	311	255	244	810
3. G.B. (including Ireland to 1920)	165½	202½	178	546

* The A.A.U. (U.S.) reinstated James F. Thorpe (1888–1953), the disqualified high scorer in the 1912 decathlon and pentathlon events on October 12, 1973, but no issue of medals has yet been authorized by the International Olympic Committee. If allowed, this would give the U.S. 2 more gold medals.

Longest Span. The longest competitive span of any Olympic competitor is 40 years by Dr. Ivan Osiier (Denmark) (1888–1965), who competed as a fencer in 1908, 1912 (silver medal), 1920, 1924, 1928, 1932 and 1948, and by Magnus Konow (Norway) (1887–1972) in yachting, 1908–20 and 1936–48. The longest span for a woman is 24 years (1932–56) by the Austrian fencer Ellen Müller-Preiss. Raimondo d'Inzeo (born February 8, 1925) competed for Italy in equestrian events in a record eight celebrations (1948–1976), gaining one gold medal, two silver and three bronze medals. Janice Lee York Romary (born August 6, 1928), the U.S. fencer, competed in all six Games from 1948 to 1968, and Lia Manoliu (Rumania) (born April 25, 1932) competed from 1952 to 1972, winning the discus title in 1968.

Largest Crowd. The largest crowd at any Olympic site was 150,000 at the 1952 ski-jumping at the Holmenkollen, outside Oslo, Norway. Estimates of the number of spectators of the marathon race through Tokyo, Japan, on October 21, 1964, have ranged from 500,000 to 1,500,000.

Most Competitors. The greatest number of competitors in any summer Olympic Games has been 7,147 at Munich in 1972. A record 122 countries competed in the 1972 Munich Games. The fewest was 311 competitors from 13 countries in 1896. In 1904 only 12 countries participated. The largest team was 880 men and 4 women from France at the 1900 Games in Paris.

Most Participations. Five countries have never failed to be represented at the 19 Celebrations of the Games: Australia, Greece, Great Britain, Switzerland and the United States of America.

Parachuting

Origins. Parachuting became a regulated sport with the institution of world championships in 1951. A team title was introduced in 1954, and women's events were included in 1956.

FALLING STAR: Jacqueline Smith landed a new world record in winning the world championship for parachute jumping accuracy in 1978.

Most Titles. The U.S.S.R. won the men's team titles in 1954–58–60–66–72–76 and the women's team titles in 1956–58–66–68–72–76. No individual has ever won a second world overall title.

Greatest Accuracy. Jacqueline Smith (G.B.) (b. March 29, 1951) scored ten consecutive dead center strikes (4-inch disk) in the World Championships at Zagreb, Yugoslavia, September 1, 1978. At Yuma, Arizona, in March, 1978, Dwight Reynolds scored a record 105 daytime dead centers, and Bill Wenger and Phil Munden tied with 43 nighttime DCs, competing as members of the U.S. Army team, the Golden Knights.

Most Jumps. The greatest number of consecutive jumps completed in 24 hours is 233 by David Parchment at Shobdon Airfield, Hereford, England, on June 19, 1979.

Pigeon Racing

Earliest References. Pigeon Racing developed from the use of homing pigeons for carrying messages—a quality utilized in the ancient Olympic Games (776 B.C.–393 A.D.). The sport originated in Belgium. The earliest major long-distance race was from London to Antwerp in 1819, involving 32 pigeons. The earliest recorded occasion on which 500 miles was flown in a day was by "Motor," owned by G. P. Pointer, which was released on June 30, 1896, from Thurso, Scotland, and covered 501 miles at an average speed of 49½ m.p.h.

Longest Flights. The greatest recorded homing flight by a pigeon was made by one owned by the 1st Duke of Wellington (1769–1852). Released from a sailing ship off the Ichabo Islands,

West Africa, on April 8, it dropped dead a mile from its loft at Nine Elms, London, England, on June 1, 1845, 55 days later, having flown an airline route of 5,400 miles, but an actual distance of possibly 7,000 miles to avoid the Sahara Desert.

Highest Speeds. In level flight in windless conditions it is very doubtful if any pigeon can exceed 60 m.p.h. The highest race speed recorded is one of 3,229 yards per minute (110.07 m.p.h.) in East Anglia, England, on May 8, 1965, when 1,428 birds were backed by a powerful south southwest wind. The winner was owned by A. Vidgeon & Son.

The highest race speed recorded over a distance of more than 1,000 kilometers is 82.93 m.p.h. by a hen pigeon in the Central Cumberland Combine Race over 683 miles 147 yards from Murray Bridge, South Australia, to North Ryde, Sydney, on October 2, 1971.

The world's longest reputed distance in 24 hours is 803 miles (velocity 1,525 yards per minute) by E. S. Peterson's winner of the 1941 San Antonio (Texas) Racing Club event.

Lowest Speed. *Blue Clip*, a pigeon belonging to Harold Hart, released in Rennes, France, arrived home in its loft in Leigh, England, on September 29, 1974, 7 years 2 months later. It had covered the 370 miles at an average speed of 0.00589 m.p.h., which is slower than the world's fastest snail.

Most First Prizes. Owned by R. Green, of Walsall Wood, West Midlands, England, *Champion Breakaway* had won a record 56 first prizes from 1972 to May, 1979.

Highest Priced Bird. The highest recorded price paid for a pigeon is approximately $48,000 by a Japanese fancier for *De Wittslager* to Georges Desender (Belgium) in October, 1978.

Polo

Earliest Games. Polo is usually regarded as being of Persian origin, having been played as *Pulu c.* 525 B.C. Other claims have come from Tibet and the Tang dynasty of China 250 A.D.

The earliest club of modern times was the Kachar Club (founded in 1859) in Assam, India. The game was introduced into England from India in 1869 by the 10th Hussars at Aldershot, Hampshire, and the earliest match was one between the 9th Lancers and the 10th Hussars on Hounslow Heath, west of London, in July, 1871. The earliest international match between England and the U.S. was in 1886.

Playing Field. The game is played (by two teams of four) on the largest field of any ball game in the world. The ground measures 300 yards long by 160 yards wide with side-boards or, as in India, 200 yards wide without boards.

Highest Handicap. The highest handicap based on eight 7½-minute "chukkas" is 10 goals, introduced in the U.S. in 1891 and in the United Kingdom and in Argentina in 1910. The latest of the 39 players to have received 10-goal handicaps are Alberto Heguy and Alfredo Harriot of Argentina, and in England, Eduardo Moore (Argentina). A match of two 40-goal handicap teams was staged for the first time ever at Palermo, Buenos Aires, Argentina, in 1975.

Highest Score. The highest aggregate number of goals scored in an international match is 30, when Argentina beat the U.S. 21–9 at Meadowbrook, Long Island, New York, in September, 1936.

Most Olympic Medals. Polo has been part of the Olympic program on five occasions: 1900, 1908, 1920, 1924 and 1936. Of the 21 gold medalists, a 1920 winner, John Wodehouse, the 3rd Earl of Kimberley (b. 1883–d. 1941) uniquely also won a silver medal (1908).

Most Internationals. Thomas Hitchcock, Jr. (1900–44) played five times for the U.S. vs. England (1921–24–27–30–39) and twice vs. Argentina (1928–36).

Oldest Pony. *Rustum*, a Barb gelding from Stourhead, England, was still playing regularly at the age of 36.

Largest Trophy. Polo claims the world's largest sporting trophy —the Bangalore Limited Handicap Polo Tournament Trophy. This massive cup standing on its plinth is 6 feet tall and was presented in 1936 by the Indian Raja of Kolanka.

Largest Crowd. Crowds of more than 50,000 have watched flood-lit matches at the Sydney, Australia, Agricultural Shows.

A crowd of 40,000 watched a game played at Jaipur, India, in 1976, when elephants were used instead of ponies. The length of the polo sticks used has not been ascertained.

Powerboat Racing

Origins. The earliest application of the gasoline engine to a boat was by Jean Joseph Etienne Lenoir (1822–1900) on the River Seine, Paris, in 1865. The sport was given impetus by the presentation of a championship cup by Sir Alfred Harmsworth of England in 1903, which was also the year of the first offshore race from Calais to Dover.

Harmsworth Cup. Of the 25 contests from 1903 to 1961, the U.S. has won the most with 16.

The greatest number of wins has been achieved by Garfield A. Wood (U.S.) with 8 (1920–21, 1926, 1928–29–30, 1932–33). The only boat to win three times is *Miss Supertest III*, owned by James G. Thompson (Canada), driven by Jack Regas (Canada), in 1959–60–61. This boat also achieved the record speed of 119.27 m.p.h. at Picton, Ontario, Canada, in 1961. The trophy is now awarded to the British Commonwealth driver with the highest points in the World Offshore Championships.

LONGEST POWERBOAT JUMP: Jerry Comeaux jumped his boat 110 feet in the air for the film "Live and Let Die."

Gold Cup. The Gold Cup (instituted 1903) has been won 7 times by Bill Muncey (1956–57–61–62–72–77–78). The record speed attained is 128.338 m.p.h. for a 2½-mile lap by the unlimited hydroplane *Atlas Van Lines*, driven by Bill Muncey in a qualifying round on the Columbia River, Washington, in July, 1977, and again in July, 1978.

Highest Speeds. The fastest offshore record, as recognized by the Union Internationale Motonautique, is 92.99 m.p.h. by a Class IIID Frode, driven by Mikael Frode (Sweden) on November 5, 1977.

The R6 inboard engine record of 128.375 m.p.h. was set by the hydroplane *Vladivar I*, driven by Tony Fahey (G.B.) on Lake Windermere, Cumbria, England, on May 23, 1977.

The Class ON record is 136.38 m.p.h. by J. F. Merten (U.S.) in 1973.

Longest Race. The longest race has been the Port Richborough (London) to Monte Carlo Marathon Offshore International event. The race extended over 2,947 miles in 14 stages on June 10–25, 1972. It was won by *H.T.S.* (G.B.), driven by Mike Bellamy, Eddie Chater and Jim Brooks in 71 hours 35 minutes 56 seconds (average 41.15 m.p.h.).

Longest Jump. The longest jump achieved by a powerboat has been 110 feet by Jerry Comeaux, 29, in a Glastron GT-150 with a 135-h.p. Evinrude Starflite off a greased ramp on an isolated waterway in Louisiana, in mid-October, 1972. The takeoff speed was 56 m.p.h. The jump was required for a sequence in the eighth James Bond film, *Live and Let Die.*

Dragsters. The first drag boat to attain 200 m.p.h. was Sam Kurtovich's *Crisis* which attained 200.44 m.p.h. in California in

October, 1969, at the end of a one-way run. *Climax* has since been reported to have attained 205.19 m.p.h.

Longest Journey. The Dane, Hans Tholstrup, 25, circumnavigated Australia (11,500 miles) in a 17-foot Caribbean Cougar fiberglass runabout with a single 80-h.p. Mercury outboard motor from May 11 to July 25, 1971.

Rodeo

Origins. Rodeo, which developed from 18th century *fiestas*, came into being with the early days of the North American cattle industry. The earliest reference to the sport is at Santa Fe, New Mexico, on June 10, 1847. Steer wrestling began with Bill Pickett (Texas) in 1900. The other events are calf roping, bull riding, saddle and bareback bronco riding.

The largest rodeo in the world is the Calgary Exhibition and Stampede at Calgary, Alberta, Canada. The record attendance has been 1,069,830, July 8–17, 1977. The record for one day is 141,670 on July 13, 1974. The oldest continuously-held rodeo is that at Payson, Arizona, first held in August, 1887.

Champion Bull. The top bucking bull was probably *Honky Tonk*, an 11-year-old Brahma, who unseated 187 riders in an undefeated eight-year career to his retirement in September, 1978.

Champion Bronc. Traditionally a bronc called *Midnight* owned by Jim McNab of Alberta, Canada, was never ridden in 12 appearances at the Calgary Stampede.

Most World Titles. The record number of all-round titles is 6 by Larry Mahan (b. November 21, 1943) (1966–67–68–69–70–73). Jim Shoulders (b. 1928) of Henryetta, Oklahoma, won a record 16 world championships between 1949 and 1959. The record figure for prize money in a single season is $128,434 by Tom Ferguson, of Miami, Oklahoma, in 1978.

Youngest Champion. The youngest winner of a world title is Metha Brorsen of Oklahoma, who was only 11 years old when she won the International Rodeo Association Cowgirls barrel racing event in 1975.

Time Records. Records for timed events, such as calf roping and steer wrestling, are meaningless, because of the widely varying conditions due to the size of arenas and amount of start given the stock. The fastest time recently recorded for roping a calf is 7.5 seconds by Junior Garrison of Marlow, Oklahoma, at Evergreen, Colorado, in 1967, and the fastest time for overcoming a steer is 2.4 seconds by James Bynum of Waxahachie, Texas, at Marietta, Oklahoma, in 1955.

The standard required time to stay on in bareback, saddle bronc and bull riding events is 8 seconds. In the now discontinued ride-to-a-finish events, rodeo riders have been recorded to have survived 90 minutes or more, until the mount had not a buck left in it.

Roller Skating

Origin. The first roller skate was devised by Joseph Merlin of Huy, Belgium, in 1760, and was first worn by him in public in London. James L. Plimpton of New York City produced the present four-wheeled type and patented it in January, 1863. The first indoor rinks were opened in London in 1857. The great boom periods were 1870–75, 1908–12, 1948–54 and 1978 to the present, each originating in the U.S.

Largest Rink. The largest indoor rink ever to operate was located in the Grand Hall, Olympia, London, England. It had an actual skating area of 68,000 square feet. It first opened in 1890 for one season, then again from 1909 to 1912.

The largest rink now in operation is the Fireside Roll-Arena in Hoffman Estates, Illinois, which has a total skating surface of 29,859 square feet.

Roller Hockey. Roller hockey was first introduced in England as Rink Polo, at the old Lava rink, Denmark Hill, London, in the late 1870's. The Amateur Rink Hockey Association was formed in 1905, and in 1913 became the National Rink Hockey (now Roller Hockey) Association. Britain won the inaugural World Championship in 1936, and since then Portugal has won the most with 11 titles from 1947 to 1973.

Most Titles. Most world speed titles have been won by Alberta Vianello (Italy) with 16 between 1953 and 1965. Most world pair titles have been taken by Dieter Fingerle (W. Germany) with four in 1959–65–66–67. The records for figure titles are 5 by Karl Heinz Losch in 1958–59–61–62–66 and 4 by Astrid Bader, also of West Germany, in 1965 to 1968.

Speed Records. The fastest speed (official world's record) is 25.78 m.p.h. by Giuseppe Cantarella (Italy) who recorded 34.9 seconds for 440 yards on a road at Catania, Italy, on September 28, 1963. The mile record on a rink is 2 minutes 25.1 seconds by Gianni Ferretti (Italy). The greatest distance skated in one hour on a rink by a woman is 21.995 miles by Marisa Danesi at Inzell, West Germany, on September 28, 1968. The men's record on a track is 23.133 miles by Alberto Civolani (Italy) at Inzell, West Germany, on September 28, 1968. He went on to skate 50 miles in 2 hours 20 minutes 33.1 seconds.

Marathon Record. The longest recorded continuous roller skating marathon was one of 322 hours 20 minutes by Randy Reed of Springfield, Oregon, June 12–26, 1977.

The longest reported skate was by Clinton Shaw (Canada) from Victoria, British Columbia, to St. John's, Newfoundland (4,900 miles) on the Trans-Canadian Highway *via* Montreal from April 1 to November 11, 1967.

On April 23, 1979, at Savannah, Georgia, Jackie Jacobs (21 years old) completed a coast-to-coast 2,389-mile skate, having started in San Diego, California, on March 18. Her longest stint in a day was 110 miles on April 17.

Rowing

Oldest Race. The Sphinx stela of Amenhotep II (1450–1425 B.C.) records that he *stroked* a boat for some three miles. The earliest established sculling race is the Doggett's Coat and Badge, first rowed on August 1, 1716 from London Bridge to Chelsea, and still contested annually. Although rowing regattas were held in Venice in 1300, the first English regatta probably took place on the Thames by the Ranelagh Gardens near Putney, London, in 1775. Boating began at Eton, England, in 1793. The oldest club, the Leander Club, was formed in *c.* 1818.

Olympic Games. Since 1900 there have been 119 Olympic finals of which the U.S. has won 26, Germany (now West Germany) 15 and Great Britain 14. Four oarsmen have won 3 gold medals: John B. Kelly (U.S.) (1889–1960), father of Princess Grace of Monaco, in the sculls (1920) and double sculls (1920 and 1924); his cousin Paul V. Costello (U.S.) (b. December 27, 1899) in the double sculls (1920, 1924 and 1928); Jack Beresford, Jr. (G.B.) (1899-1977) in the sculls (1924), coxless fours (1932) and double sculls (1936) and Vyacheslav Ivanov (U.S.S.R.) (b. July 30, 1938) in the sculls (1956, 1960 and 1964). Beresford competed in five games, winning an additional two silver medals.

Sculling. The record number of wins in the Wingfield Sculls (instituted on the Thames in 1830) is seven by Jack Beresford, Jr., from 1920 to 1926. The fastest time (Putney to Mortlake) has been 21 minutes 11 seconds by Leslie Southwood in 1933. The record number of world professional sculling titles (instituted 1831) won is seven by William Beach (Australia) between 1884 and 1887.

Highest Speed. Speeds in tidal or flowing water are of no comparative value. The highest recorded speed for 2,000 meters on non-tidal water by an eight is 5 mins. 32.17 secs. (13.46 m.p.h.) by East Germany at the Montreal Olympics on July 18, 1976. A team from the Penn A.C. (U.S.) was timed in 5 minutes 18.8 seconds (14.03 m.p.h.) in the F.I.S.A. Championships on the Meuse River, Liège, Belgium, on August 17, 1930.

Longest Race. The longest annual rowing race is the Ringvaart Regatta, a 62-mile contest for eights held at Delft, Netherlands. The record time is 7 hours 3 minutes 29 seconds by the Njord team on May 31, 1979.

Cross-Channel Row. The fastest row across the English Channel is 3 hours 50 minutes by Rev. Sidney Swann (b. 1862) in 1911.

WORLD RECORDS

MEN—Fastest times over 2,000 m course

	min sec	Country	Place	Date
Single Sculls	6:52.46	Sean Drea (Ireland)	Montreal, Canada	July 23, 1976
Double Sculls	6:12.48	Norway	Montreal, Canada	July 23, 1976
Coxed Pairs	6:56.94	East Germany	Copenhagen, Denmark	Aug. — 1971
Coxless Pairs	6:33.02	East Germany	Montreal, Canada	July 23, 1976
Coxed Fours	6:09.17	East Germany	Amsterdam, Netherlands	June 30, 1979
Coxless Fours	5:53.65	East Germany	Montreal, Canada	July 23, 1976
Quadruple Sculls	5:47.83	U.S.S.R.	Montreal, Canada	July 18, 1976
Eights	5:32.17	East Germany	Montreal, Canada	July 18, 1976

WOMEN—Fastest times over 1,000 m course

Single Sculls	3:34.31	Christine Scheiblich (East Germany)	Amsterdam, Netherlands	Aug. 21, 1977
Double Sculls	3:16.83	East Germany	Amsterdam, Netherlands	Aug. 21, 1977
Coxless Pairs	3:26.32	East Germany	Amsterdam, Netherlands	Aug. 21, 1977
Coxed Fours	3:14.5	U.S.S.R.	Mannheim, West Germany	May 20, 1979
Quadruple Sculls	3:08.49	East Germany	Montreal, Canada	July 19, 1976
Eights	2:59.00	U.S.S.R.	Mannheim, West Germany	May 19, 1979

Shooting

Earliest Club. The Lucerne Shooting Guild (Switzerland) was formed *c.* 1466, and the first recorded shooting match was held at Zurich in 1472.

Olympic Games. The record number of gold medals won is five by seven marksmen: Carl Osburn (U.S.) (1912–1924); Konrad Stäheli (Switz.) (1900 and 1906); Willis Lee (U.S.) (1920); Louis Richardet (Switz.) (1900 and 1906); Ole Andreas Lilloe-Olsen (Norway) (1920–1924); Alfred Lane (U.S.) (1912 and 1920) and Morris Fisher (U.S.) (1920 and 1924). Osburn also won 4 silver and 2 bronze medals for a record total of 11. The only marksman to win 3 individual gold medals has been Gulbrandsen Skatteboe (Norway) (b. July 18, 1875) in 1906–1908–1912.

WORLD RECORDS
Possible Score

Free Pistol	50 m. 6 × 10 shot series	600—	577	Moritze Minder (Switz.) Seoul, Korea, 1978
Free Rifle	300 m. 3 × 40 shot series	1,200—1,160		Lones W. Wigger, Jr. (U.S.) Seoul, Korea, 1978
Small-Bore Rifle	50 m. 3 × 40 shot series	1,200—1,170*		Sven Johansson (Sweden) Suhl, E. Germany, 1979
Small-Bore Rifle	50 m. 60 shots prone	600—	599	Eight men
Rapid-Fire Pistol	25 m. silhouettes 60 shots	600—	600	Weissenberger (W. Germany) Suhl, E. Germany, 1979 Ian Corneliu (Rumania) Bucharest, 1977
Running (Boar) Target	50 m. 60 shots "normal runs"	600—	581	Thomas Pfeffer (E. Ger.) Seoul, Korea, 1978
Trap	200 birds	200—	199	Angelo Scalzone (Italy) Munich, 1972 Michel Carrega (France) Thun, Switzerland, 1974
Skeet	200 birds	200—	200	Yevgeniy Petrov (U.S.S.R.) Phoenix, Ariz., 1970 Yuri Tzuranov (U.S.S.R.) Bologna, Italy, 1971 Tariel Zhgenti (U.S.S.R.) Turin, Italy, 1973 Kield Rasmussen (Denmark) Vienna, 1975 Wieslaw Gawlikowski (Poland) Vienna, 1975
Center-Fire Pistol	25 m. 60 shots	600—	597	Thomas D. Smith (U.S.) Sao Paulo, Brazil, 1963

*Awaiting ratification.

Record Heads. The world's finest head is the 23-pointer stag head in the Maritzburg collection, Germany. The outside span is 75½ inches, the length 47½ inches and the weight 41⅝ lbs. The greatest number of points is probably 33 (plus 29) on the stag shot in 1696 by Frederick III (1657–1713), the Elector of Brandenburg, later King Frederick I of Prussia.

Largest Shoulder Guns. The largest bore shoulder guns made were 2-bore. Less than a dozen of these were made by two English wildfowl gunmakers in *c.* 1885. Normally the largest guns made are double-barrelled 4-bore weighing up to 26 lbs. which can be handled only by men of exceptional physique. Larger smooth-bore guns have been made, but these are for use as punt-guns.

Bench Rest Shooting. The smallest group on record at 1,000 yards is 6.125 inches by Kenneth A. Keefer, Jr., with a 7 m.m.-300 Remington Action in Williamstown, Pennsylvania, on September 22, 1974.

Small-Bore Rifle Shooting. Richard Hansen shot 5,000 bull's-eyes in 24 hours at Fresno, California, on June 13, 1929.

Clay Pigeon Shooting. The record number of clay birds shot in an hour is 1,904 by Tom Kreckman, 36, at Cresco, Pennsylvania, on a Skeet range, September 28, 1975. Jerry Teynor shot 1,735 birds on a trapshooting range at Bucyrus, Ohio, on July 30, 1977.

Most world titles have been won by S. De Lamniczer (Hungary) in 1929, 1933 and 1939. The only woman to win two world titles has been Gräfin von Soden (West Germany) in 1966–67.

Biggest Bag. The largest animal ever shot by any big game hunter was a bull African elephant (*Loxodonta africana africana*) shot by E. M. Nielsen of Columbus, Nebraska, 25 miles north-northeast of Mucusso, Angola, on November 7, 1974. The animal, brought down by a Westley Richards 0.425, stood 13 feet 8 inches at the shoulder.

In November, 1965, Simon Fletcher, 28, a Kenyan farmer, claims to have killed two elephants with one 0.458 bullet.

The greatest recorded lifetime bag was 556,000 birds, including 241,000 pheasants, by the 2nd Marquess of Ripon (1852–1923) of England. He himself dropped dead on a grouse moor after shooting his 52nd bird on the morning of September 22, 1923.

Trick Shooting. The greatest rapid-fire feat was that of Ed McGivern (U.S.), who twice fired from 15 feet in 0.45 of a second 5 shots which could be covered by a silver half dollar piece at the Lead Club Range, South Dakota, on August 20, 1932.

McGivern also, on September 13, 1932, at Lewiston, Montana, fired 10 shots in 1.2 seconds from two guns at the same time double action (no draw), all 10 shots hitting two 2¼ by 3½ inch playing cards at 15 feet.

The most renowned trick shot of all time was Annie Oakley (*née* Mozee) (1860–1926). She demonstrated the ability to shoot 100 of 100 in trap shooting for 35 years, aged between 27 and 62. At 30 paces she could split a playing card end-on, hit a dime in mid-air or shoot a cigarette from the lips of her husband—one Frank Butler.

FASTEST GUN: Bob Munden, well-known claimant to the title of "World's Fastest Gun," has drawn and fired in just 0.0175 seconds.

Air Weapons. The individual world record for air rifle (40 shots at 10 meters) is 393 by Olegario Vazquez (Mexico) at Mexico City in 1975, and for air pistol (40 shots at 10 meters) is 394 by Uwe Potteck (b. May 1, 1955) (East Germany) at Graz, Austria, in March, 1979.

Rapid Firing. Using a Soper single-loading rifle, Private John Warrick, 1st Berkshire Volunteers, loaded and fired 60 rounds in one minute at Basingstoke, England, in April, 1870.

Skiing

Origins. The most ancient ski in existence was found well preserved in a peat bog at Höting, Sweden, dating from *c.* 2500 B.C. A rock carving of a skier at Bessovysledki, U.S.S.R., dates from 6000 B.C. The earliest recorded military use was in Norway, in 1199, though it did not grow into a sport until 1843 at Tromsø. The Trysil Shooting and Skiing Club (founded 1861), in Norway, claims to be the world's oldest. Skiing was not introduced in the Alps until 1883, though there is some evidence of earlier use in the Carniola district. The earliest formal downhill race was staged at Montana, Switzerland, in 1911. The first Slalom event was run at Mürren, Switzerland, on January 21, 1922. The International Ski Federation (F.I.S.) was founded on February 2, 1924. The Winter Olympics were inaugurated on January 25, 1924.

Highest Speed. The highest speed ever claimed for any skier is 124.412 m.p.h. by Steve McKinney (U.S.) (b. 1953) at Portillo, Chile, on October 1, 1978. The fastest by a woman is 103.084 m.p.h. by Catherine Breyton (France) at Portillo on October 1, 1978.

The average race speed by 1976 Olympic Downhill champion Franz Klammer (born December 3, 1953) of Austria on the Iglis-Patscherkofel course, Innsbruck, Austria, was 63.894 m.p.h. on February 5, 1976.

Duration. The longest non-stop Nordic skiing marathon was one that lasted 48 hours by Onni Savi, aged 35, of Padasjoki, Finland, who covered 305.9 kilometers (190.1 miles) between noon on April 19 and noon on April 21, 1966.

Ahti Nevada (Finland) covered 174.5 miles in 24 hours at Rovaniemi, Finland, on March 30, 1977.

Pat Purcell and John McGlynn (U.S.) completed 81 hours 12 minutes of Alpine skiing at Holiday Mountain, Monticello, New York, on February 1–4, 1979.

Most World Titles. The World Alpine Championships were inaugurated at Mürren, Switzerland, in 1931. The greatest number of titles won is 12 by Christel Cranz (born July 1, 1914), of Germany, with four Slalom (1934–37–38–39), three Downhill (1935–37–39) and five Combined (1934–35–37–38–39). She also won the gold medal for the Combined in the 1936 Olympics. The most titles won by a man is seven by Anton ("Toni") Sailer (born November 17, 1935), of Austria, who won all four in 1956 (Giant Slalom, Slalom, Downhill and the non-Olympic Alpine Combination) and the Downhill, Giant Slalom and Combined in 1958.

In the Nordic events Sixten Jernberg (Sweden) (b. February 6, 1929) won eight titles, 4 at 50 km., one at 30 km., and 3 in relays, in 1956–64. Johan Grottumsbraaten (1899–1942), of Norway, won six individual titles (two at 18 kilometers and four Combined) in 1926–32. The most by a woman is nine by Galina Koulakova (U.S.S.R.) (b. April 29, 1942) from 1968 to 1978. The record for a jumper is five by Birger Ruud (b. August 23, 1911), of Norway, in 1931–32 and 1935–36–37.

The Alpine World Cup, instituted in 1967, has been won four times by Gustavo Thoeni (Italy) (b. February 28, 1931) in 1971–72–73–75. The women's cup has been won six times by the 5-foot-6-inch 150-lb. Annemarie Moser (née Proell) (Austria) in 1971–72–73–74–

75–79. In 1973, she completed a record sequence of 11 consecutive downhill victories and in ten seasons, 1970–1979, has won a total of 62 individual events. The most individual events won by a man is 42 by Ingemar Stenmark (Sweden) in 1974–79, including a record 14 in one season in 1979.

The Nordic World Cup, instituted in 1979, was first won by Oddvar Braa (Norway) with the women's title won by Galina Koulakova (U.S.S.R.).

Most Olympic Victories. The most Olympic gold medals won by an individual for skiing is four (including one for a relay) by Sixten Jernberg (born February 6, 1929), of Sweden, in 1956–60–64. In addition, Jernberg has won three silver and two bronze medals. The only woman to win four gold medals is Galina Koulakova (b. 1942) of U.S.S.R., who won the 5 kilometers and 10 kilometers (1972) and was a member of the winning 3 × 5 kilometers relay team in 1972 and the 4 × 5 kilometers team in 1976. Koulakova also has won one silver and two bronze medals, in 1968 and 1976.

The most Olympic gold medals won in men's alpine skiing is three, by Anton ("Toni") Sailer in 1956 and Jean-Claude Killy in 1968.

Longest Jump. The longest ski jump ever recorded is one of 181 meters (593 feet 10 inches) by Bogdan Norcic (Yugoslavia) who fell on landing at Planica, Yugoslavia, in February 1977.

The official record is 176 meters (577 feet 5 inches) by Toni Innauer (Austria) (b. April 1, 1958) at Oberstdorf, West Germany, on March 6, 1976.

The women's record is 321 feet 6 inches by Anita Wold of Norway, at Okura, Sapporo, Japan, on January 14, 1975.

WORLD CUP WINNER: Ingemar Stenmark of Sweden won 42 Alpine World Cup events in the 1974–79 seasons.

The longest jump achieved in the Olympics is 111 meters (364 feet) by Wojciech Fortuna (Poland) at Sapporo on February 11, 1972.

Cross-Country. The world's greatest Nordic ski race is the "Vasa Lopp," which commemorates an event of 1521 when Gustavus Vasa (1496–1560), later King of Sweden, skied 85.8 kilometers (53.3 miles) from Mora to Sälen, Sweden. The re-enactment of this journey in the reverse direction is an annual event, with a record 11,596 starters on March 5, 1978. The record time is 4 hours 5 minutes 58 seconds by Ola Hassis (Sweden) on March 4, 1979.

Steepest Descent. Sylvain Saudan (b. Lausanne, Switzerland, September 23, 1936) achieved a descent of Mont Blanc on the northeast side down the Couloir Gervasutti from 13,937 feet on October 17, 1967, skiing gradients in excess of 60 degrees.

Greatest Descent. The greatest reported elevation descended in 12 hours is 416,000 feet by Sarah Ludwig, Scott Ludwig, and Timothy B. Gaffney, at Mt. Brighton, Michigan, on February 16, 1974.

Sylvain Saudan (Switzerland) skied down the 23,400-foot Nun peak in the Ladakh Himalayas on June 26, 1977.

Highest Altitude. Yuichiro Miura (Japan) skied 1.6 miles down Mt. Everest on May 6, 1970, starting from 26,200 feet.

Longest Run. The longest all-downhill ski run in the world is the Weissfluhjoch-Küblis Parsenn course (7.6 miles long), near Davos, Switzerland. The run from the Aiguille du Midi top of the Chamonix lift (vertical lift 8,176 feet) across the Vallée Blanche is 13 miles.

Backflip on Skis. Twenty-one skiers at Mont St. Saveur, Quebec, Canada, performed a simultaneous back somersault while holding hands on March 12, 1977.

Longest Lift. The longest chair lift in the world is the Alpine Way to Kosciusko Châlet lift above Thredbo, near the Snowy Mountains, New South Wales, Australia. It takes from 45 to 75 minutes to ascend the 3.5 miles, according to the weather. The highest is at Chacaltaya, Bolivia, rising to 16,500 feet. The longest gondola ski lift, at Killington, Vermont, is 3.4 miles long.

Ski Parachuting. The greatest recorded vertical descent in parachute ski-jumping is 3,300 feet by Rick Sylvester (b. 1943) (U.S.), who on July 28, 1976, skied off the 6,600-foot summit of Mt. Asgard in Auyuittuq National Park, Baffin Island, Canada, landing on the Turner Glacier. The jump was made for a sequence in the James Bond film "The Spy Who Loved Me."

Ski-Bob. The ski-bob was invented by a Mr. Stevens of Hartford, Connecticut, and patented (No. 47334) on April 19, 1892, as a "bicycle with ski-runners." The Fédération Internationale de Skibob was founded on January 14, 1961, in Innsbruck, Austria. The first World Championships were held at Bad Hofgastein, Austria, in 1967.

The highest speed has been 103.4 m.p.h. by Erich Brenter (Austria) at Cervinia, Italy, in 1964. The only ski-bobbers to retain world championships are Gerhilde Schiffkorn (Austria) who won the women's title in 1967 and 1969, Gertrude Geberth, who won in 1971 and 1973 and Alois Fischbauer (Austria) who won the men's title in 1973 and 1975.

Snowmobiling. The record speed for a snowmobile was increased to 135.93 m.p.h. by Donald J. Pitzen (U.S.) at Union Lake, Michigan, on February 27, 1977.

The longest snowmobile journey to date was the cross-country trip from Westport, Washington to Lubec, Maine, a distance of 5,004.5 miles, completed by driver Fritz Sprandel of Schnecksville, Pennsylvania, on his Scorpion 440 Whip snowmobile, accompanied by mechanic Ed Kazmierski, from December 4, 1977 to February 6, 1978. (See photo, page P.)

Soccer

Origins. A game with some similarities termed *Tsu-chu* was played in China in the 3rd and 4th centuries B.C. One of the earliest references to the game in England refers to the accidental death of a goalkeeper on February 23, 1582, in Essex. The earliest clear representation of the game is in a print from Edinburgh, Scotland, dated 1672–73. The game became standardized with the formation of the Football Association in England on October 26, 1863. A football game, *Calcio*, existed in Italy in 1410. The world's oldest club is Sheffield F.C. of England, formed on October 24, 1857. Eleven on a side was standardized in 1870.

Highest Scores

Teams. The highest score recorded in any first-class match is 36. This occurred in the Scottish Cup match between Arbroath and Bon Accord on September 5, 1885, when Arbroath won 36–0 on their home ground. But for the lack of nets, the playing time might have been longer and the score possibly even higher.

The highest goal margin recorded in any international match is 17. This occurred in the England vs. Australia match at Sydney on June 30, 1951, when England won 17–0. This match is not listed by England as a *full* international.

Individuals. The most goals scored by one player in a first-class match is 16 by Stephan Stanis (*né* Stanikowski, b. Poland, July 15, 1913) for Racing Club de Lens vs. Aubry-Asturies, in Lens, France, on December 13, 1942.

The record number of goals scored by one player in an international match is 10 by Gottfried Fuchs for Germany, which beat Russia 16–0 in the 1912 Olympic tournament (consolation event) in Sweden.

Artur Friedenreich (1892–1969) (Brazil) scored an undocumented 1,329 goals in a 43-year first-class football career. The most goals scored in a specified period is 1,216 by Edson Arantes do Nascimento

(b. Baurú, Brazil, October 23, 1940), known as Pelé, the Brazilian inside left, from September 7, 1956, to October 2, 1974 (1,254 games). His best year was 1958 with 139. His *milesimo* (1,000th) came in a penalty for his club, Santos, in the Maracaña Stadium, Rio de Janeiro, on November 19, 1969, when he was playing in his 909th first-class match. He came out of retirement in 1975 to add to his total with the New York Cosmos of the North American Soccer League. By his retirement on October 1, 1977 his total had reached 1,281 in 1,363 games. Franz ("Bimbo") Binder (b. 1911) scored 1,006 goals in 756 games in Austria and Germany between 1930 and 1950.

Fastest Goals

The record for an international match is 3 goals in 3½ minutes by Willie Hall (Tottenham Hotspur) for England against Ireland on November 16, 1938, at Old Trafford, Manchester, England.

The fastest goal in World Cup competition was one in 30 seconds by Olle Nyberg for Sweden vs. Hungary, in Paris, June 16, 1938.

Most Appearances

Robert ("Bobby") Moore of West Ham United and Fulham set a new record of full international appearances by playing in his 108th game for England vs. Italy on November 14, 1973 at Wembley, London. His first appearance was vs. Peru on May 20, 1962, and he retired on May 14, 1977, on his 1,000th appearance.

Most Successful National Coach

Helmut Schoen (born 1915) of West Germany coached his teams to victory in the 1972 European championship and the 1974 World Cup, as well as finishing second in the 1966 World Cup and 1976 European championships, and third in the 1970 World Cup.

Longest Match

The world duration record for a first-class match was set in the Copa Libertadores championship in Santos, Brazil, on August 2–3, 1962, when Santos drew 3–3 with Peñarol F.C. of Montevideo, Uruguay. The game lasted 3½ hours (with interruptions), from 9:30 p.m. to 1 a.m.

A match between the Simon Fraser University Clansmen and the Quincy College Hawks lasted 4 hours 25 minutes (221 minutes 43 seconds playing time) at Pasadena, California, in November, 1976.

Crowds

The greatest recorded crowd at any football match was 205,000 (199,854 paid) for the Brazil vs. Uruguay World Cup final in Rio de Janeiro, Brazil, on July 16, 1950.

Transfer Fees

The world's highest reported transfer fee is £922,300 ($2,305,750) for the Ajax Amsterdam striker Johan Cruyff, signed by F.C. Barcelona of Spain, announced on August 20, 1973.

**WORLD CUP
SCORING RECORD:**
Gerd Müller of West
Germany scored 14 goals
in the 1970 and
1974 World Cup finals.

World Cup

The *Fédération Internationale de Football* (F.I.F.A.) was founded in Paris on May 21, 1904, and instituted the World Cup Competition in 1930, in Montevideo, Uruguay.

The only country to win three times has been Brazil (1958–1962–1970). Brazil was also third in 1938 and 1978, and second in 1950, and is the only one of the 45 participating countries to have played in all 11 competitions.

The record goal scorer has been Just Fontaine (France) with 13 goals in 6 games in the final stages of the 1958 competition. The most goals scored in a final is 3 by Geoffrey Hurst (West Ham United) for England vs. West Germany on July 30, 1966. Gerd Müller (West Germany) scored 14 goals in two World Cup finals (1970 and 1974).

Antonio Carbajal (b. 1923) played for Mexico in goal in the competitions of 1950–54–58–62 and 1966.

Receipts

The greatest receipts at a World Cup final were £204,805 ($573,454) from an attendance of 96,924 for the match between England and West Germany at the Empire Stadium, Wembley, Greater London, on July 30, 1966.

Heaviest Goalkeeper

The biggest goalie on record was Willie J. ("Fatty") Foulke of England (1874–1916) who stood 6 feet 3 inches and weighed 311 lbs. By the time he died, he tipped the scales at 364 lbs. He once stopped a game by snapping the cross bar.

Soccer (Amateur)

Most Olympic Wins. The only country to have won the Olympic football title three times is Hungary in 1952, 1964 and 1968.

The United Kingdom won in 1908 and 1912 and also the unofficial tournament of 1900. These contests have now virtually ceased to be amateur. The highest Olympic score is Denmark 17 vs. France "A" 1 in 1908.

Largest Crowd. The highest attendance at any amateur match is 120,000 at Senayan Stadium, Djakarta, Indonesia, on February 26, 1976, for the Pre-Olympic Group II Final between North Korea and Indonesia.

Heading. The highest recorded number of repetitions for heading a ball is 12,100 in 54 minutes 22 seconds by Michael Helliwell, 17, of Elland, England, on December 14, 1973.

Ball Control. Adrian Walsh (aged 34) juggled a regulation soccer ball for 4 hours 3 minutes 43 seconds non-stop at The Town Park, Mallow, County Cork, Ireland, on June 24, 1979. He hit the ball 23,547 times with his feet, legs and head without ever letting the ball touch the ground.

Marathons. The longest recorded 11-a-side soccer marathon is 49 hours by two teams from Blackett United F.C. at Haber Park, N.S.W., Australia, on October 20–22, 1978.

The longest recorded authenticated 5-a-side games have been (outdoors) 62 hours 51 minutes by two teams (no substitutes) from St. Albans United F.C., at Belmont Hill, St. Albans, England, June 22–24, 1979, and (indoors) 91 hours 45 minutes by two teams (no substitutes) from Liverpool Polytechnic, Merseyside, England, February 16–20, 1978.

Softball

Origins. Softball, as an indoor derivative of baseball, was invented by George Hancock at the Farragut Boat Club of Chicago, in 1887. Rules were first codified in Minneapolis in 1895 as Kitten Ball. International rules were set in 1933 when the name Softball was officially adopted. The I.S.F. was formed in 1952 as governing body for both fast pitch and slow pitch.

World Championships

Most Titles. The U.S. has won the men's world championship (instituted in 1966) three times, 1966, 68.and 76 (shared). Japan has won the women's title (instituted in 1965) in 1970 and 74.

Individual Records. Joan Joyce set a pair of records by pitching 2 perfect games and notching 76 strikeouts for the U.S. women's team in the 1974 world championships at Stratford, Connecticut. In the same competition, Naruse of Japan set three batting records with 17 hits, a .515 batting average and 11 RBIs (shared with two others). In the men's competition at Wellington, New Zealand, in 1976, pitcher Ty Stofflet (U.S.) struck out a record 98 batters. Burrows of Canada hit the most-ever home runs with 4, and tied a record with 14 RBIs.

Marathon. The longest fast-pitch marathon is 55 hours 50 minutes by two teams of nine (no substitutes) from the Y.C.W. Softball

Association, Melbourne, Australia, on December 16–18, 1978. The longest for slow pitch is 72 hours 3 seconds by two teams of 10 players from the U.S. Navy in Singapore, December 28–31, 1977.

Squash

(Note: "1971," for example, refers to the 1971–72 season.)

Earliest Champion. Although racquets with a soft ball was played in 1817 at Harrow School (England), there was no recognized champion of any country until J. A. Miskey of Philadelphia won the American Amateur Singles Championship in 1906.

World Title. Australia has won the team title four times. Geoffrey B. Hunt (Australia) took the individual title in 1967, 1969 and 1971.

The World Open championship, instituted in 1976, has been won twice by Geoffrey B. Hunt (Australia), in 1976 and 1977.

Most Victories

Open Championship. The most wins in the Open Championship (amateur or professional), held annually in Britain, is seven by Hashim Khan (Pakistan) in 1950–51–52–53–54–55 and 1957. He also twice won the Vintage title, in 1977 and 78.

Amateur Championship. The most wins in the Amateur Championship is six by Abdel Fattah Amr Bey (Egypt), later appointed Ambassador in London, who won in 1931–32–33 and 1935–36–37.

Longest and Shortest Championship Matches. The longest recorded match was one of 2 hours 35 minutes in the British Amateur Championships at Wembley, England, on December 12, 1976, when Murray Lilley (New Zealand) beat Barry O'Connor (G.B.) 9–3, 10–8, 2–9, 7–9, 10–8. The second game lasted 58 minutes and there were a total of 98 lets called in the match.

WOMEN'S SQUASH CHAMPION: Heather McKay won 16 titles in the annual women's championships.

Sue Cogswell beat Teresa Lawes in only 16 minutes in a British Women's title match at Dallington, North Hampshire, on December 12, 1977.

Most Victories in the Women's Championship. The most wins in the Women's Squash Rackets Championship is 16 by Heather McKay (*née* Blundell) of Australia, 1961 to 1976. She also won the first World Open title in 1978. Since 1961 she has not lost a match.

Marathon Record. The longest squash marathon has been 110 hours 3 minutes by S.A.C. Graham Shepperdson at R.A.F. Rheindahlen, Germany, on May 26–30, 1979. George Deponselle and William de Bruin played for 106 hours 43 minutes at Sutterheim Country Club, Cape Province, South Africa, on October 1–5, 1978. (*This category will in the future be confined to two players only.*)

Surfing

Origins. The traditional Polynesian sport of surfing in a canoe (*ehorooe*) was first recorded by the British explorer, Captain James Cook (1728–79) on his third voyage to Tahiti in December, 1771. Surfing on a board (*Amo Amo iluna ka lau oka nalu*) was first described ("most perilous and extraordinary . . . altogether astonishing, and is scarcely to be credited") by Lt. (later Capt.) James King of the Royal Navy in March, 1779, at Kealakekua Bay, Hawaii Island. A surfer was first depicted by the voyage's official artist, John Webber. The sport was revived at Waikiki by 1900. Hollow boards came in in 1929 and the plastic-foam type in 1956.

Highest Waves Ridden. Makaha Beach, Hawaii, provides reputedly the best consistently high waves for surfing, often reaching the rideable limit of 30–35 feet. The highest wave ever ridden was the *tsunami* of "perhaps 50 feet," which struck Minole, Hawaii, on April 3, 1868, and was ridden to save his life by a Hawaiian named Holua.

Longest Ride. About 4 to 6 times each year rideable surfing waves break in Matanchen Bay near San Blas, Nayarit, Mexico, which make rides of *c.* 5,700 feet possible.

World Champions. World Championships were inaugurated in 1964 at Sydney, Australia. The first surfer to win two titles has been Joyce Hoffman (U.S.) in 1965 and 1966.

Swimming

Earliest References. Swimming in schools in Japan was ordered by Imperial edict of Emperor Go-Yoozei as early as 1603, but competition was known from 36 B.C. Sea water bathing was fashionable at Scarborough, North Yorkshire, England, as early as 1660. Com-

FASTEST SWIMMER: American Joe Bottom covered 50 yards in 19.70 seconds in March, 1977.

petitive swimming originated in London *c.* 1837, at which time there were five or more pools, the earliest of which had been opened at St. George's Pier Head, Liverpool, in 1828.

Largest Pools. The largest swimming pool in the world is the salt-water Orthlieb Pool in Casablanca, Morocco. It is 480 meters (1,547 feet) long, 75 meters (246 feet) wide, and has an area of 8.9 acres.

The largest land-locked swimming pool with heated water was the Fleishhacker Pool on Sloat Boulevard, near Great Highway, San Francisco. It measures 1,000 feet by 150 feet (3.44 acres), is up to 14 feet deep, and can contain 7,500,000 gallons of water. It was opened on May 2, 1925, but has now been abandoned to a few ducks.

The world's largest competition pool is at Osaka, Japan. It accommodates 13,614 spectators.

Fastest Swimmer. Excluding relay stages with their anticipatory starts, the highest speed reached by a swimmer is 5.19 m.p.h. by Joe Bottom (U.S.), who recorded 19.70 seconds for 50 yards in a 25-yard pool at Cleveland, Ohio, on March 24, 1977.

The fastest by a woman is 4.42 m.p.h. by Sue Hinderaker (U.S.) who clocked 23.14 seconds for 50 yards in Pittsburgh, Pennsylvania, on March 16, 1979.

Most World Records. Men: 32, Arne Borg (Sweden) (b. 1901), 1921–29. Women: 42, Ragnhild Hveger (Denmark) (b. December 10, 1920), 1936–42.

World Titles. In the world swimming championships (instituted in 1973), the greatest number of medals won is ten (8 gold, 2 silver) by Kornelia Ender of East Germany. The most by a man is seven (6 gold, 1 bronze) by James Montgomery (U.S.).

The most medals in a single championships is six by Tracy Caulkins (U.S.) (b. January 11, 1963) in 1975 with five golds and a silver.

SWIMMING—WORLD RECORDS—MEN

At distances recognized by the Fédération Internationale de Natation Amateur as of August, 1979. F.I.N.A. no longer recognizes any records made for non-metric distances. Only performances set up in 50-meter pools are recognized as World Records.

Distance	min. sec.	Name and Nationality	Place	Date
FREE-STYLE				
100 meters	49.44	Jonty Skinner (South Africa)	Philadelphia, Pennsylvania	Aug. 14, 1976
200 meters	1:49.83*	Serge Kopliakov (U.S.S.R.)	Potsdam, E. Germany	April 7, 1979
400 meters	3:51.41	Vladimir Salnikov (U.S.S.R.)	Potsdam, E. Germany*	April 6, 1979
800 meters	7:56.49	Vladimir Salnikov (U.S.S.R.)	Minsk, U.S.S.R.	Mar. 23, 1979
1,500 meters	15:02.40	Brian Goodell (U.S.)	Montreal, Canada	July 20, 1976
4×100 Relay	3:19.74	U.S. National Team	West Berlin, W. Germany	Aug. 22, 1978
		(Jack Babashoff, Ambrose Gaines, David McCagg, James Montgomery)		
4×200 Relay	7:20.82	U.S. National Team	West Berlin, W. Germany	Aug. 24, 1978
		(Bruce Furniss, William Forrester, Bobby Hackett, Ambrose Gaines)		
BREAST STROKE				
100 meters	1:02.86	Gerald Moerken (W. Germany)	Jönköping, Sweden	Aug. 17, 1977
200 meters	2:15.11	David Wilkie (G.B.)	Montreal, Canada	July 24, 1976
BUTTERFLY STROKE				
100 meters	54.18	Joseph Bottom (U.S.)	East Berlin, E. Germany	Aug. 27, 1977
200 meters	1:59.23	Michael Bruner (U.S.)	Montreal, Canada	July 18, 1976
BACK STROKE				
100 meters	55.49	John Naber (U.S.)	Montreal, Canada	July 19, 1976
200 meters	1:59.19	John Naber (U.S.)	Montreal, Canada	July 24, 1976
INDIVIDUAL MEDLEY				
200 meters	2:03.29	Jesse Vassallo (U.S.)	San Juan, Puerto Rico	July 6, 1979
400 meters	4:20.05	Jesse Vassallo (U.S.)	West Berlin, W. Germany	Aug. 22, 1978
MEDLEY RELAY				
		(Back Stroke, Breast Stroke, Butterfly Stroke, Free-Style)		
4×100 meters	3:42.22	U.S. National Team	West Berlin, W. Germany	Aug. 22, 1978
		(John Naber, John Hencken, Matthew Vogel, James Montgomery)		

*First leg of relay

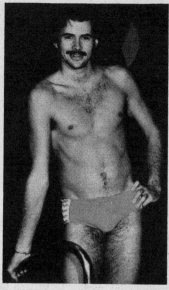

BACK STROKE STREAK (above):
John Naber set world records at 100
and 200 meters at the 1976 Olympics.
**FASTEST 200-METER BREAST
STROKE (right):** David Wilkie set
his record mark at the Montreal
Olympics as well.

Olympic Swimming Records

Most Olympic Gold Medals. The greatest number of Olympic
gold medals won is 9 by Mark Andrew Spitz (U.S.) (b. February 10,
1950), as follows:

100 meter free-style	1972
200 meter free-style	1972
100 meter butterfly	1972
200 meter butterfly	1972
4 × 100 meter free-style relay	1968 and 1972
4 × 200 meter free-style relay	1968 and 1972
4 × 100 meter medley relay	1972

All but one of these performances (the 4 × 200 meter relay of 1968)
were also new world records at the time.

The record number of gold medals won by a woman is 4 shared by
Mrs. Patricia McCormick (*née* Keller) (U.S.) (b. May 12, 1930)
with the High and Springboard Diving double in 1952 and 1956
(also the women's record for individual golds); by Dawn Fraser
(later Mrs. Gary Ware) (Australia) (b. September 4, 1937) with the
100 meter free-style (1956–60–64) and the 4 × 100 meter free-style
relay (1956); and by Kornelia Ender (East Germany) with the 100
and 200 meter free-style (1976), the 100 meter butterfly (1976) and
the 4 × 100 meter medley relay (1976). Dawn Fraser is the only
swimmer to win the same event on three successive occasions.

Most Olympic Medals. The most medals won is 11 by Spitz,
who in addition to his 9 golds (see above), won a silver (100 m.
butterfly) and a bronze (100 m. free-style), both in 1968.

DIVING MEDALIST:
Klaus Dibiasi of Italy has
dominated men's diving
competition with 5
Olympic medals and 4
World championship
medals between
1964 and 1976.

The most medals won by a woman is 8 by Dawn Fraser, who in addition to her 4 golds (see above) won 4 silvers (400 m. free-style 1956, 4 × 100 m. free-style relay 1960 and 1964, 4 × 100 m. medley relay 1960); by Shirley Babashoff (U.S.) who won 2 golds (4 × 100 m. free-style relay 1972 and 1976) and 6 silvers (100 m. free-style 1972, 200 m. free-style 1972 and 1976, 400 m. and 800 m. free-style 1976, and 400 m. medley 1976); and by Kornelia Ender (E. Germany) who, in addition to her 4 golds (see above), won 4 silvers (200 m. individual medley 1972, 4 × 100 m. medley 1972, 4 × 100 m. free-style 1972 and 1976).

Most Individual Gold Medals. The record number of individual gold medals won is 4 shared by four swimmers: Charles M. Daniels (U.S.) (1884–1973) (100 m. free-style 1906 and 1908, 220 yard free-style 1904, 440 yard free-style 1904); Roland Matthes (E. Germany) (b. November 17, 1950) with 100 m. and 200 m. backstroke 1968 and 1972 and Spitz and McCormick (see above).

Closest Verdict. The closest victory in the Olympic Games was in the Munich 400-meter individual medley final on August 30, 1972, when Gunnar Larsson (Sweden) won by 2/1,000ths of a second in 4 minutes 31.981 seconds over Tim McKee (U.S.)—a margin of less than ⅛ inch, or the length grown by a fingernail in 3 weeks.

Diving

Olympic Medals. Klaus Dibiasi (Italy) won a total of 5 medals (3 gold, 2 silver) in four Games from 1964 to 1976. He is also the only diver to win the same event (highboard) at three successive Games (1968, 1972, and 1976). Pat McCormick (see above) won 4 gold medals.

World Titles. Phil Boggs (U.S.) (b. December 29, 1949) has won three gold medals in 1973, 75 and 78, but Klaus Dibiasi of Italy won four medals (2 gold and 2 silver) in 1973 and 1975. Trina Kalinina (U.S.S.R.) (b. February 8, 1959) won five medals (three gold, one silver, one bronze) in 1973, 75 and 78.

Perfect Dive. In the 1972 U.S. Olympic Trials, held in Chicago, Michael Finneran (b. September 21, 1948) was awarded a score of 10 by all seven judges for a backward $1\frac{1}{2}$ somersault $2\frac{1}{2}$ twist free dive from the 10-meter board, an achievement without precedent.

Long Distance Swimming

A unique achievement in long distance swimming was established in 1966 by the cross-Channel swimmer Mihir Sen of Calcutta, India. These were the Palk Strait from Sri Lanka to India (in 25 hours 36 minutes on April 5–6); the Straits of Gibraltar (Europe to Africa in 8 hours 1 minute on August 24); the Dardanelles (Gallipoli, Europe, to Sedulbahir, Asia Minor, in 13 hours 55 minutes on September 12) and the entire length of the Panama Canal in 34 hours 15 minutes on October 29–31. He had earlier swum the English Channel in 14 hours 45 minutes on September 27, 1958.

The longest recorded ocean swim is one of 128.8 miles by Walter Poenisch (U.S.) (b. 1914) from Havana, Cuba to Little Duck Key, Florida (in a shark cage and wearing flippers) in 34 hours 15 minutes on July 11–13, 1978.

The greatest recorded distance ever swum is 1,826 miles down the Mississippi from Ford Dam, near Minneapolis, to Carrollton Avenue, New Orleans, July 6 to December 29, 1930, by Fred P. Newton, then 27, of Clinton, Oklahoma. He was in the water a total of 742 hours, and the water temperature fell as low as 47° F. He protected himself with petroleum jelly.

The longest duration swim ever achieved was one of 168 continuous hours, ending on February 24, 1941, by the legless Charles Zibbelman, *alias* Zimmy (born 1894), of the U.S., in a pool in Honolulu, Hawaii.

The longest duration swim by a woman was 87 hours 27 minutes in a salt water pool at Raven Hall, Coney Island, New York by Mrs. Myrtle Huddleston of New York City, in 1931. Margaret "Peggy" Byrne (U.S.) (b. December 17, 1949), a Minnesota State Representative, swam 60 hours 15 minutes in a freshwater pool at Saint Paul, Minnesota, on December 18–20, 1978.

The greatest distance covered in a continuous swim is 292 miles by Joe Maciag (b. March 26, 1956) from Billings to Glendive, Montana, in the Yellowstone River in 64 hours 50 minutes, July 1–4, 1976.

Channel Swimming

Earliest Man. The first man to swim across the English Channel (without a life jacket) was the merchant navy captain Matthew Webb (1848–83) (G.B.), who swam breaststroke from Dover,

SWIMMING—WORLD RECORDS—WOMEN

(As of August, 1979)

Distance	min. sec.	Name and Nationality	Place	Date
FREE-STYLE				
100 meters	55.41	Barbara Krause (E. Germany)	East Berlin, E. Germany	July 5, 1978
200 meters	1:58.43	Cynthia Woodhead (U.S.)	San Juan, Puerto Rico	July 4, 1979
400 meters	4:06.28	Tracey Wickham (Australia)	West Berlin, W. Germany	Aug. 24, 1978
800 meters	8:24.62	Tracey Wickham (Australia)	Edmonton, Canada	Aug. 5, 1978
1,500 meters	16:06.63	Tracey Wickham (Australia)	Perth, Australia	Feb. 25, 1979
4 × 100 Relay	3:43.43	U.S. National Team	West Berlin, W. Germany	Aug. 27, 1978
		(Tracy Caulkins, Stephanie Elkins, Jill Sterkel, Cynthia Woodhead)		
BREAST STROKE				
100 meters	1:10.31	Julia Bogdanova (U.S.S.R.)	West Berlin, W. Germany	Aug. 22, 1978
200 meters	2:28.36	Lina Kachushite (U.S.S.R.)	Potsdam, E. Germany	Apr. 6, 1979
BUTTERFLY STROKE				
100 meters	59.46	Andrea Pollack (E. Germany)	East Berlin, E. Germany	July 3, 1978
200 meters	2:09.77	Mary Meagher (U.S.)	San Juan, Puerto Rico	July 7, 1979
BACK STROKE				
100 meters	1:01.51	Ulrike Richter (E. Germany)	East Berlin, E. Germany	June 5, 1976
200 meters	2:11.93	Linda Jezek (U.S.)	West Berlin, W. Germany	Aug. 24, 1978
INDIVIDUAL MEDLEY				
200 meters	2:14.07	Tracy Caulkins (U.S.)	West Berlin, W. Germany	Aug. 20, 1978
400 meters	4:40.83	Tracy Caulkins (U.S.)	West Berlin, W. Germany	Aug. 23, 1978
MEDLEY RELAY (Back Stroke, Breast Stroke, Butterfly Stroke, Free-Style)				
4 × 100 meters	4:07.95	East German National Team	Montreal, Canada	July 18, 1976
		(Ulrike Richter, Hannelore Anke, Andrea Pollack, Kornelia Ender)		

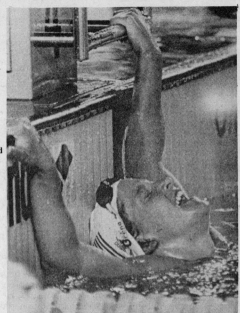

NEW 200 METER MARK: Cynthia Woodhead set a new women's world record at the Pan American Games in San Juan, Puerto Rico, on July 4, 1979.

England, to Calais Sands, France, in 21 hours 45 minutes on August 24–25, 1875. Webb swam an estimated 38 miles to make the 21-mile crossing. Paul Boyton (U.S.) had swum from Cap Gris Nez to the South Foreland in his patent lifesaving suit in 23 hours 30 minutes on May 28–29, 1875. There is good evidence that Jean-Marie Saletti, a French soldier, escaped from a British prison hulk off Dover by swimming to Boulogne in July or August, 1815. The first crossing from France to England was made by Enrico Tiraboschi, a wealthy Italian living in Argentina, who crossed in 16 hours 33 minutes on August 12, 1923, to win a $5,000 prize.

Woman. The first woman to succeed was Gertrude Ederle (U.S.) who swam from Cap Gris Nez, France, to Deal, England, on August 6, 1926, in the then record time of 14 hours 39 minutes. The first woman to swim from England to France was Florence Chadwick of California, in 16 hours 19 minutes on September 11, 1951.

Youngest. The youngest conqueror is Karl Beniston (b. December 9, 1964) of Blackpool, England, who swam from Dover to Wissant, France, in 12 hours 25 minutes, when he was aged 13 years 233 days. The youngest woman was Abla Adel Khairi (b. Egypt, September 26, 1960), aged 13 years 326 days when she swam from England to France in 12 hours 30 minutes on August 17, 1974.

Oldest. The oldest conqueror of the 21-mile crossing has been William E. (Ned) Barnie, who was 55 when he swam from France to England in 15 hours 1 minute on August 16, 1951. The oldest woman to conquer the Channel was Stella Taylor (born Bristol, Avon, England, December 20, 1929), aged 45 years 350 days when she swam it in 18 hours 15 minutes on August 26, 1975.

Fastest. The official Channel Swimming Association record is 7 hours 40 minutes by Penny Dean (b. March 21, 1955) of California, who swam from Shakespeare Beach, Dover, England to Cap Gris Nez, France on July 29, 1978.

Slowest. The slowest crossing was the third ever made, when Henry Sullivan (U.S.) swam from England to France in 26 hours 50 minutes, August 5–6, 1923. It is estimated that he swam some 56 miles.

Relays. The two-way record is 16 hours 5½ minutes by six Saudi Arabian men on August 11, 1977. They completed the return journey from France to England in a record 7 hours 58 minutes.

First Double Crossing. Antonio Abertondo (Argentina), aged 42, swam from England to France in 18 hours 50 minutes (8:35 a.m. on September 20 to 3:25 a.m. on September 21, 1961) and after about 4 minutes' rest returned to England in 24 hours 16 minutes, landing at St. Margaret's Bay at 3:45 a.m. on September 22, 1961, to complete the first "double crossing" in 43 hours 10 minutes.

Fastest Double Crossing. Cynthia Nicholas, a 19-year-old from Canada, became the first woman to complete a double crossing of the English Channel on September 7–8, 1977. Her astonishing time of 19 hours 55 minutes was more than 10 hours faster than the previous mark.

Most Conquests. The greatest number of Channel conquests is 13 by Desmond Renford (born 1927) (Australia) from August 9, 1970 to August 22, 1978. Cindy Nicholas made her first crossing of the Channel on July 29, 1975, and her sixth on August 27, 1978.

Underwater. The first underwater cross-Channel swim was achieved by Fred Baldasare (U.S.), aged 38, who completed a 42-mile swim from France to England with scuba in 18 hours 1 minute on July 10–11, 1962.

Relay Records

The longest recorded mileage in a 24-hour relay swim (team of 5) is 83 miles 620 yards by a team from the Topeka Swimming Association, Topeka, Kansas, on September 30–October 1, 1977.

The fastest time recorded for 100 miles in a pool by a team of 20 swimmers is 22 hours 38 minutes at the Atlantis Swim Centre, Plympton Park, Australia, on October 14–15, 1978.

Treading Water

The duration record for treading water (vertical posture in an 8-foot square without touching the lane markers) is 64 hours by Norman Albert at Pennsylvania State University on November 1–4, 1978.

Table Tennis

Earliest Reference. The earliest evidence relating to a game resembling table tennis has been found in the catalogues of London sporting goods manufacturers in the 1880's. The old Ping-Pong Association was formed there in 1902, but the game proved only a temporary craze until resuscitated in 1921.

Fastest Rallying. The record number of hits in 60 seconds is 162 by Nicky Jarvis and Desmond Douglas in London, England, on December 1, 1976. This was equaled by Douglas and Paul Day at Blackpool, England, on March 21, 1977. The most by women is 148 by Linda Howard and Melodi Ludi at Blackpool, Lancashire, England, on October 11, 1977.

With a paddle in each hand, Gary O. Fisher of Olympia, Washington, completed 5,000 consecutive volleys over the net in 44 minutes 28 seconds on June 25, 1979.

Longest Rally. In a 1936 Swaythling Cup match in Prague between Alex Ehrlich (Poland) and Paneth Farcas (Rumania), the opening rally lasted 2 hours 12 minutes.

Robert Siegel and Donald Peters of Stamford, Connecticut, staged a rally lasting 8 hours 33 minutes on July 30, 1978.

Longest Match. In the Swaythling Cup final match between Austria and Rumania in Prague, Czechoslovakia, in 1936, the play lasted for 25 or 26 hours, spread over three nights.

Marathon. The longest recorded time for a marathon singles match by two players is 132 hours 31 minutes by Danny Price and Randy Nunes in Cherry Hill, New Jersey, August 20-26, 1978.

The longest doubles marathon by 4 players is 101 hours 1 minute 11 seconds by Lance, Phil and Mark Warren and Bill Weir at Sacramento, California, on April 9–13, 1979.

Highest Speed. No conclusive measurements have been published, but in a lecture M. Sklorz (W. Germany) stated that a smashed ball had been measured at speeds up to 105.6 m.p.h.

Youngest International. The youngest international (probably in any sport) was Joy Foster, aged 8, the 1958 Jamaican singles and mixed doubles champion.

Tennis

Origins. The modern game of lawn tennis is generally agreed to have evolved as an outdoor form of Royal Tennis. "Field Tennis" was mentioned in an English magazine (*Sporting Magazine*) on September 29, 1793. The earliest club for such a game, variously called Pelota or Lawn Rackets, was the Leamington Club, founded in 1872 by Major Harry Gem. In February, 1874, Major Walter Clopton Wingfield of England (1833–1912) patented a form called "sphairistike," but the game soon became known as lawn tennis.

Amateurs were permitted to play with and against professionals in Open tournaments starting in 1968.

Oldest Courts. The oldest court for Royal Tennis is one built in Paris in 1496. The oldest of 17 surviving tennis courts in the British Isles is the Royal Tennis Court at Hampton Court Palace, which was built by order of King Henry VIII in 1529–30, and rebuilt by order of Charles II in 1660.

Greatest Crowd. The greatest crowd at a tennis match was the 30,472 who came to the Houston Astrodome in Houston, Texas, on September 20, 1973, to watch Billie Jean King beat Bobby Riggs, over 25 years her senior, in straight sets in the so-called "Tennis Match of the Century."

The record for an orthodox match is 25,578 at Sydney, Australia, on December 27, 1954, in the Davis Cup Challenge Round vs. the U.S. (1st day).

Most Davis Cup Victories. The greatest number of wins in the Davis Cup (instituted 1900) has been (inclusive of 1978) by the United States with 25.

Individual Davis Cup Performance. Nicola Pietrangeli (Italy) played 164 rubbers, 1954 to 1972, winning 120. He played 110 singles (winning 78) and 54 doubles (winning 42). He took part in 66 ties.

Greatest Domination. The "grand slam" is to hold at the same time all four of the world's major championship titles: Wimbledon, the U.S. Open, Australian and French championships. The first time this occurred was in 1935 when Frederick John Perry (U.K.) (b. 1909) won the French title, having won Wimbledon (1934), the U.S. title (1933–34) and the Australian title (1934).

The first player to hold all four titles simultaneously was J. Donald Budge (U.S.) (b. 1915), who won the championships of Wimbledon (1937), the U.S. (1937), Australia (1938), and France (1938). He subsequently retained Wimbledon (1938) and the U.S. (1938). Rodney George Laver (Australia) (b. August 9, 1938) achieved this grand slam in 1962 as an amateur and repeated as a professional in 1969 to become the first two-time grand slammer.

Two women players also have won all these four titles in the same tennis year. The first was Maureen Catherine Connolly (U.S.). She won the United States title in 1951, Wimbledon in 1952, retained the U.S. title in 1952, won the Australian in 1953, the French in 1953 and Wimbledon again in 1953. She won her third U.S. title in 1953, her second French title in 1954, and her third Wimbledon title in 1954. Miss Connolly (later Mrs. Norman Brinker) was seriously injured in a riding accident shortly before the 1954 U.S. championships; she died in June, 1969, aged only 34.

The second woman to win the "grand slam" was Margaret Smith Court (Australia) (b. July 16, 1942) in 1970.

Olympic Medals. Lawn tennis was part of the program at the first eight celebrations of the Games (including 1906). The winner of the most medals was Max Decugis (1882–1978) of France, with six (a record four gold, one silver and one bronze) in the 1900, 1906 and 1920 tournaments.

GRAND SLAM WINNERS: The only men to win all four major titles in the same year were Rod Laver (left) of Australia who performed the feat twice in 1962 and 1969, and Don Budge (right) of the U.S. who did it once in 1937-38.

The most medals won by a woman is five by Kitty McKane (later Mrs. L. A. Godfree) of Great Britain, with one gold, two silver and two bronze in 1920 and 1924. Five different women won a record two gold medals.

Wimbledon Records

The first Championship was in 1877. Professionals first played in 1968. From 1971 the tie-break system was introduced, which effactually prevents sets proceeding beyond a 17th game, i.e., 9–8.

Most Appearances. Arthur W. Gore (1868–1928) of the U.K. made 36 appearances between 1888 and 1927, and was in 1909 at 41 years the oldest singles winner ever. In 1964, Jean Borotra (born August 13, 1898) of France made his 35th appearance since 1922. In 1977, he appeared in the Veterans' Doubles, aged 78.

Most Wins. Six-time singles champion Billie Jean King (*née* Moffitt) has also won ten women's doubles and four mixed doubles during the period 1961 to 1979, to total a record 20 titles.

The greatest number of singles wins was eight by Helen N. Moody (*née* Wills) (b. October 6, 1905) (U.S.), who won in 1927, 1928, 1929, 1930, 1932, 1933, 1935 and 1938.

The greatest number of singles wins by a man since the Challenge Round (wherein the defending champion was given a bye until the final round) was abolished in 1922 is four, by Rod Laver in 1961, 1962, 1968 and 1969, and consecutively by Bjorn Borg (Sweden) (b. June 6, 1956) in 1976–1979. The all-time men's record was seven by William C. Renshaw in 1881–2–3–4–5–6–9.

The greatest number of doubles wins by men was 8 by the brothers Doherty (G.B.)—Reginald Frank (1872–1910) and Hugh Lawrence (1875–1919). They won each year from 1897 to 1905 except for 1902. Hugh Doherty also won 5 singles titles (1902–06) and holds the record for most men's titles with 13.

The most wins in women's doubles was 12 by Elizabeth "Bunny" Ryan (U.S.) (1894–1979).

The greatest number of mixed doubles wins was 7 by Elizabeth Ryan (U.S.). The men's record is four wins, shared by Elias Victor Seixas (b. August 30, 1923) (U.S.) in 1953–54–55–56, Kenneth N. Fletcher (b. June 15, 1940) (Australia) in 1963–65–66–68, and Owen Keir Davidson (Australia) (b. October 4, 1943) in 1967–71–73–74.

Youngest Champions. The youngest champion ever at Wimbledon was Charlotte Dod (1871–1960), who was 15 years 9 months old when she won in 1887.

The youngest male singles champion was Wilfred Baddeley (born January 11, 1872), who won the Wimbledon title in 1891 at the age of 19 years 175 days.

Richard Dennis Ralston (born July 27, 1942), of Bakersfield, California, was 25 days short of his 18th birthday when he won the men's doubles with Rafael H. Osuna (1938–69), of Mexico, in 1960.

The youngest-ever player at Wimbledon is reputedly Miss Mita Klima (Austria), who was 13 years old in the 1907 singles competition. The youngest of modern times is Tracy Austin (U.S.) (b. December 12, 1962) who was only 14 years 7 months in the 1977 tournament.

Greatest Attendance. The record crowd for one day at Wimbledon is 38,295 on June 27, 1979. The total attendance record was set at the 1975 Championships with 338,591.

Professional Tennis

Highest Prize Money. The greatest reward for playing a single match is the $500,000 won by Jimmy Connors (U.S.) (born September 2, 1952) when he beat John Newcombe (Australia) (born May 23, 1944) in a challenge match at Caesars Palace Hotel, Las Vegas, Nevada, April 26, 1975.

The record winnings for a year, not including special restricted events and team tennis salaries, is $800,642 by Guillermo Vilas (Argentina) (born August 17, 1952) in 1977. (See photo, page 647).

Christine Marie Evert (now Lloyd) (U.S.) (born December 21, 1954), the 1976 Wimbledon champion, earned a record $454,486 in 1978.

Tennis Marathons

The longest recorded non-stop tennis singles match is one of 105 hours by Ricky Tolston and Jeff Sutton at Bill Faye Park, Kinston, North Carolina, on May 7–11, 1979.

The duration record for doubles is 77 hours by Mark B. Rainford and Peter Wachtel *vs.* Roland W. Wachtel and Damian L. Dorrough at Tyalgum, Australia, on September 14–17, 1978.

A PROFITABLE RACKET: Chris Evert Lloyd (left) and Guillermo Vilas (right) have had the most financially successful single years in women's and men's tennis.

Longest Game. The longest known singles game was one of 37 deuces (80 points) between Anthony Fawcett (Rhodesia) and Keith Glass (G.B.) in the first round of the Surrey championships at Surbiton, Surrey, England, on May 26, 1975. It lasted 31 minutes.

Fastest Service. The fastest service ever *measured* was one of 163.6 m.p.h. by William Tatem Tilden (1893–1953) (U.S.) in 1931. The American professional Scott Carnahan, 22, was electronically clocked at 137 m.p.h. at Pauley Pavilion in Los Angeles, California, during the third annual "Cannonball Classic" sponsored by *Tennis* magazine, and reported in the fall of 1976.

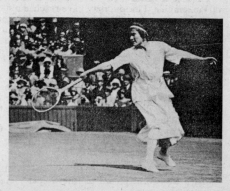

WIMBLEDON DOUBLES CHAMPION: Elizabeth "Bunny" Ryan won the greatest number of women's doubles and mixed doubles titles, and was second only to Billie Jean King in overall wins at Wimbledon.

Some players consider the service of Robert Falkenburg (U.S.) (born January 29, 1926), the 1948 Wimbledon champion, as the fastest ever produced.

Longest Career. The championship career of C. Alphonso Smith (born March 18, 1909) of Charlottesville, Virginia, extended from winning the U.S. National Boy's title at Chicago on August 14, 1924, to winning the National 65-and-over title at Aptos, California (exactly 50 years to the day later) on August 14, 1974.

Track and Field

Earliest References. Track and field athletics date from the ancient Olympic Games. The earliest accurately known Olympiad dates from July, 776 B.C., at which celebration Coroibos won the foot race. The oldest surviving measurements are a long jump of 23 feet 1½ inches by Chionis of Sparta in *c.* 656 B.C. and a discus throw of 100 cubits (*c.* 152 feet) by Protesilaus.

Oldest Race. The oldest continuously held foot race is the "Red Hose Race" held at Carnwath, Scotland, since 1507. First prize is a pair of hand-knitted knee-length red stockings.

Earliest Landmarks. The first time 10 seconds ("even time") was bettered for 100 yards under championship conditions was when John Owen recorded 9⅘ seconds in the A.A.U. Championships at Analostan Island, Washington, D.C., on October 11, 1890. The first recorded instance of 6 feet being cleared in the high jump was when Marshall Jones Brooks jumped 6 feet 0⅛ inch at Marston, near Oxford, England, on March 17, 1876. The breaking of the "4 minute barrier" in the one mile was first achieved by Dr. Roger Gilbert Bannister (born Harrow, England, March 23, 1929), when he recorded 3 minutes 59.4 seconds on the Iffley Road track, Oxford, at 6:10 p.m. on May 6, 1954.

Fastest Runners. Robert Lee Hayes (born December 20, 1942), of Jacksonville, Florida, may have reached a speed of over 27 m.p.h. at St. Louis, on June 21, 1963, in his world record 9.1 sec. 100 yards. Marlies Göhr (*née* Oelsner) (b. East Germany, March 21, 1958) reached a speed of over 24 m.p.h. in her world record 100 meters in 10.88 seconds at Dresden, East Germany, on July 1, 1977.

World Record Breakers

Oldest. The greatest age at which anyone has broken a standard world record is 41 years 196 days in the case of John J. Flanagan (1868–1938), who set a world record in the hammer throw on July 24, 1909. The female record is 35 years 255 days for Dana Zátopkova (*née* Ingrova) (born September 19, 1922) of Czechoslovakia, who broke the women's javelin record with 182 feet 10 inches at Prague, Czechoslovakia, on June 1, 1958.

Youngest. Ulrike Meyfarth (b. May 4, 1956) (W. Germany) equaled the world record for the women's high jump at 6 feet 3½ inches winning the gold medal at the Munich Olympics, 1972, when she was aged 16 years 123 days. Barbara Jones (see Oldest and Youngest Olympic Champions, page 658) was aged 15 years 123 days when she was part of a record-setting team.

Most Records in a Day. The only athlete to have his name entered in the record book 6 times in one day was J. C. "Jesse" Owens (U.S.) who at Ann Arbor, Michigan, on May 25, 1935, equaled the 100-yard running record with 9.4 secs. at 3:15 p.m.; long-jumped 26 feet 8¼ inches at 3:25 p.m.; ran 220 yards (straight away) in 20.3 secs. at 3:45 p.m.; and 220 yards over low hurdles in 22.6 secs. at 4 p.m. The two 220-yard runs were also ratified as 200 meter world records.

Running Backwards. The fastest time recorded for running 100 yards backwards is 13.3 seconds by Paul Wilson at Hastings, New Zealand, on April 10, 1977.

Three-Legged Race. The fastest recorded time for a 100-yard three-legged race is 11.0 seconds by Harry L. Hillman and Lawson Robertson in Brooklyn, New York City, on April 24, 1909.

Ambidextrous Shot Put. Allan Feuerbach (U.S.) has put a 16-lb. shot a total of 121 feet 6¾ inches (51 feet 5 inches with his left hand and 70 feet 1¾ inches with his right) at Malmö, Sweden, on August 24, 1974.

Standing Long Jump. Joe Darby (1861–1937), the famous Victorian professional jumper from Dudley, Worcestershire, England, jumped a measured 12 feet 1½ inches *without* weights at Dudley Castle, on May 28, 1890. Johan Christian Evandt (Norway) achieved 11 feet 11¾ inches as an amateur in Reykjavik, Iceland, on March 11, 1962.

Standing High Jump. The best amateur standing high jump is 5 feet 10¾ inches by Rune Almen (Sweden) at Örebro, Sweden, on December 8, 1974. Joe Darby (see above), the professional, reportedly cleared 6 feet with his ankles tied at Church Cricket Ground, Dudley, England, on June 11, 1892.

Highest Jumper. There are several reported instances of high jumpers exceeding the official world record height of 7 feet 8 inches. The earliest of these came from unsubstantiated reports of Watusi tribesmen in Central Africa clearing up to 8 feet 2½ inches, definitely, however, from inclined take-offs. The greatest height cleared above an athlete's own head is 23¼ inches by Franklin Jacobs (U.S.), who cleared 7 feet 7¼ inches despite a physical height of only 5 feet 8 inches at New York on January 28, 1978.

The greatest height cleared by a woman above her own head is 10¼ inches by Tamami Yagi (Japan) (b. November 15, 1958), who stands 5 feet 4½ inches tall and jumped 6 feet 2¾ inches at Matsumoto, Japan, on October 19, 1978.

Longest Career. Duncan McLean (born Gourock, Scotland, December 3, 1884) won the South African 100-yard title in February,

WORLD RECORDS—MEN

The complete list of World Records for the 32 scheduled men's events (excluding the 6 walking records, see under Walking) passed by the International Amateur Athletic Federation as of August 16, 1979. Those marked with an asterisk* are awaiting ratification. Note: On July 27, 1976, I.A.A.F. eliminated all records for races measured in yards, except for the mile (for sentimental reasons). All distances up to (and including) 400 meters must be electrically timed to be records. When a time is given to one-hundredth of a second, it represents the official electrically-timed record. In one case, a professional performance has bettered or equaled the I.A.A.F. mark, but the same highly rigorous rules as to timing, measuring and weighing are not necessarily applied.

RUNNING

Event	min. sec.	Name and Nationality	Place	Date
100 meters	9.95	James Ray Hines (U.S.)	Mexico City, Mexico	Oct. 14, 1968
200 meters (turn)	19.83	Tommie C. Smith (U.S.)	Mexico City, Mexico	Oct. 16, 1968
400 meters	43.86	Lee Edward Evans (U.S.)	Mexico City, Mexico	Oct. 18, 1968
800 meters	1:42.4*	Sebastian Newbold Coe (G.B.)	Oslo, Norway	July 5, 1979
1,000 meters	2:13.9	Richard Wohlhuter (U.S.)	Oslo, Norway	July 30, 1974
1,500 meters	3:21.1	Sebastian Newbold Coe (G.B.)	Zurich, Switzerland	Aug. 15, 1979
1 mile	3:49.0*	Sebastian Newbold Coe (G.B.)	Oslo, Norway	July 17, 1979
2,000 meters	4:51.4	John Walker (N.Z.)	Oslo, Norway	June 30, 1976
3,000 meters	7:32.1	Henry Rono (Kenya)	Oslo, Norway	June 27, 1978
5,000 meters	13:08.4	Henry Rono (Kenya)	Berkeley, California	April 8, 1978
10,000 meters	27:22.5	Henry Rono (Kenya)	Vienna, Austria	June 11, 1978
20,000 meters	57:24.2	Jos Hermens (Netherlands)	Papendal, Netherlands	May 1, 1976
25,000 meters	1 hr. 14:11.8	William Rodgers (U.S.)	Saratoga, California	Feb. 21, 1979
30,000 meters	1 hr. 31:30.4	James Noel Carroll Alder (U.K.)	Crystal Palace, London	Sept. 5, 1970
1 hour	13 miles 24⅓ yards	Jos Hermens (Netherlands)	Papendal, Netherlands	May 1, 1976

FASTEST 100 METERS (left): The record set at the 1968 Olympic Games by Jim Hines has now stood for over 10 years. FOUR RECORDS fell to Henry Rono in three months, as he set new marks at 3,000, 5,000, 10,000 meters and 3,000 meters steeplechase in spring 1978.

GREATEST HOURLY RUN: Jos Hermens of the Netherlands (number 5) ran a record 13 miles 24⅔ yards in one hour.

WORLD RECORDS—MEN (Continued)

HURDLING

Event	min. sec.	Name and Nationality	Place	Date
110 meters (3' 6")	13.00	Renaldo Nehemiah (U.S.)	Westwood, California	May 6, 1979
400 meters (3' 0")	47.45	Edwin Corley Moses (U.S.)	Westwood, California	June 11, 1977
3,000 meters Steeplechase	8:05.4	Henry Rono (Kenya)	Seattle, Washington	May 13, 1978

FIELD EVENTS

Event	ft.	in.	Name and Nationality	Place	Date
High Jump	7	8†	Vladimir Yashchenko (U.S.S.R.)	Tbilisi, U.S.S.R.	June 16, 1978
Pole Vault	18	8¼	David Roberts (U.S.)	Eugene, Oregon	June 22, 1976
Long Jump	29	2½	Robert Beamon (U.S.)	Mexico City, Mexico	Oct. 18, 1968
Triple Jump	58	8½	Joao de Oliveira (Brazil)	Mexico City, Mexico	Oct. 15, 1975
Shot Put	72	8	Udo Beyer (East Germany)	Gothenburg, Sweden	July 6, 1978
Discus Throw	233	5	Wolfgang Schmidt (E. Germany)	East Berlin, East Germany	Aug. 9, 1978
Hammer Throw	263	6	Karl Hans Riehm (West Germany)	Heidenheim, West Germany	Aug. 6, 1978
Javelin Throw	310	4	Miklos Nemeth (Hungary)	Montreal, Canada	July 26, 1976

Note: One professional performance which was equal or superior to the I.A.A.F. marks, but where the same highly rigorous rules as to timing, measuring and weighing were not necessarily applied, was the Shot Put of 75 feet by Brian Ray Oldfield (U.S.), at El Paso, Texas, on May 10, 1975.

† Yashchenko cleared 7 feet 8¼ inches indoors in Milan, Italy, on March 12, 1978.

HIGH JUMP:
Vladimir Yashchenko
has cleared
7 feet 8 inches outdoors,
and a half inch
higher indoors.

1904, in 9.9 seconds, and at age 91 set a world age-group record for 100 meters in 21.7 seconds in August, 1977—more than 72 years later.

Dimitrion Yordanidis completed a marathon race in 7 hours 33 minutes at the age of 98 in Athens, Greece, on October 10, 1976.

Blind 100 Meters. The fastest time recorded for 100 meters by a blind man is 11.4 seconds by Graham Henry Salmon (b. September 5, 1952) of Loughton, Essex, England, at Grangemouth, Scotland, on September 2, 1978.

One-Legged High Jump. Arnie Boldt (b. 1958), of Saskatchewan, Canada, cleared a height of 6 feet 6¾ inches indoors in 1977, in spite of the fact that he has only one leg.

Longest Race. The longest race ever staged was the 1929 Trans-continental Race (3,665 miles) from New York City to Los Angeles. The Finnish-born Johnny Salo (1893–1931) was the winner in 79 days, from March 31 to June 18. His elapsed time of 525 hours 57 minutes 20 seconds gave a running average of 6.97 m.p.h. His margin of victory was only 2 minutes 47 seconds.

Endurance. Mensen Ernst (1799–1846), of Norway, is reputed to have run from Istanbul, Turkey, to Calcutta, in West Bengal, India, and back in 59 days in 1836, so averaging an improbable 92.4 miles per day. The greatest non-stop run recorded is 186 miles in 31 hours 33 minutes 38 seconds by Max Telford (b. Hawick, Scotland, on February 2, 1935) of New Zealand at Wailuku, Hawaii, on

WORLD RECORDS—MEN

RELAYS

Event	min.sec.	Team	Place	Date
4×100 meters	38.03	United States Team	Düsseldorf, West Germany	Sept. 3, 1977
		(William Collins, Steven Earl Riddick, Clifford Wiley, Steven Williams)		
4×200 meters	1:20.3†	University of Southern California (U.S.)	Tempe, Arizona	May 27, 1978
		(Joel Andrews, James Sanford, William Mullins, Clancy Edwards)		
4×400 meters	2:56.1	United States Olympic Team	Mexico City, Mexico	Oct. 20, 1968
		(Vincent Matthews, Ronald Freeman, G. Lawrence James, Lee Edward Evans)		
4×800 meters	7:08.1	U.S.S.R. Team	Podolsk, U.S.S.R.	Aug. 12, 1978
		(Vladimir Podoliakov, Nikolai Kirov, Vladimir Malosemlin, Anatoli Reschetniak)		
4×1,500 meters	14:38.8	West German Team	Cologne, West Germany	Aug. 17, 1977
		(Thomas Wessinghage, Harald Hudak, Michael Lederer, Karl Fleschen)		

† The time of 1:20.2 achieved by the Tobias Striders at Tempe, Arizona on May 27, 1978 was not ratified as the team was composed of varied nationalities.

DECATHLON

8,618 points		Bruce Jenner (U.S.)	Montreal, Canada	July 29-30, 1976

(First day: 100 meters, 10.94 sec.; long jump, 23 ft. 8¼ in.; shot put, 50 ft. 4¼ in.; high jump, 6 ft. 8 in.; 400 meters, 47.51 sec. Second day: 110-meter hurdles, 14.84 sec.; discus, 164 ft. 2 in.; pole vault, 15 ft. 9 in.; javelin, 224 ft. 10 in.; 1,500 meters, 4 min. 12.61 sec.)

THE MARATHON

There is no official marathon record because of the varying severity of courses. The best time over 26 miles 385 yards (standardized in 1924) is 2 hours 08 minutes 33.6 seconds (av. 12.24 m.p.h.) by Derek Clayton (b. 1942 at Barrow-in-Furness, England) of Australia, at Antwerp, Belgium, on May 30, 1969.

The fastest time by a female is 2 hours 32 minutes 30 seconds (av. 10.31 m.p.h.) by Grete Waitz (Norway) (b. October 1, 1953) in New York City on October 22, 1978.

March 19–20, 1977. No rest breaks were taken. Telford ran 5,110 miles from Anchorage, Alaska, to Halifax, Nova Scotia, in 106 days 18 hours, 45 minutes from July 25 to November 9, 1977.

The 24-hour running record (on a standard track) is 161 miles 545 yards by Ron Bentley, 43, at Walton-on-Thames, Surrey, England, November 3–4, 1973.

The fastest recorded time for 100 miles is 11 hours 30 minutes 51 seconds by Donald Ritchie (b. July 6, 1944) at Crystal Palace, London, on October 15, 1977. The best by a woman is 16 hours 50 minutes 47 seconds by Ruth Anderson (b. 1929) at Woodside, California, on June 15–16, 1978.

The greatest distance covered by a man in six days (*i.e.* the 144 permissible hours between Sundays in Victorian times) was 623¾ miles by George Littlewood (England), who required only 141 hours 57½ minutes for this feat on December 3–8, 1888, at the old Madison Square Garden, New York City.

The fastest time for the cross-America run is 53 days, 7 minutes for 3,046 miles by Tom McGrath (N. Ireland) from August 29 to October 21, 1977.

The greatest racing mileage is the 5,926 miles in 192 races of marathon distance or more by Ted Corbitt (U.S.) (b. January 31, 1920) from April, 1951, to the end of 1978.

The greatest lifetime mileage recorded by any runner is 195,855 miles by Earle Littlewood Dilks (b. 1884) of New Castle, Pennsylvania, through 1977.

Most Olympic Gold Medals. The most Olympic gold medals won is 10 (an absolute Olympic record) by Ray C. Ewry (U.S.) (b. October 14, 1873, d. September 29, 1937) with:

Standing High Jump	1900, 1904, 1906, 1908
Standing Long Jump	1900, 1904, 1906, 1908
Standing Triple Jump	1900, 1904

The most gold medals won by a woman is 4, a record shared by Francina E. Blankers-Koen (Netherlands) (b. April 26, 1918) with 100 m., 200 m., 80 m. hurdles and 4 × 100 m. relay (1948) and Betty Cuthbert (Australia) (b. April 20, 1938) with 100 m., 200 m., 4 × 100 m. relay (1956) and 400 m. (1964).

Most Olympic Medals. The most medals won is 12 (9 gold and 3 silver) by Paavo Johannes Nurmi (Finland) (1897–1973) with:

1920 Gold: 10,000 m.; Cross-Country, Individual and Team; silver: 5,000 m.

1924 Gold: 1,500 m.; 5,000 m.; 3,000 m. Team; Cross-Country, Individual and Team.

1928 Gold: 10,000 m.; silver: 5,000 m.; 3,000 m. steeplechase.

The most medals won by a woman athlete is 7 by Shirley de la Hunty (*née* Strickland) (Australia) (b. July 18, 1925) with 3 gold, 1 silver and 3 bronze in the 1948, 1952 and 1956 Games. A recently discovered photo-finish indicates that she finished third, not fourth, in the 1948 200 m. event, thus unofficially increasing her total to 8. Irena Szewinska (*née* Kirszenstein) of Poland has also won 7 medals (3 gold, 2 silver, 2 bronze) in 1964, 1968, 1972 and 1976. She is the only woman ever to win Olympic medals in track and field in four successive Games.

WORLD RECORDS—WOMEN

RUNNING

Event	min. sec.	Name and Nationality	Place	Date
100 meters	10.88	Marlies Oelsner (now Göhr) (East Germany)	Dresden, East Germany	July 1, 1977
200 meters (turn)	21.71	Marita Koch (East Germany)	Karl Marx Stadt, East Germany	June 10, 1979
400 meters	48.94	Marita Koch (East Germany)	Prague, Czechoslovakia	Aug. 31, 1978
800 meters	1:54.9	Tatyana Kazankina (U.S.S.R.)	Montreal, Canada	July 26, 1976
1,500 meters	3:56.0	Tatyana Kazankina (U.S.S.R.)	Podolsk, U.S.S.R.	June 28, 1976
1 mile	4:22.1	Natalia Marasescu (née Andrei) (Rumania)	Auckland, New Zealand	Jan 27, 1979
3,000 meters	8:27.2	Ludmila Bragina (U.S.S.R.)	College Park, Maryland	Aug. 7, 1976

HURDLES

Event	min. sec.	Name and Nationality	Place	Date
100 meters (2' 9")	12.48	Grazayna Rabsztyn (Poland)	Fürth, West Germany	June 10, 1978
400 meters (2' 6")	54.89	Tatyana Zelentsova (U.S.S.R.)	Prague, Czechoslovakia	Sept. 2, 1978

FIELD EVENTS

Event	ft.	in.	Name and Nationality	Place	Date
High Jump	6	7	Sara Simeoni (Italy)	Brescia, Italy	Aug. 4, 1978
Long Jump	23	3¼	Vilma Bardauskiene (U.S.S.R.)	Prague, Czechoslovakia	Aug. 29, 1978
Shot Put	73	2¼†	Helena Fibingerova (Czechoslovakia)	Nitra, Czechoslovakia	Aug. 20, 1977
Discus Throw	232	0	Evelin Jahl (née Schlaak) (East Germany)	Dresden, East Germany	Aug. 12, 1978
Javelin Throw	228	1	Ruth Fuchs (née Gamm) (East Germany)	Dresden, East Germany	June 13, 1979

† Fibingerova set an indoor record of 73 feet 10 inches at Jablonec, Czechoslovakia, on February 19, 1977.

PENTATHLON

4,839 points (with 800 m.)	Nadezda Tkachenko (U.S.S.R.)	Lille, France	Sept. 18, 1977

(100 meter hurdles, 13.49 sec.; shot, 52 ft. 3½ in.; high jump, 5 ft. 10¼ in.; long jump, 21 ft. 3½ in.; 800 meters, 2 min. 10.62 sec.)

RELAYS

Event	min. sec.	Team	Place	Date
4 × 100 meters...	42.09	East Germany (Romy Schneider, Ingrid Auerswald, Marlies Göhr, Marita Koch)	Karl Marx Stadt, E. Germany	June 10, 1979
4 × 200 meters ...	1:31.6	British Team (Verona Elder, Donna Hartley, Sharon Colyear, Sonia Lannaman)	Crystal Palace, England	Aug. 20, 1977
4 × 400 meters ...	3:19.2	East German National Team (Doris Maletzki, Brigitte Rohde, Ellen Streidt, Christina Brehmer)	Montreal, Canada	July 31, 1976
4 × 800 meters ...	7:52.3	U.S.S.R. National Team (Tatyana Providokhina, Valentina Gerasimova, Svetlana Styrkina, Tatyana Kazankina)	Podolsk, U.S.S.R.	Aug. 16, 1976

FASTEST AT 3,000 METERS: Ludmila Bragina set the women's record at 3,000 meters in Maryland in 1976.

800 METER AND 1,500 METER CHAMPION: Tatyana Kazankina of the U.S.S.R. (leading here) set new marks for these distances in 1976.

Most Wins at One Games. The most gold medals at one celebration is 5 by Nurmi in 1924 (see above) and the most individual is 4 by Alvin C. Kraenzlein (U.S.) (1876–1928) in 1900 with 60 m., 110 m. hurdles, 200 m. hurdles and long jump.

Oldest and Youngest Olympic Champions. The oldest athlete to win an Olympic title was Irish-born Patrick J. "Babe" McDonald (U.S.) (1878–1954) who was aged 42 years 26 days when he won the 56-lb. weight throw at Antwerp, Belgium, on August 21, 1920. The oldest female champion was Lia Manoliu (Rumania) (b. April 25, 1932) aged 36 years 176 days when she won the discus at Mexico City on October 18, 1968.

The youngest gold medalist was Barbara Jones (U.S.) (b. March 26, 1937) who was a member of the winning 4 × 100 meter relay team, aged 15 years 123 days, at Helsinki, Finland, on July 27, 1952. The youngest male champion was Robert Bruce Mathias (U.S.) (b. November 17, 1930) aged 17 years 263 days when he won the decathlon at London on August 5–6, 1948.

Mass Relay Record. The record for 100 miles by 100 runners belonging to one club is 7 hours 56 minutes 55.6 seconds by Shore A.C. of New Jersey, on June 5, 1977.

The women's mark is 10 hours 47 minutes 9.3 seconds by a team from the San Francisco Dolphins Southend Running Club, on April 3, 1977.

The best time for a 100 × 400 meter relay is 1 hour 29 minutes 11.8 seconds (average 53.5 seconds) by the Physical Training Institute, Leuven, Belgium, on April 19, 1978.

A 13-man relay team from the Los Angeles Police Revolver and Athletic Club ran from the steps of the Capitol, Washington, D.C., to Los Angeles City Hall (3,871.6 miles) in 20 days 5 hours 20 minutes in May, 1974.

The longest relay ever run, and the one with the most participants, was by 1,607 students and teachers who covered 6,014.65 miles at Trondheim, Norway, from October 21 to November 23, 1977.

Pancake Race Record. The annual Housewives Pancake Race at Olney, Buckinghamshire, England, was first mentioned in 1445. The record for the winding 415-yard course (three tosses mandatory) is 61.0 seconds, set by Sally Ann Faulkner, 16, on February 26, 1974. The record for the counterpart race at Liberal, Kansas, is 58.5 seconds by Sheila Turner in the 1975 competition.

Trampolining

Origin. The sport of trampolining (from the Spanish word *trampolin*, a springboard) dates from 1936, when the prototype "T" model trampoline was developed by George Nissen (U.S.). Trampolines were used in show business at least as early as "The Walloons" of the period, 1910–12.

Marathon Record. The longest recorded trampoline bouncing marathon is one of 1,248 hours (52 days) set by a team of 6 in Phoenix, Arizona, from June 24 to August 15, 1974. The solo record is 179 hours (with 5-minute breaks per hour permissible) by Geoffrey Morton of Broken Hill, N.S.W., Australia, March 7–14, 1977.

Most Titles. Four men have won a world title (instituted 1964) twice; Dave Jacobs (U.S.) in 1967–68, Wayne Miller (U.S.) in 1966 and 1970, Richard Tison (France) in 1974 and 1976, and E. Janes (U.S.S.R.), 1976 (shared) and 1978. Judy Wills won 5 women's titles (1964–65–66–67–68).

Volleyball

Origin. The game was invented as Minnonette in 1895 by William G. Morgan at the Y.M.C.A. gymnasium at Holyoke, Massachusetts. The International Volleyball Association was formed in Paris in April, 1947. The ball travels at a speed of up to 70 m.p.h. when smashed over the net, which measures 7 feet 11½ inches. In the women's game it is 7 feet 4¼ inches.

World Titles. World Championships were instituted in 1949. The U.S.S.R. has won five men's titles (1949, 1952, 1960, 1962 and 1978). The U.S.S.R. won the women's championship in 1952, 1956, 1960 and 1970. The record crowd is 60,000 for the 1952 world title matches in Moscow, U.S.S.R.

Most Olympic Medals. The sport was introduced to the Olympic Games for both men and women in 1964. The only volleyball player to win four medals is Inna Ryskal (U.S.S.R.) (b. June 15, 1944), who won a silver medal in 1964 and 1976 and golds in 1968 and 1972.

The record for medals for men is held by Yuriy Poyarkov (U.S.S.R.), who won gold medals in 1964 and 1968, and a bronze in 1972.

Marathon. The longest recorded volleyball marathon by two teams of six is 70 hours 33 minutes by the 2nd Military Hospital at Ingleburn, N.S.W., Australia, on May 4–7, 1979.

Walking

Longest Annual Race. The Strasbourg-Paris event (instituted in 1926 in the reverse direction) over 313 to 344 miles is the world's longest annual walk event. Gilbert Roger (France) has won 6 times (1949–53–54–56–57–58). The fastest performance is by Robert Rinchard (Belgium) who walked 325 miles in the 1974 race in 63 hours 29 minutes, so (deducting 4 hours of compulsory stops) averaging 5.12 m.p.h.

Longest in 24 hours. The best performance is 142 miles 448 yards by Jesse Castañeda (U.S.) at the New Mexico State Fair in Albuquerque, September 18–19, 1976. The best by a woman is 116.6 miles by Ann Sayer (G.B.) at Rouen, France, on April 28–29, 1979.

Most Olympic Medals. Walking races have been included in the Olympic schedule since 1906, but walking matches have been known since 1589. The only walker to win three gold medals has been Ugo Frigerio (Italy) (1901–68) with the 3,000 m. and 10,000 m. in 1920 and the 10,000 m. in 1924. He also holds the record of most medals with four (having additionally won the bronze medal in the 50,000 m. in 1932), which total is shared with Vladimir Golubnitschiy (U.S.S.R.) (b. June 2, 1936), who won gold medals for the 10,000 m. in 1960 and 1968, the silver in 1972 and the bronze in 1964.

Most Titles. Four-time Olympian Ronald Owen Laird (b. May 31, 1938) of the New York Athletic Club, won a total of 65 U.S. National titles from 1958 to 1976, plus 4 Canadian championships.

OFFICIAL WORLD RECORDS (Track Walking)
(As recognized by the International Amateur Athletic Federation)

Distance	hr.	min.	sec.	Name and Nationality	Date	Place
20,000 meters	1	20	58.6	Domingo Colin (Mexico)	May 26, 1979	Norway
30,000 meters	2	08	00.0	José Marin (Spain)	Apr. 8, 1979	Spain
50,000 meters	3	41	39.0	Raul Gonzalez (Mexico)	Apr. 8, 1979	Norway
2 hours		17 miles 881 yards		José Marin (Spain)	May 25, 1979	Spain

Road Walking. The world's best road performances are: 20,000 meters, 1 hour 22 minutes 16 seconds by Daniel Bautista (Mexico) at Valencia, Spain, on May 19, 1979; 50,000 meters, 3 hours 41 minutes 19.2 seconds by Raul Gonzalez (Mexico) at Podebrady, Czechoslovakia on June 11, 1978.

DIFFERENT WALKS OF LIFE: Dimitru Dan (left) of Rumania was the only finisher in a walking race of 100,000 kilometers (62,137 miles). Plennie Wingo (right) walked 8,000 miles backwards in 1931–32. He used special glasses to see where he was going.

Greatest Mileage. Dimitru Dan (born July 13, 1890, *fl.* 1976) of
Rumania was the only man of 200 entrants to succeed in walking
100,000 kilometers (62,137 miles), in a contest organized by the
Touring Club de France on April 1, 1910. By March 24, 1916, he had
covered 96,000 kilometers (59,651 miles), averaging 27.24 miles
per day.

Walking Backwards. The greatest exponent of reverse pe-
destrianism has been Plennie L. Wingo (b. 1895) then of Abilene,
Texas, who started on his 8,000-mile transcontinental walk on April
15, 1931, from Santa Monica, California, to Istanbul, Turkey, and
arrived on October 24, 1932. He celebrated the walk's 45th anniversary by covering the 452 miles from Santa Monica to San
Francisco, California, backwards, in 85 days, aged 81 years.

The longest distance recorded for walking backwards in 24 hours
is 80.5 miles by Veikko Matias (b. April 23, 1941) of Kangasala,
Finland, at Kankaapää Airfield, Niinisalo, Finland, on October
7–8, 1978.

"Non-Stop" Walking. Thomas Patrick Benson (b. 1933) of
Great Britain walked 314.33 miles at Moor Park, Preston, England,
in 123 hours 28 minutes, April 11–16, 1977. He did not permit
himself any stops for resting and was moving 99.41 per cent of the
time.

Walking Around the World. The first person reported to have
"walked around the world" is George M. Schilling (U.S.) from
August 3, 1897–1904, but the first verified achievement was by David
Kunst, who started with his brother John from Waseca, Minnesota,

on June 10, 1970. John was killed by Afghani bandits in 1972. David arrived home after walking 14,500 miles on October 5, 1974.

Tomas Carlos Pereira (b. Argentina, November 16, 1942) spent 10 years, April 6, 1968, through April 8, 1978, walking 29,825 miles around all five continents.

The Trans-Asia record is 238 days for 6,800 miles from Riga, Latvia, to Vladivostok, U.S.S.R., by Georgyi Bushuyev, 50, in 1973–74.

Walking Across America. John Lees, 27, of Brighton, England, on April 11–June 3, 1972, walked 2,876 miles across the U.S. from City Hall, Los Angeles, to City Hall, New York City, in 53 days 12 hours 15 minutes (53.746 miles per day).

Walking Across Canada. The record trans-Canada (Halifax to Vancouver) walk of 3,764 miles is 96 days by Clyde McRae, 23, from May 1 to August 4, 1973.

Water Polo

Origins. Water polo was developed in England as "Water Soccer" in 1869 and was first included in the Olympic Games in Paris in 1900.

Olympic Victories. Hungary has won the Olympic tournament most often with six wins, in 1932, 1936, 1952, 1956, 1964 and 1976. Five players share the record of three gold medals: George Wilkinson (1879–1946) in 1900–08–12, Paulo (Paul) Radmilovic (1886–1968) and Charles Sidney Smith (1879–1951) in 1908–12–20—all G.B.; and the Hungarians Deszö Gyarmati (b. October 23, 1927) and György Kárpáti (b. June 23, 1935) in 1952–56–64.

Radmilovic also won a gold medal for the 4×200 m. free-style relay in 1908.

Most International Appearances. The greatest number of internationals is 244 by Ozren Bonacic for Yugoslavia between 1964 and September, 1975.

Marathon. The longest match on record is one of 67 hours 36 minutes between two teams of 15 from the Townsville Amateur Water Polo Association, Queensland, Australia, on December 1–4, 1978.

Water Skiing

Origins. The origins of water skiing lie in plank gliding or aquaplaning. A 19th century treatise on sorcerers refers to Eliseo of Tarentum who, in the 14th century, "walks and dances" on the water. The first report of aquaplaning was from the Pacific coast of the U.S. in the early 1900's.

A photograph exists of a "plank-riding" contest in a regatta won by a Mr. H. Storry at Scarborough, Yorkshire, England, on July 15, 1914. Competitors were towed on a *single* plank by a motor launch. The present-day sport of water skiing was pioneered by Ralph W.

Samuelson on Lake Pepin, Minnesota, on two curved pine boards in the summer of 1922, though claims have been made for the birth of the sport on Lake Annecy (Haute Savoie), France, in 1920. The first World Water Ski Organization was formed in Geneva, Switzerland, on July 27, 1946.

Jumps. The first recorded jump on water skis was by Ralph W. Samuelson, off a greased ramp at Lake Pepin in 1925. The longest jump recorded is one of 181 feet by Sammy Duvall, 20, (U.S.) at Callaway Gardens, Pine Mountain, Georgia, July 15, 1979. A minimum margin of 8 inches is required for sole possession of the world record.

The women's record is 128 feet by Linda Giddens (U.S.) at Miami, Florida, on August 22, 1976.

Slalom. The world record for slalom on a particular pass is 4 buoys (with a 37-foot rope) at 36 m.p.h. by Kris LaPoint (U.S.) at Horton Lake, near Barstow, California, on July 15, 1975, and also by his brother, Bob LaPoint, in Miami in August, 1976.

The women's record is 3 buoys on a 39-foot line by Cindy Hutcherson Todd (U.S.) at Groveland, Florida, on July 16, 1977.

Tricks. The highest official point score for tricks is 7,080 points by Carlos Suarez (Venezuela) at Milan, Italy, on September 3, 1977.

The women's record of 5,570 points was set by Maria Victoria Carrasco (Venezuela) at Milan, Italy, on September 3, 1977.

Longest Run. The greatest distance traveled non-stop is 1,124 miles by Will Coughey (New Zealand) on Lake Karapiro, New Zealand, in 30 hours 34 minutes, February 26–27, 1977.

Highest Speed. The water skiing speed record is 125.69 m.p.h. recorded by Danny Churchill (U.S.) at the Oakland Marine Stadium, California, in 1971. A claim of 134.33 m.p.h. by Grant Torrens (Australia) in February, 1978, is awaiting ratification. Donna Patterson Brice (b. 1953) set a feminine record of 111.11 m.p.h. at Long Beach, California, on August 21, 1977.

Most Titles. World overall championships (instituted 1949) have been twice won by Alfredo Mendoza (U.S.) in 1953–55, Mike Suyderhoud (U.S.) in 1967–69, and George Athans (Canada) in 1971 and 1973, and three times by Mrs. Willa McGuire (née Worthington) of the U.S., in 1949–50 and 1955, and Elizabeth Allan-Shetter (U.S.) in 1965, 1969, and 1975.

Allan-Shetter has also won a record eight individual championship events.

Barefoot. The first person to waterski barefoot is reported to be Dick Pope, Jr., at Lake Eloise, Florida, on March 6, 1947. The barefoot duration record is 2 hours 42 minutes 39 seconds by Billy Nichols (U.S.) (born 1964) on Lake Weir, Florida, on November 19, 1978. The backwards barefoot record is 39 minutes by Paul McManus (Australia). The best officially recorded barefoot jump is 52 feet by Keith Donnelly at Baronscourt, Northern Ireland, on July 9, 1978.

The official barefoot speed record (two runs) is 110.02 m.p.h. by Lee Kirk (U.S.) at Firebird Lake, Phoenix, Arizona, on June 11, 1977. His fastest run was 113.67 m.p.h. The fastest by a woman is 61.39 by Haidee Jones (now Lance) (Australia).

Weightlifting

Origins. Amateur weightlifting is of comparatively modern origin, and the first "world" championship was staged at the Café Monico, Piccadilly, London, on March 28, 1891. Prior to that time, weightlifting consisted of professional exhibitions in which some of the advertised poundages were open to doubt. The first to raise 400 lbs. was Karl Swoboda (1882–1933) (Austria) in Vienna, with 401¼ lbs. in 1910, using the Continental clean and jerk style.

Greatest Lift. The greatest weight ever raised by a human being is 6,270 lbs. in a back lift (weight raised off trestles) by the 364-lb. Paul Anderson (U.S.) (b. 1932), the 1956 Olympic heavyweight champion, at Toccoa, Georgia, on June 12, 1957. (The heaviest Rolls-Royce, the Phantom VI, weighs 5,936 lbs.) The greatest by a woman is 3,564 lbs. with a hip and harness lift by Mrs. Josephine Blatt (née Schauer) (U.S.) (1869–1923) at the Bijou Theatre, Hoboken, New Jersey, on April 15, 1895.

The greatest overhead lifts made from the ground are the clean and jerks achieved by super-heavyweights which now exceed 560 lbs. (see table on page 667).

The greatest overhead lift ever made by a woman is 286 lbs. in a continental jerk by Katie Sandwina, née Brummbach (Germany) (born January 21, 1884, died as Mrs. Max Heymann in New York City, in 1952) in c. 1911. This is equivalent to seven 40-pound office typewriters. She stood 5 feet 11 inches tall, weighed 210 lbs., and is reputed to have unofficially lifted 312½ lbs. and to have once shouldered a 1,200-lb cannon taken from the tailboard of a Barnum & Bailey circus wagon.

Power Lifts. Paul Anderson as a professional has bench-pressed 627 lbs., achieved 1,200 lbs. in a deep-knee bend, and dead-lifted 820 lbs., making a career aggregate of 2,647 lbs.

Ronald Collins (G.B.) with a 1,655-lb. lift in Liverpool, England, on December 15, 1973, when his body weight was 165 lbs., became the first man to lift a total 10 times his own body weight. Since then 9 other lifters have achieved this, but only Collins has repeated in more than one weight division.

The newly instituted two-man dead lift record was raised to 1,439 lbs. by Clay and Doug Patterson in El Dorado, Arkansas, on March 3, 1979.

Hermann Görner (Germany) performed a one-handed dead lift of 734½ lbs. in Dresden on July 20, 1920. He once raised 24 men weighing 4,123 lbs. on a plank with the soles of his feet and also

STRONGEST WOMAN:
Jan Suffolk Todd has
raised 463 lbs. in the
two-handed dead lift in
competition.

carried on his back a 1,444-lb. piano for a distance of 52½ feet on June 3, 1921. Görner is also reputed to have once lifted 14 bricks weighing 123½ lbs. horizontally, using only lateral pressure.

Peter B. Cortese (U.S.) achieved a one-arm dead lift of 370 lbs. —22 lbs. over triple his body weight—at York, Pennsylvania, on September 4, 1954.

The highest competitive two-handed dead lift by a woman is 463 lbs. by Jan Suffolk Todd (born May 22, 1952) (U.S.) at Honolulu, Hawaii, on May 4, 1979. She also holds the three-lift record total of 1,125 lbs. set at Stephenville Crossing, Newfoundland, Canada, on June 24, 1978.

It was reported that a hysterical 123-lb. woman, Mrs. Maxwell Rogers, lifted one end of a 3,600-lb. car which, after the collapse of a jack, had fallen on top of her son at Tampa, Florida, on April 24, 1960. She cracked some vertebrae.

A dead lift record of 2,100,000 lbs. in 24 hours was set by a 10-man team in relay at the Darwen Weightlifting Club, Darwen, England on August 19, 1978.

Most Olympic Gold Medals. Of the 90 Olympic titles at stake, the U.S.S.R. has won 26, the U.S. 15 and France 9. Ten lifters have succeeded in winning an Olympic gold medal in successive Games. Of these, three have also won a silver medal.

Most Olympic Medals. Winner of most Olympic medals is Norbert Schemansky (U.S.) with four: gold, middle-heavyweight 1952; silver, heavyweight 1948; bronze, heavyweight 1960 and 1964.

Schemansky achieved a world record (heavyweight snatch of 361½ lbs. on April 28, 1962, at Detroit) at the record age of 37 years 10 months.

FLYWEIGHT
CHAMPION: Alexander
Voronin of the U.S.S.R.
holds all 3 world records
in his weight class.

OFFICIAL WORLD WEIGHTLIFTING RECORDS

(As of December, 1978)

Flyweight
(114¼ lb.–52 kg.)

Snatch	243½	Alexander Voronin (U.S.S.R.)	Bulgaria	May 19, 1979
Jerk	313	Alexander Voronin (U.S.S.R.)	Bulgaria	May 19, 1979
Total	545½	Alexander Voronin (U.S.S.R.)	W. Germany	Sept. 18, 1977

Bantamweight
(123¼ lb.–56 kg.)

Snatch	267¼	Anton Kodiabashev (Bulgaria)	Bulgaria	July 9, 1979
Jerk	335	Anton Kodiabashev (Bulgaria)	Bulgaria	July 9, 1979
Total	584¼	Anton Kodiabashev (Bulgaria)	Bulgaria	July 9, 1979

Featherweight
(132¼ lb.–60 kg.)

Snatch	286½	Gyorgyi Todorov (Bulgaria)	Bulgaria	May 25, 1976
Jerk	365¾	Nikolai Kolesnikov (U.S.S.R.)	Bulgaria	May 21, 1979
Total	644½	Nikolai Kolesnikov (U.S.S.R.)	Bulgaria	May 21, 1979

Lightweight
(148¾ lb.–67.5 kg.)

Snatch	324	Yanko Rusev (Bulgaria)	Bulgaria	July 10, 1979
Jerk	402½	Yanko Rusev (Bulgaria)	Bulgaria	July 10, 1979
Total	716½	Yanko Rusev (Bulgaria)	Bulgaria	July 10, 1979

Middleweight
(165¼ lb.–75 kg.)

Snatch	347	Yordan Vardanyan (U.S.S.R.)	U.S.S.R.	May 7, 1977
Jerk	433	Alexander Logoutov (U.S.S.R.)	U.S.S.R.	Nov. 16, 1978
Total	766	Yordan Vardanyan (U.S.S.R)	U.S.S.R.	May 7, 1977

Light-heavyweight
(181¼ lb.–82.5 kg.)

Snatch	385¾	Blagoi Blagoiev (Bulgaria)	Bulgaria	July 10, 1979
Jerk	468¼	Yurik Vardanyan (U.S.S.R.)	U.S.S.R.	June 4, 1979
Total	848¾	Yurik Vardanyan (U.S.S.R.)	U.S.S.R.	June 4, 1979

Middle-heavyweight
(198¼ lb.–90 kg.)

Snatch	398	David Rigert (U.S.S.R.)	Czech.	June 16, 1978
Jerk	490½	Rolf Milser (West Germany)	Bulgaria	May 25, 1979
Total	881¾	David Rigert (U.S.S.R.)	U.S.S.R.	May 14, 1976

(220½ lb.–100 kg.)

Snatch	396¾	David Rigert (U.S.S.R.)	Bulgaria	May 26, 1979
Jerk	507	Viktor Kanonov (U.S.S.R.)	U.S.S.R.	June 9, 1979
Total	887¼	David Rigert (U.S.S.R.)	Bulgaria	May 26, 1979

Heavyweight
(242½ lb.–110 kg.)

Snatch	407¾	Valentin Khristov (Bulgaria)	E. Germany	Apr. 10, 1976
Jerk	523½	Valentin Khristov (Bulgaria)	U.S.S.R.	Sept. 22, 1975
Total	920¼	Valentin Khristov (Bulgaria)	U.S.S.R.	Sept. 22, 1975

Super-heavyweight
(Over 242½ lb.–110 kg.)

Snatch	442	Sultan Rakhmanov (U.S.S.R.)	U.S.S.R.	Apr. 25, 1978
Jerk	564¼	Vasili Alexeev (U.S.S.R.)	U.S.S.R.	Nov. 1, 1977
Total	981	Vasili Alexeev (U.S.S.R.)	U.S.S.R.	Sept. 1, 1977

SELECTED POWERLIFTING RECORDS

(*as recognized by the International Powerlifting Federation as of July 1, 1979*)

Body Weight Class	Lift	Lbs.	Name and Country
114½ lb.	Squat	479½	Chuck Dunbar (U.S.)
	Bench Press	297½	Chuck Dunbar (U.S.)
	Dead Lift	494¾	Hideaki Inaba (Japan)
	Total	1,218	Hideaki Inaba (Japan)
132¼ lb.	Squat	534½	Eddie Pengelley (G.B.)
	Bench Press	358¼	Yoshinobu Tominaga (Japan)
	Dead Lift	622¾	Lamar Gant (U.S.)
	Total	1,416¼	Eddie Pengelley (G.B.)
181¾ lb.	Squat	733	Ron Collins (G.B.)
	Bench Press	508	Mike McDonald (U.S.)
	Dead Lift	749½	Vince Anello (U.S.)
	Total	1,857¼	Ron Collins (G.B.)
Over 242½ lb.	Squat	931¼	Don Reinhoudt (U.S.)
	Bench Press	611¼	Doug Young (U.S.)
	Dead Lift	881¾	Don Reinhoudt (U.S.)
	Total	2,419½	Don Reinhoudt (U.S.)

MOST SUCCESSFUL OLYMPIC WEIGHTLIFTERS

Louis Hostin (France)	Gold, light-heavyweight 1932 and 1936; Silver, 1928.
John Davis (U.S.)	Gold, heavyweight 1948 and 1952.
Tommy Kono (Hawaii/U.S.)	Gold, lightweight 1952; Gold, light-heavyweight 1956; Silver, middleweight 1960.
Charles Vinci (U.S.)	Gold, bantamweight 1956 and 1960.
Arkady Vorobyov (U.S.S.R.)	Gold, middle-heavyweight 1956 and 1960.
Yoshinobu Miyake (Japan)	Gold, featherweight 1964 and 1968; Silver, bantamweight 1960.
Waldemar Baszanowski (Poland)	Gold, lightweight 1964 and 1968.
Leonid Zhabotinsky (U.S.S.R.)	Gold, heavyweight 1964 and 1968.
Vasili Alexeev (U.S.S.R.)	Gold, super-heavyweight 1972 and 1976.
Norair Nourikian (Bulgaria)	Gold, featherweight 1972; Gold, bantamweight 1976.

Wrestling

Earliest References. The earliest depictions of wrestling holds and falls on the walls of the tomb of Ptahhotep (5th Dynasty Egypt) indicate that organized wrestling dates from before *c.* 2350 B.C.. It was introduced into the ancient Olympic Games in the 18th Olympiad in *c.* 708 B.C. The Graeco-Roman style is of French origin and arose about 1860. The International Amateur Wrestling Federation (F.I.L.A.) was founded in 1912.

Sumo Wrestling. The sport's origins in Japan certainly date from *c.* 23 B.C. The heaviest performers were probably Dewagatake, a wrestler of the 1920's who was 6 feet 7¾ inches tall and weighed up to 430 lbs., and Odachi, of the 1950's, who stood 6 feet 7½ inches and weighed about 441 lbs. Weight is amassed by over-eating a high protein stew called *chankonabe.* The tallest was probably Ozora, an early 19th century performer, who stood 7 feet 3 inches tall. The most successful wrestlers have been Koki Naya (born 1940), *alias* Taiho ("Great Bird"), who won 32 Emperor's Cups until his retirement in 1971; Sadaji Akiyoshi (b. 1912), *alias* Futabayama, who won 69 consecutive bouts in the 1930's; Totaro Koe, *alias* Umegatani I, who had the highest winning percentage among grand champions of .951 in the 1880's; and the *ozeki* Torokichi, *alias* Raiden, who in 21 years (1789–1810) won 240 bouts and lost only ten.

The youngest of the 56 men to attain the rank of *Yokozuna* (Grand Champion) was Toshimitsu Obata (*alias* Kitanoumi) in July, 1974, aged 21 years 2 months. Jesse Kuhaulva (b. Hawaii, June 16, 1944), *alias* Takamiyama, was the first non-Japanese to win an official tournament, in July, 1972.

Best Records. In international competition, Osamu Watanabe (b. October 21, 1940) (Japan), the 1964 Olympic free-style featherweight champion, was unbeaten and unscored-upon in 187 consecutive matches.

Wade Schalles (U.S.) has won 615 bouts from 1964 to the end of 1977.

Most World Championships. The greatest number of world championships won by a wrestler is ten by the free-styler Aleksandr Medved (U.S.S.R.), with the light-heavyweight titles in 1964 (Olympic) and 1966, the heavyweight 1967 and 1968 (Olympic), and the super-heavyweight title 1969, 1970, 1971 and 1972 (Olympic). The only wrestler to win the same title in 6 successive years has been Abdollah Movahed (Iran) in the lightweight division in 1965–70. The record for successive Graeco-Roman titles is five by Roman Rurua (U.S.S.R.) with the featherweight 1966, 1967, 1968 (Olympic), 1969 and 1970.

Most Olympic Titles. Three wrestlers have won three Olympic titles. They are:

Carl Westergren (Sweden) (1895–1958)		Ivar Johansson (Sweden) (b. Jan. 31, 1903)	
Graeco-Roman Middleweight A	1920	Free-style Middleweight	1932
Graeco-Roman Middleweight B	1924	Graeco-Roman Welterweight	1932
Graeco-Roman Heavyweight	1932	Graeco-Roman Middleweight	1936

Free-style Light-heavyweight   1964
Free-style Heavyweight   1968
Free-style Super-heavyweight   1972

The only wrestler with more medals is Imre Polyák (Hungary) who won the silver medal for the Graeco-Roman featherweight class in 1952, 56–60 and the gold in 1964.

Heaviest Heavyweight. The heaviest wrestler in Olympic history is Chris Taylor (b. U.S., June 13, 1950), bronze medallist in the super-heavyweight class in 1972, who stood 6 feet 5 inches tall and weighed over 420 lbs.

Longest Bout. The longest recorded bout was one of 11 hours 40 minutes between Martin Klein (Estonia, representing Russia) and Alfred Asikáinen (Finland) in the Graeco-Roman middleweight "A" event in the 1912 Olympic Games in Stockholm, Sweden. Klein won.

Yachting

Origin. Yachting in England dates from the £100 (now $200) stake race between King Charles II of England and his brother, James, Duke of York, on the Thames River, on September 1, 1661, over 23 miles, from Greenwich to Gravesend. The earliest club is the Royal Cork Yacht Club (formerly the Cork Harbour Water Club), established in Ireland in 1720. The word "yacht" is from the Dutch, meaning to hunt or chase.

Most Successful. The most successful racing yacht in history was the British Royal Yacht *Britannia* (1893–1935), owned by King Edward VII while Prince of Wales, and subsequently by King George V, which won 231 races in 625 starts.

Highest Speed. The official world sailing speed record is 33.4 knots (38.46 m.p.h.) achieved by the 73½-foot *Crossbow II* over a 500-meter (547-yard) course off Portland Harbor, Dorset, England, on October 4, 1977. The vessel, with a sail area of 1,400 square feet, was designed by Rod McAlpine-Downie and owned and steered by Timothy Colman. In an unsuccessful attempt on the record in October, 1978, *Crossbow II* is reported to have momentarily attained a speed of 45 knots (51 m.p.h.).

The fastest 24-hour single-handed run by a sailing yacht was recorded by Nick Keig (b. June 13, 1936), of the Isle of Man, who covered 340 nautical miles in a 37½-foot trimaran, *Three Legs of Mann I*, during the Falmouth to Punta, Azores, race on June 9–10, 1975, averaging 14.16 knots (16.30 m.p.h.). The fastest bursts of speed reached were about 25 knots (28.78 m.p.h.).

Longest Race. The longest regularly contested yacht race is the biennial Los Angeles-Tahiti Trans-Pacific event which is over 3,571 miles. The fastest time has been 8 days 13 hours 9 minutes by Eric Taberley's *Pen Duick IV* (France) in 1969.

Most Competitors. 1,261 sailing boats started the 233-mile Round Zealand (Denmark) race in June, 1976.

America's Cup. The America's Cup was originally won as an outright prize by the schooner *America* on August 22, 1851, at Cowes, England, but was later offered by the New York Yacht Club as a challenge trophy. On August 8, 1870, J. Ashbury's *Cambria* (G.B.) failed to capture the trophy from the *Magic*, owned by F. Osgood (U.S.). Since then the Cup has been challenged by Great Britain in 15 contests, by Canada in two contests, and by Australia four times, but the United States holders have never been defeated. The closest race ever was the fourth race of the 1962 series, when the 12-meter sloop *Weatherly* beat her Australian challenger *Gretel* by about 3½ lengths (75 yards), a margin of only 26 seconds, on September 22, 1962. The fastest time ever recorded by a 12-meter boat for the triangular course of 24 miles is 2 hours 46 minutes 58 seconds by *Gretel* in 1962.

Little America's Cup. The catamaran counterpart to the America's Cup was instituted in 1961 for International C-class catamarans. Great Britain has won 8 times from 1961 to 1968.

Admiral's Cup. The ocean racing series to have attracted the largest number of participating nations (three boats allowed to each nation) is the Admiral's Cup held by the Royal Ocean Racing Club in the English Channel in alternate years. Up to 1977, Britain had won 7 times, U.S. twice and Australia and West Germany once each. A record 19 nations competed in 1975, 1977 and 1979.

Olympic Victories. The first sportsman ever to win individual gold medals in four successive Olympic Games has been Paul B. Elvström (b. February 24, 1928) (Denmark) in the Firefly class in 1948 and the Finn class in 1952, 1956 and 1960. He has also won 8 other world titles in a total of 6 classes.

The lowest number of penalty points by the winner of any class in an Olympic regatta is 3 points [6 wins (1 disqualified) and 1 second in 7 starts] by *Superdocius* of the Flying Dutchman class sailed by Lt. Rodney Stuart Pattison (b. August 5, 1943), British Royal Navy, and Ian Somerled Macdonald-Smith (b. July 3, 1945), in Acapulco Bay, Mexico, in October, 1968.

Largest Sail. The largest sail ever made was a parachute spinnaker with an area of 18,000 square feet (more than two-fifths of an acre) for Harold S. Vanderbilt's *Ranger* in 1937.

Largest Marina. The largest marina in the world is that of Marina Del Rey, Los Angeles, California, which has 7,500 berths.

Highest Altitude. The greatest altitude at which sailing has been conducted is 16,109 feet on Laguna Huallatani, Bolivia, by Peter Williams, Brian Barrett, Gordon Siddeley and Keith Robinson in *Mirror Dinghy No. 55448* on November 19, 1977.

LATE RECORDS

The following pages include records which were received and verified too late to be included in the main sections of this book.

Chapter 1

Tallest Giants. The circus giant Gabriel Monjane was credited with a new measurement of 8 feet 8⅓ inches by his promoters in 1979, but his true height is believed to be closer to 8 feet ¾ inch.

Heaviest Man. In July, 1979, an unconfirmed weight of 856 pounds was reported for T.J. Albert, known as "Fat Albert" in his work as a sideshow attraction. He is reputed to be able to cover 100 yards in an improbable 23 seconds.

Earliest Life Form. Traces of yeast-like cells called *isuasphaera* from cherty layers of quartzite from southwest Greenland dated to 3,800,000,000 years ago were announced on August 9, 1979.

Most Proximate Births and Shortest Pregnancies. Mrs. Gloria Kuehn of Lemay, Missouri, gave birth to a daughter, Amy Elizabeth, on June 9, 1978, and a son, Gregory Charles, on January 19, 1979, only 224 days later.

Fire-Eating. Darryl Hayden extinguished 2,509 flaming torches successively in his mouth in 1 hour 52 minutes at The Dolphin, Kingston-upon-Thames, Surrey, England, on April 15, 1979.

Longest Operations. James Boydston, 24 years old, underwent arterial surgery for 47 hours at the Veterans Administration Hospital, Des Moines, Iowa, June 15-17, 1979.

Fasting. Andreas Mihavecz, 18 years old, was put into a holding cell on April 1, 1979, in a local government building in Hochst, Austria, and was totally forgotten by the police. On April 18, 1979, he was discovered close to death, having had neither food nor water during his incarceration. He had been a passenger involved in a car crash.

Memorizing Pi. Creighton Carvello of Cleveland, England, recited the value of pi to 15,186 places from memory on July 12, 1979.

Chapter 2

Highest-Flying Birds. Thirty Whooper swans (*Cygnus c. cygnus*) flying in from Iceland were spotted by an airplane over the Outer Hebrides at an altitude of 27,000 feet on December 9, 1967. The height was also confirmed by air traffic control in Northern Ireland after they picked up the skein of swans on radar.

Chicken Flying. The greatest recorded distance flown by a chicken is 302 feet 8 inches by Lola B., owned by Sherwood Costen of Point Pleasant, West Virginia, at the 8th Annual International Chicken Flying Contest, held in Rio Grande, Ohio, on May 19, 1979.

Longest-Lived Mollusk. According to a recent American study, the Quahog (*Venus mercenaria*), a thick-shelled clam found in the North Atlantic, lives 100-150 years.

Largest Wreath. The largest wreath ever constructed was the wreath built by the Interflora Australian Unit Ltd., District 4 at Mt. Lawley, W. Australia, in May, 1979. It measured 43.8 feet in diameter.

Chapter 3

Northernmost Land. On July 26, 1978, Uffe Petersen of the Danish Geodetic Institute observed an as-yet-unnamed islet measuring 100 feet across, located 1,487 yards *north* of Kaffedlubben Oyen, off Pearyland, Greenland, in Longitude 83° 40′ 32.5″ N., Latitude 30° 40′ 10.1″ W.

Highest Waterspout. The Spithead waterspout off Ryde, Isle of Wight, England, was measured by sextant to be "about a mile" in height on August 21, 1878.

Chapter 4

Longest Manned Space Flight. Cosmonauts Valery Ryumin, 40 years old, and Lieutenant Colonel Vladimir Lyakhov, 38 years old, returned to earth on August 19, 1979, having remained in space for a record 175 days on the *Soyuz 34* mission.

Chapter 5

Most Expensive Wine. A bottle of 1806 Château Lafite-Rothschild was bought by Charles F. Maras for $28,000 at the 11th annual Heublein Premiere National Auction of Rare Wines, held on May 24, 1979. There is allegedly only one other bottle surviving.

Miniature Bottles. Mrs. Ivy Grant of Sussex, England, has an unduplicated collection of 2,307 as of August 1, 1979.

Precious Stone Records, Sapphire. A star sapphire weighing 63,000 carats (27 lbs. 12¼ oz.) was found near Mogok, Upper Burma, in 1966.

Highest Prime Number. A new record value of $2^{44497}-1$ was announced on May 30, 1979, after a two-month-long run on a CRAY-1 computer at the University of California's Lawrence Livermore Laboratory, by Harry Nelson, age 47, and David Slowinski, age 25.

Chapter 6

Smallest Painting. Jose M. Salas executed an "oil painting" with a diameter of 1/231 of an inch in April, 1979, in Orillia, Ontario, Canada.

Largest Poster. A poster 800 feet long and 10 feet wide was painted by 400 artists for the British Safety Council at South Bank, London, July 28-August 6, 1979.

Longest Crossword Puzzle. A crossword puzzle based on the Guinness Book of World Records, published by Onsworld Ltd. with over 1,200 clues, measures 7 feet 2 inches in length.

Largest Library. The New York Public Library now has 9,210,630 volumes, 10,993,975 manuscripts and 331,804 maps.

Movie-Going. In 1977, the highest rate of motion picture attendance was on Mauritius, with 18.9 visits per head per year. This figure compares with 1.9 in the United Kingdom, and 0.1 in Ghana and Zaire.

Most Gold Records. Paul McCartney's total of RIAA gold record awards reached 60 with his album *Back to the Egg* in August, 1979.

Smallest TV Set. Sinclair Radionics now manufactures a TV set weighing 20 ounces with dimensions of 3½ × 2 × 7 inches, a screen measuring 2 inches diagonally, and costing $200 plus tax in England.

Highest TV Commercial Contract. Brooke Shields (b. May 31, 1965) was reportedly paid $250,000 for one minute of film by a Japanese TV commercial film maker in 1979. Faye Dunaway was reported in May, 1979, to have been paid $900,000 for uttering 6 words for a Japanese department store TV commercial.

Chapter 7

Deepest Drilling. A drilling 6.04 miles deep on the Kola Peninsula, U.S.S.R., was announced in July, 1979. The plan is to continue until the total depth reaches 34,450 feet.

Largest Oil Spill. The slick from the Mexican marine blow-up in Campeche Bay, Gulf of Mexico, on June 3, 1979, reached 400 miles by August, 1979, and was still growing.

Chapter 8

Highest-Priced License Plates. On December 9, 1978, Sir Run Run Shaw bid HK $330,000 ($70,650) for a "Good Fortune" license plate at a Hong Kong Government charity auction.

Fastest Car. A three-wheeled jet car, the 36-foot-1-inch-long Khadi-9, designed to be the first land speed record car to better Mach 1 (760.98 miles per hour), was exhibited by the Kharkov Motor and Highways Institute in the U.S.S.R. in December, 1978.

Most Expensive Car. The Rolls-Royce *Camargue* retailed in the U.S. for $130,000 in July, 1979.

Most on One Motorcycle. At the Brisbane Show Grounds, Australia, on May 18, 1979, Sgt. John Patrick Toohey drove a Kawasaki 1,000-c.c. motorcycle, with 18 other policemen mounted on it, a distance of 880 yards. The weight of the motorcycle was 790 lbs. and the weight of the policemen was 3,838 lbs., making a total all-up weight of 4,628 lbs.

Most Takeoffs and Landings. Al Yates and Bob Phoenix of Texas made 193 takeoffs and daylight landings in 14 hours 57 minutes in a Piper Seminole on June 15, 1979.

Thinnest Watch. Eterna of Grenchen, Switzerland, manufactures a watch 1/16 inch thick.

Chapter 9

Largest Take-Over Bid. A bid of $1,125,000,000 made by Brascan Ltd. of Canada for an interest in F.W. Woolworth Co. was still being resisted in May, 1979. Exxon Corporation bid $1,165,000,000 for Reliance Electric Co. in May, 1979.

Largest Rag Doll. Children stuffed a Raggedy Ann doll 27 feet long for display in the Guinness Exhibit Hall in the Empire State Building in New York City at Macy's "Clowning Around" day on August 26, 1979.

Largest Jig-Saw Puzzle. A styrofoam puzzle measuring 28 × 52 feet, but with only 364 large pieces, was put together by children in Herald Square, New York City, as part of Macy's "Clowning Around" day on August 26, 1979.

Chapter 10

Mass Suicide. The final total of the mass cyanide poisoning of the People's Temple cult near Port Kaituma, Guyana, on November 18, 1978, was 910. The leader was the paranoid "Reverend" Jim Jones of San Francisco, California, who had reportedly deposited "millions of dollars" overseas.

Gold Reserves. The country with the greatest monetary gold reserve is West Germany, whose Treasury had $38,000,000,000 on hand in February, 1979.

Largest Treasure Trove. A hoard of 56,500 Roman coins was found at Cunetio, near Marlborough, Wiltshire, England, on October 15, 1978.

Most Expensive Coffee. In August, 1979, French Haymarket coffee was retailing in New York City for $7 per pound.

Energy Consumption. With only 5.3 per cent of the world's population, the U.S. comsumes 28.6 per cent of the world's gasoline and 32.9 percent of the world's electric power.

National Hourly Wage Rates. Comparative data from the world's 12 most highly industrialized countries, published in May, 1979, showed that Japan was the leader with $6.70 per hour. The U.S. was fifth with $5.63.

Chapter 11

Brick Lifting. Toby Hoffman of Santa Monica, California, while working on the set of the "Guinness Game" TV show during a rehearsal on August 10, 1979, inadvertently set a record by laterally lifting 16 bricks (weighing a total of 96 lbs.) using only the palms of his hands. He was showing a contender for a record on the television show how it should be done. The contender could not duplicate the feat.

Dancing, Disco. J.C. Stare, age 22, spent his last days with the U.S. Marine Corps on leave, disco dancing for 332 hours from August 1 to August 15, 1979, in New York City, to raise funds for the Muscular Dystrophy Associaton.

Longest Desert Walk. The longest desert walk ever recorded is one of 316 miles by Bill Collins (b. October 22, 1923) of Las Vegas, through Death Valley, California, in 10 days 10 hours, July 28-August 6, 1972.

Diving, Highest Shallow. Henri La Mothe set a new record by diving into 12⅜ inches of water, but from only 28 feet up, in Northridge, California, on April 7, 1979. He struck the water chest first at a speed of more than 25 miles per hour.

Egg Throwing. William Cole and Jonathan Heller successfully completed a 350-foot toss on their 58th exchange in Central Park, New York City, on March 17, 1979.

Frisbee Throwing. Charles Duvahl threw a regulation Frisbee at a speed of 60 miles per hour and his teammate Steve McClean made a clean catch of the throw on the "Guinness Game" TV show on August 1, 1979.

Foot Juggling. Chester Cable of Hossapple, Pennsylvania, turned a 10-foot-long, 130-lb. aluminum table 30 revolutions in less than 60 seconds, lying on his back and using only his feet, on the "Guinness Game" TV show on August 1, 1979.

Riding in Armor. The longest recorded ride in full armor is one of 167 miles from Edinburgh to Dumfries, Scotland, in 3 days (total riding time 28 hours 30 minutes) by Dick Brown, age 48, on June 13-15, 1979.

Skateboarding. The highest recorded speed on a skateboard under U.S.

Skateboard Association rules is 71.79 miles per hour on a course at Mt. Baldy, California in a prone position, by Richard K. Brown, age 33, on June 17, 1979.

Highest Jumping Somersault. Donny Evins, a gymnastics teacher from Fullerton, California, completed a back somersault over a high bar set at 6 feet 4 inches on the "Guinness Game" TV show on August 13, 1979.

Tire Changing. A team of five men from Modesto, California, weighing in at a total of 1,195 lbs., changed all four tires on a 2,220-lb. Datsun 510 *without the aid of a jack* within 90 seconds, led by Ron Edward, on the "Guinness Game" TV show on August 1, 1979.

Wire Climb, Steepest. Steven McPeak of Las Vegas, Nevada, broke his own record by climbing a wire 45 feet high at a 40° angle at the top, with the use of a pole. He took 71 seconds to make the ascent on August 10, 1979.

Greatest Bankruptcy. William G. Stern (b. Hungary, 1936), a U.S. citizen since 1957, who set up Wilstar Group Holding Co. in the London Property Market in 1971, was declared bankrupt for $208,780,496 in February, 1979.

Chapter 12

Auto Racing. Fastest Circuits. The highest average lap speed attained on any closed circuit is 250.958 m.p.h. in a trial by Dr. Hans Liebold (b. October 12, 1929) (Germany), who lapped the 7.85-mile-high speed track at Nardo, Italy, in 1 minute 52.67 seconds in a Mercedes-Benz C111-IV experimental coupe on May 5, 1979. The car was powered by a V8 engine with two KKK turbochargers with an output of 500 h.p. at 6,200 r.p.m.

Auto Racing. Indianapolis 500. The record prize fund is $1,271,954 for the 63rd race, held on May 27, 1979. The individual prize record is $290,363 by Al Unser on May 28, 1978.

Badminton. Doubles Marathon. Richard and Margarette Jones, Sarah Moss and Neelam Sarpal played for 50 hours at Ilkley Grammar School, West Yorkshire, England, August 1-3, 1979.

Basketball. Most Points. Pearl Moore of Francis Marion College, Florence, South Carolina, scored 4,061 points in her college career.

Billiards. Pool Marathon. The greatest number of balls pocketed in 24 hours is 11,700 (an average of one every 7.5 seconds) by Gary Mounsey (b. 1947) in Hamilton, New Zealand, June 30-July 1, 1979.

Fishing. Marathon. John Reader fished for 552 hours at Hunstrete Lake, Weston-super-Mare, Avon, England, July 7-30, 1979.

Gymnastics. Parallel Bar Dips. Peter Herbert (aged 33) performed a record 294 consecutive dips on July 11, 1979, at Haverfordwest Sports Centre, Dyfed, Wales.

Gymnastics. Push-Ups. Tommy Gildert did 9,105 consecutive push-ups at the Burnley Boys Club, Lancashire, England, on July 1, 1979. On the same day he also performed 269 one-arm push-ups in 10 minutes.

Gymnastics. Sit-Ups. Darryl Hyek, age 18, recorded 125 sit-ups in 2 minutes at the Golden Triangle Health Spa, Tarentum, Pennsylvania, on May 31, 1979, on a hard surface without feet pinned or knees bent.

Horse Racing. Most Valuable Horse. The highest price paid for a yearling has been $1,600,000 for a colt by Hoist the Flag—Royal Dowry bought on July 25, 1979, in Keeneland, Kentucky, by two Japanese buyers.

Ice Skating. Speed Records. Eric Heiden (U.S.) skated 1,000 meters in 1 minute 14.99 seconds at Inzell, West Germany, on February 17, 1979.

Jai-Alai. Fastest Throw. Jose Areitio recorded a speed of 188 m.p.h. for a throw of the pelota at the Newport Jai-Alai, Rhode Island, on August 3, 1979.

Rodeo. Most World Titles. The record figure for prize money in a single season is $131,233 for Tom Ferguson in 1978.

Rodeo. Time Records. The fastest time for roping a calf is 5.7 seconds by Bill Reeder in Assiniboia, Saskatchewan, Canada, in 1978.

Soccer. Ball Control. Istvan Halaszi (b. Hungary, July 24, 1957) headed a regulation soccer ball non-stop for 79 minutes 24 seconds (12,374 repetitions) at the Jewish Community Center, Milwaukee, Wisconsin, on April 29, 1979.

Swimming. Women's Records
   1,500 meter free-style in 16 minutes 4.49 seconds by Kim Linehan in Fort Lauderdale, Florida, on August 20, 1979.
   200 meter butterfly in 2 minutes 07.01 seconds by Mary Meagher in Fort Lauderdale, Florida, on August 17, 1979.

Swimming. Channel Swimming. The youngest person ever to swim the English Channel is Markus Hooper (b. June 14, 1967) of Eltham, Kent, England who swam from Dover to Sangatte, France in 14 hours 37 minutes, August 5-6, 1979, when he was 12 years 53 days old.
   The fastest double crossing of the Channel was accomplished by Cynthia Nicholas on August 4-5, 1979, in 19 hours 12 minutes. This brought her women's record total to 8 crossings.
   The greatest number of crossings by a man is 14 by Des Renford as of August 4, 1979.

Tennis. Doubles Marathon. Paul Blackburn, Terry Mabbitt, Nigel Johnson and Rod Wiley played for 80 hours at Ilkley Tennis Club, Yorkshire, England, June 13-16, 1979.

Track and Field. Women's Records
   400 meters in 48.60 seconds by Maritta Koch (East Germany) in Turin, Italy, on August 4, 1979.
   400 meter hurdles in 54.78 seconds by Marina Makeyeva (U.S.S.R.) in Moscow, U.S.S.R., on July 27, 1979.
   4 × 200 meter relay in 1 minute 30.8 seconds by the Ukraine, U.S.S.R. team (Raisa Maklova, Nina Zuskova, Tatyana Prorochenko, Maria Kulchunova) in Moscow, U.S.S.R., on July 29, 1979.

Walking. Non-Stop. Fred Jago of Great Britain walked 317.155 miles in 148 hours 31 minutes, July 13-19, 1979, at Vivary Park, Taunton, Somerset, England. He was moving 98.3 per cent of the time.

Water Skiing. Tricks. The men's record is 7,840 points by Cory Pickos (U.S.) (b. 1963) in Lakeland, Florida, on May 6, 1979. The women's record is 5,880 in Lakeland on May 6, 1979.

Weightlifting. Lightweight Jerk. 410 lbs. by Todorov in Leningrad, U.S.S.R., on July 29, 1979.

Yachting. Admiral's Cup. As of the 1979 contest, Great Britain had won seven times, the U.S. and Australia twice each.

INDEX

An asterisk at the end of an entry indicates that further information in that category will be found in the Late Records section.

Cherry Pie, largest 414
Cherry Tomato, greatest yield 122
Chess, origins, world champions 575, winning streak, longest games, marathon, most opponents 576
Chest Measurement, largest 20, 36
Chicken, population 84, largest, longest flight 89, highest egg-laying rate 368, eating 489*
Chicken Plucking 370
Chicken Ranch, largest 366
Children, most by one mother 29, most descendants 30, multiple births 31–35; see also Babies
Chimney, tallest 256, most massive 257
Chimpanzee, strength of 69
Chin-ups, most 591
Chocolate Easter Egg, largest 414
Chocolate Factory, largest 343
Choir Marathon 480
Choir Service, longest 432
Chorus Line, longest 239
Christianity, see Religion
Christmas Cards, earliest, most sent 224
Christmas Tree, tallest 126
Church, oldest 427, largest, smallest 429, tallest spires 430, attendance 432
Cigar, largest, most expensive 354, most voracious smoker 355
Cigarette, largest plant 349, simultaneous smoker, consumption, largest collection, packs 355, rarest, most popular, longest and shortest, most expensive lighter, cards 356
Cinematography, see Motion Pictures
Circle, sitting unsupported in a 487
Circular Storm, worst 433
Circulation, highest paper 225, highest magazine 226
Circumnavigation, fastest automobile, by amphibious vehicle 306, motorcycle 309, by air 316–317, polar 317, fastest flight on scheduled airlines 440, marine records 444–445, walking 661
Circum-Polar Flight, first 317
Circus, largest 262, cycling 454, other records 456
Citadel, see Castle
Cities, most populous, largest not on water, oldest, largest, highest capital 374, lowest, northernmost and southernmost, most remote from sea 375
Civil Engineering Structures, tallest, tower 266, bridges 267–269, aqueduct 268, canals 269–270, locks 270–271, dams 271–273, reservoir 272, polder, levees 273, tunnels 273–274
Civil War, bloodiest 384
Clam, slowest growing animal 59, longest-lived, largest shell 110, eating record 489
Clapping 454
Clergy, largest 427
Cliffs, highest sea 153
Climate, see Weather
Clock, earliest, oldest 337, largest, public, largest four-faced, tallest four-faced clock, most accurate and complicated 338
Cloth, finest, most expensive 356
Cloud, highest, lowest, greatest vertical range 155
Clover, Fourteen-Leafed 124
Club Swinging 455
Clusters and Gold Stars, most 497
Coach, fastest 297
Coal, carrying, shoveling 455

Coastline, shortest 371
Cobras, see Snake
Coffee, greatest drinkers, most expensive 417*
Coffin, heaviest gold 359
Coin Balancing 455
Coinless Country 408
Coins, oldest, smallest, heaviest, coinless countries, highest, lowest denomination 408, most expensive, rarest, greatest collection, largest auction, largest treasure trove 409, largest mint 410*
Coin Snatching 455
Cold, see Temperature
Cold, Common 39
Collision, largest between ships 296
Colony, smallest 371
Color, sensitivity, blindness 46
Column, tallest 276, monumental 278
Coma, longest 41
Comet, earliest, closest approach, largest 166, shortest and longest periods 167
Comic Strip, longest-lived, earliest, most syndicated cartoonist 222
Commerce, 340–349, land 349–350, stock exchanges 350–351, banks 351–352, manufactured articles 352–365
Commercials, see Advertising Rates*
Communication, telephones 421–422, postal services 421, stamps 422–424, postal addresses, telegrams 424
Communist Parties, largest 382
Community Garden, largest 366
Company, oldest, greatest assets, sales and capital, profit and loss 340, biggest work force, largest take-over, largest write-off 341
Compensation, greatest 392
Complainer, most successful 393
Composer, most prolific 230, most prolific symphonist, most rapid 231
Composition, Musical, longest symphony, longest piano composition 231, longest silence 232; see also Opera and Hymns
Compounds, see Chemical Compounds
Computer, human 50, fastest, largest, most powerful 200, company 343
Computer Fraud, greatest 403
Concert, greatest classical attendance, greatest pop festival attendance 230, loudest pop 252
Concrete, largest structure 271
Condiment, rarest 416
Conga Dancing 458
Congress, see Parliaments
Conjunction, solar system 168
Consonants, most and least in a language 209
Constellations, largest and smallest 171
Contest Winnings, largest 455
Continent, largest, smallest 141
Contracts, largest television 244
Conveyor Belt, longest 336
Cooling Tower, largest 258
Copper, most productive mine, largest underground 287
Cork Flight, champagne 185
Corn, greatest yield 366
Countries, total sovereign and non-sovereign 371, richest, poorest 406
Country, largest, smallest, smallest colony, smallest republic 371, smallest state, flattest and most elevated, frontiers 372, coinless 408
Court, most appearances 400, largest 403

Energy (power), consumption 417*
Engagement, longest, "faux pas" 448
Engine, car, first 297, fastest rocket, jet, gas-turbine 298, piston, diesel 299, largest 302, oldest steam 331, military 389
Engineering 332–339
English Channel, first flight 316, first human-powered flight 327, canoe crossing 545, rowing 622, swimming 639, 641–642*
English Language, oldest words 207, commonest language, most irregular verbs, largest vocabulary 208, word with most consecutive vowels, oldest and youngest letters 209, longest word, longest palindrome 210, commonest words, most over-worked word, most homophones, worst tongue-twister, shortest holoalphabetic sentence, longest acronym 211, anagrams, sentence 212; see also Names
Enrollment, highest university 425
Entertainment, see Arts
Epidemic, worst 433
Eponymous Record 495
Equestrian Sports, origin 553, most Olympic medals, world titles, jumping records 554, longest ride, marathon 555
Equity, largest 351
Eruption, greatest volcanic 133, geyser 135
Escalators, first 335, longest 336
Escape, longest prison 400
Escapology 463
Eskimo Rolls 545
Espionage, industrial 401
Estuary, longest 146
Evacuation, greatest 384
Excavation, greatest 287, manual 288
Excavator, largest, dragline 333
Executions, greatest ritualistic, last guillotinings 398, largest hanging, most attempts 399
Expansion, highest and lowest elemental 181, lowest chemical compound 182
Explosion, greatest volcanic 134, largest conventional 390, worst 434
Extinct Animals, largest, heaviest 112–113, largest predator 113, longest tusks, heaviest tusks, longest antlers, most brainless, largest mammal, largest flying creature 114, largest mammoth, largest dinosaur eggs, largest bird, largest marine reptile, largest crocodile 115, largest chelonians, largest fish 116, earliest animal by type, longest snake 117, largest amphibian, largest arachnid, insect, shelled mollusk, most southerly 118
Extrasensory Perception 52
Eye, acuteness 45, color sensitivity, color blindness 46, largest animal 59, acuteness, bird 87

Fabric, oldest, most expensive 357
Factory, see Company and Plant
Fair, earliest 264, largest, record attendance 265
Falconet, smallest bird of prey 84
Fall, longest without parachute 475
Families, richest 494
Family Tree, largest 464
Famine, worst 433
Fangs, longest snake 94
Farms, largest, largest fields, wheat, hops, vineyard, cattle station 365, sheep, chicken, turkey, piggery, mushroom, community garden 366

Fashion Show, longest 464
Fasting, record 49*
Father, of most children 29
Fauna, see Animal Kingdom
Feathers, longest 88, most 89
Feline, largest 65, smallest 66; see also Cat
Feminine Beauty 464
Fence, longest 281
Fencing, origins 555, most Olympic, world titles 556
Fern, largest 128, smallest 129
Ferris Wheel, largest 265
Ferris Wheel Riding 464
Ferry, Car, largest 293
Fiction, highest sales 220
Fiddler, most durable 459
Field, largest oil 284, sports 502
Field Hockey, origins, earliest international, highest international score, longest game, marathon 557
Figure Skating, see Ice Skating
Filibusters, longest Senate 380, legislative 381
Film, see Motion Pictures
Finance, largest budget, foreign aid, highest tax rate, least taxed country, national debts, biggest savers 405, richest, poorest countries, gross national product, gold reserves, worst inflation 406, currency 406–407, check 407, bond 408
Financial Transactions (Stock Exchange), highest index, trading volume, Dow Jones decline, paper loss, daily increase 350, largest transaction, largest stock trade, largest security offering, greatest market value 351; see also Stock Exchanges
Fines 403
Fingers, most, longest nails 38, touch sensitivity 38
Fire, worst 434
Fireball, brightest 161
Fire-Eating 45*
Fire Engine, most powerful 304
Fire Pumping 464
Fire Pump Pull 464
Fire-Walking, hottest 45
Fireworks, largest 357, worst disaster 434
Fisheries, world catches, largest fishmongers, largest net 345
Fishes, greatest size difference between sexes 59, largest sea 97, largest freshwater 98, smallest sea and freshwater, fastest 99, longest-lived, oldest goldfish, shortest-lived, deepest, most venomous, most and least eggs, most electric 100, largest extinct 116, earliest 117
Fishing, smallest catch possible 99, largest net 345, largest catches 557, sea and freshwater fish records (table) 558, smallest catch, spear-fishing, record casts, longest fight, marathon 559*
Fjord, longest 150
Flag, largest, oldest 357
Flagpole, tallest 277
Flamenco (dance) 459
Flare, greatest gas 285
Flea, largest, longest jump 107
Fleet, largest taxi 307
Flight, fastest bird 57, 86, fastest bat 67, longest, highest bird 86, most airborne bird 87, longest chicken 89, fish 100, fastest insect 106, earliest flying creature 117, space 175–178, champagne cork 185, earliest airplane 315, cross-Channel, transat-

Lighthouse, brightest, most powerful, greatest visible light range, tallest 280
Lightning, length, speed, most powerful 156, worst disaster 435, most lightning-struck person 471
Light-Year, speed 159
Limbo (dance) 459
Limousine, longest 301
Liner, Passenger, largest, longest and most expensive 290
Linguist, greatest, living 209
Lion, heaviest 65
Lion Taming, greatest feat 471
Liqueur, most expensive 184
Liquid-Fuel Rocket, first 173
Liquor, see Alcoholic Consumption, Distillery, Drink
Literacy, lowest rate 424
Litigation, most protracted 391, greatest damages, highest settlement 392, largest suit 393
Litter, largest mammal 63, dogs 79, cats 82, pigs 367
Livestock Prices 369–370
Living Thing, oldest, largest 125, smallest 131
Lizard, largest, oldest 91, extinct 112
Load, heaviest hauled by horses 77, dog 78, truck 304, train 313
Lobster, heaviest, largest, smallest, longest-lived 104
Locks (canal), largest single, deepest 270, highest elevator 271, (padlock), largest 334
Locomotive, first, steam, most powerful 311
Locust, largest swarm 106
Logo, largest 284
Log Rolling 472
Longevity, human 25–29, animal 56, 92, bacteria 56, 131, mammal 61, tree 124, average human 376
Loss, greatest weight 21, greatest commercial 340, stock market, on paper 495, gambling 571*
Lugeing, origins 533, most world titles, highest speed 534
Lunar Conquest 178, 437
Lynching 400

Machinery, oldest 332
Mach Scale 315
Mafia 396
Magazines, see Periodical
Magnet, most magnetic and non-magnetic metal 182, strongest and weakest magnetic fields, heaviest 197
Magnitudes, stellar 159, 170, planetary 168
Mail, see Postal Services
Mammals, largest, heaviest 59, largest land, smallest, fastest 60, slowest, tallest, longest-lived 61, rarest, longest hibernation, highest living, largest herd, longest and shortest gestation periods 62, largest litter 63, youngest breeder 64, carnivores 64–66, pinnipeds 66–67, bats 67–68, primates 68–70, rodents, insectivores 70, antelope 71, deer 72, tusks and horns 72–73, blood temperatures 73, most valuable furs, ambergris, marsupials 74, domesticated horses 75–77, dogs 77–81, cats 81–82, rabbits 82–83, hares, guinea pigs, gerbil, house mouse, hamster, rat 83, extinct, largest 114, earliest 117
Mammoth, heaviest tusks 114, largest 115

Man (male), tallest 11–14, shortest 16–19, lightest, heaviest 20, earliest 23–25, oldest 25–29, first in space 175, most traveled 439; see also Human Being, Humans*
Manual Excavation, largest 288
Manufactured Articles 352–365
Manufacturing, see Company
Manuscript, highest price 215
Map, oldest, earliest printed 224
Marble, largest slab 188
March, most rapid 389
Marching Band, largest 230
Marijuana, largest haul, raids 402
Marine Disaster, worst 434
Marine Mammal, largest 55, smallest 60, largest toothed 64, prehistoric 114
Marine Records, see Circumnavigation, Transatlantic, Diving and Swimming
Marine Reptile, largest prehistoric 115
Market, largest 348
Marriage, ages 376, longest engagement, engagement "faux pas" 448, greatest number, oldest bride and bridegroom, longest 449, most married couple, largest mass ceremony 450, biggest dowry 494
Marsupials, largest, smallest, rarest, longest-lived, highest and longest jump 74
Massacres, see Killings
Masts, radio, television 254, 266, most on sailing ship 294
Matadors, see Bullfighting
Matchbox Labels, oldest, longest 360
Maternity Hospital, busiest 377
Mathematics, human ability at 50
Mayoralty, longest 383
Maze, largest 282
Meanings, most word 211
Measures, Weights, earliest system 193, time, longest, shortest 194, most accurate balance 196, most accurate timekeeper 339
Meat, greatest and least eaters 412, largest pie 414, eating record 490
Mechanic, most successful racing 307
Mechanical World, ships 289–297, road vehicles 297–310, coaches 297, cars 297–308, motorcycles 308–309, bicycles 309–310, railroads 311–314, aircraft 315–329, power producers 330–331, engineering 332–339
Mechanism, slowest moving designed 338
Medals, most expensive 361, U.S. 496, most bemedalled person 497, Olympic 614
Medical Center, largest 377
Medicine, most pill taking 44, most powerful drug, analgesic drug, most prescribed 183
Meeting, record attendance, stockholders 340
Melons, largest 120
Melting Points, elements, lowest, highest 181
Membership, largest 346
Memory, Human, 49, places of Pi 50
Mental Calculation, fastest 50
Mental Hospital, largest, longest stay 377
Merchandise, fastest-moving 344
Merchandiser, largest 346
Merry-Go-Round Marathon 472
Message in a Bottle 472
Metals, lightest, densest, most expensive 180, least stable, most isotopes, most ductile, highest melting point, lowest ex-

Index prepared by Stephen Topping

PICTURE CREDITS

The editors and publishers wish to thank the following people and organizations for pictures which they supplied: